Photoshop® 4
for Windows® 95 Bible

Photoshop® 4 for Windows® 95 Bible

by Deke McClelland

Revised by Julie King

Foreword by Mark Hamburg

Technical Review by Marc Pawliger

IDG Books Worldwide, Inc.
An International Data Group Company

Foster City, CA ◆ Chicago, IL ◆ Indianapolis, IN ◆ Southlake, TX

Photoshop® 4 for Windows® 95 Bible

Published by
IDG Books Worldwide, Inc.
An International Data Group Company
919 E. Hillsdale Blvd., Suite 400
Foster City, CA 94404

http://www.idgbooks.com (IDG Books Worldwide Web site)
http://www.dummies.com (Dummies Press Web site)

Library of Congress Catalog Card No.: 97-73217

ISBN: 0-7645-4032-7

Printed in the United States of America

10 9 8 7 6 5 4 3 2 1

IB/QZ/QW/ZX/FC

Distributed in the United States by IDG Books Worldwide, Inc.

Distributed by Macmillan Canada for Canada; by Contemporanea de Ediciones for Venezuela; by Distribuidora Cuspide for Argentina; by CITEC for Brazil; by Ediciones ZETA S.C.R. Ltda. for Peru; by Editorial Limusa SA for Mexico; by Transworld Publishers Limited in the United Kingdom and Europe; by Academic Bookshop for Egypt; by Levant Distributors S.A.R.L. for Lebanon; by Al Jassim for Saudi Arabia; by Simron Pty. Ltd. for South Africa; by Pustak Mahal for India; by The Computer Bookshop for India; by Toppan Company Ltd. for Japan; by Addison Wesley Publishing Company for Korea; by Longman Singapore Publishers Ltd. for Singapore, Malaysia, Thailand, and Indonesia; by Unalis Corporation for Taiwan; by WS Computer Publishing Company, Inc. for the Philippines; by WoodsLane Pty. Ltd. for Australia; by WoodsLane Enterprises Ltd. for New Zealand. Authorized Sales Agent: Anthony Rudkin Associates for the Middle East and North Africa.

For general information on IDG Books Worldwide's books in the U.S., please call our Consumer Customer Service department at 800-762-2974. For reseller information, including discounts and premium sales, please call our Reseller Customer Service department at 800-434-3422.

For information on where to purchase IDG Books Worldwide's books outside the U.S., please contact our International Sales department at 415-655-3023 or fax 415-655-3299.

For information on foreign language translations, please contact our Foreign & Subsidiary Rights department at 415-655-3021 or fax 415-655-3281.

For sales inquiries and special prices for bulk quantities, please contact our Sales department at 415-655-3200 or write to the address above.

For information on using IDG Books Worldwide's books in the classroom or for ordering examination copies, please contact our Educational Sales department at 800-434-2086 or fax 817-251-8174.

For press review copies, author interviews, or other publicity information, please contact our Public Relations department at 415-655-3000 or fax 415-655-3299.

For authorization to photocopy items for corporate, personal, or educational use, please contact Copyright Clearance Center, 222 Rosewood Drive, Danvers, MA 01923, or fax 508-750-4470.

is a trademark under exclusive license to IDG Books Worldwide, Inc., from International Data Group, Inc.

ABOUT IDG BOOKS WORLDWIDE

Welcome to the world of IDG Books Worldwide.

IDG Books Worldwide, Inc., is a subsidiary of International Data Group, the world's largest publisher of computer-related information and the leading global provider of information services on information technology. IDG was founded more than 25 years ago and now employs more than 8,500 people worldwide. IDG publishes more than 275 computer publications in over 75 countries (see listing below). More than 60 million people read one or more IDG publications each month.

Launched in 1990, IDG Books Worldwide is today the #1 publisher of best-selling computer books in the United States. We are proud to have received eight awards from the Computer Press Association in recognition of editorial excellence and three from *Computer Currents'* First Annual Readers' Choice Awards. Our best-selling *...For Dummies*® series has more than 30 million copies in print with translations in 30 languages. IDG Books Worldwide, through a joint venture with IDG's Hi-Tech Beijing, became the first U.S. publisher to publish a computer book in the People's Republic of China. In record time, IDG Books Worldwide has become the first choice for millions of readers around the world who want to learn how to better manage their businesses.

Our mission is simple: Every one of our books is designed to bring extra value and skill-building instructions to the reader. Our books are written by experts who understand and care about our readers. The knowledge base of our editorial staff comes from years of experience in publishing, education, and journalism — experience we use to produce books for the '90s. In short, we care about books, so we attract the best people. We devote special attention to details such as audience, interior design, use of icons, and illustrations. And because we use an efficient process of authoring, editing, and desktop publishing our books electronically, we can spend more time ensuring superior content and spend less time on the technicalities of making books.

You can count on our commitment to deliver high-quality books at competitive prices on topics you want to read about. At IDG Books Worldwide, we continue in the IDG tradition of delivering quality for more than 25 years. You'll find no better book on a subject than one from IDG Books Worldwide.

IDG BOOKS WORLDWIDE

John Kilcullen
CEO
IDG Books Worldwide, Inc.

Steven Berkowitz
President and Publisher
IDG Books Worldwide, Inc.

Eighth Annual Computer Press Awards ≥1992

Ninth Annual Computer Press Awards ≥1993

Tenth Annual Computer Press Awards ≥1994

Eleventh Annual Computer Press Awards ≥1995

About the Author

Deke McClelland is a contributing editor to *Macworld* and *Publish* magazines. He has authored more than 30 books on desktop publishing and the Macintosh computer, and his work has been translated into more than 20 languages. Deke also hosts *Digital Gurus,* a syndicated TV show about personal computing, from his home base in Colorado. He started his career as artistic director at the first service bureau in the United States.

Deke won a Society of Technical Communication Award in 1994, an American Society for Business Press Editors Award in 1995, and the Ben Franklin Award for Best Computer Book in 1989. He also won the prestigious Computer Press Association Award in 1990, 1992, 1994, and 1995.

Deke is the author of the following books for IDG Books Worldwide: *CorelDRAW 7 For Dummies*, *Macworld FreeHand 7 Bible*, *PageMaker 6 For Windows For Dummies*, and *Photoshop 4 For Dummies*. He is also the author of *Real World Illustrator 7* (Peachpit Press).

Credits

Acquisitions Editor
Nancy E. Dunn

Development Editor
Amy Thomas

Copy Editor
Marcia Baker

Technical Editor
Marc Pawliger

Project Coordinator
Susan Parini

Production Staff
Kurt Krames
Christopher Pimentel
Dina Quan
Mark Schumann

Proofreader
Melissa Buddendeck

Indexer
Liz Cunningham

Cover Design
Peter Kowaleszyn

Foreword

If you are reading this foreword, it probably means you've purchased a copy of Adobe Photoshop 4.0 and, for that, I, and the rest of the Photoshop team at Adobe, thank you.

If you own a previous edition of the *Photoshop Bible*, you probably know what to expect. If not, then get ready for an interesting trip.

I have long felt the best way to learn Photoshop is through exploration. Rather than just offering a set of canned effects, it offers a broad collection of tools for a wide range of imaging tasks. Becoming a skilled Photoshop user involves getting to know those tools, how they interact, and when to use them. The best way I've found to do that is through use, exploration, and play.

On the other hand, because Photoshop enables one to do so much, it can be difficult to know where to begin. It's like opening a watch maker's tool chest: The screwdrivers are pretty obvious, but what about all those other strange and mysterious instruments?

In Photoshop 4.0, one of our main goals was trying to eliminate many of the inconsistencies and arcana that had accreted in Photoshop over the years. At the expense of changing some of the ways in which people had become used to working — ways we often felt were excessively awkward — we think we've come a long way. Those changes should make Photoshop easier to learn and use from the standpoint that what you learn in one place is more likely to apply in another. The program, however, still spans so much territory that it can be difficult to know where to begin.

This is where Deke McClelland comes in.

The *Photoshop 4 for Windows 95 Bible* is a guided tour through Photoshop with a guide who has been over the territory many times. (I've been involved with Photoshop for six years and, for essentially as long as I can remember, I've had Deke looking over my shoulder.)

Deke takes you through most of Photoshop and covers a lot of areas in impressive depth. Not only does Deke show you the features in Photoshop — after all, you have the manual to do this — he shows you how to use them to solve issues that look almost like real-world problems. This is the *Photoshop Bible,* not the *Photoshop Encyclopedia,* hence, it tells stories, rather than just presenting information. Those stories take the form of looking at complex problems — like dealing with hair — and showing how you can use Photoshop's tools to solve those problems.

A second thing you'll get from this book is a lot of commentary. Deke isn't shy about letting you know how he feels about various features. I don't always agree with his opinions on these matters, but I think Deke's openness makes the book much richer. If you become a routine user of Photoshop, you will almost certainly develop your own opinions, some of which will probably match Deke's, and some of which probably won't. It's valuable to get his opinions during the tour, however, because, even if you end up disagreeing with them, they give you more to think about.

Finally, the most invigorating aspect of this book is the enthusiasm Deke brings to the tour. You'll note I include *play* in my list of strategies for coming to know Photoshop; I think just having fun with the program is really one of the best things you can do when starting out. Deke almost relentlessly conveys that sense of excitement and fun, and for that, I thank him.

So, fasten your seat belts, put on your pith helmets, and get ready. It's a fascinating trip ahead.

Mark Hamburg
Principal Scientist and Architect for Adobe Photoshop
Adobe Systems Incorporated

Preface

I have no idea where you are as you read this. You might be sitting in front of your computer, lounging on a beach in Martinique, or curled up under the covers with a flashlight. But there's a chance you're standing in a bookstore with a clerk behind you asking if you need any help. If so, you're at what we in the book biz like to call *the point of purchase* (POP). From my perspective, the POP is a dangerous place, fraught with ambiguities and temptations. There's a chance — however infinitesimal — that you might put this book back where you found it and buy a competing title. I shudder to think of it.

So for the benefit of you POPers, I'm about to lay it on a bit thick.

The *Photoshop Bible*, in its *Macworld* incarnation, is not only the number-one selling guide to Adobe Photoshop, but one of the two or three most successful books on any electronic publishing topic ever printed. You can find localized translations in China, France, Japan, Korea, Poland, Russia, Spain, and the Netherlands. But my favorite story is the earliest: When the first printing hit the market at the Boston Macworld Expo in August 1993, it sold an unprecedented 500 copies in three days — one book every three minutes.

Now, we all know *best seller* doesn't necessarily translate to *best* — I needn't remind you Air Supply sold a lot of albums in its day. But the *Photoshop Bible* seems to have touched a chord. Based on the letters I've received over the years, most readers find the book informative, comprehensive, and entertaining. (Okay, one woman summed up the book as "violent, satanic, and blasphemous" — cross my heart, it's true — but now that we've removed all the backward lyrics, I think we've addressed that problem.) Knowing people not only buy the book, but actually read it and find it pleasurable, gives me more satisfaction than I can say.

The driving philosophy behind the *Photoshop 4 for Windows 95 Bible* is: Even the most intimidating topic can be made easy if it's explained properly. This goes double when the subject of the discussion is something as modest as a piece of software. Photoshop isn't some remarkable work of nature that defies our comprehension — Photoshop is nothing more than a commercial product designed by a bunch of regular people like you for the express purpose of being understood and put to use by a bunch of regular people like you. If I can't explain something already this inherently straightforward, then shame on me.

I've made it my mission to address every topic head on — no cop-outs, no apologies. Everything's here, from the practical benefits of creating accurate masks to the theoretical wonders of designing your own custom filters. I wasn't born with this knowledge, and times occur when I'm learning with you. But if I don't know how something works, I do the research and figure it out, sometimes discussing features directly with the programmers, sometimes taking advantage of other sources. My job is to find out the answers, make sure they make sense, and pass them along to you as clearly as I can.

I also provide background, opinions, and humor. A dry listing of features followed by ponderous discussions of how they work doesn't mean squat unless I explain why the feature is there, where it fits into your workflow, and — on occasion — whether it's the best solution. I am alternatively cranky, excited, and just plain giddy as I explain Photoshop, and I make no effort to contain my criticisms or enthusiasm.

This book is me walking you through the program as subjectively as I would explain it to a friend.

But before I brag any more about the book, it's possible you're not even sure what Photoshop is, much less why you'd need a book on the subject. Just so we're all clear, let's take a peek at the program.

What Is Photoshop?

Photoshop is software for Macintosh and Windows-based computers that enables you to edit photos and artwork scanned to disk and to print your results. Here's an example: Your job is to take a picture of Mr. High-and-Mighty CEO, touch up his crow's feet, and publish his smiling face on the cover of the annual report. No problem. Just shoot the photo, have it digitized to a Photo CD or some other high-tech gizmo, open Mr. H & M inside Photoshop, dab on the digital wrinkle cream, fix his toupee (and for heaven's sake, do something about those jowls), and there you go. The man looks presentable no matter how badly the company is doing.

Photoshop, then, is about changing reality. And it goes beyond just reducing the distance between two Giza pyramids on the cover of *National Geographic* or plopping a leaning Tom Cruise, photographed in Hawaii, onto the supportive shoulder of Dustin Hoffman, photographed in New York, for a *Newsweek* spread (both duller-than-fiction applications of photo-editing software). Photoshop brings you full-tilt creativity. Picture a diver leaping from the summit of Mount Everest, or a bright violet zebra galloping toward a hazel-green sunset, or an architectural rendering with wallpaper that looks exactly like the surface of the moon. Photoshop enables you to paint snapshots from your dreams. The sky's the limit.

About This Book

If you're familiar with previous editions of this book, this one represents your everyday average humongous renovation. I've hacked out an interesting, but long-winded, chapter about compositing, and I added three chapters, one each for shortcuts and scripting, layering (which used to be peppered throughout the book), and Web graphics. I've also expanded my discussions of masking, transformations, color corrections, blend modes, and digital cameras.

Naturally, I also devote much room to Photoshop 4's new capabilities, including the Navigator and Actions palettes, enhanced gradations, grids and guides, adjustment layers, and the more than 40 new filters. But the most significant change to Photoshop 4 is the interface. Frankly, if you're familiar with Versions 3 and earlier, you may feel a little lost and confused inside the new program. Not to worry. I explain every change, tell you why Adobe did it, and do everything within my power to make you more productive than you were in the past.

Images, color and otherwise

More than half the figures and images in this book are new. If only for the sake of variety, I've taken out images that have been staples of previous editions and traded them for new photographs from stock-image vendors Digital Stock and PhotoDisc, as well as stuff I've shot myself with the latest digital cameras.

As in the past, the book includes 32 pages of color images, with hundreds of color images and artwork available for your perusal on the CD. Of course, that still leaves a lot of grayscale images, which begs the question, why isn't this book printed in full-color throughout? The answer is a simple and irrefutable matter of economics. A full-color book of this size would cost nearly $150. With volume discounts, we could probably pull it off at something in the $85 to $90 range. But even so, this is a little steep for a book that will sit on your desk and get coffee stains and pen marks all over it, don't you think? We did, too, and so we opted to forego full-color throughout the book and concentrate on giving you what you really need: tons of useful information at an affordable price.

That silver Frisbee in the back of the book

In the back of this book, you'll find a CD-ROM containing hundreds of pieces of original artwork and stock photography in full, natural color. I've included most of the pivotal images from this book so you can follow along with my examples (if you see fit). The CD holds 650MB of data — and we took full advantage of it.

Wendy Sharp, formerly head of the reviews department at *Macworld* magazine, spent nearly as much time compiling the CD as I spent writing the book. Rather than limiting herself to the same old plug-ins you find in every book, Wendy knocked herself out to make sure this CD was valuable in and of itself. You'll find software from Adobe, Extensis, Alien Skin, Andromeda, Xaos Tools, DataStream Imaging, and others. Also included is a digital article of direct interest to Photoshop users from *Macworld* magazine; stunning digital artwork from some of the best around, including Jeff Brice, Steve Campbell, Christopher Ching, Kevin Curry, Diane Fenster, Larry Goode, Ranulfo Ponce, and Greg Vander Houwen; and royalty-free stock photos from PhotoDisc and Digital Stock.

**Cross
Reference** Read Appendix E, "Using the CD-ROM," for a complete listing of the contents of the
CD-ROM.

The Guts of the Book

As far as the actual pages in this massive tome are concerned, well, there are lots
of them. But, remember, I don't cover every command or option available in
Photoshop. That's the job of the Photoshop manual. My job is to explain the
features that really count and to explore capabilities you won't easily glean on
your own. I also look at Photoshop's place in the larger electronic design scheme
and examine how best to approach Photoshop in ways that will yield the most
efficient and accurate results.

 Caution This is a big, fat book, so exercise caution. Those of you who like to read in-flight,
remember to stow the book under the seat in front of you after you board the
plane. It'll damage less luggage than if you try to stick it in the overhead
compartment. If you plan on using the book for self-defense, be sure to spar with a
partner armed with a volume of equal size. And please, take out the CD before
using the book to prop up a youngster at the dinner table. That way, you can use
the CD as a coaster in case of spills.

To enhance your enjoyment of Photoshop's mouth-watering capabilities, I sliced
the task into five tasty parts and then diced those parts into a total of 18 digestible
chapters. Bon appetite.

Part I: Welcome to Photoshop 4

Here's all the basic stuff you need to know about Photoshop. I explain the new
Photoshop 4 interface, give you an overview of the low-level functions that have
changed, and show you how to work with Photoshop from the keyboard. Whether
you're new to Photoshop or an old hand, you'll find a lot you didn't know in these
first three chapters.

 Note If you're experienced with Photoshop and you're familiar with the previous edition
of this book, read the last section of Chapter 1 and all of Chapters 2 and 3. Then
skip to the beginning of Part III and keep reading.

Chapter 1: Getting to Know Photoshop, explains how Photoshop fits into the
larger experience of using the PC to produce printed pages and onscreen
presentations. I also list all the new features in Photoshop 4 in case you're trying
to decide whether to upgrade.

Chapter 2: Inside Photoshop, introduces you to Version 4's revamped working environment and examines Photoshop's generous supply of tools, cursors, multipaneled palettes, and preference settings.

Chapter 3: Shortcuts and Scripts, keeps you apprised of time-saving techniques and makes you more productive. Roughly half of Photoshop's key-based techniques have changed in Photoshop 4, as I explain in Table 3-1. This is also where I tell all about Photoshop 4's new Actions palette, which enables you to design your own shortcuts and batch-process images.

Part II: Understanding Digital Imagery

This part of the book examines the core image editing process, taking you from composition and construction to color theory and output. You learn how to change the size and resolution of an image, how to define colors and navigate among color channels, and, finally, how to print the image to paper or film.

Chapter 4: Image Fundamentals, describes what it means to be a digitized image and how file formats, such as TIFF and JPEG, affect the content of an image and its size on disk. You also learn how to resample and crop images within Photoshop.

Chapter 5: Defining Colors, covers the fundamentals of editing colors on a computer screen. I explain how you can manipulate common color models to display predictable results. I also examine the differences and similarities between the commercial printing standards Pantone and Trumatch.

Chapter 6: Navigating Channels, looks at color channels, which are the building blocks of color images, and examines how they work. In a nutshell, channels are so important that even beginning Photoshop users should become comfortable with editing them.

Chapter 7: Printing Images, starts off with a glossary of printing terms that will help you better communicate with the folks at your service bureau or commercial print house. Following this, I explain how to print grayscale and color composites, four-color separations, and duotones, tritones, and quadtones.

Part III: Painting and Retouching Images

Every month or so, some fraudulent photo sparks a new flame of public scorn and scrutiny. Now it's your chance to give people something to talk about. These chapters show you how to exchange fact with a modicum of fantasy.

Chapter 8: Painting and Editing, shows you how to use Photoshop's brush tools to enhance and augment photographic images. It also explores ways to paint images from scratch using pressure-sensitive tablets. The chapter ends with an in-depth analysis of brush modes and how they add to everyday living.

Chapter 9: Filling and Stroking, shows how to paint the interiors and outlines of images with solid colors and gradations. It also steps you through the processes of creating drop shadows, halos, and translucent, gradient arrows (of all things). There's a lot more to Photoshop's straightforward fill and stroke functions than meets the eye.

Chapter 10: Duplicating and Reverting, details the operation of the rubber stamp tool, the most versatile and, possibly, the most frequently overlooked editing tool available to Photoshop users. In addition, you learn how to create seamless repeating patterns and textures in Photoshop for use with the rubber stamp and other tools. And, finally, you learn how to revert images to their original appearance using the eraser tool.

Part IV: Selections, Layers, and Text

Selections are Photoshop's most important capability. They enable you to limit the area you edit, as well as lift foreground images and combine them with other backgrounds. I also cover text in this section because text in Photoshop is no more than character-shaped selection outlines.

Chapter 11: Selections and Paths, covers absolutely everything you ever wanted to know about the magic wand and the path tools, antialiasing and feathering, expanding, and growing. You also learn about the new role of the move tool, which is now the only way to move selections in Photoshop 4.

Chapter 12: Creating Masks, documents the inherent advantages of masks over the rest of the selection tools. I explain how to paint inside selection masks, how to work in the quick mask mode, how to generate selections automatically using the Color Range command, how to save masks to a separate channel, and how to create your own highly accurate masks.

Chapter 13: Layers and Transformations, tells how layers work in Photoshop 4. Pasting, dragging and dropping, creating text, and several other operations now automatically result in new layers. You can also scale, rotate, and skew layers with more control than ever before. If you've shied away from layers in the past, read this chapter.

Chapter 14: Amazing Text Stuff, tells you how to create word art, including gradient text, characters with tiger stripes, raised letters, custom logos, and a whole mess of other effects guaranteed to make jaws drop and eyes boggle.

Part V: Filters and Special Effects

Making manual artistic enhancements is all well and good, but it's easier to let your computer do the work. These chapters show ways to produce highly entertaining and effective results using fully automated operations.

Chapter 15: Corrective Filtering, covers how to get the most out of Photoshop's most commonly used filters, including Unsharp Mask, Gaussian Blur, Add Noise, and High Pass. I'll also explain how to clean up a photograph from a digital camera and how to lessen the effects of a filter with the new Fade command.

Chapter 16: Full-Court Filtering, describes the old and new special effects filters available in Photoshop 4. I also document a series of specific applications for Photoshop's abundant supply of plug-in filters.

Chapter 17: Constructing Homemade Effects, investigates the exact workings of the Custom and Displace filters, which multiply and shift pixels to create user-definable effects. If you're feeling brave, you can program your own effects using the Filter Factory.

Part VI: Corrections, Composites, and the Web

Here's where you learn what you can do with Photoshop's most powerful color correction commands, how to composite images using overlay modes and channel operations, and how to create images specifically for the World Wide Web.

Chapter 18: Mapping and Adjusting Colors, explores ways to change the color balance in scanned photographs to represent real life more accurately — or to depart from it more radically. You learn how to make use of the straightforward Variations options, how to modify specific colors with Hue/Saturation, and how to adjust brightness values using Levels and Curves. I also document Photoshop's fantastic new adjustment layers.

Chapter 19: The Wonders of Blend Modes, describes everything you need to know about mixing images from different layers or even different windows. I answer such burning questions as how blend modes work, how to drop out colors in a layer and force through colors from underneath, and what you do when channel operations fail to provide sufficient control.

Chapter 20: Creating Graphics for the Web, tells you how to create images you'll be proud to post on the World Wide Web. I explain how to account for differences in screen brightness, how to save progressive JPEG images, and how to downsize the color palette for GIF graphics. I also tell you all about the hottest new Web format, PNG.

Part VII: Appendixes

Five — count 'em, five — appendixes follow Chapter 20. The first two provide some information about hardware and software issues related to Photoshop 4 and Windows 95; the third explains how to install Photoshop onto your hard drive; the fourth provides complete information about the photographers, image collections, and news services that contributed images to this book; and the fifth explains the expansive contents of the CD-ROM in the back of the book.

Last, but not least, is an astonishingly comprehensive index. It'll knock your socks off, should you be wearing any.

Conventions

Every computer book seems to conform to a logic all its own, and this one's no exception. Although I try to avoid pig latin — *ellway, orfay hetay ostmay artpay* — I do subscribe to a handful of conventions you may not immediately recognize.

Vocabulary

Call it computerese, call it technobabble, call it the synthetic jargon of propeller heads. The fact is, I can't explain Photoshop in graphic and gruesome detail without reverting to the specialized language of the trade. To help you keep up, however, I italicized vocabulary words (as in *random-access memory*) with which you may not be familiar or that I use in an unusual context. An italicized term is followed by a definition.

If you come across a strange word that is *not* italicized (that bit of italics was for emphasis), look it up in the index to find the first reference to the word in the book.

Commands and options

To distinguish the literal names of commands, dialog boxes, buttons, and so on, I capitalize the first letter in each word (for example, click the Cancel button). The only exceptions are option names, which can be six or seven words long and filled with prepositions like *to* and *of.* Traditionally, prepositions and articles (*a, an, the*) don't appear in initial caps, and this book follows that time-honored rule, too.

When discussing menus and commands, I use an arrow symbol to indicate hierarchy. For example, Choose File ➪ Open means to choose the Open command from the File menu. If you have to display a submenu to reach a command, I list the command used to display the submenu between the menu name and the final command. Choose Image ➪ Adjust ➪ Invert means to choose the Adjust command from the Image menu and then choose the Invert command from the Adjust submenu.

Version numbers

A new piece of software comes out every 15 minutes. That's not a real statistic, mind you, but I bet I'm not far off. Photoshop currently has advanced to Version 4.0. But by the time you read this, the version number may be seven hundredths of a percentage point higher. So know that when I write Photoshop 4, I mean any version of Photoshop short of 5 (if that ever occurs).

Similarly, when I write Photoshop 3, I mean Versions 3.0, 3.0.1, 3.0.3, 3.0.4, and 3.0.5. Photoshop 2.5 means 2.5 and 2.5.1; Photoshop 2 means 2.0 and 2.01; and Photoshop 1 means anything up to Version 1.0.7.

Icons

Like nearly every computer book currently available on your green grocer's shelves, this one includes alluring icons that focus your eyeballs smack dab on important information. The icons make it easy for folks who like to skim books to figure out what the heck's going on. Icons serve as little insurance policies against short attention spans. On the whole, the icons are self-explanatory, but I'll explain them anyway.

 The Caution icon warns you a step you're about to take may produce disastrous results. Well, perhaps *disastrous* is an exaggeration. Inconvenient, then. Uncomfortable. For heaven's sake, use caution.

 The Note icon highlights some little tidbit of information I've decided to share with you that seemed at the time remotely related to the topic. I might tell you how an option came into existence, why a feature is implemented as it is, or how things used to be better back in the old days.

 The Photoshop 4 icon explains an option, command, or other feature that is brand spanking new to this latest revision. If you're already familiar with previous versions of Photoshop, you might want to plow through the book looking for Photoshop 4 icons and see what new stuff is out there.

 This book is bursting with tips and techniques. If I were to highlight each of them, whole pages would be gray with icons popping out all over the place. The Tip icon calls attention to shortcuts that are specifically applicable to the Photoshop application. For the bigger, more useful power tips, I'm afraid you'll actually have to read the text.

 The New Technology icon highlights every one of those weird pieces of software and hardware that have managed to change the way we work completely. You may not have these products yet, but you might want to look into them.

 The Cross-Reference icon tells you where to go for information related to the current topic. I included one a few pages back and you probably read it without thinking twice. This means you're either sharp as a tack or an experienced computer book user. Either way, you won't have any trouble with this icon.

I thought of including one more icon to alert you to every new bit of information — whether Photoshop 4-dependent or not — included in this book. But I found myself using it in every other paragraph. Besides, that would have robbed you of the fun of discovering the new stuff yourself.

About operating systems

Photoshop 4 runs on Windows 95, Windows 3.1, and Windows NT. As you probably deduced from the title of this book, I focus primarily on Windows 95. But that isn't to say I neglect the other versions of Windows — at least, not totally. You'll find some information relevant to Windows 3.1 and Windows NT scattered here and there. (Whenever I say Windows 3.1, by the way, I mean Windows 3.1 and Windows for Workgroups 3.11).

How to Bug Me

Even though this book is in its second edition and has been scanned by hundreds of thousands of readers' eyes and scanned about 60 times by the eyes of my editor, I'll bet someone, somewhere will still manage to locate errors and oversights. If you notice those kinds of things and you have a few spare moments, please let me know what you think. I always appreciate readers' comments.

If you want to share your insights, comments, or corrections, please contact me over the Internet at dekemc@internetMCI.com. Or try me on America Online at plain old DekeMc. (Sorry, my old CompuServe account is finis.) Don't fret if you don't hear from me for a few days, or months, or ever. I read every letter and try to implement nearly every idea anyone bothers to send me.

I also urge you to visit my Web site, the infamous http://www.dekemc.com. There you'll find news and excerpts about my books, tips for various graphics products, and other goofy online stuff. Let me know what you think.

Now, without further ado, I urge you to turn the page and advance forward into the great untamed frontier of image editing. But, remember, this book can be a dangerous tool if wielded unwisely. Don't set it on any creaky card tables or let your children play with it without the assistance of a stalwart adult, preferably an All-Star Wrestler or that guy who played the Incredible Hulk on TV. And no flower pressing. The little suckers would be pummeled to dust by this monstrously powerful colossus of a book.

Acknowledgments

Thank you to the following people and companies for their assistance in providing me with the information and product loans I needed to complete this book.

Mark Hamburg, Russell Preston Brown, Sonya Schaefer, Patricia Pane, and Andrei Herasimchuk at Adobe Systems

Charles Smith at Digital Stock

Tom Hughes and Sophia McShea at PhotoDisc

John Palmer and Dan Patrick at Palmers

Kevin Hurst at Extensis

Sumeet Pasricha at Andromeda

Jeff Butterworth at Alien Skin Software

Paul Badger, Chris Cox, and Hugh Kawahara

Steve Zahm at DigitalThink

Burton Holmes at Burton Holmes Associates

Bruce Berkoff at Umax

and my excellent technical editor, Marc Pawlinger at Adobe

Additional kudos to the artists who contributed their work to this book: Jeff Brice, Steve Campbell, Christopher Ching, Kevin Curry, Diane Fenster, Larry Goode, Ranulfo Ponce, and Greg Vander Houwen.

A very special thank you to Amy Thomas, Wendy Sharp, Nancy Dunn, Marjorie Baer, Mark Collen, Denise McClelland, Russell McDougal, John Kilcullen, Matt Wagner, and Robert Swirksy-Warner.

Last, but not least, thanks a dozen times over to Julie King for another fine job in adapting this edition for the Windows platform.

Contents at a Glance

Contents

Welcome to Photoshop 4

Getting to Know Photoshop

What Is Photoshop?

Adobe Photoshop is the most popular image-editing application available for use on Macintosh and Windows-based computers. Despite hefty competition from programs such as Macromedia xRes, Wright Design, and others, Adobe Systems, Inc., reports that Photoshop's sales account for more than 80 percent of the image-editing market. (The estimate includes Fractal Design Painter, an image-creation program that does not strictly compete with Photoshop.) This makes Photoshop four times more popular than all its competitors combined.

Note The term *application* — as in *image-editing application* — is just another word for computer program. Photoshop satisfies a specific purpose, so programmers abuse the language by calling it an application. The word is also used in the conventional sense throughout the book, as in "Photoshop has many applications." Hopefully, you won't become hopelessly confused.

Photoshop 4.0 If you're already familiar with Photoshop and you just want to scope out its new capabilities, skip to the section "Fast Track to Version 4."

Photoshop's long-term advantage

Photoshop's historically lopsided sales advantage provides Adobe with a clear incentive to reinvest in Photoshop and regularly enhance — even overhaul — its capabilities. Meanwhile, other vendors have had to devote smaller resources to playing catch-up. Although competitors provide interesting and sometimes amazing capabilities, the sums of their parts remain inferior to Photoshop.

As a result, Photoshop rides a self-perpetuating wave of industry predominance. Photoshop hasn't always been the best image editor, and it wasn't the earliest one either. But its deceptively straightforward interface, combined with a few terrific core functions, made it a hit from the moment of its first release. More than half a decade later — thanks to substantial capital injections and highly creative programming on the part of Adobe's staff and Photoshop originators, Thomas and John Knoll — Photoshop has evolved into the most popular program of its kind.

A brief history of image editing

Image editing really began on the Macintosh in the late 1980s. The first image editor for the Mac was ImageStudio, a grayscale program from Fractal Design, creator of ColorStudio and Painter. The first Macintosh image editor to feature color was an Avalon Development Group entry called PhotoMac, now all but forgotten. Rumor had it the best photo editor during this time was Lumena from Time Arts, a DOS-based program that ran on IBM PCs and compatibles.

Meanwhile, Photoshop began as Tom Knoll's graduate school project. If brother John hadn't quickly put Photoshop to work within the hallowed walls of George Lucas's Industrial Light and Magic, the program might never have seen the light of day, much less become the dominant player in computer graphics. Even when Adobe purchased the product in 1990, Photoshop was viewed as a modest-selling companion piece for the company's bread and butter, Illustrator. Little did anyone guess the tail would end up wagging the dog, with Illustrator, Macromedia FreeHand, and every other drawing program on the planet scurrying to ride the coattails of Photoshop.

Image-Editing Theory

Having used mirrors, dry ice, and some rather titillating industry analysis to convince you of Photoshop's prowess, I will now answer that burning question: What the heck does Photoshop do?

Like any image editor, Photoshop enables you to alter photographs and other scanned artwork. You can retouch an image, apply special effects, swap details between photos, introduce text and logos, adjust color balance, and even add color to a grayscale scan. Photoshop also provides the tools you need to create images from scratch. These tools are fully compatible with pressure-sensitive tablets, so you can create naturalistic images that look for all the world like watercolors and oils.

Bitmaps versus objects

Image editors fall into the larger software category of *painting programs.* In a painting program, you draw a line, and the application converts it to tiny square dots called *pixels.* The painting itself is called a *bitmapped image,* but *bitmap* and *image* are equally acceptable terms. Every program discussed so far is a painting program. Other examples include Corel Photo-Paint, Micrografx Picture Publisher, and Ulead PhotoImpact.

Note

Photoshop uses the term *bitmap* exclusively to mean a black-and-white image, the logic being that each pixel conforms to one bit of data, 0 or 1 (off or on). To avoid ad hoc syllabic mergers like pix-map — and because forcing a distinction between a painting with exactly two colors and one with anywhere from 4 to 16 million colors is entirely arbitrary — the term bitmap is used more broadly to mean any image composed of a fixed number of pixels, regardless of the number of colors involved.

What about other graphics applications, such as Adobe Illustrator and Macromedia FreeHand? Illustrator, FreeHand, CorelDRAW, and others fall into a different category of software called *drawing programs.* Drawings comprise objects, which are independent, mathematically defined lines and shapes. For this reason, drawing programs are sometimes said to be *object-oriented.* Some folks prefer the term *vector-based,* but I hate that because vector implies the physical components — direction and magnitude — generally associated with straight lines. Besides, my preference suggests an air of romance, as in, "Honey, I'm bound now for the Object Orient."

Illustrator and FreeHand are sometimes called *illustration programs,* though this is more a marketing gimmick — you know, like Father's Day — than a legitimate software category. The idea is Illustrator and FreeHand provide a unique variety of features unto themselves. In reality, their uniqueness extends little beyond more reliable printing capabilities and higher prices.

The ups and downs of painting

Painting programs and drawing programs each have their strengths and weaknesses. The strength of a painting program is it offers an extremely straightforward approach to creating images. For example, although many of Photoshop's features are complex — exceedingly complex on occasion — its core painting tools are as easy to use as a pencil. You alternately draw and erase until you reach a desired effect, just as you've been doing since grade school. (Of course, for all I know, you've been using computers since grade school. If you're pushing 20, you probably managed to log in many happy hours on paint programs in your formative years. Then again, if you're under 20, you're still in your formative years. Shucks, we're all in our formative years. Wrinkles, expanding tummies, receding hairlines . . . if that's not a new form, I don't know what is.)

In addition to being simple to use, each of Photoshop's core painting tools is fully customizable. It's as if you have access to an infinite variety of crayons, colored pencils, pastels, airbrushes, watercolors, and so on, all of which are entirely erasable. Doodling on the phone book was never so much fun.

The downside of a painting program is it limits your *resolution* options. Because bitmaps contain a fixed number of pixels, the resolution of an image — the number of pixels per inch — is dependent upon the size at which the image is printed, as demonstrated in Figure 1-1. Print the image small and the pixels become tiny, which increases resolution; print the image large and the pixels grow, which decreases resolution. An image that fills a standard 13-inch screen (640 × 480 pixels) prints with smooth color transitions when reduced to, say, half the size of a postcard. But if you print that same image without reducing it, you may be able to distinguish individual pixels, which means you can see jagged edges and blocky transitions. The only way to remedy this problem is to increase the number of pixels in the image, which dramatically increases the size of the file on disk.

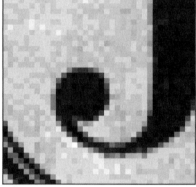

Figure 1-1: When printed small, a painting appears smooth (left). But when printed large, it appears jagged (right).

Cross Reference

Remember, this is a simplified explanation of how images work. For a more complete description that includes techniques for maximizing image performance, refer to the "How Images Work" section of Chapter 4.

The downs and ups of drawing

Painting programs provide tools reminiscent of traditional art tools. A drawing program, on the other hand, features tools with no real-world counterparts. The process of drawing might more aptly be termed *constructing*, because you actually build lines and shapes point by point, and then stack them on top of each other to create a finished image. Each object is independently editable — one of the few structural advantages of an object-oriented approach — but you're still faced with the task of building your artwork one chunk at a time.

Nevertheless, because a drawing program defines lines, shapes, and text as mathematical equations, these objects automatically conform to the full resolution of the output device, whether it's a laser printer, imagesetter, or film recorder. The drawing program sends the math to the printer and the printer renders the math to paper or film. In other words, the printer converts the drawing program's equations to printer pixels. Your printer offers far more pixels than your screen — a 300 dots-per-inch (dpi) laser printer, for example, offers 300 pixels per inch (dots equal pixels) whereas most screens offer 72 pixels per inch. So the printed drawing appears smooth and sharply focused, regardless of the size at which you print it, as shown in Figure 1-2.

Another advantage of drawings is they take up relatively little room on disk. The file size of a drawing depends on the quantity and complexity of the objects the drawing contains. Thus, the file size has almost nothing to do with the size of the printed image, which is the opposite of the way bitmapped images work. A thumbnail drawing of a garden containing hundreds of leaves and petals consumes several times more disk space than a poster-sized drawing containing three rectangles.

Figure 1-2: Small or large, a drawing prints smoothly, but it's a pain to create. This one took more than an hour of my day and, as you can see, I didn't even bother with the letters around the perimeter of the design.

When to use Photoshop

Thanks to their specialized methods, painting programs and drawing programs fulfill distinct and divergent purposes. Photoshop and other painting programs are best suited to creating and editing the following kinds of artwork:

✦ Scanned photos, including photographic collages and embellishments that originate from scans

✦ Realistic artwork that relies on the play between naturalistic highlights, midranges, and shadows

✦ Impressionistic-type artwork and other images created for purely personal or aesthetic purposes

✦ Logos and other display type featuring soft edges, reflections, or tapering shadows

✦ Special effects that require the use of filters and color enhancements you simply can't achieve in a drawing program

✦ Nearly any graphic or photograph you intend to post on the World Wide Web

When to use a drawing program

You're probably better off using Illustrator, FreeHand, or some other drawing program if you're interested in creating more stylized artwork, such as the following:

✦ Poster art and other high-contrast graphics that heighten the appearance of reality

✦ Architectural plans, product designs, or other precise line drawings

✦ Business graphics, such as charts and other *infographics* that reflect data or show how things work

✦ Traditional logos and text effects that require crisp, ultrasmooth edges (Drawing programs are unique because they enable you to edit character outlines to create custom letters and symbols)

✦ Brochures, flyers, and other single-page documents that mingle artwork, logos, and standard-sized text (such as the text you're reading now)

If you're serious about computer graphics, you should own at least one painting program and one drawing program. If I had to rely exclusively on two graphics applications, I would probably choose Photoshop and Illustrator. Both are Adobe products, and the two function together almost without a hitch. Much to its credit, though, FreeHand also works remarkably well in combination with Photoshop.

The Computer Design Scheme

If your aspirations go beyond image editing into the larger world of computer-assisted design, you'll soon learn Photoshop is a single cog in a mighty wheel of programs used to create artwork, printed documents, and presentations.

The natural-media paint program Fractal Design Painter emulates real-world tools, such as charcoal, chalk, felt-tip markers, calligraphic pen nibs, and camel-hair brushes as deftly as a synthesizer mimics a thunderstorm. Three-dimensional drawing applications such as Caligari trueSpace and Ray Dream Designer enable you to create hyper-realistic objects with depth, lighting, shadows, surface textures, reflections, refractions — you name it. These applications can import images created in Photoshop, as well as export images, which you can then enhance and adjust with Photoshop.

Page-layout programs such as Adobe PageMaker and QuarkXPress from Quark, Inc., enable you to integrate images into newsletters, reports, books (such as this one), and nearly any other kind of document you can imagine. If you prefer to transfer your message to slides, you can use Adobe Persuasion or Microsoft PowerPoint to add impact to your images through the use of charts and diagrams.

With Adobe Premiere, you can merge images with video sequences recorded in the QuickTime format. You can even edit individual frames in Premiere movies with Photoshop. Macromedia Director makes it possible to combine images with animation, QuickTime movies, and sound to create multimedia presentations you can show on a screen or record on videotape.

The latest rage in screen design is the World Wide Web. Using Adobe PageMill, Microsoft FrontPage, or Netscape Navigator, you can create Web pages that include lots of fast-loading screen images. The Web is single-handedly breathing new life and respectability into low-resolution images.

Photoshop Scenarios

All the programs just described run on the PC with Windows. But the number of programs you decide to purchase and how you decide to use them is up to you. The following list outlines a few specific ways to use Photoshop alone and in tandem with other products:

✦ After scanning and adjusting an image inside Photoshop, use PageMaker or QuarkXPress to place the image into your monthly newsletter, and then print the document from the page-layout program.

✦ After putting the finishing touches on a lovely tropical vista inside Photoshop, import the image for use as an eye-catching background inside

PowerPoint. Then save the document as a self-running screen presentation or print it to overhead transparencies or slides from the presentation program.

✦ Capture an onscreen image (by pressing the Print Screen key or by using a screen capture utility). Then open the screen shot and edit it in Photoshop. Place the corrected image into Illustrator or FreeHand, annotate the screen shot using arrows and labels, and print it from the drawing program.

✦ Paint an original image inside Photoshop using a Wacom pressure-sensitive tablet. Use the image as artwork in a document created in a page-layout program or print it directly from Photoshop.

✦ Snap a photo with a digital camera, such as Kodak's DC50 or Epson's PhotoPC. Correct the focus and brightness in Photoshop (as explained in Chapters 15 and 18). Then add the photo to your personal Web site using PageMill or a similar program.

✦ Scan a surface texture, such as wood or marble, into Photoshop and edit it to create a fluid, repeating pattern (as explained in Chapter 10). Import the image for use as a texture map in a three-dimensional drawing program. Render the 3D graphic to an image file, open the image inside Photoshop, and retouch as needed.

✦ Create a repeating pattern, save as a .BMP format file, and use it as Windows wallpaper.

✦ Take a problematic Illustrator EPS file that keeps generating errors when you try to print it, open the file inside Photoshop, and render it as a high-resolution bitmap. Then place the image in a document created in a page-layout program or print it directly from Photoshop. Many top drawing programs, including FreeHand and CorelDRAW, support the Illustrator format.

✦ Start an illustration in a drawing program and save it as an Illustrator EPS file. Open the file in Photoshop and use the program's unique tools to add textures and tones that are difficult or impossible to create in a vector-based drawing program.

✦ Record a QuickTime movie in Premiere and export it to the Filmstrip format. Open the file inside Photoshop and edit it one frame at a time by drawing on the frame or by applying filters. Finally, open the altered Filmstrip file in Premiere and convert it back to the QuickTime format.

Obviously, few folks have the money to buy all these products and even fewer have the energy or inclination to implement every one of these ideas. But, quite honestly, these are only a handful of projects I can list off the top of my head. Hundreds of uses must exist for Photoshop that involve no outside applications whatsoever. So far as I can figure, there's no end to the number of design jobs you can handle in whole or in part using Photoshop.

Simply put, this is a versatile and essential product for any designer or artist who currently uses or plans to purchase a Macintosh or Windows-based computer. I, for one, wouldn't remove Photoshop from my hard drive for a thousand bucks. (Of course, that's not to say I wouldn't consider higher offers. For $1,500, I'd gladly swap it to a Jaz cartridge.)

Fast Track to Version 4

Photoshop 4.0

If it seems like you've been using Photoshop 3 for the better part of your professional career and you're itching to strap on the new version and ride, the following list explains everything. Here I've compiled a few of the most prominent features new to Photoshop 4, in rough order of importance. I also point you to the chapter where you can rocket on to more information.

✦ **Adjustment layers (Chapter 18):** In the old days, you had to color-correct each layer independently. But in Photoshop 4, you can create an adjustment layer that affects every layer under it. This means you can modify the brightness, contrast, and color balance of multiple layers at one time. Plus, these modifications are temporary, so you can come back and revise the settings any time you like. You can even paint in affected and protected areas using a layer mask. It's a little bit of Live Picture in Photoshop.

✦ **Good-bye floating selections (Chapter 13):** Photoshop 3 introduced layers, but Version 4 forces you to use them. The type tool creates a new layer, the Paste command creates a new layer, even Ctrl+J creates a new layer. In fact, floating selections are, for all practical purposes, dead. Taking their place are a host of layer-management and merging capabilities that make working with layers much easier.

✦ **Advanced transformation capabilities (Chapter 13):** Photoshop's rotation and resizing capabilities used to be so lame, I didn't even bother to document them in this book. But this changed with Photoshop 4. You can now experiment with moving, scaling, and rotating a selection all at the same time without making permanent changes to the image. You can even apply numerical transformations. It's about time.

✦ **Expanded support for Web graphics (Chapter 20):** According to Adobe, more than half of Photoshop artists use the program to create Web graphics, and this number is growing. That's why Photoshop 4 provides built-in support for Mac, Windows, and Web color palettes. You can also save images in a variety of Web formats — including interlaced GIF, progressive JPEG, PNG, and PDF — using the standard Save command. Chapter 20 of this book is your guide to creating Web graphics in Photoshop.

✦ **Enhanced navigation capabilities (Chapter 2):** Photoshop 4 adds new keyboard shortcuts for magnifying and reducing your image onscreen. It also introduces the Navigator palette, which enables you to scroll and zoom large images by dragging inside a miniature thumbnail. And if this doesn't satisfy your needs, you can zoom with 0.01-percent accuracy.

✦ **Scripting and batch processing (Chapter 3):** The Commands palette has spun a cocoon and metamorphosed into the Actions palette. This new palette not only enables you to assign keyboard shortcuts to commands, but also group commands into repeatable sequences. You can even have Photoshop batch-process entire folders full of images while you go out for lunch. The Actions palette isn't perfect, but it's easy to use and a heck of an improvement over its predecessor.

✦ **Fading filters (Chapter 15):** I've been yammering about the benefits of mixing a filtered image with the unfiltered original for years now; I guess someone at Adobe decided to listen. After you apply a filter like Unsharp Mask or Gaussian Blur, you can mix the result with the original by choosing Filter ➪ Fade (or pressing Ctrl+Shift+F). You gotta love it.

✦ **Better layer masks (Chapter 13):** Most Photoshop users don't pay much attention to layer masks, but you have new reasons to check them out in Photoshop 4. First of all, some commands — such as Paste Inside — automatically generate layer masks. Second, adjustment layers use masks to determine which areas are affected and which are not. Third, you can now create layer masks with the click of a button. And fourth, you can load layer masks as selection outlines and convert selections to masks. I'm not normally one for predictions, but I'm guessing layer masks are going to be bigger than the "Macarena."

✦ **Grids and guides (Chapter 13):** Also look to lucky Chapter 13 for the straight dope on Photoshop's new grids and guides. You can drag guides from the ruler, specify a grid, and otherwise establish a structured working environment. And don't be thinking these new features are just for looks — these grids and guides snap like turtles.

✦ **Improved gradients (Chapter 9):** Now you can create custom gradients that contain three or more colors, much as in sibling Illustrator. You can also assign transparency to a gradient, something you could only do with third-party plug-ins in the past. The new gradients aren't as robust as those in, say, Kai's Power Tools, but they come close.

✦ **Linking layers (Chapter 13):** You could always move two or more layers together. But now you can link layers together so they rotate, resize, flip, skew, distort, and otherwise transform as a group. (Don't confuse this new linking feature with the confusingly named Group command, which merely creates a clipping group.)

✦ **Improved distortion previews (Chapter 16):** The distortion filters — under the Filter ➪ Distort submenu — were the first Photoshop filters to offer previews. But after the other filters added previews in Photoshop 3, the puny little zoomed-out distortion thumbnails appeared comically inaccurate and provided only a hint of the effect you could expect to achieve. This changes in Photoshop 4. Although you can't preview an effect in the Image window, the dialog box previews are finally up to snuff.

✦ **The more prominent move tool (Chapter 11):** The move tool used to be reserved for moving whole layers. Now you must use the move tool to move or clone any pixel, whether in a selection or on a layer. You can temporarily access the move tool when another tool is active by pressing the Ctrl key. But this upsets old Ctrl+key tasks, such as subtracting from a selection outline, which have mutated into Alt+key tasks. This is extremely confusing at first but, ultimately, it makes a good deal of sense. I walk you through the entire thorny issue in Chapter 11.

✦ **Revised interface (Chapter 2):** Photoshop 4 is packed with little interface enhancements that go a long way toward making the program more consistent. For example, you can tab through option boxes in the palettes and even jump from one palette to the next. You can adjust values in the Colors palette numerically, access all tools from the Toolbox, hide and show paths, and bring up context-sensitive pop-up menus by right-clicking. The downside is much of this housekeeping comes at the expense of age-old techniques that are second nature for many of us. For the experienced user, Photoshop 4.0 takes some serious adjustment.

✦ **New type mask tool (Chapter 14):** In Photoshop, text is simply a bunch of filled selection outlines in the shape of familiar characters. Now you can bag the fill and create the selection outlines directly. Just use the new type mask tool, available in the type tool pop-up menu.

✦ **Stacking order shortcuts (Chapter 13):** You can now send layers forward and backward using keyboard shortcuts and menu commands. You can still drag layer names up and down in the Layers palette, but the shortcuts are more convenient. And you never know — these same keystrokes might pop up in Illustrator and PageMaker.

✦ **More amenable sanitation service (Chapter 3):** You can now click the trash can icon in the Layers, Channels, Paths, and Actions palettes to delete the selected item. Photoshop displays an alert box to make certain your click wasn't a mistake. To bypass the message, Alt+click the trash can icon.

✦ **Hot link to Adobe's Web site (Chapter 2):** Choose Help ➪ Adobe Photoshop Home Page to open an HTML file Photoshop automatically installs on your hard disk. If you have a live connection to the Internet, you can then click the hypertext (underlined text) in the HTML page to link to various pages in Adobe's Web site. This is a great way to find information about the latest Photoshop upgrades and documentation.

For you special effects nuts, Version 4 integrates the 48 filters from the old Gallery Effects collection (as I explain in Chapter 16). You also get three new blend modes (covered in Chapters 8 and 19), a few handy Delete-key techniques (Chapter 9), a new image-caching scheme (Chapter 2), and a special polygonal lasso tool to make up for the wacky revisions to Alt+clicking (Chapter 11).

Frankly, this isn't the most dramatic upgrade to Photoshop, but it may be the most bewildering. Instead of a few big modifications, we have loads of little ones. Watch for the Photoshop 4.0 icon in this book to get you over the hump and back into the image-editing groove again.

Inside
Photoshop

The New Look and Feel of Photoshop 4

This chapter introduces Photoshop's tools, palettes, and other interface ingredients. Normally, I would recommend these pages as essential reading to new Photoshop users. (In fact, if you are a new user, skip to "The Photoshop Desktop" section and dive right in.) But you experienced folks should browse through the "Customizing the Interface" section only if you're trying to decipher some weird new preference setting, like the Use Cache for Histograms check box.

Photoshop 4 is not your typical upgrade, though. This is one version of the program that's likely to challenge experienced users nearly as much as their novice counterparts. Photoshop 4 offers a numerical magnification option, three new zoom commands, and a full-blown Navigator palette. The crop tool is now grouped with the marquee tools, the path tools have moved into the Toolbox, and two variations exist for each of the lasso and type tools. One menu has disappeared, another menu has moved, and two new ones have sprouted up. The cursors have changed, the Scratch palette is dead, and the Preferences dialog box is completely revamped. In short, your Photoshop world has turned upside down.

Adobe has restructured Photoshop from the ground up, sometimes bravely forging ahead for the long-term good, sometimes recklessly trampling over time-honored techniques. But whatever your take on the new version, it is the way it is. Adobe is unlikely to go back to the old ways — regardless of the inevitable grumbling — because of its internal mandate to homogenize features among Photoshop, Illustrator, and PageMaker. You can go back to Photoshop 3 — and, undoubtedly, some will — but don't expect things in Photoshop 5, 6, or 7 to return to the way they were in earlier versions.

In this regard, Photoshop 4 is less an enhancement than an immutable force of nature. Do what you would do if your work was interrupted by a power outage or a similar inconvenience: Buck up and adapt. Start by skimming this chapter, watching for the Photoshop 4 icon. Then proceed to Chapter 3 and read it, too. (If you think the interface has changed, wait until you get a load of the keyboard modifiers. The shortcuts are shaken, not stirred.) When you finish, your head may still be spinning, but at least the initial seasickness will have gone.

The Photoshop Splash Screen

Shortly after you launch Photoshop, the Photoshop splash screen appears. Shown at the top of Figure 2-1, the splash screen explains the launching process by telling you which plug-in modules are loading. Any time you run Photoshop, you can access the splash screen by choosing Help ➪ About Photoshop.

If you need help installing Photoshop, see Appendix C, "Installing Photoshop 4."

I know no one cares about the splash screen. In fact, the only reason I even mention it is Photoshop 4 offers a few splash screen-related tips and tricks:

✦ If it's too much effort to choose Help ➪ About Photoshop, you can display the splash screen by clicking that little eyeball icon at the top of the Toolbox.

✦ If you Alt+click the Toolbox icon, you display the double-secret Big Electric Cat screen. (You can also press Alt when choosing the About Photoshop command.)

✦ In the Mac version of Photoshop, you can click the cat's nose to make him belch. Sadly, the Windows version offers no such amusement.

✦ Click the Adobe icon in the upper-left corner of the splash screen to open the Adobe Web page in your favorite browser (most likely Netscape Navigator). If you have Internet access, you can navigate from the page into Adobe's online Web site. (You can accomplish the same thing by choosing Help ➪ Adobe Photoshop Home Page.)

Figure 2-1: The splash screen from Photoshop 4, as well as its hidden companion

After the splash screen or Big Electric Cat screen has been displayed for a few seconds, the list of programmers and copyright statement at the bottom of the splash screen begins to scroll. Press the Alt key to make the list scroll more quickly. The final line of the scrolling message thanks you, of all people, for being "one of our favorite customers."

To make the splash screen go away, click it.

The Photoshop Desktop

After the launch process is complete, the Photoshop desktop consumes the foreground. Figure 2-2 shows the Photoshop 4 desktop as it appears when an image is open and all palettes are visible.

Many of the elements that make up the Photoshop desktop are well-known to folks familiar with the Windows environment. For example, the menu bar provides access to menus and commands. You can drag the Title bar to move the Image window. And the scroll bars enable you to view hidden portions of the image.

Other elements of the Photoshop desktop work as follows:

✦ **Image window:** You can open as many images in Photoshop as RAM and virtual memory allow. Each open image resides inside its own window.

✦ **Status bar:** As in other Windows programs, the Status bar provides information about the currently selected tool and active image. (If the Status bar doesn't appear on your screen, choose Windows ⇨ Show Status Bar.) The left corner of the Status bar window features a Magnification box, which tells you the current view size, and a Preview box that lists the size of the foreground image in memory.

For complete information on the Magnification box, read the "Navigating Inside Photoshop 4" section later in this chapter. I explain the Preview box in the following section.

✦ **Toolbox:** The Toolbox offers 20 tool icons. The tools are organized into logical groups, starting with the selection tools on top; then the painting and editing tools; the path, type, and fill tools; and the two navigation tools at the bottom. To select a tool, click its icon. Then use the tool by clicking or dragging with it inside the Image window.

The lower third of the Toolbox features three sets of controls. The color controls enable you to change the colors with which you paint; the mask controls enable you to enter and exit the quick mask mode; and the Image window controls enable you to change the state of the foreground window on the desktop.

✦ **Floating palettes:** Like its predecessors, Photoshop 4 offers floating palettes, as labeled in Figure 2-2. *Floating* refers to each palette being independent of the Image window and of other palettes. The palettes contain multiple panels, which offer related, but independent, options. Read "The floating palettes" section later in this chapter for a brief overview of each of the palettes and their panels.

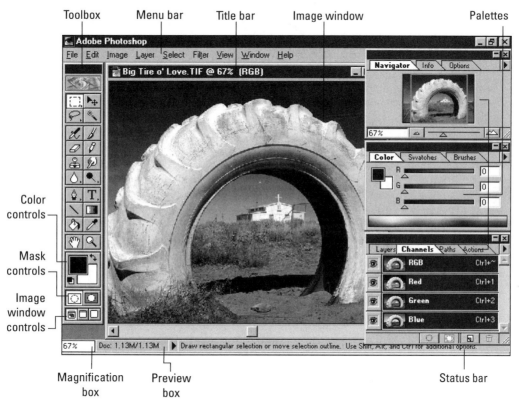

Figure 2-2: The Photoshop 4 desktop in all its glory

The Preview box

By default, the Preview box contains two numbers divided by a slash. The first number is the size of the base image in memory. Photoshop calculates this value by multiplying the height and width of the image (both in pixels) by the *bit depth* of the image, which is the size of each pixel in memory. A full-color RGB image takes up 3 bytes per pixel; a grayscale image takes up 1 byte per pixel; and a black-and-white image consumes 1 bit (or ⅛ byte) per pixel. This means a 640 × 480-pixel RGB image takes up 640 × 480 × 3 = 921,600 bytes, which is exactly 900K. (Exactly 1,024 bytes are in 1 kilobyte, and 1,024K are in 1 megabyte.)

The number after the slash takes into account any additional layers in your image. Photoshop measures the opaque pixels in each layer only; transparent pixels are ignored. If you transfer a 160×320-pixel selection of an RGB image to a new layer, for example, that layer consumes only $160 \times 320 \times 3$ = 153,600 bytes = 150K, even if the base image is much larger. If the image contains one layer only, the numbers before and after the slash are the same.

Click and hold on the Preview box to display a pop-up window that shows the placement of the image on the printed page. The preview even shows the approximate placement of crop marks and other elements requested in the Page Setup dialog box (File ➪ Page Setup).

Tip   Press Alt and mouse down on the Preview box to view the size and resolution of the image.

You can also Ctrl+click the Preview box to see the tile sizes. Photoshop uses *tiles* to calculate pixel manipulations. If you confine your work to a single tile, it will probably go faster than if you slop a little over into a second tile. But who cares? Unless you're some kind of tile-reading robot, this technical information is rarely of any practical use.

Click the right-pointing arrowhead next to the Preview box to display a pop-up menu of four options. The first option — Document Sizes — is selected by default. Document Sizes displays the image size values previously described.

Tip   The prefix displayed before the values in the Preview box indicates which of the four options is active: Doc indicates Document Sizes is selected; Scr, Scratch Sizes; and Eff, Efficiency. When the Timing option is active, an *s* appears after the numerical value.

The following sections explain how the three remaining options work.

Scratch sizes

When you select Scratch Sizes, Photoshop changes the values in the Preview box to represent memory consumption and availability. The first value is the amount of room required to hold all open images in RAM. This value is generally equal to about $3\,1/2$ times the sum total of all images, including layers. The value constantly updates, however, depending on the operations you perform, growing as large as five times the image size when floating images and complex operations are involved.

The second Preview box value indicates the amount of RAM space available to images after the Photoshop application is loaded. This value does not change unless you choose File ➪ Preferences ➪ Memory and Image Cache and change the Physical Memory Usage value.

If the value before the slash in the Preview box is larger than the value after the slash, Photoshop has to take advantage of virtual memory to display the open images. Virtual memory makes Photoshop run more slowly because the program must swap portions of the image on and off your hard disk. To speed the application, close one or more images until the first value is smaller than the second value. (If this isn't possible, don't sweat it. Virtual memory is an occasional fact of life when using Photoshop.)

You can do a number of things to improve performance, though. You should regularly run ScanDisk (if you're in the pre-Windows 95 world, Chkdsk) to search for and remove stray bits and pieces in your scratch disk partition. You should search for .TMP files, especially after Photoshop has crashed. Even when Photoshop hasn't crashed, you should still search for .TMP files. Under normal circumstances, Photoshop should clean up after itself; if you're finding .TMP files and haven't been crashing, your system needs some tweaking.

You can also improve efficiency by increasing the amount of free space available for the scratch disk. You can't restrict Photoshop. Set its scratch disk to a partition and Photoshop will gobble what it finds. Note: This must be free contiguous space — when you have a lot of fragmentation, Photoshop will only see the largest free contiguous block for its scratch disk. Hence, the value of dedicating one entire partition to the scratch disk and religiously checking it. When you must have the scratch disk in a partition where other files are located, regularly defragment and optimize/pack the free space. What you want is drive space at least five times the size of the image on which you plan to work. This is the ideal — you can work with only three times the size or even less.

Photoshop defaults to your startup partition (typically C:) for its scratch disk. I recommend you change it ASAP. Windows 95 uses that partition for its own virtual memory management. I can't prove you will have problems if you let Photoshop in there too, but you should do better with Photoshop doing its scratching elsewhere.

You may wish to set your scratch disk to removable media, such as a Jaz or Syquest drive. I don't recommend this, though, because those drives are substantially slower than your hard drive, meaning scratch disk operations will be substantially slower. Still, enough people have asked how to do this, so it's worth covering here. In your ...\Photoshop\Prefs\PHOTOS40.INI file, add a line that reads `AllowRemovableScratch=1` (the default for off is 0). When this switch is enabled, removable drives (including floppy drives) appear as possible scratch disk choices. Obviously, this may cause problems for Photoshop if media is removed at startup.

Background You may wonder why Photoshop uses a scratch disk rather than the main Windows virtual memory scheme like other Windows applications. Here's why. Photoshop originated on the Macintosh, which has a slow virtual memory scheme. So a private, improved virtual memory scheme (the scratch disk) was built into Photoshop from the start. An enormous code overhaul would have been required to change this setup for Photoshop's move to the Windows environment. And having a private scratch disk, even under Windows, allows Photoshop to operate faster because it doesn't have to share with anyone else.

Nevertheless, Photoshop is aware of the Windows virtual memory scheme. Under earlier versions, you needed a Permanent Swapfile equal to the amount of physical RAM on your system or Photoshop wouldn't open. This changed with Version 3.04. When the available physical RAM plus the Swapfile equal 21MB or greater, the program opens without complaint. Why? Obviously, it was bizarre (to say the least) for a machine with 64MB of RAM to need 64MB of swapfile on the hard drive. But the physical RAM isn't quite what you think. On, say, a 16MB machine, Photoshop will report about 8MB of RAM available. This happens because after loading, the program reserves a certain amount of RAM for various other processes. This algorithm is hardwired; you can't change it. So, to continue the 16MB example, if you have Windows 3.1/Windows for Workgroups and set the Permanent Swapfile to 13MB, you won't have a memory warning message. In Windows 95, you probably won't have to do this, if you accepted the default (Settings ⇨ Control Panel ⇨ System ⇨ Performance ⇨ Virtual Memory) to let Windows 95 manage your virtual memory. If you're running pre-Windows 95 and find Windows complains when you try to set your Permanent Swapfile to a larger size, ignore the complaint. This is an acknowledged bug. You can set it to the larger size — look in SYSTEM.INI afterward, and you'll see Windows has accepted your setting.

Note The various Distort filters perform their operations entirely in physical memory. The scratch disk may hold terabytes, but it won't do you any good. One workaround is performing those filter operations a channel at a time. If you're running under Windows 3.1 or Windows for Workgroups, 16MB is the largest block of memory that can be allocated — this is a limitation of the Win32s subsystem and, hence, a Microsoft issue. No such limitation exists under Windows 95 or Windows NT.

Efficiency

When you select the Efficiency option, Photoshop lists the amount of time it spends running operations in RAM compared with swapping data back and forth between the hard disk. A value of 100 percent is the best-case scenario. It means Photoshop never has to rely on virtual memory. Low values indicate higher reliance on the hard disk and, as a result, slower operations. Adobe recommends that if the value falls below 75 percent, you should either assign more memory to Photoshop or purchase more RAM for your computer.

The Efficiency option is a reality check. If it seems Photoshop is dragging its feet, and you hear it writing a little too often, you can refer to the Efficiency rating to see if things are as bad as you suspect. Remember, hearing Photoshop occasionally write to disk is not, in and of itself, cause for concern. All versions of Photoshop since 3.0 automatically copy open images to a disk buffer in case virtual memory is later warranted. In fact, this is the reason Adobe added the Efficiency option to Version 3.0.1 — to quash fears that a few sparks from your hard drive indicated anything less than peak performance.

Timing

The final option — Timing — is new to Photoshop 4. When selected, Timing tells how long Photoshop took to perform the last operation (including background tasks, such as transferring an image to the system Clipboard). Adobe may have added this option to help testing facilities run their Photoshop tests. But built-in timing helps you as well.

For example, suppose you're trying to decide whether to purchase a new computer. You read a magazine article comparing the newest super-fast system. You can run the same filters with the same settings on your computer and see how much slower your results are, all without picking up a stopwatch.

At the risk of starting interoffice feuding, the Timing option also provides you with a mechanism for testing your computer against those of coworkers and friends. The Timing option serves as a neutral arbitrator, enabling you and an associate to test identical operations over the phone. Like Efficiency, Timing is a reality check. If you and your associate own similarly configured computers and your Timing values are vastly different, something's wrong.

The tools

The new Photoshop 4 Toolbox shows only 20 of its 33 tools at any one time. The other tools are hidden inside pop-up menus. Any tool icon that includes a tiny right-pointing triangle harbors a pop-up menu with one or more alternate tools. As demonstrated in Figure 2-3, just drag on a tool to display the pop-up menu.

Tip

You can also Alt+click a tool icon to switch to the next tool in the pop-up menu.

Also, when you hover your cursor over a tool, Photoshop 4 tells you the name of the tool and how to select it from the keyboard. For example, *marquee tool (M)* means you can press the M key to get the marquee tool. I explain more about keyboard shortcuts in Chapter 3.

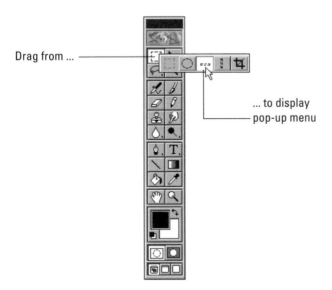

Drag from ...

... to display
pop-up menu

Figure 2-3: Drag from any tool icon with a triangle to
display a pop-up menu of alternates.

**Cross
Reference**

If you find the tool tips irritating, you can turn them off using File ➪ Preferences ➪
General (Ctrl+K). I explain more about this and other preference settings in the
"General preferences" section later in this chapter.

Despite the cosmetic changes to the Toolbox, most of the tools work just as they
did in Photoshop 3. The exceptions are the selection tools, which have changed
fairly dramatically thanks to the new role of the move tool. I touch on the
differences in the following brief descriptions but, for a complete analysis, read
Chapter 11.

Note

I've catalogued each tool in the following lengthy list, with tool icons, pithy
summaries, and the chapter to which you can refer for more information. No need
to read the list word for word; just use it as a reference to get acquainted with the
new program. Incidentally, unless otherwise noted, each of the following
descriptions tells how to use the tool inside the Image window. For example, if an
item says drag, you click the tool's icon to select the tool, and then drag in the
Image window; you don't drag on the tool icon itself.

⌐⌐ **Rectangular marquee (Chapter 11):** Drag with this tool to enclose a portion
of the image in a rectangular *marquee,* which is a pattern of moving dash
marks indicating the boundary of a selection.

Shift+drag to add to a selection; Alt+drag to delete from a selection (versus Ctrl+drag in Photoshop 3). The same goes for the other marquee tools, as well as the lasso and magic wand.

Elliptical marquee (Chapter 11): Drag with the elliptical marquee tool to enclose a portion of the window in an oval marquee.

Single-row marquee (Chapter 11): Click with the single-row marquee to select an entire horizontal row of pixels that stretches all the way across the image. You can also drag with the tool to position the selection. You'll rarely need it.

Single-column marquee (Chapter 11): Same as the single-row marquee, except the single-column marquee selects an entire vertical column of pixels. Again, not a particularly useful tool.

Crop (Chapter 4): Drag with the crop tool to enclose the portion of the image you want to retain in a rectangular boundary. The crop boundary sports several square handles you can drag to resize the cropped area.

Drag outside the boundary to rotate it. Drag inside the boundary to move it. Press Enter to crop away the portions of the image that lie outside the boundary; press Escape to cancel.

Move (Chapter 11): Drag to move the selected portion of an image. If no portion of the image is selected, dragging with the move tool moves the entire layer.

In Photoshop 4, the move tool is the exclusive means for moving and cloning selected portions of an image. (You can also Ctrl+drag selections with other tools, but only because Ctrl temporarily accesses the move tool.)

Lasso (Chapter 11): Drag with the lasso tool to select a free-form portion of the image. You can also Alt+click with the lasso to create a straight-sided selection outline.

Polygonal lasso (Chapter 11): Click hither and yon with this tool to draw a straight-sided selection outline (just like Alt+clicking with the standard lasso). Each click sets a corner point in the selection.

Magic wand (Chapter 11): Click with the magic wand tool to select a contiguous area of similarly colored pixels. To select discontiguous areas, click in one area and then Shift+click in another.

Airbrush (Chapter 8): Drag with the airbrush tool to spray diffused strokes of color that blend into the image, just the thing for creating shadows and highlights.

Paintbrush (Chapter 8): Drag with the paintbrush tool to paint soft lines, which aren't as jagged as those created with the pencil, but aren't as fluffy as those created with the airbrush.

✐   **Eraser (Chapter 10):** Drag with the eraser tool to paint in the background color or erase areas in a layer to reveal the layers below. Alt+drag to access the "magic" eraser, which changes portions of the image back to the way they appeared when last saved.

Tip   Four styles of erasers exist in all — paintbrush, airbrush, pencil, and square (called "block"). You can cycle through them by Alt+clicking the eraser tool icon in the Toolbox.

✏   **Pencil (Chapter 8):** Drag with the pencil tool to paint jagged lines.

♟   **Rubber stamp (Chapter 10):** The rubber stamp tool serves many functions, but you usually use it to copy one portion of the image onto another. Alt+click the part of your image you want to clone, and then drag to clone that area to another portion of the image.

Tip   You also can use the rubber stamp tool to paint with a pattern or to change portions of an image to the way they looked when last saved. To cycle through the seven alternative settings, Alt+click the rubber stamp tool icon in the Toolbox.

🖐   **Smudge (Chapter 8):** Drag with this tool to smear colors inside the image.

◊   **Blur (Chapter 8):** Drag with the blur tool to diffuse the contrast between neighboring pixels, which blurs the focus of the image. You can also Alt+drag to sharpen the image.

△   **Sharpen (Chapter 8):** Drag with this tool to increase the contrast between pixels, which sharpens the focus. Alt+drag when this tool is active to blur the image.

✦   **Dodge (Chapter 8):** Drag with the dodge tool to lighten pixels in the image. Alt+drag to darken the image.

✆   **Burn (Chapter 8):** Drag with the burn tool to darken pixels. Alt+drag to lighten.

◉   **Sponge (Chapter 8):** Drag with the sponge tool to decrease the amount of saturation in an image so the colors appear dimmer and, eventually, gray. You can also increase color saturation by changing the setting of the first pop-up menu in the Toning Tool Options palette from Desaturate to Saturate.

♙   **Pen (Chapter 11):** Once available only from the Paths palette, the pen tool and its cohorts are now included in the Toolbox. Use the pen tool by clicking and dragging to set points in the Image window. Photoshop draws an editable path outline — much like a path in Illustrator — that you can convert to a selection outline or stroke with color.

▷   **Direct selection (Chapter 11):** Use this tool — which I generally call the arrow tool — to edit a path drawn with the pen tool. You can drag points or control handles. Alt+click a path to select all its points and move the path as a whole.

Insert point (Chapter 11): Click a segment with this tool to insert a point in the path.

Remove point (Chapter 11): Click a point to remove the point without interrupting the outline of the path. Photoshop automatically draws a new segment between the neighboring points.

Convert point (Chapter 11): Points in a path come in different varieties, some indicating corners and others indicating smooth arcs. The convert point tool enables you to change one kind of point to another. Drag a point to convert it from a corner to an arc. Click a point to convert it from an arc to a sharp corner.

T **Type (Chapter 14):** Click with the type tool to display the Type Tool dialog box, which enables you to enter and format text. Note, you can't use the type tool to edit existing text as you would in a page-layout or drawing program. (Like any other image, type is just a bunch of colored dots. If you misspell a word, you have to erase it and try again.)

4.0 In Photoshop 4, the type tool creates text on a new layer. This way, you can edit the text and adjust the letter spacing using the selection tools without harming other parts of the image.

Type mask (Chapter 14): As with the standard type tool, clicking with the type mask tool brings up the Type Tool dialog box. But when you exit the dialog box, Photoshop creates the letters as transparent selection outlines. If you don't want to add a new layer, this is the type tool to use.

Line (Chapter 9): Drag with the line tool to create a straight line. Click the Start or End option in the Line Tool Options palette to add arrowheads.

Gradient (Chapter 9): Drag with this tool to fill a selection with a gradual transition of colors, commonly called a *gradient*.

4.0 By default, the gradient fades from the foreground color to the background color. But in Photoshop 4, you can create custom gradients by clicking the Edit button in the Gradient Tool Options palette.

Paint bucket (Chapter 9): Click with the paint bucket tool to fill a contiguous area of similarly colored pixels with the foreground color or a predefined pattern.

Eyedropper (Chapter 5): Click with the eyedropper tool on a color in the Image window to make that color the foreground color. Alt+click a color in the image to make that color the background color.

Hand (Chapter 2): Drag an image with the hand tool to scroll the window so you can see a different portion of the image. Double-click the hand tool icon to magnify or reduce the image so it fits on the screen in its entirety.

⬗ **Zoom (Chapter 2):** Click with the zoom tool to magnify the image so you can see individual pixels more clearly. Alt+click to step back from the image and take in a broader view. Drag to enclose the specific portion of the image you want to magnify. And, finally, double-click the zoom tool icon to restore the image to 100 percent view size.

Tip You can modify the performance of the active tool by adjusting the settings in the Options palette. To display this palette, double-click the tool icon in the toolbox. Or press the Enter key. Only the type tools lack palette options.

The cursors

Every version of Photoshop witnesses a cursor explosion, and Photoshop 4 is no exception. The cursor population has grown from a little over 50 in Photoshop 3 to nearly 100 in the current version. Most of these cursors are related to selection actions. A few correspond to a specific tool. And every one of them conveys special meaning.

You may think reading about every cursor amounts to a waste of time. And certainly my descriptions don't qualify as literary treats. But you must realize the cursor is Photoshop's way of communicating with you. Each cursor is a different visual cue in the program's onscreen vocabulary.

So don't read the entire list if you don't want to, but keep it close by as a handy reference. If you can't figure out what Photoshop is trying to say, look here to get the gist.

▲ **Arrow:** The left-pointing arrow appears any time the cursor is outside the Image window. You can select a tool, set palette options, or choose a command when this cursor is visible.

✛ **Marquee:** The cross appears when any of the marquee tools is active and the cursor is outside the selected area. If a marquee tool is active and no part of the image is selected, Photoshop shows you this cursor no matter what keys you press.

✛₊ **Add marquee:** When you press the Shift key to add to a selection with one of the marquee tools, you get this cursor.

✛₋ **Subtract marquee:** Press the Alt key and drag with one of the marquee tools to subtract from a selection.

✛ₓ **Intersect marquee:** When you Shift+Alt+drag with a marquee tool, you find the intersection of the dragged area and the previous selection outline. I explain this in more detail in Chapter 11.

◗ **Lasso:** The lasso cursor works the same way as the marquee cursor, except it indicates the lasso tool is selected.

Add lasso: Shift+drag with the lasso tool to get this cursor. It tells you Photoshop intends to add to your selection.

Subtract lasso: Alt+drag with the lasso tool to carve bits out of a selection.

Intersect lasso: Shift+Alt+drag with the lasso tool to find the intersection of the dragged area and the previous selection outline.

Polygonal lasso: When the polygonal lasso tool is selected and the cursor is positioned outside a selection, you get this cursor. It tells you Photoshop is ready to draw a new selection outline.

Add polygonal lasso: Shift+click with the polygonal lasso tool to add to a selection.

Subtract polygonal lasso: Alt+click with the polygonal lasso tool to clip away selected portions of the image.

Intersect polygonal lasso: Shift+Alt+click with the polygonal lasso tool to find the intersection of the enclosed area and the previous selection outline.

Close polygonal lasso: When you position the polygonal lasso cursor over the first point in the shape — the point at which you first clicked — you get this cursor. It tells you that clicking now will close the shape and finish the selection outline.

Wand: This cursor tells you Photoshop is ready to start a new magic wand selection the moment you click. Naturally, the magic wand tool must be selected and the cursor must be positioned over a deselected area in the image.

Add wand: Shift+click with the magic wand tool to add an area of contiguous color to a selection.

Subtract wand: Alt+click with the magic wand tool to remove a chunk from the selection.

Intersect wand: When you Shift+Alt+click with the magic wand, Photoshop selects an area of contiguous color that falls inside the previous selection.

Move selection outline: If you're familiar with previous versions of Photoshop, this may be the first of the new cursors to catch your attention. You get it when you previously got the right arrow — that is, when a selection tool is active and you move the cursor inside a selected portion of the image. But rather than moving the selected area, dragging with this cursor moves only the selection outline and leaves the image unchanged. You must use the move tool to modify the image.

Float and move: This is the cursor you want to see when preparing to move a selected area in an image. Either select the move tool or press the Ctrl key along with one of the other tools. Drag with this cursor to move the selection so it floats in front of some other portion of the image.

▶   **Move floater:** After the selection is floating, you can drag it with the move tool or any of the selection tools. This cursor tells you it's safe to drag. Don't click outside the floating selection, however, or you'll defloat the selection. (You also get this cursor when moving points in a path.)

▶   **Clone:** Alt+drag with the move tool to clone the selected portion of an image. If some other tool is selected, Ctrl+Alt+drag. (This cursor also appears when you clone a path by Alt+dragging it with the arrow tool.)

▶   **Move layer:** If you position the move tool cursor over a deselected portion of an image, you get this cursor. It tells you Photoshop is prepared to drag the selection or — if no portion of the image is selected — the entire layer.

⊄   **Crop:** This cursor appears when the crop tool is selected and remains onscreen until you marquee the portion of the image you want to retain.

↕   **Scale vertical:** After you draw the crop boundary, you can change its size by dragging one of the square handles. Drag the top or bottom handle to scale the boundary vertically. (This cursor and the three that follow also appear when scaling a selection using Layer ➪ Free Transform.)

↔   **Scale horizontal:** Drag the left or right handle to scale the crop boundary horizontally.

↘   **Scale top left/bottom right:** Drag the top-left or bottom-right handle to scale the crop boundary horizontally and vertically at the same time.

↗   **Scale top right/bottom left:** You can also scale the crop boundary both horizontally and vertically by dragging the top-right or bottom-left handle.

↻   **Rotate from right:** Position the cursor outside the crop boundary to get one of 12 rotate cursors. This one appears when the cursor is to the right of the boundary. Drag up to rotate counterclockwise; drag down to rotate clockwise. (All 12 rotate cursors also appear when rotating a selection using Layer ➪ Free Transform.)

↻   **Rotate from bottom right:** Again, this cursor appears when you position the crop tool outside the boundary, this time under the bottom-right corner. Drag to rotate.

↪   **Rotate from bottom:** This cursor appears when you move the crop tool under the boundary. Drag left to rotate clockwise; drag right to rotate counterclockwise.

↳   **Rotate from bottom left:** I'm guessing . . .

↺   **Rotate from left:** . . . that by now . . .

↱   **Rotate from top left:** . . . you're beginning . . .

↩   **Rotate from top:** . . . to get . . .

↱   **Rotate from top right:** . . . the idea.

Distort: Photoshop 4's new Free Transform command enables you to scale, rotate, move, skew, and otherwise distort a selection or layer in one continuous operation. After choosing Layer ➪ Free Transform, Ctrl+drag a corner handle to get this cursor. Photoshop distorts the image.

Skew vertical: Ctrl+Shift+drag the left or right handle of the transformation boundary to skew the image vertically.

Skew horizontal: You might care to Ctrl+Shift+drag the top or bottom handle of the transformation boundary to skew the image horizontally.

Skew top left/bottom right: After a few skews and distorts, the transformation boundary may get pretty twisted around. What was once a top side becomes a diagonal edge. But no matter — Photoshop updates the skew cursor to keep up with the new inclination.

Skew top right/bottom left: Here's yet another wacky skew cursor you may spy when Ctrl+Shift+dragging a transformation boundary.

Type: The common I-beam cursor indicates the type tool is selected and ready to use. You also get this cursor when using the type mask tool. Click to display the Type Tool dialog box.

Add type mask: As far as Photoshop is concerned, the type mask tool is just another selection tool. Shift+click with the tool to add the character outlines to the previous selection.

Subtract type mask: Alt+click with the type mask tool to carve letter-shaped holes out of the previous selection.

Intersect type mask: You can also Shift+Alt+click with the type mask tool to find the intersection of a few characters and the previous selection outline.

Pen: This cursor appears when the pen tool is selected, enabling you to start a new path or add points to the current path.

Insert point: When a small plus (+) sign accompanies the pen cursor, you can click a segment in a path to insert a point.

Remove point: When this cursor is active, click a point in a path to delete it. A new segment joins the remaining points to prevent a break in the path.

Close path: When you position your cursor over the first point in an open path, this cursor appears. Click with the cursor to close the path.

Arrow: Press the Ctrl key when using the pen tool to access the arrow cursor, which enables you to move a point or adjust a control handle. This cursor also appears when the direct selection tool is active.

Convert point: Use this cursor to convert a corner in a path to an arc or an arc to a corner. Click a point to change it to a corner; drag from a point to change it to an arc.

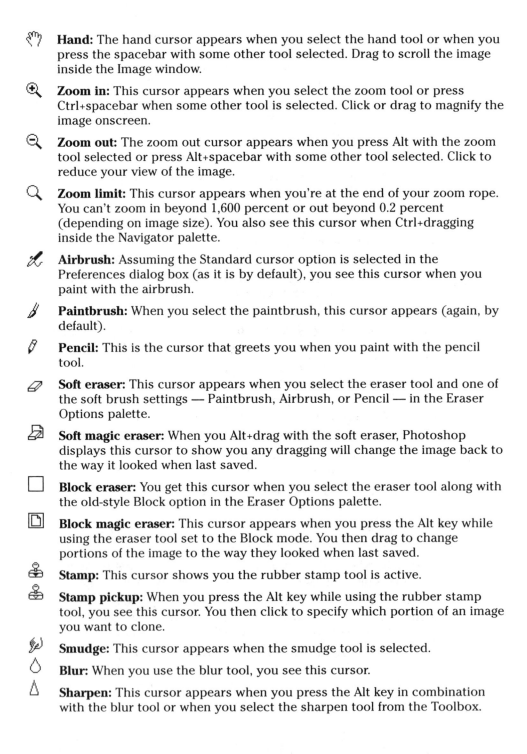

Hand: The hand cursor appears when you select the hand tool or when you press the spacebar with some other tool selected. Drag to scroll the image inside the Image window.

Zoom in: This cursor appears when you select the zoom tool or press Ctrl+spacebar when some other tool is selected. Click or drag to magnify the image onscreen.

Zoom out: The zoom out cursor appears when you press Alt with the zoom tool selected or press Alt+spacebar with some other tool selected. Click to reduce your view of the image.

Zoom limit: This cursor appears when you're at the end of your zoom rope. You can't zoom in beyond 1,600 percent or out beyond 0.2 percent (depending on image size). You also see this cursor when Ctrl+dragging inside the Navigator palette.

Airbrush: Assuming the Standard cursor option is selected in the Preferences dialog box (as it is by default), you see this cursor when you paint with the airbrush.

Paintbrush: When you select the paintbrush, this cursor appears (again, by default).

Pencil: This is the cursor that greets you when you paint with the pencil tool.

Soft eraser: This cursor appears when you select the eraser tool and one of the soft brush settings — Paintbrush, Airbrush, or Pencil — in the Eraser Options palette.

Soft magic eraser: When you Alt+drag with the soft eraser, Photoshop displays this cursor to show you any dragging will change the image back to the way it looked when last saved.

Block eraser: You get this cursor when you select the eraser tool along with the old-style Block option in the Eraser Options palette.

Block magic eraser: This cursor appears when you press the Alt key while using the eraser tool set to the Block mode. You then drag to change portions of the image to the way they looked when last saved.

Stamp: This cursor shows you the rubber stamp tool is active.

Stamp pickup: When you press the Alt key while using the rubber stamp tool, you see this cursor. You then click to specify which portion of an image you want to clone.

Smudge: This cursor appears when the smudge tool is selected.

Blur: When you use the blur tool, you see this cursor.

Sharpen: This cursor appears when you press the Alt key in combination with the blur tool or when you select the sharpen tool from the Toolbox.

Dodge: This cursor appears when you select the dodge tool. Drag to lighten an image.

Burn: If you prefer to darken portions of an image, press the Alt key while using the dodge tool or select the burn tool from the Toolbox. Either way, you get this handy cursor.

Sponge: Drag with the sponge tool cursor to decrease or increase the saturation of colors in the image.

Brush size: This cursor varies in size to show you the exact diameter of the brush you're using when dragging with any of the paint or edit tools, from the airbrush to the sponge. You can request this special cursor by selecting the Brush Size radio button in the Preferences dialog box, as I explain later in this chapter.

Crosshair: You see this cursor when you press the Caps Lock key while using any selection, painting, or editing tool. Caps Lock is a particular blessing when using the rubber stamp or smudge tool because, otherwise, the big cursors can prevent you from seeing what you're doing.

Line/gradient: This cursor appears when you select either the line or gradient tool. Drag with the cursor to determine the angle and length of a prospective straight line or gradient fill.

Paint bucket: This cursor appears when the paint bucket tool is selected. Click to fill an area with the foreground color.

Eyedropper: This cursor appears when you select the eyedropper tool, or when you press Alt while using the type tool, paint bucket tool, gradient tool, or any of the painting tools except the eraser. Click to lift a color from the image window.

Crosshair pickup: If the eyedropper cursor prevents you from seeing what you're doing, press the Caps Lock key to display a crosshair cursor that zeroes in on an exact pixel. This specific crosshair appears when you use the eyedropper tool or when you Alt+click with the rubber stamp tool while Caps Lock is down.

Black eyedropper: This cursor and the two that follow are available only when you work in the Levels and Curves dialog boxes. Click a color in the Image window to change that color to black.

Gamma eyedropper: Click a color with this cursor to change the color to medium gray (sometimes called the *gamma*).

White eyedropper: Use this cursor to click a color in the Image window and change it to white.

Eyedropper plus: This cursor and the next are available only when using the Color Range and Replace Color commands. Click with this cursor to add colors to the temporary mask. For complete information about these commands, read Chapters 12 and 18, respectively.

Eyedropper minus: Click with this cursor to remove colors from the temporary mask in the Color Range and Replace Color dialog box.

Palette hand: This cursor appears when working in the Layers, Channels, or Paths palette. Drag with the cursor to move a selected item above or below other items listed in the palette.

Palette selection: In Photoshop 4, you can convert a layer, channel, or path to a selection outline by Ctrl+clicking it. When you do, you see this cursor.

Add palette selection: If you can convert layers, channels, and paths to selections, it only makes sense that you can add the new selection outline to the previous one. Just Ctrl+Shift+click an item to see this cursor.

Subtract palette selection: When you Ctrl+Alt+click a palette item, you subtract it from the previous selection.

Intersect palette selection: You can also Ctrl+Shift+Alt+click a layer, channel, or path name to find the intersection of the item with the previous selection.

Move palette item: When you drag a layer, channel, or path, the palette hand changes to the move palette item cursor.

Vertical guide: Drag from the vertical ruler into the Image window to create a vertical guide in Photoshop 4. When creating or moving a vertical guide, you see this cursor.

Horizontal guide: Drag from the horizontal ruler along the top of the Image window to create a horizontal guide.

Group layers: Press the Alt key and position the cursor over the horizontal line between two layers in the Layers palette to get this cursor. Then click to group the layers divided by that line.

Ungroup layers: When two layers are grouped, the horizontal line between them becomes dotted. Alt+click the dotted line to ungroup the two layers.

Not available: If you try to click a palette icon that is not applicable to the current state of affairs, Photoshop tells you the icon is off limits with this cursor.

Hourglass: The hourglass cursor is the universal Windows symbol for *hurry up and wait.* When you see this cursor inside Photoshop, you can either sit on your idle hands, waiting for the devil to start playing with them, or you can switch to another application and try to get some work done. Windows 95 enables you to change the hourglass to something less lethal (or more lethal) in appearance — you can even switch to an animated cursor. I didn't illustrate the hourglass cursor here for two reasons: First, you've probably seen it often enough on your screen. Second, you may have changed it to something else in Windows 95.

The Toolbox controls

You have to love lists. They're fun to write and a joy to read.

All right, so I'm lying. Making your way through lists of information is a monstrous chore, whether you're on the giving or receiving end. But these particular lists happen to contain essential reference information. So on we go with the most astonishing list yet — the one that explains the controls at the bottom of the Toolbox.

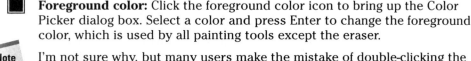 **Foreground color:** Click the foreground color icon to bring up the Color Picker dialog box. Select a color and press Enter to change the foreground color, which is used by all painting tools except the eraser.

 Note I'm not sure why, but many users make the mistake of double-clicking the foreground or background color icons when they first start using Photoshop. A single click is all that's needed.

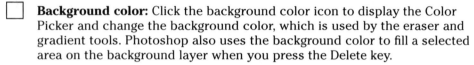 **Background color:** Click the background color icon to display the Color Picker and change the background color, which is used by the eraser and gradient tools. Photoshop also uses the background color to fill a selected area on the background layer when you press the Delete key.

↰ **Switch colors:** Click the switch colors icon to exchange the foreground and background colors.

Default colors: Click this icon to change the foreground color automatically to black and the background color to white.

Tip At any time, you can quickly make the foreground color white by clicking the default colors icon and then clicking the switch colors icon.

 Marching ants: Click this icon to exit Photoshop's quick mask mode and view selection outlines as animated dotted lines that look like marching ants, hence the name. (Adobe calls this the "standard" mode, but I think marching ants mode better describes how it works.)

Quick mask: Click here to enter the quick mask mode, which allows you to edit selection boundaries using painting tools. The marching ants vanish and the image appears half covered by a translucent layer of red, like a rubylith in traditional pasteup. The red layer covers the deselected — or masked — portions of the image. Paint with black to extend the masked areas, thereby subtracting from the selection. Paint with white to erase the mask, thereby adding to the selection.

 Cross Reference The quick mask mode is too complex a topic to sum up in a few sentences. If you can't wait to find out what it's all about, check out Chapter 12.

 Standard window: Click this icon to display the foreground image in a standard window, as shown earlier in Figure 2-2. By default, every image opens in the standard window mode.

☐ **Full screen with menu bar:** If you can't see enough of your image inside a standard window, click this icon. The Title bar and scroll bars disappear, as do all background windows and the Windows 95 taskbar, but the menu bar and palettes remain visible, as in Figure 2-4. (You can still access other open images by choosing their names from the Window menu.) A light gray background fills any empty area around the image.

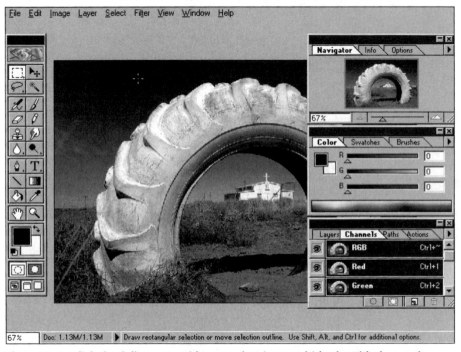

Figure 2-4: Click the full screen with menu bar icon to hide the Title bar and scroll bars.

☐ **Absolute full screen:** If you still can't see enough of your image — or the light gray area in the image is too distracting — click the rightmost of the Image window icons to see the photo set against a neutral black background. The menu bar disappears, limiting your access to commands (though you still can choose some commands using keyboard shortcuts). Only the Toolbox and palettes remain visible, as shown in Figure 2-5.

Tip   If the palettes get in your way, you can hide all palettes — including the Toolbox — by pressing the Tab key. To bring the Toolbox back into view, press Tab again.

In Photoshop 4, you can hide the palettes but leave the Toolbox up onscreen by pressing Shift+Tab. Press Shift+Tab again to bring the palettes back. (Pressing Tab while the palettes are gone hides the Toolbox.)

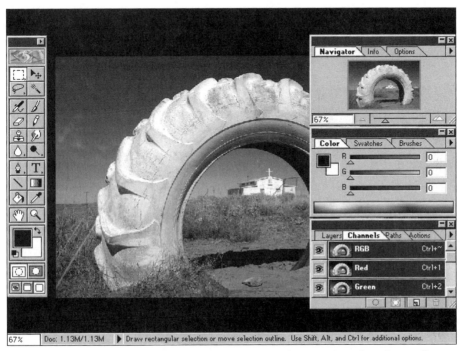

Figure 2-5: Click the absolute full screen icon to hide everything but the Toolbox, floating palettes, and image.

The floating palettes

The palettes in Photoshop 4 have seen their fair share of changes, but they include the same basic elements as their predecessors from Version 3. That is, the palettes offer most or all of the elements labeled in Figure 2-6. (Some panels lack scroll bars, others lack size boxes.)

Many palette elements are miniature versions of the elements that accompany any window. For example, the Close button and Title bar work identically to their Image-window counterparts. The Title bar lacks a title, but you can still drag it to move the palette to another location onscreen. Photoshop automatically snaps palettes into alignment with other palettes.

Tip

To snap a palette to the edge of the screen, Shift+click its Title bar. You can also Shift+drag the Title bar to move the palette around the perimeter of the screen, or to snap the palette from one edge of the screen to the other. (This tip also works with the Toolbox.)

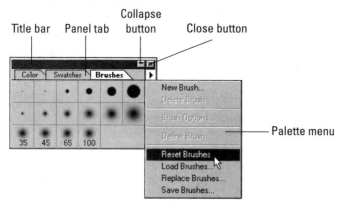

Figure 2-6: Most palettes include the same basic elements as the Brushes palette, shown here.

Four elements are unique to floating palettes:

✦ **Palette options:** Each floating palette offers its own collection of options. These options may include tools, icons, pop-up menus, slider bars, you name it.

✦ **Palette menu:** Click the right-pointing arrowhead icon to display a menu of commands specific to the palette. These commands enable you to manipulate the palette options and adjust preference settings.

✦ **Panel tabs:** Click a panel tab to switch from one panel to another inside a palette. (You can also switch panels by selecting the palette commands from the Window menu, but it's more convenient to click a tab.)

✦ **Collapse button:** Click the collapse button to decrease the onscreen space consumed by the palette. If you previously enlarged the palette by dragging the size box, your first click reduces the palette back to its default size. After that, clicking the collapse box hides all but the most essential palette options.

Tip

In most cases, collapsing a palette hides all options and leaves only the panel tabs visible. But in the case of the Options, Color, and Layers palettes, clicking the collapse box leaves a sliver of palette options intact, as demonstrated in the middle example of Figure 2-7. To eliminate all options for these panels — as in the last example — Alt+click the collapse box. You can also double-click one of the panel tabs, or in the empty area to the right of the tabs. These tricks work even if you've enlarged the palette by dragging the size box.

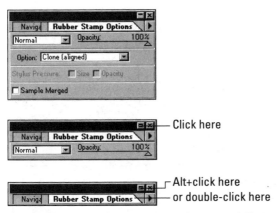

— Click here

┌ Alt+click here
└ or double-click here

Figure 2-7: The Options palette shown at full size (top), partially collapsed (middle), and fully collapsed (bottom)

Tabbing through the options

I mentioned earlier that you can hide the palettes by pressing Shift+Tab and hide both palettes and Toolbox by pressing Tab. But this keyboard trick doesn't work if an option box is active.

For example, suppose you click inside the R option box in the Color palette. This activates the option. Now press Tab. Rather than hiding the palettes, Photoshop advances you to the next option box in the palette. To move backward through the options, press Shift+Tab.

To apply an option box value and return focus to the Image window, press Enter. This deactivates the palette options. If an option box remains active, certain keyboard tricks — such as pressing a key to select a tool — won't work properly. Photoshop either ignores the shortcut or beeps at you for pressing a key the option box doesn't like. For more information on shortcuts, read Chapter 3.

Tip You can also return focus to the palette options from the keyboard by pressing the Enter key. When you press Enter, Photoshop displays the Options palette for the active tool. Assuming the Options palette for that tool offers an option box, Photoshop highlights the contents of the option box. You can then tab around to reach the option you want to change, enter a new value, and press Enter to get out.

Shuffling panels

Photoshop enables you to separate and group panels into palettes as you see fit. To separate a panel into its own palette, drag the panel tab away from the palette, as demonstrated in the left example in Figure 2-8. To combine a panel with a different palette, drag the panel tab onto the palette so the palette becomes highlighted, and then release. The middle and right examples in the figure show off this technique.

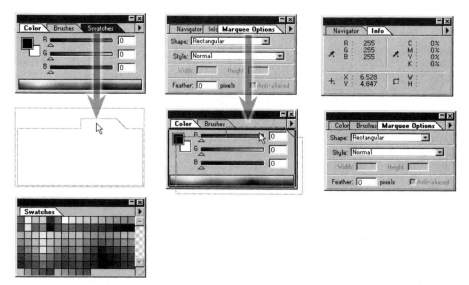

Figure 2-8: Dragging a panel off a palette (left) results in a new panel (middle). Dragging a panel onto another palette (middle) adds that panel to the palette (right).

Tip If you ever completely muck up the palettes — or a palette somehow gets stuck under the menu bar — press Ctrl+K and click the Reset Palette Locations to Default button in the Preferences dialog box. For more information, read the "General preferences" section later in this chapter.

Navigating Inside Photoshop 4

All graphics and desktop publishing programs provide a variety of navigational tools and functions that enable you to scoot around the screen, visit the heartlands and nether regions, examine the fine details, and take in the big picture. And Photoshop is no exception. In fact, Photoshop's navigation tools would make Magellan drool (were he inclined to edit an image or two).

Tip The truth is, Photoshop 3 provided more navigational tricks per square pixel than just about any other graphics program, and the navigation controls have nearly doubled in Version 4. So hold onto your hats, folks. We're going to be zooming and scrolling with a fair amount of gusto in the next few pages.

The view size

You can change the view size — the size at which an image appears onscreen — so you can either see more of an image or concentrate on individual pixels. Each change in view size is expressed as a *zoom ratio,* which is the ratio between screen pixels and image pixels. Photoshop 4 displays the zoom ratio as a percentage value in the Title bar. The 100 percent zoom ratio shows one image pixel for each screen pixel, and is, therefore, equivalent to the old 1:1 zoom ratio in Photoshop 3. A 200 percent zoom ratio doubles the size of the image pixels onscreen, and so on.

Actual pixels

Photoshop 4 calls the 100 percent zoom ratio the *actual-pixels* view. This is the most accurate view size because you can see the image as it really is. Reduced view sizes drop pixels; magnified view sizes stretch pixels. Only the actual-pixels view displays each pixel without a trace of screen distortion.

You can switch to this most accurate of view sizes at any time using one of the following techniques:

✦ Choose View ➪ Actual Pixels.

✦ Press Ctrl+Alt+0. (That's a zero, not the letter *O.*)

✦ Double-click the zoom tool icon in the Toolbox.

Fit-on screen

When you first open an image, Photoshop displays it at the largest zoom ratio (up to 100 percent) that permits the entire image to fit onscreen. Assuming you don't change the size of the image, you can return to this "fit-on screen" view size in one of the following ways:

✦ Choose View ➪ Fit-on Screen.

✦ Press Ctrl+0.

✦ Double-click the hand tool icon in the Toolbox.

Strangely, any of these techniques may magnify the image beyond the 100 percent view size. When working on a very small image, for example, Photoshop 4 enlarges the image to fill the screen, even if this means maxing out the zoom to 1,600 percent. Personally, I prefer to use the fit-on screen view only when working on very large images.

Caution

If you're thoroughly accustomed to pressing Ctrl+0 to switch to the color composite view, as in earlier versions of Photoshop, note this shortcut now zooms the window. To switch to the color composite view, you must press Ctrl+tilde (the ~ key in the upper-left corner of the keyboard). Old habits die hard.

Print size

You can switch to yet another predefined view size by choosing View ➪ Print Size. New to Photoshop 4, this command displays the image onscreen at the size it will print. (You set the print size using Image ➪ Image Size, as I explain in Chapter 4.)

That's the theory, anyway. In practice, the "print-size" view isn't particularly reliable. Photoshop assumes your monitor displays exactly 72 pixels per inch. Although this is the most common setting, monitor resolutions simply aren't that dependable. High-end monitors enable you to change screen resolutions without Photoshop even noticing.

The long and the short is this: Don't expect to hold up your printed image and have it exactly match the print-size view onscreen. It's a rough approximation, designed to show you how the image will look when imported into QuarkXPress, PageMaker, or some other publishing program.

The zoom tool

Obviously, the aforementioned zoom ratios aren't the only ones available to you. You can zoom in as close as 1,600 percent and zoom out to 0.2 percent.

The easiest way to zoom in and out of your image is to use the zoom tool:

✦ Click in the Image window with the zoom tool to magnify the image in preset increments — from 33.33 percent to 50 to 66.67 to 100 to 200 and so on. Photoshop tries to center the zoomed view at the point where you clicked (or come as close as possible).

✦ Alt+click with the zoom tool to reduce the image incrementally — 200 to 100 to 66.67 to 50 to 33.33 and so on. Again, Photoshop tries to center the new view on the click point.

 Tip Drag with the zoom tool to draw a rectangular marquee around the portion of the image you want to magnify. Photoshop magnifies the image so the marqueed area fits just inside the Image window. (If the horizontal and vertical proportions of the marquee do not match those of your screen — for example, if you draw a tall, thin marquee or a really short, wide one — Photoshop favors the smaller of the two possible zoom ratios to avoid hiding any detail inside the marquee.)

✦ If you like, you can instruct Photoshop to resize the window when you click with the zoom tool. Press Enter when the zoom tool is active to display the Zoom Options palette and then select the Resize Windows to Fit check box. (Turn off this option to zoom without resizing the window, as in Photoshop 3 and earlier.)

Tip

To access the zoom tool temporarily when some other tool is selected, press and hold the Ctrl and spacebar keys. Release both keys to return control of the cursor to the selected tool. To access the zoom out cursor, press Alt with the spacebar. These keyboard equivalents work from inside many dialog boxes, enabling you to modify the view of an image while applying a filter or color correction.

The zoom commands

You can also zoom in and out using the following commands and keyboard shortcuts:

✦ Choose View ➪ Zoom In or press Ctrl+plus (+) to zoom in. This command works exactly like clicking with the zoom tool except you can't specify the center of the new view size. Photoshop merely centers the zoom in keeping with the previous view size.

✦ Choose View ➪ Zoom Out or press Ctrl+minus (-) to zoom out.

By default, the keyboard shortcuts do not resize the window as they magnify. To override this, press Alt. Press Ctrl+Alt+plus to zoom in and resize the window; press Ctrl+Alt+minus to zoom out and resize the window. If you want to swap the performance of the zoom shortcut keys — so Ctrl+plus and minus resize the window — add the line *SwapZoomKeys* to the Photoshop\Prefs\Photos40.ini file.

In Photoshop 3, the Alt+key shortcuts would zoom to the maximum and minimum view sizes, respectively. No one found these operations terribly useful, so they're now extinct.

The Magnification box

Another way to zoom in and out without changing the window size is to enter a value into the Magnification box, located in the lower-left corner of the Photoshop window. Select the magnification value, enter a new one, and press Enter. Photoshop zooms the view without zooming the window.

In Figure 2-9, I started with a specially sized window at actual-pixels view. I then entered two different zoom ratios into the Magnification box — 156.7 percent and 60.4 percent — alternately enlarging and reducing the image within the confines of a static window.

You might like to know several other things about the Magnification box:

✦ If you later decide you want to change the dimensions of the window to fit the image exactly, press Ctrl+plus or Ctrl+minus to zoom image and window together.

Figure 2-9: To zoom an image without changing the window size, enter a zoom ratio into the Magnification box and press Enter.

✦ You can enter values in the Magnification box and in the Navigator palette (explained later in this chapter) in several ways. To switch to a zoom value of 250 percent, for example, you can enter 250%, 5:2, 750/3, or 2.5X.

✦ You can specify a zoom value in increments as small as .01 percent. So if a zoom value of 250.01 doesn't quite suit your fancy, you can try 250.02. I seriously doubt you'll need this kind of precision, but isn't it great to know it's there?

Tip   When you press Enter after entering a magnification value, Photoshop changes the view size and returns focus to the Image window. If you aren't exactly certain what zoom ratio you want to use, press Shift+Enter instead. This changes the view size while keeping the magnification value active; this way you can enter a new value and try again.

Creating a reference window

In the old days, paint programs provided a cropped view of your image at the actual-pixels view size to serve as a reference when you worked in a magnified view. Because it's so doggone modern, Photoshop does not, but you can easily create a second view of your image by choosing View ⇨ New View, as in Figure 2-10. Use one window to maintain a 100 percent view of your image while you zoom and edit inside the other window. Both windows track the changes to the image.

Figure 2-10: You can create multiple windows to track the changes made to a single image by choosing the New View command from the View menu.

Scrolling inside the window

In the standard window mode, you have access to scroll bars, just as you do in the vast majority of Windows applications. But as you become more proficient with Photoshop, you'll use the scroll bars less and less. One way to bypass the scroll bars is to use the keyboard equivalents listed in Table 2-1.

Table 2-1	
Scrolling from the Keyboard	
Scrolling Action	*Extended Keyboard*
Up one screen	Page Up
Up slightly	Shift+Page Up
Down one screen	Page Down
Down slightly	Shift+Page Down
To upper-left corner	Home
To lower-right corner	End

Unfortunately, you can't scroll exclusively left or right from the keyboard. But who cares? You won't be scrolling from the keyboard that often anyway. Most of the time, you'll use the hand tool.

Tip To access the hand tool temporarily when some other tool is selected, press and hold the spacebar. Releasing the spacebar returns the cursor to its original appearance. This keyboard equivalent even works from inside many dialog boxes.

The Navigator palette

I saved the best for last. Shown in Figure 2-11, the Navigator palette is the best thing to happen to zooming and scrolling since Photoshop was first introduced. If you routinely work on large images that extend beyond the confines of your relatively tiny screen, you'll want to get up and running with this palette as soon as possible.

If the Navigator palette isn't visible, choose Window ➪ Show Navigator. You can then use the palette options as follows:

✦ **View box:** Drag the view box inside the image thumbnail to reveal some hidden portion of the photograph. Photoshop dynamically tracks your adjustments in the image window. Isn't it great?

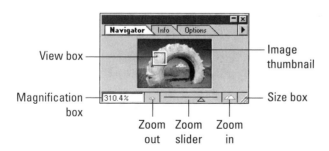

View box

Image thumbnail

Magnification box

310.4%

Size box

Zoom out   Zoom slider   Zoom in

Figure 2-11: The Navigator palette is the best thing to happen to zooming and scrolling since Photoshop 1.0.

Tip

But wait, it gets better. Press Ctrl to get a zoom cursor in the Navigator palette. Then Ctrl+drag to resize the view box and zoom the photo in the image window. Awesome!

You can also Shift+drag to constrain dragging the view box to only horizontal or vertical movement.

You can change the color of the view box by choosing the Palette Options command from the palette menu. My favorite setting is yellow, but it ultimately depends on the colors in your image. Ideally, you want something that stands out. To lift a color from the image itself, move the cursor outside the dialog box and click in the image window with the eyedropper.

✦ **Magnification box:** This value works like the one in the lower-left corner of the Image window. Just enter a new zoom ratio and press Enter.

✦ **Zoom out:** Click the zoom out button to reduce the view size in the same predefined increments as the zoom tool. The difference is this button doesn't alter the size of the Image window. So it works like the zoom tool used to work.

✦ **Zoom slider:** Give the slider triangle a yank and see where it takes you. Drag to the left to zoom out, drag right to zoom in. Again, Photoshop dynamically tracks your changes in the Image window. Dang, it's nice to zoom on the fly.

✦ **Zoom in:** Click the big mountains to magnify incrementally the view of the image without altering the window size.

✦ **Size box:** Drag the size box to enlarge the palette if necessary.

Customizing the Interface

Every program gives you access to a few core settings so you can modify the program to suit your personal needs. These settings are known far and wide as *preferences.* Photoshop ships with certain recommended preference settings already in force — known coast-to-coast as *factory defaults* — but just because these settings are recommended doesn't mean they're right. In fact, I disagree with quite a few of them. But why quibble when you can change the preferences according to your merest whim?

You can modify preference settings in two ways: You can make environmental adjustments using File ➪ Preferences ➪ General, or you can change the operation of specific tools by adjusting settings in the Options palette. Photoshop remembers environmental preferences, tool settings, and even the file format under which you saved the last image by storing this information to a file called PHOTOS40.PSP in the Prefs folder inside the Photoshop folder.

Tip

To restore Photoshop's factory default settings, delete the PHOTOS40.PSP file when the application is not running. The next time you launch Photoshop, it creates a new preferences file automatically.

Deleting the preferences file is also a good idea if Photoshop starts acting funny. Photoshop's preferences file has always been highly susceptible to corruption, possibly because the application writes to it so often. Whatever the reason, if Photoshop starts behaving erratically, quit the program, delete the PHOTOS40.PSP file, and relaunch Photoshop. You'll have to reset your preferences, but a smooth-running program is worth the few minutes of extra effort. Be careful, though, because in addition to resetting all your preferences, you must re-create all your scripts that were on the Actions palette. Save those Actions separately.

Tip

After you get your preferences set as you like them, you can prevent Photoshop from altering them further by locking the file. In the Windows 95 Explorer, right-click the PHOTOS40.PSP file and choose Properties from the pop-up menu that appears. (Or, in Windows 3.1 File Manager, select the file, and then choose File ➪ Properties.) In the Properties dialog box, select the Read Only check box, and then press Enter. From now on, Photoshop will start up with a consistent set of default settings.

Personally, I don't use this tip because I periodically modify settings and I want Photoshop to remember the latest and greatest. Instead, I make a backup copy of my favorite settings. After a few weeks of working in the program and getting things to a more or less acceptable level, copy the preferences file to a separate disk. Or just stick a copy in the same folder as the Photoshop application file. Then, if the preferences file becomes corrupt, you can replace it quickly with your backup.

The preference panels

Photoshop **4.0**

Photoshop 4 includes a long list of commands in the File ➪ Preferences submenu. As it turns out, you needn't choose any of these commands if you'll remember a simple keyboard shortcut: Ctrl+K. This shortcut brings up the Preferences dialog box, which provides access to eight panels of options, representing every one of the File ➪ Preferences commands. Select the desired panel from the pop-up menu in the upper-left corner of the dialog box, as demonstrated in Figure 2-12. Or press the Ctrl key equivalent for the panel as listed in the pop-up menu. You can also click the Prev and Next buttons (or press Alt+P and Alt+N, respectively) to cycle from one panel to the next.

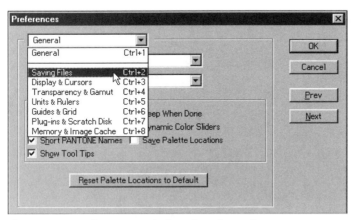

Figure 2-12: Select a panel of options from the pop-up menu, or click the Prev and Next buttons to advance from one panel to the next.

Tip

Photoshop always displays the first panel, General, when you press Ctrl+K. If you prefer to go to the panel you were last using, press Ctrl+Alt+K.

To accept your settings and exit the Preferences dialog box, press Enter. Or press Escape or click Cancel to cancel your settings. Okay, so you already knew this, but here's one you might not know: Press and hold the Alt key to change the Cancel button to Reset. Then click the button to restore the settings that were in force before you entered the dialog box.

The following sections examine each of the Preferences panels, in the order they appear in the Figure 2-12 pop-up menu. Out of context like this, Photoshop's preference settings can be a bit confusing. In future chapters, I'll try to shed some additional light on the settings you may find most useful.

General preferences

The General panel, shown in Figure 2-13, contains a miscellaneous supply of what are arguably the most important Preferences options. In the following list, I explain how each option works. I also include what I consider the optimal setting in parentheses:

✦ **Color Picker (Photoshop):** When you click the foreground or background color control icon in the Toolbox, Photoshop displays one of two color pickers: its own or the one provided by Windows. You may be tempted to use the latter one, but don't. Photoshop's color picker is more versatile.

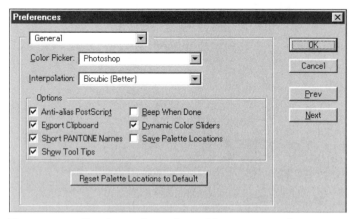

Figure 2-13: The General panel provides access to the most important environmental preference settings.

✦ **Interpolation (Bicubic):** When you resize an image using Image ⇨ Image Size or transform it using Layer ⇨ Free Transform or one of the commands in the Layer ⇨ Transform submenu, Photoshop has to make up — or *interpolate* — pixels to fill in the gaps. You can change how Photoshop calculates the interpolation by choosing one of three options from the Interpolation submenu.

If you select Nearest Neighbor, Photoshop simply copies the next-door pixel when creating a new one. This is the fastest setting, but it invariably results in jagged effects.

The second option, Bilinear, smoothes the transitions between pixels by creating intermediate shades. Photoshop averages the color of each pixel with four neighbors — the pixel above, the one below, and the two to the left and right. Bilinear takes more time but, typically, the softened effect is worth it.

Still more time intensive is the default setting, Bicubic, which averages the color of a pixel with its eight closest neighbors — one up, one down, two on the sides, and four in the corners. The Bicubic setting boosts the amount of contrast between pixels to offset the blurring effect that generally accompanies interpolation.

Tip

The moral is this: Select Bicubic to turn Photoshop's interpolation capabilities on, and select Nearest Neighbor to turn them off. The Bilinear setting is a poor compromise between the two — too slow for roughing out effects, but too remedial to waste your time.

✦ **Anti-alias PostScript (on):** Photoshop enables you to import object-oriented graphics from Illustrator and 3D drawing program Adobe Dimensions (included with Illustrator 6 and 7). Either copy the objects in Illustrator or Dimensions and paste them into Photoshop, or drag the objects from Illustrator and drop them into an open Photoshop Image window. Either way, the Anti-alias PostScript option softens the edges of PostScript objects. If you prefer jagged edges, turn off this check box.

✦ **Export Clipboard (off):** When selected, this option tells Photoshop to transfer a copied image from the program's internal Clipboard to the system's Clipboard whenever you switch applications. This enables you to paste the image into another running program. Turn this option off if you plan to use copied images only within Photoshop and you want to reduce the lag time that occurs when you switch from Photoshop to another program. Even with this option off, you can paste images copied from other programs into Photoshop.

✦ **Short Pantone Names (on):** Generally speaking, Photoshop doesn't support Pantone-brand spot colors. In fact, you can assign Pantone colors only when printing a grayscale image as a duotone (as explained in Chapter 7). Otherwise, feel free to ignore this option completely.

For those of you who will create duotones, Photoshop supports the most recent Pantone naming conventions. This is great for printing duotones directly from Photoshop, but if you plan to import a Pantone duotone into a desktop publishing or drawing package, you must select the Short Pantone Names check box to ensure the receiving application properly recognizes the color names. (Actually, naming conventions vary from one application to the next — PageMaker 6 and FreeHand 7 default to long names, for example — but because all programs support the short names, short is safest.)

✦ **Show Tool Tips (on):** When on, this option displays little labels and keyboard shortcuts when you hover your cursor over a tool or palette option. The tool tips don't impede Photoshop's performance, so I see no reason to turn off this option.

✦ **Beep When Done (off):** You can instruct Photoshop to beep at you whenever it finishes an operation that displays a Progress window. This option may be useful if you doze off during particularly time-consuming operations. But I'm a firm believer that computers should be seen and not heard.

✦ **Dynamic Color Sliders (on):** When selected, this option instructs Photoshop to preview color effects within the slider bars of the Color palette. When the option is turned off, the slider bars show the same colors regardless of your changes. Unless you're working on a slow computer, leave this option on. Photoshop takes a fraction of a second longer to calculate the color effects, but it's worth it.

✦ **Save Palette Locations (on):** When this option is selected, Photoshop remembers the location of the Toolbox and floating palettes from one session to the next. If you turn off this check box, Photoshop restores the default palette positions the next time you restart the program.

✦ **Reset Palette Locations to Default:** Occasionally palettes go haywire. They can get stuck under menu bars. And, if you change monitor resolutions, a palette can even disappear off the screen. If this happens, click this button and Photoshop will restore the palettes to their original "safe" positions.

Saving files

When in the Preferences dialog box, press Ctrl+2 to advance to the Saving Files panel, shown in Figure 2-14. Every one of these options affects how Photoshop saves images to disk. The following list explains how the options work and the recommended settings:

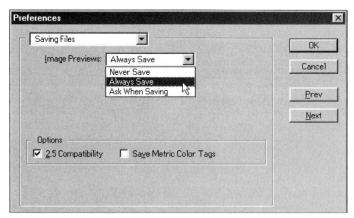

Figure 2-14: The Saving Files options tell Photoshop how to save your images to disk.

✦ **Image Previews (Always Save):** Photoshop 4 can save thumbnail previews of images along with your image files. These previews then appear in the Open dialog box. The three options in the Image Preview pop-up menu, shown in Figure 2-14, enable you to decide whether you want Photoshop always to save the previews, never to save the previews, or to ask you for permission to save a preview each time you save a file.

If you choose Never Save, by the way, you can still save a preview for an individual file by selecting the Save Thumbnail check box in the Save As dialog box when you save the file. The Always Save option automatically selects the option for you. I recommend you turn on the Always Save option; then you have one less worry.

✦ **2.5 Compatibility (off):** This option enables backward compatibility between Photoshop 4 and Photoshop 2.5, but it comes at a steep price. Here's the story: The only file format that retains layers is the Photoshop format. Even though Photoshop 2.5 does not support layers, it can open a flattened version of the image in which all the layers are fused together, as long as the 2.5 Compatibility check box is on. This is because Photoshop inserts an additional flattened version of the image into the file, which takes up a considerable amount of disk space. On the other hand, if you don't need to open your images in Photoshop 2.5, you can reduce the file size by as much as 50 percent by turning off this check box. Granted, old versions of Photoshop cannot open the image but, unless you're working with folks who are behind the times, backward compatibility doesn't matter.

Note

If you are saving a grayscale file for use as a displacement map or patter, however, you must turn on 2.5 Compatibility, as discussed in Chapter 10, in the section "How to create patterns."

✦ **Save Metric Color Tags (off):** If you use EFI's EfiColor for Photoshop to help with screen and printer calibration and you import and print most of your images inside QuarkXPress, turn on this option. Photoshop then references the active EfiColor separation table when saving an image in the TIFF or EPS file format, making the table available to XPress and, thus, maintaining consistent color between the two applications. If you don't use EfiColor — as most folks don't — leave the option off.

Display & Cursors

Press Ctrl+3 to saddle up to the Display & Cursors options, which appear in Figure 2-15. These options affect the way colors and cursors appear onscreen. Here's how the options work, along with recommended settings:

✦ **CMYK Composites (Faster):** Your monitor mixes red, green, and blue light to create colors onscreen. This is the *RGB color mode.* An opposite color mode known as *CMYK* (cyan, magenta, yellow, and black) is used to print colors on paper. As a result, when you edit a CMYK image, Photoshop has to convert the colors to their RGB equivalents.

For those who spend much time editing CMYK images, Photoshop provides a control for specifying the accuracy of the CMYK-to-RGB conversion. If you select the Smoother option, Photoshop preserves the actual CMYK color values and converts them on the fly to your RGB display — a precise but slow process. If you opt instead for the Faster option, Photoshop cheats by converting the colors in an image to their nearest RGB equivalents according to a predefined look-up table (known as an *LUT*), which speeds the screen display, but sacrifices a small amount of color accuracy.

Unless your monitor is precisely calibrated, the Smoother option won't do you much good. And if you own a calibrated monitor, you may also want to invest in a piece of CMYK acceleration hardware. This makes the Smoother option run nearly as fast as Faster. Otherwise, select the Faster radio button and enjoy the speed savings.

✦ **Color Channels in Color (off):** An individual color channel contains just 8 bits of data per pixel, which makes it equivalent to a grayscale image. Photoshop provides you with the option of colorizing the channel according to the primary color it represents. For example, when this option is turned on, the red color channel looks like a grayscale image viewed through red acetate. Most experts agree the effect isn't helpful, though, and it does more to obscure your image than make it easier for you to see what's happening. Leave this check box turned off and read Chapter 6 for more information.

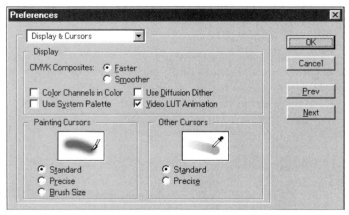

Figure 2-15: The Display & Cursors options control the way images and cursors look onscreen.

✦ **Use System Palette (off):** If you're working on an 8-bit monitor that displays no more than 256 colors at a time, this option matters to you. Otherwise, give it the slip.

To simulate the 16 million-color spectrum on a 256-color screen, Photoshop automatically jumbles colored pixels using a technique called *dithering.* By default, Photoshop selects 256 colors best suited to your image. In doing so, however, it must switch to a new set of 256 colors every time you bring a new document to the foreground. If you want all open documents to conform to the same set of colors — namely, the so-called "system palette" built into your system — select this check box. But for the most accurate display, leave the option turned off and live with the periodic screen fluctuations.

✦ **Use Diffusion Dither (on):** Here's another option for you folks working on 8-bit screens. While the previous option controls the colors used, this option controls the pattern of dithered pixels. Photoshop offers a naturalistic "diffusion" dither that looks nice onscreen. But because the diffusion dither follows no specific pattern, you sometimes see distinct edges between selected and deselected portions of your image after applying a filter or some other effect. You can eliminate these edges and resort to a more geometric dither pattern by turning off this check box.

Tip

Turning off the Use Diffusion Dither check box is an awfully drastic (not to mention ugly) solution, though. The better way to eliminate the occasional visual disharmony is to force Photoshop to redraw the entire image. You can press Ctrl+Alt+0 or perform some other zoom function.

✦ **Video LUT Animation (off):** Most Photoshop users can ignore this option. It works only if you're using some brands of video cards or if you've set your monitor to display only 256 colors. In that scenario, you can see video look-up table (LUT) animation in progress if you turn off the Preview check box inside one of Photoshop's color correction dialog boxes — such as Levels or Curves — and turned off the Preview check box, you've seen Photoshop's video look-up table animation in progress. Photoshop changes the LUT on the fly according to your specifications, in effect applying the color correction to the entire screen. It's not a real preview — in fact, it's pretty lousy. Video LUT animation doesn't account for selections, and it doesn't properly preview CMYK images. Turn this option off.

✦ **Painting Cursors (Brush Size):** When you use a paint or edit tool, Photoshop can display one of three cursors. The default Standard cursor looks like a paintbrush, airbrush, finger, or whatever. These cursors are great if you have problems keeping track of what tool you selected, but otherwise they border on childish.

The Precise and Brush Size options are more functional. Precise displays crosshairs, the same ones that appear when you press the Caps Lock key (as explained back in "The cursors" section earlier in this chapter).

Brush Size shows the actual size of the brush up to 300 screen pixels in diameter. This means if the zoom ratio is 50 percent and the brush size is 500 pixels wide, the brush only appears 250 pixels wide onscreen. But if you switch to the actual-pixels view, the brush size is too large to display, and the standard cursor appears instead. In the final analysis, the Brush Size option is the setting of choice.

Tip

When Standard or Brush Size is selected, pressing the Caps Lock key displays the precise crosshair cursors. But when Precise is selected, pressing Caps Lock displays the actual brush size.

✦ **Other Cursors (Standard):** Again, you can select Standard to get the regular cursors or Precise to get crosshairs. I prefer to leave this option set to Standard, because you can easily access the crosshairs by pressing Caps Lock. The Precise option locks you into crosshairs whether or not you like it.

Transparency & Gamut

Press Ctrl+4 to switch to the Transparency & Gamut panel shown in Figure 2-16. The options in this panel change how Photoshop displays two conceptual items — transparent space behind layers and RGB colors that can't be expressed in CMYK printing.

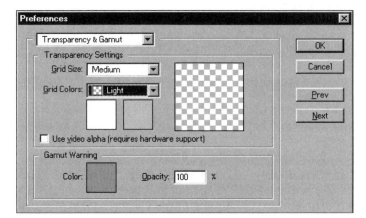

Figure 2-16: The options in this panel affect how Photoshop represents transparency and out-of-gamut colors onscreen.

The options are arranged into two groups — Transparency Settings and Gamut Warning — as explained in the following sections.

Transparency settings

Just as the Earth spins around in empty space, a Photoshop image rests on a layer of absolute transparency. By default, Photoshop represents this transparency as a gray checkerboard pattern. (What better way to demonstrate nothingness? I might have preferred a few lines from a Jean-Paul Sartre play, but no matter.) You may get a brief glimpse of this checkerboard when you first open an image or switch to Photoshop from another application.

When you view a layer independently of others, Photoshop fills the see-through portions of the layer with the checkerboard. So having the checkerboard stand out from the layer itself is essential. You can customize the size of the checkers and the color of the squares using the Grid Size and Grid Colors pop-up menus. You can also click the color swatches to define your own colors.

Tip

To lift colors from the Image window, move your cursor outside the Preferences dialog box to get the eyedropper. Click a color to change the color of the white checkers; Alt+click to change the gray ones.

If you own a TrueVision NuVista+ board or some other 32-bit device that enables chroma keying, you can select the Use Video Alpha check box to view a television signal in the transparent area behind a layer. Unless you work in video production, you needn't worry about this option.

Gamut warning

If Photoshop can display a color onscreen but can't accurately print the color, the color is said to be *out of gamut.* You can choose View ▷ Gamut Warning to coat all out-of-gamut colors with gray. I'm not a big fan of this command — View ▷ CMYK Preview is much more useful — but if you use it, you don't have to accept gray as the out-of-gamut coating. Change the color by clicking the Gamut Warning Color swatch, and lower the Opacity value to request a translucent coating.

Units & Rulers

The Units & Rulers panel is the fifth panel in the Preferences dialog box, hence, you reach the panel by pressing Ctrl+5. Shown in Figure 2-17, this panel offers options that enable you to change the predominant system of measurement used throughout the program.

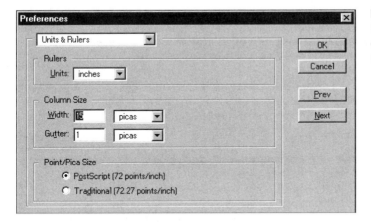

Figure 2-17: Go to the Units & Rulers panel to change the system of measurement.

Tip   Whenever the rulers are visible, the Units & Rulers panel is only a double-click away. Choose View ▷ Show Rulers (Ctrl+R) to see the rulers onscreen and then double-click either the horizontal or vertical ruler.

Rulers

Start by selecting the desired unit of measure from the Units pop-up menu. When you're first learning Photoshop, going with inches or picas is tempting, but experienced Photoshop artists use pixels. Because you can change the resolution of an image at any time, the only constant is pixels. An image measures a fixed number of pixels high by a fixed number of pixels wide — you can print those pixels as large or as small as you want. (To learn more about resolution, read Chapter 4.)

Column size

The Column Size options enable you to size images according to columns in a newsletter or magazine. Just enter the width of your columns and the size of the gutter into the Width and Gutter option boxes. Then use File ➪ New or Image ➪ Image Size to specify the number of columns assigned to the width of the image. I explain these commands in more detail in Chapter 4.

Point/pica size

The last option in the Units & Rulers panel may be the most obscure of all Photoshop options. In case you aren't familiar with points and picas, exactly 12 points are in a pica, and about 6.06 picas are in an inch.

Well, because picas are almost evenly divisible into inches, the folks who came up with the PostScript printing language decided to bag the difference and to define a pica as exactly $\frac{1}{6}$ inch. This makes a point exactly $\frac{1}{72}$ inch.

But a few purists didn't take to it. They found their new electronic documents weren't quite matching their old paste-up documents and, well, I guess life pretty much lost its meaning. So Adobe had to go back and add the Traditional (72.27 points/inch) option to keep everyone happy.

I prefer the nontraditional PostScript definition of points. This way, a pixel onscreen translates to a point on paper when you print an image at 72 ppi (the standard screen resolution). Call me a soulless *technodweeb*, but computer imaging makes more sense when you can measure points and pixels without resorting to a calculator. The old ways are dead; long live the $\frac{1}{72}$-inch point!

Guides & Grid

Photoshop 4.0

Someone at Adobe said, "Let the preference settings continue." And, lo, there was Guides & Grid, which could be accessed by all who pressed Ctrl+6 and viewed by all who cast an eye on Figure 2-18. This panel enables you to modify the colors of Photoshop 4's new guides and specify the size of Photoshop 4's new grid.

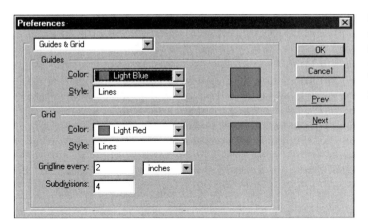

Figure 2-18: Use these options to adjust the size of the grid and change the way both the grid and ruler guides appear onscreen.

Tip

You can display the Preferences dialog box and go directly to the Guides & Grid panel by double-clicking a guide with the move tool or Ctrl+double-clicking with another tool. (To create a guide, drag from the horizontal or vertical ruler into the image.)

I explain these options in more detail in Chapter 13 but, for the moment, here are some brief descriptions.

Guides
Select a color for horizontal and vertical ruler guides from the Color pop-up menu. To lift a color from the image, move your cursor outside the Preferences dialog box and click in the Image window with the eyedropper. You can also view guides as solid lines or dashes by selecting an option from the Style pop-up menu.

Grid
Select a color for the grid from the Color menu, or Alt+click in the Image window to lift a color from the image. Then decide how the grid lines look by selecting a Style option. The Dots setting is the least intrusive.

The Gridline Every value determines the increments for the visible grid marks onscreen. But the Subdivisions value sets the real grid. For example, if you request a grid mark every two inches with four subdivisions — as in Figure 2-18 — Photoshop snaps selections and layers in half-inch increments (two inches divided by four).

Plug-ins & Scratch Disk
Press Ctrl+7 to advance to the panel shown in Figure 2-19. Each time you launch Photoshop, the program searches for plug-in modules and identifies one or more scratch disks. You have to tell Photoshop where the plug-ins can be found and where the temporary scratch files should go.

The settings in this panel don't take effect until the next time you launch Photoshop. This means you must quit Photoshop and restart the program.

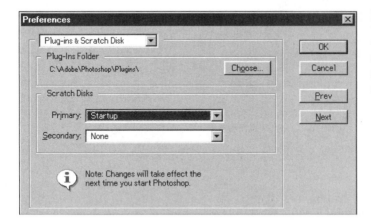

Figure 2-19: Tell Photoshop where to find plug-ins and where to put scratch files using these options.

Plugins folder

By default, the plug-ins are located in a folder called Plug-Ins, which resides in the same folder as the Photoshop application. But you can rename this folder and put it anywhere you like. You can even organize your plug-ins into multiple folders, loading one folder of plug-ins one day, and another folder the next.

If you do change the location of the plug-ins, tell Photoshop where to find them by clicking the Choose button and locating the desired folder on disk.

Scratch disks

By default, Photoshop assumes you have only one hard disk, so Photoshop stores its temporary virtual memory documents — called *scratch files* — on the same disk that contains your system software. If you have more than one drive available, though, you might want to tell Photoshop to look elsewhere. You have to restart Photoshop before the new scratch disks take effect.

For example, one of my computers is equipped with two internal hard drives: one 1GB drive that contains the system, and one 4GB drive that contains applications and workaday files. The 4GB drive is partitioned into two 2GB segments, called PowerShrine.1 and PowerShrine.2. (Let's face it, I spend most of my time praying my computer will work, so I decided to make this official.) Because PowerShrine.1 has the most free space, I selected it from the Primary pop-up menu. On the off chance that my images get so huge Photoshop has to look for another drive, I selected PowerShrine.2 from the Secondary pop-up menu.

Caution Adobe advises against using removable media, such as SyQuest and Zip drives, as a scratch disk. Removable media is typically less reliable and slower than a permanent drive. Using a removable drive on an occasional basis isn't the end of the world but, if you use it regularly, you'll probably want to add a new hard drive.

Cross Reference For more information about scratch disks, see the section "Scratch sizes" earlier in this chapter.

Image cache

Ever since Photoshop 3 came out, Adobe has received a fair amount of flack from high-end users who demand faster image handling. Programs like Live Picture and xRes take seconds to apply complex operations to super-huge photographs, while Photoshop putters along for a minute or more. Granted, Live Picture and xRes aren't nearly as capable as Photoshop, but they are faster.

Unfortunately, Photoshop 4 isn't quite the speed breakthrough many had hoped it would be. In fact, rumor is the big speed bump awaits us in Version 5. But while we wait, Photoshop 4 has made modest improvements. The program sports a new caching scheme that speeds operations at reduced view sizes. You can adjust this feature by pressing Ctrl+8 in the Preferences dialog box. This displays the Memory & Image Cache panel, shown in Figure 2-20.

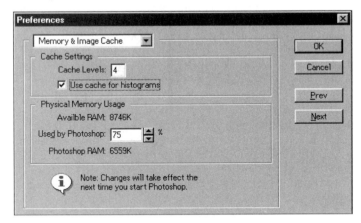

Figure 2-20:
Photoshop's new caching capabilities speed the processing of very large images.

Cache levels

Photoshop has been criticized for its lack of a "pyramid-style" file format, such as Live Picture's IVUE or xRes' LRG. Both IVUE and LRG store an image several times over at progressively smaller and smaller image sizes, called *downsamplings*. For example, the program would save a full view of the image, a 50 percent view, a 25 percent view, and so on. Live Picture or xRes can then load and edit only the portion of the image visible onscreen, greatly accelerating functions.

Photoshop's alternative is image caching. Rather than saving the downsamplings to disk, Photoshop generates the reduced images in RAM. By default, the Cache Levels value is set to 4, the medium value. This means Photoshop can cache up to four downsamplings — at 100, 50, 25, and 12.5 percent — which permits the program to apply operations more quickly at reduced view sizes. For example, if you choose a color correction command at the 50 percent view size, it previews much faster than normal because Photoshop has to modify a quarter as many pixels onscreen.

The downside is Photoshop must cache downsamplings in RAM, which takes away memory that could be used to hold the image. If you have lots of RAM (60MB or more) and you frequently work on large images (20MB or larger), you'll probably want to raise the value to the maximum, 8. The lost memory is worth the speed boost. If you have little RAM (say, 16MB or less) and you usually work on small images (4MB or smaller), you may want to reduce the Cache Levels value. When files are small, RAM is better allocated to storing images rather than caching them.

Use cache for histograms

The Use Cache for Histograms check box tells Photoshop whether to generate the histograms that appear in the Levels and Threshold dialog boxes based on the cached sampling or the original image. As I explain in Chapter 18, a *histogram* is a bar graph of the colors in an image. When you choose a command like Image ⇨ Adjust ⇨ Levels, Photoshop must spend a few seconds graphing the colors. If you turn the Use Cache for Histograms check box on, Photoshop graphs the colors in the reduced screen view, which takes less time, but is also less accurate. Turn the check box off for slower, more accurate histograms.

Generally speaking, I say leave the option on. A histogram is just a visual indicator; most folks will be unable to judge the difference between a downsampled histogram and a fully accurate one.

Again, if you're working in very large images and you have the Cache Levels value maxed out at 8, you should probably leave this check box selected. But if you have to reduce the Cache Levels value, turn off the check box. Histograms are the first thing that can go.

Annotating an Image

If you work for a stock agency or you distribute your work by some other means, you'll be interested in Photoshop's image-annotation feature. You can attach captions, credits, bylines, photo location and date, copyright, and other information, as prescribed by the IPTC (International Press Telecommunications Council). We're talking official worldwide guidelines here.

Choose File ➪ File Info to display the six-paneled File Info dialog box, shown in Figure 2-21. You switch from one panel to another by pressing Ctrl+1 through Ctrl+6 or choosing the panel name from the Section pop-up menu. Alt+N and Alt+P will also go to the next and previous panel, respectively. The first panel, the Caption panel, appears in Figure 2-21.

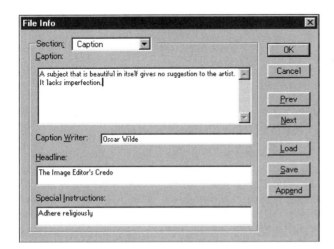

Figure 2-21: You can document your image in encyclopedic detail using the wealth of options in the File Info dialog box.

Although sprawling with options, this dialog box is pretty straightforward. For example, if you want to create a caption, travel to the Caption panel and enter your caption into the Caption option box, which can hold up to 2,000 characters. The Keywords panel enables you to enter a list of descriptive words that will help folks find the image if it's part of a large electronic library. Just enter the desired word and press Enter (or click the Add button) to add the keyword to the list. Or you can replace a word in the list by selecting it, entering a new word, and pressing Enter (or clicking Replace). Likewise, you can delete a selected keyword by clicking Delete. Browser utilities enable you to search images by keyword, as do some dedicated image servers.

The Categories panel, shown in Figure 2-22, may seem foreign to anyone who hasn't worked with a news service. Many large news services use a system of three-character categories to file and organize stories and photographs. If you're familiar with this system, you can enter the three-character code into the Category option box and even throw in a few supplemental categories up to 32 characters long. Finally, use the Urgency pop-up menu to specify the editorial timeliness of the photo. The High option tells editors around the world to hold the presses and holler for their copy boys. The Low option is for celebrity mug shots that can be tossed in the morgue to haul out only if the subject of the photograph decides to do something diverting, like lead police on a nail-biting tour of the Los Angeles freeway system.

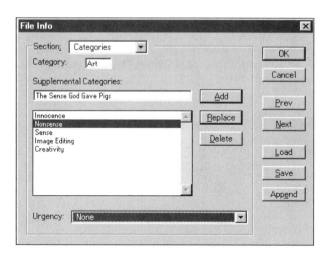

Figure 2-22: Large news services use the options found in the Categories panel to aid in organizing photographs.

The new Copyright & URL panel enables you to add a copyright notice to your image. If you check the Mark as Copyrighted check box, a copyright symbol (©) will appear in the window Title bar and in the status box at the bottom of the screen. This symbol tells people viewing the image they can go to the Copyright & URL panel to get more information about the owner of the image copyright.

You can also include a World Wide Web address (if you have one). Then, when folks have your image open in Photoshop 4, they can come to this panel and click the Go to URL button to launch their Web browser and jump to the URL. The Help ➪ Open Image URL command accomplishes the same thing as the Go to URL button.

File information is only saved in file formats that support saving extra data with the file. For Photoshop for Windows, this means only Photoshop (.PSD) format, JPEG (.JPG), Encapsulated PostScript (.EPS), and TIFF (.TIF) files retain the extra information. Because you cannot format the text in the File Info dialog box, it consumes little space on disk — 1 byte per character — meaning all the text in Figure 2-20 doesn't even take up 1K.

You can also save the information from the File Info dialog box by clicking the Save button. Or open information saved to disk previously by clicking Load. To add the information from a saved file to the information you've already entered into the File Info dialog box, click the Append button.

Shortcuts and Scripts

Keystrokes and Modifiers

Unlike most graphics programs, Photoshop invests a lot of its capabilities in the keyboard. Literally hundreds of functions are available exclusively at the press of a key. For example, Photoshop offers no command that adds the next selection outline you draw to the previous one. No command exists that fills only the opaque areas of a selection with the background color, and there is no command that brings up the last-used color correction settings. In fact, every one of these options is out of your reach if you don't know the right key. The keyboard may seem like an unlikely artistic tool, but it is both a powerful and an essential ally in Photoshop.

Two basic varieties of keyboard tricks exist. Some keystroke combinations produce immediate effects. For example, pressing Ctrl and Backspace together fills the selection with the background color. Other keys change the behavior of a tool or command. Pressing Shift while dragging with the lasso tool adds the lassoed area to the previous selection. As a result, Shift, Alt, and Ctrl are known collectively as *modifiers*.

Photoshop 4.0 offers one more kind of keyboard trick you'll want to check out. *Scripts* are collections of commands Photoshop can play over and over again in a specified order and with specified settings. You create scripts using the new Actions palette, which I explain at length later in this chapter. After creating a script, you can assign a keyboard equivalent to it, or you can play the script by Alt+double-clicking it. Even the shortcuts have shortcuts.

But wonderful as all this may sound, I feel compelled to share one significant bit of bad news, which may cast a cloud on your otherwise sunny day. If you're familiar with previous versions of Photoshop, many of the shortcuts you know don't work anymore. It's an exaggeration to say that every technique involving the Ctrl or Alt key has changed, but it's not far from the truth. For example, when using the marquee tool, you now Alt+drag to subtract from a selection, Ctrl+drag to move the selection, and Ctrl+Alt+drag to clone the selection. Photoshop 4 turns your world upside down.

But never fear. This chapter addresses new and old users alike. If you're having problems making the keyboard transition to Photoshop 4, skim through this chapter, practice a few of the techniques, and then take a much-deserved rest in your favorite Barco-Lounger. After a few hours of uninterrupted downtime, the initial shock should pass, and you'll be ready to tackle the rest of the book with an open mind.

Hidden Shortcuts and Modifiers

Shortcuts enable you to initiate operations without resorting to the laborious task of choosing commands from menus or clicking some tool icon until your arm falls off. Many shortcuts are fairly obvious. For example, Photoshop lists keyboard equivalents for its commands next to the command in the menu. You can choose File ➪ New by pressing Ctrl+N, choose Edit ➪ Undo by pressing Ctrl+Z, choose Select ➪ All by pressing Ctrl+A, and so on. But most of Photoshop's shortcuts are hidden. And, wouldn't you know it, the hidden ones are the most essential.

Alt+key combos

Tip

As in other Windows programs, you can also choose commands using so-called *hot keys,* which are the underlined letters you see in menu, command, and dialog box option names. To access a menu or dialog box option, press Alt plus the underlined letter in the menu or option name. To choose a command from a menu, you can simply press the hot key — no Alt key required.

Right-clicking

The best hidden trick in Photoshop 4 is right-clicking. Go ahead, try it: Right-click in the Image window. Up pops a menu of commands. For example, if you right-click with the lasso tool while a selection is active, you get the list of commands shown in Figure 3-1. Although you can apply other commands to a selection, these commands are some of the most common.

The right-click pop-up menu is *context-sensitive,* which means it changes to suit the active tool and the current state of the image (selected or not). You can also right-click items such as brushes and layers in the palettes.

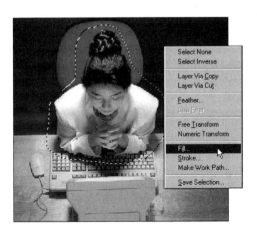

Figure 3-1: If you get stuck, right-click to bring up a pop-up menu of helpful commands. This is more productive than praying to your computer.

Toolbox shortcuts

Usability has always been one of Photoshop's great strengths. One of the ways Photoshop expedites your workflow is to enable you to select tools from the keyboard. This way, you can use one tool, press a key, and immediately start in with another tool without losing your place in the image.

Tip

Best of all, the shortcuts work even when the Toolbox is hidden. The only reason I even look at the Toolbox is to monitor which tool is selected, so I don't get confused.

Figure 3-2 tells the whole, wonderful story. Press the appropriate key, as shown in the figure — no Ctrl, Alt, or other modifiers required. Many of the shortcuts make sense. *M* selects the marquee tool, *L* is for lasso tool. But then there are the weird ones, like *K* for paint bucKet, *O* for dOdge, *U* for smUdge, and my favorite, *I* for I-dropper. The only alphabetical key that goes unused is *J*.

Photoshop 4.0

If you're used to Photoshop 3, you'll notice three changes to Version 4: The Y, T, and P keys have changed. *Y* used to select the type tool, now *T* selects that tool. *T* used to select the pen tool, now you press *P*. And *P* used to select the pencil, but now *Y* does the job. Is it possible someone at Adobe is using a pYncYl?

The keys that appear in bold type in Figure 3-2 act as toggles. For example, if you press *M* once, you get the last marquee tool used (rectangular by default). Press *M* again to select the other marquee tool. Other toggles work as follows:

✦ **L** switches between the standard lasso tool we all know and love from the ancient days of MacPaint, and the new polygonal lasso tool.

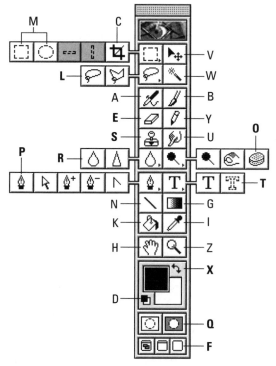

Figure 3-2: Press these keys to select tools and activate controls in Photoshop 4.

✦ **E** changes between the four styles of eraser — paintbrush, airbrush, pencil, and block. You can monitor the active style by pressing Enter to display the Eraser Options panel.

✦ **S** cycles through the various stamp tool modes.

✦ **R** switches between the blur and sharpen tools.

✦ **O** toggles between the dodge, burn, and sponge tools.

✦ **P** switches between the five path tools — from the pen tool to the arrow tool and so on down the list.

✦ **T** selects the standard type tool or the new type mask tool.

✦ **X** swaps the foreground and background colors and then swaps them back again.

✦ **Q** enters the quick mask mode and then exits it.

✦ **F** takes you from one window mode to the next.

Palette shortcuts

Photoshop also enables you to access a few palette options from the keyboard. I've documented these options in Figure 3-3. But the figure is sufficiently peculiar that I thought I'd back it up with the following list. And as with the tool keys, each of these shortcuts works even when the palette is hidden:

✦ Press the bracket keys [and] to decrease and increase the brush shape when a paint or edit tool is selected.

✦ Press Shift+[to select the first brush shape (generally the single-pixel brush). Press Shift+] to select the last brush shape.

✦ When a paint, edit, or fill tool is selected, press a number key to change the Opacity, Pressure, or Exposure setting assigned to that tool in the Alts palette. Lowered values enable you to create translucent strokes and fills. Press 1 to change the value to 10 percent, 2 for 20 percent, all the way up to 0 for 100 percent. Or enter the exact value — such as 15 percent — by typing 1-5 right in a row.

✦ When any other tool is selected — whether a selection, navigation, type, or eyedropper tool — pressing a number key changes the Opacity value assigned to a floating selection or layer. Again, press one number to modify the Opacity setting in 10-percent increments; press two numbers to specify an exact Opacity setting.

✦ Press the forward slash key (/) to turn on and off the Preserve Transparency check box. This is easily one of the least-known shortcuts in all of Photoshop. But it's useful, as I explain further in Chapter 13.

✦ Press Alt+] to ascend through the layers. Press Alt+[to descend. (Experienced users note: The old Photoshop 3 shortcuts — Ctrl+] and Ctrl+[— now change the order of the active layer.)

✦ Press Shift+Alt+] to activate the top layer in the image. Press Shift+Alt+[to go all the way down to the background layer.

The Great Grandmother of All Shortcut Tables

As I wrote the Mac version of this book, Saddam Hussein was back in the news. Chances are, he's in the news as you're reading this, too. He's a compulsive invader. I mean, can you imagine living next door to the guy? You'd wake up one day and find out he'd taken over your garage. Anyway, I know he's not a popular fellow — what with being a bloodthirsty dictator and all — but you have to give him credit for that "mother of all battles" thing. He really added to our language. I'm sure we'll be joking about the mothers of all this and that for years to come.

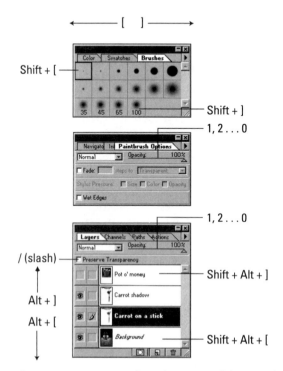

Figure 3-3: You can take advantage of these palette shortcuts even when the palettes themselves are hidden.

But still, the phrase doesn't quite do justice to Table 3-1. Here's a list covering every keystroke and modifier available to Photoshop 4. So far, we've barely scratched the surface — tons of shortcuts are left to discuss. Add to it that about half these shortcuts are new to Photoshop 4, and we face a monumental challenge. So I've done something you probably won't find in any other book. I've created a table that tells you both the old Photoshop 3 keyboard shortcut and the new Photoshop 4 equivalent. If the shortcut has changed in Version 4, I've indicated it in **bold type** so you can more quickly scan the list.

For key combinations involving a character that normally requires the Shift key (like ", which is usually ' + Shift), you needn't hold down the Shift key. Just press the key with the shortcut character on it. For example, the shortcut for Show Grid is listed as Ctrl+ ", but to use that shortcut, you only have to press Ctrl and the ' (single quote) key. This leaves one more finger free for wiggling, pointing, or whatever.

Remember, a shortcut won't make much sense if you aren't familiar with the feature it facilitates. I explain both features and their shortcuts in context in later chapters. The intent of the table is to serve as a reference you can revisit as your knowledge of Photoshop grows. The more you learn, the more useful the table becomes.

So fold the corner of this page, tag it with a sticky note, or stab it with a bayonet. This isn't your everyday average mother of all shortcuts table. This table is so huge and all-encompassing, it skips two whole generations. Table 3-1 is a great grandmother — and you know how powerful grandmothers can be!

Table 3-1 Photoshop's Hidden Shortcuts and Modifiers		
Operation	*Old Photoshop 3 shortcut*	*New Photoshop 4 shortcut*
Menu commands		
Actual Pixels	*new command*	**Ctrl+Alt+zero (0)**
Auto Levels	*none*	**Ctrl+Shift+L**
Brightness/Contrast	Ctrl+B	*none*
Bring Layer Forward	*new command*	**Ctrl+]**
Bring Layer to Front	*new command*	**Ctrl+Shift+]**
Clear	Delete	Delete
Close	Ctrl+W	Ctrl+W
CMYK Preview	*none*	**Ctrl+Y**
Color Balance	Ctrl+Y	**Ctrl+B**
Color Balance, with last settings	Ctrl+Alt+Y	**Ctrl+Alt+B**
Copy	Ctrl+C	Ctrl+C
Copy Merged	*none*	**Ctrl+Shift+C**
Curves	Ctrl+M	Ctrl+M
Curves, with last settings	Ctrl+Alt+M	Ctrl+Alt+M
Cut	Ctrl+X	Ctrl+X
Desaturate	*none*	**Ctrl+Shift+U**
Defloat	Ctrl+J	**Ctrl+E**
Equalize	Ctrl+E	*none*
Fade Filter	*new command*	**Ctrl+Shift+F**
Feather Selection	none	**Ctrl+Shift+D**

(continued)

Table 3-1
Photoshop's Hidden Shortcuts and Modifiers (*continued*)

Operation	Old Photoshop 3 shortcut	New Photoshop 4 shortcut
Menu commands		
Fill dialog box	Shift+Delete or Shift+F5	**Shift+Backspace** or Shift+F5
Filter, repeat last	Ctrl+F	Ctrl+F
Filter, repeat with new settings	Ctrl+Alt+F	Ctrl+Alt+F
Fit onscreen	*new command*	**Ctrl+zero (0)**
Float Selection	Ctrl+J	**Ctrl+Alt+arrow**
Free Transform	*new command*	**Ctrl+T**
Gamut Warning	*none*	**Ctrl+Shift+Y**
Grid, show or hide	*new command*	**Ctrl+quote (')**
Group with Previous Layer	*new command*	**Ctrl+G**
Grow Selection	Ctrl+G	***none***
Guides, show or hide	*new command*	**Ctrl+semicolon (;)**
Hide Edges	Ctrl+H	Ctrl+H
Hide Path	*new command*	**Ctrl+Shift+H**
Hue/Saturation	Ctrl+U	Ctrl+U
Hue/Saturation, with last settings	Ctrl+Alt+U	Ctrl+Alt+U
Inverse Selection	*none*	**Ctrl+Shift+I**
Invert	Ctrl+I	Ctrl+I
Layer Via Copy	*new command*	**Ctrl+J**
Layer Via Cut	*new command*	**Ctrl+Shift+J**
Levels	Ctrl+L	Ctrl+L
Levels, with last settings	Ctrl+Alt+L	Ctrl+Alt+L
Lock Guides	*new command*	**Ctrl+Alt+semicolon (;)**
Merge Down	*none*	**Ctrl+E**
Merge Visible	*none*	**Ctrl+Shift+E**
New	Ctrl+N	Ctrl+N
New, with default settings	Ctrl+Alt+N	Ctrl+Alt+N

Operation	Old Photoshop 3 shortcut	New Photoshop 4 shortcut
	Menu commands	
Numeric Transform	*new command*	**Ctrl+Shift+T**
Open	Ctrl+O	Ctrl+O
Page Setup	*none*	**Ctrl+Shift+P**
Paste	Ctrl+V	Ctrl+V
Paste Into	*none*	**Ctrl+Shift+V**
Preferences	Ctrl+K	Ctrl+K
Preferences, last panel	*none*	**Ctrl+Alt+K**
Print	Ctrl+P	Ctrl+P
Quit	Ctrl+Q	Ctrl+Q
Redo	Ctrl+Z	Ctrl+Z
Revert	F12	F12
Rulers, show or hide	Ctrl+R	Ctrl+R
Save	Ctrl+S	Ctrl+S
Save As	*none*	**Ctrl+Shift+S**
Save a Copy	*none*	**Ctrl+Alt+S**
Select All	Ctrl+A	Ctrl+A
Select None	Ctrl+D	Ctrl+D
Send Layer Backward	*new command*	**Ctrl+[**
Send Layer to Back	*new command*	**Ctrl+Shift+[** ⌃
Toggle Snap to Grid	*new command*	**Ctrl+Shift+quote (')**
Toggle Snap to Guides	*new command*	**Ctrl+Shift+semicolon (;)**
Threshold	Ctrl+T	***none***
Undo	Ctrl+Z	Ctrl+Z
Ungroup Layers	*new command*	**Ctrl+Shift+G**
Zoom In, not resizing window	*none*	**Ctrl+plus (+)**
Zoom In, resizing window	Ctrl+plus (+)	Ctrl+Alt+plus (+)
Zoom In, all the way	Ctrl+Alt+plus (+)	***none***
Zoom Out, not resizing window	*none*	Ctrl+minus (-)

(continued)

Table 3-1
Photoshop's Hidden Shortcuts and Modifiers *(continued)*

Operation	Old Photoshop 3 shortcut	New Photoshop 4 shortcut
Menu commands		
Zoom Out, resizing window	Ctrl+minus (-)	Ctrl+Alt+minus (-)
Zoom Out, all the way	Ctrl+Alt+minus (-)	*none*
Navigation		
Scroll image with hand tool	spacebar+drag	spacebar+drag **or drag in Navigator palette**
Scroll up or down one screen	press Page Up or Page Down	press Page Up or Page Down
Scroll up or down slightly	Shift+Page Up or Shift+Page Down	Shift+Page Up or Shift+Page Down
Scroll up or down exactly one frame in Filmstrip file	Shift+Page Up or Shift+Page Down	Shift+Page Up or Shift+Page Down
Switch to upper-left corner	press Home key	press Home key
Switch to lower-right corner	press End key	press End key
Zoom in without changing window size	Ctrl+spacebar+click	Ctrl+spacebar+click **or Ctrl+plus (+)** **[*Ctrl+Alt+plus (+)]**
Magnify to custom zoom ratio	Ctrl+spacebar+drag	Ctrl+spacebar+drag **or Ctrl+drag in Navigator palette**
Zoom in and change window size to fit	Ctrl+plus (+)	Ctrl+Alt+plus (+) **[*Ctrl+plus (+)]**
Zoom out without changing window size	Alt+spacebar+click	Alt+spacebar+click **or Ctrl+minus (-)** **[*Ctrl+Alt+minus (-)]**
Zoom out and change window size to fit	Ctrl+minus (-)	Ctrl+Alt+minus (-) **[*Ctrl+minus (-)]**
Zoom to 100%	double-click zoom tool icon	**Ctrl+Alt+zero (0)** or double-click zoom tool icon
Fit image onscreen	double-click hand tool icon	**Ctrl+zero (0)** or double-click hand tool icon

Operation	Old Photoshop 3 shortcut	New Photoshop 4 shortcut
Navigation		
Apply zoom value but keep magnification box active	*new feature*	**Shift+Enter**
Painting and editing		
Display Options palette	Double-click tool icon	Double-click tool icon **or Enter**
Display crosshair cursor	Caps Lock	Caps Lock
Revert image with magic eraser	Alt+drag with eraser	Alt+drag with eraser
Cycle through eraser styles	Alt+click eraser tool icon or press E key	Alt+click eraser tool icon or press E key
Specify an area to clone	Alt+click with rubber stamp	Alt+click with rubber stamp
Cycle through rubber stamp options	*none*	**Alt+click rubber stamp tool icon or press S key**
Dip into the foreground color when smearing	Alt+drag with smudge tool	Alt+drag with smudge tool
Cycle through focus tools	Alt+click focus tool icon or press R key	Alt+click focus tool icon or press R key
Sharpen with the blur tool or blur with the sharpen tool	Alt+drag	Alt+drag
Cycle through toning tools	Alt+click toning tool icon or press O key	Alt+click toning tool icon or press O key
Darken with the dodge tool or lighten with the burn tool	Alt+drag	Alt+drag
Paint or edit in a straight line	click and then Shift+click	click and then Shift+click
Change opacity, pressure, or exposure in 10% increments	press number key (1 through 0)	press number key (1 through 0)
Change opacity, pressure, or exposure in 1% increments	*none*	**press two number keys in a row**
Change brush mode	select mode from Options palette	select mode from Options palette
Display or hide Brushes palette	F5	F5

(continued)

Table 3-1
Photoshop's Hidden Shortcuts and Modifiers (continued)

Operation	Old Photoshop 3 shortcut	New Photoshop 4 shortcut
Painting and editing		
Cycle through brush shapes	press bracket key, [or]	press bracket key, [or]
Switch to first shape in Brushes palette	Shift+[	Shift+[
Switch to last shape in Brushes palette	Shift+]	Shift+]
Delete shape from Brushes palette	Ctrl+click brush shape	Ctrl+click brush shape
Create new brush shape	click in empty area of palette	click in empty area of palette
Edit brush shape	double-click brush shape	double-click brush shape
Applying colors		
Lift foreground color from image	Alt+click with paint tool or click with eyedropper	Alt+click with paint tool or click with eyedropper
Lift background color from image	Alt+click with eyedropper	Alt+click with eye-dropper
Lift foreground color from color bar at bottom of Color palette	click color bar	click color bar
Lift background color from color bar	Alt+click color bar	Alt+click color bar
Display or hide Color palette	F6	F6
Cycle through color bars	Shift+click color bar	Shift+click color bar
Specify new color bar	Ctrl+click color bar	Ctrl+click color bar
Lift foreground color from Swatches palette	click swatch	click swatch
Lift background color from Swatches palette	Alt+click swatch	Alt+click swatch
Delete swatch from palette	Ctrl+click swatch	Ctrl+click swatch
Replace swatch with foreground color	Shift+click swatch	Shift+click swatch

Operation	Old Photoshop 3 shortcut	New Photoshop 4 shortcut
	Applying colors	
Add new swatch to palette	click in empty area of palette or Shift+Alt+click swatch	click in empty area of palette or Shift+Alt+click on swatch
Fill selection or layer with foreground color	Alt+Delete	**Alt+Backspace**
Fill layer with foreground color but preserve transparency	*none*	**Shift+Alt+Backspace**
Fill selection on background layer with background color	Delete	Delete
Fill selection on any layer with background color	*none*	**Ctrl+Backspace**
Fill layer with background color but preserve transparency	*none*	**Shift+Ctrl+Backspace**
Display Fill dialog box	Shift+Delete	**Shift+Backspace**
	Selections	
Select everything	Ctrl+A	Ctrl+A
Deselect everything	Ctrl+D	Ctrl+D
Hide or show marching ants	Ctrl+H	Ctrl+H
Feather the selection	*none*	**Ctrl+Shift+D or Shift+F6**
Reverse the selection	*none*	**Ctrl+Shift+I or Shift+F7**
Draw out from center with marquee tool	Alt+drag	Alt+drag
Constrain marquee to square or circle	press Shift while drawing shape	press Shift while drawing shape
Move shape with marquee tool	*none*	**press spacebar while drawing shape**
Draw straight-sided selection outline	Alt+click with lasso tool	Alt+click with lasso tool **or press L to switch to polygonal lasso tool**
Add to selection	Shift+drag or Shift+click with selection tool	Shift+drag or Shift+click with selection tool

(continued)

Table 3-1
Photoshop's Hidden Shortcuts and Modifiers (*continued*)

Operation	Old Photoshop 3 shortcut	New Photoshop 4 shortcut
	Selections	
Subtract from selection	Ctrl+drag or Ctrl+click with selection tool	**Alt+drag or Alt+click with selection tool**
Retain intersected portion of selection	Shift+Ctrl+drag or Shift+Ctrl+click with selection tool	**Shift+Alt+drag or Shift+Alt+click with selection tool**
Temporarily access magic wand	press Ctrl when selection tool is active	*none*
Add character outlines to a selection	*new feature*	**Shift+click with type mask tool**
Cut letter-shaped holes into a selection	*new feature*	**Alt+click with type mask tool**
Retain areas where character outlines and selection intersect	*new feature*	**Shift+Alt+click with type mask tool**
Temporarily access move tool	*none*	**Ctrl**
Move selection	drag with selection or move tool	drag with move tool **or Ctrl+drag with other tool**
Constrain movement vertically or horizontally	press Shift while dragging selection	press Shift while dragging selection
Move selection in 1-pixel increments	press any arrow key	**Ctrl+arrow key**
Move selection in 10-pixel increments	Shift+arrow key	**Ctrl+Shift+arrow key**
Clone selection	Alt+drag with selection or move tool	Alt+drag with move tool **or Ctrl+Alt+drag with other tool**
Clone selection in 1-pixel increments	Alt+arrow key	**Ctrl+Alt+arrow key**
Clone selection in 10-pixel increments	Shift+Alt+arrow key	**Ctrl+Shift+Alt+arrow key**
Clone selection to different image	drag selection from one window and drop it into another	**Ctrl+drag selection from one window and drop it into another**
Move selection outline independently of its contents	Ctrl+Alt+drag with selection or move tool	**drag with selection tool**

Operation	Old Photoshop 3 shortcut	New Photoshop 4 shortcut
	Selections	
Move selection outline in 1-pixel increments	Ctrl+Alt+arrow key	**press any arrow key when selection tool is active**
Move selection outline in 10-pixel increments	Ctrl+Shift+Alt+ arrow key	**Shift+arrow key when selection tool is active**
Copy empty selection outline to different image	*none*	**drag selection from one window into another with selection tool**
Float selection in place	Ctrl+J	**Ctrl+Alt+up arrow then press down arrow key**
Drop floating selection	Ctrl+J	**Ctrl+E**
Drop fragment of floating selection	Ctrl+drag with type tool	***none***
Change opacity of floating selection in 10% increments	press number key (1 through 0) when selection tool is active	press number key (1 through 0) when selection tool is active
Change opacity of floating selection in 1% increments	*none*	**press two number keys in a row when selection tool is active**
Paste image into selection	*none*	**Ctrl+Shift+V**
Paste image behind selection	press Alt and choose Edit ⇨ Paste Into	**Ctrl+Shift+Alt+V**
	Layers	
Display or hide Layers palette	F7	F7
View single layer by itself	Alt+click eyeball icon in Layers palette	Alt+click eyeball icon in Layers palette
Create new empty layer	click new layer icon at bottom of Layers palette	click new layer icon at bottom of Layers palette
Clone selection to new layer	*none*	**Ctrl+J**
Convert selection to new layer and leave hole behind	*none*	**Ctrl+Shift+J**
Convert floating selection to new layer	double-click Floating Selection	double-click Floating Selection **or Ctrl+Shift+J** item in Layers palette

(continued)

Table 3-1
Photoshop's Hidden Shortcuts and Modifiers *(continued)*

Operation	Old Photoshop 3 shortcut	New Photoshop 4 shortcut
Layers		
Clone entire layer to new layer	drag layer name onto page icon	drag layer name onto page icon **or Ctrl+A, Ctrl+J**
Ascend one layer	Ctrl+]	**Alt+]**
Descend one layer	Ctrl+[	**Alt+[**
Ascend to top layer	Ctrl+Alt+]	**Shift+Alt+]**
Descend to background layer	Ctrl+Alt+[	**Shift+Alt+[**
Go directly to layer that contains specific image	Ctrl+click image with move tool	**Ctrl+Alt+right-click image with any tool**
Preserve transparency of layer	press slash (/) key	press slash (/) key
Convert layer's transparency mask to selection outline	Ctrl+Alt+T	**Ctrl+click layer name in Layers palette**
Add transparency mask to selection	*none*	**Ctrl+Shift+click layer name**
Subtract transparency mask from selection	*none*	**Ctrl+Alt+click layer name**
Retain intersection of transparency mask and selection	*none*	**Ctrl+Shift+Alt+click layer name**
Move entire layer	drag with move tool	drag with move tool **or Ctrl+drag with other tool**
Move entire layer in 1-pixel increments	press any arrow key when move tool is active	**Ctrl+arrow key**
Move entire layer in 10-pixel increments	Shift+arrow key when move tool is active	**Ctrl+Shift+arrow key**
Bring layer forward one level	drag layer name in palette	**Ctrl+]**
Bring layer to front of file	drag layer name in palette	**Ctrl+Shift+]**
Send layer backward one level	drag layer name in palette	**Ctrl+[**
Send layer to back, just above the background layer	drag layer name in palette	**Ctrl+Shift+[**

Operation	Old Photoshop 3 shortcut	New Photoshop 4 shortcut
	Layers	
Link layer with active layer	click in front of layer name	click in front of layer name
Change opacity of active layer in 10% increments	press number key (1 through 0) when selection tool is active	press number key (1 through 0) when selection tool is active
Change opacity of active layer in 1% increments	none	**press two number keys in a row when selection tool is active**
Edit blend options for layer	double-click layer name in Layers palette	double-click layer name in Layers palette
Adjust "fuzziness" in Layer Options dialog box	Alt+drag slider triangle	Alt+drag slider triangle
Merge layer with next layer down	none	**Ctrl+E**
Merge linked layers	none	**Ctrl+E**
Merge all visible layers	none	**Ctrl+Shift+E**
Copy merged version of selection to Clipboard	none	**Ctrl+Shift+C**
Clone contents of layer into next layer down	none	**Ctrl+Alt+E**
Clone contents of linked layers to active layer	none	**Ctrl+Alt+E**
Clone contents of all visible layers to activate layer	Alt+choose Merge Layers from Layers palette menu	**Alt+choose Layer ➪ Merge Visible**
Group neighboring layers	Alt+click horizontal line in Layers palette	Alt+click horizontal **or press Ctrl+G**
Ungroup neighboring layers	Alt+click dotted line in Layers palette	Alt+click dotted line **or press Ctrl+Shift+G**
Create adjustment layer	new feature	**Ctrl+click page icon at bottom of Layers palette**
Save flattened copy of layered image	none	**Ctrl+Alt+S**

(continued)

Table 3-1
Photoshop's Hidden Shortcuts and Modifiers (continued)

Operation	Old Photoshop 3 shortcut	New Photoshop 4 shortcut
Channels and masks		
Switch between independent color and mask channels	Ctrl+1 through Ctrl+9	Ctrl+1 through Ctrl+9
Switch to composite color channel	Ctrl+zero (0)	**Ctrl+tilde (~)**
Activate or deactivate color channel	Shift+click channel name in Channels palette	Shift+click channel name in Channels palette
Create channel mask from selection outline	click mask icon at bottom of Channels palette	click mask icon at bottom of Channels palette
View channel mask and image together	click eyeball in front of hidden channel	click eyeball in front of hidden channel
Convert channel mask to selection outline	press Ctrl and Alt with number key or Alt+click channel name in Channels palette	press Ctrl and Alt with number key **or Ctrl+click channel name in Channels palette**
Add channel mask to selection	Shift+Alt+click channel name	**Ctrl+Shift+click channel name**
Subtract channel mask from selection	Ctrl+Alt+click channel name	Ctrl+Alt+click channel name
Retain intersection of channel mask and selection	Ctrl+Shift+Alt+click channel name	Ctrl+Shift+Alt+click channel name
Enter or exit quick mask mode	press Q key	press Q key
Toggle quick mask color over masked or selected area	Alt+click quick mask icon in Toolbox	Alt+click quick mask icon in Toolbox
Change quick mask color overlay	double-click quick mask icon in Toolbox	double-click quick mask icon in Toolbox
View quick mask independently of image	click topmost eyeball in Channels palette	click topmost eyeball in Channels palette
Create layer mask filled with white	choose Add Layer Mask from Layers palette menu	**click mask icon at bottom of Layers palette**

Operation	Old Photoshop 3 shortcut	New Photoshop 4 shortcut
	Channels and masks	
Create layer mask filled with black	*none*	**Alt+click mask icon**
Create layer mask from selection outline	*none*	**click mask icon**
Create layer mask that hides selection	*none*	**Alt+click mask icon**
Switch focus from layer mask to image	Ctrl+zero (0)	**Ctrl+tilde (~)**
Switch focus from image to layer mask	Ctrl+tilde (~)	**Ctrl+backslash (\)**
View layer mask independently of image	Alt+click layer mask thumbnail in Layers palette	Alt+click layer mask thumbnail in Layers palette
View layer mask and image together	Shift+click layer mask thumbnail	**Shift+Alt+click layer mask thumbnail**
Disable layer mask	Ctrl+click layer mask thumbnail	Shift+click layer mask thumbnail
Toggle link between layer and layer mask	none	click between layer and mask thumbnails in Layers palette
Convert layer mask to selection outline	Ctrl+Alt+tilde (~)	**Ctrl+Alt+backslash (\) or Ctrl+click layer mask thumbnail**
Add layer mask to selection	*none*	**Ctrl+Shift+click layer mask thumbnail**
Subtract layer mask from selection	*none*	**Ctrl+Alt+click layer mask thumbnail**
Retain intersection of layer mask and selection	*none*	**Ctrl+Shift+Alt+click layer mask thumbnail**
	Transformations	
Select crop tool	press C key	press C key
Move cropping boundary	Ctrl+drag boundary handle	**drag inside boundary**

(continued)

Table 3-1
Photoshop's Hidden Shortcuts and Modifiers *(continued)*

Operation	Old Photoshop 3 shortcut	New Photoshop 4 shortcut
Transformations		
Resize cropping boundary	drag boundary handle	drag boundary handle
Rotate cropping boundary	Alt+drag boundary handle	**drag outside boundary**
Accept crop	click inside boundary	**press Enter**
Cancel crop	click outside boundary	**press Escape**
Transform selection or layer numerically	*new feature*	**Ctrl+Shift+T**
Freely transform selection or layer	*new feature*	**Ctrl+T**
Move transformation boundary	*new feature*	**drag inside boundary**
Resize transformation boundary	*new feature*	**drag boundary handle**
Rotate transformation boundary	*new feature*	**drag outside boundary**
Distort transformation boundary	*new feature*	**Ctrl+drag boundary handle**
Symmetrically distort adjacent corners	*new feature*	**Ctrl+Alt+drag boundary handle**
Filters		
Repeat filter with last-used settings	Ctrl+F	Ctrl+F
Repeat filter with different settings	Ctrl+Alt+F	Ctrl+Alt+F
Scroll preview box in corrective filter dialog boxes	drag in preview box or click in Image window	drag in preview box or click in Image window
Zoom preview box in corrective filter dialog boxes	Ctrl+spacebar+click and Alt+spacebar+click	**Ctrl+click and Alt+click**
Increase selected option-box value by 1 (or 0.1)	up arrow	up arrow
Decrease value by 1 (or 0.1)	down arrow	down arrow
Increase value by 10 (or 1)	Shift+up arrow	Shift+up arrow
Decrease value by 10 (or 1)	Shift+down arrow	Shift+down arrow

Operation	Old Photoshop 3 shortcut	New Photoshop 4 shortcut
Transformations		
Adjust Angle value (where offered) in 15° increments	Shift+drag in Angle wheel	Shift+drag in Angle wheel
Reset options inside corrective filter dialog boxes	Alt+click Cancel button	Alt+click Cancel button
Clone light in Lighting Effects dialog box	Alt+drag light	Alt+drag light
Delete Lighting Effects light	press Delete key	press Delete key
Adjust size of footprint without affecting angle of light	Shift+drag handle	Shift+drag handle
Adjust angle of light without affecting size of footprint	Ctrl+drag handle	Ctrl+drag handle
Paths		
Select pen tool	press T key	**press P key**
Cycle between path tools	*none*	**press P key**
Move selected points	drag point with arrow tool or Ctrl+drag with pen tool	drag point with arrow tool or Ctrl+drag with pen tool
Select multiple points in path	Shift+click point with arrow or Ctrl+Shift+click with pen	Shift+click point with arrow or Ctrl+Shift+click with pen
Select entire path	Alt+click path with arrow or Ctrl+Alt+click with pen	Alt+click path with arrow or Ctrl+Alt+click with pen
Clone path	Alt+drag path with arrow or Ctrl+Alt+drag with pen	Alt+drag path with arrow or Ctrl+Alt+drag with pen
Convert corner to arc	Ctrl+drag point with arrow	Ctrl+drag point arrow
Convert arc to corner	Ctrl+click with arrow	Ctrl+click with arrow
Convert arc to cusp or cusp to arc	Ctrl+drag handle with arrow	Ctrl+drag handle with arrow
Insert point in path	Ctrl+Alt+click segment with arrow tool	Ctrl+Alt+click segment with arrow tool

(continued)

Table 3-1
Photoshop's Hidden Shortcuts and Modifiers *(continued)*

Operation	Old Photoshop 3 shortcut	New Photoshop 4 shortcut
Paths		
Remove point from path	Ctrl+Alt+click point with arrow tool	Ctrl+Alt+click point with arrow tool
Convert path to selection outline	press Enter on keypad when selection or path tool is active	press Enter on keypad when selection or path tool is active **or Ctrl+click path name in Paths palette**
Add path to selection	Shift+Enter on keypad when selection or path tool is active	Shift+Enter on keypad **or Ctrl+Shift+ click path name**
Subtract path from selection	Ctrl+Enter on keypad when selection or path tool is active	**Alt+Enter on keypad or Ctrl+Alt+ click path name**
Retain intersection of path and selection	Ctrl+Shift+Enter on keypad when selection or path tool is active	**Shift+Alt+Enter on keypad or Ctrl+Shift+Alt+ click path name**
Apply brushstroke around perimeter of path	press Enter when paint or edit tool is active	press Enter on numeric keypad when paint or edit tool is active
Revert around perimeter of path	press Alt+Enter when eraser tool is active	press Alt+Enter on numeric keypad when eraser tool is active
Save path for future use	double-click Work Path item in Paths palette	double-click Work Path item in Paths palette
Hide path (it remains active)	*none*	**Ctrl+Shift+H**
Deactivate path	click in empty portion of Paths palette	click in empty portion of Paths palette
Rulers and guides		
Display or hide rulers	Ctrl+R	Ctrl+R
Display or hide Info palette	F8	F8
Change unit of measure	drag from X,Y pop-up in Info palette	drag from X,Y pop-up in Info palette **or double-click ruler**

Operation	Old Photoshop 3 shortcut	New Photoshop 4 shortcut
Rulers and guides		
Display or hide guides	*new function*	**Ctrl+semicolon (;)**
Create guide	*new function*	**drag from ruler**
Move guide	*new function*	**drag guide with move tool or Ctrl+drag with other tool**
Toggle horizontal guide to vertical or vice versa	*new function*	**press Alt while dragging guide**
Snap guide to ruler tick marks	*new function*	**press Shift while dragging guide**
Toggle guide magnetism	*new function*	**Ctrl+Shift+semicolon (;)**
Lock or unlock guides	*new function*	**Ctrl+Alt+semicolon (;)**
Display or hide grid	*new function*	**Ctrl+quote (″)**
Toggle grid magnetism	*new function*	**Ctrl+Shift+quote (″)**
Edit guide color and grid increments	*new function*	**double-click guide with move tool or Ctrl+double-click with other tool**
Miscellaneous		
Display or hide Actions palette (Commands palette for 3.0)	F9	F9
Display or hide all palettes, Toolbox, and Status bar	Tab	Tab
Display or hide palettes but not Toolbox and Status bar	*none*	Shift+Tab
Hide Toolbox and Status bar	Alt+Tab	**Tab, Shift+Tab**
Move a panel out of a palette	drag panel tab	drag panel tab
Snap palette to edge of screen	Shift+click palette Title bar	Shift+click palette Title bar
Fully collapse palette	Alt+click collapse box or double-click panel tab	Alt+click collapse box or double-click panel tab
Delete item in Layers, Channels, Paths, or Actions palette	drag item to trash can icon at bottom of palette	**Alt+click trash can icon at bottom of palette**
Preview how image sits on printed page	click preview box	click preview box

(continued)

Table 3-1
Photoshop's Hidden Shortcuts and Modifiers *(continued)*

Operation	Old Photoshop 3 shortcut	New Photoshop 4 shortcut
Miscellaneous		
View size and resolution of image	Alt+click preview box	Alt+click preview box
Change the preference settings	Ctrl+K	Ctrl+K
Display last used Preferences dialog box panel	*none*	**Ctrl+Alt+K**
Bring up dialog box with last-used settings	Alt+choose command from Image ➪ Adjust submenu	Alt+choose command from Image ➪ Adjust submenu
Duplicate image and bypass dialog box	press Alt and choose Image ➪ Duplicate	press Alt and choose Image ➪ Duplicate
Exit Type Tool dialog box	Enter	Enter
Cancel the current operation	Ctrl+period	**Escape**

Note: An asterisk (*) indicates a Version 4.0.1 shortcut.

Creating Scripts

So much for the shortcuts built into Photoshop 4. But while Table 3-1 may be the longest shortcuts list you've ever seen in your life, it's possible the list isn't long enough. You still must choose quite a few common commands from the menus. Image Size, Unsharp Mask, Variations, CMYK Color, and Color Range are a few of the commands I dearly wish included keyboard equivalents. Frankly, I used all five a heck of a lot more often than Show Rulers, Color Balance, and Gamut Warning, all of which Photoshop has endowed with shortcuts.

Back in Version 3, Photoshop provided the nifty Commands palette, which enabled you to assign function-key shortcuts to as many as 30 commands. Photoshop 4 has dispensed with this palette and substituted the Actions palette, which is at once better and worse than its predecessor.

The Actions palette is an improvement in that it enables you to create *scripts*, which are sequences of operations you can apply en masse. You can also *batch-process* images, which means to apply a script to an entire folder of files while you go off and have one of those power lunches you've heard about so often. If you spend a lot of your time performing repetitive tasks, scripts can help you automate your workaday routine; then you can devote your creative energies to something more important, like a nap.

If you took advantage of the Commands palette in Photoshop 3, the bad news boils down to a lack of continuity. The Actions palette can't open Version 3 Commands palette files, so you must create your old shortcuts from scratch. And the Actions palette lacks many of the modifiers that made the Commands palette so easy to use.

In fact, the only similarity between the Actions and Commands palette is the keystrokes you can assign to your scripts. You can assign the function keys F1 through F12, as well as these same keys with Shift. So, like Version 3 before it, Photoshop 4 tops out at 24 user-defined shortcuts. Frankly, I think this artificial limitation is stupid — I for one could use twice as many custom shortcuts — but nobody asked me.

Cross Reference

For examples of real scripts, read Chapters 15 and 18. Both chapters contain recipes for correcting pictures you've shot with a digital camera or downloaded from the Web.

Recording a script

Choose Window ➪ Show Actions to view the Actions palette. The icons along the bottom of the palette — labeled in Figure 3-4 — enable you to record commands and manage your recorded scripts. A script can include only a single command, as in the case of the Grayscale and RGB Color items listed near the top of the palette in the figure. Or you can record many commands in a row, as in the case of the Digital Pix Fix example. Photoshop divides one script from the next with a horizontal line.

Figure 3-4: The Actions palette enables you to record a sequence of commands and assign a keyboard shortcut.

If you've ever used a macro editor like QuicKeys or Tempo, the Actions palette isn't much different. (If you've never even heard of these utilities, not a problem. No experience required.) Here's a basic rundown of how you record a script.

Steps: Recording a Script

1. **Create a new script.** Click the new script icon — the one that looks like a little page — at the bottom of the Actions palette. Photoshop responds with the New Action dialog box, shown in Figure 3-6.

   Tip If you don't care about naming your script and assigning a function key, you can Alt+click the new script icon to skip the dialog box in Figure 3-5 and proceed directly to Step 4.

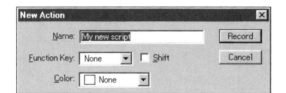

Figure 3-5: You can assign a name, function key, and color to a new script.

2. **Enter a name for your script.** You can also assign a function key, with or without Shift, and a color. Don't get too worked up about this stuff. You can always change the name, function key, and color later.

3. **Press Enter to start recording.** The circular record icon at the bottom of the Actions palette turns red to show you Photoshop is now observing your every action.

   Remember two things as you proceed into the next steps. First, if you mess up, keep going. Photoshop enables you to insert and reorder commands later. Second, there's no rush. You can take all day to figure out what you're doing. You can start to choose a command and then change your mind. You can even enter a dialog box and cancel out of it. Photoshop ignores your hesitations and false starts. All it cares about are commands.

4. **Choose a command.** If a dialog box comes up, enter some settings and press Enter. Nearly any command will do, but you must work with commands or use shortcuts that access commands. For example, Photoshop records you if you press Ctrl+A because that's the same as choosing Select ➪ All. But Photoshop ignores you if you change the opacity of a layer or paint with the airbrush because neither of these operations requires a command.

At this point, some of you automation enthusiasts — especially you folks who are familiar with Visual Basic — might be grumbling this is pretty lame scripting. And, in truth, it is. The Actions palette is easy to use, but it's not very powerful. Sometimes, you must be creative to get around its limitations.

After you complete the command, Photoshop adds it to the Actions palette. The program constantly keeps you apprised of what it's recording. If you perform an action and Photoshop doesn't add it to the palette, you have officially been ignored.

5. **Choose a few more commands.** Add as many as you like. Remember to watch the Actions palette so you know Photoshop is keeping up.

Note

If Photoshop ignores a command — as it may well do on occasion — don't fret. You can force Photoshop to add an uncooperative command after you finish recording the script. I'll show you how shortly.

6. **Click the square stop icon at the bottom of the Actions palette.**

That's it, you've now successfully recorded a script.

Tip

Photoshop not only records your commands in the Actions palette, it also applies them to whatever image you have open. (If you open an image while recording, Photoshop adds the Open command to the script.) For this reason, it's usually a good idea to have a dummy image open. When you're finished recording, you can choose File ➪ Revert to restore the original, unmolested image.

If your script includes a Save operation, try to use File ➪ Save As or File ➪ Save a Copy. This way, the original file will remain intact.

Caution

Be careful when you play a script that contains the Image Size command, discussed in Chapter 4. The command *always* uses the Resample Image setting that was in force the last time you issued the command. For example, if you resize an image with Resample Image turned on and then run a script that includes the Image Size command, the command is carried out with Resample Image turned on, even if you recorded the action with the check box turned off. So always check the setting of Resample Image before you run a script involving the Image Size command.

Oh, and one other thing: If you assigned a color to the script back in Step 2, you'll notice the conspicuous absence of color in the Actions palette. The color is visible only in the button mode, which I discuss in "Playing scripts and commands" later in this chapter.

Editing a script

You probably have about a 50/50 chance of recording your script right the first time. But no matter, Photoshop offers the following options to help you get it exactly right:

✦ **Adding more commands:** To add more commands at the end of a script, select the script and click the round record icon. Then start choosing those commands. When you finish, click again on the stop icon. If you selected the script before recording, Photoshop automatically adds the new commands to the end of the script. Or you can click a specific command name and then begin recording. In this case, the new command appears immediately after the command you clicked.

✦ **Moving a command:** To change the order of a command, drag the command up or down in the list. You can even drag a command from one script into another if you like.

✦ **Copying a command:** To make a copy of a command, Alt+drag it to a different location. Again, you can Alt+drag commands between scripts.

✦ **Investigating a command:** If you can't remember what setting you entered in a dialog box, or you don't recognize what a command name like Set means, click the triangle before the command name to expand it. Figure 3-6 shows an example of a Set command expanded to show that Photoshop has set the selection to all. This is Actions palette code for Select ➪ All.

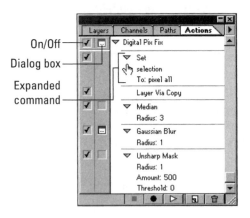

Figure 3-6: Click the little triangles to expand the commands and view their settings.

✦ **Changing a setting:** If the command name includes an embossed square to the left of it — in the column marked Dialog box in Figure 3-6 — the command brings up a dialog box. When you expand the command, Photoshop tells you the settings entered into that dialog box. In the case of the Median item in the figure, for example, the Radius value in the Median dialog box has been set to 3. To change the setting, double-click the command name to display the dialog box, and then revise the settings and press Enter.

Tip

Photoshop will go ahead and apply the settings to your image. If this is a problem, press Ctrl+Z to undo the command. This reverses the settings applied to the image, but has no effect on the changed settings in the script. The Actions palette ignores Edit ➪ Undo. (You can force the palette to accept the Undo command, however, as explained in a few paragraphs.)

✦ **Leaving a setting open:** Not all images are alike, and not all images will need the same settings applied to them. If you want to enter your own settings as the script plays, click the faint square in front of the command name in the dialog box column. A little dialog box icon appears, which shows you must be on hand when the script is played. In Figure 3-6, for example, a dialog box icon appears before the Gaussian Blur item. When I play the script, Photoshop leaves the Gaussian Blur dialog box up onscreen until I enter a setting and press Enter. Then the program continues playing the script through to completion.

Tip

Alt+click in front of a command name in the dialog box column to display a dialog box icon in front of that one command and hide all others. To bring up dialog boxes for everybody, Alt+click the same dialog box icon again, or click the red dialog box icon in front of the script name.

✦ **Forcing Photoshop to record a command:** If Photoshop ignored one of the commands you tried to record, choose Insert Menu Item from the Actions palette menu (the right-pointing triangle below the Title bar). Photoshop displays the dialog box shown in Figure 3-7, which asks you to choose a command. Go ahead and do it — the dialog box won't interfere with your progress. Then press Enter to add the command to the script. If the command brings up a dialog box, the Actions palette will probably ignore it, requiring you to enter settings manually and to press Enter when you play back the script.

Tip

If you want to force Photoshop to record the Undo command, by the way, type **Undo** into the Insert Menu Item dialog box. If you choose the Undo command from the Edit menu, Photoshop undoes your typing.

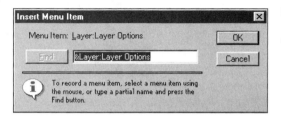

Figure 3-7: This dialog box forces Photoshop to record your command, whether or not it likes it.

✦ **Inserting a stop:** A *stop* is a pause in the action. You can't do anything when the script is paused — not in Photoshop anyway. You can switch to a different application, but Photoshop's options are off limits until you cancel or complete the script. The only real purpose of a stop is to give you the chance to see how the commands have progressed so far. To add a stop, choose the Insert Stop command from the Actions palette menu. Then enter the message you want to appear when the stop occurs. Select the Allow Continue check box to enable you to continue the script during playback.

✦ **Changing the name and function key:** To change the name, shortcut, or color assigned to a script, double-click the script name. Up comes the Action Options dialog box, which contains the same options as appeared back in Figure 3-5. Change the settings as you like. Any function keys assigned to other scripts appear dimmed.

✦ **Deleting a command:** To Delete a command, drag it to the trash can icon at the bottom of the Actions palette. Or easier still, select the command you want to Delete, and then Alt+click the trash can icon. (You can also merely click the icon, but Photoshop will display an irritating alert message. Alt+clicking skips the message.)

Playing scripts and commands

When it comes time to play your script, you can play all of it or just a single command. The simplest way to play back an entire script is to press the function key you assigned to it.

If you don't like to fill your brain with ephemeral nonsense like what function key does what, you might prefer to switch to the button mode. To do so, choose the Button Mode command from the Actions palette menu, as shown in Figure 3-8. You can now see the colors you assigned to the scripts, as well as the function keys. Click the button for the script you want to play.

Figure 3-8: Choose the Button Mode command to view each script as an independent button.

But the button mode has its drawbacks. All you can do is click buttons. You can't edit scripts, you can't change the order of scripts, you can't assign new function keys to scripts, and you can't play individual commands. This is a great mode if you want to protect your scripts from less adept users, but it's an awful mode if you want to modify your scripts and create new ones.

So, choose the Button Mode command again to return to the normal palette setup. Then try some of these less-restrictive script-playing techniques:

✦ To play a selected script, click the play icon at the bottom of the palette. You can also play a script by Ctrl+double-clicking the script name.

✦ To play a script from a certain command on, select that command name in the palette, and then click the play icon.

✦ To play a single command and no more, drag the command name onto the play icon. Or Ctrl+double-click the command name.

✦ You can tell Photoshop which commands to play and which to skip using the check marks in the on/off column (labeled back in Figure 3-7). Click a check mark to turn off the corresponding command.

✦ Alt+click a check mark to turn that one command on and the rest off. To turn all the commands in the script on again, Alt+click the check mark again, or click the red check mark by the script name.

Batch-Processing Images

Batch-processing is one of those scary terms you hear bandied about by experts on a fairly regular basis. But it's actually relatively easy, especially with Photoshop 4's Batch command.

The following steps walk you through the task of batch-processing a bunch of files. This isn't the only way to batch-process files — Photoshop offers several additional variations you can experiment with on your own. But these steps represent the best way.

Steps: Batch-Processing Files

1. **Create the script you want to apply.** The last step in the script should be File ⇨ Save As. This saves the completed image to disk without saving over the original. Use whatever format you like (as discussed in Chapter 4).

2. **Round up the images to which you want to apply the script.**

You can put all the images in a single folder. Or, if you own a digital camera from which Photoshop can open images directly — anything from the $3,000 Polaroid PDC-2000 to the $300 Kodak DC20 — you should plug the camera into your PC and turn it on.

3. **Create a folder to collect the images once Photoshop is done processing them.** If you're opening images from a folder, you can have Photoshop save to the same folder, but this will save over the original files (even with File ⇨ Save As). It's a good precaution to save the files elsewhere so you can refer to the originals if you're not pleased with the scripted results.

4. **Choose the Batch command from the Actions palette menu.** Photoshop displays the dialog box shown in Figure 3-9. The dialog box offers many options, but it's a peach once you get to know it.

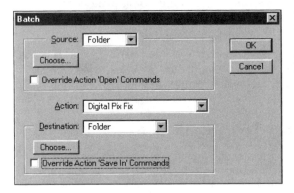

Figure 3-9: Here I have the Batch command all set up to open images stored in one folder, run the Digital Pix Fix script, and save the images in another folder.

5. **Select a source for the images.** Select Import from the Source pop-up menu if you want to acquire the images from a digital camera. Then select the acquire module you generally use to communicate with the camera from the From pop-up menu.

   To open images from a folder, select Folder from the Source pop-up menu. Then click the Choose button and locate the folder on disk.

6. **Select your script from the Action pop-up menu.** Photoshop selects the active script by default, but you can select any script you like.

7. **Select the destination folder.** First, select the Folder option from the Destination pop-up menu. Then click the Choose button and locate the destination folder on disk.

   The Destination pop-up menu offers two other options — None, which collects the images onscreen without saving them, and Save and Close, which saves the images over the originals and closes them. One clogs up RAM and slows performance, while the other eliminates your backup images. Boo to both.

8. **Turn on the Override Action "Save In" Commands check box.** If you worked all day, I don't think you could come up with a more confusing name for a check box. (Why didn't Adobe name it *Gibberish* and be done with it?) But it has an important purpose. It overrides the folder destination and file name included with the Save As command in your script. The script instead retains the original name of the image and saves it to the folder you requested in the last step. Photoshop still saves the image in the file format you specified with the Save As command.

9. **Press Enter.** Photoshop begins batch-processing your images, starting with the first images in alphabetical order.

You might want to watch the first image from start to finish to make sure everything goes smoothly, particularly the save operation. (Photoshop should close each image after it finishes saving it.) But after the first image, you should probably leave Photoshop and your PC alone to work their wonders. A watched pot never boils and a watched batch defeats the purpose. You're supposed to be out there engaging in interesting carbon-based activities while Photoshop slaves away in your absence. So get out of here!

Understanding Digital Imagery

P A R T

In This Part

◆ ◆ ◆ ◆

Image Fundamentals

How Images Work

Think of a bitmapped image as a mosaic made from square tiles of various colors. When you view the mosaic up close, it looks like something you might use to decorate your bathroom. You see the individual tiles, not the image itself. But if you back a few feet away from the mosaic, the tiles lose their definition and merge together to create a recognizable work of art, presumably Medusa getting her head whacked off or some equally appetizing thematic classic.

Similarly, *images* are colored pixels pretending to be artwork. If you enlarge the pixels, they look like an unrelated collection of colored squares. Reduce the size of the pixels, and they blend together to form an image that looks to all the world like a standard photograph. Photoshop deceives the eye by borrowing from an artistic technique older than Mycenae or Pompeii.

Of course, differences exist between pixels and ancient mosaic tiles. Pixels come in 16 million distinct colors. Mosaic tiles of antiquity came in your basic granite and sandstone varieties, with an occasional chunk of lapis lazuli thrown in for good measure. Also, you can resample, color separate, and crop electronic images. We know from the time-worn scribblings of Dionysius of Halicarnassus that these processes were beyond the means of classical artisans.

But I'm getting ahead of myself. I won't be discussing resampling, cropping, or Halicarnassus for several pages. Meanwhile, I'll address the inverse relationship between image size and resolution.

Size versus resolution

If you haven't already guessed, the term *image size* describes the physical dimensions of an image. *Resolution* is the number of pixels per linear inch. I say linear because you measure pixels in a straight line. If the resolution of an image is 72 *ppi* — that is, pixels per inch — you get 5,184 pixels per square inch (72 pixels wide × 72 pixels tall = 5,184).

Assuming the number of pixels in an image is fixed, increasing the size of an image decreases its resolution and vice versa. An image that looks good when printed on a postage stamp, therefore, probably will look jagged when printed as an 11 × 17-inch poster.

Figure 4-1 shows a single image printed at three different sizes and resolutions. The smallest image is printed at twice the resolution of the medium-sized image; the medium-sized image is printed at twice the resolution of the largest image.

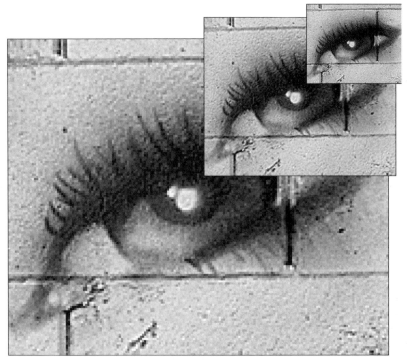

Figure 4-1: These three images contain the same number of pixels, but are printed at different resolutions. Doubling the resolution of an image reduces it to 25 percent of its original size.

One inch in the smallest image includes twice as many pixels vertically and twice as many pixels horizontally as an inch in the medium-sized image, for a total of four times as many pixels per square inch. Therefore, the smallest image covers one-fourth of the area of the medium-sized image.

The same relationships exist between the medium-sized image and the largest image. An inch in the medium-sized image comprises four times as many pixels as an inch in the largest image. Consequently, the medium-sized image consumes one-fourth the area of the largest image.

Changing the printing resolution

When printing an image, a higher resolution translates to a sharper image with greater clarity. Photoshop enables you to change the resolution of a printed image in one of two ways:

✦ Choose Image ➪ Image Size to access the controls that enable you to change the pixel dimensions and resolution of an image. Then enter a value into the Resolution option box, either in pixels per inch or pixels per centimeter.

Caution

A good idea (although not essential) is to turn off the Resample Image check box, as demonstrated in Figure 4-2. If you leave it on, Photoshop may add or subtract pixels, as discussed in the "Resampling and Cropping" section later in this chapter.

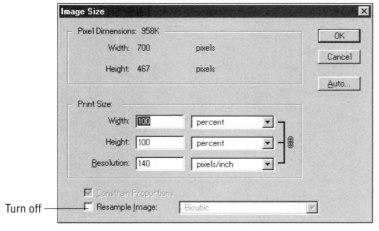

Figure 4-2: Turn off the Resample Image check box to maintain a constant number of pixels in an image and to change only the printed resolution.

✦ Or you can instruct Photoshop to scale an image during the print cycle by choosing File ➪ Page Setup (Ctrl+Shift+P), clicking the Properties button, and entering a percentage value into the Scaling option box, found on the Graphics tab of the Properties dialog box. Note, this option isn't available for some lower-end printers.

Both the Resolution and Scaling settings are saved with an image. Together, the two determine the printed resolution. Photoshop divides the Resolution value in the Image Size dialog box by the Scaling percentage in the Page Setup dialog box. For example, if the image resolution is set to 72 ppi and you reduce the image to 48 percent, then the final printed image has a resolution of 150 ppi (72 divided by .48).

Note At the risk of boring some of you, I'll briefly remind the math haters in the audience that whenever you use a percentage in an equation, you first convert it to a decimal. For example, 100 percent is 1.0, 64 percent is .64, 5 percent is .05, and so on.

Tip To avoid confusion, most folks rely exclusively on the Resolution value and leave Scaling set to 100 percent. The only exception is when printing proofs. Because proof printers offer lower-resolution output, you may find it helpful to print images larger so you can see more pixels. Raising the Scaling value enables you to accomplish this without upsetting the Resolution value. Just be sure to restore the Scaling value to 100 percent after you print the proof.

Changing the page-layout resolution

The Scaling value has no effect on the size and resolution of an image imported into an object-oriented application, such as QuarkXPress or Illustrator. But these same applications do observe the Resolution setting.

Specifying the resolution in Photoshop is a handy way to avoid resizing operations and printing complications in your page-layout program. For example, I preset the resolution of all the images in this book so the production team had only to import the images and print away.

Tip Always remember: Photoshop is as good or better at adjusting pixels than any other program with which you work. So prepare an image as completely as possible in Photoshop before importing the image into another program. Ideally, you should never have to resize, rotate, or crop an image in any other program.

Screen resolution

Regardless of the Resolution and Scaling values, Photoshop displays each pixel onscreen according to the zoom ratio (as discussed in Chapter 2). If the zoom ratio is 100 percent, for example, each image pixel takes up a single screen pixel. Zoom ratio and printer output are unrelated.

When creating an image for a screen presentation or display, you want the image size to fit inside the prospective monitor at the 100-percent zoom ratio. I say *prospective* monitor because although you may use a 17-inch monitor when you create the image, you may want to display the final image on a 13-inch monitor. In this case, you would set the image size no larger than 640 × 480 pixels (the standard resolution of a 13-inch monitor) with no concern for the size the image appears on your 17-inch monitor.

Many monitors conform to specific default resolutions, as listed in Table 4-1. But more and more graphics cards enable you to change the resolution of the monitor so a 640 × 480-pixel image may shrink or grow onscreen. For this reason, many Web and screen artists prepare for the worst-case scenario, typically 640 × 480. (Old-model Macs have lower screen resolutions, but it's safe to say few folks who are still using Classics are out surfing the Web.)

I discuss Web graphics in more detail in Chapter 20. Meanwhile, Table 4-1 lists a few common DOS-based PC and Macintosh screen sizes. If you care, flag the pages as a resource. If you don't, rip them out and wrap a few fish.

Table 4-1 Macintosh and PC Monitor Standards		
Monitor	**Pixels wide**	**Pixels tall**
IBM compatibles		
Old monochrome Hercules cards	720	348
16-color EGA cards	640	350
Old MCGA cards	640	480
VGA and XGA cards	640	480
SuperVGA	800	600
8514/a or TIGA cards	1,024	768
High-end graphics cards	1,280	1,024
Professional-level cards	1,600	1,200
Macintosh		
13-inch screens	640	480
15-inch portrait screens	640	870
17-inch screens	832	624
19-inch screens	1,024	768
21-inch (two-page) screens	1,152	870
High-end graphics cards	1,360	1,024
Professional-level cards	1,600	1,200

Remember, only a representative few of the kinds of monitors and graphics cards exist. And modern video cards enable you to switch between different resolutions. For example, the S3 Vision card installed in my current Pentium PC can accommodate 640 × 480, 800 × 600, 1,024 × 768, or 1,280 × 1,024 pixels, depending on how many colors I want to display.

Even so, the values in Table 4-1 are indicative of the basic resolution settings available and the inherent differences between platforms. Both Macs and PCs support 640 × 480 and 1,024 × 768. But while the medium Mac setting is 832 × 624, the medium PC setting is 800 × 600. This small discrepancy can mean the difference between an image fitting onscreen or being cut short.

How to Open, Duplicate, and Save Images

Before you can work on an image in Photoshop — whether you're creating a brand new document or opening an image from disk — you must first load the image into an Image window. Here are the four basic ways to create an Image window:

✦ **File ➪ New:** Create a new window by choosing File ➪ New (Ctrl+N). After you fill out the desired size and resolution specifications in the New dialog box, Photoshop confronts you with a stark, white, empty canvas. You then face the ultimate test of your artistic abilities — painting from scratch. Feel free to go nuts and cut off your ear.

✦ **File ➪ Open:** Open an image saved to disk or CD-ROM by choosing File ➪ Open (Ctrl+O). Of the four ways to create an Image window, this method is the one you'll probably use most often. You can open images scanned in other applications, images purchased from stock photo agencies, slides and transparencies digitized to a Kodak Photo CD, or an image you previously edited in Photoshop.

✦ **Edit ➪ Paste:** Photoshop automatically adapts a new Image window to the contents of the Clipboard (provided those contents are bitmapped). So if you copy an image inside a different application or in Photoshop, and then choose File ➪ New, Photoshop enters the dimensions and resolution of the image into the New dialog box. All you must do is accept the settings and choose Edit ➪ Paste (Ctrl+V) to introduce the image into a new window. This technique is useful for testing filtering effects on a sample of an image without harming the original.

Note

You might also think this method would be useful for editing screen shots captured to the Clipboard via Alt+Print Screen. There's just one problem. After you open the first Clipboard image, Photoshop refuses to replace this image with the next screen shot you capture, even though the Clipboard Viewer confirms you have, indeed, successfully captured a new screen. You can solve the problem in one of two ways: First, you can add a line to your

PHOTOS40.INI file: ALWAYSIMPORTCLIP=1 (the default is 0) and then restart Photoshop. Second, you can use an add-on utility that enables you to capture multiple Clipboard images — remember, natively the Clipboard will replace whatever is on it with your latest capture. I heartily recommend the shareware program Clipmate, widely available online and on the CD-ROM that comes with IDG Books' *Windows 95 SECRETS*.

Photoshop 4.0

Photoshop 4 automatically pastes an image to a new layer. This means you can save the resulting file exclusively in the native Photoshop format (as I explain later in this chapter). To flatten the pasted image so you can save it in some other format, choose Layer ➪ Merge Down or press Ctrl+E.

✦ **File ➪ Import:** If you own a scanner or digital camera, it may include a plug-in module that enables you to transfer an image directly into Photoshop. Just copy the module into Photoshop's Plugins folder and then run or relaunch the Photoshop application. To initiate a scan or to load an image into Photoshop, choose the plug-in module from the File ➪ Import submenu.

For example, to load an image from my Polaroid PDC-2000 — the best camera currently under $5,000 — I cable the camera to my Adaptec SCSI card. Then I turn the camera on and choose File ➪ Import ➪ PDC-2000. A dialog box appears showing thumbnails of all the images I've shot. I select the images I want to edit, click the Transfer button, and the images open directly inside Photoshop.

Creating a new image

Whether you're creating an image from scratch or transferring the contents of the Clipboard to a new Image window, choose File ➪ New or press Ctrl+N to bring up the New dialog box shown in Figure 4-3. If the Clipboard contains an image, the Width, Height, and Resolution option boxes show the size and resolution of this image. Otherwise, you can enter your own values in one of five units of measurement: pixels, inches, centimeters, picas, or points. If you're uncertain exactly what size image you want to create, enter a rough approximation. You can always change your settings later.

Tip

Although Photoshop matches the contents of the Clipboard by default, you can also match the size and resolution of other images:

✦ Press Alt when choosing File ➪ New, or press Ctrl+Alt+N to override the contents of the Clipboard. Photoshop displays the size and resolution of the last image you created, whether or not it came from the Clipboard. Use this technique when creating many same-sized images in a row.

✦ You can also match the size and resolution of the new image to any other open image. While the New dialog box is open, choose the name of the image you want to match from the Window menu. It's that simple.

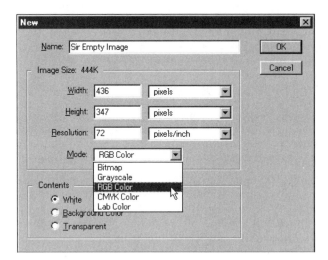

Figure 4-3: Use the New dialog box to specify the size, resolution, and color mode of your new image.

Units of measure

The Width and Height pop-up menus contain the five common units of measure mentioned earlier: pixels, inches, centimeters, points, and picas. But the Width pop-up menu offers one more, called Columns. If you want to create an image that fits exactly within a certain number of columns when it's imported into a desktop publishing program, select this option. You can specify the width of a column and the gutter between columns by pressing Ctrl+K and Ctrl+5 for the Units & Rulers preferences. Then enter values into the Column Size option boxes.

The Gutter value affects multiple-column images. Suppose you accept the default setting of a 15-pica column width and a 1-pica gutter. If you specify a one-column image in the New dialog box, Photoshop makes it 15 picas wide. If you ask for a two-column image, Photoshop adds the width of the gutter to the width of the two columns and creates an image 31 picas wide.

The Height pop-up menu in the New dialog box lacks a Column option because vertical columns have nothing to do with an image's height.

Tip

You can change the default unit of measure that appears in the Width and Height pop-up menus by pressing Ctrl+K, Ctrl+5, and selecting a different option from the Units pop-up menu. Easier still, bring up the Info palette by pressing the F8 key. Then click or drag on the little cross icon in the palette's lower-left corner. Up comes a pop-up menu of units, as demonstrated in Figure 4-4.

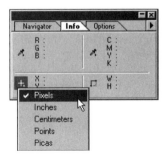

Figure 4-4: You can select a default unit of measure from the coordinates pop-up menu in the lower-left corner of the Info palette.

New image size

In most cases, the onscreen dimensions of an image depend on your entries in the Width, Height, and Resolution option boxes. If you set both the Width and Height values to 10 inches and the Resolution to 72 ppi, the new image will measure 720 × 720 pixels. The exception occurs if you choose pixels as your unit of measurement, as in Figure 4-4. In this case, the onscreen dimensions depend solely on the Width and Height options, and the Resolution value determines the size at which the image prints.

Color mode

Use the Mode pop-up menu to specify the number of colors that can appear in your image. Choose Bitmap to create a black-and-white image and choose Grayscale to access only gray values. RGB Color, CMYK Color, and Lab Color all provide access to the full range of 16 million colors, although their methods of doing so differ.

Cross Reference

RGB stands for red-green-blue, CMYK for cyan-magenta-yellow-black, and Lab for luminosity and two abstract color variables: a and b. To learn how each of these color modes works, read the "Working in Different Color Modes" section of Chapter 5.

Background color

The New dialog box also provides three Contents radio buttons that enable you to change the color of the background for the new image. You can fill the new image with white, with the current background color (assuming, of course, the background color is something other than white), or with no color at all. This last setting, Transparent, results in a floating layer with no background image whatsoever, which can be useful when editing one layer independently of the rest of an image, or when preparing a layer to be composited with an image. (For an in-depth examination of the more nitty-gritty aspects of layering, see Chapter 13.)

If you do select a transparent background, you must later flatten the layer by choosing Layer ➪ Flatten Image if you want to save the image to any format other than native Photoshop. The advantage of the Transparent setting, however, is Photoshop doesn't create a new layer when you press Ctrl+V to paste the contents of the Clipboard. In the long run, this doesn't make much difference — you still must flatten the image before you save it — but at least you needn't fuss around with two layers, one of which is completely empty.

Naming the new image

The New dialog box provides a Name option. If you know what you want to call your new image, enter the name now. Or don't. It doesn't matter. Either way, when you choose File ➪ Save, Photoshop asks you to specify the location of the file and confirm the file's name, just as in previous versions. So don't feel compelled to name your image anything. The only reason for this option is to help you keep your images organized onscreen. Lots of folks create temporary images they never save; Photoshop offers a way to assign temporary images more meaningful names than Untitled-4, Untitled-5, Untitled-6, and so on.

Caution

You may be tempted to go hog-wild with long filenames (LFNs), which Windows 95 and Photoshop allow — after all, the Mac has offered this option for years. Be careful! If you're sending your file to someone who doesn't use Windows 95, the long filename gets truncated (cut off) to the old-style Windows naming convention (eight characters followed by a three-letter file extension). The cut-off filenames can lead to some confusion down the line, so you're better off to stick with the old file-naming conventions unless you're sure you won't exchange files with pre-Windows 95 users. And for heaven's sake, ignore the advice you may hear from computer gurus about editing the Windows 95 Registry to address this problem. Doing so can play havoc with some programs.

Opening an existing image

If you want to open an image stored on disk, choose File ➪ Open or press Ctrl+O to display the Open dialog box. The Open dialog box behaves just like the ones in other Windows applications, with a folder pop-up menu, scrolling list of files, and other standard navigation options.

The scrolling list contains the names of documents Photoshop recognizes it can open. If you can't find the file you want, type ***.*** into the File Name option box and press Enter. If you're lucky, you'll see a file that makes sense, along with a file extension that probably makes no sense, or no extension at all.

Note

The lack of an extension typically arises in either of two ways. Sometimes files transmitted electronically (via the Internet, for example) lose their extensions en route. The problem can be compounded if the person sending the file uses a Mac. The Macintosh doesn't use file extensions; the file type information is saved internally. That is, your Mac friend may have produced a PSD file and named it Deke's Unmentionable File. On the Mac side, the file opens perfectly in Photoshop.

But on the PC, Photoshop won't touch the file with a ten-foot pole. Solution? Rename the file Deke's Unmentionable File.PSD, and all will be well.

But, you say, *I don't see file extensions when I go trolling in the Windows 95 Explorer.* The reason you don't see them is you probably have the option selected that hides the extensions of registered file types. Uncheck the option, and your extensions appear.

Photoshop's Open dialog box goes the extra mile by offering an option other dialog boxes lack — namely, a thumbnail preview of the selected image. The thumbnail appears at the bottom of the dialog box, as shown in Figure 4-5. Beneath the thumbnail, Photoshop shows the file size of the image.

A preview appears, however, only if the Save Thumbnail check box was selected in the Save As dialog box when you saved the image to disk in Photoshop 4.0 (as discussed in the "Saving Files" section of Chapter 2 and in "Saving an image to disk" later in this chapter). If the image was last saved using an earlier version of Photoshop, no thumbnail preview will appear — this feature is new in Version 4.0.

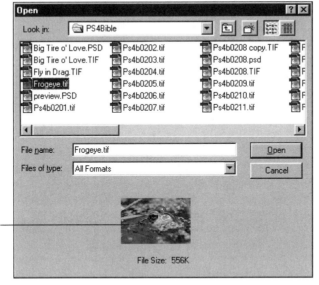

Image Preview

Figure 4-5: If you selected the Save Thumbnail check box when saving your image, you can see a preview of the image in the Open dialog box.

Previewing outside Photoshop

Tip

In Windows 95, the Open dialog box isn't the only place you can preview an image before you open it. In fact, you can preview an image without even opening Photoshop. Right-click an image saved in the native Photoshop format — either in Windows Explorer, a folder window, or on the desktop — and choose Properties from the pop-up menu that appears. When the Properties dialog box opens, click the Photoshop Image tab to look at your image, as shown in Figure 4-6. On the other tabs of the dialog box, you can view the caption, keywords, credits, and other file information, if any.

If you select any of the Icon Thumbnails radio buttons on the Photoshop Image tab except Don't Generate, Windows also displays a tiny thumbnail on the General tab of the dialog box. You can see this same thumbnail on the desktop (if the image file is stored there), in the folder window, and next to the file name in Explorer (you must choose View ➪ Large Icons to see the thumbnail in Explorer). Right-click the icon and choose Properties to get to the Properties dialog box and the larger preview.

Unfortunately, this trick works only for images saved in the native Photoshop 4 format. But, even so, it's a heck of a trick. And it works regardless of whether you select the Save Thumbnail option when saving the image in Photoshop.

Figure 4-6: You can preview files saved in the Photoshop 4 native format via the Windows 95 Properties dialog box.

Duplicating an image

Have you ever wanted to try an effect without permanently damaging an image? Certainly, you can undo the last action performed in Photoshop (by choosing Edit ➪ Undo), but what if the technique involves multiple steps? And what if you want to apply two or more effects to an image independently and compare them side by side? And later maybe even merge them? This is a job for image duplication.

To create a new window with an independent version of the foreground image, choose Image ➪ Duplicate. A dialog box appears, requesting a name for the new image. Just like the Name option in the New dialog box, the option is purely an organizational tool you can use or ignore. If your image contains multiple layers, Photoshop will, by default, retain all layers in the duplicate document. Or you can merge all visible layers into a single layer by selecting the Merged Layers Only check box. (Hidden layers remain independent.) Press Enter to create your new, independent image. (This image is unsaved; you need to choose File ➪ Save to save any changes to disk.)

Tip

If you're happy to let Photoshop automatically name your image and you don't care what it does with the layers, press Alt while choosing Image ➪ Duplicate. This bypasses the Duplicate Image dialog box and immediately creates a new window.

Saving an image to disk

The first rule of storing an image on disk is to save it frequently. If the foreground image is untitled, as it is when you work on a new image, choosing File ➪ Save (Ctrl+S) displays the Save dialog box, enabling you to name the image, specify its location on disk, and select a file format. As mentioned earlier, in the section "Naming the new image," avoid using Windows 95 long filenames unless you're certain you won't be sharing the image with someone who doesn't use Windows 95.

Be sure to check the Save Thumbnail option box if you want to view a thumbnail of your image in the Open dialog box. The check box is selected automatically if you choose the Always Save option from the Image Preview pop-up menu on the Saving Files panel of the Preferences dialog box, as discussed in Chapter 2. The check box is turned off by default if you have the Never Save option selected. As for the Ask When Saving option, well, it's no different than the Always Save option. The Save Thumbnail option box is turned on automatically; it's up to you to turn the check box off if you don't want a thumbnail.

After you save the image once, choosing the Save command updates the file on disk without bringing up the Save dialog box. Choose File ➪ Save As or press Ctrl+Shift+S to change the name, location, or format of the image stored on disk. By the way, if your only reason for choosing the Save As command is to change the file format, it's perfectly acceptable to overwrite (save over) the original document, assuming you no longer need the previous copy of the image. Granted, your computer could crash during the Save As operation, in which case you would lose both the new document and the original. But the chance of crashing during a Save As is extremely remote — no more likely than crashing during any other save operation.

Tip

To speed the save process, I usually save an image in Photoshop's native format until I'm finished working on it. Before I close the image, I choose File ➪ Save As and save the image in the compressed TIFF or JPEG format. By using this method, I compress each image only once during a session.

Saving a copy

The final save command — File ➪ Save a Copy (Ctrl+Alt+S) — enables you to save a copy of the current image without changing that special relationship between the image and its original on disk. This is like duplicating the image, saving it, and closing the duplicate all in one step.

The whole purpose of the Save a Copy command is to save a flattened version of a layered image or to dump the extra channels in an image that contains masks. Just select the file format you want to use and let Photoshop do the flattening and dumping automatically.

When you choose the Save a Copy command, Photoshop displays two extra check boxes at the bottom of the standard Save dialog box, as shown in Figure 4-7.

✦ **Flatten Image:** Photoshop activates this check box whenever you select a format other than the native Photoshop format. Because no other format supports layers, the check box must turn on to show the layers will fuse together when the image is saved.

✦ **Don't Include Alpha Channels:** "Alpha channel" is Photoshop's techy name for a mask. As discussed in Chapter 12, a *mask* is a method for defining highly accurate selections. But only a few formats — Photoshop, TIFF, and Raw — support masks. Other formats abandon them. Again, Photoshop automatically activates this check box when you select a no-mask format.

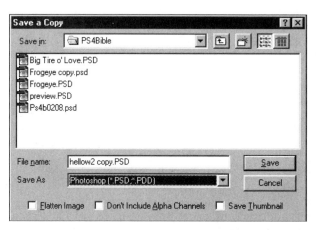

Figure 4-7: Choose the Save a Copy command to save a separate, flattened copy of a layered image. This way, you can continue to adjust the layers in the future.

The Save a Copy command is perfect for when you want to export a layered image for use in another program. A page-layout application like QuarkXPress doesn't support Photoshop's native format, but you don't want to flatten the image and permanently lose your layers. So here's your compromise: Keep one copy with layers in the Photoshop format and create a flattened copy for QuarkXPress.

Cross Reference

The whole issue of formats is too large to discuss here. In fact, it takes up the majority of this chapter, starting with the "File Format Roundup" section coming up next.

File Format Roundup

Photoshop 4 supports more than 20 file formats from inside its Open and Save dialog boxes. It can support even more through the addition of plug-in modules, which attach commands to the File ⇨ Save As, File ⇨ Import and File ⇨ Export submenus.

File formats represent different ways to save a file to disk. Some formats provide unique image-compression schemes, which save an image in a manner that consumes less space on disk. Other formats enable Photoshop to trade images with different applications on the Mac and on different platforms.

The native format

Like most programs, Photoshop offers its own *native format* — that is, a format optimized for Photoshop's particular capabilities and functions. This format saves every attribute you can apply in Photoshop, including layers, and is compatible with Versions 3 and later of the program.

Tip

Also worth noting is Photoshop 4 can open and save in its native format more quickly than in any other format and it also offers image compression. Like TIFF's compression, the Photoshop compression scheme does not result in any loss of data.

In addition, the Version 4 Photoshop format is compatible with Photoshop 2.5 if the 2.5 Compatibility check box is selected inside the Preferences dialog box (which you reach by pressing Ctrl+K and then Ctrl+2). If this check box is turned off, Photoshop 2.5 will be unable to open a layered image saved in the modern Photoshop format.

After that explanation, you may be surprised when I tell you I leave the 2.5 Compatibility check box turned off. Now that we're two versions beyond Photoshop 2.5, it's safe to assume the overwhelming majority of folks have upgraded at least as far as Version 3. More importantly, you save disk space by turning the 2.5 Compatibility option off, particularly if your image involves layers.

If you are creating single-channel grayscale images to be used as displacement maps with the Displace filter, however, you must have the 2.5 Compatibility check box turned on. Otherwise the Displace filter won't *see* the grayscale image.

Cross-platform formats

Photoshop 4 provides several formats for saving an image you want to transfer to a different computer or to post on the World Wide Web. If your clients or coworkers use painting applications other than Photoshop, you'll find these formats essential.

The GIF, PDF, and PNG formats have special significance for Web designers. I discuss all three, as well as compression champ JPEG, in Chapter 20.

Microsoft Paint's BMP

BMP (Windows Bitmap) is the native format for Microsoft Paint (included with Windows) and is supported by a variety of Windows, DOS, and OS/2 applications. Photoshop supports BMP images with up to 16 million colors. You also can use Run-Length Encoding (RLE), a lossless compression scheme specifically applicable to the BMP format.

The term *lossless* refers to compression schemes such as BMP's RLE and TIFF's LZW (Lempel-Ziv-Welch) that enable you to save space on disk without sacrificing any data in the image. The only reasons not to use lossless compression are it slows down the open and save operations and it may prevent less-sophisticated applications from opening an image. Lossy compression routines, such as JPEG, sacrifice a user-defined amount of data to conserve even more disk space.

The most common use of BMP is to create images for use in help files and Windows wallpaper. In fact, rolling your own wallpaper is a fun way to show off your Photoshop skills, which is exactly what I did in Color Plate 4-2. Remember, you may want to save your wallpaper image in indexed color format; a high-color wallpaper displayed in 256-color video looks, well, excruciating. And you can get great effects with an 8-bit palette. Color Plate 4-2, for example, contains just 256 colors. See Chapter 20 for further details on indexed color.

Also, if you want Windows to find and recognize your wallpaper file automatically, don't use RLE. If you use RLE, you have to direct Windows toward the specific wallpaper file unless you're using a third-party wallpaper-management utility.

CompuServe's GIF

Originally, CompuServe supported GIF (pronounced *jiff,* short for Graphics Interchange Format) as a means of compressing files so you could quickly transfer photographs via modem to and from the company's commercial bulletin board service. Like TIFF, GIF uses LZW compression, but unlike TIFF, GIF can't handle more than 256 colors.

With the advent of the World Wide Web, though, GIF graphics have become more sophisticated. Two varieties of GIF currently exist, known by the helpful codes 87a and 89a. GIF87a supports strictly opaque pixels, while GIF89a enables some pixels to be transparent. You can open either kind of image using File ➪ Open. You can save an image to the GIF87a format by choosing File ➪ Save and selecting CompuServe GIF from the Save As pop-up menu. To save a GIF89a file with transparent pixels, choose File ➪ Export ➪ GIF89a Export.

Cross Reference Before saving a GIF image, use Image ➪ Mode ➪ Indexed Color to lower the number of colors to 256 or fewer. In fact, the GIF format doesn't appear in the Save As pop-up menu if your image has more than 256 colors. For complete information about creating and saving GIF images for the Web, see Chapter 20.

PC Paintbrush's PCX

PCX doesn't stand for anything. Rather, it's the extension PC Paintbrush assigns to images saved in its native file format. Although the format is losing favor, many PCX images are still in use today, largely because PC Paintbrush is the oldest painting program for DOS. Photoshop supports PCX images with up to 16 million colors. You can find an enormous amount of art, usually clip art, in this format. But don't save files to PCX unless a client specifically demands it. Other formats are better.

Adobe's paperless PDF

The Portable Document Format (PDF) is a variation on the PostScript printing language that enables you to view electronically produced documents onscreen. This means you can create a publication in QuarkXPress or PageMaker, export it to PDF, and distribute it without worrying about color separations, binding, and other printing costs. Using a program called Adobe Acrobat, you can open PDF documents, zoom in and out of them, and follow hypertext links by clicking highlighted words. Adobe distributes Mac, Windows, and UNIX versions of the Acrobat Reader free, so about anyone with a computer can view your stuff in full, natural color.

Photoshop offers only limited support for the PDF format. You can't open full PDF documents created in QuarkXPress or PageMaker; you can only open and save PDF images saved by Photoshop. And, frankly, little reason exists to save an image to PDF. Although the PDF format supports JPEG compression, you have no way to change the amount of compression applied (as you do when saving JPEG images, discussed later in the "JPEG" section of this chapter). Unless you want to save an image for use in Acrobat Exchange — which is restricted to PDF images — you'll probably want to use some other format instead.

Pixar workstations

Pixar has created some of the most memorable computer-animated movies and commercials in recent memory. Examples include the desk lamps playing with a beach ball from *Luxo, Jr.,* the run-amok toddler from the Oscar-winning *Tin Toy,* and the commercial adventures of a Listerine bottle that boxes gingivitis one day and swings Tarzan-like through a spearmint forest the next. But Pixar really made the grade with the feature-length *Toy Story,* which provided Disney with enough merchandising options to last a lifetime.

Pixar works its 3D magic using mondo-expensive workstations. Photoshop enables you to open a still image created on a Pixar machine or to save an image to the Pixar format so you can integrate it into a 3D rendering. The Pixar format supports grayscale and RGB images.

PNG for the Web

Pronounced *ping,* the PNG format enables you to save 16 million color images without compression for use on the Web. Only a few browsers currently support PNG, including Netscape Navigator 3.0. But for those folks who want full-color images without the pesky visual compression artifacts you get with JPEG, PNG may well be a big player in the future.

PNG was invented for the World Wide Web, and I've never seen anyone use it for a purpose other than the Web. So, like all things *Webby,* you'll find more information about PNG in Chapter 20.

Scitex image-processors

Some high-end commercial printers use Scitex printing devices to generate color separations of images and other documents. Photoshop can open images digitized with Scitex scanners and save the edited images to the Scitex CT (Continuous Tone) format. Because you need special hardware to transfer images from the PC to a Scitex drive, you'll probably want to consult with your local Scitex service bureau technician before saving to the CT format. The technician may prefer that you submit images in the native Photoshop, TIFF, or JPEG format. The Scitex CT format supports grayscale, RGB, and CMYK images.

TrueVision's TGA

TrueVision's Targa and NuVista video boards enable you to overlay computer graphics and animation onto live video. The effect is called *chroma keying* because, typically, a key color is set aside to let the live video show through. TrueVision designed the TGA (Targa) format to support 32-bit images that include 8-bit alpha channels capable of displaying the live video. Support for TGA is widely implemented among professional-level color and video applications on the PC.

PICT

PICT (Macintosh Picture) is the Macintosh system software's native graphics format. Based on the QuickDraw display language the system software uses to convey images onscreen, PICT is one of the few file formats that handles object-oriented artwork and bitmapped images with equal aplomb. It supports images in any bit depth, size, or resolution. PICT even supports 32-bit images, so you can save a fourth masking channel when working in the RGB mode.

PICT is obviously popular with the Macintosh crowd. So if you share a lot of files with Mac-type people, you may occasionally be asked to supply images in the

PICT format. If you want to save an image in a format your mom can open on her Mac, for example, PICT is a better choice than JPEG. Heck, you can open PICT files inside a word processor. When you save RGB images to the PICT format, Photoshop enables you to choose from 16-bit or 32-bit resolution. For grayscale images, the options are 2—, 4—, or 8-bits per pixel resolution. You should always stick with the default resolution, however, which is the highest resolution available for the particular image. *Don't* mess around with these options.

On the flip side, you may need to open a PICT file a Mac friend sends you. Photoshop 4 can do this, but one thing may trip you up: On the Mac, you have the option of saving PICT files with QuickTime JPEG compression. Unless you have QuickTime installed on your PC — and few Windows users do — you won't be able to open images saved with this compression option turned on.

Interapplication formats

In the name of interapplication harmony, Photoshop supports a few software-specific formats that enable you to trade files with programs that run on the PC, including such popular object-oriented programs as Illustrator and QuarkXPress. Photoshop can also trade images directly with two painting pioneers, MacPaint and PixelPaint. And, finally, you can use Photoshop to edit frames from a QuickTime movie created with Adobe Premiere.

Rasterizing an Illustrator or FreeHand file

Photoshop supports object-oriented files saved in the EPS format. EPS is specifically designed to save object-oriented graphics that you intend to print to a PostScript output device. Every drawing program and most page-layout programs enable you to save EPS documents.

Prior to Version 4, Photoshop could interpret only a small subset of EPS operations supported by Illustrator. But Photoshop 4 now offers a full-blown EPS translation engine, capable of interpreting EPS illustrations created in FreeHand, Canvas, CorelDraw, and more. You can even open EPS drawings that contain imported images, something else Photoshop 3 could not do. This is one of those extremely important, but little-known, advances that should make your life much easier in the future.

When you open an EPS illustration, Photoshop *rasterizes* (or renders) the artwork — that is, it converts the artwork from a collection of objects to a bitmapped image. During the open operation, Photoshop presents the Rasterize Generic EPS Format dialog box (see Figure 4-8), which enables you to specify the size and resolution of the image, just as you can in the New dialog box. Assuming the illustration contains no imported images, you can render it as large or as small as you want without any loss of image quality.

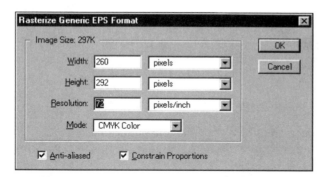

Figure 4-8: You can specify the size and resolution at which Photoshop renders an EPS illustration.

Tip

If the EPS illustration does contain an imported image or two, you need to know the resolution of the images and factor this information into the Rasterize Generic EPS Format dialog box. Select anything but Pixels from both the Width and Height pop-up menus, and leave the suggested values unchanged. Then enter the setting for the highest-resolution imported image into the Resolution option box. (If all the images are low-rez, you may want to double or triple the Resolution value to ensure the objects render smoothly.)

You should always select the Anti-aliased check box unless you're rendering a very large image — say, 300 ppi or higher. *Anti-aliasing* blurs pixels to soften the edges of the objects so they don't appear jagged. When you're rendering a very large image, the difference between image and printer resolution is less noticeable, so anti-aliasing is unwarranted.

Photoshop renders the illustration to a single layer against a transparent background. Before you can save the rasterized image to a format other than native Photoshop, you must eliminate the transparency by choosing Layer ➪ Flatten Image. Or save a flattened version of the image to a separate file by choosing File ➪ Save a Copy.

Tip

Rendering an EPS illustration is an extremely useful technique for resolving printing problems. If you regularly work in Illustrator or FreeHand, you, no doubt, have encountered *limitcheck errors,* which occur when an illustration is too complex for an imagesetter or other high-end output device to print. If you're frustrated with the printer and tired of wasting your evening trying to figure out what's wrong (sound familiar?), use Photoshop to render the illustration at 300 ppi and print it. Nine times out of ten, this technique works flawlessly.

If Photoshop can't *parse* the EPS file — a techy way of saying Photoshop can't break down the individual objects — it attempts to open the PICT (Mac) or TIFF (Windows) preview. This exercise is usually useless, but you may want to take an occasional quick look at an illustration to, say, match the placement of elements in an image to those in the drawing.

Placing an EPS illustration

If you want to introduce an EPS graphic into the foreground image rather than to render it into a new Image window of its own, choose File ➪ Place. Unlike other File menu commands, Place supports only EPS illustrations.

After you import the EPS graphic, it appears inside a box with a great big X across it. Photoshop enables you to move, scale, and rotate the illustration into position before rasterizing it to pixels. Drag a corner handle to resize the image, drag outside the image to rotate it. You can also nudge the graphic into position by pressing the arrow keys. When everything is the way you want it, press Enter to rasterize the illustration. Or double-click inside the box. If the placement isn't perfect, not to worry. The graphic appears on a separate layer, so you can move it with complete freedom. To cancel the Place operation, press Escape instead of Enter.

Saving an EPS image

Illustrator 7 now supports a wide range of file formats, including TIFF (finally). But its implementation is pretty awful, especially where large images are concerned. If you import an image saved in any format but EPS, Illustrator takes forever to import and to print, and it swells the size of your illustration like a balloon. Unlike FreeHand, which smartly tags a TIFF file on disk, Illustrator insists on importing every pixel. And Illustrator is not adept at dealing with pixels.

So if you want to import an image into Illustrator, your best bet remains EPS. Illustrator tags EPS images on disk, so they don't slow down the program and they print quickly. Unfortunately, EPS is not an efficient format for saving images. An EPS image may be three to four times larger than the same image saved to the TIFF format with LZW compression. This is the price we pay.

To save an image in the EPS format, choose Photoshop EPS from the Save As pop-up menu in the Save dialog box. After you press Enter, Photoshop displays the dialog box shown in Figure 4-9. The options in this dialog box work as follows:

✦ **Preview:** Technically, an EPS document comprises two parts: a pure Post-Script-language description of the graphic for the printer and a bitmapped preview that enables you to see the graphic onscreen. Select the TIFF (8 bits/pixel) option from the Preview pop-up menu to save a 256-color TIFF preview of the image. The 1-bit options provide black-and-white previews only, which are useful if you want to save a little room on disk. Select the None option to include no preview and save even more disk space.

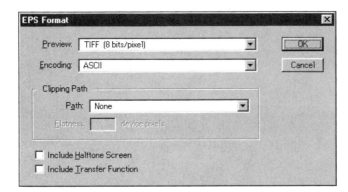

Figure 4-9: When you save an image in the EPS format, you can specify the type of preview and tack on some printing attributes.

✦ **Encoding:** If you're exporting an image for use with Illustrator, QuarkXPress, or some other established program, select the Binary encoding option (also known as *Huffman encoding*), which compresses an EPS document by substituting shorter codes for frequently used characters. The letter *a,* for example, receives the 3-bit code 010, rather than its standard 8-bit ASCII code, 01100001 (the binary equivalent of what we humans call 97). Some programs don't recognize Huffman encoding, in which case you must select the ASCII option. (*ASCII* stands for American Standard Code for Information Interchange, which is fancy jargon for text-only. In other words, you can open and edit an ASCII EPS document in a word processor, provided you know how to read and write PostScript.)

Tip

Actually, this can be a useful technique if you have a Mac file that won't open, especially if the file was sent to you electronically. Chances are a Mac-ish header got into the works. Open the file in a word processor and look at the beginning. You should see these four characters: %!PS. Delete any garbage that comes before (that is, the Mac-ish header), save the file in text format, and try to reopen your file in Photoshop.

Caution

Select one of the JPEG options only if you plan to print your final artwork to a PostScript Level 2 printer. Earlier PostScript devices do not support EPS artwork with JPEG compression. JPEG compression not only results in smaller files on disk, but it also degrades the quality of the image. Select JPEG (Maximum Quality) to invoke the least degradation. For more information, read the "JPEG" section later in this chapter.

✦ **Clipping Path:** These options enable you to select a path you created using the path tool and saved in the Paths palette. You can then use this path to mask the contents of the EPS image. For complete information about clipping paths, see the final section in Chapter 11.

✦ **Include Halftone Screen:** EPS does have one significant advantage over other image formats: It can retain printing attributes. If you specified a custom halftone screen using the Screens button inside the Page Setup dialog box, you can save this setting with the EPS document by selecting the

Include Halftone Screen check box. For information on halftone screens, see Chapter 7.

✦ **Include Transfer Function:** As described in Chapter 7, you can change the brightness and contrast of a printed image using the Transfer button inside the Page Setup dialog box. To save these settings with the EPS document, select the Include Transfer Function check box.

✦ **Transparent Whites:** When saving black-and-white EPS images in Photoshop, the two check boxes previously discussed drop away, replaced by Transparent Whites. Select this option to make all white pixels in the image transparent.

Although Photoshop EPS is the only format that offers the Transparent Whites option, many programs — including Illustrator 7 — treat white pixels in black-and-white TIFF images as transparent as well.

QuarkXPress DCS

Quark developed a variation on the EPS format called Desktop Color Separation (DCS). When you work in QuarkXPress, this format enables you to print color separations of imported artwork. If you save a CMYK image in the EPS format, Photoshop displays the additional Desktop Color Separation options shown in Figure 4-10. When you save to the DCS format, Photoshop creates five files on disk: one master document plus one file each for the cyan, magenta, yellow, and black color channels. Select Off (Single File) to save the image as a single standard EPS document. Select one of the three On options to save the separations as five independent DCS files.

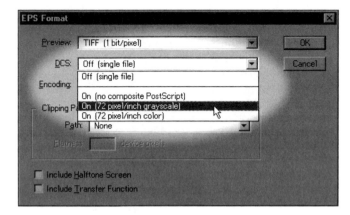

Figure 4-10: Photoshop offers four DCS options when you save a CMYK image in the EPS format.

Photoshop also gives you the option of saving a 72-ppi PostScript-language version of the image inside the DCS master document. Independent from the bitmapped preview — which you specify as usual by selecting a Preview option — the 72-ppi composite image enables you to print a low-resolution version of a DCS image imported into QuarkXPress or PageMaker to a consumer-quality printer. If you're using a black-and-white printer, select the 72 pixel/inch grayscale option; if you're using a color printer, select the final option. Note: The composite image significantly increases the size of the master document on disk.

Caution

You convert an image to the CMYK mode by choosing Image ➪ Mode ➪ CMYK Color. Do not choose this command casually. Converting back and forth between RGB and CMYK results in a loss of color information. Use the CMYK Color command only if you want to convert an image to CMYK color for good. For more information, see Chapter 5.

Premiere Filmstrip

Adobe Premiere is the foremost QuickTime movie-editing application for both Mac and PC. The program is a wonder when it comes to fades, frame merges, and special effects, but it offers no frame-by-frame editing capabilities. For example, you can neither draw a mustache on a person in the movie nor can you make brightly colored brush strokes swirl about in the background — at least, not inside Premiere.

You can export the movie to the Filmstrip format, though, which is a file-swapping option exclusive to Photoshop and Premiere. A Filmstrip document organizes frames in a long vertical strip, as shown on the left side of Figure 4-11. The right side of the figure shows the movie after each individual frame was edited in ways not permitted by Premiere. (I believe the Constitution states somewhere that a brother has the right to edit his sister's face in bizarre and unusual ways.)

A gray bar separates each frame. The number of each frame appears on the right; the Society of Motion Picture and Television Engineers (SMPTE) time code appears on the left. The structure of the three-number time code is minutes:seconds:frames, with 30 frames per second.

Caution

If you change the size of a Filmstrip document inside Photoshop in any way, you cannot save the image back to the Filmstrip format. Feel free to paint and apply effects, but stay the heck away from the Image Size and Canvas Size commands.

Tip

I don't really delve into the Filmstrip format anywhere else in this book, so I want to pass along a few quick Filmstrip tips right here and now:

✦ First, you can scroll up and down exactly one frame at a time by pressing Shift+Page Up or Shift+Page Down, respectively.

✦ Second, you can move a selection exactly one frame up or down by pressing Ctrl+Shift+up arrow or Ctrl+Shift+down arrow.

✦ If you want to clone the selection as you move it, press Ctrl+Shift+Alt+up arrow or Ctrl+Shift+Alt+down arrow.

Figure 4-11: Four frames from a QuickTime movie as they appear in the Filmstrip format before (left) and after (right) editing the frames in Photoshop

And finally — here's the great one — you can select several sequential frames and edit them simultaneously by following these steps:

Steps: Selecting Sequential Frames in a Movie

1. **Select the first frame you want to edit.** Select the rectangular marquee tool by pressing the M key. Then drag around the area you want to edit in the movie. (This is the only step that takes any degree of care or coordination whatsoever.)

2. **Switch to the quick mask mode by pressing the Q key.** The areas around the selected frame are overlaid with pink.

3. **Set the magic wand Tolerance value to 0.** Double-click the magic wand tool icon in the Toolbox to display the Magic Wand Options palette. Enter 0 for the Tolerance value and deselect the Anti-aliased check box.

4. **Click inside the selected frame (the one that's not pink) with the magic wand tool.** This selects the unmasked area inside the frame.

5. **Press Ctrl+Shift+Alt+down arrow to clone the unmasked area to the next frame in the movie.** When you exit the quick mask mode, both this frame and the one above it will be selected.

6. **Repeat several times.** Keep Ctrl+Shift+Alt+down arrowing until you're rid of the pink stuff on all the frames you want to select.

7. **Exit the quick mask mode by pressing the Q key again.** All frames appear selected.

8. **Edit the frames to your heart's content.**

Cross Reference

If you're new to Photoshop, half of these steps, if not all of them, probably sailed over your head like so many extraterrestrial spaceships. If you want to learn more about selections and cloning, see Chapter 11. In Chapter 12, I explore the quick mask mode and other masking techniques in-depth. After you finish reading those chapters, return to this section to see if it doesn't make a little more sense.

The process of editing individual frames as just described is sometimes called *rotoscoping,* named after the traditional technique of combining live-action film with animated sequences. You also can try out some scratch-and-doodle techniques, which is where an artist scratches and draws directly on frames of film. If this isn't enough, you can emulate *xerography,* in which an animator makes Xerox copies of photographs, enhances the copies using markers or whatever else is convenient, and shoots the finished artwork, frame by frame, on film. In a nutshell, Photoshop extends Premiere's functionality by adding animation to its standard supply of video-editing capabilities.

You can save an image in the Filmstrip format only if you opened the image as a Filmstrip document and did not change the size of the image. To do so, press Ctrl+S.

The mainstream formats

The formats discussed so far are mighty interesting and they all fulfill their own niche purposes. But the following formats — JPEG and TIFF — are the all-stars of PC imagery. You'll use these formats the most because of their outstanding compression capabilities and almost universal support among graphics applications.

JPEG

Photoshop supports the JPEG format, named after the folks who designed it, the Joint Photographic Experts Group. JPEG is the most efficient and essential compression format currently available and is likely to be the compression standard for years to come. JPEG is a lossy compression scheme, which means it sacrifices image quality to conserve space on disk. You can control how much data is lost during the save operation, however.

When you save an image in the JPEG format, Photoshop displays the dialog box in Figure 4-12, which offers a total of 11 compression settings. (That's seven more than Photoshop 3 offered, and two more than Photoshop 2.5.) Just select an option from the Quality pop-up menu or drag the slider triangle from 0 to 10 to specify the quality setting. Of the named options, Low takes the least space on disk, but distorts the image rather severely; Maximum retains the highest amount of image quality, but consumes more disk space. Of the numbered options, 0 is the most severe compressor and 10 does the least damage.

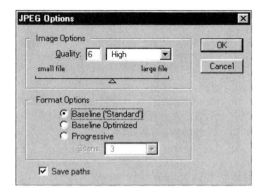

Figure 4-12: The new JPEG Options dialog box provides a total of 11 compression settings, ranging from 0 (heaviest compression) to 10 (best quality), as well as some new Web options.

Note

JPEG evaluates an image in 8 × 8-pixel blocks, using a technique called *Adaptive Discrete Cosine Transform* (or ADCT, as in "Yes, I'm an acronym ADCT"). It averages the 24-bit value of every pixel in the block (or 8-bit value of every pixel in the case of a grayscale image). ADCT then stores the average color in the upper-left pixel in the block and assigns the remaining 63 pixels smaller values relative to the average.

Next, JPEG divides the block by an 8 × 8 block of its own called the *quantization matrix,* which homogenizes the pixels' values by changing as many as possible to zero. This process saves the majority of disk space and loses data. When Photoshop opens a JPEG image, it can't recover the original distinction between the zero pixels, so the pixels become the same, or similar, colors. Finally, JPEG applies lossless Huffman encoding to translate repeating values to a single symbol.

In most instances, I recommend you use JPEG only at the Maximum quality setting (8 or higher), at least until you gain some experience with it. The smallest amount of JPEG compression saves more space on disk than any non-JPEG compression format and still retains the most essential detail from the original image. Figure 4-13 shows a grayscale image saved at each of the four compression settings.

The samples are arranged in rows from highest image quality (upper left) to lowest quality (lower right). Below each sample is the size of the compressed document on disk. Saved in the only moderately compressed native Photoshop format, the image consumes 116K on disk. From 116K to 28K — the result of the lowest-quality JPEG setting — is a remarkable savings, but it comes at a price.

I've taken the liberty of sharpening the focus of strips in each image so you can see more easily how JPEG averages neighboring pixels to achieve smaller file sizes. The first strip in each image appears in normal focus, the second strip is sharpened once by choosing Filter ➪ Sharpen ➪ Sharpen More, and the third strip is sharpened twice. I also adjusted the gray levels to make the differences even more pronounced. You can see that although the lower-image quality setting leads to a dramatic saving in file size, it also excessively gums up the image. The effect, incidentally, is more obvious onscreen. And believe me, after you familiarize yourself with JPEG compression, you can spot other people's overly compressed JPEG images a mile away. This isn't something you want to exaggerate in your images.

Cross Reference

To see the impact of JPEG compression on a full-color image, check out Color Plate 4-1. The original image consumes 693K in the native Photoshop format, but 116K when compressed at the JPEG module's Maximum setting. To demonstrate the differences between different settings better, I enlarged one portion of the image and oversharpened another.

Caution

JPEG is a *cumulative compression scheme,* meaning Photoshop recompresses an image every time you save it in the JPEG format. No disadvantage exists to saving an image to disk repeatedly during a single session, because JPEG always works from the onscreen version. But if you close an image, reopen it, and save it in the JPEG format, you inflict a small amount of damage. Use JPEG sparingly. In the best of all possible worlds, you should only save to the JPEG format after you finish all work on an image. Even in a pinch, you should apply all filtering effects before saving to JPEG, because these have a habit of exacerbating imperfections in image quality.

Figure 4-13: Four JPEG settings applied to a single image, with the highest image quality setting illustrated at the upper left and the lowest at the bottom right.

JPEG is best used when compressing continuous-tone images (images in which the distinction between immediately neighboring pixels is slight). Any image that includes gradual color transitions, as in a photograph, qualifies for JPEG compression. JPEG is not the best choice for saving screen shots, line drawings (especially those converted from EPS graphics), and other high-contrast images. These are better served by a lossless compression scheme such as TIFF with LZW. The JPEG format is available when you are saving grayscale, RGB, and CMYK images.

Occupying the bottom half of the JPEG Options dialog box are three radio buttons, designed to optimize JPEG images for the World Wide Web. When creating images for print media, select the first option, Baseline ("Standard"). For information on the other two radio buttons, see Chapter 20.

The Save Paths check box determines whether any paths in your image are saved along with the file. Photoshop uses an "application marker" to store paths and other Photoshop-specific data so other programs that accept JPEG can open the image. This option does increase the file size, however; if this is an issue, leave the option turned off. If your image doesn't have any paths, the setting of the check box is irrelevant.

TIFF

Developed by Aldus in the early days of the Mac to standardize an ever-growing population of scanned images, TIFF (Tag Image File Format) is the most widely supported image printing format across both the Macintosh and PC platforms. Unlike PICT, it can't handle object-oriented artwork and it doesn't support JPEG compression. But, otherwise, it's unrestricted. In fact, TIFF offers a few tricks of its own worth mentioning. When you save an image in the TIFF format, Photoshop displays the TIFF Options dialog box (see Figure 4-14), which offers these options:

✦ **Byte Order:** Leave it to Photoshop to name a straightforward option in the most confusing way possible. Byte Order? No, this option doesn't have anything to do with how you eat your food. Rather, because Macintosh TIFF and PC TIFF are two slightly different formats, this option enables you to specify whether you want to use the image on the Mac or on an IBM PC-compatible machine. I'm sure this has something to do with the arrangement of 8-bit chunks of data, but who cares? You want Mac or you want PC? It's that simple.

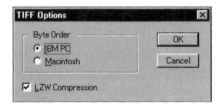

Figure 4-14: Photoshop enables you to save TIFF files in either the Mac or PC format and to compress the image using LZW.

✦ **LZW Compression:** Like Huffman encoding (previously described in the "Saving an EPS image" section), the LZW (Lempel-Ziv-Welch) compression scheme digs into the computer code that describes an image and substitutes frequently used codes with shorter equivalents. But instead of substituting characters, as Huffman does, LZW substitutes strings of data. Because LZW doesn't so much as touch a pixel in your image, it's entirely lossless. Most image editors and desktop publishing applications — including FreeHand, PageMaker, and QuarkXPress — import LZW-compressed TIFF images, but a few still have yet to catch on.

Note

If names like Huffman and LZW ring a faint bell, it may be because these are the same compression schemes used by PKZIP, WinZip, and other compression utilities. For this reason, using an additional utility to compress a TIFF image that was already compressed using LZW makes no sense. Neither do you want to compress a JPEG image, because JPEG takes advantage of Huffman encoding. You may shave off a few K, but this isn't enough space to make it worth your time and effort.

In Photoshop, the TIFF format supports up to 24 channels, the maximum number permitted in any image. In fact, TIFF is the only format other than "raw" and the native Photoshop format that can save more than four channels. To save a TIFF file without extra mask channels, choose File ⇨ Save a Copy and select the Don't Include Alpha Channels check box. (For complete information on channels, read Chapter 6.)

Tip

If you have limited RAM, or you're working with a very large TIFF image, you can open an isolated detail of the image using File ⇨ Import ⇨ Quick Edit. Photoshop displays a small preview of the image. Drag in the preview to select the area you want to open and press Enter. Photoshop opens only that isolated portion of the file. To save the detail back into the larger TIFF image, choose File ⇨ Export ⇨ Quick Edit.

I must admit, I have a love/hate thing going with Quick Edit. I appreciate Quick Edit enabling you to open small chunks of an image at a time. But I hate that you can open uncompressed TIFF images only, and that Quick Edit doesn't support any format other than TIFF. It doesn't even support the native Photoshop format. What a stinker.

The oddball formats

Can you believe it? After plowing through a half-million formats, I still haven't covered them all. The last three are the odd men out. Few programs other than Photoshop support these formats, so you won't be using them to swap files with other applications. Also, these formats don't enable you to compress images, so you can't use them to conserve disk space. What can you do with these formats? Read the following sections and find out.

Photo CD YCC images

Photoshop can open Eastman Kodak's Photo CD and Pro Photo CD formats directly. A Photo CD contains compressed versions of every image in each of the five scan sizes provided on Photo CDs — from 128 × 192 pixels (72K) to 2,048 × 3,072 pixels (18MB). The Photo CD format uses the YCC color model, a variation on the CIE (Commission Internationale de l'Eclairage) color space discussed in the next chapter. YCC provides a broader range of color — theoretically, every color your eye can see.

The Pro Photo CD format can accommodate each of the five sizes included in the regular Photo CD format, plus one additional size — 4,096 × 6,144 pixels (72MB) — that's four times as large as the largest image on a regular Photo CD. As a result, Pro Photo CDs hold only 25 scans; standard Photo CDs hold 100. Like their standard Photo CD counterparts, Pro Photo CD scanners can accommodate 35mm film and slides. But they can also handle 70mm film and 4 × 5-inch negatives and transparencies. The cost might knock you out, though. While scanning an image to a standard Photo CD costs between $1 and $2, scanning it to a Pro Photo CD costs about $10. This goes to show you, once you gravitate beyond consumerland, everyone expects you to start coughing up the big bucks.

By opening Photo CD files directly, you can translate the YCC images directly to Photoshop's Lab color mode, another variation on CIE color space that ensures no color loss. The Photo CD files are found inside the Images folder inside the Photo_CD folder on the Photo CD, as shown in Figure 4-15.

For more information on the relationship between YCC, Lab, and every other color mode you ever thought you might want to learn about, see Chapter 5.

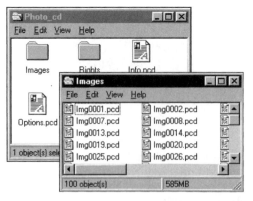

Figure 4-15: On a Photo CD disk, the YCC documents are in the Images folder inside the Photo_CD folder.

Photoshop 4 includes the latest Kodak Color Management Software (CMS), which tweaks colors in Photo CD images based on the kind of film from which they were scanned. When you open a Photo CD image, Photoshop displays the dialog box shown in Figure 4-16. Here you can specify the image size you want to open by selecting an option from the Resolution pop-up menu. The dialog box even shows you a preview of the image. But the options that make a difference are the Source and Destination buttons:

✦ **Source:** Click this button to specify the kind of film from which the original photographs were scanned. You can select from two specific Kodak brands — Ektachrome and Kodachrome — or settle for the generic Color Negative Film option. Your selection determines the method by which Photoshop transforms the colors in the image.

✦ **Destination:** After clicking this button, select an option from the Device pop-up menu to specify the color model you want to use. Select Adobe Photoshop RGB to open the image in the RGB mode; select Adobe Photoshop CIELAB to open the image in the Lab mode.

Note A CMYK profile can be purchased separately from Kodak. Some stock photo agencies also include special color profiles. For example, Digital Stock currently provides its excellent image library on Photo CDs. The company offers a source profile for its particular drum-scanning technology, as well as CMYK destination profiles.

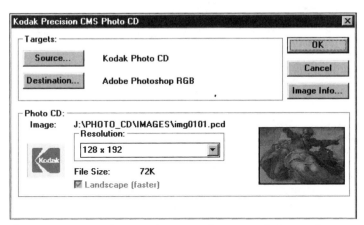

Figure 4-16: Use these options to select a resolution and to calibrate the colors in the Photo CD image.

To access Photo CD images, you need a single-session or multisession CD-ROM device and the proper drivers. If you purchased your CD-ROM drive in the last three years, you're probably set; older drives may not be compatible.

Photoshop cannot save to the Photo CD format. And frankly, there's little reason you'd want to do so. Photo CD is strictly a means for transferring slides and film negatives onto the world's most ubiquitous and indestructible storage medium, the CD-ROM.

Opening a raw document

A *raw document* is a plain binary file stripped of all extraneous information. It contains no compression scheme, specifies no bit depth or image size, and offers no color mode. Each byte of data indicates a brightness value on a single color channel, and that's it. Photoshop offers this function specifically so you can open images created in undocumented formats, such as those created on mainframe computers.

To open an image of unknown origin, choose File ➪ Open and select All Formats from the Files of Type pop-up menu. Then select the desired image and choose Raw from the Files of Type pop-up menu. After you press Enter, the dialog box shown in Figure 4-17 appears, featuring these options:

✦ **Width, Height:** If you know the dimensions of the image in pixels, enter the values in these option boxes.

✦ **Swap:** Click this button to swap the Width value with the Height value.

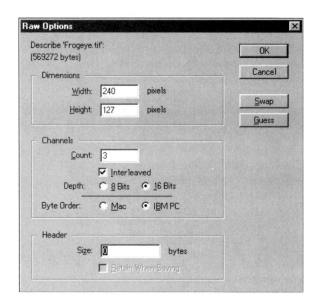

Figure 4-17: Photoshop requires you to specify the size of an image and the number of color channels when you open an image that does not conform to a standardized file format.

✦ **Count:** Enter the number of color channels in this option box. If the document is an RGB image, enter 3; if it is a CMYK image, enter 4.

✦ **Interleaved:** Select this value if the color values are stored sequentially by pixels. In an RGB image, the first byte represents the red value for the first pixel, the second byte represents the green value for that pixel, the third the blue value, and so on. If you turn this check box off, the first byte represents the red value for the first pixel, the second value represents the red value for the second pixel, and so on. When Photoshop finishes describing the red channel, it describes the green channel and then the blue channel.

✦ **Depth:** Select the number of bits per color channel. Most images contain 8 bits per channel, but scientific scans from mainframe computers may contain 16.

✦ **Byte Order:** If you specify 16 bits per channel, you must tell Photoshop whether the image comes from a Mac or a PC.

✦ **Header:** This value tells Photoshop how many bytes of data at the beginning of the file comprise header information it can ignore.

✦ **Retain Header When Saving:** If the Header value is greater than zero, you can instruct Photoshop to retain this data when you save the image in a different format.

✦ **Guess:** If you know the Width and Height values, but you don't know the number of bytes in the header — or vice versa — you can ask Photoshop for help. Fill in either the size or header information and then click the Guess button to ask Photoshop to take a stab at the unknown value. Photoshop estimates all this information when the Raw Options dialog box first appears. Generally speaking, if it doesn't estimate correctly the first time around, you're on your own. But, hey, the Guess button is worth a shot.

Tip

If a raw document is a CMYK image, it opens as an RGB image with an extra masking channel. To display the image correctly, choose Image ⇨ Mode ⇨ Multichannel to free the four channels from their incorrect relationship. Then recombine them by choosing Image ⇨ Mode ⇨ CMYK Color.

Saving a raw document

Photoshop also enables you to save to the raw document format. This capability is useful when you create files you want to transfer to mainframe systems or output to devices that don't support other formats, such as the Kodak XL7700.

Caution

Do not save 256-color indexed images to the raw format or you will lose the color lookup table and, therefore, lose all color information. Be sure to convert such images first to RGB or one of the other full-color modes before saving.

When you save an image in the raw document format, Photoshop presents the dialog box shown in Figure 4-18. The dialog box options work as follows:

✦ **File Type:** This option is a carry-over from the Macintosh, because only Macs use this code. The option is grayed out in the Windows version of Photoshop.

✦ **File Creator:** Ditto. The default code 8BIM is selected for you and the option is grayed out.

✦ **Header:** Enter the size of the header in bytes. If you enter any value but zero, you must fill in the header using a data editor such as Norton Disk Editor.

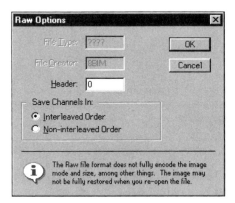

Figure 4-18: When saving a raw document, enter file type and creator codes and specify the order of data in the file.

✦ **Save Channels In:** Select the Interleaved Order option to arrange data sequentially by pixels, as described earlier. To group data by color channel, select Non-interleaved Order.

Still can't get that file open?

File format specs are continually evolving. As a result, programs that provide support for a particular format may not support the specific version of the format used to save the file you're trying to open. For example, Adobe Illustrator 4 and 4.1 can't handle the TIFF 6 spec, but Illustrator 7 can. At the other end, neither can handle some early TIFF files. JPEG is notorious for causing problems (there were several private implementations). Some JPEGs can only be read by the originating application.

If you can't open a file in Photoshop, you may have another program that can read and write the problem format. Try the problem file in every program you have — and every program your friends have. After all, what are friends for?

You may also want to try a program like HiJaak or TransverterPro. Current predictions are DeBabelizer, a terrific format converter from Equilibrium, formerly available on the Mac only, may soon be available for Windows.

Still out of it? Go online and check such forums as ADOBEAPPS on CompuServe. The Usenet newsgroups `comp.graphics.apps.photoshop` and `rec.photo.digital` are other good resources. Post a question about your problem; chances are good someone may have an answer for you.

Resampling and Cropping

After you bring up an image — whether you created it from scratch or opened an existing image stored in one of the five billion formats discussed in the preceding pages — its size and resolution are established. Neither size nor resolution is set in stone, however. Photoshop provides two methods for changing the number of pixels in an image: resampling and cropping.

Resizing versus resampling

Typically, when folks talk about *resizing* an image, they mean enlarging or reducing it without changing the number of pixels in the image, as previously demonstrated in Figure 4-1. By contrast, *resampling* an image means scaling it so the image contains a larger or smaller number of pixels. With resizing, an inverse relationship exists between size and resolution — size increases when resolution decreases, and vice versa. But resampling affects either size or resolution independently. Figure 4-19 shows an image resized and resampled to 50 percent of its original dimensions. The resampled and original images have identical resolutions, while the resized image has twice the resolution of its companions.

Resizing an image

To resize an image, use one of the techniques discussed in the "Changing the printing resolution" section near the beginning of this chapter. To recap briefly, the best method is to choose Image ⇨ Image Size, turn off the Resample Image check box, and enter a value into the Resolution option box. See Figure 4-2 to refresh your memory.

Resampling an image

You also use Image ⇨ Image Size to resample an image. The difference is you leave the Resample Image check box turned on, as shown in Figure 4-20. As its name implies, the Resample Image check box is the key to resampling.

When Resample Image is selected, the Resolution value is independent of both sets of Width and Height values. (The only difference between the two sets of options is the top options work in pixels and the bottom options work in relative units of measure like percent and inches.) You can increase the number of pixels in an image by increasing any of the five values in the dialog box; you can decrease the number of pixels by decreasing any value. Photoshop stretches or shrinks the image according to the new size specifications.

At all times, you can see the new number of pixels Photoshop will assign to the image, as well as the increased or decreased file size. In Figure 4-20, for example, the Pixel Dimensions value at the top of the dialog box reads 362K (was 1.13M), which shows the file size has decreased. You can also look to the Print Size values, which are set to 56 percent. All these indicators show I'm about to dump pixels.

To calculate the pixels in the resampled image, Photoshop must use its powers of interpolation, as explained in the "General preferences" section of Chapter 2. The interpolation setting defaults to the one chosen in the Preferences dialog box. But you can also change the setting right inside the Image Size dialog box. Simply select the desired method from the Resample Image pop-up menu. Bicubic results in the smoothest effects. Bilinear is faster. And Nearest Neighbor turns off interpolation so Photoshop merely throws away the pixels it doesn't need or duplicates pixels to resample up.

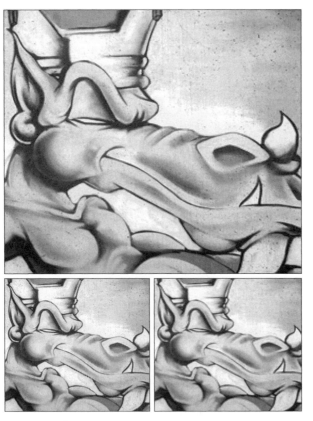

Resized   Resampled

Figure 4-19: An image (top) resized (bottom left) and resampled (bottom right) down to 50 percent. The resized image sports a higher resolution; the resampled image contains fewer pixels.

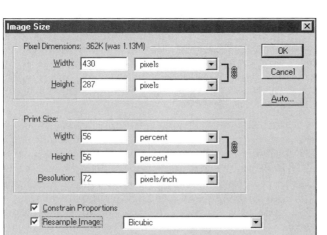

Figure 4-20: With the Resample Image check box turned on, you can modify the number of pixels in your image.

Here are a few more random items you should know about resampling with the Image Size dialog box:

✦ This may sound odd, but you generally want to avoid adding pixels. When you resample up, you're asking Photoshop to make up details from thin air, and the program isn't that smart. Simply put, an enlarged image almost never looks better than the original; it merely takes up more disk space and prints slower.

Tip

✦ Resampling down, on the other hand, is a useful technique. It enables you to smooth away photo grain, halftone patterns, and other scanning artifacts. One of the most tried-and-true rules is to scan at the maximum resolution permitted by your scanner, and then resample the scan down to, say, 72 or 46 percent (with the interpolation set to Bicubic, naturally). By selecting a round value other than 50 percent, you force Photoshop to jumble the pixels into a regular, homogenous soup. You're left with fewer pixels, but these remaining pixels are better. And you have the added benefit that the image takes up less space on disk.

✦ To make an image tall and thin or short and fat, you must first turn off the Constrain Proportions check box. This enables you to edit the two Width values entirely independently of the two Height values.

Tip

✦ You can resample an image to match precisely the size and resolution of any other open image. While the Image Size dialog box is open, choose the name of the image you want to match from the Window menu.

If you ever get confused inside the Image Size dialog box, and you want to return to the original size and resolution settings, press the Alt key to change the Cancel button to Reset. Then click the Reset button to start from the beginning.

Caution

Photoshop remembers the setting of the Resample Image check box and uses this same setting the next time you open the Image Size dialog box. This can trip you up if you record a script for the Actions palette, as discussed in Chapter 3. Suppose you create a script to resize images, turning Resample Image off. If you later resample an image — turning on Resample Image — the check box stays selected when you close the dialog box. The next time you run the script, you end up resampling instead of resizing. Always check the status of the check box before you apply the Image Size command or run any scripts containing the command.

Cropping

Another way to change the number of pixels in an image is to crop it, which means to clip away pixels around the edges of an image without harming the remaining pixels. (The one exception occurs when you rotate a cropped image, in which case Photoshop has to interpolate pixels to account for the rotation.)

Cropping enables you to focus on an element in your image. For example, Figure 4-21 shows a bit of urban graffiti from a Digital Stock CD. I like this fellow's face — good chiaroscuro — but I can't quite figure out what's going on with this guy. I mean, what's with the screw? And is that a clown hat or what? All I do is crop around the guy's head to delete all the extraneous image elements and focus on his sleepy features, as shown in Figure 4-22.

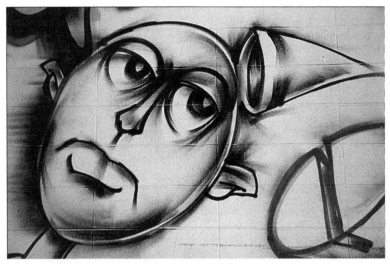

Figure 4-21: This image contains too much extraneous information. Where should my eye go? I'm so confused.

Figure 4-22: Cropping enables you to clean up the background junk and focus on the essential foreground image.

Changing the canvas size

One way to crop an image is to choose Image ➪ Canvas Size, which displays the Canvas Size dialog box shown in Figure 4-23. The options in this dialog box enable you to scale the imaginary canvas on which the image rests separately from the image itself.

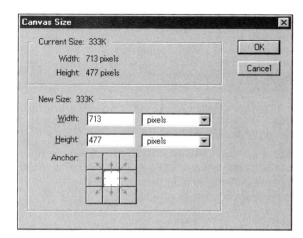

Figure 4-23: Choose Image ➪ Canvas Size to crop an image or to add empty space around the perimeter of an image.

If you enlarge the canvas, Photoshop surrounds the image with a white background (assuming the background color is white). If you reduce the canvas, you crop the image.

Click inside the Anchor grid to specify the placement of the image on the new canvas. For example, if you want to add space to the bottom of an image, enlarge the canvas size and then click inside the upper-middle square. If you want to crop away the upper-left corner of an image, create a smaller canvas size and then click the lower-right square. Photoshop 4 offers new little arrows to show how the canvas will shrink or grow.

Using the crop tool

Generally speaking, the Canvas Size command is most useful for enlarging the canvas or shaving a few pixels off the edge of an image. If you want to crop away a large portion of an image, using the crop tool is a better choice.

To crop the image, select the crop tool by pressing the C key. (Selecting the tool manually is quite inconvenient in Photoshop 4, so get used to pressing the C key.) Then drag with the crop tool to create a rectangular marquee that surrounds the portion of the image you want to retain.

Tip

As you drag, you can press the spacebar to move the crop boundary temporarily on the fly. To stop moving the boundary and return to resizing it, release the spacebar. This excellent technique is new to Photoshop 4.

If you don't get the crop marquee right the first time, you can move, scale, or rotate it at will. These operations have been changed in Photoshop 4, significantly for the better, in my opinion. But they may come as a shock to Version 3 users. Here's what you do:

✦ Drag inside the crop marquee to move it.

✦ Drag one of the square handles to resize the marquee. You can Shift+drag a handle to scale the marquee proportionally (the same percentage vertically and horizontally).

✦ Drag outside the crop marquee to rotate it. This may strike you as weird at first, but it works wonderfully.

When the marquee surrounds the exact portion of the image you want to keep, press Enter or double-click inside the marquee. Photoshop clips away all pixels except those that lie inside and along the border of the crop marquee.

If you change your mind about cropping, you can cancel the crop marquee by pressing Escape.

Rotating the crop marquee

As I said, you can rotate an image by dragging outside the crop marquee. Straightening out a crooked image can be a little tricky, however. I wish I had a certified check for every time I thought I had the marquee rotated properly, only to find the image was still crooked after I pressed Enter. If this happens to you, choose Edit ➪ Undo (Ctrl+Z) and try again. Do not try using the crop tool a second time to rotate the already rotated image. If you do, Photoshop sets about interpolating between already interpolated pixels, resulting in more lost data. Every rotation gets farther away from the original image.

Tip

A better solution is to do it right the first time. Locate a line or general axis in your image that should be straight up and down. Rotate the crop marquee so it aligns exactly with this axis. In Figure 4-24, I rotated my crop marquee so one edge bisects the graffiti guy's egg-shaped head. Don't worry because this isn't how you want to crop the image — you're just using the line as a reference. After you arrive at the correct angle for the marquee, drag the handles to size and position the boundary properly. As long as you don't drag outside the marquee, its angle remains fixed throughout.

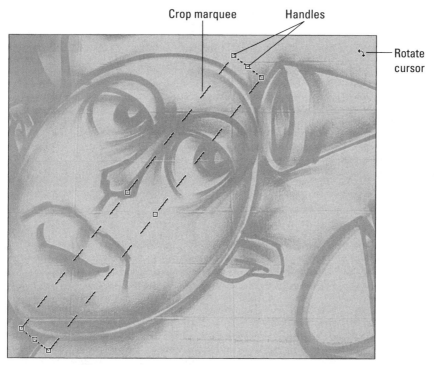

Figure 4-24: Align the crop marquee with an obvious axis in your image to determine the proper angle of rotation.

Cropping an image to match another

Two ways exist to crop an image so it matches the size and resolution of another:

✦ Bring the image you want to crop forward and choose Image ➪ Canvas Size. Then, while inside the Canvas Size dialog box, select the name of the image you want to match from the Window menu.

Tip   This method doesn't give you much control when cropping an image, but it's a great way to enlarge the canvas and add empty space around an image.

✦ Better yet, use the crop tool. First, bring the image you want to match to the front. Then select the crop tool and press Enter to display the Cropping Tool Options palette, pictured in Figure 4-25. Select the Fixed Target Size check box and click the Front Image button. Photoshop loads the size and resolution values into the palette's option boxes.

✦ Now bring the image you want to crop to the front and drag with the crop tool as normal. Photoshop constrains the crop marquee to the proportions of the targeted image. After you press Enter, Photoshop crops, resamples, and rotates the image as necessary.

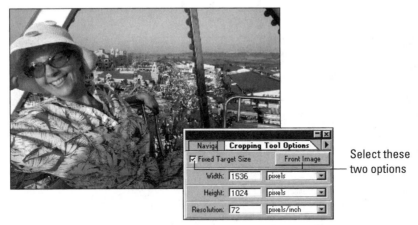

Select these
two options

Figure 4-25: Bring the image you want to target to the front, and click each of the two options at the top of the Cropping Tool Options palette.

Cropping a selection

Another way to crop an image is to create a rectangular selection and then choose Image ➪ Crop. One advantage of this technique is you needn't switch back and forth between the marquee and crop tools. One tool is all you need to select and crop. (If you're as lazy as I am, the mere act of selecting a tool can prove more effort than it's worth.) And, as with the crop tool, you can now press the spacebar while you draw a marquee to move it on the fly. It's no trick to get the placement and size exactly right — the only thing you can't do is rotate.

Another advantage of the Crop command is flexibility. You can draw a selection, switch windows, apply commands, and generally use any function you like prior to choosing Image ➪ Crop. The crop tool, by contrast, is much more demanding. After drawing a cropping marquee, you can't do anything but adjust the marquee until you press Enter to accept the crop or Escape to dismiss it.

And finally, Image ➪ Crop enables you to crop the canvas to the boundaries of an image pasted from the Clipboard or dragged and dropped from another Image window. As long as the boundaries of the pasted image are rectangular, as in the case of an image copied from a different application, you can choose Edit ➪ Paste, Ctrl+click the new layer in the Layers palette to regain the selection outline, and then choose Image ➪ Crop. Photoshop replaces the former image and crops the window to fit the new image.

Defining Colors

Selecting and Editing Colors

Occasionally, the state of computer graphics technology reminds me of television in the early 1950s. Only the upper echelon of Photoshop artists can afford to work exclusively in the wonderful world of color. The rest of us print most of our images in black and white.

Cross Reference

Some of you might be thinking, "Wait a second, what about the equalizing force of the Internet? It brings color to all of us!" Well, I concur wholeheartedly. So read on, yon color user, paying special attention to RGB and little to CMYK. Then advance to Chapter 20, and learn how you can reduce color palettes and otherwise prepare your images for the bold new challenges of the World Wide Web.

Regardless of who you are — print person or Web head — color is a prime concern. Even gray values, after all, are colors. Many folks have problems accepting this premise — I guess we're all so used to separating the worlds of grays and other colors in our minds that never the two shall meet. But gray values are only variations on what Noah Webster used to call "The sensation resulting from stimulation of the retina of the eye by light waves of certain lengths." (Give the guy a few drinks and he'd spout off 19 more definitions, not including the meanings of the transitive verb.) Just as black and white represent a subset of gray, gray is a subset of color. In fact, you'll find that using Photoshop involves a lot of navigating through these and other colorful subsets.

Specifying colors

First off, Photoshop provides four color controls in the Toolbox, as shown in Figure 5-1. These icons work as follows:

> ✦ **Foreground color:** The foreground color icon indicates the color you apply when you use the type, paint bucket, line, pencil, airbrush, or paintbrush tool, or if

you Alt+drag with the smudge tool. The foreground color also begins any gradation created with the gradient tool. You can apply the foreground color to a selection by choosing Edit ➪ Fill or Edit ➪ Stroke or by pressing Alt+Backspace. To change the foreground color, click the foreground color icon to display the Color Picker dialog box, select a new color in the Color palette, or click an open image window with the eyedropper tool.

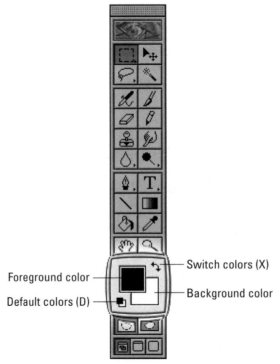

Foreground color

Default colors (D)

Switch colors (X)

Background color

Figure 5-1: The color controls provided with Photoshop (along with keyboard shortcuts in parentheses, where applicable)

✦ **Background color:** The active background color indicates the color you apply with the eraser tool. The background color also ends any gradation created with the gradient tool. To change the background color, click the background color icon to display the Color Picker dialog box, use the Color palette, or Alt+click any open image window with the eyedropper tool.

As in earlier versions of Photoshop, you can apply the background color to a selection by pressing Delete. But if the selection is floating or exists on any layer except the background layer, Delete actually deletes the selection instead of filling it. For complete safety, avoid the Delete key and use Ctrl+Backspace to fill a selection with the background color instead.

✦ **Switch colors:** Click this icon (or press X) to exchange the foreground and background colors.

✦ **Default colors:** Click this icon (or press D) to make the foreground color black and the background color white, according to their factory default settings. If you're editing a layer mask or adjustment layer, the default colors are reversed, as explained in Chapter 13.

Using the Color Picker

When you click the foreground or background color icon, Photoshop displays the Color Picker dialog box. (This assumes Photoshop is the active option in the Color Picker pop-up menu in the General Preferences dialog box. If you select the Windows option, the generic Windows Color Picker appears; see Chapter 2 on why you shouldn't select this option.) Figure 5-2 labels the wealth of elements and options in the Color Picker dialog box, which work as follows:

✦ **Color slider:** Use the color slider to home in on the color you want to select. Drag up or down on either of the slider triangles to select a color from a particular 8-bit range. The colors represented inside the slider correspond to the selected radio button. For example, if you select the H (Hue) radio button, which is the default setting, the slider colors represent the full 8-bit range of hues. If you select S (Saturation), the slider shows the current hue at full saturation at the top of the slider, down to no saturation — or gray — at the bottom of the slider. If you select B (Brightness), the slider shows the 8-bit range of brightness values, from solid color at the top of the slider to absolute black at the bottom. You also can select R (Red), G (Green), or B (Blue), in which case the top of the slider shows you what the current color looks like when subjected to full-intensity red, green, or blue (respectively), and the bottom of the slider shows every bit of red, green, or blue subtracted.

Cross Reference

For a proper introduction to the HSB and RGB color models, including definitions of specific terms such as hue, saturation, and brightness, read the "Working in Different Color Modes" section later in this chapter.

✦ **Color field:** The color field shows a 16-bit range of variations on the current slider color. Click inside it to move the color selection marker and, thereby, select a new color. The field graphs colors against the two remaining attributes not represented by the color slider. For example, if you select the H (Hue) radio button, the field graphs colors according to brightness vertically and saturation horizontally, as demonstrated in the first example of Figure 5-3. The other examples show what happens to the color field when you select the S (Saturation) and B (Brightness) radio buttons.

Color field   Color slider   Current color

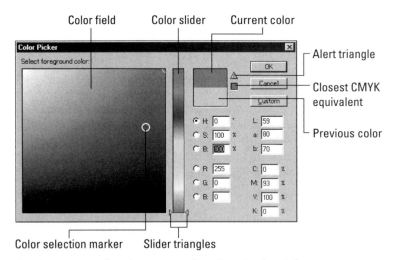

Alert triangle

Closest CMYK
equivalent

Previous color

Color selection marker   Slider triangles

Figure 5-2: Use the elements and options in the Color
Picker dialog box to specify a new foreground or
background color from the 16-million-color range.

Likewise, Figure 5-4 shows how the field graphs colors when you select the
R (Red), G (Green), and B (Blue) radio buttons. Obviously, it would help to
see these images in color, but you probably couldn't afford this big, fat
book if we'd printed it in full color. So I recommend you experiment with the
Color Picker inside your version of Photoshop or refer to Color Plate 5-1 to
see how the dialog box looks when the H (Hue), S (Saturation), and B
(Brightness) options are selected.

Note   Slider and field always work together to represent the entire 16 million color
range. The slider displays 256 colors, and the field displays 65,000 variations
on the slider color; 256 times 65,000 is 16 million. No matter which radio
button you select, you have access to the same colors; only your means of
accessing them changes.

✦ **Current color:** The color currently selected from the color field appears in
the top rectangle immediately to the right of the color slider. Click the OK
button or press Enter to make this the current foreground or background
color (depending on which color control icon in the Toolbox you originally
clicked to display the Color Picker dialog box).

✦ **Previous color:** The bottom rectangle to the right of the color slider shows
how the foreground or background color — whichever one you are in the
process of editing — looked before you displayed the Color Picker dialog
box. Click the Cancel button or press Escape to leave this color intact.

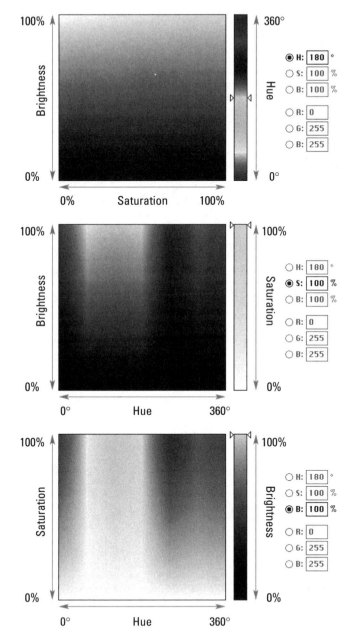

Figure 5-3: The color field graphs colors against the two attributes not represented in the slider. Here you can see how color is laid out when you select (top to bottom) the H (Hue), S (Saturation), and B (Brightness) radio buttons.

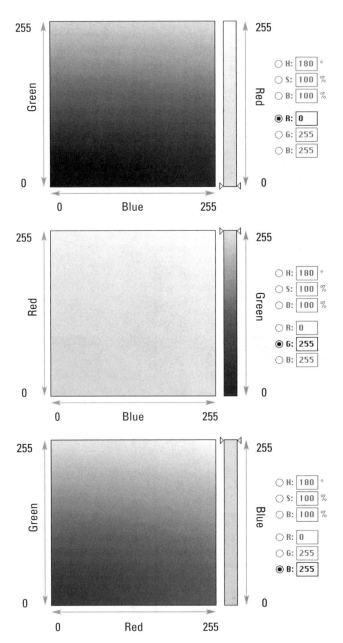

Figure 5-4: The results of selecting (top to bottom) the R (Red), G (Green), and B (Blue) radio buttons

✦ **Alert triangle:** The alert triangle appears when you select a bright color that Photoshop can't print using standard process colors. The box below the triangle shows the closest CMYK equivalent, invariably a duller version of the color. Click either the triangle or the box to bring the color into the printable range.

Entering numeric color values

In addition to selecting colors using the slider and color field, you can enter specific color values in the option boxes in the lower-right region of the Color Picker dialog box. Novices and intermediates may find these options less satisfying to use than the slider and field. These options, however, enable artists and print professionals to specify exact color values, whether to make controlled adjustments to a color already in use or to match a color used in another document. The options fall into one of four camps:

✦ **HSB:** These options stand for hue, saturation, and brightness. Hue is measured on a 360 degree circle. Saturation and brightness are measured from 0 to 100 percent. These options permit access to more than 3 million color variations.

✦ **RGB:** You can change the amount of the primary colors red, green, and blue by specifying the brightness value of each color from 0 to 255. These options enable access to more than 16 million color variations.

✦ **Lab:** This acronym stands for luminosity, measured from 0 to 100 percent, and two arbitrary color axes, a and b, whose brightness values range from 128 to 127. These options enable access to more than 6 million color variations.

✦ **CMYK:** These options display the amount of cyan, magenta, yellow, and black ink required to print the current color. In fact, when you click the alert triangle, these are the only values that don't change, because these values make up the closest CMYK equivalent.

In my opinion, the numerical range of these options is bewildering. For example, numerically speaking, the CMYK options enable you to create 100 million unique colors, whereas the RGB options enable the standard 16 million variations, and the Lab options enables a scant 6 million. Yet Lab is the largest color space, theoretically encompassing all colors from both CMYK and RGB. The printing standard CMYK provides by far the fewest colors, the opposite of what you might expect. What gives? Misleading numerical ranges. How do these weird color models work? Keep reading and you'll find out.

Working in Different Color Modes

The four sets of option boxes inside the Color Picker dialog box represent color models — or, if you prefer, color modes (one less letter, no less meaning, perfect for you folks who are trying to cut down in life). *Color models* are different ways to define colors both onscreen and on the printed page.

Outside the Color Picker dialog box, you can work inside any one of these color models by choosing a command from the Image ➪ Mode submenu. In doing so, you generally change the colors in your image by dumping a few hundred, or even thousand, colors with no equivalents in the new color model. The only exception is Lab, which in theory encompasses every unique color your eyes can detect.

Rather than discuss the color models in the order in which they occur in the Mode submenu, I cover them in logical order, starting with the most common and widely accepted color model, RGB. Also note, I don't discuss the duotone or multichannel modes now. Image ➪ Mode ➪ Duotone represents an alternative method for printing grayscale images, so it is discussed in Chapter 7. The multichannel mode, meanwhile, is not even a color model. Rather, Image ➪ Mode ➪ Multichannel enables you to separate an image into entirely independent channels, which you then can swap around and splice back together to create special effects. For more information, see the "Using multichannel techniques" section of Chapter 6.

RGB

RGB is the color model of light. RGB comprises three primary colors — red, green, and blue — each of which can vary between 256 levels of intensity (called brightness values, as discussed in previous chapters). The RGB model is also called the *additive primary model,* because a color becomes lighter as you add higher levels of red, green, and blue light. All monitors, projection devices, and other items that transmit or filter light, including televisions, movie projectors, colored stage lights, and even stained glass, rely on the additive primary model.

Red, green, and blue light mix as follows:

✦ **Red and green:** Full-intensity red and green mix to form yellow. Subtract some red to make chartreuse; subtract some green to make orange. All these colors assume a complete lack of blue.

✦ **Green and blue:** Full-intensity green and blue with no red mix to form cyan. If you try hard enough, you can come up with 65,000 colors in the turquoise/jade/sky blue/sea green range.

✦ **Blue and red:** Full-intensity blue and red mix to form magenta. Subtract some blue to make rose; subtract some red to make purple. All these colors assume a complete lack of green.

✦ **Red, green, and blue:** Full-intensity red, green, and blue mix to form white, the absolute brightest color in the visible spectrum.

✦ **No light:** Low intensities of red, green, and blue plunge a color into blackness.

As far as image editing is concerned, the RGB color model is ideal for editing images onscreen because it provides access to the entire range of 24-bit screen colors. Furthermore, you can save an RGB image in every file format supported by Photoshop, except GIF. As shown in Table 5-1, grayscale is the only other color mode compatible with a wider range of file formats.

Table 5-1 File-Format Support for Photoshop 4's Color Models							
	Bitmap	*Grayscale*	*Duotone*	*Indexed*	*RGB*	*Lab*	*CMYK*
Photoshop	yes	yes	yes	yes	yes	yes	yes
BMP	yes	yes	no	yes	yes	no	no
EPS	yes	yes	yes	yes	yes	yes	yes
GIF	yes	yes	no	yes	no	no	no
JPEG	no	yes	no	no	yes	no	yes
PCX	yes	yes	no	yes	yes	no	no
PICT	yes	yes	no	yes	yes	no	no
PNG	yes	yes	no	yes	yes	no	no
Scitex CT	no	yes	no	no	yes	no	yes
TIFF	yes	yes	no	yes	yes	yes	yes

Note Table 5-1 lists color models in the order they appear in the Image ➪ Mode submenu. Again, I left out the multichannel mode because it is not a color model. (Also, the multichannel mode can only be saved in the Photoshop and raw formats.)

On the negative side, the RGB color model provides access to a wider range of colors than you can print. If you are designing an image for full-color printing, therefore, you can expect to lose many of the brightest and most vivid colors in your image. The only way to avoid such color loss entirely is to scan your image and edit it in the CMYK mode, which can be an exceptionally slow proposition. The better solution is to scan your images to Photo CDs and edit them in the Lab mode, as explained in the upcoming "CIE's Lab" section.

HSB

Back in Photoshop 2, the Modes menu provided access to the HSB — hue, saturation, brightness — color model, now relegated to the Color Picker dialog box and the Color palette (discussed later in this chapter). *Hue* is pure color, the stuff rainbows are made of, measured on a 360-degree circle. Red is located at 0 degrees, yellow at 60 degrees, green at 120 degrees, cyan at 180 degrees (midway around the circle), blue at 240 degrees, and magenta at 300 degrees. This is basically a pie-shaped version of the RGB model at full intensity.

Saturation represents the purity of the color. A zero saturation value equals gray. White, black, and any other colors you can express in a grayscale image have no saturation. Full saturation produces the purest version of a hue.

Brightness is the lightness or darkness of a color. A zero brightness value equals black. Full brightness combined with full saturation results in the most vivid version of any hue.

CMYK

In nature, our eyes perceive pigments according to the *subtractive color model*. Sunlight contains every visible color found on Earth. When sunlight is projected on an object, the object absorbs (subtracts) some of the light and reflects the rest. The reflected light is the color you see. For example, a fire engine is bright red because it absorbs all non-red — meaning all blue and green — from the white-light spectrum.

Pigments on a sheet of paper work the same way. You can even mix pigments to create other colors. Suppose you paint a red brush stroke, which absorbs green and blue light, over a blue brush stroke, which absorbs green and red light. You get a blackish mess with only a modicum of blue and red light left, along with a smidgen of green because the colors weren't absolutely pure.

But wait — every child knows red and blue mix to form purple. So what gives? What gives is what you learned in elementary school is only a rude approximation of the truth. Did you ever try mixing a vivid red with a canary yellow only to produce an ugly orange-brown gloop? The reason you didn't achieve the bright orange you wanted is obvious. Red starts out darker than bright orange, which means you must add a great deal of yellow before you arrive at orange. And even then, the yellow had better be an incredibly bright lemon yellow, not some deep canary yellow with a lot of red in it.

Commercial subtractive primaries

The subtractive primary colors used by commercial printers — cyan, magenta, and yellow — are for the most part very light. Cyan absorbs only red light, magenta absorbs only green light, and yellow absorbs only blue light. On their own, these colors unfortunately don't do a good job of producing dark colors. In fact, at full intensities, cyan, magenta, and yellow all mixed together don't get much beyond a muddy brown. That's where black comes in. Black helps to accentuate shadows, deepen dark colors, and, of course, print real blacks.

In case you're wondering how colors mix in the CMYK model, it's basically the opposite of the RGB model. Because pigments are not as pure as primary colors in the additive model, though, some differences exist:

✦ **Cyan and magenta:** Full-intensity cyan and magenta mix to form a deep blue with a little violet. Subtract some cyan to make purple; subtract some magenta to make a dull medium blue. All these colors assume a complete lack of yellow.

✦ **Magenta and yellow:** Full-intensity magenta and yellow mix to form a brilliant red. Subtract some magenta to make vivid orange; subtract some yellow to make rose. All these colors assume a complete lack of cyan.

✦ **Yellow and cyan:** Full-intensity yellow and cyan mix to form a bright green with a hint of blue. Subtract some yellow to make a deep teal; subtract some cyan to make chartreuse. All these colors assume a complete lack of magenta.

✦ **Cyan, magenta, and yellow:** Full-intensity cyan, magenta, and yellow mix to form a muddy brown.

✦ **Black:** Black pigmentation added to any other pigment darkens the color.

✦ **No pigment:** No pigmentation results in white (assuming white is the paper color).

Editing in CMYK

If you're used to editing RGB images, editing in the CMYK mode can require some new approaches, especially when editing individual color channels. When you view a single color channel in the RGB mode (as discussed in the following chapter), white indicates high-intensity color, and black indicates low-intensity color. It's the opposite in CMYK. When you view an individual color channel, black means high-intensity color, and white means low-intensity color.

This doesn't mean RGB and CMYK color channels look like inverted versions of each other. In fact, because the color theory is inverted, they look much the same. But if you're trying to achieve the full-intensity colors mentioned in the preceding section, you should apply black to the individual color channels, not white as you would in the RGB mode.

Should I edit in CMYK?

RGB doesn't accurately represent the colors you get when you print an image because RGB enables you to represent many colors — particularly very bright colors — that CMYK can't touch. This is why when you switch from RGB to CMYK, the colors appear duller. (If you're familiar with painting, RGB is like oils and CMYK is like acrylics. The latter lacks the depth of color provided by the former.)

For this reason, many folks advocate working in the CMYK mode, but I do not. Although working in CMYK eliminates color disappointments, it is also much slower because Photoshop has to convert CMYK values to your RGB screen on the fly.

Furthermore, your scanner and monitor are RGB devices. No matter how you work, a translation from RGB to CMYK color space must occur at some time. If you pay the extra bucks to purchase a commercial drum scan, for example, you simply make the translation at the beginning of the process — Scitex has no option but to use RGB sensors internally — rather than at the end. Every color device on Earth, in fact, is RGB except the printer.

You should wait to convert to the CMYK mode until right before you print. After your artwork is finalized, choose Image ➪ Mode ➪ CMYK and make whatever edits you deem necessary. For example, you might want to introduce a few color corrections, apply some sharpening, and even retouch a few details by hand. Photoshop applies your changes more slowly in the CMYK mode, but at least you're only slowed down at the end of the job, not throughout the entire process.

Cross Reference

Before converting an image to the CMYK color space, make certain Photoshop is aware of the monitor you're using and the printer you intend to use. These two items can have a pronounced effect on how Photoshop generates a CMYK image. I discuss how to set up the monitor and printer in the "Creating Color Separations" section of Chapter 7.

Previewing the CMYK color space

This isn't to say you can't edit in the RGB mode and still get a picture of what the image will look like in CMYK. If you choose View ➪ CMYK Preview or press Ctrl+Y, Photoshop displays colors in the CMYK color space onscreen while enabling you to continue working in the larger world of RGB.

View ➪ Gamut Warning (Ctrl+Shift+Y) is a companion command that covers so-called "out-of-gamut" colors — RGB colors with no CMYK equivalents — with gray. I personally find this command less useful because it demonstrates a problem without suggesting a solution. You can desaturate the grayed colors with the sponge tool (which I explain in Chapter 8), but this merely accomplishes what Photoshop will do automatically. A CMYK preview is much more serviceable and representative of the final CMYK image.

Tip You can choose both the CMYK Preview and Gamut Warning commands while inside Photoshop's Color Picker dialog box. CMYK Preview shows how all colors will appear in the CMYK color space, regardless of which options you use to define the color. And Gamut Warning takes on new meaning, enabling you to mask out colors that won't print. It's also an excellent way to glean a little color theory.

CIE's Lab

RGB isn't the only mode that responds quickly and provides a bountiful range of colors. Photoshop's Lab color space comprises all the colors from RGB and CMYK and is every bit as fast as RGB. Many high-end users prefer to work in this mode, and I certainly advocate this if you're brave enough.

Whereas the RGB mode is the color model of your luminescent computer screen and the CMYK mode is the color model of the reflective page, Lab is independent of light or pigment. Perhaps you've already heard the bit about how in 1931, an international color organization called the Commission Internationale d'Eclairage (CIE) developed a color model that, in theory, contains every single color the human eye can see. (Gnats, iguanas, fruit bats, go find your own color models; humans, you have CIE. Mutants and aliens — maybe CIE, maybe not, too early to tell.) Then, in 1976, the significant birthday of our nation, the CIE celebrated by coming up with two additional color systems. One of those systems was Lab, and the other was shrouded in secrecy. Well, at least I don't know what the other one was. Probably something that measures how the entire visible spectrum of color can bounce off your retina when using flash photography and come out looking the exact shade of red one normally associates with lab (not Lab) rabbits. But this is just a guess.

The beauty of the Lab color model is it fills in gaps in both the RGB and CMYK models. RGB, for example, provides an overabundance of colors in the blue-to-green range, but is stingy on yellows, oranges, and other colors in the green-to-red range. Meanwhile, the colors missing from CMYK are enough to fill the holes in the Albert Hall. Lab gets everything right.

Understanding Lab anatomy

The Lab mode features three color channels, one for luminosity and two others for color ranges, known simply by the initials *a* and *b*. (The Greeks would have called them alpha and beta, if that's any help.) Upon hearing luminosity, you might think, "Ah, just like HSL." Well, to make things confusing, Lab's *luminosity* is like HSB's brightness. White indicates full-intensity color.

Meanwhile, the *a* channel contains colors ranging from deep green (low-brightness values) to gray (medium-brightness values) to vivid pink (high-brightness values). The *b* channel ranges from bright blue (low-brightness values) to gray to burnt yellow (high-brightness values). As in the RGB model, these colors mix together to produce lighter colors. Only the brightness values in the luminosity channel darken the colors. So you can think of Lab as a two-channel RGB with brightness thrown on top.

To get a glimpse of how it works, try the following simple experiment.

Steps: Testing Out the Lab Mode

1. **Create a new image in the Lab mode — say, 300 × 300 pixels.**

2. **Press the D key to return the default colors to the Toolbox.** The foreground color is now black and the background color is white.

3. **Press Ctrl+2. This takes you to the *a* channel.**

4. **Double-click the gradient tool in the Toolbox.** Or press Enter. Either approach displays the Gradient Tools Options palette. Make sure you see the words Normal, Foreground to Background, and Linear in the palette. If these words aren't visible, select them from the first, second, and third pop-up menus, respectively.

5. **Shift+drag with the gradient tool from the top to the bottom of the window.** This creates a vertical black-to-white gradation.

6. **Press Ctrl+3. This takes you to the *b* channel.**

7. **Shift+drag from left to right with the gradient tool.** Photoshop paints a horizontal gradation.

8. **Press Ctrl+tilde (~) to return to the composite display.** Now you can see all channels at once. If you're using a 24-bit monitor, you should be looking at a window filled with an incredible array of super bright colors. In theory, these are the brightest shades of all the colors you can see. In practice, however, the colors are limited by the display capabilities of your RGB monitor.

9. **If you really want a sobering sight, choose View ➪ CMYK Preview and watch those bright colors disappear.** Aagh, isn't it pitiful? Luckily, CMYK is capable of doing a slightly better job than this. Choose Image ➪ Adjust ➪ Auto Levels (or press Ctrl+Shift+L). That's better — quite a bit better, in fact — but it's still muted compared with its Lab counterpart.

Using Lab

Because it's device independent, you can use the Lab mode to edit any image. Editing in the Lab mode is as fast as editing in the RGB mode and several times faster than editing in the CMYK mode. If you plan on printing your image to color separations, you may want to experiment with using the Lab mode instead of RGB, because Lab ensures no colors are altered when you convert the image to CMYK, except to change colors that fall outside the CMYK range. In fact, any time you convert an image from RGB to CMYK, Photoshop automatically converts the image to the Lab mode as an intermediate step.

Tip

If you work with Photo CDs often, open the scans directly from the Photo CD format as Lab images. Kodak's proprietary YCC color model is nearly identical to Lab, so you can expect an absolute minimum of data loss; some people claim no loss whatsoever occurs.

Grayscale

Grayscale is possibly my favorite color mode. *Grayscale* frees you from all the hassles and expense of working with color and provides access to every bit of Photoshop's power and functionality. Anyone who says you can't do as much with grayscale as you can with color, missed out on *Citizen Kane, L'Aventura, To Kill a Mockingbird,* and *Raging Bull.* You can print grayscale images to any laser printer, reproduce them in any publication, and edit them on nearly any machine. Besides, they look great, they remind you of old movies, and they make a hefty book like this one affordable. What could be better?

Other than extolling its virtues, however, there isn't a whole lot to say about grayscale. You can convert an image to the grayscale mode regardless of its current mode, and you can convert from grayscale to any other mode just as easily. In fact, choosing Image ➪ Mode ➪ Grayscale is a necessary step in converting a color image to a duotone or black-and-white bitmap.

Search your channels before converting

When you convert an image from one of the color modes to the grayscale mode, Photoshop normally weights the values of each color channel in a way that retains the apparent brightness of the overall image. For example, when you convert an image from RGB, Photoshop weights red more heavily than blue when computing dark values. This is because red is a darker-looking color than blue (much as that might seem contrary to popular belief).

Tip

If you choose Image ➪ Mode ➪ Grayscale while viewing a single color channel, though, Photoshop retains all brightness values in that channel only and abandons the data in the other channels. This can be an especially useful technique for rescuing a grayscale image from a bad RGB scan.

So before switching to the grayscale mode, be sure to look at the individual color channels — particularly the red and green channels (the blue channel frequently contains substandard detail) — to see how each channel might look on its own. To browse the channels, press Ctrl+1 for red, Ctrl+2 for green, and Ctrl+3 for blue. Or

Ctrl+1 for cyan, Ctrl+2 for magenta, Ctrl+3 for yellow, and Ctrl+4 for black. Or even Ctrl+1 for luminosity, Ctrl+2 for *a*, and Ctrl+3 for *b*. Chapter 6 describes color channels in more detail.

Dot gain interference

You should be aware of a little item that might throw off your gray value calculations. If the Use Dot Gain for Grayscale Images check box in the Printer Inks Setup dialog box (File ➪ Color Settings ➪ Printer Inks Setup) is turned on, Photoshop figures in *dot gain* when calculating the lightness and darkness of grayscale images.

Cross Reference Dot gain is more thoroughly discussed in the "Printer calibration" section of Chapter 7, but the basic concept is this: Printed images are made up of tiny dots of ink called *halftone cells*. During the printing process, the halftone cells expand — sort of like what happens to drops of water plopped onto a paper towel. The Use Dot Gain for Grayscale Images check box lightens the gray values in an image, which reduces the size of the halftone cells, thereby giving the dots some room to bleed.

Suppose you click the foreground color icon and change the B (Brightness) value in the Color Picker dialog box to 50 percent. Later, after applying the 50 percent gray to the current image, you move your cursor over some of the medium gray pixels while the Info palette is displayed. You notice the Info palette interprets the pixels as 56 percent gray, 6 percentage points darker than the color you specified. This happens because Photoshop automatically darkens the colors in your image to reflect how they will print subject to the dot gain specified in the Printer Inks Setup dialog box.

Note At this point, let me give you two bits of information to avoid (or perhaps enhance) confusion. First, as long as the S (Saturation) value is 0, the B (Brightness) value is the only Color Picker option you need to worry about when editing grayscale images. Second, although the B (Brightness) value measures luminosity, ranging from 0 percent for black to 100 percent for white, the K value in the Info dialog box measures ink coverage, thus reversing the figures to 100 percent for black and 0 percent for white. Ignoring dot gain for a moment, this means a 50 percent brightness translates to 50 percent ink coverage, a 40 percent brightness translates to 60 percent ink coverage, a 30 percent brightness translates to 70 percent ink coverage, and so on.

In theory, automatic dot gain compensation is a good idea but, in practice, it frequently gets in the way. Fortunately, this option is turned off by default. But you never know when the person using Photoshop ahead of you might go in there and snap it on.

Black and white (bitmap)

Choose Image ➪ Mode ➪ Bitmap to convert a grayscale image to exclusively black-and-white pixels. This may sound like a boring option, but it can prove useful for gaining complete control over the printing of grayscale images. After all, output devices, such as laser printers and imagesetters, render grayscale images as a series of tiny dots. Using the Bitmap command, you can specify the size, shape, and angle of those dots.

When you choose Image ➪ Mode ➪ Bitmap, Photoshop displays the Bitmap dialog box, shown in Figure 5-5. Here you specify the resolution of the black-and-white image and select a conversion process. The options work as follows:

✦ **Output:** Specify the resolution of the black-and-white file. If you want control over every single pixel available to your printer, raise this value to match your printer's resolution. As a rule of thumb, try setting the Output value somewhere between 200 to 250 percent of the Input value.

✦ **50% Threshold:** Select this option to make every pixel that is darker than 50 percent gray black and every pixel that is 50 percent gray or lighter white. Unless you are working toward some special effect — for example, overlaying a black-and-white version of an image over the original grayscale image — this option most likely isn't for you. (And if you're working toward a special effect, Image ➪ Adjust ➪ Threshold is the better alternative.)

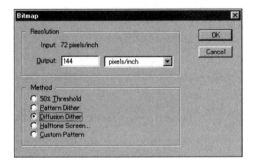

Figure 5-5: The Bitmap dialog box converts images from grayscale to black and white.

✦ **Pattern Dither:** To *dither* pixels is to mix them up to emulate different colors. In this case, Photoshop mixes up black and white pixels to produce shades of gray. The Pattern Dither option dithers an image using a geometric pattern. Unfortunately, the results are pretty ugly, as demonstrated in the top example in Figure 5-6. And the space between dots has a tendency to fill in, especially when you output to a laser printer.

✦ **Diffusion Dither:** Select this option to create a mezzotint-like effect, as demonstrated in the second example in Figure 5-6. Again, because this option converts an image into thousands of stray pixels, you can expect your image to darken dramatically when output to a low-resolution laser printer and when reproduced. So be sure to lighten the image with something like the Levels command (as described in Chapter 18) before selecting this option.

Figure 5-6: The results of selecting the Pattern Dither option (top) and the much more acceptable Diffusion Dither option (bottom)

✦ **Halftone Screen:** When you select this option and press Enter, Photoshop displays the dialog box shown in Figure 5-7. These options enable you to apply a dot pattern to the image, as demonstrated in Figure 5-8. Enter the number of dots per inch in the Frequency option box and the angle of the dots in the Angle option box. Then select a dot shape from the Shape pop-up menu. Figure 5-8 shows examples of four shapes, each with a frequency of 24 lines per inch.

✦ I cover screen patterns and frequency settings in more depth in the "Changing the halftone screen" section of Chapter 7.

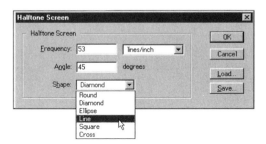

Figure 5-7: This dialog box appears when you select the Halftone Screen option in the Bitmap dialog box.

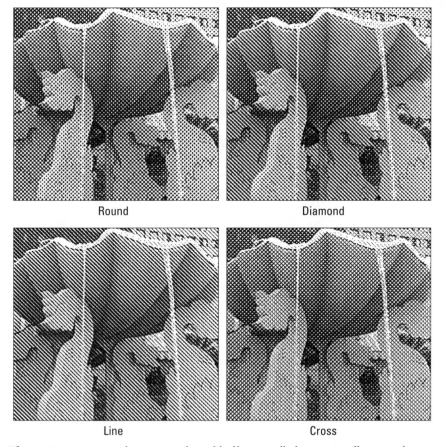

Round   Diamond

Line   Cross

Figure 5-8: Four random examples of halftone cell shapes. In all cases, the Frequency value was set to 24.

✦ **Custom Pattern:** If you have defined a repeating pattern by choosing Edit ➪ Define Pattern, you can use it as a custom dither pattern. Figure 5-9 shows two custom examples. The first pattern was created using the Twirl Pattern file, stored in the Dispmaps folder. (Dispmaps is stored inside the Filters folder, which is stored in the Plugins folder.) I created the second pattern manually using the Add Noise, Emboss, and Ripple filters (as discussed in the "Creating texture effects" section of Chapter 17).

Cross Reference

For a complete guide to creating and defining patterns in Photoshop, see the "Applying Repeating Patterns" section of Chapter 10.

Figure 5-9: Two examples of employing repeating patterns (created with Edit ➪ Define Pattern) as custom halftoning patterns

Caution Photoshop enables you to edit individual pixels in the so-called bitmap mode, but that's about the extent of it. After you go to black-and-white, you can neither perform any serious editing nor expect to return to the grayscale mode and restore your original pixels. So be sure to finish your image editing before choosing Image ➪ Mode ➪ Bitmap. Even more important, make certain to save your image before converting it to black-and-white. Frankly, saving is a good idea when performing any color conversion.

Using Photoshop's Other Color Selection Methods

In addition to the Color Picker dialog box, Photoshop provides a handful of additional techniques for selecting colors. The sections that finish out this chapter explain how to use the Custom Colors dialog box, the Colors palette, and the eyedropper tool. None of this information is terribly exciting, but it will enable you to work more efficiently and conveniently.

Predefined colors

If you click the Custom button inside the Color Picker dialog box, Photoshop displays the Custom Colors dialog box shown in Figure 5-10. In this dialog box, you can select from a variety of predefined colors by choosing the color family from the Book pop-up menu, moving the slider triangles up and down the color slider to specify a general range of colors and, ultimately, selecting a color from the color list on the left. If you own the swatchbook for a color family, you can locate a specific color by entering its number on the keyboard.

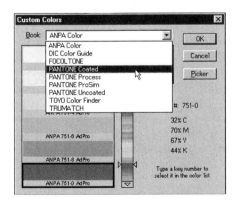

Figure 5-10: The Custom Colors dialog box enables you to select predefined colors from brand-name libraries.

The color families represented in the Book pop-up menu fall into six brands: ANPA (now NAA), DIC, Focoltone, Pantone, Toyo, and Trumatch, all of which get a big kick out of capitalizing their names in dialog boxes. I honestly think one of these companies would stand out better if its name weren't capitalized. Anyway, at the risk of offending a few of these companies, you're likely to find certain brands more useful than others. The following sections briefly introduce the brands in order of their impact on the American market — forgive me for being ethnocentric in this regard — from smallest to greatest impact.

The number-one use for predefined colors in Photoshop is in the creation of duotones, tritones, and quadtones (described in Chapter 7). You can also use predefined colors to match the colors in a logo or some other important element in an image to a commercial standard.

Focoltone, DIC, and Toyo

Focoltone, Dianippon Ink and Chemical (DIC), and Toyo fall into the negligible impact category. All are foreign color standards with followings abroad. Focoltone is an English company; not English speaking — although they probably do — but English living, as in commuting-to-France-through-the-Chunnel England. DIC and Toyo are popular in the Japanese market, but have next to no subscribers outside Japan.

Newspaper Association of America

American Newspaper Publishers Association (ANPA) recently changed its name to NAA, which stands for Newspaper Association of America, and updated its color catalog. NAA provides a small sampling of 33 process colors (mixes of cyan, magenta, yellow, and black ink) plus 5 spot colors (colors produced by printing a single ink). The idea behind the NAA colors is to isolate the color combinations that reproduce most successfully on inexpensive newsprint and to provide advertisers with a solid range of colors from which to choose, without allowing the color choices to get out of hand. You can purchase a Pocket Tint Chart from NAA for $175. Members pay $100.

Trumatch

Trumatch remains my personal favorite process-color standard. Designed entirely using a desktop system and created especially with desktop publishers in mind, the Trumatch Colorfinder swatchbook features more than 2,000 process colors, organized according to hue, saturation, and brightness. Each hue is broken down into 40 tints and shades. Tints are created by reducing the saturation in 15 percent increments; shades are created by adding black ink in 6 percent increments. The result is a guide that shows you exactly which colors you can attain using a desktop system. If you're wondering what a CMYK blend will look like when printed, you need look no further than the Trumatch Colorfinder.

As if the Colorfinder weren't enough, Trumatch provides the ColorPrinter Software utility, which automatically prints the entire 2,000-color library to any PostScript-compatible output device. The utility integrates EfiColor and PostScript Level 2, thereby enabling design firms and commercial printers to test the entire range of capabilities available to their hardware. Companies can provide select clients with swatches of colors created on their own printers, guaranteeing what you see is darn well what you'll get.

Pantone

On the heels of Trumatch, Pantone released a 3,006-color Process Color System Guide (labeled Pantone Process in the Book pop-up menu) priced at $75, $10 less than the Trumatch Colorfinder. Pantone also produces the foremost spot color swatchbook, the Color Formula Guide 1000. Then there's the Process Color Imaging Guide, which enables you to figure out quickly if you can closely match a Pantone spot color using a process-color blend or if you ought to give it up and stick with the spot color.

Pantone spot colors are ideal for creating duotones, as discussed in Chapter 7. Furthermore, Pantone is supported by every computer application that aspires to the color prepress market. As long as the company retains the old competitive spirit, you can, most likely, expect Pantone to remain the primary color printing standard for years to come.

The Color palette

Another means of selecting colors in Photoshop is to use the Color palette, shown in Figure 5-11. If you're willing to sacrifice onscreen real estate for the convenience of defining colors on the spot, without having to call the Color Picker dialog box, the Color palette is a useful tool indeed.

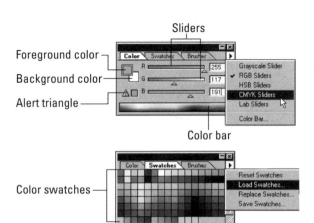

Figure 5-11: The Color and Swatches palettes enable you to edit colors without having to display the Color Picker dialog box.

To display the palette, choose Window ➪ Show Color. You then can use the elements and options inside the palette as explained in the upcoming list.

Tip

You can hide and show the Color palette from the keyboard by pressing the F6 key. (This assumes you haven't assigned F6 to a script in the Actions palette, as explained in Chapter 3.)

✦ **Foreground color/background color:** Click the foreground or background color icon in the Color palette to specify the color you want to edit. If you click the foreground or background color icon when it's already highlighted — as indicated by a double-line frame — Photoshop displays the Color Picker dialog box.

✦ **Slider bars:** Drag the triangles in the slider controls to edit the highlighted color. By default, the sliders represent the red, green, and blue primary colors when a color image is open. You can change the slider bars by choosing a different color model from the palette menu.

Photoshop 4.0

In Photoshop 4, you can also enter numerical values into the option boxes to the right of the sliders. It's about time! Press Tab to advance from one option box to the next; press Shift+Tab to go to the previous option.

✦ **Alert triangle:** Photoshop displays the alert triangle when a color falls outside the CMYK color gamut. The color swatch to the right of the triangle shows the closest CMYK equivalent. Click the triangle or the color swatch to replace the current color with the CMYK equivalent.

✦ **Color bar:** The bar along the bottom of the Color palette displays all colors contained in the CMYK spectrum. Click or drag inside the color bar to lift a color and make it the current foreground or background color (depending on whether the foreground or background icon is selected above). The sliders update as you drag. Alt+click or drag to lift the background color if the foreground icon is selected or the foreground color if the background color is selected.

✦ **Color Bar option:** You needn't accept the CMYK spectrum in the color bar. To change to a different spectrum, select the Color Bar command from the palette menu. The resulting dialog box enables you to change to the RGB spectrum or to select a black-to-white gradation (Grayscale Slider). If you select Current Colors, the color bar is filled with a gradation from the current foreground color to the current background color. The color bar continuously updates to represent the newest foreground and background colors.

Tip

Here are some neat shortcuts that enable you to change color bars without the trouble of choosing the Color Bar command from the palette menu. Just right-click the color bar to bring up a pop-up menu containing the same options found in the Color Bar dialog box. Or better yet, Shift+click the bar to cycle from one color bar to the next.

The Swatches palette

As shown in Figure 5-11, the Color palette offers an additional panel called Swatches. (A third panel, Scratch, was dropped from Photoshop 4 because of a complete lack of user interest in the function.) The Swatches palette enables you to collect colors for future use, sort of like a favorite color reservoir.

Here's how to use the swatches in the reservoir:

✦ Click a color swatch to make that color the foreground color. Alt+click to set the background color.

✦ To add the current foreground color to the reservoir, Shift+click an existing color swatch to replace the old color or click an empty swatch to append the new color. In either case, your cursor temporarily changes to a paint bucket.

✦ To insert a color anywhere in the palette, Shift+Alt+click a swatch. The other colors scoot over to make room.

✦ To delete a color from the panel, Ctrl+click a color swatch. Your cursor changes to a pair of scissors and cuts the color away.

You can also save and load color palettes on disk using options in the pop-up menu. The Load Swatches option adds the colors in the file to the current set of swatches; Replace Swatches replaces the current swatches with the ones in the file. The Palettes folder, located inside the same folder that contains the Photoshop application, contains palettes for the major color libraries from Pantone, Trumatch, and others. When one of these palettes is loaded, positioning your cursor over a color swatch makes the name of that color appear in place of the word Swatches in the panel tab.

The eyedropper tool

The eyedropper tool — which you can select by pressing the I key — provides the most convenient and straightforward means of selecting colors in Photoshop. This is so straightforward, in fact, it's hardly worth explaining. But quickly, here's how the eyedropper tool works:

✦ **Selecting a foreground color:** To select a new foreground color, click the desired color inside any open Image window with the eyedropper tool. (This assumes the foreground icon in the Color palette is selected. If the background icon is selected, Alt+click with the eyedropper tool to lift the foreground color.) You can even click inside a background window to lift a color without bringing that window to the foreground.

✦ **Selecting a background color:** To select a new background color, Alt+click the desired color with the eyedropper tool. (Again, this assumes the foreground icon is selected in the Color palette. If the background icon is selected, click with the eyedropper to lift the background color.)

✦ **Skating over the color spectrum:** You can animate the foreground color control box by dragging with the eyedropper tool in the Image window. As soon as you achieve the desired color, release your mouse button. To animate the background color icon, Alt+drag with the eyedropper tool. The icon color changes as you move the eyedropper tool.

✦ **Sampling multiple pixels:** Normally, the eyedropper tool selects the color from the single pixel on which you click. If you prefer to average the colors of several neighboring pixels, however, press Enter or double-click the eyedropper icon in the Toolbox to display the Eyedropper Options palette. Then select a different option from the Sample Size pop-up menu. Or right-click with the eyedropper to bring up a convenient pop-up menu of sampling options.

Tip

To access the eyedropper tool temporarily when using the type, paint bucket, gradient, line, pencil, airbrush, or paintbrush tool, press Alt. The eyedropper cursor remains in force for as long as the Alt key is down. The eyedropper lifts whatever color is active in the Color palette (foreground or background). To lift the other color, switch to the eyedropper tool by pressing the I key and then Alt+click an Image window.

CHAPTER

6

Navigating Channels

Introducing Color Channels

Have you ever seen a set of separated CMYK transparencies? Certainly print professionals see these all the time, but even if you're an absolute beginner, you may have come in contact with them — perhaps on your grade school field trip to the print shop. Some nebulous adult — life was a stream of nebulous adults back then — held up four sheets of acetate. One sheet showed a cyan picture, another showed the same picture in magenta, a third showed it in yellow, and the last depicted the scene in a rather washed-out black. By themselves, the pictures appeared exceedingly light and rather sparse in the detail department. But when they were put together — one layered in front of another — you saw a full-color picture. Pretty cool stuff.

Sound familiar? Whether it does or not — hey, I can't spend all day conjuring up these little slices of nostalgia — those sheets of acetate have a functional equivalent inside Photoshop: channels. In a CMYK image, for example, there is one cyan channel, one magenta channel, one yellow channel, and one black channel. They mix onscreen to form a full-color image. The RGB mode features a red channel, a green channel, and a blue channel. Because RGB is the color model of light, the three images mix together like three differently colored slides in different projectors aimed at the same screen. In other words, regardless of color mode, channels are distinct planes of primary color.

Note Channels frequently correspond to the structure of an input or output device. Each channel in a CMYK image, for example, corresponds to a different printer's plate when the document goes to press. The cyan plate is inked with cyan, the magenta plate is inked with magenta, and so on. Each channel in an RGB image corresponds to a pass of the red, green, or blue scanner sensor over the original photograph or artwork. Only the Lab mode is device-independent, so its channels don't correspond to any piece of hardware.

Why you should care

But so what, right? Who cares how many planes of color an image comprises? You want to edit the photograph, not dissect it. "Dammit, Jim, I'm an artist, not a doctor!" Well, even if you don't like to rebuild car engines or poke preserved frog entrails with sharp knives, you'll get a charge from editing channels. The fact is, channels provide you with yet another degree of selective control over an image.

Consider this example: Your client scanned an image he wants you to integrate into some goofy ad campaign for his car dealership. Unfortunately, the scan is downright rotten. Maybe it looked good on his computer, but on your screen it looks like dried . . . well, perhaps I shouldn't get too graphic here. Still, you don't want to offend the guy. The image is a picture of his favorite daughter, after all (come on, I'm making this up as I go along), so you praise him on his fine scan and say something to the effect of, "No problem, boss." But after you take his scan back to your office and load it into Photoshop, you break out in a cold sweat. You try swabbing at it with the edit tools, applying a few filters, and even attempting some scary-looking color-correction commands, but the image continues to look like the inside of a garbage disposal. (Not that I've ever seen the inside of a garbage disposal, but it can't be attractive.)

Suddenly, it occurs to you to look at the channels. What the heck, it can't hurt. With little effort, you discover the red and green channels look okay, but the blue channel looks like it's melting. Big gobs of gooey detail slide off the kid's face like some kind of mobile acne. Her mouth is sort of mixed in with her teeth, her eyes look like an experiment in expressionism, and her hair has a slightly geometric appearance. (If you think this is a big exaggeration, look at a few blue channels from low-end scanners. They're frequently ripe with tattered edges, random blocks of color, stray pixels, and other so-called digital artifacts.)

The point is, you've located the cancer, Doctor. You don't have to waste your time trying to perform surgery on the entire image; in fact, doing so may very well harm the channels that are in good shape. You merely have to fix this one channel. A wave of the Gaussian Blur filter here, an application of the Levels command there, and some selective rebuilding of missing detail borrowed from the other channels — all of which I'll get to in future sections or chapters — result in an image that resembles a living, breathing human being. It may not be absolute perfection, but it's solid enough to pass muster.

How channels work

Photoshop devotes 8 bits of data to each pixel in each channel, thus permitting 256 brightness values, from 0 (black) to 255 (white). Therefore, each channel is actually an independent grayscale image. You may be thrown off by this at first. If an RGB image is made up of red, green, and blue channels, why do all the channels look gray?

Photoshop provides an option in the Display & Cursors panel of the Preferences dialog box (Ctrl+K, then Ctrl+3) called Color Channels in Color. When selected, this function displays each channel in its corresponding primary color. Although this feature can be reassuring — particularly to novices — it is equally counterproductive.

When you view an 8-bit image composed exclusively of shades of red, for example, it's easy to miss subtle variations in detail that may appear obvious when you print the image. You may have problems accurately gauging the impact of filters and tonal adjustments. I mean, face it, red isn't a friendly shade to stare at for half an hour of intense editing. So leave the Color Channels in Color option off and temporarily suspend your biological urge for onscreen color. With a little experience, you can better monitor your adjustments and predict the outcome of your edits in plain old grayscale.

Tip Just because you're editing a single channel doesn't mean you must work wearing blinders. At any time, you can see how your changes affect the full-color image. Simply create a new view of your image by choosing View ➪ New View. Leave this window set to the standard composite view (presumably RGB, but it could be CMYK, Lab, or any other color mode) and edit away on the individual channel in the first image. (Don't worry, I explain how to switch channels in the next section.)

Images that include 256 or fewer colors can be expressed in a single channel and, therefore, do not include multiple channels you can edit independently. A grayscale image, for example, includes a single channel. A black-and-white image permits only one bit of data per pixel, so a single channel is more than enough to express it. Duotones are the really weird ones. Although duotones may contain two, three, or four plates of color, Photoshop treats them as a single channel of 8-bit color. Duotones are explained in detail in Chapter 7.

Cross Reference You can add channels above and beyond those required to represent a color or grayscale image for the purpose of storing masks, as described in Chapter 12. But, even then, each channel is typically limited to 8 bits of data per pixel — meaning it's just another grayscale image. Mask channels do not affect the appearance of the image onscreen or when it is printed. Rather, they serve to save selection outlines, as Chapter 12 explains.

How to switch and view channels

To access channels in Photoshop, display the Channels palette by choosing Window ➪ Show Channels. Every channel in the image appears in the palette — including any mask channels — as shown in Figure 6-1. Photoshop even shows little thumbnail views of each channel so you can see what it looks like.

Eyeball icon

Selection to channel

Channel to selection

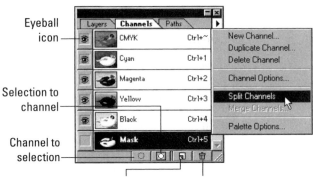

New channel   Delete channel

Figure 6-1: Photoshop displays tiny thumbnails of each color and mask channel in the Channels palette.

To switch to a different channel, click a channel name in the Channels palette. The channel name becomes highlighted — like the Mask channel in Figure 6-1 — showing you can now edit it independently of other channels in the image.

Tip

To edit more than one channel at a time, click one channel name and then Shift+click another. You can also Shift+click an active channel to deactivate it independently of any others.

When you select a channel, Photoshop normally displays the channel you want to edit onscreen. You can view additional channels beyond those you want to edit, though. To specify which channels appear onscreen, click in the far left column of the Channels palette. Click an eyeball icon to make it disappear and, hence, hide that channel. Click where no eyeball is to display one and, thus, display the channel.

When only one channel is visible, that channel appears as a grayscale picture in the Image window (possibly colorized in accordance with the Color Channels in Color check box in the Preferences dialog box). When more than one channel is visible, however, you always see color. If both the blue and green channels are visible, for example, the image appears blue-green. If the red and green channels are visible, the image has a yellow cast, and so on. If a mask channel and some other channel are visible, the mask appears by default as a pink overlay. (The color of the mask can be changed.) For more information on viewing two or more individual channels simultaneously — and why in the world you'd want to — read the "Viewing mask and image" section of Chapter 12.

In addition to the individual channels, Photoshop provides access to a composite view that displays all colors in an RGB, CMYK, or Lab image at once. (The composite view does not show mask channels; you have to specify their display separately.) The composite view is listed first in the Channels palette and is displayed by default. Notice when you select the composite view, all the names of the individual color channels in the Channels palette become highlighted along with the composite channel. This shows all the channels are active. The composite view is the one in which you will perform the majority of your image editing.

Press Ctrl plus a number key to switch between color channels. Depending on the color mode you're working in, Ctrl+1 takes you to the red (RGB), cyan (CMYK), or luminosity (Lab) channel; Ctrl+2 takes you to the green, magenta, or *a* channel; and Ctrl+3 takes you to the blue, yellow, or *b* channel. In the CMYK mode, Ctrl+4 displays the black channel. Other Ctrl+key equivalents — up to Ctrl+9 — take you to mask channels (if there are any).

New to Photoshop 4, Ctrl+tilde (~) takes you to the composite view. (The tilde is the key to the left of 1.) You should stop pressing Ctrl+0 — the old shortcut — pretty darn fast. That shortcut now zooms the image to fit onscreen.

The shortcuts are slightly different when you're working on a grayscale image. You access the image itself by pressing Ctrl+1. Ctrl+2 and higher take you to the mask channels.

Note   Don't freak or in any way feel inadequate if your images don't contain mask channels. You must create masks manually and, as I mentioned earlier, we won't be talking about masks until Chapter 12. Meanwhile, I'm trying to make sure I leave no stone unturned as I explain the various nuances of this many-splendored topic.

Trying Channels on for Size

Feeling a little mystified? Need some examples? Fair enough. Color Plate 6-1 shows a woman in a bright yellow swimsuit on a bright red floatation device set against a bright green ocean beneath a bright blue sky. These colors — yellow, red, green, and blue — cover the four corners of the color spectrum; therefore, you can expect to see a lot of variation among the images in the independent color channels.

RGB channels

Suppose the sunbathing woman is an RGB image. Figure 6-2 compares a grayscale composite of this same image (created by choosing Image ➪ Mode ➪ Grayscale) compared with the contents of the red, green, and blue color channels from the original color image. The green channel is similar to the grayscale composite because green is an ingredient in all colors in the image, except for the red of the raft. The red and blue channels differ more significantly. The pixels in the red channel are lightest in the swimsuit and raft because they contain the highest concentrations of red. The pixels in the blue channel are lightest in the sky and water because — you guessed it — the sky and water are rich with blue.

Notice how the channels in Figure 6-2 make interesting grayscale images in and of themselves? The red channel, for example, looks like the sky darkening above our bather, even though the sun is blazing down.

I mentioned this as a tip in the previous chapter, but it bears a bit of casual drumming into the old noggin. When converting a color image to grayscale, you have the option of calculating a grayscale composite or simply retaining the image exactly as it appears in one of the channels. To create a grayscale composite, choose Image ➪ Mode ➪ Grayscale when viewing all colors in the image in the composite view, as usual. To retain a single channel only, switch to that channel and then choose Image ➪ Mode ➪ Grayscale. Instead of the usual *Discard color information?* message, Photoshop displays the message *Discard other channels?* If you click the OK button, Photoshop chucks the other channels into the electronic abyss.

Grayscale composite   Red

Green   Blue

Figure 6-2: This is a grayscale composite of the image from Color Plate 6-1, followed by the contents of the red, green, and blue color channels.

CMYK channels

In the name of fair and unbiased coverage, Figures 6-3 and 6-4 show the channels from the image after it was converted to other color modes. In Figure 6-3, I converted the image to the CMYK mode and examined its channels. Here, the predominant colors are cyan (sky and water) and yellow (in the swimsuit and raft). Because this color mode relies on pigments rather than light, as explained in the "CMYK" section of Chapter 5, dark areas in the channels represent high-color intensity. For this reason, the sky in the cyan channel is dark, whereas it is light in the blue channel back in Figure 6-2.

Cyan   Magenta

Yellow   Black

Figure 6-3: Here are the contents of the cyan, magenta, yellow, and black channels from the image shown in Color Plate 6-1.

Notice how similar the cyan channel in Figure 6-3 is to its red counterpart in Figure 6-2. Same with the magenta and green channels, and the yellow and blue channels. The CMY channels have more contrast than the RGB pals, but the basic brightness distribution is the same. Here's another graphic demonstration of color theory. In a perfect world, the CMY channels would be identical to the RGB channels — one color model would simply be the other turned on its head. But because this is not a perfect world (you might have noticed this as you've traveled life's bitter highway), Photoshop has to boost the contrast of the CMY channels and throw in black to punch up those shadows.

Lab channels

To create Figure 6-4, I converted the image in Color Plate 6-1 to the Lab mode. The image in the luminosity channel looks similar to the grayscale composite because it contains the lightness and darkness values for the image. The a channel maps the greens and magentas, while the b channel maps the yellows and blues, so both channels are working hard to provide color information for this photograph. Certainly differences exist — the a channel is hotter in the raft, while the b channel offers more cloud detail — but the two channels carry roughly equivalent amounts of color information.

Grayscale composite　　　　　　　　　Luminosity

a (black is green, white is magenta)　　b (black is blue, white is yellow)

Figure 6-4: The grayscale composite followed by the contents of the luminosity channel and the a and b color channels after converting the image shown in Color Plate 6-1 to the Lab mode

You can achieve some entertaining effects by applying commands from the Image ➪ Adjust submenu to the *a* and *b* color channels. For example, if I go to the *a* channel in Figure 6-4 and reverse the brightness values by choosing Image ➪ Adjust ➪ Invert (Ctrl+I), the water turns a sort of salmon red and the raft turns green, as demonstrated in the first example of Color Plate 6-2. If I apply Image ➪ Adjust ➪ Auto Levels (Ctrl+Shift+L) to the *b* channel, the sky lights up with brilliant blue without altering so much as a color in the woman or her raft, as in the second example. The third example in Color Plate 6-2 shows what happens when I apply both Invert and Auto Levels to both the *a* and *b* channels. Now there's the way I want to vacation — on a different planet!

Other Channel Functions

In addition to viewing and editing channels using any of the techniques discussed in future chapters of this book, you can choose commands from the Channels palette menu and select icons along the bottom of the palette (labeled back in Figure 6-1). The following items explain how the commands and icons work.

Cross Reference

You'll notice I say "see Chapter 12" every so often when explaining these options, because many of them are specifically designed to accommodate masks. This list is designed to introduce you to all the options in the Channels palette, even if you'll need more background to use a few of them. After I introduce the options, I'll revisit the ones with a direct effect on managing the colors in your image.

✦ **Palette Options:** Even though this is the last command in the menu, it's the easiest, so I'll start here. When you choose Palette Options, Photoshop displays four Thumbnail Size radio buttons, enabling you to change the size of the thumbnail previews that appear along the left side of the Channels palette. Figure 6-5 shows the four thumbnail settings — nonexistent, small, medium, and large.

✦ **New Channel:** Choose this command to add a mask channel to the current image. The Channel Options dialog box appears, enabling you to name the channel. You also can specify the color and translucency Photoshop applies to the channel when you view it with other channels. I explain how these options work in the "Changing the red coating" section of Chapter 12. An image can contain no more than 24 total channels, regardless of color mode.

Tip

You can also create a new channel by clicking the new channel icon at the bottom of the Channels palette. (It's the one that looks like a little page.) Photoshop creates the channel without displaying the dialog box. To force the dialog box to appear onscreen, Alt+click the page icon.

✦ **Duplicate Channel:** Choose this command to create a duplicate of the selected channel, either inside the same document or as part of a new document. (If the composite view is active, the Duplicate Channel command is dimmed, because you can only duplicate one channel at a time.) The most common reason to use this command is to convert a channel into a mask. Again, you can find real-life applications in Chapter 12.

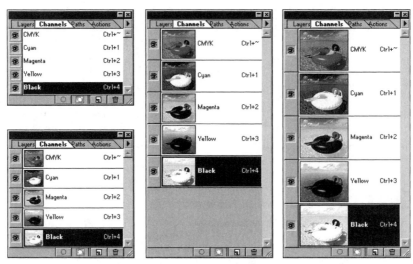

Figure 6-5: The Channels Palette Options dialog box enables you to select among four thumbnail preview options.

You can also duplicate a channel by dragging the channel name onto the new channel icon. No dialog box appears; Photoshop merely names the channel automatically. To copy a channel to a different document, drag the channel name and drop it into an open Image window. Photoshop automatically creates a new channel for the duplicate.

✦ **Delete Channel:** To delete a channel from an image, click the channel name in the palette and choose this command. You can delete only one channel at a time. The Delete Channel command is dimmed when any essential color channel is active or when more than one channel is selected.

If choosing a command is too much effort, drag the channel onto the delete channel icon (the little trash can icon in the lower-right corner of the Channels palette). In Photoshop 4, you can also merely click the trash can icon, in which case Photoshop asks you if you really want to delete the channel. To bypass this warning, Alt+click the trash can icon.

✦ **Channel Options:** Choose this command or double-click the channel name in the palette's scrolling list to change the name, color, and translucency settings of a mask channel, as described in the "Viewing mask and image" section of Chapter 12. The Channel Options command is dimmed when any of the color channels is active. This command is applicable to mask channels only.

✦ **Split Channels:** When you choose this command, Photoshop splits off each channel in an image to its own independent grayscale image window. As demonstrated in Figure 6-6, Photoshop automatically appends the channel color initial to the end of the window name. The Split Channels command is useful as a first step in redistributing channels in an image prior to choosing Merge Channels (as demonstrated later in this chapter).

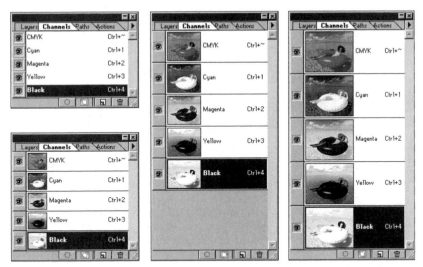

Figure 6-6: When you choose the Split Channels command, Photoshop relocates each channel to an independent image window.

✦ **Merge Channels:** Choose this command to merge several images into a single multichannel image. The images you want to merge must be open, they must be grayscale, and they must be absolutely equal in size — the same number of pixels horizontally and vertically. When you choose Merge Channels, Photoshop displays the Merge Channels dialog box, shown in Figure 6-7. Then Photoshop assigns a color mode for the new image based on the number of open grayscale images that contain the same number of pixels as the foreground image.

You can override Photoshop's choice by selecting a different option from the Mode pop-up menu. (Generally, you won't want to change the value in the Channels option box; doing so causes Photoshop to select Multichannel automatically from the Mode pop-up menu. I explain multichannel images in the upcoming "Using multichannel techniques" section.)

After you press Enter, Photoshop displays a second dialog box, which also appears in Figure 6-7. In this dialog box, you can specify which grayscale image goes with which channel by choosing options from pop-up menus. When working from an image split with the Split Channels command, Photoshop automatically organizes each window into a pop-up menu according to the color appended to the window's name. For example, Photoshop associates the window Float_C.TIF with the Cyan pop-up menu.

✦ **Convert selection:** Click the channel-to-selection icon — the one in the bottom-left corner of the Channels palette — to convert a selected channel to a selection outline. You can also click the next icon to the right to convert a selection outline to a new mask channel. For the complete story on these options, read Chapter 12.

Figure 6-7: The two dialog boxes that appear after you choose Merge Channels enable you to select a color mode for the merged image (top) and to associate images with color channels (bottom).

Color Channel Effects

Now that you know how to navigate among channels and apply commands, permit me to suggest a few reasons for doing so. The most pragmatic applications for channel effects involve the restoration of bad color scans. If you use a color scanner, know someone who uses a color scanner, or just have a bunch of color scans lying around, you can be sure some of them look like dog meat. (Nothing against dog meat, mind you. I'm sure Purina has some lovely dog meat scans in its advertising archives.) With Photoshop's help, you can turn those scans into filet mignon — or at the least, into an acceptable Sunday dinner roast.

Improving the appearance of color scans

The following are a few channel-editing techniques you can use to improve the appearance of poorly scanned full-color images. Remember, these techniques don't work miracles, but they can retrieve an image from the brink of absolute ugliness into the realm of tolerability.

Note Don't forget, you can choose View ➪ New View to maintain a constant composite view. Or you can click the eyeball icon in front of the composite view in the Channels palette to view the full-color image, even when you're editing a single channel.

✦ **Aligning channels:** Occasionally, a scan may appear out of focus even after you use Photoshop's sharpening commands to try to correct the problem, as discussed in Chapter 15. If on closer inspection you can see slight shadows or halos around colored areas, one of the color channels is probably out of alignment. To remedy the problem, switch to the color channel that corresponds to the color of the halos. Then select the move tool (by pressing the V key) and use the arrow keys to nudge the contents of the channel into alignment. Use the separate composite view (created by choosing View ➪ New View) or click the eyeball in front of the composite channel to monitor your changes.

✦ **Channel focusing:** If all channels seem in alignment (or, at least, as aligned as they're going to get), one of your channels may be poorly focused. Use the Ctrl+key equivalents to search for the responsible channel. When and if you find it, use the Unsharp Mask filter to sharpen it as desired. You may also find blurring a channel is helpful, as when trying to eliminate moiré patterns in a scanned halftone. (For a specific application of these techniques, see the "Cleaning up Scanned Halftones" section in Chapter 15.)

✦ **Bad channels:** In your color channel tour, if you discover a channel is not so much poorly focused as simply rotten to the core — complete with harsh transitions, jagged edges, and random brightness variations — you may be able to improve the appearance of the channel by overlaying the other channels on top of it. Suppose the blue channel is awful, but the red and green channels are in fairly decent shape. First, save your image to disk in case this technique does more to harm than help the image. Then switch to the red channel (Ctrl+1), select the entire image (Ctrl+A), and copy it (Ctrl+C). Switch back to the blue channel (Ctrl+3) and paste the contents of the Clipboard (Ctrl+V). Photoshop pastes the channel as a floating selection, permitting you to mix it with the underlying pixels. Change the opacity of the floating red channel to somewhere in the neighborhood of 30 to 50 percent by adjusting the Opacity slider bar in the Layers palette. Next, switch to the green channel (Ctrl+2) and repeat the process. The colors in the composite view will change slightly or dramatically depending on the range of colors in your image. But if you can live with the color changes, the appearance of the image will improve dramatically.

Cross Reference

As discussed in Chapter 19, Image ➪ Calculations serves as an alternate method for blending one channel with another. At first glance, the dialog box might appear sufficiently complicated to make you feel a mild twinge of panic. But if you give the dialog box a chance, you'll find it works faster than transferring images via the Clipboard, particularly when editing very large images. Meanwhile, don't worry about it. Chapter 19 will come soon enough.

Using multichannel techniques

The one channel function I've ignored so far is Image ➪ Mode ➪ Multichannel. When you choose this command, Photoshop changes your image so channels no longer have a specific relationship to one another. They don't mix to create a full-color image; instead, they exist independently within the confines of a single image. The multichannel mode is generally an intermediary step for converting between different color modes without recalculating the contents of the channels.

For example, normally when you convert between the RGB and CMYK modes, Photoshop maps RGB colors to the CMYK color model, changing the contents of each channel as demonstrated back in Figures 6-2 and 6-3. But suppose, as an experiment, you want to bypass the color mapping and, instead, transfer the exact contents of the red channel to the cyan channel, the contents of the green channel to the magenta channel, and so on. You convert from RGB to the multichannel mode and then from multichannel to CMYK as described in the following steps.

Steps: Using the Multichannel Mode as an Intermediary Step

1. **Open an RGB image.** If the image is already open, make sure it is saved to disk.

2. **Choose Mode ⇨ Multichannel.** This eliminates any relationship among the formerly red, green, and blue color channels.

3. **Click the new channel icon at the bottom of the Channels palette.** Or choose the New Channel command from the palette menu and press Enter to accept the default settings. Either way, you add a mask channel to the image. This empty channel will serve as the black channel in the CMYK image. (Photoshop won't let you convert from the multichannel mode to CMYK with less than four channels.)

4. **Press Ctrl+I.** Unfortunately, the new channel comes up black, which would make the entire image black. To change it to white, press Ctrl+I or choose Image ⇨ Adjust ⇨ Invert.

5. **Choose Mode ⇨ CMYK.** The image looks washed out and a tad bit dark compared to its original RGB counterpart, but the overall color scheme of the image remains more or less intact. This is because the red, green, and blue color channels each have a respective opposite in the cyan, magenta, and yellow channels.

6. **Press Ctrl+Shift+L.** Or choose Image ⇨ Adjust ⇨ Auto Levels. This punches up the color a bit by automatically correcting the brightness and contrast.

7. **Convert the image to RGB, and then back to CMYK again.** The problem with the image is it lacks any information in the black channel. So, although it may look okay onscreen, the image will lose much of its definition when printed. To fill in the black channel, choose Image ⇨ Mode ⇨ RGB Color, and then choose Image ⇨ Mode ⇨ CMYK Color. Photoshop automatically generates an image in the black channel, in keeping with the standards of color separations (as explained in Chapter 7).

Remember, these steps are by no means a recommended procedure for converting an RGB image to a CMYK image; they are intended to suggest one way to experiment with channel conversions to create a halfway-decent image. You can, likewise, experiment with converting between the Lab, multichannel, and RGB modes, or Lab, multichannel, and CMYK.

Replacing and swapping color channels

If you truly want to abuse the colors in an RGB or CMYK image, there's nothing like replacing one color channel with another to produce spectacular effects. Color Plate 6-3 shows a few examples applied to an RGB image. In the first example, I copied the image in the blue channel (Ctrl+3, Ctrl+A, Ctrl+C) and pasted it into the red channel (Ctrl+1, Ctrl+V). The result is a green woman floating in a green sea under a purple sky. To achieve the next example (starting again from the original RGB image), I copied the red channel and pasted it into the green channel. The result this time is a yellow woman against a deep blue background. To create the purple woman in a green world on the right side of Color Plate 6-3, I copied the red channel and pasted it into the blue channel.

Again, instead of copying and pasting, you can transfer images between channels without upsetting the contents of the Clipboard by choosing Image ➪ Calculations. I discuss this and other applications for this command in Chapter 19.

You can create more interesting effects by swapping the contents of color channels. For example, in the lower-left example of Color Plate 6-3, I swapped the contents of the red and blue channels to create a blue woman on a green sea under an orange sky. To accomplish this, I chose the Split Channels command from the Channels palette menu. I then chose the Merge Channels command and accepted the default settings in the Merge Channels dialog box. When the Merge RGB Channels dialog box appeared, I selected the blue channel from the Red pop-up menu and the red channel from the Blue pop-up menu.

The next two examples along the bottom of Color Plate 6-3 show the results of swapping the red and green channels (for a bright green woman) and the green and blue channels. Because the green and blue channels contain relatively similar data, this produces the most subtle effect, mostly switching the sea and sky colors and turning the swimsuit pink.

When experimenting, a good idea is to keep the original contents of each color channel nearby in case you don't like the results. I recommend using the Duplicate Channel command to save each color channel in the image to a separate mask channel. For example, when editing an RGB image, create three duplicates, one each for duplicates of the red, green, and blue channels, for a total of six channels in the image. You then can replace channels with impunity, knowing you have backups if you need them.

Printing Images

Welcome to Printing

On one hand, printing can be a straightforward topic. You choose the Print command, press Enter, wait for something to come out of your printer, and admire yet another piece of forestry that you've destroyed. On the other hand, printing can be a ridiculously complicated subject, involving dot gain compensation, hardware calibration, under color removal, toxic processor chemicals, separation table generation, and so many infinitesimal color parameters, you're liable to spend half your life trying to figure out what's happening.

This chapter is about finding a middle ground. Although it is in no way intended to cover every possible facet of printing digitized images, this chapter walks you through the process of preparing and printing the three major categories of output: composites, color separations, and duotones. By the end of the chapter, you'll be familiar with all of Photoshop's printing options. You'll also be prepared to communicate with professionals at your service bureau or commercial printer, if need be, and to learn from their input and expertise.

Note　Before stepping into the printing abyss, I should make one final preparatory comment. The Windows platform is in flux (what isn't?) and printing complications can arise because of this. Some people use Windows 3.1 to run Photoshop via the Win32s subsystem. This subsystem is constantly evolving and, as it does, newer versions break the latest printer drivers for a particular printer model. Not a pretty sight. Users are forced either to return to an earlier printer driver — assuming they haven't scrapped it — or return to an earlier version of Win32s.

On Windows 95, matters can be equally convoluted. Although most printer manufacturers now offer Windows 95 drivers, those drivers aren't always perfected. Sometimes you must get seriously down and dirty by using an older printer DLL (dynamic link library, one of the basic components of Windows anything) with a later printer driver. These nightmares are definitely not what the people in Adobe's Press Relations department had in mind when they came up with the slogan *If you can dream it, you can do it.*

If you encounter a Windows-related printing problem, your first cry for help should be to your printer manufacturer. If the manufacturer's tech support staff can't solve the problem, check online forums and newsgroups, such as CompuServe's ADOBEAPPS forum. Your service bureau can also be an excellent source for technical advice. Chances are, you're not the first person to experience the problem, and someone, somewhere, should have a fix for you.

Understanding Printing Terminology

I'm not a big believer in glossaries. Generally, they contain glib, jargony, out-of-context definitions — about as helpful in gaining understanding of a concept as a seminar in which all the presenters speak pig latin. But before I delve into the inner recesses of printing, I want to introduce, in a semilogical, sort of random order, a smattering of the printing terms you'll encounter. *Ood-gay uck-lay:*

✦ **Service bureau:** A *service bureau* is a shop filled with earnest young graphic artists (at least they were young and earnest when *I* worked there), printer operators, and about a billion dollars' worth of hardware. A small service bureau is usually outfitted with a few laser printers, photocopiers, and self-service computers. Big service bureaus offer scanners, imagesetters, film recorders, and other varieties of professional-quality input and output equipment.

Service bureaus once relied exclusively on the Macintosh. This has changed, but a substantial number of Mac-based service bureaus remain. Some service bureaus are equally ready to help Photoshoppers on both PC and Mac platforms, but some will take your Photoshop file and run it through a Mac. Nothing is wrong with this, but cross-platform problems can crop up sometimes. All other things being equal, I recommend you make sure your service bureau can output from Photoshop for Windows and has the requisite technical skills to do so.

✦ **Commercial printer:** Generally speaking, a *commercial printer* takes up where the service bureau leaves off. Commercial printers reproduce black-and-white and color pages using offset presses, web presses, and a whole bunch of other age-old technology I don't cover in this miniglossary (or anywhere else in this book, for that matter). The process is less expensive than photocopying when you're dealing with large quantities, say, more than 100 copies, and it delivers professional-quality reproductions.

✦ **Output device:** This is just another way to say *printer*. Rather than writing *Print your image from the printer,* which sounds repetitive and a trifle obvious, I write *Print your image from the output device. Output devices* also include laser printers, imagesetters, film recorders, and a whole bunch of other machines.

✦ **Laser printer:** A *laser printer* works much like a photocopier. First, it applies an electric charge to a cylinder, called a *drum,* inside the printer. The charged areas, which correspond to the black portions of the image being printed, attract fine, petroleum-based dust particles called *toner.* The drum transfers the toner to the page, and a heating mechanism fixes the toner in place. Most laser printers have resolutions of at least 300 dots (or *printer pixels*) per inch. The newer printers offer higher resolutions, such as 600 and 1,200 dots per inch (*dpi*).

✦ **Color printers:** *Color printers* fall into three categories. Generally speaking, ink-jet and thermal-wax printers are at the low end, and dye-sublimation printers occupy the high end. *Ink-jet printers* deliver colored dots from disposable ink cartridges. *Thermal-wax printers* apply wax-based pigments to a page in multiple passes. Both kinds of printers mix cyan, magenta, yellow, and, depending on the specific printer, black dots to produce full-color output. If you want photographic quality prints — the kind you'd be proud to hang on your wall — you must migrate up the price ladder to *dye-sublimation printers*. Dye-sub inks permeate the surface of the paper, literally dying it different colors. Furthermore, the cyan, magenta, yellow, and black pigments mix in varying opacities from one dot to the next, resulting in a continuous-tone image that appears nearly as smooth on the page as it does onscreen.

✦ **Imagesetter:** A typesetter equipped with a graphics page-description language such as PostScript is called an *imagesetter.* Unlike a laser printer, an imagesetter prints photosensitive paper or film by exposing the portions of the paper or film that correspond to the black areas of the image. The process is like exposing film with a camera, but an imagesetter only knows two colors: black and white. The exposed paper or film collects in a light-proof canister. In a separate step, the printer operator develops the film in a *processor* that contains two chemical baths — developer and fixer — a water bath to wash away the chemicals, and a heat dryer to dry off the water. Developed paper looks like a typical glossy black-and-white page. Developed film is black where the image is white and transparent where the image is black. Imagesetters typically offer resolutions between 1,200 and 3,600 dpi. But the real beauty of imageset pages is blacks are absolutely black (or transparent), as opposed to the irregular gray you get with laser-printed pages.

✦ **Film recorder:** The *film recorder* transfers images to full-color 35mm and 4×5 slides perfect for professional presentations. Slides also can be useful to provide images to publications and commercial printers. Many publications can scan from slides, and commercial printers can use slides to create color separations. So, if you're nervous a color separation printed from Photoshop won't turn out well, ask your service bureau to output the image to a 35mm slide. Then have your commercial printer reproduce the image from the slide.

✦ **PostScript:** The *PostScript* page-description language was the first project developed by Adobe — the same folks who sell Photoshop — and is now a staple of hundreds of brands of laser printers, imagesetters, and film recorders. A *page-description language* is a programming language for defining text and graphics on a page. PostScript specifies the locations of points, draws line segments between them, and fills in areas with solid blacks or *halftone cells* (dot patterns that simulate grays). PostScript Level 2, an updated version of the original PostScript, speeds output time and provides improved halftoning options, better color separations, automated antialiasing of jagged images, and direct support for Lab images (discussed in the "CIE's Lab" section of Chapter 5).

✦ **Spooling:** Printer *spooling* enables you to work on an image while another image prints. Rather than communicating directly with the output device, Photoshop describes the image to the system software. Under Windows 3.1, the Print Manager controls this. Under Windows 95, you set spooling options via the Printer Properties dialog box. Choose Settings ➪ Printers, right-click the icon for your specific printer, and choose Properties from the pop-up menu. Inside the printer's Properties dialog box, click the Details tab and click the Spool Settings button. When Photoshop finishes describing the image — a relatively quick process — you are free to resume working while the system software prints the image in the background.

✦ **Calibration:** Traditionally, *calibrating* a system means synchronizing the machinery. In the context of Photoshop, however, calibrating means to adjust or compensate for the color displays of the scanner, monitor, and printer so what you scan is what you see onscreen, which in turn is what you get from the printer. Colors match from one device to the next. Empirically speaking, this is impossible; a yellow image in a photograph won't look exactly like the onscreen yellow or the yellow printed from a set of color separations. But calibrating is designed to make the images look as much alike as possible, taking into account the fundamental differences in hardware technology. Expensive hardware calibration solutions seek to change the configuration of scanner, monitor, and printer. Less expensive software solutions, including those provided by Photoshop, manipulate the image to account for the differences between devices.

✦ **Brightness values/shades:** As described in Chapter 5, a fundamental difference exists between the way your screen and printer create gray values and colors. Your monitor shows colors by lightening an otherwise black screen; the printed page shows colors by darkening an otherwise white piece of paper. Onscreen colors, therefore, are measured in terms of *brightness values.* High values equate to light colors; low values equate to dark colors. On the printed page, colors are measured in percentage values called *shades* or, if you prefer, *tints.* High-percentage values result in dark colors, and low-percentage values result in light colors.

✦ **Composite:** A *composite* is a page that shows an image in its entirety. A black-and-white composite printed from a standard laser printer or imagesetter translates all colors in an image to gray values. A color composite printed from a color printer or film recorder shows the colors as they actually appear. Composites are useful any time you want to proof an image or print a final grayscale image from an imagesetter, an overhead projection from a color printer, or a full-color image from a film recorder.

✦ **Proofing:** To *proof* an image is to see how it looks on paper before the final printing. Laser printers are considered low-end proofing devices because they lack sufficient quality or resolution to output final images. Color printers aren't necessarily proofing devices because commercial printers can't reproduce from any color composite output except slides. (Well, they can reproduce from other kinds of color composites, but you don't get the same quality results.) Professional-level proofing devices include the 3M Rainbow dye-sublimation printer, which prints images of photographic quality, and the IRIS, which uses a special variety of ink-jet technology to create, arguably, the most accurate electronic proofs in the business.

✦ **Bleeds:** Simply put, a *bleed* is an area that can be printed outside the perimeter of a page. You use a bleed to reproduce an image all the way to the edge of a page, as in a slick magazine ad. For example, this book includes bleeds. Most of the pages — like the page you're reading — are encircled by a uniform 2-pica margin of white space. This margin keeps the text and figures from spilling off into oblivion. A few pages, however — including the parts pages and the color plates in the middle of the book — print all the way to the edges. In fact, the original artwork goes 2 picas beyond the edges of the paper. This ensures that if the paper shifts when printing — as it invariably does — you won't see any thin white edges around the artwork. This 2 picas of extra artwork is the bleed. In Photoshop, you create a bleed by clicking the Bleed button in the Page Setup dialog box.

✦ **Color separations:** To output color reproductions, commercial printers require *color separations* (or slides, which they can convert to color separations for a fee). A color-separated image comprises four printouts, one each for the cyan, magenta, yellow, and black primary printing colors. The commercial printer transfers each printout to a *plate,* which is used in the actual reproduction process.

✦ **Duotone:** A grayscale image in Photoshop can contain as many as 256 brightness values, from white on up to black. A printer can convey significantly fewer shades. A typical laser printer, for example, provides 26 shades at most. An imagesetter typically provides from 150 to 200 shades, depending on resolution and screen frequency. And this assumes perfect printing conditions. You can count on at least 30 percent of those shades to get lost in the reproduction process. A *duotone* helps to retain the depth and clarity of detail in a grayscale image by printing with two inks. The number of shades available to you suddenly jumps from 150 to 22,000 (150^2). Photoshop also enables you to create *tritones* (three inks) and *quadtones* (four inks). Note, using more inks translates to higher printing costs. Color Plate 7-1 shows a quadtone.

Printing Composites

Now that you've picked up some printer's jargon, you're ready to learn how to put it all together. This section explores the labyrinth of options available for printing composite images. Later in this chapter, I cover color separations and duotones.

Like any Windows 95 application, Photoshop can print composite images to nearly any output device you hook up to your PC. Assuming your printer is turned on, properly attached, and in working order, printing a composite image from Photoshop is a five-step process, as shown in the following sections that describe each step in detail.

Steps: Printing a Composite Image

1. **Choose your printer.** Use Settings ⇨ Printers to select your output device. If your computer is not part of a network that includes multiple printers, you probably rely on a single output device, in which case you can skip this step.

2. **Right-click the printer icon and select Properties.** Click the Paper tab to specify the page size and size and orientation of the image on the page. You can access this same tab inside Photoshop by choosing File ⇨ Page Setup (Ctrl+Shift+P) and then clicking the Properties button. (You can also use Image ⇨ Image Size to control the size of the image by changing its resolution, as explained in the "Changing the printing resolution" section of Chapter 4.)

3. **Adjust the halftone screens, if needed.** Inside the Page Setup dialog box (File ⇨ Page Setup), click the Screens button to change the size, angle, and shape of the halftone screen dots. This step is purely optional, useful mostly for creating special effects.

4. **Adjust the transfer function, again, if needed.** Click the Transfer button to map brightness values in an image to different shades when printed. This step is also optional, though frequently useful.

5. **Choose File ⇨ Print (Ctrl+P).** Photoshop prints the image according to your specifications.

If you already have your printer set up to your satisfaction, you may be thinking about drag-and-drop printing (drag the file from Explorer and drop it onto the printer icon). The file will print, using the application for which the file type is registered. If you're using a native Photoshop file (PSD), everything should be okay. But if you want to print, say, a TIFF image from Photoshop, you may be in for a surprise; Windows 95 prints from the application for which TIFF is a registered file format. Upon installation, Photoshop 4 registers itself as the application for opening TIFF files. But if you later install another paint program, that program may register *itself* as the TIFF application of choice. Windows will then open and print your image from this newly installed program rather than from Photoshop. For this reason, doing all your printing directly from Photoshop is best.

Figuring out where to change what setting

As mentioned in the preceding section, you can access certain printer settings in two ways: You can right-click a printer icon in the Windows 95 Printers window (Settings ➪ Printers), or you can click the Properties button inside the Photoshop Page Setup dialog box (File ➪ Page Setup).

Figure 7-1 shows the Windows 95 Properties dialog box for a PostScript printer. The dialog box offers several tabs, which vary depending on your printer and PC configuration. Inside Photoshop, you usually have access to some, but not all, of the same tabs. Again, the tabs available inside Photoshop depend on your printer setup.

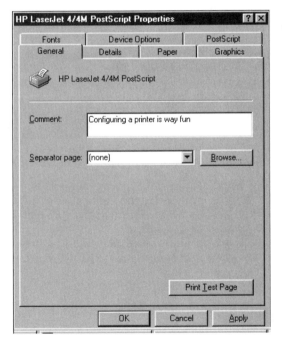

Figure 7-1: The Properties dialog box for a PostScript printer in Windows 95

Caution Just because you can access the overlapping tabs from two places doesn't mean you get the same results from both routes. As a rule, settings you establish in Windows 95, rather than from inside Photoshop, become the default settings for *any* future print jobs — whether you're printing from Photoshop or from some other program. Settings you establish inside Photoshop generally affect Photoshop print jobs only.

Suppose you want to do a landscape print job — that is, print your document sideways on the page. If you choose the landscape setting on the Paper tab in Photoshop, the setting is applied to that print job only. When you exit Photoshop, no more landscape printing. But you can also configure a landscape print job on that same Paper tab out in Windows 95. Of course, you'll get your landscape orientation in Photoshop. But suppose some minor distractions arise — the cats decide to have a game on your monitor or the shingles blow off your roof. Time passes. You need to print a letter from your word processor. Surprise — it comes out sideways on the paper. Because you set landscape printing as the default in Windows 95, your word processor used that setting.

Tip   Adobe actually made all this rather idiotproof. The options available on the tabs inside Photoshop are precisely the options that can mess you up if you set them globally outside Photoshop.

Note   Remember, when you change your default print settings out in Windows 95, the new settings aren't reflected in the Photoshop Page Setup dialog box or Properties dialog box until the next time you start Photoshop.

Choosing a printer

To select a printer, bring up the Control Panel from the Start menu and select Printers or choose Start ➪ Settings ➪ Printers. Right-click your printer of choice and select Set As Default on the resulting pop-up menu, as shown in Figure 7-2. If you want to add a printer, double-click the Add Printer icon, and be sure to have either your Windows 95 CD-ROM (or floppies) or a drivers disk from your printer manufacturer.

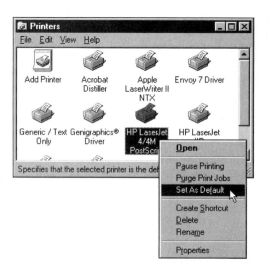

Figure 7-2: Specify your default printer from inside the Printers window.

Printer drivers help the PC hardware, Windows 95, and Photoshop translate the contents of an image to the printer hardware and the page-description language it uses. You'll generally want to select the driver for your specific model of printer. But you can, if necessary, prepare an image for output to a printer that isn't currently hooked up to your computer. For example, you can use this technique prior to submitting a document to be output on an imagesetter at a service bureau.

Starting with Windows 3.1, certain applications (such as PageMaker) could take advantage of *PostScript printer description* (*PPD*) files. A single driver can't account for the myriad differences between different models of PostScript printers, so each PPD serves as a little guidance file, customizing the driver to accommodate a specific printer model. Basically, each printer manufacturer writes its PPD file and sends it to Adobe for *blessing* (this isn't a throwaway term — it's what they call the process). Windows 95 now enables you to attach a PPD file globally to your PostScript printer, for which you need both the PPD file and the INF file to tell Windows 95 what to install. (Adobe offers its own printer setup program, available via the Adobe Web site, that doesn't require INF files. The setup program works only for Adobe-licensed PostScript printers, however.)

Setting up the page

The next step is to define the relationship between the current image and the page on which it prints. Choosing File ⇨ Page Setup (or pressing Ctrl+Shift+P) displays the Page Setup dialog box. Click the Properties button to open the Properties dialog box for the selected printer. Figure 7-3 shows the dialog box for a PostScript printer.

The dialog box may include slightly different options depending upon your printer. For example, most non-PostScript printers have a Device options tab but no PostScript tab. A few PostScript printers have both. Color printers can have different Graphics tabs. I'm tempted to do a screen shot to illustrate all the different variations, but that would add a pound or two to the weight of this book. If you like, you can investigate the many varieties of printer options by installing some printers and playing around with the various tabs. Don't worry — you're not messing up your system. When you're done having a good look around, simply delete those extra printers.

Note, the Device Options tab, as its name suggests, contains options related to your specific printer. You'll have to consult your printer manual for guidance on these options. I wish I were psychic enough to know which printer you have so I could cover the options available to you but, sadly, I'm not that psychic. The options on the other three tabs are available for most PostScript printers, however, and they are covered in the following sections.

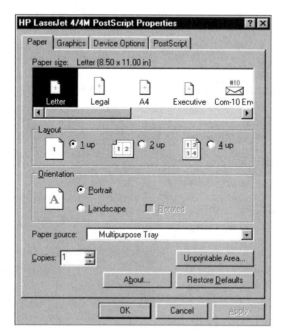

Figure 7-3: Use this tab to specify the relationship between the printed image and the page on which it appears.

The Paper tab

The Paper tab provides the following options related to page setup:

✦ **Paper Size:** From the scrolling window of paper sizes, select the option that corresponds to the size of the paper loaded into your printer's paper tray. The paper size you select determines the imageable area of a page — that is, the amount of the page Photoshop can use to print the current image. For example, the Letter option calls for a page that measures 8.5 × 11 inches, but only 7.7 × 10.2 inches is imageable.

✦ **Layout:** The layout options enable you to print more than one page per each sheet of paper. For example, if you want to proof the layout of a 16-page QuarkXPress document, you can select the 4 up option to print four quarter-sized versions of each page per each piece of paper. You save paper, kill fewer trees, and even waste a little less time. Because no such thing as a multipage document exists in Photoshop, however, this option serves no purpose. For example, if you select the 4 up option, you simply get one image reduced to 25 percent its normal size in the upper-left corner of the printed page. So always leave this option set to 1 up when printing from Photoshop.

✦ **Orientation:** You can specify whether an image prints upright on a page (called the *portrait setting*) or on its side (called the *landscape setting*) by selecting the corresponding Orientation icon. The landscape setting is useful when an image is wider than it is tall.

The Graphics tab

On the Graphics tab, you can usually find these page setup options:

✦ **Resolution:** In most cases, you don't want to tinker with the resolution setting. But exceptions exist. For example, some ink-jet printers use different resolution in different printing modes.

✦ **Halftoning:** Don't touch these settings. Instead, apply halftoning settings as discussed later in this chapter.

✦ **Special:** These options enable you to print a negative or mirror image. You may find this option of some use, but you can accomplish the same results by using Photoshop's image-editing commands. Why bother fooling with these options?

✦ **Scaling:** Enter a percentage value into this option box to enlarge or reduce the size of the image when printed. For more information on this option, see Chapter 3.

After specifying the Scaling percentage and Orientation icon, you can check to see how the image fits on the page. To do so, press Enter twice to exit the Page Setup dialog box, and then click and hold on the Preview box in the lower-left corner of the Photoshop window. The rectangle with the inset X that appears inside the pop-up window represents the image on the page. If the rectangle extends outside the page, you need to reduce the image further or to change the page orientation.

The PostScript tab

✦ **PostScript output format:** This option can be useful. Typically, you'll want to optimize for speed if you're printing directly to a printer. You may want to consider optimizing for portability using the Adobe Document Structuring Convention (ADSC) if you're printing to file and taking that file elsewhere. But don't choose this option on a regular basis — only if the need arises or your service bureau requests it. Click the little question-mark icon at the top of the dialog box, and then click the PostScript Output Format option to see what Microsoft has to say on the subject — it's a pretty good summary.

On to the special Photoshop printing options

Figure 7-4 offers a look at the Page Setup dialog box (File ➪ Page Setup or Ctrl+Shift+P). The options at the bottom of the dialog box are specific to Photoshop. First I'll describe how to use the buttons on the left, and then I'll explain the check boxes on the right:

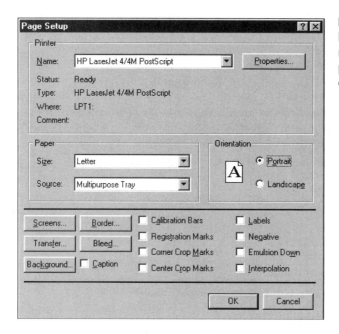

Figure 7-4: Use this dialog box to specify the relationship between the printed image and the page on which it appears.

✦ **Screens:** Click this button to enter a dialog box that enables you to change the size, angle, and shape of the printed halftone cells, as described in the upcoming "Changing the halftone screen" section.

✦ **Transfer:** The dialog box that appears when you click this button enables you to redistribute shades in the printed image, as explained in the upcoming section, "Specifying a transfer function."

✦ **Background:** To assign a color to the area around the printed image, click this button and select a color from the Color Picker dialog box, described in more detail in Chapter 5. This button and the one that follows (Border) are designed specifically for use when printing slides from a film recorder.

✦ **Border:** To print a border around the current image, click this button and enter the thickness of the border into the Width option box. The border automatically appears in black.

✦ **Bleed:** This button enables you to print outside the imageable area of the page when outputting to an imagesetter. (Imagesetters print to huge rolls of paper or film, so you can print far outside the confines of standard page size. Most other printers use regular old sheets of paper; any bleed — were the printer to acknowledge it — would print off the edge of the page.) Click the Bleed button and enter the thickness of the bleed into the Width option box. Two picas (24 points) is generally a good bet. (Bleeds are defined in the "Understanding Printing Terminology" glossary at the beginning of this chapter.)

Now for the check boxes in the lower-middle and right-hand sections of the dialog box. Most of these options — all except Negative, Emulsion Down, and Interpolation — append special labels and printer marks to the printed version of the image. These labels and marks are demonstrated in Figure 7-5.

By the way, Figure 7-5 shows the actual labels and marks exactly as they print. This may not sound like much but, in the past, such printer's marks have been difficult to capture because no way existed to save them in a reliable file format. A book writer like me either had the option of printing the file to disk as an EPS file — which might or might not print accurately when placed into a page-layout program — or simply printing the page independently and manually pasting it up into the book. But, because Illustrator 6 opens EPS files created in any application, I could create an editable version of the printed image.

In the name of full disclosure — my job is to pass along information, not store trade secrets — here's how I accomplished this smallish feat: I first printed the Photoshop image to disk as an EPS file (as described in the "Printing pages" section later in this chapter) — labels, printer's marks, and all. I then used Illustrator to open the EPS file and assign the callouts — those little labels like "Calibration bar" and "Modern youngster."

Here's how the check box options work:

✦ **Caption**: To print a caption beneath the image, select this option. Then press Enter to exit this dialog box, choose File ➪ File Info, and enter a caption into the File Info dialog box. The caption prints in 9-point Helvetica. This is strictly an image-annotation feature, something to help you 17 years down the road, when your brain starts to deteriorate and you can't remember why you printed the darn thing. (You might also use the caption to keep images straight in a busy office where hundreds of folks have access to the same images, but I don't like this alternative as much because I can't make fun of it.)

✦ **Calibration Bars:** A calibration bar is a 10-step grayscale gradation beginning at 10 percent black and ending at 100 percent black. The function of the calibration bar is to ensure all shades are distinct and on target. If not, the output device isn't properly calibrated, which is a fancy way of saying the printer's colors are out of whack and need realignment by a trained professional armed with a hammer and hacksaw. When you print color separations, the Calibration Bars check box instructs Photoshop to print a gradient tint bar and progressive color bar, also useful to printing professionals.

✦ **Registration Marks:** Select this option to print eight crosshairs and two star targets near the four corners of the image. Registration marks are imperative when you print color separations; they provide the only reliable means to ensure exact registration of the cyan, magenta, yellow, and black printing plates. When printing a composite image, however, you can ignore this option.

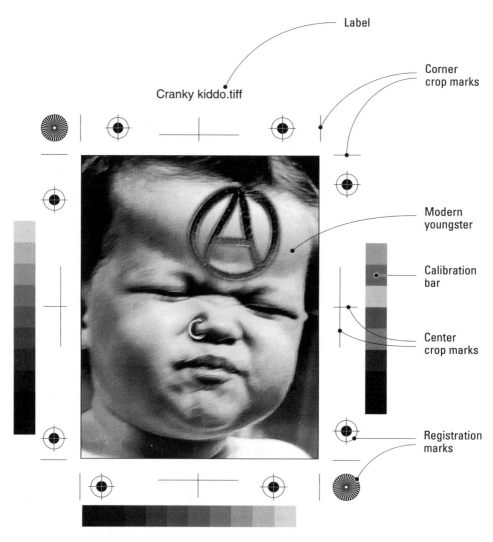

Figure 7-5: An image printed with nearly all the Page Setup check boxes turned on.

✦ **Corner Crop Marks:** Select this option to print eight hairline *crop marks* — two in each of the image's four corners — which indicate how to trim the image in case you anticipate engaging in a little traditional paste-up work.

✦ **Center Crop Marks:** Select this option to print four pairs of hairlines that mark the center of the image. Each pair forms a cross. Two pairs are located on the sides of the image, the third pair is above it, and the fourth pair is below the image.

✦ **Labels:** When you select this check box, Photoshop prints the name of the image and the name of the printed color channel in 9-point Helvetica. If you process many images, you'll find this option extremely useful for associating printouts with documents on disk.

✦ **Negative:** When you select this option, Photoshop prints all blacks as white and all whites as black. In-between colors switch accordingly. For example, 20 percent black becomes 80 percent black. Imagesetter operators use this option to print composites and color separations to film negatives.

✦ **Emulsion Down:** The *emulsion* is the side of a piece of film on which an image is printed. When the Emulsion Down check box is turned off, film prints from an imagesetter emulsion side up; when the check box is turned on, Photoshop flips the image so the emulsion side is down. Like the Negative option, this option is useful only when you print film from an imagesetter and should be set in accordance with the preferences of your commercial printer.

✦ **Interpolation:** If you own an output device equipped with PostScript Level 2, you can instruct Photoshop to antialias the printed appearance of a low-resolution image by selecting this option. The output device resamples the image up to 200 percent, and then reduces the image to its original size using bicubic interpolation (as described in the "General preferences" section of Chapter 2), thereby creating a less-jagged image. This option has no effect on older-model PostScript devices.

Changing the halftone screen

Before I proceed, let me explain more about how printing works. To keep costs down, commercial printers use as few inks as possible to create the appearance of a wide variety of colors. Suppose you want to print an image of a pink flamingo wearing a red bow tie. Your commercial printer could print the flamingos in one pass using pink ink, let that color dry, and then load the red ink and print all the bow ties. But why go to all this trouble? After all, pink is only a lighter shade of red. Why not imitate the pink by lightening the red ink?

Unfortunately, with the exception of dye-sublimation printers, high-end ink jets, and film recorders, output devices can't print lighter shades of colors. They recognize only solid ink and the absence of ink. So how do you print the lighter shade of red necessary to represent pink?

The answer is *halftoning*. The output device organizes printer pixels into spots called *halftone cells*. Because the cells are so small, your eyes cannot quite focus on them. Instead, the cells appear to blend with the white background of the page to create a lighter shade of an ink. Figure 7-6 shows a detail of an image enlarged to display the individual halftone cells.

The cells grow and shrink to emulate different shades of color. Large cells result in dark shades; small cells result in light shades. Cell size is measured in printer pixels. The maximum size of any cell is a function of the number of cells in an inch, called the *screen frequency*.

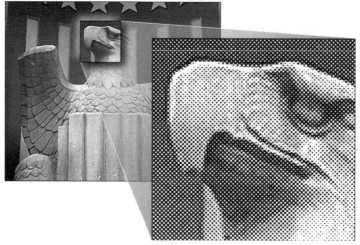

Figure 7-6: A detail from an image (left) is enlarged so you can see the individual halftone cells (right).

For example, suppose the default frequency of your printer is 60 halftone cells per linear inch and the resolution is 300 printer pixels per linear inch. Each halftone cell must, therefore, measure 5 pixels wide × 5 pixels tall ($300 ÷ 60 = 5$), for a total of 25 pixels per cell (5^2). When all pixels in a cell are turned off, the cell appears white; when all pixels are turned on, you get solid ink. By turning on different numbers of pixels — from 0 up to 25 — the printer can create a total of 26 shades, as demonstrated in Figure 7-7.

Photoshop enables you to change the size, angle, and shape of the individual halftone cells used to represent an image on the printed page. To do so, click the Screens button in the Page Setup dialog box. The Halftone Screens dialog box shown in Figure 7-8 appears.

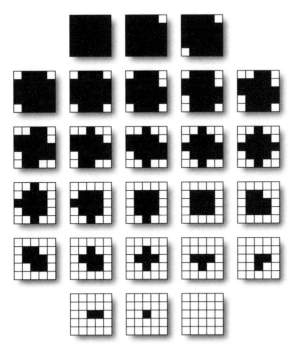

Figure 7-7: 5 × 5-pixel halftone cells with different numbers of pixels activated, ranging from 25 (top left) to 0 (bottom right). Each cell represents a unique shade from 100 to 0 percent black.

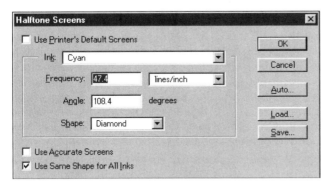

Figure 7-8: Use the Halftone Screens dialog box to edit the size, angle, and shape of the halftone cells for any one ink.

In the dialog box, you can manipulate the following options:

✦ **Use Printer's Default Screens:** Select this check box to accept the default size, angle, and shape settings built into your printer's ROM. All other options in the Halftone Screens dialog box automatically become dimmed to show they are no longer in force.

✦ **Ink:** If the current image is in color, you can select the specific ink you want to adjust from the Ink pop-up menu. When you work with a grayscale image, no pop-up menu is available.

✦ **Frequency:** Enter a new value into this option box to change the number of halftone cells that print per linear inch. A higher value translates to a larger quantity of smaller cells; a smaller value creates fewer, larger cells. Frequency is traditionally measured in *lines-per-inch*, or *lpi* (as in lines of halftone cells), but you can change the measurement to lines per centimeter by selecting Lines/cm from the pop-up menu to the right of the option box.

Tip

Higher screen frequencies result in smoother-looking printouts. Raising the Frequency value, however, also decreases the number of shades an output device can print because it decreases the size of each halftone cell and, likewise, decreases the number of printer pixels per cell. Fewer printer pixels means fewer shades. You can calculate the precise number of printable shades using the following formula:

Number of shades = (printer resolution ÷ frequency)^2 + 1

✦ **Angle:** To change the orientation of the lines of halftone cells, enter a new value into the Angle option box. In the name of accuracy, Photoshop accepts any value between negative and positive 180 degrees.

Caution

When printing color composites to ink-jet and thermal-wax printers, and when printing color separations, Photoshop calculates the optimum Frequency and Angle values required to print seamless colors. In such a case, you should change these values only if you know exactly what you're doing. Otherwise, your printout may exhibit weird patterning effects. When printing grayscale images, though, you can edit these values to your heart's content.

✦ **Shape:** By default, most PostScript printers rely on roundish halftone cells. You can change the appearance of all cells for an ink by selecting one of six alternate shapes from the Shape pop-up menu. For a demonstration of four of these shapes, see Figure 5-8 in the "Black and white (bitmap)" section of Chapter 5. If you know how to write PostScript code, you can select the Custom option to display a text-entry dialog box and code away.

✦ **Use Accurate Screens:** If your output device is equipped with PostScript Level 2, select this option to subscribe to the updated screen angles for full-color output. Otherwise, don't worry about this option.

✦ **Use Same Shape for All Inks:** Select this option if you want to apply a single set of size, angle, and shape options to the halftone cells for all inks used to represent the current image. Unless you want to create some sort of special effect, leave this check box deselected. The option is unavailable when you are printing a grayscale image.

✦ **Auto:** Click this button to display the Auto Screens dialog box, which automates the halftone editing process. Enter the resolution of your output device in the Printer option box. Then enter the screen frequency you want to use in the Screen option box. After you press Enter to confirm your change, Photoshop automatically calculates the optimum screen frequencies for all inks. This technique is most useful when you print full-color images — because Photoshop does the work for you, you can't make a mess of things.

✦ **Load/Save:** You can load and save settings to disk in case you want to reapply the options to other images. These buttons are useful if you find a magic combination of halftone settings that results in a really spectacular printout.

Tip

You can change the default size, angle, and shape settings Photoshop applies to all future images by Alt+clicking the Save button. When you press Alt, the Save button changes to read ⇨ Default. To restore the default screen settings at any time, Alt+click the Load button (Default).

Cross Reference

The Halftone Screens dialog box settings don't apply only to printing images directly from Photoshop. You can export these settings along with the image for placement in QuarkXPress or some other application by saving the image in the Photoshop EPS format. Make sure you turn on the "Include Halftone Screen" check box in the EPS Format dialog box, as discussed in the "Saving an EPS image" section of Chapter 4. This also applies to transfer function settings, explained in the following section.

Caution

If you do decide to include the halftone screen information with your EPS file, be sure the settings are compatible with your intended output device. You don't want to specify a low Frequency value such as 60 lpi when printing to a state-of-the-art 3,600-dpi imagesetter, for example. If you have any questions, make certain to call your service bureau or printer before saving the image. You don't want both a last-minute surprise and a hefty bill, to boot.

Specifying a transfer function

A *transfer function* enables you to change the way onscreen brightness values translate — or *map* — to printed shades. By default, brightness values print to their nearest shade percentages. A 30 percent gray onscreen pixel (which equates to a brightness value of roughly 180) prints as a 30 percent gray value.

Problems arise, however, when your output device prints lighter or darker than it should. For example, in the course of using a LaserWriter NTX over the past five years or so — I know it's going to die one day but, until then, it keeps chugging along — I've discovered all gray values print overly dark. Dark values fill in and become black; light values appear a dismal gray, muddying up any highlights. The problem increases if I try to reproduce the image on a photocopier.

To compensate for this overdarkening effect, I click the Transfer button in the Page Setup dialog box and enter the values shown in Figure 7-9. Notice I lighten 30 percent onscreen grays to 10 percent printer grays. I also lighten 90 percent screen grays to 80 percent printer grays. The result is a smooth, continuous curve that maps each gray value in an image to a lighter value on paper.

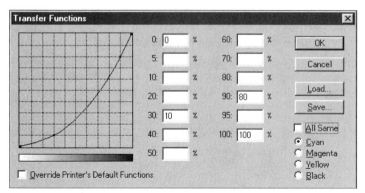

Figure 7-09: The transfer function curve enables you to map onscreen brightness values to specific shades on paper.

The options in the Transfer Functions dialog box work as follows:

✦ **Transfer graph:** The *transfer graph* is where you map onscreen brightness values to their printed equivalents. The horizontal axis of the graph represents onscreen brightness values; the vertical axis represents printed shades. The *transfer curve* charts the relationship between onscreen and printed colors. The lower-left corner is the origin of the graph — the point at which both onscreen brightness value and printed shade are white. Move to the right in the graph for darker onscreen values; move up for darker printed shades. Click in the graph to add points to the line. Drag up on a point to darken the output; drag down to lighten the output.

Cross Reference

For a more comprehensive explanation of how to graph colors on a curve, read about the incredibly powerful Curves command, covered in Chapter 18.

✦ **Percentage option boxes:** The option boxes are labeled according to the onscreen brightness values. To lighten or darken the printed brightness values, enter higher or lower percentage values in the option boxes. Note: A direct correlation exists between changes made to the transfer graph and the option boxes. For example, if you enter a value in the 50 percent option box, a new point appears along the middle line of the graph.

✦ **Override Printer's Default Functions:** As an effect of printer calibration, some printers have custom transfer functions built into their ROM. If you have problems making your settings take effect, select this check box to instruct Photoshop to apply the transfer function you specify, regardless of the output device's built-in transfer function.

✦ **Load/Save:** Use these buttons to load and save settings to disk. Alt+click the buttons to retrieve and save default settings.

✦ **Ink controls:** When you print a full-color image, five options appear in the lower-right corner of the Transfer Functions dialog box. These options enable you to apply different transfer functions to different inks. Select the All Same check box to apply a single transfer function to all inks. To apply a different function to each ink, deselect the check box, and then select one of the radio buttons and edit the points in the transfer graph as desired.

Printing pages

When you finish slogging your way through the mind-numbingly extensive Page Setup options, you can initiate the printing process by choosing File ⇨ Print (Ctrl+P). The Print dialog box appears, shown in its RGB and CMYK forms in Figure 7-10.

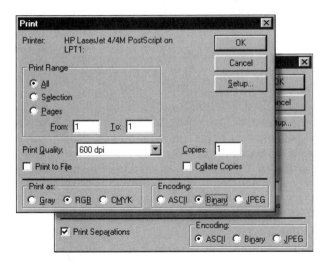

Figure 7-10: The Print dialog box as it appears when printing an RGB (top) and CMYK (bottom) image

Most of the options of this dialog box are a function of Windows 95, but a few at the bottom of the dialog box are exclusive to Photoshop. The options work as follows:

✦ **Copies:** Enter the number of copies you want to print in this option box. You can print up to 999 copies of a single image, although why you would want to do so is beyond me.

✦ **Print Range:** No such thing as a multipage document exists in Photoshop, so you can ignore these options for the most part. If you select an image area with the rectangular marquee tool, though, you can print only the selection by choosing the Selection radio button. You may want to use this option to divide an image into pieces when it's too large to fit on a single page.

✦ **Paper Source:** If you want to print your illustration on a letterhead or other special piece of paper, click the Setup button, and then click Properties in the Page Setup dialog box. In the resulting Properties dialog box, choose Manual Feed from the Paper Source pop-up menu.

✦ **Print to File:** This option enables you to generate a PostScript-language definition of the file on disk rather than to print it directly to your printer. Deselect the option to print the image to an output device as usual. Because Photoshop offers its own EPS option via the Save dialog box, you'll probably want to ignore this option. In fact, the only reason to select Print to File is to capture printer's marks, as I did back in Figure 7-5. If you select this option, a second dialog box appears, asking where you want to save the EPS file. You can navigate just as in the Open and Save dialog boxes. For the best results, select the Binary radio button.

✦ **Print As:** Select one of these radio buttons to specify the type of composite image Photoshop prints. Select the first radio button to print the image as a grayscale composite. Select the second radio button to enable the printer to translate the colors from the current color mode to CMYK, or to print an image to an RGB film recorder. Select the third radio button to instruct Photoshop to convert the image to CMYK colors during the print process. These options are unavailable when you print a grayscale image. (When printing a CMYK image, the Print As options change to a single Print Separations check box, which is described in the following section.)

Relying on the output device to translate colors can result in printing errors, thanks to the low-memory capabilities of most printers. If an image refuses to print, try selecting either the Gray or CMYK radio button. Use the first option when you print to black-and-white devices, such as laser printers and imagesetters; use the last option when printing to color printers.

✦ **Encoding:** If your network doesn't support binary encoding or your printer is attached only through the local parallel printer port, instead of the network, select the ASCII option to transfer data in the text-only format. The printing process takes much longer to complete, but at least it's possible. If your printer supports PostScript Level 2, you can also choose to use JPEG compression to reduce the amount of data sent to the printer.

✦ **Setup:** This button takes you to the Page Setup dialog box, discussed previously.

Press Enter inside the Print dialog box to start the printing process on its merry way. To cancel a print in progress, your best bet is to choose Settings ➪ Printers from the Windows 95 Start menu to display the Printers dialog box. Right-click the printer icon for the printer you're using, and then click Open. Or you can double-click the little printer icon that appears on the Windows 95 taskbar when you send a file to the printer. Either way, Windows shows you a window listing the current print jobs in progress. You can pause or cancel the selected print job by choosing a command from the Document menu.

Creating Color Separations

If printing a composite image is moderately complicated, printing color separations is a terrific pain in the behind. Printer manufacturers and software developers are working to simplify this process but, for the present, Photoshop requires you to stagger through a maze of variables and obtuse options. The upcoming steps explain how to muddle your way through the color-separation process. You'll recognize many of the steps from the process described for printing a grayscale or color composite.

Steps: Printing CMYK Color Separations

1. **Choose your printer.** If your computer is part of a network that includes many printers, select the printer you want to use, as described previously in the "Choosing a printer" section.

2. **Calibrate your system.** Make sure your monitor and printer are in sync using File ⇨ Color Settings ⇨ Monitor Setup and File ⇨ Color Settings ⇨ Printing Inks Setup. You only need to complete this step once for each time you switch hardware. If you always use the same monitor and printer combination, you need to repeat this step rarely, say once every six months, to account for screen and printer degradation.

3. **Adjust the CMYK separation setting.** Use File ⇨ Color Settings ⇨ Separation Setup to control how Photoshop converts RGB and Lab colors to CMYK color space. Again, you need to perform this step only when you want to compensate for a difference in the output device or if you simply want to fine-tune Photoshop to create better separations.

4. **Convert the image to the CMYK color space.** Choose Image ⇨ Mode ⇨ CMYK Color to convert the image from its present color mode to CMYK. The CMYK mode is explained in the "CMYK" section of Chapter 5.

5. **Adjust the individual color channels.** Switching color modes can dramatically affect the colors in an image. To compensate for color and focus loss, you can edit the individual color channels as described in the "Color Channel Effects" section of Chapter 6.

6. **Trap your image, if necessary.** If your image features many high-contrast elements and you're concerned your printer might not do the best job of registering the cyan, magenta, yellow, and black color plates, you can apply Image ⇨ Trap to prevent your final printout from looking like the color funnies.

7. **Turn on a few essential printer marks.** Choose File ⇨ Page Setup to specify the size of the pages and the size and orientation of the image on the pages, as described earlier in this chapter. Also be sure to select — at the very least — the Calibration Bars, Registration Marks, and Labels check boxes.

8. **Adjust the halftone and transfer functions as needed.** Click the Screen and Transfer buttons to modify the halftone screen dots and map brightness values for each of the CMYK color channels, as described earlier in the "Changing the halftone screen" and "Specifying a transfer function" sections. This step is optional.

9. **Choose File ⇨ Print (Ctrl+P).** Select the Print Separations check box in the lower-left corner of the dialog box (see Figure 7-10). Photoshop then prints the color separations according to your specifications.

Steps 1 and 7 through 9 are repeats of concepts explained in previous sections of this chapter. To understand Steps 4 and 5 fully, read the larger color theory discussions contained in Chapters 5 and 6. This leaves Steps 2, 3, and 6, which I describe in detail in the following sections.

You also can create color separations by importing an image into a desktop publishing program like PageMaker or QuarkXPress. To do so, convert the image to the CMYK color space and export the image in the DCS format, as described in the "QuarkXPress DCS" section of Chapter 4. Then print the separations directly from the desktop publishing program. Because DCS is a subset of the EPS format, it enables you to save halftone screen and transfer function settings.

Monitor calibration

Choose File ⇨ Color Settings ⇨ Monitor to display the Monitor Setup dialog box shown in Figure 7-11. The Monitor Setup dialog box provides options that directly affect the conversion of scanned colors to their CMYK equivalents. These options advise Photoshop that certain onscreen color distortions are in effect and instruct the program to make accommodations when converting between the RGB and CMYK color modes.

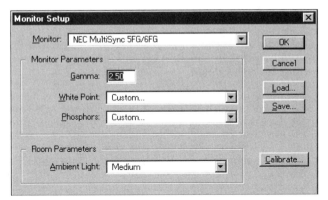

Figure 7-11: The options in the Monitor Setup dialog box tell Photoshop how to compensate for onscreen colors when preparing color separations.

The options in the Monitor Setup dialog box work as follows:

✦ **Monitor:** In the best of all possible worlds, you can select your exact model of monitor from this pop-up menu. Photoshop automatically changes the settings in the Monitor Parameters box — Gamma, White Point, and Phosphors — in accordance with the recommendations of the monitor's manufacturer. If you can't find your exact model, look for a model made by the same manufacturer and whose only difference from your model is screen size. If you can't find a suitable model, select the Other option.

Caution

Do not assume all monitors from the same vendor are basically alike. Most vendors sell screens manufactured by different companies. Refresh rates can differ, and screen technology can differ. Do not select a monitor other than the one you use unless the only difference in the name is screen size — and even then, be careful.

✦ **Gamma:** This value represents the brightness of medium colors onscreen. Low values down to 0.75 darken the printed image to compensate for an overly light screen; high values up to 3.00 lighten the image to compensate for an overly dark screen. Generally speaking, 1.8 is the ideal value. When you use an NTSC television monitor — as when editing video images using TrueVision's NuVista+ — set Gamma to 2.2.

✦ **White Point:** This value represents the temperature of the lightest color your screen can produce. Measured on the Kelvin temperature scale, it refers to the heat at which a so-called "black body" would turn to white. So, theoretically, if you took the Maltese Falcon and heated it to 6,500 degrees Kelvin, it would turn white (if it didn't catch on fire first). The only way to achieve the correct value for this option is to consult the technical support department for your make of monitor or to use a hardware testing device.

✦ **Phosphors:** This pop-up menu enables you to select the kind of screen used in your monitor. Select the NTSC option if you are using a television monitor. Otherwise, consult your vendor's technical support department. The technician may be willing to supply you with precise chromacity coordinates, which you enter by choosing the Custom option.

✦ **Ambient Light:** Select the amount of light in your office or studio from this pop-up menu. In a dark room, Photoshop slightly darkens the image. In a light room, Photoshop lightens the image so you can see it clearly despite the ambient light.

✦ **Calibrate:** Click this button to display the Calibrate dialog box, which you can use to make what you see onscreen jibe with your printer output. For example, if your images look fine onscreen but come out of the printer too dark, use the Gamma control to adjust the monitor display so the onscreen image more closely resembles the printed image. Click Preview to see the results of your changes. If you have a color printer, you can use the Color Balance options in the same way. Don't worry about the other dialog box options.

When you finish messing with the Monitor Setup options, press Enter to close the dialog box. Photoshop takes a moment or two to recalculate the display of any CMYK images open onscreen.

Printer calibration

To prepare an image for reproduction on a commercial offset or web press, choose File ➪ Color Settings ➪ Printing Inks Setup to display the Printing Inks Setup dialog box shown in Figure 7-12.

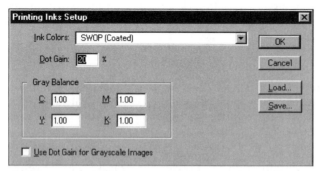

Figure 7-12: Use the options in the Printing Inks Setup dialog box to prepare an image for printing on a commercial offset or web press.

Like the Monitor Setup options, these settings are highly technical and can be properly set only with the assistance of your commercial printer. But so you have an inkling about inks, here's how the options work:

✦ **Ink Colors:** Select the specific variety of inks and paper stock that will be used to reproduce the current image. (Consult your commercial printer for this information.) Photoshop automatically changes the settings of the Dot Gain and Gray Balance options to the most suitable values.

✦ **Dot Gain:** Enter any value from -10 to 40 percent to specify the amount by which you can expect halftone cells to shrink or expand during the printing process, a variable known as *dot gain*. When printing to newsprint, for example, you can expect halftone cells to bleed into the page and expand by about 30 percent. When you convert to the CMYK color mode, Photoshop automatically adjusts the brightness of colors to compensate for the dot gain.

✦ **Gray Balance:** Assuming the inks are up to snuff, equal amounts of cyan, magenta, yellow, and black ink should produce gray. But inks can fade and become impure over time. To compensate for this, you can vary the amount of ink that mixes to produce medium gray by entering values from 0.50 to 2.00 in the Gray Balance option boxes. Think of this as a recipe — 0.75 parts cyan mixed with 1.50 parts magenta, and so on. Again, consult with your commercial printer before changing these values.

✦ **Use Dot Gain for Grayscale Images:** When this option is turned off, the Dot Gain value only affects the creation and editing of CMYK images. If you select this check box, however, you also can apply the value to grayscale images. Then, any time you select a gray value, Photoshop automatically treats the value as if it were lighter or darker, depending on whether the Dot Gain value is negative or positive, respectively.

Caution

Rather than getting 50 percent gray when you select 50 percent gray, for example, you may get 58 percent gray. This can cause problems when you want to create displacement maps, create precise gradations, or simply achieve exact brightness values. I strongly recommend you turn this check box off unless you have some specific reason for turning it on, like you've suddenly taken leave of your senses.

How to prepare CMYK conversions

After you tell Photoshop how to compensate for the foibles of your screen and commercial printer, you need to explain what kind of separation process you intend to use. To do this, choose File ➪ Color Settings ➪ Separation Setup to display the Separation Setup dialog box, shown in Figure 7-13. Unlike the options in the Printing Inks Setup dialog box, which describe the specific press belonging to your commercial printer, these options describe a general printing process. Even so, you'll probably find consulting with your commercial printer helpful before you change the settings.

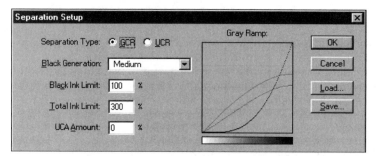

Figure 7-13: Describe the printing process using the options inside the Separation Setup dialog box.

The options in the Separation Setup dialog box work as follows:

✦ **Separation Type:** When the densities of cyan, magenta, and yellow inks reach a certain level, they mix to form a muddy brown. The GCR (*gray component replacement*) option avoids this unpleasant effect by overprinting these colors with black to the extent specified with the Black Generation option. If you select the UCR (*under color removal*) option, Photoshop removes cyan, magenta, and yellow inks where they overlap black ink. Generally speaking, GCR is the setting of choice except when you're printing on newsprint.

✦ **Black Generation:** Available only when the GCR option is active, the Black Generation pop-up menu enables you to specify how dark the cyan, magenta, and yellow concentrations must be before Photoshop adds black ink. Select Light to use black ink sparingly; select Heavy to apply it liberally. The None option prints no black ink whatsoever, while the Maximum option prints black ink over everything. You may want to use the UCA Amount option to restore cyan, magenta, and yellow ink if you select the Heavy or Maximum option.

✦ **Black Ink Limit:** Enter the maximum amount of black ink that can be applied to the page. By default, this value is 100 percent, which is solid ink coverage. If you raise the UCA Amount value, you'll probably want to lower this value by a similar percentage to prevent the image from overdarkening.

✦ **Total Ink Limit:** This value represents the maximum amount of all four inks permitted on the page. For example, assuming you use the default Black Ink Limit and Total Ink Limit values shown in Figure 7-13, the darkest printable color contains 100 percent black ink. The sum total of cyan, magenta, and yellow inks, therefore, is 200 percent. (You subtract the Black Ink Limit value from the Total Ink Limit value to get the sum total of the three other inks.)

✦ **UCA Amount:** The opposite of UCR, UCA stands for *under color addition*, which enables you to add cyan, magenta, and yellow inks to areas where the concentration of black ink is highest. For example, a value of 20 percent raises the amount of cyan, magenta, and yellow inks applied with black concentrations between 80 and 100 percent. This option is dimmed when the UCR radio button is active.

The Gray Ramp graph demonstrates the effects of your changes to any option in the Separation Setup dialog box. Four lines — one in each color — represent the four inks. Although you can't edit the colored lines in this graph by clicking and dragging them, as you can in the Transfer Functions dialog box, you can observe the lines to gauge the results of your settings. If you choose Custom from the Black Generation pop-up menu when GCR is on, you can directly edit the black curve and see how it will affect the C, M, and Y curves.

Color trapping

If color separations misalign slightly during the reproduction process (a problem called *misregistration*), the final image can exhibit slight gaps between colors. Suppose an image features a 100 percent cyan chicken against a 100 percent magenta background. (Pretty attractive image idea, huh? Go ahead, you can use it if you like.) If the cyan and magenta plates don't line up exactly, you're left with a chicken with a white halo around it. Yuck.

A *trap* is a little extra bit of color that fills in the gap. For example, if you choose Image ⇨ Trap and enter 4 into the Width option box, Photoshop outlines the chicken with an extra 4 pixels of cyan and the background with an extra 4 pixels of magenta. Now the registration can be off a full 8 pixels without any halo occurring.

Continuous-tone images, such as photographs and natural-media painting, don't need trapping because no harsh color transitions occur. In fact, trapping will actually harm such images by thickening up the borders and edges, smudging detail, and generally dulling the focus.

The only reason to use the Trap command, therefore, is to trap rasterized Illustrator drawings. Some state-of-the-art prepress systems trap documents by first rasterizing them to pixels and then modifying the pixels. Together, Photoshop and Illustrator constitute a more rudimentary but, nonetheless, functional trapping system. When you open an Illustrator document in Photoshop, the latter converts the illustration into an image according to your size and resolution specifications, as described in the "Rasterizing an Illustrator or FreeHand file" section of Chapter 4. Once the illustration is rasterized, you can apply Image ⇨ Trap to the image as a whole. Despite the command's simplicity, it handles nearly all trapping scenarios, even going so far as to reduce the width of the trap incrementally as the colors of neighboring areas grow more similar.

Caution If you plan on having a service bureau trap your files for you, do not apply Photoshop's Trap command. You don't want to see what happens when someone traps an image that's already been trapped. If you're paying the extra bucks for professional trapping, leave it to the pros.

Printing Duotones

It's been a few pages since the "Understanding Printing Terminology" section, so here's a quick recap: A duotone is a grayscale image printed with two inks. This technique expands the depth of the image by allowing additional shades for highlights, shadows, and midtones. If you've seen one of those glossy Calvin Klein magazine ads, you've seen a duotone. Words like *rich, luxurious,* and *palpable* come to mind.

Photoshop also enables you to add a third ink to create a tritone and a fourth ink to create a quadtone. Color Plate 7-1 shows an example of an image printed as a quadtone. Figure 7-14 shows a detail from the image printed in its original grayscale form. See the difference?

Figure 7-14: This salute to all-around athlete Jim Thorpe by artist Mark Collen looks pretty good, but if you want to see great, check out the quadtone in Color Plate 7-1.

Creating a duotone

To convert a grayscale image to a duotone, tritone, or quadtone, choose Image ➪ Mode ➪ Duotone. Photoshop displays the Duotone Options dialog box shown in Figure 7-15. By default, Monotone is the active Type option, and the Ink 2, Ink 3, and Ink 4 options are dimmed. To access the Ink 3 option, select Tritone from the Type pop-up menu; to access both Ink 3 and Ink 4, select Quadtone from the pop-up menu.

You specify the color of each ink you want to use by clicking the color box associated with the desired ink option. The first time you define colors, Photoshop displays the Color Picker dialog box. You can either define colors in the Color Picker or click Custom Colors to select a color from the Custom Colors dialog box, as described in the "Predefined colors" section of Chapter 5.

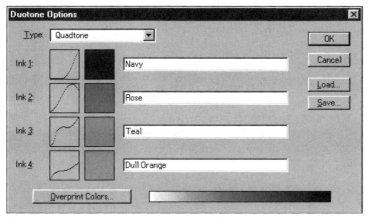

Figure 7-15: The Duotone Options dialog box enables you to apply multiple inks to a grayscale image.

The next time you create a duotone, Photoshop displays the same colors you defined in your last visit to the Duotone Options dialog box. If you previously defined colors in the Custom Colors dialog box, clicking a color box brings up that same dialog box (click Picker to get to the Color Picker dialog box).

When creating duotones, tritones, and quadtones, prioritize your inks in order — from darkest at the top to lightest at the bottom — when you specify them in the Duotone Options dialog box. Because Photoshop prints inks in the order they appear in the dialog box, the inks will print from darkest to lightest. This ensures rich highlights and shadows and a uniform color range.

After selecting a color, you can use either of two methods to specify how the differently colored inks blend. The first and more dependable way is to click the transfer function box associated with the desired ink option. Photoshop then displays the Transfer Functions dialog box, described back in the "Specifying a transfer function" section of this chapter. This enables you to emphasize specific inks in different portions of the image according to brightness values.

For example, Figure 7-16 shows the inks and transfer functions assigned to the quadtone in Color Plate 7-1. The Navy Blue color is associated only with the darkest brightness values in the image; Rose peaks at about 80 percent gray and then descends; Teal covers the midtones in the image; Dull Orange is strongest in the light values. The four colors mix to form an image whose brightness values progress from light orange to olive green to brick red to black.

The second method for controlling the blending of colors is to click the Overprint Colors button. An Overprint Colors dialog box appears, showing how each pair of colors will mix when printed. Other color swatches show how three and four colors mix, if applicable. To change the color swatch, click it to display the Color Picker dialog box.

The problem with this second method is it complicates the editing process. Photoshop doesn't actually change the ink colors or transfer functions in keeping with your new specifications; it just applies the new overprint colors without any logical basis. And you lose all changes made with the Overprint Colors dialog box when you adjust any of the ink colors or any of the transfer functions.

To return and change the colors or transfer functions, choose Image ➪ Mode ➪ Duotone again. Instead of reconverting the image, the command now enables you to edit the existing duotone, tritone, or quadtone.

Reproducing a duotone

If you want a commercial printer to reproduce a duotone, tritone, or quadtone, you must print the image to color separations, just like a CMYK image. Because you already specified which inks to use and how much of each ink to apply, however, you needn't mess around with all those commands in the File ➪ Color Settings submenu. Just take the following familiar steps:

Steps: Printing a Duotone, Tritone, or Quadtone

1. **Choose the printer you want to use.** Select a printer as described previously in the "Choosing a printer" section.

2. **Turn on the printer marks.** Choose File ➪ Page Setup (Ctrl+Shift+P) to specify the size of the pages and the size and orientation of the image on the pages, as described earlier in this chapter in the "Setting up the page" section. Be sure to select the Registration Marks option.

3. **Adjust the halftone screens, if desired.** If you're feeling inventive, click the Screens button to change the size, angle, and shape of the halftone screen dots for the individual color plates, as described previously in the "Changing the halftone screen" section.

4. **Choose File ➪ Print (Ctrl+P).** Select the Print Separations check box in the lower-left corner of the dialog box to print each ink to a separate sheet of paper or film.

To prepare a duotone to be imported into QuarkXPress, Illustrator, or some other application, save the image in the EPS format, as described in the "Saving an EPS image" section of Chapter 4. As listed back in Table 5-1 of Chapter 5, EPS (and its DCS variation) is the only file format other than the native Photoshop format that supports duotones, tritones, and quadtones.

If you'll print your duotone using CMYK colors and you can't quite get the effect you want inside the Duotone Options dialog box, you can convert the duotone to the CMYK mode (by choosing Image ➪ Mode ➪ CMYK). Not only will all the duotone shades remain intact, but you'll also have the added advantage of being able to tweak colors and to add color using Photoshop's standard color-correction commands and editing tools. You can even edit individual color channels, as described in Chapter 6.

Spot-Color Separations

Photoshop 4 offers no new capability that accommodates spot-color printing. Photoshop is, after all, designed for creating and editing continuous-tone images and, although spot colors work well for printing duotones, they more often lend themselves to high-contrast artwork created in drawing and page-layout programs.

But what if you want to add a spot-color highlight to an image? For example, suppose you have a full-color image of a jet ski. The logo along the side of the boat is fully visible, just as the client wants it, but the color is off. Normally, the logo appears in Pantone 265 purple. But the CMYK equivalent for this color looks about three shades darker, four shades redder, and several times muddier. The only solution is to assign the proper spot color — Pantone 265 — to the logo. But how do you do it? Here are your options:

✦ Paint over the logo in the actual image. Then import the image into Illustrator or FreeHand and re-create the logo as object-oriented text. Then assign the text Pantone 265 and export the document in the EPS format or print it directly from the drawing program. The logo will appear on its own separation.

✦ Select the logo using the magic wand tool (or some more exacting method, as described in Chapters 11 and 12) and remove it using Edit ➪ Cut (Ctrl+X). Then create a new channel by choosing the New Channel command from the Channels palette menu. After the Channel Options dialog box appears, click the Color swatch and change it to a color that matches Pantone 265 as closely as possible. Press Enter or click OK twice to create the new channel, and then press Ctrl+I to invert the channel and to make it white. Paste in the logo art (Edit ➪ Paste or Ctrl+V). As long as your selection outline is still intact, the logo is pasted in the exact position as in the original image. To see the logo and image together, click the eyeball icon in front of the CMYK composite view to show all channels at once. The logo will automatically appear in the purple color you selected in the Channel Options dialog box. Edit the CMYK image and logo as desired.

If you opt for the second option, you can print the image directly from Photoshop in two passes. First, you switch to the CMYK composite view (Ctrl+tilde) and print the traditional four-color separation. Second, you switch to the logo channel (Ctrl+5) and print this channel independently.

You cannot import the image into QuarkXPress or some other publishing program, however. Photoshop doesn't offer any file formats that support more than four color channels, except the native Photoshop format (which most other programs don't support and certainly not for the purpose of printing quality separations). If you were to save the image to the EPS or DCS format, for example, Photoshop would simply jettison the logo channel.

Windows 95 and Color

Given all the convolutions of color models and color spaces and calibrations, what's a poor Photoshopper to do? Microsoft is attempting to offer a solution in Windows 95 through Image Color Matching (ICM). ICM is designed to use a color profile from the manufacturer of a given device. That profile should allow ICM to map colors from Windows' logical color space to the color capabilities of the given output device — thus the device's drivers work in conjunction with the system to perform color matching. Finally, ICM is implemented as a Dynamic Link Library (DLL), and more than one can be loaded at a time for maximum flexibility.

Sounds pretty good, doesn't it? It may well be. But just try to find a color profile in the International Color Consortium (ICC) format — or an application that uses it. Of course, things change rapidly in computing, and the situation may well have changed by the time you read this. Definitely something to watch for the future.

Painting and Retouching Images

Painting and Editing

Paint and Edit Tool Basics

Here it is, Chapter 8 and I'm finally getting around to explaining how to use Photoshop's painting tools. You must feel like you're attending some kind of martial arts ritual where you have to learn to run away, cry, beg, and attempt bribery before you get to start karate-chopping bricks and kicking your instructor. "The wise person journeys through the fundamentals of image editing before painting a single brushstroke, Grasshoppa." *Wang, wang, wang.* (That's a musical embellishment, in case you didn't recognize it. Man, I hate to have to explain my jokes. Especially when they're so measly.) Now that you've earned your first belt or tassel or scouting patch or whatever it is you're supposed to receive for slogging this far through the book, you're as prepared as you'll ever be to dive into the world of painting and retouching images.

You may think these tools require artistic talent. In truth, each tool provides options for about any level of proficiency or experience. Photoshop offers get-by measures for novices who want to make a quick edit and put the tool down before they make a mess of things. If you have a few hours of experience with other painting programs, you'll find Photoshop's tools provide at least as much functionality and, in many cases, more. (The one exception is Painter, which is several times more capable than Photoshop in the painting department.) And if you're a professional artist — well, come on now — you'll have no problems learning how to make Photoshop sing. No matter who you are, you'll find electronic painting and editing tools more flexible, less messy, and more forgiving than their traditional counterparts.

Cross Reference If you screw something up in the course of painting your image, stop and choose Edit ➪ Undo (or press Ctrl+Z). If this doesn't work, try one of the reversion techniques described in the "Selectively Undoing Changes" section of Chapter 10. As long as a previous version of the image is saved on disk, you have a way out.

Meet your tools

Photoshop provides three paint tools: the pencil, paintbrush, and airbrush. You also get six edit tools: smudge, blur, sharpen, burn, dodge, and sponge. Figure 8-1 shows all these tools. The keyboard equivalent for each tool appears in parentheses.

 Cross Reference In case you're wondering about all the other tools, Figure 8-2 segregates tools by category and lists the chapter in which you can find more information.

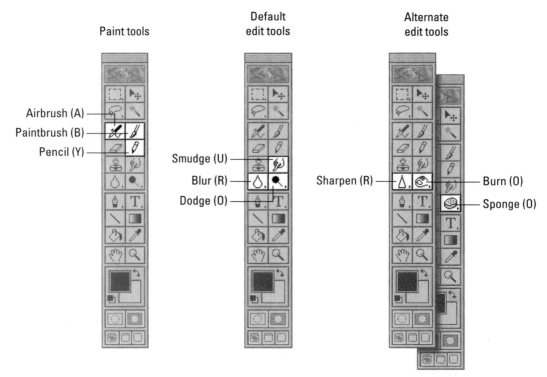

Figure 8-1: The three paint tools, the three edit tools that appear in the Toolbox by default, and the three alternative edit tools.

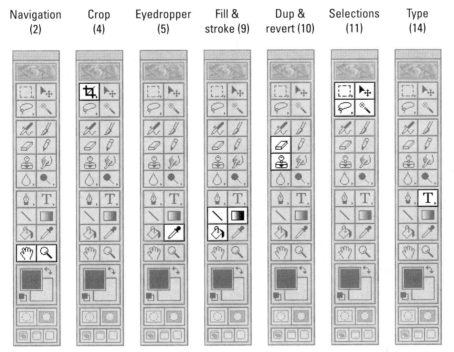

Navigation (2)	Crop (4)	Eyedropper (5)	Fill & stroke (9)	Dup & revert (10)	Selections (11)	Type (14)

Figure 8-2: The rest of Photoshop's tools fall into the categories listed above each Toolbox. The chapter in which I discuss each category of tools appears in parentheses.

The paint tools

The paint tools apply paint in the foreground color. In this and other respects, they work like their counterparts in other painting programs, but a few exceptions exist:

✦ **Pencil:** Unlike pencil tools found in most other painting programs — which paint lines 1-pixel thick — Photoshop's pencil paints a hard-edged line of any thickness. Figure 8-3 compares the default single-pixel pencil line with a fatter pencil line, a paintbrush line, and an airbrush line.

If you're used to selecting the pencil tool by pressing the P key, get used to being confused. You now select the pencil by pressing *Y*, as in "Boys and Girls, get your *yellow* number 2 pencils."

Photoshop **4.0**

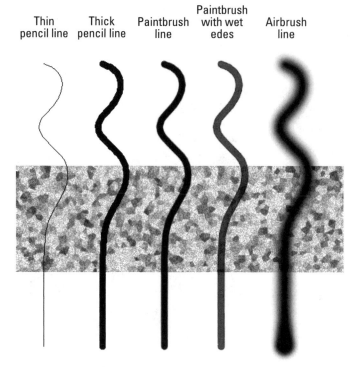

Thin pencil line | Thick pencil line | Paintbrush line | Paintbrush with wet edes | Airbrush line

Figure 8-3: Five lines painted in black with the pencil, paintbrush, and airbrush tools. The Wet Edges option (second from right) causes the line to appear translucent. Notice I held the airbrush tool in place for a few moments at the end of the rightmost line.

✦ **Paintbrush:** The paintbrush works like the pencil tool, except it paints an anti-aliased line that blends in with its background.

The paintbrush offers a Wet Edges option. (Double-click the paintbrush tool icon in the Toolbox and you'll see the Wet Edges check box in the bottom left-corner of the Paintbrush Options palette.) When this option is turned on, the paintbrush creates a translucent line with darkened edges, much as if you were painting with watercolors. Soft brush shapes produce more naturalistic effects. An example of this effect is shown in Figure 8-3.

✦ **Airbrush:** Dismissing Photoshop's airbrush tool as a softer version of the paintbrush is tempting because it uses a softer brush shape by default. Photoshop's default settings also call for a lighter pressure, so the airbrush paints a translucent line. But unlike the paintbrush, which applies a continuous stream of color and stops applying paint when you stop dragging, the airbrush applies a series of colored dollops and continues to apply these dollops as long as you press the mouse button. Figure 8-3 shows the dark glob of paint that results from pressing the mouse button while holding the mouse motionless at the end of the drag.

The edit tools

The edit tools don't apply color; rather, they influence existing colors in an image. Figure 8-4 shows each of the five edit tools applied to a randomized background. The tools work as follows:

✦ **Smudge:** The smudge tool smears colors in an image. The effect is much like dragging your finger across wet paint.

✦ **Blur:** The first of the two focus tools, the blur tool blurs an image by lessening the amount of color contrast between neighboring pixels.

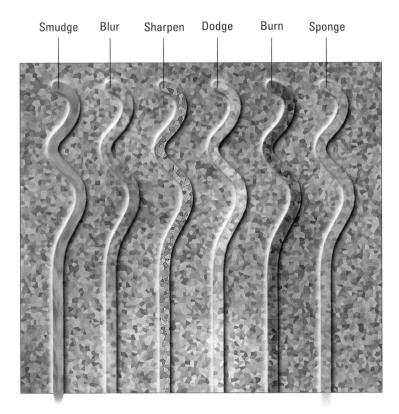

Figure 8-4: These are the effects of dragging with each of Photoshop's edit tools. The boundaries of each line are highlighted so you can clearly see the distinctions between line and background.

✦ **Sharpen:** The second focus tool selectively sharpens by increasing the contrast between neighboring pixels. Generally speaking, both the blur and sharpen tools are less useful than their command counterparts in the Filters menu. They provide less control and usually require scrubbing at an image. Maybe I've been using a computer too long, but my wrist starts to ache when I use these tools. If, unlike me, you like the basic principle behind the tools, but you want to avoid carpal tunnel syndrome, you can achieve consistent, predictable results without scrubbing by using the tools in combination with the Shift key, as described in the next section.

✦ **Dodge:** The first of three toning tools, the dodge tool enables you to lighten a portion of an image by dragging across it. Named after a traditional film exposure technique, the dodge tool is supposed to look like a little paddle thingie — you know, like one of those spoons you put over your eye at the optometrist's — that you wave over an image to diffuse the amount of light that gets to the film and, therefore, lighten the print. Thank golly we no longer have to wave little paddle thingies in our modern age.

✦ **Burn:** The burn tool enables you to darken a portion of an image by dragging over it. The effect is similar to burning a film negative, which you apparently do by holding your hand in a kind of O shape in an effort to focus the light, kind of like frying a worker ant using a magnifying glass (except not quite so smelly). At least, that's what they tell me. Sadly, I've never had the pleasure of trying it.

✦ **Sponge:** The final toning tool, the sponge tool, robs an image of both saturation and contrast. Or you can set the tool so it boosts saturation and adds contrast. For more information, stay tuned for the upcoming section "Mopping up with the sponge tool."

To access the sharpen tool temporarily when the blur tool is selected, press and hold the Alt key while using the tool. The sharpen tool remains available only as long as you press the Alt key. You also can press Alt to access the blur tool when the sharpen tool is selected, to access the burn tool when the dodge tool is selected, and to access the dodge tool when the burn tool is selected. (If the sponge tool is active, pressing the Alt key has no effect, except maybe to give your finger a cramp.)

Tip

You can replace the blur tool with the sharpen tool in the Toolbox by Alt+clicking the tool's icon. To *toggle* (switch) back to the blur tool, Alt+click the sharpen icon. Likewise, you can Alt+click the dodge tool icon to toggle between the dodge, burn, and sponge tools.

As explained in Chapter 3, the keyboard equivalents also toggle between the tools. When the blur tool is selected, press R to toggle to the sharpen tool. Another tap of the R key returns you to blur. When the dodge tool is selected, press O to toggle to the burn tool, and then press *O* again to get the sponge. Press *O* one more time to take the trail back to dodge. (What dodge tool discussion would be complete without at least one *Gunsmoke* joke?)

Tip

To modify the performance of a tool, double-click its icon in the Toolbox to display the customized Options palette. Or you can simply press Enter while the tool is selected. I discuss the options inside the various Options palettes throughout the remainder of this chapter.

Basic techniques

I know several people who claim they can't paint, and yet they create beautiful work in Photoshop. Even though they don't have sufficient hand-eye coordination to write their names onscreen, they have unique and powerful artistic sensibilities and they know lots of tricks that enable them to make judicious use of the paint and edit tools. I can't help you in the sensibilities department, but I can show you a few tricks to boost your ability and inclination to use the paint and edit tools.

Painting a straight line

You're probably already aware you can draw a straight line with the line tool. If not, try it. The line tool is the diagonal line on the left side of the Toolbox. After selecting the tool, drag with it inside the Image window to create a line. Pretty hot stuff, huh? Well, no, it's actually pretty dull. In fact, the only reason I ever use this tool is to draw arrows like those shown in the upcoming Figure 8-6. If you don't want to draw an arrow, you're better off using Photoshop's other means for creating straight lines: the Shift key.

Cross Reference

To add an arrowhead to a line drawn with the line tool, double-click the line tool icon in the Toolbox and select the Start or End check box inside the Line Tool Options palette. These options are explained in the "Applying Strokes and Arrowheads" section of Chapter 9.

To draw a straight line with any of the paint or edit tools, click one point in the image and then press Shift and click another point. Using the current tool, Photoshop draws a straight line between the two points.

To create free-form polygons, continue to Shift+click with the tool. Figure 8-5 features a photograph and a tracing I made on a separate layer (as explained in Chapter 13) exclusively by Shift+clicking with the paintbrush tool. As an academic exercise, I never dragged with the tool, I never altered the brush size, and I used just two colors: black and gray.

Figure 8-5: Starting from an image by photographer Barbara Penoyar (left), I created a stylized tracing (right) by clicking and Shift+clicking with the paintbrush tool on a separate layer.

Tip

The Shift key makes the blur and sharpen tools halfway useful. Suppose you want to edit the perimeter of the car shown in Figure 8-6. The arrows in the figure illustrate the path your Shift+clicks should follow. Figure 8-7 shows the effect of Shift+clicking with the blur tool; Figure 8-8 demonstrates the effect of Shift+clicking with the sharpen tool.

Figure 8-6: It takes one click and 24 Shift+clicks to soften or accentuate the edges around this car using the blur or sharpen tool.

Figure 8-7: These are the results of blurring the car's perimeter with the pressure set to 50 percent (top) and 100 percent (bottom). You set the pressure using the slider bar in the Focus Tools Options palette.

Figure 8-8: The results of sharpening the car with the pressure set to 50 percent (top) and 100 percent (bottom)

Painting a perpendicular line

To draw a perpendicular line — either a vertical or a horizontal line — with any of the paint or edit tools, press and hold the mouse button, press the Shift key, and begin dragging in a vertical or horizontal direction. Don't release the Shift key until you finish dragging or until you want to change the direction of the line, as shown in Figure 8-9. Notice, pressing the Shift key in middrag snaps the line back into perpendicular alignment.

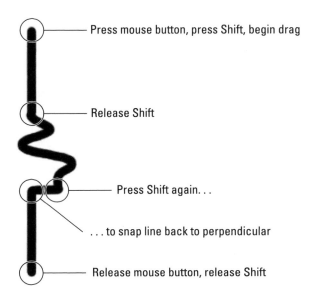

Press mouse button, press Shift, begin drag

Release Shift

Press Shift again. . .

. . . to snap line back to perpendicular

Release mouse button, release Shift

Figure 8-9: Pressing the Shift key after you start to drag with a paint or edit tool results in a perpendicular line for as long as the key is pressed.

One way to exploit the Shift key's penchant to snap to the perpendicular is to draw "ribbed" structures. Being left-handed, I dragged from right to left with the paintbrush to create both of the central outlines around the skeleton that appears at the top of Figure 8-10. I painted each rib by pressing and releasing the Shift key as I dragged with the paintbrush tool. Pressing Shift snapped the line to the horizontal axis, whose location was established by the beginning of the drag.

In the figure, I represented the axis for each line in gray. After establishing the basic skeletal form, I added some free-form details with the paintbrush and pencil tools, as shown in the middle image in Figure 8-10. I then selected a general area around the image and chose Filter ➪ Stylize ➪ Emboss to create the finished fossil image. Nobody's going to confuse my painting with a bona fide fossil — "Hey Marge, look what I done tripped over in the back forty!" — but it's not bad for a cartoon.

It's no accident Figure 8-10 features a swordfish instead of your everyday round-nosed carp. To snap to the horizontal axis, I had to establish the direction of my drag as being more horizontal than vertical. If I had, instead, dragged in a fish-faced convex arc, Photoshop would have interpreted my drag as vertical and snapped to the vertical axis.

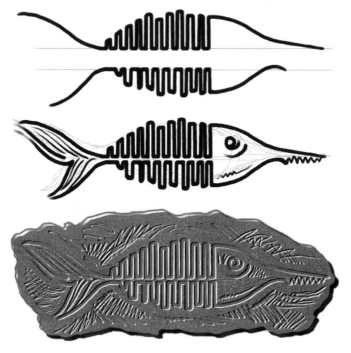

Figure 8-10: To create the basic structure for our bony pal, I periodically pressed and released the Shift key while dragging with the paintbrush (top). Then I embellished the fish using the paintbrush and pencil (middle). Finally, I applied the Emboss filter to transform fish into fossil (bottom).

Painting with the smudge tool

Many first-time Photoshop artists misuse the smudge tool to soften color transitions. In fact, softening is the purpose of the blur tool. The smudge tool *smears* colors by shoving them into each other. The process bears more resemblance to the finger painting you did in grade school than to any traditional photographic-editing technique.

In Photoshop, the performance of the smudge tool depends in part on the settings of the Pressure and Finger Painting options. Both reside in the Smudge Tool Options palette (see Figure 8-11), which you access by pressing Enter when the smudge tool is active. These two options work as follows:

✦ **Pressure:** Measured as a percentage of the brush shape, this option determines the distance the smudge tool drags a color. Higher percentages and larger brush shapes drag colors farthest. A Pressure setting of 100 percent equates to infinity, meaning the smudge tool drags a color from the beginning of your drag until the end of your drag, regardless of how far you drag. Cosmic, Daddy-O.

✦ **Finger Painting:** The folks at Adobe used to call this effect *dipping,* which I think more accurately expressed how the effect works. When you select this option, the smudge tool begins by applying a smidgen of foreground color, which it eventually blends in with the colors in the image. It's as if you dipped your finger in a color and then dragged it through an oil painting. Use the Pressure setting to specify the amount of foreground color applied. If you turn on Finger Painting and set the Pressure to 100 percent, the smudge tool behaves exactly like the paintbrush tool.

Tip You can reverse the Finger Painting setting by Alt+dragging. If the option is off, Alt+dragging dips the tool into the foreground color. If Finger Painting is turned on, Alt+dragging smudges normally.

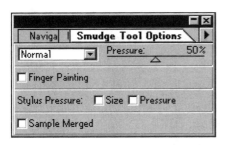

Figure 8-11: Combined with brush shape, the Pressure and Finger Painting options are the most important considerations when using the smudge tool.

For some examples of the smudge tool in action, look at Figure 8-12. The figure shows the effects of using the smudge tool set to four different Pressure percentages and with the Finger Painting option both off and on. In each instance, the brush shape is 13 pixels in diameter and the foreground color is set to black.

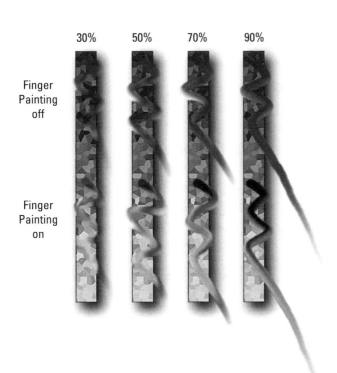

Figure 8-12: Eight drags with the smudge tool subject to different Pressure and Finger Painting settings.

The Sample Merged option in the Smudge Tool Options palette instructs the smudge tool to grab colors in all visible layers and smudge them into the current layer. Whether the option is on or off, only the current layer is affected; the background and other layers remain intact.

For example, suppose the inverted eyes of the woman at the top of Figure 8-13 are on a different layer than the rest of the face. If I use the smudge tools on the eyes layer with Sample Merged turned off, Photoshop ignores the face layer when smudging the eyes. As a result, details like the nose and teeth remain unsmudged, as you can see in the lower-left example. If I turn Sample Merged on, Photoshop lifts colors from the face layer and mixes them in with the eyes' layer, as shown in the lower-right example.

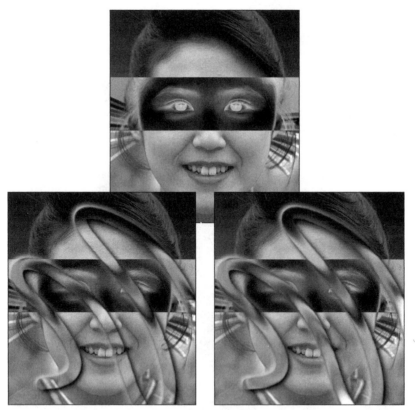

Figure 8-13: The original image (top) features inverted eyes on a layer above the rest of the face. I first smudged the eyes with Sample Merged turned off (lower left) and then with the option turned on (lower right).

Note, all this activity occurs exclusively on the eyes' layer. To give you a better look, the two lower examples on the eyes' layer are shown independently of those on the face layer in Figure 8-14. You can now clearly see the proliferation of face details mixed into the eyes in the right example. Meanwhile, the face layer remains absolutely unaffected.

Figure 8-14: The eyes' layer from the previous figure shown by itself

Incidentally, in case you're wondering where the heck the option name Sample Merged comes from, Photoshop is saying it will *sample* — that is, lift colors — as if all layers are merged into one. For more information about setting up and merging layers, read Chapter 13.

Mopping up with the sponge tool

The sponge tool is actually a pretty darn straightforward tool, hardly worth expending valuable space in a book as tiny as this one. But I'm a compulsive explainer, so here's the deal: Press Enter when the sponge tool is active to gain access to the Toning Tools Options palette. In the upper-left corner of the palette is a pop-up menu that offers two options: Desaturate and Saturate. When set to Desaturate, the tool reduces the saturation of the colors over which you drag. When editing a grayscale image, the tool reduces the contrast. If you select the Saturate option, the sponge tool increases the saturation of the colors over which you drag or increases contrast in a grayscale image. Higher Pressure settings produce more dramatic results.

Consider Color Plate 8-1. The upper-left example shows the original PhotoDisc image. The upper-right example shows the result of applying the sponge tool set to Desaturate. I dragged with the tool inside the pepper and around in the corner area. The Pressure was set to 100 percent. Notice, the affected colors are on the wane, sliding toward gray. In the lower-right example, the effect is even more pronounced. I applied the sponge tools here with great vim and vigor two additional times. Hardly any hint of color is left in these areas now.

To create the lower-left example in Color Plate 8-1, I applied the sponge tool set to Saturate. This is where things get a little tricky. If you boost saturation levels with the sponge tool in the RGB or Lab color modes, you can achieve colors of absolutely neon intensity. These high-saturation colors don't stand a snowball's chance in a microwave of printing in CMYK, however. So I recommend you choose View ➪ CMYK Preview before boosting saturation levels with the sponge tool. This way, you can accurately view the results of your edits. After you're finished, choose View ➪ CMYK Preview to turn off the CMYK preview and return to the RGB view.

Figure 8-15 shows the yellow channel from Color Plate 8-1. Because yellow is the most prevalent primary color in the image, it is the most sensitive to saturation adjustments. When I boosted the saturation in the lower-left example, the yellow brightness values deepened, adding yellow ink to the CMYK image. When I lessened the saturation in the two right examples, the amount of ink diminished.

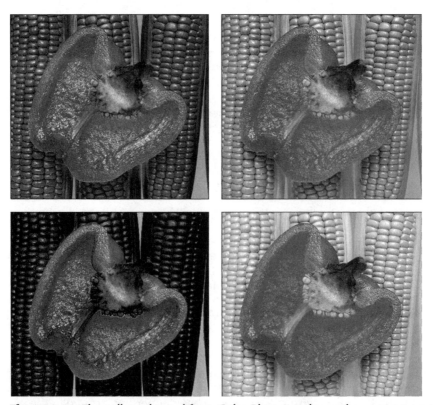

Figure 8-15: The yellow channel from Color Plate 8-1 shows the greatest amount of variation when reducing and boosting the saturation with the sponge tool.

One of Adobe's recommended purposes of the sponge tool is to reduce the saturation levels of out-of-gamut RGB colors before converting an image to the CMYK mode. I'm not too crazy about this use of the tool because it requires a lot of scrubbing. Generally, selecting the out-of-gamut area and reducing the colors using more automated controls is easier (as discussed in Chapter 16). You might prefer, instead, to use the sponge tool when a more selective, personal touch is required, as when curbing a distracting color that seems to leap a little too vigorously off the screen or boosting the saturation of a detail in the CMYK mode.

Brush Shape and Opacity

So far, I mentioned the words *brush shape* several times and I have yet to explain what the Sam Hill I'm talking about. Luckily, it's simple. The *brush shape* is the size and shape of the tip of your cursor when you use a paint or edit tool. A big, round brush shape paints or edits in broad strokes. A small, elliptical brush shape is useful for performing hairline adjustments.

Tip

Although Photoshop is not set up this way by default, it is capable of displaying a cursor whose outline reflects the selected brush shape. To access this incredibly useful cursor, press Ctrl+K to bring up the Preferences dialog box and press Ctrl+3 for the Display & Cursors panel. Then select Brush Size from the Painting Cursors radio buttons. Photoshop now shows the actual size of the brush you're using, up to 300 pixels in diameter. If the brush is bigger — as when you zoom in on the image while using a large brush — the standard tool cursor appears instead.

When using very small brushes, as when using the single-pixel pencil to do precise retouching, the cursor includes four dots around its perimeter, making the cursor easier to locate. If you need a little more help, press the Caps Lock key to access the more obvious crosshair cursor.

The Brushes palette

You access brush shapes by choosing Window ➪ Palettes ➪ Show Brushes to display the Brushes palette. Or you can press the F5 key. Figure 8-16 shows the Brushes palette with its pop-up menu wide open for your viewing pleasure.

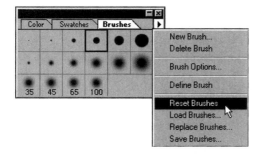

Figure 8-16: Photoshop's Brushes palette enables you to select a predefined brush shape or create one of your own.

Tip   You can switch brush shapes from the keyboard without displaying the Brushes palette. Press the left-bracket key, [, to select the previous brush shape in the palette; press the right-bracket key,], to select the next brush shape. You can also press Shift+[to select the first brush shape in the palette and Shift+] to select the last shape.

Editing a brush shape

To edit a brush shape in the Brushes palette, select the brush you want to change and choose Brush Options from the palette menu. To create a new brush shape, choose New Brush. Either way, the dialog box shown in Figure 8-17 appears. (If you choose the New Brush command, the Title bar is different, but the options are the same.)

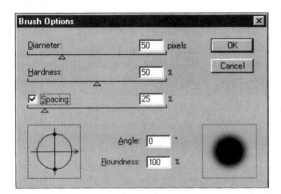

Figure 8-17: The Brush Options dialog box enables you to change the size, shape, and hardness of the brush shape.

Tip   If you hate menus — and who doesn't? — you can more conveniently edit a brush shape by simply double-clicking it. To create a new brush shape, click once on an empty brush slot, as shown in the first example in Figure 8-18. (Incidentally, you can also delete a brush from the palette. To do so, press Ctrl to display the scissors cursor — as in the second example in Figure 8-18 — then click. It's a great little housekeeping tip.)

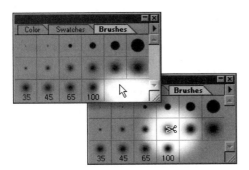

Figure 8-18: Clicking an empty brush slot (left) brings up the New Brush dialog box so you can create a new brush shape. Ctrl+clicking a brush shape (right) deletes it from the palette.

Whether you're editing an existing brush or creating a new one, you have the following options at your disposal:

✦ **Diameter:** This option determines the width of the brush shape. If the brush shape is elliptical instead of circular, the Diameter value determines the longest dimension. You can enter any value from 1 to 999 pixels. Brush shapes with diameters of 30 pixels or higher are too large to display accurately in the Brushes palette and instead appear as circles with inset Diameter values.

✦ **Hardness:** Except when you use the pencil tool, brush shapes are always anti-aliased. You can further soften the edges of a brush, however, by dragging the Hardness slider bar away from 100 percent. The softest setting, 0 percent, gradually tapers the brush from a single solid color pixel at its center to a ring of transparent pixels around the brush's perimeter. Figure 8-19 demonstrates how low Hardness percentages expand the size of a 100-pixel brush beyond the Diameter value (as demonstrated by the examples set against black). Even a 100-percent hard brush shape expands slightly because it is anti-aliased. The Hardness setting is ignored when you use the pencil tool.

✦ **Spacing:** The Spacing option controls how frequently a tool affects an image as you drag, measured as a percentage of the brush shape. Suppose the Diameter of a brush shape is 12 pixels and the Spacing is set to 25 percent (the setting for all default brush shapes). For every 3 pixels (25 percent of 12 pixels) you drag with the paintbrush tool, Photoshop lays down a 12-pixel wide spot of color. A Spacing of 1 percent provides the most coverage, but may also slow down the performance of the tool. If you deselect the Spacing check box, the effect of the tool is wholly dependent on the speed at which you drag; this can be useful for creating nonuniform or splotchy lines. Figure 8-20 shows examples.

✦ **Angle:** This option enables you to pivot a brush shape on its axes. Unless the brush is elliptical, though, this won't make a difference in the appearance of the brush shape.

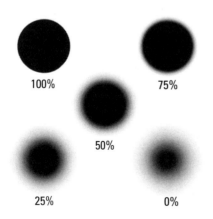

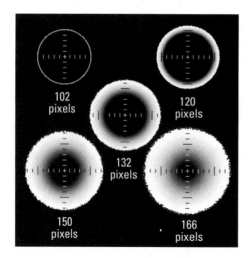

Figure 8-19: A 100-pixel diameter brush shown as it appears when set to a variety of Hardness percentages. I changed the background pixels below from white to black, so you can see the actual diameter of each brush shape. The tick marks indicate 10-pixel increments.

✦ **Roundness:** Enter a value of less than 100 percent into the Roundness option to create an elliptical brush shape. The value measures the width of the brush as a percentage of its height, so a Roundness value of 5 percent results in a long, skinny brush shape.

Tip   You can adjust the angle of the brush dynamically by dragging the gray arrow inside the box to the left of the Angle and Roundness options. Drag the handles on either side of the black circle to make the brush shape elliptical, as demonstrated in Figure 8-21.

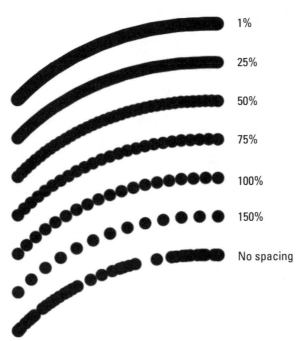

1%

25%

50%

75%

100%

150%

No spacing

Figure 8-20: Examples of lines drawn with different Spacing values in the Brush Options dialog box. Gaps or ridges generally begin to appear when the Spacing value exceeds 30 percent. The final line was created by turning off the Spacing option.

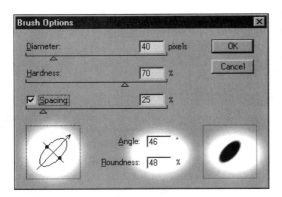

Figure 8-21: Drag the gray arrow or the black handles to change the angle or roundness of a brush, respectively. The Angle and Roundness values update automatically, as does the preview of the brush in the lower-right corner of the dialog box.

I heartily recommend you take a few moments soon to experiment at length with the Brush Options dialog box. By combining paint and edit tools with one or more specialized brush shapes, you can achieve artistic effects unlike anything permitted via traditional techniques. Starting with a PhotoDisc image lightened and filtered to serve as a template, I painted Figure 8-22 using the flat, 45-pixel brush shape shown in the dialog box. (For a color version of the effect, take a look at Color Plate 8-2.) No other brush shape or special effect was applied. Think of what you can accomplish if you don't limit yourself as ridiculously as I did.

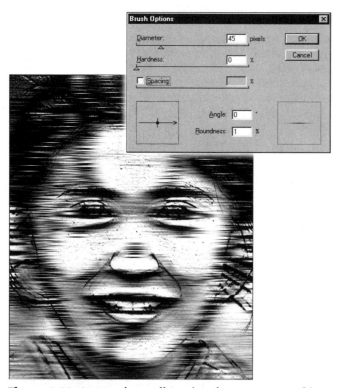

Figure 8-22: Just to show off, I painted over a scanned image with the paintbrush tool, using the brush shape shown in the dialog box at the top.

Creating and using custom brushes

You can define a custom brush shape by selecting a portion of your image that you want to change to a brush and choosing the Define Brush command from the Brushes palette pop-up menu.

In addition to giving you the flexibility to create a brush from some element in your image, Photoshop ships with a file called Assorted Brushes, which contains all kinds of little symbols and doodads you can assign as custom brush shapes. You can load the contents of the Assorted Brushes file into the Brushes palette by choosing the Replace Brushes command from the palette menu (or Load Brushes if you don't want to lose the brush shapes that currently occupy the palette). You'll find Assorted Brushes inside the Brushes folder inside the main Photoshop folder. Figure 8-23 shows an inspirational image I created using Photoshop's predefined custom brushes.

To return to the original default brush shapes, choose Reset Brushes from the palette menu. You then have the option of either replacing the existing brushes with the default brushes or simply adding the default brushes to the end of the palette.

Figure 8-23: Yes, it's Boris, the sleeping custom-brush guy. If you suspect this image is meant to suggest custom brushes are more amusing than utilitarian, you're right. The brushes from the Assorted Brushes file appear on the right.

In Photoshop, you can adjust the performance of a custom brush in the following ways:

✦ **Brush options:** Choose the Brush Options command from the palette menu or double-click the custom brush in the Brushes palette to bring up the dialog box shown in Figure 8-24. Here you can adjust the spacing of the brush shape and specify whether Photoshop antialiases (softens) the edges or leaves them as is. If the brush is sufficiently large, the Anti-aliased check box appears dimmed. All custom brushes are hard-edged when you use the pencil tool.

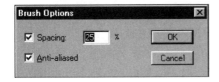

Figure 8-24: The dialog box that appears when you double-click a custom brush

✦ **Brush color:** The foreground color affects a custom brush just as it does a standard brush shape. To erase with the brush, select white as the foreground color. To paint in color, select a color.

✦ **Opacity and brush modes:** The setting of the Opacity slider bar and the brush modes pop-up menu also affect the application of custom brushes. For more information on these options, keep reading this chapter.

Tip   You can achieve some unusual and, sometimes, interesting effects by activating the smudge tool's Finger Painting option and painting in the Image window with a custom brush. At high Pressure settings, say 80 to 90 percent, the effect is rather like applying oil paint with a hairy paintbrush, as illustrated in Figure 8-25.

Figure 8-25: I created this organic, expressive image by combining the smudge tool's dipping capability with four custom brushes. I don't know what those fingerlike growths are, but they'd probably feel right at home in an aquarium.

Opacity, pressure, and exposure

The brush shapes in the Brushes palette affect two tools other than the paint and edit tools; these are the eraser and the rubber stamp, both discussed in Chapter 10. But the slider bar in the upper-right corner of the Options palette additionally affects the paint bucket, gradient, and line tools. Photoshop assigns one of three labels to this slider bar, illustrated in Figure 8-26.

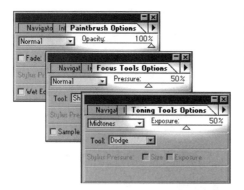

Figure 8-26: The slider bar in the upper-right corner of the Brushes palette assumes one of these functions, depending on the selected paint or edit tool.

✦ **Opacity:** The Opacity slider bar determines the translucency of colors applied with the paint bucket, gradient, line, pencil, paintbrush, eraser, or rubber stamp tool. At 100 percent, the applied colors appear opaque, completely covering the image behind them. (The one exception is the paintbrush with Wet Edges active, which is always translucent.) At lower settings, the applied colors mix with the existing colors in the image.

✦ **Pressure:** The Pressure slider bar affects different tools in different ways. When you use the airbrush tool, the slider bar controls the opacity of each spot of color the tool delivers. The effect appears unique because the airbrush lays each spot of color onto the previous spot, mixing them together. This results in a progressive effect. Meanwhile, the paintbrush and pencil tools are not progressive, so their spots blend to form smooth lines.

When you use the smudge tool, the slider bar controls the distance the tool drags colors in the image. And in the case of the blur, sharpen, or sponge tool, the slider bar determines the degree to which the tool changes the focus or saturation of the image, 1 percent being the minimum and 100 percent being the maximum.

✦ **Exposure:** If you select the dodge or burn tool, the slider bar title changes to Exposure. A setting of 100 percent applies the maximum amount of lightening or darkening to an image, which is still far short of either absolute white or black.

The factory default setting for all Exposure and Pressure slider bars is 50 percent; the default setting for all Opacity sliders is 100 percent.

Tip

As long as one of the tools listed in this section is selected, you can change the Opacity, Pressure, or Exposure setting in 10 percent increments by pressing a number key on the keyboard or keypad. Press 1 to change the setting to 10 percent, press 2 for 20 percent, and so on, all the way up to 0 for 100 percent.

Photoshop 4.0

In Photoshop 4, you can go one better. Press two keys in a row to change the Opacity, Pressure, or Exposure setting in 1 percent increments. Press 4 twice for 44 percent, 0 and 7 for 7 percent, and so on. This tip and the previous one work whether the Options palette is visible. Get in the habit of using the number keys and you'll thank yourself later.

Tapered Lines

Photoshop provides two ways to create tapering lines reminiscent of brushstrokes created using traditional techniques. You can specify the length over which a line fades by entering a value into the Fade option box, as described in the next section. Or, if you own a pressure-sensitive drawing tablet, you can draw brushstrokes that fade in and out automatically according to the amount of pressure you apply to the stylus. Both techniques enable you to introduce an element of spontaneity into what, otherwise, seems at times like an absolute world of computer graphics.

Fading the paint

All three paint tools offer Fade check boxes in their respective Options palettes, which enable you to create lines that gradually fade away as you drag. Figure 8-27 shows the Fade option as it appears in the Paintbrush Options palette, along with some examples of the effect.

After selecting the Fade check box, enter a value into the option box to specify the distance over which the color fading should occur. The fading begins at the start of your drag and is measured in brush shapes.

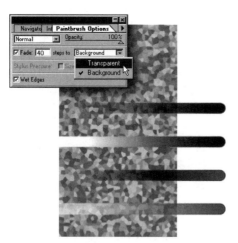

Figure 8-27: This is the Fade check box as it appears in the Paintbrush Options palette, along with four examples.

For example, assume the foreground color is black. If you enter 40 into the Fade option box — as in Figure 8-27 — Photoshop paints 40 brush shapes, the first in black and the remaining 39 in increasingly lighter shades of gray.

Cross Reference

In Photoshop, you can paint gradient lines by selecting the To Background radio button. Photoshop fades the line from the foreground color to the background color, much the same way the gradient tool fades the interior of a selection. For more information on the gradient tool, see the "Applying Gradient Fills" section of Chapter 9.

Fading and spacing

The physical length of a fading line is dependent both on the Fade value and on the value entered into the Spacing option box in the Brush Options dialog box, discussed back in the "Editing a brush shape" section earlier in this chapter.

To recap, the Spacing value determines the frequency with which Photoshop lays down brush shapes, and the Fade value determines the number of brush shapes laid down. Therefore, as demonstrated in Figure 8-28, a high Fade value combined with a high Spacing value creates the longest line.

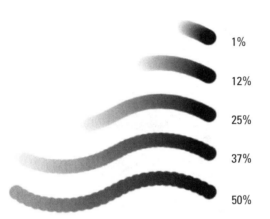

1%

12%

25%

37%

50%

Figure 8-28: Here are five fading lines drawn with the paintbrush tool. In each case, the Fade option is set to 36 brush shapes. I changed the Spacing value incrementally from 1 to 50 percent, as labeled.

Creating sparkles and comets

Fading lines may strike you as pretty ho-hum, but they enable you to create some no-brainer, cool-mandoo effects, especially when combined with the Shift key techniques discussed earlier, in the "Painting a straight line" section.

Figures 8-29 and 8-30 demonstrate two of the most obvious uses for fading straight lines: creating sparkles and comets. The top image in Figure 8-29 features two sets of sparkles, each made up of 16 straight lines emanating from the sparkle's center. To create the smaller sparkle on the right, I set the Fade value to 60 and drew each of the four perpendicular lines with the paintbrush tool. I changed the Fade value to 36 before drawing the four 45-degree diagonal lines. The eight very short lines that occur between the perpendicular and diagonal lines were drawn with a Fade value of 20. I, likewise, created the larger sparkle on the left by periodically adjusting the Fade value, this time from 90 to 60 to 42.

For comparison's sake, I used different techniques to add a few more sparkles to the bottom image in Figure 8-29. To achieve the reflection in the upper-left corner of the image, I chose Filter ➪ Render ➪ Lens Flare and selected 50-300mm Zoom from the Lens Type options. (Lens Flare works exclusively in the RGB mode, so I had to switch to RGB to apply the filter, even though Figure 8-29 is a grayscale image.)

I created the two tiny sparkles on the right edge of the bumper using a custom brush shape. I merely selected the custom brush, set the foreground color to white, and clicked once with the paintbrush tool in each location. So many sparkles make for a tremendously shiny image.

Figure 8-29: I drew the sparkles in the top image using the paintbrush tool. The second image features a reflection applied with the Lens Flare filter (upper-left corner) and two dabs of a custom brush shape (right edge of the bumper).

In Figure 8-30 — a nostalgic tribute to the days when gas was cheap and the whole family would pile in the Plymouth for a Sunday drive through space — I copied the car and pasted it on top of a NASA photograph of Jupiter. I then went nuts clicking and Shift+clicking with the paintbrush tool to create the comets — well, if you must know, they're actually cosmic rays — you see shooting through and around the car. It's so real, you can practically hear the in-dash servo unit warning, "Duck and cover!"

After masking portions of the image (a process described at length in Chapter 12), I drew rays behind the car and even one ray that shoots up through the car and out the spare tire. The three bright lights in the image — above the left fin, above the roof, and next to the right-turn signal — are more products of the Lens Flare filter in the RGB mode.

Figure 8-30: To create the threatening cosmic rays, I set the Fade option to 110 and then clicked and Shift+clicked on opposite sides of the image with the paintbrush tool.

Note I drew all the fading lines in Figures 8-29 and 8-30 with the paintbrush tool, using a variety of default brush shapes. Because I didn't edit any brush shape, the Spacing value for all lines was a constant 25 percent.

Setting up pressure-sensitive tablets

The pressure-sensitive tablet must be the single most useful piece of optional hardware available to computer artists. Not only can you draw with a penlike stylus instead of a clunky mouse, you also can dynamically adjust the thickness of lines and the opacity of colors by changing the amount of pressure you apply to the stylus. Several vendors currently manufacture pressure-sensitive *tablets,* but my favorite continues to be Wacom.

Note On some pressure-sensitive tablets, the stylus has an "eraser" on the end. When you use the eraser, Photoshop automatically switches to the eraser tool.

New Technology Of these, my favorite is Wacom's $200 ArtPad II. Measuring a diminutive 7 × 7.25 inches (with an active area of 4 × 5 inches), this thing is smaller than a standard mouse pad. The tablet offers 256 levels of pressure and a resolution of thousands of lines per inch. (Like any digital tracking device, a tablet uses pixels to communicate the location of your stylus. The higher the resolution, the smoother your mouse movements.)

Wacom's cordless stylus comes in several different varieties — illustrated in Figure 8-31 — each of which weighs less than an ounce. All of them feature both a pressure-sensitive nib and at least one side switch for double-clicking or choosing macros. My favorite stylus is the WideBody, which actually includes pencil lead or ink. This way, you can see what you're drawing both on paper and onscreen. Oh, what miracles the modern age brings!

If you're an artist and you've never experimented with this or any other pressure-sensitive tablet, I recommend you do so at your earliest convenience. You'll be amazed at how much it increases your range of artistic options. Thirty minutes after I installed my first tablet back in 1990, I had executed the cartoon you see in Figure 8-32 (and in Color Plate 8-3). Whether you like the image or not — I'll admit there's a certain troglodyte quality to the slope of his forehead, and that jaw could bust a coconut — it shows off the tablet's capability to paint tapering lines and accommodate artistic expression.

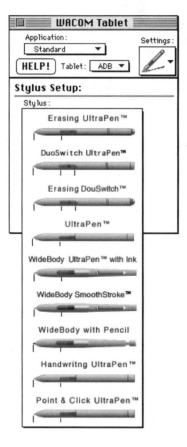

Figure 8-31: Wacom boasts the largest pressure-sensitive stylus library of any tablet vendor. You can customize the settings for your particular stylus from a pop-up menu in the central control panel.

Color Plate 4-1

This little warlock shows off the differences between the four different JPEG compression settings, from maximum quality, minimum compression (upper left) to minimum quality, maximum compression (lower right). Inspect the enlarged eye and sharpened staff for subtle erosions in detail.

Maximum   116K   High   66K

Medium   50K   Low   46K

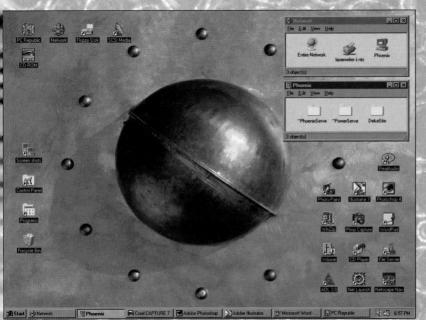

Color Plate 4-2

My personal 1024 × 768-pixel background pattern image saved as a BMP file.

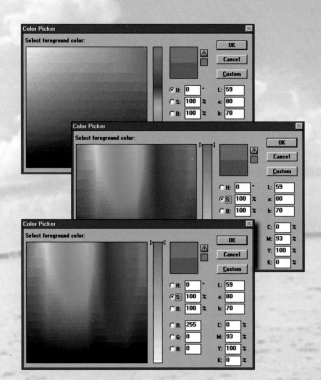

Color Plate 5-1
The colors inside the field and slider in the Color Picker dialog box change to reflect the selection of the H (Hue), S (Saturation), and B (Brightness) radio buttons.

Color Plate 6-1
This colorful image is the basis for an awful lot of channel discussions in Chapter 6. Right about now, I'm wishing I was in that inner tube instead of editing it.

Color Plate 6-2
One of the wonderful things about the Lab mode is that it allows you to edit the colors in an image independently of the brightness values. Here I've inverted and boosted the contrast of the a and b color channels to produce some startling effects, all without harming a smidgen of detail.

Invert a

Auto Levels b

Invert and Auto Levels a and b

Color Plate 6-3
You can wreak some pretty interesting havoc on the colors in an image by copying the image from one channel and pasting it into another, or by swapping the contents of two color channels.

Replace red with blue

Replace green with red

Replace blue with red

Swap red and blue

Swap red and green

Swap green and blue

Color Plate 7-1
I converted this grayscale piece by Seattle-based artist Mark Collen to a quadtone using the colors navy blue, rose, teal, and dull orange. All colors were defined and printed using CMYK pigments.

Color Plate 8-1
Starting with an image of typical saturation (upper left), I applied the sponge tool set to Desaturate to the inside of the pepper and the corn in the background (upper right). I then repeated the effect twice more to make the areas almost gray (lower right). Returning to the original image, I then selected the Saturate option and again scrubbed inside the pepper and in the corn to boost the colors (lower left).

Color Plate 8-2
To create this image, I traced an image from the PhotoDisc library using the paintbrush tool and a flat brush shape. Although Photoshop offers automated filters that you can use to create similar effects, nothing is so versatile and precise as a simple paintbrush.

Color Plate 8-3
If you've picked up a previous edition of this book, you've seen this image before. But I keep it in because it's the first thing I ever drew with a pressure-sensitive tablet. Within an hour of plugging a Wacom SD-510 tablet into my computer, I rendered this image. If I can do it, so can you.

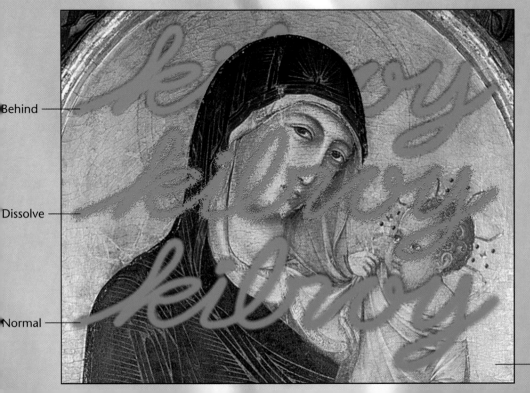

Behind

Dissolve

Normal

Color Plate 8-4
Here I've gone and desecrated a pivotal work of European iconography by scribbling the name of America's patron saint of graffiti. Reading up from the bottom, the Normal brush mode applies paint normally. The Dissolve mode scattered pixels along the fuzzy edge of the brushstroke. And the Behind mode paints behind the current layer, in this case, a layer containing the Madonna's head.

A perfectly good piece of art ruined

Multiply

Screen

Overlay

Soft Light

Hard Light

Color Dodge

Color Burn

Color Plate 8-5
Here I've painted green lines using the seven brush modes in the middle of the Options palette pop-up menu. Multiply darkens uniformly and Screen lightens uniformly. (In fact, Multiply and Screen are direct opposites.) Overlay, Soft Light, and Hard Light all multiply the darkest pixels and screen the lightest ones to produce different contrast-enhancing effects. New to Photoshop 4, Color Dodge and Color Burn work like dodge and burn tools that also add color to an image.

Color Plate 8-6
Here are the effects of the final eight entries in Photoshop 4's enormous arsenal of brush modes. Darken and Lighten are opposites, Difference and Exclusion are very closely related, and the last four apply different bits and pieces of the HSL color model. Because many of these modes produce slight effects — particularly the Saturation and Luminosity modes — I have added dark halos around the brushstrokes to offset them slightly from the background. Naturally, the halos feel right at home.

Darken

Lighten

Difference

Exclusion

Hue

Saturation

Color

Luminosity

Color Plate 9-1

Here I've used the paint bucket to colorize two oranges (top) with bright blue. First, I set the Tolerance value in the Paint Bucket Options palette to 120 and changed the brush mode to Color. Then I clicked at each of the four points marked with blue arrows (middle). After that, I changed the foreground color to green and clicked just once in the lower right corner of the image (marked with the green arrow). Unfortunately, the paint bucket isn't very precise, so I had to touch up the dimples and edges with the paintbrush, also set to the Color mode. Finally, I used the airbrush — set to the Color Burn mode — to deepen some of the blue shadows inside the fruit.

Noise × 3

Blast and Motion Blur

Color Plate 9-2

The results of filtering the three horizontal gradations by applying the Add Noise filter three times in a row (top) and then blasting the gradations with the Wind filter and applying the Motion Blur filter (bottom).

Color Plate 9-3
I started by designing a three-color gradient that fades twice into transparen as demonstrated by the checkerboard background (left). Such a gradation is meant to be blended with image, such as the piano keys (middle). So I selected the Overlay brush mode from the Gradient Tool Options palette and tickled my gradation across the ivories (right).

Color Plate 11-1
If you attempt to select this whimsical sign with the magic wand tool, you end up selecting odd little fragments of the yellow areas one at a time. However, by switching to the blue channel — in which both sign and Sasquatch appear black against a relatively light background — you can easily select both portions of the sign in two easy clicks. I then inverted the sign (right) by pressing Ctrl+I. The effect isn't perfect, but it's as good as it gets with the magic wand.

Color Plate 12-1

Two selections (top left and right) followed by their equivalent masks (middle). Here the mask is represented as a transparent red overlay, permitting you to see mask and image at the same time. Red-tinted areas are masked, representing deselected areas in the image; untinted areas are unmasked, and represent selected areas. In the final examples, I inverted the selected areas to demonstrate the full extent of the selection outlines.

Color Plate 12-2

In the left example, I drew a black-to-white gradation in the quick mask mode, extending from the base of the top row of pillars to the top of the flagpole. Then I applied the Add Noise filter to jumble up the pixels a little. Finally, I exited the quick mask mode to convert the mask to a selection, and Ctrl+ dragged the Capitol into the lava image (right).

Color Plate 12-3

Which twin has the Toni? With the help of a very precise mask, I dragged this girl in from her old environment into this new one. But despite the mask's accuracy, I managed to bring in some blue from her prior background (left). To fix this problem, I brushed in some color from the new background, and erased a few of the overly dark hairs (right).

Color Plate 13-1

After filling my layered drop shadow with a reddish orange (top), I chose the Multiply option from the blend mode pop-up menu in the Layers palette to mix the drop shadow with the underlying image (middle). Then I changed the Opacity setting to 70 percent (bottom) to create the finished colored drop shadow.

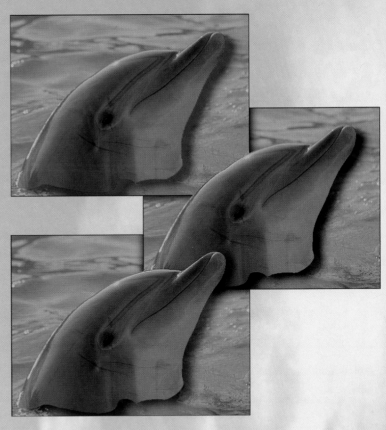

Color Plate 13-2

The popular cartoon character Neutron Mammal — what, you've never heard of Neutron Mammal? — is the result of applying both the haloing and spotlighting effects described in Chapter 13 and then setting the whole thing against an inverted background.

Color Plate 13-3

Here I've used a clipping group to fill some characters of type with a water pattern. I started by adding a couple of pool images that I shot with a digital camera to a layer above my text — which is itself on an independent layer — as demonstrated on the left. Then I just Alt+clicked on the horizontal line between the two layers in the Layers palette. Photoshop automatically assigned the type layer's transparency mask to the pool layer, filling the letters.

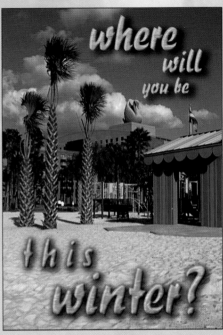

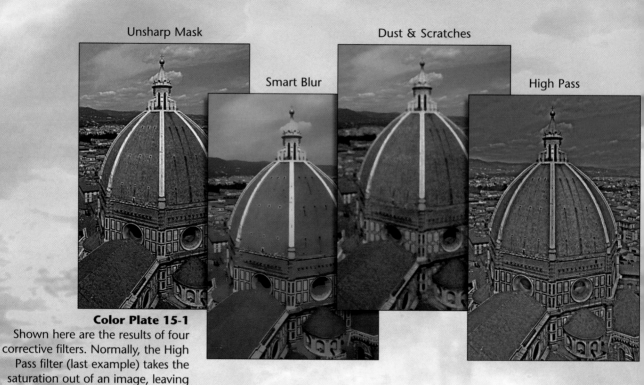

Unsharp Mask

Dust & Scratches

Smart Blur

High Pass

Color Plate 15-1
Shown here are the results of four corrective filters. Normally, the High Pass filter (last example) takes the saturation out of an image, leaving many areas gray. To restore the colors, I chose Filter ➪ Fade High Pass (Ctrl+Shift+F) and selected Luminosity from the Mode pop-up menu in the Fade dialog box.

Color Plate 15-2
Here are the effects of four destructive filters from the Filter ➪ Distort, Pixelate, Render, and Stylize submenus. Every one of these filters has a dramatic impact on the color and detail of an image. From a pixel's perspective, destructive filters are dynamite, so use with care and moderation.

ZigZag

Mezzotint

Difference
Clouds

Find Edges

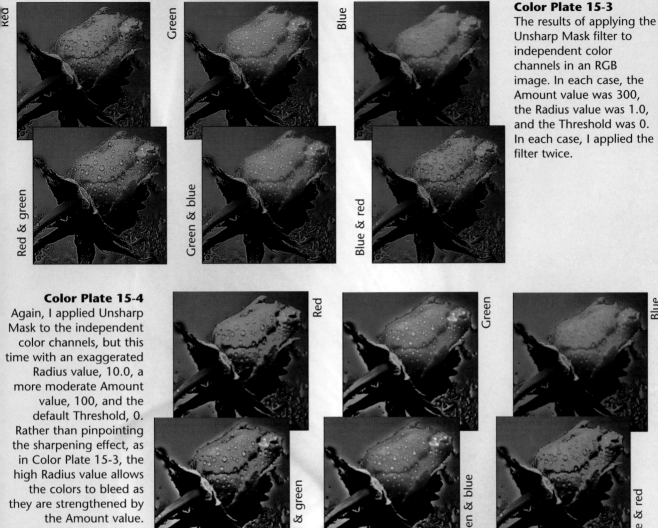

Color Plate 15-3
The results of applying the Unsharp Mask filter to independent color channels in an RGB image. In each case, the Amount value was 300, the Radius value was 1.0, and the Threshold was 0. In each case, I applied the filter twice.

Color Plate 15-4
Again, I applied Unsharp Mask to the independent color channels, but this time with an exaggerated Radius value, 10.0, a more moderate Amount value, 100, and the default Threshold, 0. Rather than pinpointing the sharpening effect, as in Color Plate 15-3, the high Radius value allows the colors to bleed as they are strengthened by the Amount value.

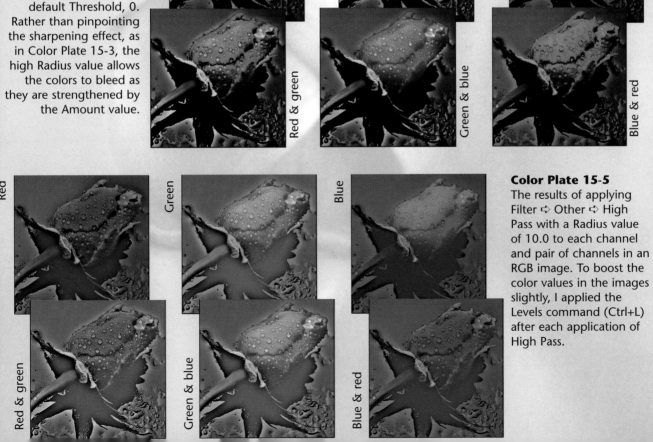

Color Plate 15-5
The results of applying Filter ⇨ Other ⇨ High Pass with a Radius value of 10.0 to each channel and pair of channels in an RGB image. To boost the color values in the images slightly, I applied the Levels command (Ctrl+L) after each application of High Pass.

Color Plate 15-6
After applying the Gaussian Blur filter with a Radius of 8.0, I used the Fade Gaussian Blur command to mix the filtered image with the original. The labels tell the blend mode and Opacity setting applied to each image.

Normal, 60%   Luminosity, 50%

Darken, 80%   Lighten, 80%

Color Plate 15-7
An image scanned from an old issue of *Macworld* magazine shown as it appears in the normal RGB mode (top right) and when each channel is viewed separately (top left). The middle images show the affects of the Dust & Scratches filter set to a Radius of 2 and a Threshold of 20. The bottom images show how the channels look after suppressing the moiré patterns with the Gaussian Blur, Median, and Unsharp Mask filters.

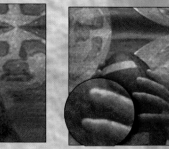
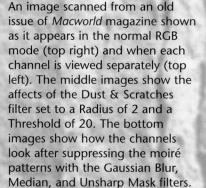

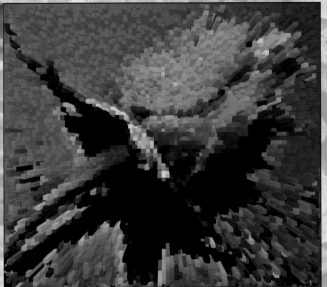

Color Plate 16-1
The result of applying the Extrude filter to the lower left rose from Color Plate 15-4. If you select the Blocks and Solid Front Faces options, the filter transforms the image into mosaic tiles and shoves the tiles out at you in 3-D space.

Color Plate 16-2
Here I applied Filter ➪ Sketch ➪ Charcoal with the foreground color set to dark green and the background color light blue (as demonstrated in the upper left inset). Then I used the Fade Charcoal command to change the blend mode to Overlay.

Color Plate 16-3
I applied the Mezzotint filter set to the Long Strokes effect in each of the RGB, Lab, and CMYK color modes (top row). After each application of the filter, I pressed Ctrl+Shift+F and faded the filtered image into the original using the Overlay mode and an Opacity setting of 40 percent (bottom row).

RGB   Lab   CMYK

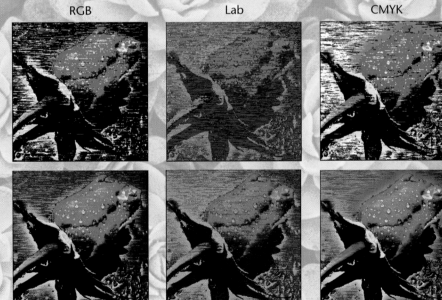

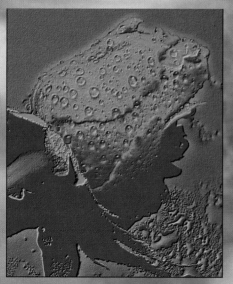

Color Plate 16-4

In both examples, I applied the Emboss filter armed with an Angle of 135 degrees, a Height value of 2, and an Amount of 300 percent. To create the left image, I used the Fade command to mix embossed and original images together using the Luminosity blend mode and an Opacity setting of 80 percent. To get the psychedelic effect on right, I selected the Difference mode and reduced the Opacity value to 40 percent.

Color Plate 16-5

After selecting an image from the PhotoDisc library (top left), I layered the image, blurred it, applied the Find Edges filter, and darkened it with the Levels command (top middle). I then composited the image using the Overlay mode and an Opacity setting of 80 percent (top right). The bottom row shows the results of applying three effects filters set to the Luminosity mode and 80 percent Opacity settings.

Original

Blur and Find Edges

Overlay, 80%

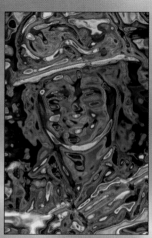

Bas Relief

Plastic Wrap

Chrome

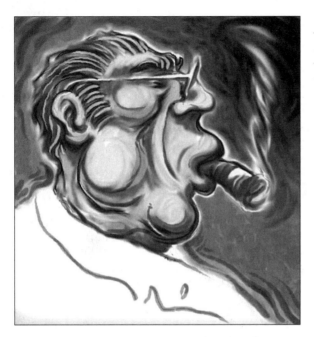

Figure 8-32: Although I painted this caricature years ago, it still demonstrates the range of artistic freedom provided by a pressure-sensitive tablet.

Undoing pressure-sensitive lines

Pressure-sensitive lines are hard to undo (especially when you have only one level of undo at your disposal, as in Photoshop). Because a Wacom or other stylus is so sensitive to gradual pressure, you can unwittingly let up and repress the stylus during what you think is a single drag. If, after doing so, you decide you don't like the line and choose Edit ➪ Undo, Photoshop deletes only the last portion of the line, because it detected a release midway. As a result, you're stuck with half a line you don't want or, worse, which visually mars your image.

Problems are even more likely to occur if you use a stylus with a side switch, as all of the modern ones do. Accidentally pressing your thumb or forefinger against the switch as you drag is easy. If you have the switch set to some separate operation, such as double-clicking, you interrupt your line. This not only creates an obvious break, but it also makes the error impossible to undo.

Tip To prepare for this eventuality — and believe me, it will happen — make sure to save your image at key points when you're content with its appearance. Or better yet, paint on a separate layer in your image (as discussed in Chapter 13). Then, if you are stuck with half a line, you can remove the line by Alt+dragging with the eraser tool- or by simply erasing within the layer — as discussed in the "Selectively Undoing Changes" section of Chapter 10.

Pressure-sensitive options

All paint and edit tools, as well as the eraser and rubber stamp, provide three check boxes for controlling Photoshop's reaction to stylus pressure (see Figure 8-33). Available from the Options palette only when a pressure-sensitive tablet is hooked up to your computer, these options include the following:

✦ **Size:** If you select the Size check box, Photoshop varies the thickness of the line. The more pressure you apply, the thicker the line. The Size check box is selected by default. Figure 8-34 shows three paintbrush lines drawn with the Size option selected. I drew the first line using a hard brush, the second with a soft brush, and the third with a hard brush and with the Wet Edges check box selected.

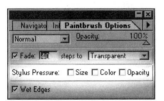

Figure 8-33: Photoshop provides three check boxes for interpreting the signals from a pressure-sensitive tablet.

✦ **Color:** Select this option to create custom gradient lines. Full pressure paints in the foreground color, slight pressure paints in the background color, medium pressure paints a mix of the two.

✦ **Opacity:** This option paints an opaque coat of foreground color at full pressure that dwindles to transparency at slight pressure.

Because Photoshop presents its pressure options as check boxes, you can select more than one option at a time. For example, you can select both Size and Color to instruct Photoshop to change both the thickness and color of a line as you bear down or lift up on the stylus.

Brush Modes

When a painting or editing tool is active, the pop-up menu in the Options palettes provides access to Photoshop's brush modes, which control how the colors applied by the tools affect existing colors in the image. Figure 8-35 shows which brush modes are available when you select various tools.

Cross Reference

With the exception of the specialized brush modes provided for the dodge, burn, and sponge tools, the brush modes and the blend modes described in Chapter 19 are varieties of the same animal. Read this section to get a brief glimpse of brush modes; read Chapter 19 for a more detailed account that should appeal to brush-mode aficionados.

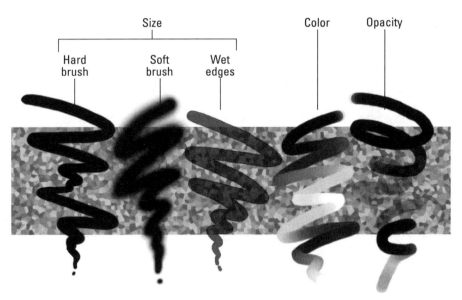

Figure 8-34: The effects of the Size, Color, and Opacity options on lines drawn with the paintbrush tool and a pressure-sensitive tablet

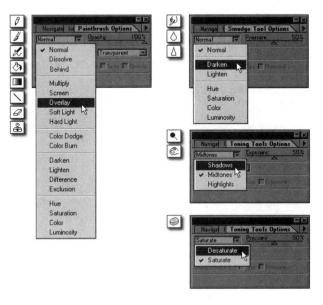

Figure 8-35: The number of options in the brush modes pop-up menu varies depending on whether you select a paint tool (left), an edit tool (top right), the dodge or burn tool (middle right), or the sponge tool (bottom right).

The 18 paint tool modes

Photoshop 4 provides a whopping 18 brush modes when you're using the pencil, paintbrush, airbrush, or any of the other tools shown along the left side of Figure 8-35. To show you what these brush modes look like when applied to an image, Color Plates 8-4, 8-5, and 8-6 illustrate all 18. In each case, I used the paintbrush tool to apply a bit of green graffiti to a work of fourteenth-century religious iconography. Who among us hasn't been tempted with the primal urge to paint "Kilroy" on something old and priceless? Now, thanks to the miracle of digital imagery, you need resist this temptation no longer.

The 18 standard brush modes work as follows:

✦ **Normal:** Choose this mode to paint or edit an image normally. A paint tool coats the image with the foreground color, and an edit tool manipulates the existing colors in an image according to the setting of the Opacity or Pressure slider bar.

✦ **Dissolve:** This mode and the six that follow are not applicable to the edit tools (though I wonder why — the Dissolve mode would be especially useful with the smudge tool). Dissolve scatters colors along the edge of a brushstroke randomly throughout the course of your drag. The Dissolve mode produces the most pronounced effects when used with soft brushes and the airbrush tool.

✦ **Behind:** This one is applicable exclusively to layers with transparent backgrounds. When Behind is selected, the paint tool applies color behind the image on the active layer, showing through only in the transparent and translucent areas. In Color Plate 8-4, for example, I painted over the Madonna's head, and yet the brushstroke appears behind her head because she is positioned on an independent layer. When you're working on an image without layers or on the background layer of a multilayered image, the Behind mode is dimmed.

✦ **Multiply:** The Multiply mode combines the foreground color with an existing color in an image to create a third color, darker than the other two. Using the multiply analogy, red times white is red, red times yellow is orange, red times green is brown, red times blue is violet, and so on. As discussed in Chapter 5, this is subtractive (CMYK) color theory at work. The effect is almost exactly like drawing with felt-tipped markers, except the colors don't bleed. Check out the first Kilroy in Color Plate 8-5 to see the Multiply mode in action.

Note

The multiply mode has no effect on the paintbrush when it's set to Wet Edges; the Wet Edges brush already multiplies.

✦ **Screen:** The inverse of the Multiply mode, Screen combines the foreground color with each colored pixel you paint over to create a third color, lighter than the other two. Red on white is white, red on yellow is off-white, red on green is yellow, and red on blue is pink. The Screen mode uses additive (RGB) color theory. If the effect has a traditional counterpart, it's like some impossibly bright, radioactive Uranium-238 highlighter, hitherto used only by G-Men to mark the pants' cuffs of Communist sympathizers.

Because the Wet Edges option always multiplies, combining it with the Screen mode must render the brush invisible. If the paintbrush tool isn't working, this could be your problem.

✦ **Overlay:** Overlay, Soft Light, and Hard Light are cousins. Each mode multiplies the dark pixels in an image and screens the light pixels as you lay down color with a paint tool. But although related, the three modes are not variations on an identical theme. In other words, you can't emulate the Soft Light mode by simply applying the Hard Light mode at 70 percent or some similar opacity.

Of the three modes, Overlay is the kindest. Overlay always enhances contrast and boosts the saturation of colors in an image. In fact, Overlay works rather like a colored version of the sponge tool set to Saturate. It mixes the colors in the image with the foreground color to come up with a vivid blend that is almost always visually pleasing. Overlay may be the most interesting and downright useful brush mode of the bunch.

✦ **Soft Light:** This mode applies a subtle glazing of color to an image. In fact, Soft Light is remarkably similar to painting a diluted acrylic wash to a canvas. Soft Light never completely covers the underlying detail — even black or white applied at 100 percent Opacity does no more than darken or lighten the image — but it does slightly diminish contrast.

✦ **Hard Light:** This mode might better be named *Obfuscate*. It's as if you were applying a thicker, more opaque wash to the image. You might think of Hard Light as Normal with a whisper of underlying detail mixed in.

For examples of Overlay, Soft Light, and Hard Light, check out the middle brushstrokes in Color Plate 8-5.

✦ **Color Dodge:** New to Photoshop 4, this brush mode lightens the pixels in an image according to the lightness or darkness of the foreground color. Color Dodge produces a harsher, chalkier effect than the Screen mode and is designed to act like a dodge tool that also adds color. At 100 percent Opacity, even painting with black has a lightening effect.

✦ **Color Burn:** If Color Dodge is like drawing with chalk, Color Burn is like drawing with coal. It darkens pixels according to the lightness or darkness of the foreground color and is designed to simulate a colored version of the burn tool. For examples of Color Dodge and Color Burn, look to the last two Kilroys in Color Plate 8-5.

✦ **Darken:** Ah, back to the old familiars. If you choose the Darken mode, Photoshop applies a new color to a pixel only if that color is darker than the present color of the pixel. Otherwise, the pixel is left unchanged. The mode works on a channel-by-channel basis, so it might change a pixel in the green channel, for example, without changing the pixel in the red or blue channel. I used this mode to create the first brushstroke of Color Plate 8-6.

✦ **Lighten:** The opposite of the previous mode, Lighten ensures that Photoshop applies a new color to a pixel only if the color is lighter than the present color of the pixel. Otherwise, the pixel is left unchanged. On or off — either you see the color or you don't.

✦ **Difference:** When a paint tool is set to the Difference mode, Photoshop subtracts the brightness value of the foreground color from the brightness value of the pixels in the image. If the result is a negative number, Photoshop simply makes it positive. The result of this complex-sounding operation is an inverted effect. Black has no effect on an image; white inverts it completely. Colors in between create psychedelic effects. In the third example of Color Plate 8-6, for example, the Difference mode inverts the green paint to create a red brushstroke.

Tip

Because the Difference mode inverts an image, it results in an outline around the brushstroke. You can make this outline thicker by using a softer brush shape. For a really trippy effect, select the paintbrush tool, turn on Wet Edges, and apply the Difference mode with a soft brush shape.

✦ **Exclusion:** Recently, I e-mailed Mark Hamburg, lead programmer for Photoshop 4 about this new brush mode. He kindly explained, and I quote, "Exclusion applies a probabilistic, fuzzy-set-theoretic, symmetric difference to each channel." Don't think about it too long — your frontal lobe will turn to boiled squash. When Mark remembered he was communicating with a lowerlife form, he explained Exclusion inverts an image in much the same way as Difference, except colors in the middle of the spectrum mix to form medium gray. Exclusion typically results in high-contrast effects with less color saturation than Difference. My suggestion is you try the Difference mode first. If you're looking for something a little different, press Ctrl+Z and try Exclusion instead. (Both Difference and Exclusion brushstrokes appear in Color Plate 8-6.)

✦ **Hue:** Understanding the next few modes requires a color theory recap. Remember how the HSL color model calls for three color channels? One is for hue, the value that explains the colors in an image; the second is for saturation, which represents the intensity of the colors; and the third is for luminosity, which explains the lightness and darkness of colors. If you choose the Hue brush mode, therefore, Photoshop applies the hue from the foreground color without changing any saturation or luminosity values in the existing image.

None of the HSL brush modes — Hue, Saturation, Color, or Luminosity — is available when painting within grayscale images.

✦ **Saturation:** If you choose this mode, Photoshop changes the intensity of the colors in an image without changing the colors themselves or the lightness and darkness of individual pixels. In Color Plate 8-6, Saturation has the effect of breathing new life into those ancient egg-tempura colors.

✦ **Color:** This mode might be more appropriately titled *Hue and Saturation*. Color enables you to change the colors in an image and the intensity of those colors without changing the lightness and darkness of individual pixels.

Tip

The Color mode is most often used to colorize grayscale photographs. Open a grayscale image and then choose Image ➪ Mode ➪ RGB Color to convert the image to the RGB mode. Then select the colors you want to use and start painting. The Color mode ensures the details in the image remain completely intact.

✦ **Luminosity:** The opposite of the Color mode, Luminosity changes the lightness and darkness of pixels, but leaves the hue and saturation values unaffected. Frankly, this mode is rarely useful. But its counterpart — the Luminosity blend mode — is exceptionally useful when applied to layers. Read Chapter 19 to find out more.

The three dodge and burn modes

Phew, that takes care of the brush modes available to the paint tools, the smudge tool, and the two focus tools. I already explained the Desaturate and Saturate modes available to the sponge tool (in the "Mopping up with the sponge tool" section of this chapter). That leaves us with the three brush modes available to the dodge and burn tools:

✦ **Shadows:** Along with the Midtones and Highlights modes (described next), Shadows is unique to the dodge and burn tools. When you select this mode, the dodge and burn tools affect dark pixels in an image more dramatically than they affect light pixels and shades in between.

✦ **Midtones:** Select this mode to apply the dodge or burn tools equally to all but the very lightest or darkest pixels in an image.

✦ **Highlights:** When you select this option, the dodge and burn tools affect light pixels in an image more dramatically than they affect dark pixels and shades in between.

Selecting Shadows when using the dodge tool or selecting Highlights when using the burn tool has an equalizing effect on an image. Figure 8-36 shows how using either of these functions and setting the Exposure slider bar to 100 percent lightens or darkens pixels in an image to nearly identical brightness values.

Dodge

Burn

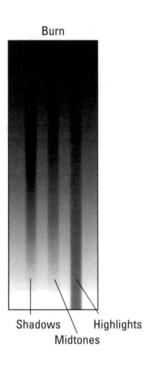

Shadows   Highlights
Midtones

Shadows   Highlights
Midtones

Figure 8-36: The dodge and burn tool applied at 100 percent Exposure settings subject to each of the three applicable brush modes.

Filling and Stroking

Filling Portions of an Image

No explanation of filling and stroking would be complete
without a definition, so here goes: To *fill* a selection or layer
is to put color inside it; to *stroke* a selection or layer is to put
color around it. Simple stuff, actually. Many of you already
knew this and are now hot under the collar because you
wasted valuable seconds reading such a flat-out obvious
sentence. And you're getting more steamed because you have
to read sentences like these that add little to your overall
understanding of Photoshop. And this sentence, well, it's
sufficient reason to write the publisher and burst a blood
vessel.

In fact — he said, miraculously veering off the shoulder of
the road and back onto the highway — Photoshop's fill and
stroke functions are so straightforward, you may have long
since dismissed them as wimpy little tools with remarkably
limited potential. But the truth is, you can do a world of stuff
with them. In this chapter, for example, I'll show you how to
fill selections in five different ways using various keyboard
shortcuts, how to create an antique framing effect, how to
make the most of Photoshop 4's new gradient editor, and
how to add an arrowhead to a curving line, all in addition to
the really basic stuff many Photoshop users already know.
Actually, come to think of it, you might even want to read
about the basic stuff on the off chance you missed some
golden nugget of information in your Photoshopic journeys
thus far.

Filling an Area with Color

You can fill an area of an image with color in four ways:

✦ **The paint bucket tool:** You can apply the foreground color or a repeating pattern to areas of related color in an image by clicking in the Image window with the paint bucket tool (known in some circles as the fill tool). For example, if you want to turn all midnight blue pixels in an image into red pixels, set the foreground color to red and then click one of the blue pixels.

✦ **The Fill command:** Select the portion of the image you want to color and then fill the entire selection with the foreground color or a repeating pattern by choosing Edit ➪ Fill.

Tip

To choose the Fill command without so much as moving the mouse, press Shift+Backspace.

✦ **Delete and Backspace key techniques:** After selecting part of the single layer image — or part of the Background layer — you can fill the selection with the background color by pressing the Delete key. On any other layer, press Ctrl+Delete or Ctrl+Backspace (new to Photoshop 4). To fill the selection with the foreground color, press Alt+Delete or Alt+Backspace.

✦ **The gradient tool:** Drag across the image with the gradient tool to fill it with a multicolor gradation. Revamped in Photoshop 4, the gradient tool is now as powerful as the ones included with high-end drawing programs Illustrator and FreeHand. The gradient tool is still so special and wide ranging in its capabilities, in fact, I devote several pages to the topic in the section "Applying Gradient Fills" later in this chapter.

The following sections discuss each of these options in-depth.

The paint bucket tool

Unlike remedial paint bucket tools in other painting programs, which apply paint exclusively within outlined areas or areas of solid color, the Photoshop paint bucket tool offers several useful adjustment options. To explore them, double-click the paint bucket icon in the Toolbox to display the Paint Bucket Options palette, shown in Figure 9-1. (Or you can press the K key to select the paint bucket tool and then press Enter to display the Options palette.)

Figure 9-1: The Paint Bucket Options palette governs the performance of the paint bucket tool.

The brush mode's pop-up menu and the Opacity slider bar work like their counterparts in the Paintbrush Options palette, which I covered at length in Chapter 8. But, in case you need a recap, here's how these and other options work, in the order they appear in the palette:

✦ **Brush modes:** Select an option from the brush mode's pop-up menu to specify how and when color is applied. For example, if you select Darken, the paint bucket tool affects a pixel in the image only if the foreground color is darker than that pixel. If you select Color, the paint bucket colorizes the image without changing the brightness value of the pixels.

Tip

In Color Plate 9-1, for example, I used the Color mode to change a few oranges to blue and the background to green, all by clicking at five different spots with the paint bucket tool. I then touched up the stray pixels the paint bucket didn't catch with the paintbrush and airbrush tools.

✦ **Opacity:** Drag the Opacity slider or press a number key to change the translucency of a color applied with the paint bucket.

✦ **Tolerance:** You can raise or lower the Tolerance value to increase or decrease the number of pixels affected by the paint bucket tool. The Tolerance value represents a range in brightness values, as measured from the pixel on which you click with the paint bucket.

Immediately after you click a pixel, Photoshop reads the brightness value of that pixel from each color channel. Next, the program calculates a color range based on the Tolerance value — which can vary from 0 to 255. The program adds the Tolerance to the brightness value of the pixel on which you clicked to determine the top of the range, and subtracts the Tolerance from the pixel's brightness value to determine the bottom of the range. For example, if the pixel's brightness value is 100 and the Tolerance value is 32, the top of the range is 132, and the bottom is 68.

After establishing a Tolerance range, Photoshop applies the foreground color to any pixel that both falls inside the range and touches some other affected pixel. (This way, the paint bucket fills an isolated area, rather than seeping out into every similarly colored pixel in the image.)

Figure 9-2 shows the result of clicking the same pixel three separate times, each time using a different Tolerance value. In Color Plate 9-1, I raised the Tolerance to 120. But even with this high setting, I had to click several times to recolor all the nooks and crannies of the oranges. The moral is, don't get too hung up on getting the Tolerance exactly right — no matter how you paint it, the bucket is not a precise tool.

Paint bucket cursor

Figure 9-2: The results of applying the paint bucket tool to the exact pixel after setting the Tolerance value to 16 (top), 32 (middle), and 64 (bottom). In each case, the foreground color is light gray.

✦ **Anti-aliased:** Select this option to soften the effect of the paint bucket tool. As demonstrated in the left-hand example of Figure 9-3, Photoshop creates a border of translucent color between the filled pixels and their unaffected neighbors. If you don't want to soften the transition, turn off the Anti-aliased check box. Photoshop then fills only those pixels that fall inside the Tolerance range, as demonstrated in the right example of the figure.

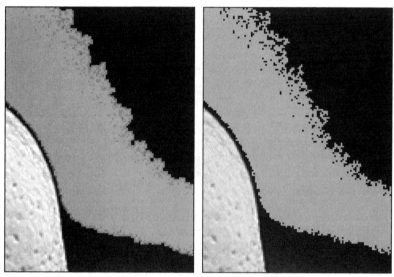

Figure 9-3: The results of turning on (left) and off (right) the Anti-aliased check box prior to using the paint bucket tool. It all depends on whether you want cottage cheese or little spiky coral edges.

✦ **Contents:** In this pop-up menu, you can choose whether you want to apply the foreground color or a repeating pattern created using Edit ➪ Define Pattern. The Define Pattern command is covered in the "Applying Repeating Patterns" section of Chapter 10.

✦ **Sample Merged:** Select this option to make the paint bucket see beyond the current layer. When the option is selected, the tool takes all visible layers into account when calculating the area to fill. Mind you, it only fills the active layer, but the way it fills an area is dictated by all layers.

For an example of Sample Merged, look no further than Figure 9-4. The dog sits on one layer and the fire hydrant rests on another layer directly below it. If I were to click the fire hydrant when the dog layer was active and the Sample Merged check box was turned off, I'd fill everything around the dog. The paint bucket couldn't see the hydrant; all the paint bucket could see would be the transparent area of the dog layer, so it would try to fill that area. To avoid this, I selected Sample Merged and then clicked the hydrant. With Sample Merged on, the paint bucket could see all layers, so it contained its fill within the hydrant, as in the second example of the figure.

Because the fill and hydrant were on separate layers, I could edit the two independently of each other. I used the airbrush to paint inside and behind the fill alternatively (using the Behind brush mode, discussed in the previous chapter). I painted the teeth and eyes with the paintbrush and used the smudge tool to mix colors around the white fill. (Naturally, I had to turn on the Sample Merged check box inside the Smudge Tool Options palette as well.) As a result, all the bizarre alterations you see in the bottom example of Figure 9-4 were applied to the dog layer. I didn't change a single pixel in the hydrant layer (which is a good thing — in light of my changes, I might like to get that hydrant back).

Tip

To limit the area affected by the paint bucket, select a portion of the image before using the tool. As when using a paint or edit tool, the region outside the selection outline is protected from the paint bucket. To see an interesting application of this, skip ahead to the "Using the paint bucket inside a selection" section later in this chapter.

Cross Reference

When working on a layer, you can, likewise, protect pixels by turning on the Preserve Transparency check box in the Layers palette. For everything you ever wanted to know about layers, read Chapter 13.

Tip

Here's one more paint bucket tip for good measure: You can use the paint bucket to color the empty window area around your image. First, make your Image window larger than your image, so you can see some blank "canvas area" around the image. Now Shift+click with the paint bucket to fill the canvas area with the foreground color. This technique can come in handy if you're creating a presentation for onscreen viewing.

The Fill command

The one problem with the paint bucket tool is its lack of precision. Although undeniably convenient, the effects of the Tolerance value are so difficult to predict, you typically have to click with the tool, choose Edit ⇨ Undo when you don't like the result, adjust the Tolerance value, and reclick with the tool several times more before you fill the image as desired. For my part, I rarely use the paint bucket for any purpose other than filling same-colored areas. On my machine, the Tolerance option is nearly always set to 0 and Anti-alias is generally off, which puts me right back in the all-the-subtlety-of-dumping-paint-out-of-a-bucket camp.

Figure 9-4: Although dog and hydrant are on separate layers (top), I can mix them together with Sample Merged. This option enables me to fill an area of the hydrant (middle), even though the dog layer is active. Then I paint in front of and behind the fill without harming the hydrant (bottom).

A better option is to select the area you want to fill and choose Edit ➪ Fill or press Shift+Backspace. In this way, you can define the exact area of the image you want to color using the entire range of Photoshop's selection tools, which are so extensive they consume all four chapters in Part IV. For example, instead of putting your faith in the paint bucket tool's Anti-aliased option, you can draw a selection outline that features hard edges in one area, anti-aliased edges elsewhere, and downright blurry edges in between.

When you choose the Fill command (or press Shift+F5), Photoshop displays the Fill dialog box shown in Figure 9-5. In this dialog box, you can apply a translucent color or pattern by entering a value into the Opacity option box. You can also choose a brush mode option from the Mode pop-up menu. In addition to its inherent precision, the Fill command maintains all the functionality of the paint bucket tool — and then some.

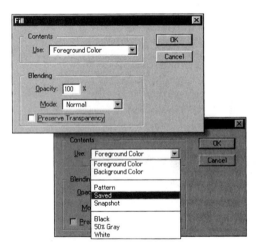

Figure 9-5: The Fill dialog box combines the Opacity and brush mode options from the Paint Bucket Options palette with an expanded collection of Contents options.

If you display the Contents pop-up menu, as shown in the lower example in Figure 9-5, you'll see a collection of things you can use to fill the selected area. Foreground Color and Pattern perform the same functions they do with the paint bucket tool. You can also fill a selection with the Background Color and such monochrome options as Black, White, and 50 percent Gray. Black and White are useful if the foreground and background colors have been changed from their defaults; 50 percent Gray enables you to access the absolute medium color without having to mess around with the Color palette. Saved and Snapshot enable you to revert the selected area to a previous appearance, as I discuss at length in the "Reverting selected areas" section of Chapter 10.

The Preserve Transparency check box works exactly like the identically named option in the Layers palette (discussed in Chapter 13). When the option is turned on, you can't fill the transparent pixels in the active layer. When Preserve Transparency is turned off, you can fill the selection outline uniformly. (The option is dimmed when you're working on the background layer or when the Preserve Transparency check box in the Layers palette is turned on already.)

Delete-key and Backspace-key techniques

Of all the fill techniques, using the Delete and Backspace keys is, by far, the most convenient and, in most respects, every bit as capable as the others. The keys' only failings are they can neither fill a selection with a repeating pattern nor revert a selection to its last saved appearance. But with the exception of those two items, you can rely on the Delete and Backspace keys for the overwhelming majority of your fill needs.

Here's how to get a ton of functionality from these two keys:

✦ **Background color, method 1:** To fill a selection on the background layer with solid background color, press Delete. The selection outline remains intact.

✦ **Background color, method 2:** The problem with pressing Delete is it's unreliable. If the selection is floating, as I explain in Chapter 11, the Delete key actually deletes it. Delete also deletes pixels on a layer. So there's no time like the present to get into a new habit — press Ctrl+Delete or Ctrl+Backspace instead. Either key combination fills the selection with the background color, no matter where it is.

✦ **Foreground color:** To fill a selection with solid foreground color, press Alt+Delete or Alt+Backspace. You can fill floating and nonfloating selections alike by pressing Alt+Delete or Alt+Backspace.

✦ **Black or white:** To fill an area with black, press D to get the default foreground and background colors and then press Alt+Delete or Alt+Backspace. To fill it with white, press D for defaults and then Ctrl+Delete or Ctrl+Backspace.

✦ **Preserve transparency:** Photoshop 4 adds two additional key tricks that will make more sense when you read Chapter 13. (Don't worry, I'll repeat the tricks then.) You can fill only the opaque pixels in a layer — whether or not Preserve Transparency is turned on — by pressing Shift. Press Shift+Alt+Delete or Shift+Alt+Backspace to fill a selection with the foreground color while preserving transparency. Press Ctrl+Shift+Delete or Ctrl+Shift+Backspace to fill the opaque pixels with the background color. This is a great technique for drop shadows, as I explain in Chapter 13.

Using the paint bucket inside a selection

So far, I've come up with two astounding generalizations: The paint bucket tool is mostly useless, and you can fill anything with the Delete and Backspace keys. Well, just to prove you shouldn't believe everything I say — some might even suggest you dismiss everything I say — the following steps explain how to create an effect you can perform only with the paint bucket tool. Doubtless, it's the only such example you'll ever discover using Photoshop — after all, the paint bucket is mostly useless and you can fill anything with the Delete and Backspace keys — but I'm man enough to eat my rules this once.

The steps explain how to create an antique photographic frame effect like the one shown in Figure 9-6.

Steps: Creating an Antique Photographic Frame

1. **Use the rectangular marquee tool to select the portion of the image you want to frame.** Make certain the image extends at least 20 pixels outside the boundaries of the selection outline. And be sure to use a photo — this effect won't look right against a plain white background.

2. **Choose Select ⇨ Feather (Ctrl+Shift+D).** Then specify a Radius value somewhere in the neighborhood of 6 to 12 pixels. I've found these values work for nearly any resolution of image. (If you enter too high a value, the color you'll add in a moment with the paint bucket will run out into the image.)

3. **Choose Select ⇨ Inverse (Ctrl+Shift+I).** This exchanges the selected and deselected portions of the image.

4. **Press the D key to make certain the background color is white.** Then press Ctrl+Delete or Ctrl+Backspace to fill the selected area with the background color.

5. **Select the paint bucket tool and press Enter to display the Paint Bucket Options palette.** Enter 20 to 30 in the Tolerance option box and turn on the Anti-aliased check box. (You can also experiment with turning off this option.)

6. **Click inside the feathered selection to fill it with black.** The result is an image fading into white and then into black, like the edges of a worn slide or photograph, as shown in Figure 9-6.

Figure 9-6: I created this antique frame effect by filling a feathered selection with the paint bucket tool.

Figure 9-7 shows a variation on this effect you can create using the Dissolve brush mode. Rather than setting the Tolerance value to 20, raise it to around 60. Then select the Dissolve option from the brush mode's pop-up menu in the Paint Bucket Options palette. When you click inside the feathered selection with the paint bucket tool, you create a frame of random pixels, as illustrated in the figure.

Figure 9-7: Select Dissolve from the Brushes palette pop-up menu to achieve a speckled frame effect.

Applying Gradient Fills

In the previous edition of this book — the one for Photoshop 3 — I berated the application for its lousy gradient tool. You could create a smooth transition of shades from the foreground color to the background color or cycle through an HSB-style color wheel, but that was about it. This goes to show you how incredibly influential this immense tome is. Oh sure, Adobe has been ignoring my complaints about Illustrator, PageMaker, and half a dozen other products for years. But when I *diss* the gradient tool in Photoshop, it gets fixed. I tell you, I'm crazy with power!

The gradient tool itself gives no hint of its new capabilities. And the Gradient Tool Options palette seems hardly changed at all. But click the Edit button, and your world comes alive. You can now add up to 32 colors to a gradient. You can name gradients and save them to disk for later use. But best of all, you can adjust the transparency of colors so they fade in and out over the course of the gradient fill, mixing in with the original colors in the image. The bad news is you're still limited to linear and radial fills — no conical fills or gradients along a path — but I, for one, can live with these limitations.

Note   If you're used to using gradients in a drawing program — like Illustrator or FreeHand — Photoshop is better. Because Photoshop is a pixel editor, it enables you to blur and mix colors in a gradation if they start *banding* — that is, if you can see a hard edge between one color and the next when you print the image. And Photoshop's gradations will never choke the printer or slow it down, no matter how many colors you add. While each band of color in an object-oriented gradation is expressed as a separate shape — so one gradation can contain hundreds, or even thousands, of objects — gradations in Photoshop are plain old colored pixels, the kind we've been editing for eight and a half chapters.

Using the gradient tool

First, the basics. A *gradation* (also called a *gradient fill*) is a progression of colors that fade gradually into one another, as demonstrated in Figure 9-8. You specify a few key colors in the gradation, and Photoshop automatically generates the hundred or so colors in between to create a smooth transition.

You apply gradations using the gradient tool (just above the eyedropper on the right side of the Toolbox). Unlike the paint bucket tool, which fills areas of similar color according to the Tolerance setting, the gradient tool affects all colors within a selection. If you don't select a portion of your image, Photoshop applies the gradation to the entire layer.

To select the gradient tool, press the G key. To use the tool, drag inside the selection, as shown in the left example of Figure 9-8. The point at which you begin dragging (upper-left corner in the figure) defines the location of the first color in

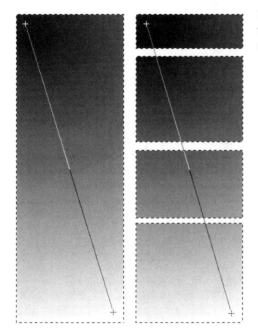

Figure 9-8: Dragging with the gradient tool within a single selection (left) and across multiple selections (right)

the gradation. The point at which you release (lower-right corner) defines the location of the last color. If multiple portions of the image are selected, the gradation fills all selections continuously, as demonstrated by the right example of Figure 9-8.

Gradient tool options

To master the gradient tool, you must fully understand how to modify its performance. Press Enter when the gradient tool is active to display the Gradient Tool Options palette, shown in Figure 9-9. This palette enables you to specify the colors in a gradation, as well as the arrangement of those colors, by using the following options:

> ✦ **Brush mode and Opacity:** These options work the same way they do in the paint and edit tool Options palettes, in the Paint Bucket Options palette, in the Fill dialog box, and everywhere else they pop up. Select a different brush mode to change how colors are applied; lower the Opacity value to make a gradation translucent. In both cases — as with all the other options in this palette — you must adjust the options before using the gradient tool. They do not affect existing gradations.

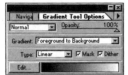

Figure 9-9: The Gradient Tool Options palette provides access to the all-important Edit button, which enables you to create custom gradations.

✦ **Gradient:** The new Gradient pop-up menu provides access to gobs of factory-predefined gradations. When you select a gradation, Photoshop displays it in the gradient preview (labeled in Figure 9-9). The first three factory gradations are dependent on the current foreground and background colors. The others contain specific colors bearing no relationship to the colors specified in the Toolbox. If you create and name your own custom gradations, they will also show up in this menu.

✦ **Type:** Select Linear or Radial from this pop-up menu to specify the variety of gradation you want to create. A *linear gradation* progresses in bands of color in a straight line between the beginning and end of your drag, like the gradation shown back in Figure 9-8. A *radial gradation* progresses outward from a central point in concentric circles, as in Figure 9-10. The point at which you begin dragging defines the center of the gradation, and the point at which you release defines the outermost circle. This means the first color in the gradation appears in the center of the fill. So to create the gradation on the right side of Figure 9-10, you must set white to the foreground color and black to the background color.

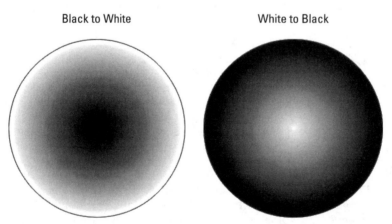

Black to White   White to Black

Figure 9-10: With Foreground to Background selected from the Gradient pop-up menu, set the foreground and background colors to their defaults to get the left-hand gradation. Press *X* to swap the colors for the gradation on the right.

✦ **Mask:** You can specify different levels of opacity throughout a gradation in Photoshop 4. For example, the Transparent Stripes effect (available from the Gradient pop-up menu) lays down a series of alternately black and transparent stripes. But you needn't use this transparency information. If you prefer to apply a series of black and white stripes instead, you can make all portions of the gradation equally opaque by turning off the Mask check box.

For example, in Figure 9-11, I applied Transparent Stripes as a radial gradation in two separate swipes, at top and bottom. Both times, I changed the Opacity setting to 50 percent, so dog and hydrant would never be obscured. (The Opacity setting works independently of the gradation's built-in transparency, providing you with additional flexibility.) In the top gradation, the Mask check box is on, so the white stripes are completely transparent. In the bottom gradation, Mask is turned off, so the white stripes become 50 percent opaque (as prescribed by the Opacity setting).

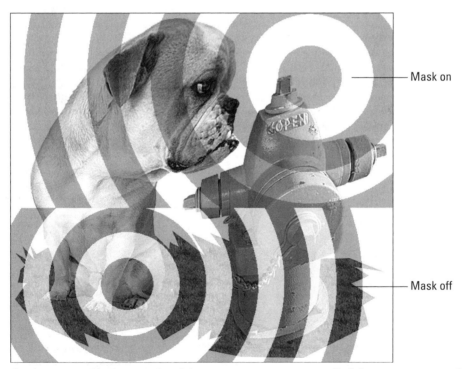

Mask on

Mask off

Figure 9-11: With the Opacity slider set to 50 percent, I applied the Transparent Stripes gradation with Mask on (top) and off (bottom). When Mask is off, the white stripes obscure the view of the underlying image.

✦ **Dither:** In the old days, Photoshop drew its gradients one band at a time. Each band was filled with an incrementally different shade of color. The potential result was banding, in which you could clearly distinguish the transition between two or more bands of color. The Dither check box helps to eliminate this problem by mixing up the pixels between bands (much as Photoshop dithers pixels when converting a grayscale image to black and white). You should leave this option turned on unless you want to use the banding to create a special effect.

Eliminating gradient banding

Despite the helpful effect of the Dither check box, banding is not necessarily completely eliminated. If you do experience banding, this section describes how to eliminate it.

As explained in Chapter 15, the Add Noise filter randomizes pixels in a selection. So when you apply Filter ➪ Noise ➪ Add Noise to a gradation, it randomly mixes the bands of color, very much like a variable dithering function. In fact, it enables you to outdither the Dither check box.

The first column in Figure 9-12 shows linear and radial gradations. In the second column, I applied the Add Noise filter three times in a row to both gradations. To make the effect as subtle as possible — you don't want the noise to be obvious — I specified an Amount value of 8 and selected the Uniform radio button inside the Add Noise dialog box. Multiple repetitions of a subtle noise effect are preferable to a single application of a more radical effect.

If noise isn't enough or if the noise appears a little too obvious, you can further mix the colors in a gradation by applying a directional blur filter. To blur a linear gradation, apply the Motion Blur filter in the direction of the gradation. In the top-right example of Figure 9-12, I applied Filter ➪ Blur ➪ Motion Blur with an Angle value of 90 degrees (straight up and down) and a Distance value of 3 pixels.

To blur a radial gradation, apply the Radial Blur filter (Filter ➪ Blur ➪ Radial Blur). To mix the noise around the center of the gradation, select the Spin option in the Radial Blur dialog box. To blend color in the bands, select the Zoom option. The lower-right example in Figure 9-12 is divided into two halves. To create the top half, I applied the Spin option with an Amount value of 10; to create the bottom half, I applied Zoom with an Amount value of 20. (If you can barely see any difference between the two — that's the idea when it comes to gradations — look closely at the perimeter of the gradients. The top one, created with the Spin option, is smooth; the bottom one, created with the Zoom option, is rougher.)

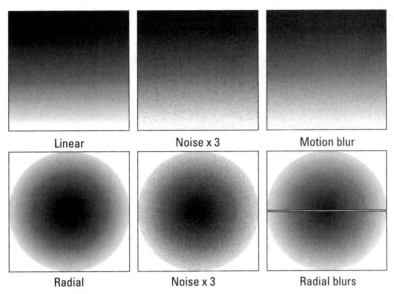

Linear	Noise x 3	Motion blur
Radial	Noise x 3	Radial blurs

Figure 9-12: The results of applying noise (middle column) and directional blur effects (right column) to linear and radial gradations.

To deemphasize color bands in a horizontal linear gradation further, you can apply the Wind filter (Filter ➪ Stylize ➪ Wind). Color Plate 9-2 shows three sample gradations subject to the Add Noise, Wind, and Motion Blur filters. In each case, I applied the Add Noise filter three times (just as in Figure 9-18), the Blast option in the Wind dialog box twice (once in each direction), and the Motion Blur filter in a horizontal direction at 10 pixels.

Cross Reference

You can get a sense of what the Add Noise, Motion Blur, Radial Blur, and Wind filters do by experimenting with them for a few minutes. If you want to learn even more, I discuss all four in Chapter 15.

Creating custom gradations

The only remaining option in the Gradient Tool Options palette is the Edit button. Click this button to create your own custom gradation or to edit one of the factory presets. Photoshop answers your request with the Gradient Editor dialog box, pictured in Figure 9-13. Because this dialog box has so much going on in it, I've lifted the most essential options and labeled them in Figure 9-14.

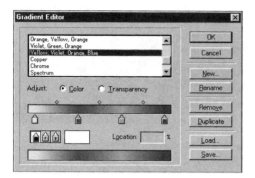

Figure 9-13: Click the Edit button in the Gradient Tool Options palette to bring up this dialog box, which allows you to design your own custom gradations.

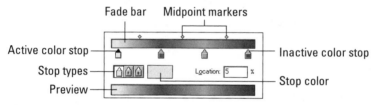

Figure 9-14: These few small options are quite powerful. Despite the array of buttons available in the Gradient Editor dialog box, these controls are where it's happening.

Select a named gradation that interests you from the scrolling list. Then click the Duplicate button to design a new gradation based on the selected one. Photoshop asks you to name the new gradient. Do so and then press Enter.

Tip Actually, one essential option for creating custom gradients isn't included in Figure 9-14: the Save button. Photoshop automatically saves your custom gradients to the Preferences file when you close the Gradient Editor. But clicking the Save button gives you the option of saving your gradients to a different location. This option can come in handy because if you ever need to dump your Preferences file — which you might want to do to restore the factory default settings — you also end up dumping all your gradients.

If you press Ctrl and Shift in conjunction with the Save button, Photoshop saves only the currently selected gradient. To select more than one gradient, click the first one and Ctrl+click the others. If you click Save without Ctrl and Shift, all gradients are saved.

Positioning colors and midpoint markers

Below the scrolling list is the *fade bar* (labeled in Figure 9-14). The starting color appears as a house-shaped *color stop* on the left; the ending color appears on the far right. Positioned between each pair of color stops along the top of the fade bar is a diamond-shaped *midpoint marker,* which represents the spot where the two colors mix in exactly equal amounts. You can change the location of any stop or marker by dragging it. Or you can click a stop or marker to select it and then enter a value into the Location option box below the fade bar. The selected stop or marker appears black.

✦ When numerically positioning a selected color stop, a value of 0 percent indicates the left end of the fade bar; 100 percent indicates the right end. Even if you add more color stops to the gradation, the values represent absolute positions along the fade bar.

✦ When repositioning a midpoint marker, the initial setting of 50 percent is smack dab between the two color stops; 0 percent is all the way over to the left stop; and 100 percent is all the way over to the right. Midpoint values are, therefore, measured relative to color stop positions. In fact, when you move a color stop, Photoshop moves the midpoint marker along with it to maintain the same relative positioning. Figure 9-15 shows four radial gradations subjected to different midpoint settings, ranging from the minimum to maximum allowed values. (If you enter a value below 13 percent or over 87, Photoshop politely ignores you.)

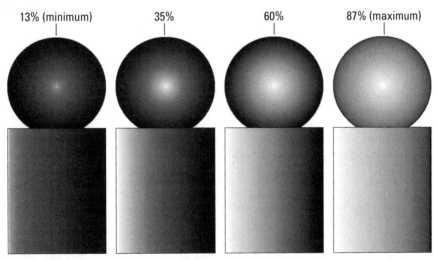

Figure 9-15: Four sets of white-to-black gradations — radial on top and linear at bottom — subject to different midpoint settings.

Caution   Pressing Enter after you enter a value into the Location option box is tempting, but don't do it. Pressing Enter takes you out of the Gradient Editor dialog box.

Adjusting the colors in a gradation

You can change the colors in a gradation by selecting a color stop and clicking the stop color box (immediately to the left of the Location option box). Photoshop displays the Color Picker dialog box. Select the desired color and press Enter.

Tip   That's the hard way. The easy way is to lift a color from the Image window. When you move the cursor outside the dialog box into the Image window, it changes to an eyedropper. Just click the color in the image you want to use. You can also click a color in the fade bar in the Gradient Editor dialog box, a color in the Color palette's color bar, or in the Swatches palette.

If you want a color stop to vary with the active foreground color, select the color stop and click the little *F* icon in the stop types area (on the left side of the dialog box, labeled back in Figure 9-14). To use the background color, select a stop and click the little *B* icon.

Adding and deleting color stops

Here are three last items you should know about color stops:

✦ As I mentioned earlier, you can add as many as 32 colors per gradation. To add a color stop, click anywhere along the bottom of the fade bar. A new stop appears right where you click. Photoshop also adds a midpoint marker between the new color stop and its neighbor.

Tip   ✦ To duplicate a color stop, Alt+drag it to a new location along the fade bar.

✦ To remove a color stop, drag the stop away from the fade bar. The stop icon vanishes and the fade bar automatically adjusts as defined by the remaining color stops.

Adjusting the transparency mask

Photoshop 4 enables you to include a *transparency mask* with each gradation, which determines where the colors are opaque and where they fade into translucency or even transparency. You create and edit this mask independently of the colors in the gradation, and you can turn it on and off using the Mask check box in the Gradient Tool Options palette (as explained earlier).

To create a transparency mask, click the Transparency radio button in the Gradient Editor dialog box. The fade bar changes to reflect the transparency settings (if any), as shown in Figure 9-16. As when editing colors, you click under the fade bar to add *transparency stops,* drag the stops to move them, and to edit the Location value to position a selected stop numerically.

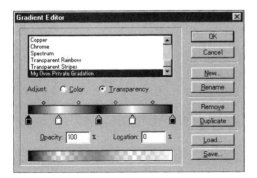

Figure 9-16: Click the Transparency radio button to switch to a different fade bar that controls how the gradation fades in and out of sight.

The difference is, instead of changing the color of the stops, you modify their opacity. By default, each new stop is 100 percent opaque. You can modify the transparency by selecting a stop and changing the Opacity value. The preview along the bottom of the dialog box updates to reflect your changes. A checkerboard pattern represents the underlying image.

Color Plate 9-3 demonstrates the effect of applying a three-color gradation to a photograph. The gradation fades from red to transparency to green to transparency and, finally, to blue. In the first example in the color plate, I dragged over a standard checkerboard pattern with the gradient tool, from the lower-left corner to the upper-right corner. The second example shows the photograph prior to applying the gradation. In the last example, I applied the gradient — again from lower left to upper right — using the Overlay brush mode. Previously, you couldn't achieve this effect in Photoshop without the help of a third-party plug-in.

Gradations and brush modes

Overlay isn't the only brush mode you can use with gradations. All 18 of the standard brush modes are available and they make a tremendous impression on the performance of the gradient tool. This section examines yet another way to apply a brush mode in conjunction with the tool. Naturally, it barely scrapes the surface of what's possible, but it may inspire you to experiment and discover additional effects on your own.

The following steps tell you how to use the Dissolve mode in combination with a radial gradation to create a supernova explosion. (At least, it looks like a supernova to me — not that I've ever seen one up close, mind you.) Figures 9-17 through 9-19 show the nova in progress. The steps offer you the opportunity to experiment with a brush mode setting and some general insight into creating radial gradations.

Cross Reference

These steps involve the use of the elliptical marquee tool. Generally speaking, it's an easy tool to use. But if you find you have problems making it work according to my instructions, you may want to read the "Geometric selection outlines" section of Chapter 11. It's only a few pages long.

Steps: Creating a Gradient Supernova

1. **Create a new image window.** Make it 500 × 500 pixels. A grayscale image is fine for this exercise.

2. **Click with the pencil tool at the apparent center of the image.** Don't worry if it's not the exact center. This point is merely intended to serve as a guide. If a single point is not large enough for you to identify easily, draw a small cross.

3. **Alt+drag from the point with the elliptical marquee tool to draw the marquee outward from the center.** You can select the elliptical marquee tool by pressing the M key twice in a row. While dragging with the tool, press and hold the Shift key to constrain the marquee to a circle. Release Shift after you release the mouse button. Draw a marquee that fills about ¾ of the window.

4. **Choose Image ➪ Adjust ➪ Invert (Ctrl+I).** This fills the marquee with black and makes the center point white.

5. **Choose Select ➪ None (Ctrl+D) to deselect the circle.**

6. **Again, Alt+drag from the center point with the elliptical marquee tool.** And, again, press Shift to constrain the shape to a circle. Create a marquee roughly 20 pixels larger than the black circle.

7. **Alt+drag from the center point with the elliptical marquee tool.** This subtracts a hole from the selection. After you begin dragging, release the Alt key (but keep that mouse button down). Then press and hold both Shift and Alt together and keep them down. Draw a marquee roughly 20 pixels smaller than the black circle. Then release the mouse button and finally release the keys. The result is a doughnut-shaped selection — a large circle with a smaller circular hole — as shown in Figure 9-17.

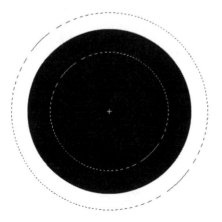

Figure 9-17: The result of creating a black circle and two circular marquees, all centered about a single point

8. **Choose Select ⇨ Feather and enter 10 for the Radius value.** Then press Enter to feather the section outline.

9. **Press the D key, and then press X.** This makes the foreground color white and the background color black.

10. **Select the gradient tool and press Enter to display the Options palette.** Select Foreground to Background from the Gradient pop-up menu. Also select the Radial option from the Type pop-up menu.

11. **Select Dissolve from the brush mode's pop-up menu on the left side of the Gradient Tool Options palette.**

12. **Drag from the center point in the image window to anywhere along the outer rim of the largest marquee.** The result is the fuzzy gradation shown in Figure 9-18.

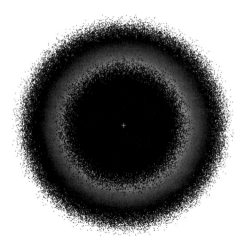

Figure 9-18: The Dissolve brush mode option randomizes the pixels around the feathered edges of the selection outlines.

13. **Choose Select ⇨ None (Ctrl+D) to deselect the image.**

14. **Choose Image ⇨ Adjust ⇨ Invert (Ctrl+I) to invert the entire image.**

15. **Press the D key to restore black and white as foreground and background colors, respectively.** Then use the eraser tool to erase the center point. The finished supernova appears in Figure 9-19.

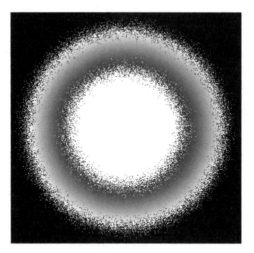

Figure 9-19: By inverting the image from the previous figure and erasing the center point, you create an expanding series of progressively lighter rings dissolving into the black void of space, an effect better known to its friends as a supernova.

Applying Strokes and Arrowheads

Photoshop is nearly as adept at drawing lines and outlines as it is at filling selections. The following sections discuss how to apply a border around a selection outline — which is practical, if not terribly exciting — and how to create arrowheads — which can yield more interesting results than you might think.

Stroking a selection outline

Stroking is useful for creating frames and outlines. Generally speaking, you can stroke an image in Photoshop in three ways:

✦ **Using the Stroke command:** Select the portion of the image you want to stroke and choose Edit ⇨ Stroke to display the Stroke dialog box shown in Figure 9-20. Enter the thickness of the stroke in pixels into the Width option box. Select a Location radio button to specify the position of the stroke with respect to the selection outline. The Stroke dialog box also includes Opacity, Mode, and Preserve Transparency options that work like those in the Fill dialog box.

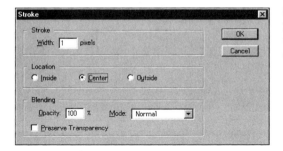

Figure 9-20: Use the options in the Stroke dialog box to specify the thickness of a stroke and its location with respect to the selection outline.

> **Tip** When in doubt, select Inside from the Location radio buttons. This setting ensures the stroke is entirely inside the selection outline in case you decide to move the selection. If you select Center or Outside, Photoshop may apply part or all of the stroke to the deselected area around the selection outline.

✦ **Using the Border command:** Select a portion of the image and choose Select ➪ Modify ➪ Border to retain only the outline of the selection. Specify the size of the border by entering a value in pixels into the Width option box and press Enter. To fill the border with the background color, press Ctrl+Delete or Ctrl+Backspace. To fill the border with the foreground color, press Alt+Delete or Alt+Backspace. To apply a repeating pattern to the border, choose Edit ➪ Fill and select the Pattern option from the Use pop-up menu. You can even apply a command under the Filter menu or some other special effect.

✦ **Framing the image:** Okay, so this one is a throwaway, but it's useful just the same. To create an outline around the entire image, change the background color (yes, the background color) to the color you want to apply to the outline. Then choose Image ➪ Canvas Size and add twice the desired border thickness to the Width and Height options in pixels. Make sure the Anchor control has the center box selected. For example, to create a 1-pixel border, add 2 pixels to the Width value (1 for the left side and 1 for the right) and 2 pixels to the Height value (1 for the top edge and 1 for the bottom). When you press Enter, Photoshop enlarges the canvas size according to your specifications and fills the new pixels around the perimeter of the image with the background color. Simplicity at its best.

Applying arrowheads

The one function missing from all the operations in the previous list is applying arrowheads. The fact is, in Photoshop, you can apply arrowheads only to straight lines drawn with the line tool. To create an arrowhead, double-click the line tool icon in the Toolbox (or press *N* to select the line tool and then press Enter) to display the Line Tool Options palette shown in Figure 9-21. Enter a value into the

Line Width option box to specify the thickness of the line — better known as the line's *weight* — and then use the Arrowheads options as follows:

✦ **Start:** Select this check box to append an arrowhead to the beginning of a line drawn with the line tool.

✦ **End:** Select this check box to append an arrowhead to the end of a line. (Like you needed me to tell you this.)

✦ **Shape:** Click the Shape button to display the Arrowhead Shape dialog box, which also appears in Figure 9-21.

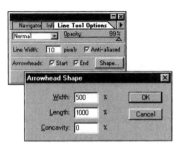

Figure 9-21: Click the Shape button in the Line Tool Options palette (top) to display the Arrowhead Shape dialog box (bottom). The line tool remains the only way to create arrowheads in Photoshop.

The Arrowhead Shape dialog box contains three options, which enable you to specify the size and shape of the arrowhead as a function of the line weight:

✦ **Width:** Enter the width of the arrowhead in pixels into this option box. The width of the arrowhead is completely independent of line weight.

✦ **Length:** Enter the length of the arrowhead, measured from the base of the arrowhead to its tip, into this option box. Again, length is measured in pixels and is independent of line weight.

✦ **Concavity:** You can specify the shape of the arrowhead by entering a value between negative and positive 50 percent into the Concavity option box. Figure 9-22 shows examples of a few Concavity settings applied to an arrowhead 50 pixels wide and 100 pixels long.

Appending arrowheads to curved lines

Applying arrowheads to straight lines is a simple matter. Double-click the line tool icon, select a few choice options, and draw a line with the line tool. Applying an arrowhead to a stroked selection outline is a little trickier, but still possible. The following steps explain the process.

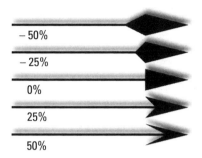

Figure 9-22: Examples of a 50 × 100-pixel arrowhead subject to five different Concavity values.

– 50%

– 25%

0%

25%

50%

Steps: Adding an Arrowhead to a Free-form Stroke

1. **Create a new layer.** Display the Layers palette by pressing the F7 key. Then click the little page icon to create a new layer.

2. **Draw and stroke a selection.** Draw any selection outline you like and stroke it by choosing Edit ➪ Stroke and applying whatever settings strike your fancy. Remember the value you enter into the Width option. In Figure 9-23, I drew a wiggly line with the lasso tool and applied a 4-pixel black stroke at 30 percent Opacity.

Figure 9-23: Here, I created a new layer, drew a free-form shape with the lasso tool, and stroked it with a 4-pixel black outline at 30 percent Opacity.

3. **Press Ctrl+D.** Or choose Select ➪ None to deselect all portions of the image.

4. **Erase the portions of the stroke you don't need.** Select the eraser tool by pressing the E key. Then drag to erase through the stroke layer without harming the layer below. Erase away the areas of the stroke at which you want to add arrowheads. I wanted to add an arrowhead behind the fly, so I erased around the fly.

5. **Double-click the line tool icon.** Up comes the Line Tool Options palette.

6. **Specify the arrowhead settings.** Enter the line weight you used when stroking the selection outline into the Line Width option box (in my case, 4 pixels). Then select the End check box and deselect the Start check box, if necessary. Then click the Shape button and specify the width, length, and concavity of the arrowhead as desired.

7. **Set the foreground color as needed.** I applied a black stroke at 30 percent Opacity, so I set the foreground color to 30 percent gray. (Click the stroke with the eyedropper to change the foreground color to the stroke color.)

8. **Zoom in on the point in the image at which you want to add the arrowhead.** You must get in close so you can see what you're doing, as in Figure 9-24.

9. **Draw a very short line exactly the length of the arrowhead at the tip of the stroke.** Figure 9-24 illustrates what I mean. This may take some practice to accomplish. Start the line a few pixels in from the end of the stroke to make sure the base of the arrowhead fits snugly. If you mess up the first time, choose Edit ➪ Undo (Ctrl+Z) and try again.

That's all there is to it. From there on, you can continue to edit the stroke as you see fit.

In Figure 9-25, I erased a series of scratches across the stroke to create a dashed-line effect, all the rage for representing cartoon fly trails. I then set the eraser brush size to the largest, fuzziest setting and erased the end of the stroke (above the dog's head) to create a gradual trailing off. That crazy fly is distracting our hero from his appointed rounds.

Figure 9-24: Use the line tool to draw a line no longer than the arrowhead to append the arrow to the end of the stroke. The view size of this image is magnified 300 percent.

Figure 9-25: I finished by erasing dashes into the line and softening the end of the trail with a large, fuzzy eraser.

Duplicating and Reverting

Introducing the Amalgamated Rubber Stamp

This chapter is primarily about one tool: the rubber stamp tool. Although the eraser figures into the reversion discussion in this chapter (and I even include a small reference to the pencil tool), the main ingredient — after you boil it down at your local editorial content refinery — is the rubber stamp tool. This tool provides four loosely related, but distinct, capabilities, every one of which deserves to be split into a tool of its own.

The name *rubber stamp* is misleading because this particular tool has nothing to do with rubber stamps. First, no tree sap is involved — let's get that sticky issue resolved right off the bat. Second, you don't use the rubber stamp tool to stamp an image. When I think of rubber stamps, I think of those things you see in stationery stores that plunk down laudatory exclamations and smiley faces and Pooh bears. Elementary school teachers and little girls use rubber stamps. I've never seen a professional image editor walking around with a rubber stamp in my life.

So remove rubber stamps entirely from your mind for now. To discover exactly what the rubber stamp tool does, select the tool and press Enter to display the Rubber Stamp Options palette, shown in Figure 10-1. In addition to the standard brush modes pop-up menu, Opacity slider, Stylus Pressure options, and Sample Merged check box you get when you use half a dozen paint and edit tools (see Chapter 8 if your memory's getting a tad fuzzy), the Rubber Stamp

Options palette includes an Option pop-up menu, shown unfurled in the bottom portion of Figure 10-1. The real heart of the tool, this pop-up menu includes the following options:

✦ **Cloning:** Select one of the two Clone options to duplicate portions of an image by dragging over it. Alt+click with the tool to specify a point of reference, and then drag in a different area of the image to begin cloning. (Don't worry, I cover the difference between the two Clone options in the upcoming "Aligned and non-aligned cloning" section.)

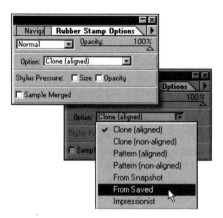

Figure 10-1: Select an option from the Option pop-up menu to define the way the rubber stamp tool works.

✦ **Pattern application:** Select one of the two Pattern options to paint an image with a repeating pattern rather than the standard foreground color. Before using this option, you must establish a pattern by selecting a portion of the image with the rectangular marquee tool and choosing Edit ➪ Define Pattern.

✦ **Reversion:** The From Snapshot option enables you to use the rubber stamp tool to revert portions of your image to the way they appeared when you last chose Edit ➪ Take Snapshot. From Saved enables you to revert portions of an image to the way they appeared when you last saved the image.

✦ **Impressionist:** The last option, Impressionist, retrieves the last saved version of the image and sort of smears it around to create a gooey, unfocused effect. You can achieve some mildly interesting and halfway useful effects — and I'm being generous here — by combining this function with the Overlay, Hard Light, or Soft Light brush modes, but it wouldn't be my first choice for any job. This is my nomination for the least useful of the rubber stamp settings, and this is the last time I'll mention it.

Note If there is a tie that binds the rubber stamp's various capabilities, it is that most rubber stamp tools enable you to paint with images. When you clone with the rubber stamp tool, for example, you paint with a displaced version of the image itself. When you paint a pattern, you paint with an image fragment. When you revert, you paint with the saved version of the image. Even the Impressionist option paints with the saved image in its own skewed sort of way. (Ah, man, I wasn't going to mention that option again.)

As you can see, a better name for the rubber stamp tool might be the "clone/pattern/revert/stupid effects tool" or maybe the "junk-drawer tool." Then again, the "mother of all mixed-up tools" has a certain ring to it. In any case, the remainder of this chapter explores every one of the rubber stamp's capabilities.

Photoshop 4.0

In Photoshop 4, you needn't visit the Rubber Stamp Options palette to switch between one Option pop-up menu option and the next. Just press the S key. Each press of *S* cycles from one option to the next — for example, from Clone (Aligned) to Clone (Non-aligned) to Pattern (Aligned), and so on and, eventually, back to the beginning again. Because so many options exist, keeping the Rubber Stamp Options palette up onscreen, so you can see which one is active, is helpful.

Cloning Image Elements

Although my take on the rubber stamp tool may sound a bit derogatory, most of its capabilities can come in handy. All except that dumb Impressionist option — which I swear, really, I'm going to stop mentioning.

Take cloning, for example. As any dyed-in-the-wool Photoshop user will tell you, the rubber stamp is an invaluable tool for touching up images if you want to remove dust fragments, hairs, and other blotches scanned with a photo or to eliminate portions of an image.

You also can use the rubber stamp to duplicate specific elements in an image, such as flowers and umbrellas, as described in the Photoshop manual. But, by all accounts, this is an inefficient use of the tool. If you want to duplicate an element, you'll have better luck if you select it and clone it, as explained in Chapter 11. By taking this approach, you can specify the exact boundaries of the element, the softness of its edges, and the precise location of the clone. Cloning an element with the rubber stamp is more of an ordeal, because it's easy to clone areas around the element accidentally and to begin a clone in the wrong location.

The cloning process

To clone part of an image, double-click the rubber stamp tool icon to display the Rubber Stamp Options palette, and then select either the Clone (Aligned) or Clone (Non-aligned) option. (The upcoming section explains the difference between the two.) Alt+click in the Image window to specify a point of reference in the portion of the image you want to clone. Then click or drag with the tool in some other region of the image to paint a cloned spot or line.

In Figure 10-2, for example, I Alt+clicked above and to the right of the bird's head, as demonstrated by the appearance of the stamp pickup cursor. I then painted the line shown inside the white rectangle. The rubber stamp cursor shows the end of my drag; the cross-shaped clone reference cursor shows the corresponding point in the original image.

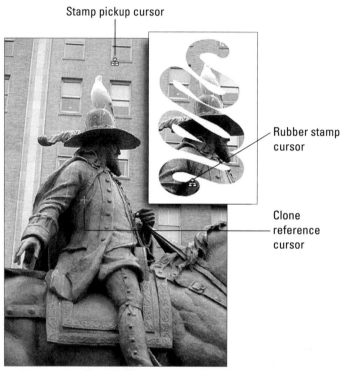

Stamp pickup cursor

Rubber stamp cursor

Clone reference cursor

Figure 10-2: After Alt+clicking at the point indicated by the stamp pickup cursor, I dragged with the rubber stamp tool to paint with the image. (The only reason I painted inside the white rectangle was to set off the line so you can see it better.)

Photoshop enables you to clone not only from within the image you're working on, but also from an entirely separate Image window. This technique enables you to merge two different images together, as demonstrated in Figure 10-3. To achieve this effect, Alt+click in one image, bring a second image to the foreground, and then drag with the rubber stamp tool to clone from the first image.

Figure 10-3: I merged the area around the horse and rider with a water image from another open window (see the upcoming Figure 10-6). The translucent effects were created by periodically adjusting the Opacity slider bar to settings ranging from 50 to 80 percent.

Aligned and non-aligned cloning

Now that I've explained how to use the tool, I'll return to the options in the Rubber Stamp Options palette:

✦ **Clone (Aligned):** To understand how this option works, think of the locations where you Alt+click and begin dragging with the rubber stamp tool as opposite ends of an imaginary straight line, as illustrated in the top half of Figure 10-4. The length and angle of this imaginary line remains fixed until you Alt+click a second time. As you drag, Photoshop moves the line, cloning pixels from one end of the line and laying them down at the other. Regardless of how many times you start and stop dragging with the stamp tool, all lines match up as seamlessly as pieces in a puzzle.

✦ **Clone (Non-aligned):** If you want to clone from a single portion of an image repeatedly, select this option. The second example in Figure 10-4 shows how the length and angle of the imaginary line change every time you paint a new line with the rubber stamp tool.

Figure 10-4: Select the Clone (Aligned) option to instruct Photoshop to clone an image continuously, no matter how many lines you paint (top). If you select Clone (Non-aligned), Photoshop clones each new line from the point at which you Alt+click.

Stamp differences

When cloning, the Photoshop 4 rubber stamp tool works like the Version 3 rubber stamp, which is different than the Version 2 stamp. I only mention this because I personally liked the Version 2 setup better. In Version 2, the rubber stamp cloned the image as it existed before you began using the tool. Even when you drag over an area containing a clone, the tool references the original appearance of the image to prevent recloning. This prevents you from creating more than one clone during a single drag and produces the effect in the first example of Figure 10-5.

In Photoshop 4, however, any changes you make to the image affect the tool as you use it, which can result in the repeating patterns like those shown in the second example of the figure. Although you can create some interesting effects, avoid cloning and recloning areas when retouching; this can result in obvious patterns that betray your adjustments.

Figure 10-5: Photoshop 2's rubber stamp tool cloned the image as it existed before you started using the tool (top). In Version 4, the tool clones and reclones images during a single drag (bottom).

Tip To avoid recloning areas in Photoshop 4, clone from a duplicate of the image. Begin by choosing Image ➪ Duplicate to create a copy of the current image (as explained back in Chapter 4). Alt+click with the rubber stamp tool somewhere in the duplicate window. Then switch to the original image and drag freely with the tool to clone from the duplicate. Because your changes don't affect the duplicate image, no chance exists of recloning.

Touching up blemishes

One of the best uses for the rubber stamp tool is to touch up a scanned photo. Figure 10-6 shows a Photo CD image desperately in need of the stamp tool's attention. Normally, Kodak's Photo CD process delivers some of the best consumer-quality scans money can buy. But this particular medium-resolution image looks like the folks at the lab got together and blew their respective noses on it. It's too late to return to the service bureau and demand they rescan the photo, so my only choice is to touch it up myself.

The best way to fix this image — or any image like it — is to use the rubber stamp over and over again, repeatedly Alt+clicking at one location and then clicking at another. Begin by selecting a brush shape slightly larger than the largest blotch. Of the default brushes, the hard-edged varieties with diameters of 5 and 9 pixels generally work best. (The soft-edged brush shapes have a tendency to cover the blemishes.)

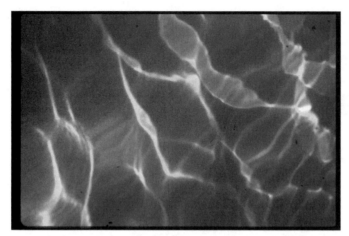

Figure 10-6: This appallingly bad Photo CD image is riddled with blotches and big hurky wads of dust that didn't exist on the original 35mm slide.

Alt+click with the stamp tool at a location that is close to the blemish and features similarly colored pixels. Then click — do not drag — directly on the blemish. The idea is to change as few pixels as possible.

If the retouched area doesn't look quite right, choose Edit ⇨ Undo (Ctrl+Z), Alt+click at a different location, and try again. If your touchup appears seamless — absolutely seamless — move on to the next blemish, repeating the Alt+click and click routine for every dust mark on the photo.

This process isn't necessarily time-consuming, but it does require patience. For example, although it took more than 40 Alt+click and click combinations (not counting 10 or so undos) to arrive at the image shown in Figure 10-7, the process itself took less than 15 minutes. Boring, but fast.

Retouching hairs is a little trickier than dust and other blobs. This is because a hair, although very thin, can be surprisingly long. The retouching process is the same, though. Rather than dragging over the entire length of the hair, Alt+click and click your way through it, bit by little bit. The one difference is brush shape. Because you'll be clicking so many times in succession, and because the hair is so thin, you'll probably achieve the least-conspicuous effects if you use a soft brush shape, such as the default 9-pixel model in the second row of the Brushes palette.

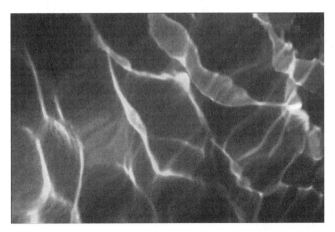

Figure 10-7: The result of Alt+clicking and clicking more than 40 times on the photo shown in Figure 10-6. Notice I also cropped the image and added a border.

Caution   At this point you might wonder, "Why go to all this work to remove dust and scratches when Photoshop provides the automated feature Filter ➪ Noise ➪ Dust & Scratches?" The reason is, quite frankly, the Dust & Scratches filter stinks. No offense to the designers of this filter: They're wonderful people, every one of them, but it doesn't produce the effect it advertises. It mucks up the detail in your image by averaging neighboring pixels, and this simply isn't an acceptable solution. Do your photograph a favor — fix its flaws manually (not to mention lovingly) with the rubber stamp tool.

Eliminating distracting background elements

Another way to apply the stamp tool's cloning capabilities is to eliminate background action that competes with the central elements in an image. For example, Figure 10-8 shows a wonderful news photo shot by Michael Probst for the Reuters image library. Although the image is well photographed and historic in its implications — in case you missed the last century, that's Comrade V. I. Lenin (Vlad to his mom) — that rear workman doesn't contribute anything to the scene; in fact, he draws your attention away from the foreground drama. I mean, hail to the worker and everything, but the image would be better off without him. The following steps explain how I eradicated the offending workman from the scene.

Note   Remember as you read the following steps, deleting an image element with the rubber stamp tool is something of an inexact science, which requires some trial and error. So regard the following steps as an example of how to approach the process of editing your image rather than as a specific procedure that works for all images. You may need to adapt the process slightly depending upon your image.

Figure 10-8: You have to love that old Soviet state-endorsed art. So bold, so angular, so politically intolerant. But you also have to lose that rear workman.

Steps: Eliminating Distracting Elements from an Image

1. I began by cloning the area around the neck of the statue with a soft brush shape. Abandoning the controlled clicks I recommended in the last section, I dragged with the tool because I needed to cover relatively large portions of the image. The apartment building (or whatever that structure is) behind the floating head is magnificently out of focus, just the thing for hiding any incongruous transitions I might create with the rubber stamp. So I warmed up to the image by retouching this area first. Figure 10-9 shows my progress.

   Notice, I covered the workman's body by cloning pixels from both his left and right sides. I also added a vertical bar where the workman's right arm used to be to maintain the rhythm of the building. Remember, variety is the key to using the rubber stamp tool: If you consistently clone from one portion of the image, you create an obvious repetition the viewer can't help but notice.

Figure 10-9: Cloning over the background worker's upper torso was fairly easy because the background building is so regular and out of focus, it provides a wealth of material from which to clone.

2. The next step was to eliminate the workman's head. This was a little tricky because it involved rubbing up against the focused perimeter of Lenin's neck. I had to clone some of the more intricate areas using a hard-edged brush. I also ended up duplicating some of the neck edges to maintain continuity. In addition, I touched up the left side of the neck (your left, not Lenin's) and removed a few white spots from his face. You see my progress in Figure 10-10.

3. Now for the hard part: eliminating the worker's legs and lower torso. See that fragment of metal the foreground worker is holding? What a pain. Its edges were so irregular, there was no way I could restore it with the rubber stamp tool if I messed up while trying to eradicate the background worker's limbs. So I lassoed around the fragment to select it and chose Select ➪ Inverse (Ctrl+Shift+I) to protect it. I also chose Select ➪ Feather (Ctrl+Shift+D) and gave it a Radius value of 1 to soften its edges slightly. This prevented me from messing up the metal no matter what edits I made to the background worker's remaining body parts.

Figure 10-10:
I eliminated the workman's head and touched up details around the perimeter of his neck.

4. From here on, it was just more cloning. Unfortunately, I barely had anything from which to clone. See the little bit of black edging between the two "legs" of the metal fragment? That's it. This was all I had to draw the strip of edging to the right of the fragment that eventually appears in Figure 10-11. To pull off this feat, I pressed the S key to switch to the Clone (Non-aligned) option. Then I Alt+clicked on the tiny bit of edging and click, click, clicked my way down the street.

5. Unfortunately, the strip I laid down in Step 4 appeared noticeably blobular — it looked for all the world like I clicked a bunch of times. Darn. To fix this problem, I clicked and Shift+clicked with the smudge tool set to about 30 percent pressure. This smeared the blobs into a continuous strip but, again, the effect was noticeable. It looked as if I had smeared the strip. So I went back and cloned some more, this time with the Opacity slider bar set to 50 percent.

Figure 10-11: After about 45 minutes of monkeying around with the rubber stamp tool — a practice declared illegal during Stalin's reign — the rear workman is gone, leaving us with an unfettered view of the dubious one himself.

6. To polish the image off, I chose Select ➪ None (Ctrl+D) and ran the sharpen tool along the edges of the metal fragment. This helped to hide that I'd retouched around it and further distinguished the fragment from the unfocused background. I also cropped away 20 or so pixels from the right side of the image to correct the balance of the image.

What I hope I demonstrated in this section is this: Cloning with the rubber stamp tool requires you to alternate between patching and whittling away. No rights and wrongs or hard-and-fast rules exist. Anything you can find to clone is fair game. As long as you avoid mucking up the foreground image, you can't go wrong (so I guess one hard-and-fast rule *does* exist). If you're careful and diligent, no one but you will notice your alterations.

Caution Any time you edit the contents of a photograph, you tread on sensitive ground. Although some have convincingly argued that electronically retouching an image is, theoretically, no different than cropping a photograph — a technique available and in use since the first daguerreotype — photographers have certain rights under copyright law that cannot be ignored. A photographer may have a reason for including an element you wish to eliminate. So, before you edit any photograph, be sure to get permission either from the original photographer or from the copyright holder (as I did for this photo).

Applying Repeating Patterns

Before you can use the rubber stamp tool to paint with a pattern, you must define a pattern by selecting a portion of the image with the rectangular marquee tool and by choosing Edit ➪ Define Pattern. For the Define Pattern command to work, you must use the rectangular marquee — no other selection tool will do. In addition, the selection cannot be feathered, smoothed, expanded, or, in any other way, altered. If the selection is altered, the command is dimmed.

Figure 10-12 shows an example of how you can apply repeating patterns. I selected the single apartment window (surrounded by marching ants) and chose Edit ➪ Define Pattern. I then applied the pattern with the rubber stamp tool at 80 percent opacity over the horse and rider statue.

Caution Like the Clipboard, Photoshop can retain only one pattern at a time and it remembers the pattern throughout a single session. Any time you choose Edit ➪ Define Pattern, you delete the previous pattern as you create a new one. Photoshop also deletes the pattern when you quit the program. Each time you launch Photoshop, therefore, you must define the pattern from scratch.

Pattern options

To paint with a pattern, double-click the rubber stamp tool icon and select either the Pattern (Aligned) or Pattern (Non-aligned) option from the Option pop-up menu in the Rubber Stamp Options palette. These options work as follows:

✦ **Pattern (Aligned):** Select this option to align all patterns you apply with the stamp tool, regardless of how many times you start and stop dragging. The two left examples in Figure 10-13 show the effects of selecting this option. The elements in the pattern remain exactly aligned throughout all the lines. I painted the top image with the Opacity slider bar set to 50 percent, which is why the lines darken when they meet.

✦ **Pattern (Non-aligned):** To allow patterns in different lines to align randomly, select this option. The positioning of the pattern within each line is determined by the point at which you begin dragging. I dragged from right to left to paint the horizontal lines and from top to bottom to paint the vertical lines. The two right examples in Figure 10-13 show how nonaligned patterns overlap.

Figure 10-12: After marqueeing a single window (top) and choosing Edit ➪ Define Pattern, I painted a translucent coat of the pattern over the statue with the rubber stamp tool (bottom).

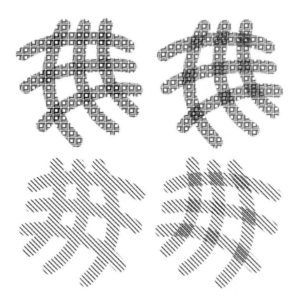

Figure 10-13: Select the Pattern (Aligned) option to align the patterns in all brush strokes painted with the stamp tool (left). If you select Pattern (Non-aligned), Photoshop aligns each pattern with the beginning of the line (right).

After you select Pattern (Aligned) or Pattern (Non-aligned), you're free to start dragging with the stamp tool. You don't need to Alt+click or make any other special provisions, as you do when cloning.

Note

As discussed in Chapter 9, you can also apply a pattern to a selected portion of an image by choosing Edit ➪ Fill and selecting the Pattern option from the Use pop-up menu. Photoshop offers another function that enables you to load an image from disk and apply it as a repeating pattern throughout the selection. Choose Filter ➪ Render ➪ Texture Fill to open any grayscale image saved in the native Photoshop format and then repeat it as many times as the selection will permit. (The image must have been saved with the 2.5 Compatibility option in the Preferences dialog box turned on, as explained later in this chapter.)

How to create patterns

The biggest difficulty with painting patterns is not figuring out the rubber stamp tool, but creating the patterns in the first place. Ideally, your pattern should repeat continuously, without vertical and horizontal seams. Here are some ways to create repeating, continuous patterns:

✦ **Load a displacement map:** Photoshop offers a Displacement Maps folder inside the Photoshop/Plugins/Filters folder. This folder contains several images, each of which represents a different repeating pattern, as illustrated in Figure 10-14. To use one of these patterns, open the image, choose Select ➪ All (Ctrl+A), and choose Edit ➪ Define Pattern. (For more information on displacement maps, see Chapter 15.)

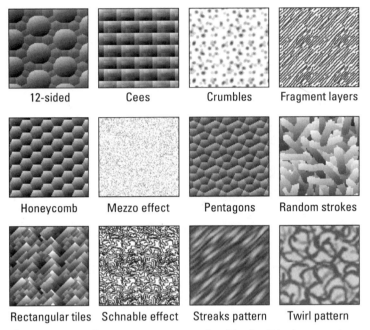

12-sided	Cees	Crumbles	Fragment layers
Honeycomb	Mezzo effect	Pentagons	Random strokes
Rectangular tiles	Schnable effect	Streaks pattern	Twirl pattern

Figure 10-14: The 12 patterns contained in the Displacement Maps folder included with Photoshop.

✦ **Illustrator patterns:** Inside the Photoshop/Patterns folder are Illustrator EPS files that contain repeating object patterns. The patterns, some of which appear in Figure 10-15, are all seamless repeaters. You can open them and rasterize them to any size you like. Then press Ctrl+A, choose Edit ➪ Define Pattern, and you have your pattern.

✦ **Using filters:** As luck would have it, you can create your own custom textures without painting a single line. In fact, you can create a nearly infinite variety of textures by applying several filters to a blank document. To create the texture shown in the bottom-right box in Figure 10-16, for example, I began by selecting a 128 × 128-pixel area. I then chose Filter ➪ Noise ➪ Add Noise, entered a value of 32, and selected the Gaussian radio button. I pressed Ctrl+F twice to apply the noise filter two more times. Finally, I chose Filter ➪ Stylize ➪ Emboss and entered 135 into the Angle option box, 1 into the Height option box, and 100 percent into the Amount option box. The result is a bumpy surface that looks like stucco. This is merely one example of the myriad possibilities filters afford. There's no end to what you can do, so experiment away.

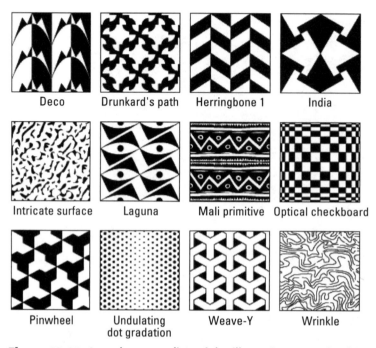

Deco   Drunkard's path   Herringbone 1   India

Intricate surface   Laguna   Mali primitive   Optical checkboard

Pinwheel   Undulating dot gradation   Weave-Y   Wrinkle

Figure 10-15: A random sampling of the illustrations contained in the PostScript Patterns folder inside the Patterns folder.

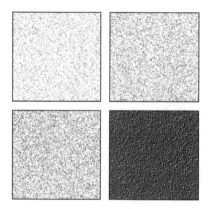

Figure 10-16: To create a stucco texture, apply Filter ➪ Noise ➪ Add Noise three times in a row (upper left, upper right, lower left). Then choose Filter ➪ Stylize ➪ Emboss and enter a Height value of 1 (lower right).

Note   If you want to save a file for use as a displacement map or pattern, it must be a grayscale file. You must also turn on the Photoshop 2.5 compatibility option on the Saving Files panel of the Preferences dialog box (File ➪ Preferences ➪ Saving Files).

For more information on using Add Noise, see Chapter 15. For information about Emboss and other filter commands, see Chapter 16.

✦ **Marquee and clone:** You can use the rectangular marquee and rubber stamp tools to transform a scanned image into a custom pattern. Because this technique is more complicated, as well as more rewarding, than the others, I explain it in the upcoming section, "Steps: Building a Repeating Pattern from a Scanned Image."

The following steps describe how to change a scanned image into a seamless, repeating pattern. To illustrate how this process works, Figures 10-17 through 10-20 show various stages in a project I completed. You need only two tools to carry out these steps: the rectangular marquee tool and the rubber stamp tool with the Clone (Aligned) option active.

Even so, these steps do involve a few selection and layering techniques I haven't yet discussed (for those of you reading sequentially). If you become confused, you can find out more about selecting, moving, and cloning images in Chapter 11.

Steps: Building a Repeating Pattern from a Scanned Image

1. **Begin by marqueeing a portion of your scanned image and copying it to the Clipboard.** For best results, specify the exact size of your marquee by double-clicking the rectangular marquee icon in the Toolbox, selecting Fixed Size from the Style pop-up menu (in the Marquee Options palette), and entering specific values into the Width and Height option boxes. This way, you can easily reselect a portion of the pattern in the steps that follow and use the fixed-size marquee to define the pattern when you finish. To create the patterns shown in the example, I set the marquee to 128 × 128 pixels.

2. **Choose File ⇨ New (Ctrl+N) and triple the values Photoshop offers as the default image dimensions.** In my case, Photoshop offered 128 × 128 pixels because this was the size of the image I copied to the Clipboard. So I changed the image size to 384 × 384 pixels.

3. **Paste the marqueed image into the new Image window.** When you press Ctrl+V, Photoshop pastes the image smack dab in the center of the window, which is exactly where you want it. This image will serve as the central tile of your repeating pattern. Unfortunately, Photoshop 4 pastes the image on a new layer, so you must recover the selection outline and flatten the image. The following steps tell how.

4. **Ctrl+click the item labeled Layer 1 in the Layers palette.** This brings back the selection outline. Hooray.

5. **Press Ctrl+E.** This merges the layer with the background, in effect, flattening it. Or you can choose Layer ⇨ Flatten Image. Either way, the selection outline remains intact.

6. **Clone the selection by Ctrl+Alt+dragging it a total of eight times.** The idea is to fill the window with a 3 × 3-tile grid, as shown in Figure 10-17. First, Ctrl+Alt+drag up, and then keep going around the perimeter of the image. Incidentally, making the edges match up exactly is important, so take care when cloning. Feel free to use the arrow keys to nudge the selection, if necessary.

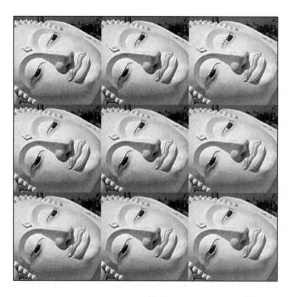

Figure 10-17: To build the repeating pattern shown in Figure 10-20, I started by creating a grid of nine image tiles. As you can see, the seams between the tiles in this grid are harsh and unacceptable.

7. **Press Ctrl+D to deselect the image.** Once you clone the image a few times, you need to deselect it so you can clone freely with the rubber stamp.

8. **Drag the Title bar of the new Image window to position it so you can see the portion of the image you copied in the original Image window.** If necessary, drag the Title bar of the original Image window to reposition it, as well. After you have your windows arranged, click the Title bar of the new Image window to make it the active window.

9. **Select the Clone (Non-aligned) option.** First select the rubber stamp by pressing the S key. Then press Enter to display the Rubber Stamp Options palette. If Clone (Non-aligned) is not selected in the Option pop-up menu, press the S key until it is selected.

10. **Specify the image you want to clone by Alt+clicking in the original Image window.** No need to switch out of the new window. Alt+click an easily identifiable pixel that belongs to the portion of the image you copied. The exact pixel you click is very important. If you press the Caps

Lock key, you get the crosshair cursor, which enables you to narrow in on a pixel. In my case, I clicked the corner of the Buddha's mouth. (At least, I assume that's Buddha. What a narrow-minded, Western-bred ignoramus I must be.)

11. **Now click with the stamp tool on the matching pixel in the central tile of the new window.** If you clicked the correct pixel, the tile should not change one iota. If it shifts at all, press Ctrl+Z (Edit ➪ Undo) and try again. Because Clone (Non-aligned) is the active stamp setting, you can keep undoing and clicking over and over again without resetting the clone-from point in the original image.

12. **Switch the Alt setting to Clone (Aligned).** Once you click in the image without seeing any shift, select the Clone (Aligned) option from the pop-up menu in the Rubber Stamp Options palette to lock in the alignment between clone-from and clone-to points.

13. **Use the stamp tool to fill in portions of the central tile.** For example, in Figure 10-18, I extended the Buddha's cheek and neck down into the lower row of tiles. I also extended the central forehead to meet the Buddha on the left.

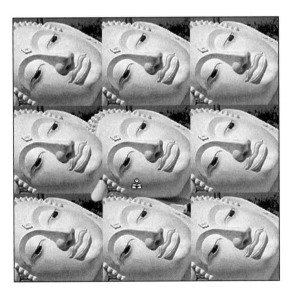

Figure 10-18: I used the rubber stamp's cloning capability to extend the features in the central face toward the left and downward.

14. **After you establish one continuous transition between two tiles in any direction — up, down, left, or right — select a portion of the image with the rectangular marquee tool and clone the selection repeatedly to fill out a single row or column.** In my case, I managed to create a smooth transition between the central and bottom tiles. Therefore, I selected a region that includes half the central tile and half

the tile below it. Because I fixed the rectangular marquee to a 128 ×
128-pixel square, I only had to click an area to select it. (Drag to position
the marquee exactly where you want it.) I then cloned that selection
along the entire width of the image.

15. **Press Ctrl+D to deselect the image.** Again, you need to deselect the
    image so you can clone freely.

16. **If you started by creating a horizontal transition, use the rubber
    stamp tool to create a vertical transition now.** Likewise, if you started
    vertically, now go horizontally. You may well need to press the S key to
    switch to the Clone (Non-aligned) setting again. This enables you to
    change the location of the clone-to point and build on one of the
    perimeter tiles. In my case, I shifted the clone-to point several times —
    alternatively building on the central Buddha, the right-hand one, and the
    middle one in the bottom row. Each time you get the clone-to point
    properly positioned, select the Clone (Aligned) option again to lock in
    the alignment. Then clone away.

    As long as you get the clone-from and clone-to points properly aligned,
    you can't make a mistake. If you change your mind, realign the clone
    points and try again. In my case, I cloned the long, droopy earlobe down
    into the face of the Buddha below. (What's a long, droopy earlobe
    between identical cousins?) I also cloned the god's chin onto the
    forehead of the one to the right, ultimately achieving the effect shown
    in Figure 10-19.

17. **After you build up one set of both horizontal and vertical
    transitions, you can select a portion of the image and choose
    Edit ⇨ Define Pattern.** Figure 10-19 shows where I positioned my
    128 × 128-pixel selection boundary. This includes parts of each of four
    neighboring heads, including the all-important droopy earlobe. (Didn't
    Buddha realize once the droopy earlobe fad passed, he would be stuck
    with it for the rest of his life?) Don't worry if the image doesn't appear
    centered inside the selection outline. What counts is the selection
    repeats seamlessly when placed beside itself.

18. **Select the Pattern (Aligned) option inside the Rubber Stamp
    Options palette.** To confirm the pattern is, indeed, seamless and every
    bit as lovely as you hoped, drag around inside the current image with
    the rubber stamp tool and a large brush shape. Figure 10-20 shows the
    seamless results of my dragging. If you see any flaws, cover them more
    with the Clone (Aligned) and Clone (Non-aligned) settings, as explained
    previously.

19. **Press Ctrl+S to save your completed image.** You don't want to go to
    all this trouble for nothing.

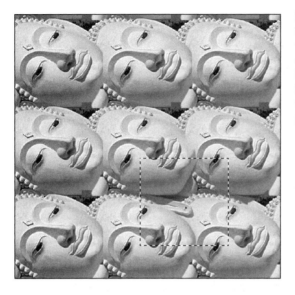

Figure 10-19: After completing a smooth transition between the central tile and the tiles below and to the right of it, I selected a portion of the image and chose Edit ⇨ Define Pattern.

Figure 10-20: This Eastern montage is the result of applying the Buddha pattern. Buddha sure looks serene and comfortable, especially considering he's resting on his own head.

Selectively Undoing Changes

Welcome to the second act of this chapter. It's a short act — more like a scene, really — so you'll have to forgo the intermission.

Now that I've explained the cloning and related patterning attributes of the rubber stamp tool, it's time to turn your attention — come on, turn, turn, just a little more, there you go — to a new topic. The rest of this chapter deals with *reversion*, which is a fancy word for returning your image to the way it looked before you went and made an unholy mess of it.

Using the traditional undo functions

Before I dive into the rubber stamp's reversion capabilities, allow me to introduce the more traditional reversion functions found in nearly all paint applications, including Photoshop:

✦ **Undo:** To restore an image to the way it looked before the last operation, choose Edit ➪ Undo (Ctrl+Z). You can undo the effect of a paint or edit tool, a change made to a selection outline, or a special-effect or color-correction command. You can't undo disk operations, such as opening or saving. Photoshop does enable you to undo an edit after printing an image, though. You can test out an effect, print it, and then undo it if you think the effect looks awful.

Photoshop 4.0

Photoshop still offers only one level of Undo. This is fast becoming unacceptable. Adobe will, hopefully, remedy this most obvious of all possible oversights in the next version. If it doesn't — well, I'll be plenty steamed, that's all.

✦ **Revert:** Choose File ➪ Revert to reload an image from disk. Most folks think of this as the last-resort function, the command you choose after everything else has failed. But really, it's quite useful as a stop-gap measure. Suppose you're about to embark on a series of filtering operations that may or may not result in the desired effect. You're going to perform multiple operations, so you can't undo them if they don't work. Before choosing your first filter, choose File ➪ Save. Now you're ready for anything. You can wreak a degree of havoc on your image that no user in his or her right mind would dare. If everything doesn't go exactly as you planned or hoped, you can simply choose File ➪ Revert and you're back in business.

✦ **The eraser tool:** Drag with the eraser tool to paint in white or some other background color. This enables you to revert portions of your image back to bare canvas.

Actually, this is just the beginning of the eraser tool's capabilities. Once a piddly little tool of little consequence, the eraser has grown muscles over the years. That's why I explain it in so much detail in the next section.

Using the eraser tool

Select the eraser tool by pressing the E key. Then press Enter to display the Eraser Options palette, shown in Figure 10-21. The palette offers a pop-up menu of four eraser styles: Paintbrush, Airbrush, Pencil, and Block. *Block* is the old 16 × 16-pixel square eraser that's great for hard-edged touch-ups. The other options work exactly like the tools for which they're named.

Tip You needn't go to the trouble of selecting the options from the pop-up menu. When the eraser is selected, pressing the E key cycles through the different eraser styles.

Figure 10-21: The eraser tool can now paint like the paintbrush, the airbrush, the pencil, or the old eraser (Block). The only question is, why didn't Adobe do this long ago?

As if this weren't enough, the eraser is pressure sensitive, it responds to Opacity settings, and you can create fading eraser strokes. For cryin' in a bucket, you even have access to the Wet Edges check box described back in Chapter 8. The only thing missing is the brush modes menu, which I'm afraid you'll have to live without.

Here are a few things to know and love about the eraser:

✦ **Erasing on a layer:** By now, some of you are probably thinking, "Why does Photoshop even have an eraser? If all it does is paint in the background color, who needs it? You can do that with any paint tool by pressing the X key." What makes Photoshop's eraser tool unique is layers. When working on a layer with the Preserve Transparency check box turned off, the eraser tool actually removes paint and exposes portions of the underlying image. The eraser tool suddenly performs like a real eraser.

Caution If the Preserve Transparency check box is turned on, Photoshop won't let the eraser bore holes in the layer and, instead, paints in the background color. For more information on Preserve Transparency and its other pals in the Layers palette, read Chapter 13.

✦ **Erasing lightly:** Change the Opacity setting in the Eraser Options palette to make portions of a layer translucent in inverse proportion to the Opacity value. For example, if you set the Opacity to 90 percent, you remove 90 percent of the opacity from the layer and, therefore, leave 10 percent of the opacity behind. The result is a nearly transparent stroke through the layer.

✦ **The eraser compared with layer masks:** As described in the "Creating layer-specific masks" section of Chapter 13, you can also erase holes in a layer using a layer mask. But unlike the eraser — which eliminates pixels for good — a layer mask doesn't do any permanent damage. On the other hand, using the eraser tool doesn't increase the size of your image, as a layer mask does. It's a trade-off.

✦ **Erasing everything:** In case you're curious, you now restore the entire Image window to the background color by clicking the Erase Image button in the Eraser Options palette. When you're working on a layer, the button changes to Erase Layer and erases the current layer only. Considering how often most folks need to start over at square one — that is, never — this isn't a function you're likely to use often.

✦ **Erasing with the pencil:** If you double-click the pencil icon in the Toolbox and select the Auto Erase check box in the Pencil Options palette, the pencil draws in the background color any time you click or drag on a pixel colored in the foreground color. This can be useful when you're drawing a line against a plain background. Set the foreground color to the color of the line; set the background color to the color of the background. Then use the pencil tool to draw and erase the line until you get it just right.

Note   Unlike the eraser, the pencil always draws either in the foreground or background color, even when used on a layer.

Reverting to the last saved image

The traditional reversion functions just described are all very well and good. But they don't hold a candle to Photoshop's selective reversion functions, which allow you to restore specific portions of an image to the way they looked when you last saved the image to disk.

The most convenient selective reversion function is the magic eraser tool. To access the magic eraser, press the Alt key while using the standard eraser tool. (You can also select the Erase to Saved check box in the Eraser Options palette, in which case dragging with the eraser reverts and Alt+dragging paints in the background color.) If you set your cursor display to Standard in the Preferences dialog box (File ➪ Preferences ➪ Display & Cursors), you see a tiny page icon behind the eraser cursor. Alt+drag with the magic eraser to paint with the last saved image or, if you prefer to think of this in a different way, to scrape away paint laid down since the last time you saved the image to disk. The process is demonstrated in Figure 10-22.

Figure 10-22: After making a dreadful mistake (top), I Alt+dragged with the eraser tool to restore the image to the way it looked when I last saved it (bottom).

Tip

Before Photoshop can begin to revert an image selectively, it must load the last saved version of the image into memory. This operation takes some time — the same amount of time, in fact, Photoshop took to open the image in the first place. You probably won't want to hold the mouse button down for the entire time. So, if this is the first time you've selectively reverted inside the current image, Alt+click with the eraser tool, and then wait for Photoshop to load the image. Your click won't effect the image in the slightest. After the load operation is completed, Alt+drag with the eraser as described earlier.

Reverting with the rubber stamp tool

Thanks to the improved performance of the eraser tool in Photoshop 3, the rubber stamp tool offers only two advantages over the magic eraser. First, you can take advantage of brush modes. By choosing a different brush mode from the pop-up menu in the upper-left corner of the Rubber Stamp Options palette, you can mix pixels from the changed and saved images to achieve interesting and, sometimes, surprising effects.

Second, you can revert to one of two different images. Either choose From Saved from the Option pop-up menu in the Rubber Stamp Options palette to revert to the last image saved to disk, or choose From Snapshot to revert to the last image stored in memory as a snapshot.

To store the current version of an image in memory, choose Edit ➪ Take Snapshot. The operation takes no time to complete because the image is already in memory. By choosing the Take Snapshot command, you merely instruct Photoshop not to eliminate this image.

There's no waiting when you use the tool, either. When you drag with the rubber stamp tool set to From Snapshot, you needn't wait for the image to load into memory as you do when reverting to a saved version, because it's already there. The function works instantaneously.

Photoshop can remember only one snapshot at a time. So when you choose the Take Snapshot command, you not only capture the current image, you also abandon any snapshot previously stored in memory. You cannot undo the Take Snapshot command; be careful how you use it.

Reverting selected areas

As I explained briefly in the previous chapter, you can also revert selected areas of an image. After selecting the portion of the image you want to revert, choose Edit ➪ Fill (or press Shift+Backspace) to display the Fill dialog box. Then select the Saved or Snapshot option from the Use pop-up menu and press Enter. The selected area reverts to the saved image or snapshot, according to your choice.

Because you're actually filling the selected area with the saved image or snapshot, all the selection operations I mention in Chapter 11 are equally applicable to reversions. You can revert a feathered or antialiased selection, you can revert an area selected with the pen tool, and you can even revert the contents of a layer and apply overlay modes from the Layers palette. (The Fill dialog box offers its own Mode pop-up menu, but it's easier to apply the overlay modes from the Layers palette because you can preview the results as they occur.)

Reversion limitations

Photoshop doesn't enable you to revert an image selectively from disk if you have in any way changed the number of pixels in the image since it was last saved. Neither the Fill command nor the eraser and rubber stamp will revert if you have chosen Image ➪ Image Size or Image ➪ Canvas Size or if you have used the crop tool or Image ➪ Crop command.

Photoshop also can't revert an image if you haven't yet saved the image or if it can't read the document from disk (as when the image is saved in a format that requires conversion or can only be opened by means of a plug-in module).

You can, however, work around the image-size problem by taking the following steps.

Steps: Selectively Reverting a Resized Image

1. **Select the entire image and copy it to the Clipboard.**

2. **Alt+click the Preview box in the lower-left corner of the window to view the size of the document in pixels.** Write this information down or assign it to memory (the memory in your head, that is).

3. **Choose File ⇨ Revert.** Photoshop loads the last-saved version of the image into the Image window.

4. **Choose Image ⇨ Canvas Size.** Resize the image to the dimensions you noted when Alt+clicking the Preview box in Step 2.

5. **Save the image to disk.**

6. **Paste the copied changes back into the Image window.** Photoshop pastes the changes as a new layer.

7. **Press Ctrl+E or choose Layer ⇨ Flatten Image to merge the new layer with the existing background layer.** You can then use the rubber stamp or magic eraser to revert the image selectively.

That's all there is to it. In fact, it's so simple, Photoshop should revert from a resized image without your help. Sometimes computers are so stupid. But what can you do? I guess this is why it's a good thing we're here to help them occasionally. We're lucky, really. The day computers are smart enough to take care of themselves, we'll all be obsolete.

Selections, Layers, and Text

Selections and Paths

Selection Fundamentals

Selections direct and protect. If it weren't for Photoshop's selection capabilities, you and I would be flinging paint on the canvas for all we're worth, like so many Jackson Pollock and Vasily Kandinsky wannabes, without any means to constrain, discriminate, or otherwise regulate the effects of our actions. Without selections, there'd be no filters, no color corrections, and no layers. In fact, we'd all be dangerously close to real life, that dreaded environment we've spent so much time and money to avoid.

That's the first reason this chapter is one of the most important in the book. The second reason is everything changes under Photoshop 4. If you're familiar with previous versions of the mighty image editor, get ready to see your world change.

Photoshop 4.0

This is a classic domino effect. To forge greater consistency with other Adobe applications (Illustrator, PageMaker, and the like), you now must use the move tool — previously used only with layers — to move and clone selections. Because this is such a pain in the keister, Photoshop 4 enables you to access the move tool temporarily by pressing and holding the Ctrl key (the same key used to access the arrow tool in Illustrator). This means old techniques that used to involve Ctrl+dragging, such as subtracting from selection outlines, have been reassigned to the Alt key. Old Alt key techniques change to Ctrl+Alt, and old Ctrl+Alt techniques change to . . . well, it gets pretty gnarly.

If the last paragraph went by a little quickly, not to worry. I explain every selection technique — new or old — in the following pages. Be aware, though, if you try to sit down and select images in Photoshop 4 the same way you used to select them in Version 3, you're likely to encounter quite a few surprises. My suggestion is you read through this chapter before you attempt anything important. Or at least skim the next few pages for the telltale Photoshop 4 icon.

How selections work

Before you can edit a portion of an image, you must first *select* it, which is computerese for marking the boundaries of the area you want to edit. To select part of an image in a painting program, you must surround it with a selection outline or *marquee;* this tells Photoshop where to apply your editing instructions. The selection outline appears as a moving pattern of dash marks, lovingly termed marching ants by doughheads who've been using the computer too long. (See Figure 11-1 for the inside story.)

Figure 11-1: A magnified view of a dash mark in a selection outline reveals a startling discovery.

Photoshop 4 provides eight tools for drawing selection outlines, which are described in the following list. You can access most of the tools from the keyboard, as noted in the parentheses:

✦ **Rectangular marquee (M):** The rectangular marquee tool has long been a staple of painting programs. This tool enables you to select rectangular or square portions of an image.

✦ **Elliptical marquee (M again):** The elliptical marquee tool works like the rectangular marquee except it selects elliptical or circular portions of an image. (Pressing the M key switches between the rectangular and elliptical marquee tools.)

✦ **Single-row/single-column:** The single-row and single-column tools enable you to select a single row or column of pixels that stretches the entire width or height of the image. These are the only tools in all of Photoshop you can't access from the keyboard.

✦ **Lasso (L):** The lasso tool enables you to select a free-form portion of an image. You simply drag with the lasso tool around the area you want to edit. Unlike the lasso tools in most painting programs, which shrink selection outlines to disqualify pixels in the background color, Photoshop's lasso tool selects the exact portion of the image you enclose in your drag.

✦ **Polygonal lasso (L again):** Click different points in your image to set corners in a straight-sided selection outline. This is a great way to select free-form if you're not good at wielding the mouse or your wrists are a tad sore. (You can achieve this same effect by Alt+clicking with the lasso tool, but I'll explain this more in the "Free-form outlines" section later in this chapter.)

✦ **Magic wand (W):** First introduced by Photoshop, this tool enables you to select a contiguous region of similarly colored pixels by clicking inside it. For example, you might click inside the boundaries of a face to isolate it from the hair and background elements. Novices tend to gravitate toward the magic wand because it seems like such a miracle tool but, in fact, it's the least predictable and, ultimately, the least useful of the bunch.

✦ **Pen (P):** Now available in the main Toolbox, the pen tool is both the most difficult to master and the most accurate and versatile of the selection tools. You use the pen tool to create a *path*, which is a special breed of selection outline. You click and drag to create individual points in the path. You can edit the path after the fact by moving, adding, and deleting points. You can even transfer a path via the Clipboard or by dragging and dropping to or from Illustrator 7 or FreeHand 7. For a discussion of the pen tool, read the "How to Draw and Edit Paths" section later in this chapter.

Photoshop 4's new type mask tool is also technically a selection tool because Photoshop converts each character of type to a selection outline. But type involves other issues that would merely confuse the content of this chapter. I've awarded type its own chapter (Chapter 14).

If this were all you needed to know to use the selection tools in Photoshop, the application would be on par with the average paint program. Part of what makes Photoshop exceptional, however, is it provides literally hundreds of little tricks to increase the functionality of every selection tool.

Furthermore, all of Photoshop's selection tools work together in perfect harmony. You can exploit the specialized capabilities of all eight tools (and the type mask tool, as well) to create a single selection boundary. After you understand which tool best serves which purpose, you can isolate any element in an image, no matter how complex or how delicate its outline.

Geometric selection outlines

The default tool in the upper-left corner of the Toolbox is the rectangular marquee tool. You can access the elliptical marquee tool by Alt+clicking on the marquee tool icon or by pressing the M key when the rectangular marquee tool is already selected. Pressing *M* again returns you to the rectangular marquee tool. Alt+clicking cycles through the single-row and single-column tools, as well.

The marquee tools are more versatile than they may appear at first glance. You can adjust the performance of each tool as follows:

✦ **Constraining to a square or circle:** Press and hold Shift *after* beginning your drag to draw a perfect square with the rectangular marquee tool or a perfect circle with the elliptical marquee tool. (Pressing Shift *before* dragging also works if no other selection is active; otherwise, this adds to a selection, as I explain later in the "Ways to Change Selection Outlines" section.)

✦ **Drawing a circular marquee:** When perusing an online forum a while back, someone asked how to create a perfect circular marquee. Despite more than a month of helpful suggestions — some highly imaginative — no one offered the easiest suggestion of all (well, I ultimately did, but I'm a know-it-all). So remember to press Shift after you begin to drag and you'll be one step ahead of the game.

✦ **Drawing out from the center:** Press and hold the Alt key after you begin dragging to draw the marquee from the center outward instead of from corner to corner. (Again, pressing Alt before dragging works if no selection outline is active; otherwise, this subtracts from the selection.) This technique is especially useful when you draw an elliptical marquee. Locating the center of the area you want to select is frequently easier than locating one of its corners — particularly because ellipses don't have corners.

✦ **Moving the marquee on the fly:** Here's the slickest addition to marquees in Photoshop 4. While drawing a marquee, press and hold the spacebar to move the marquee rather than to resize it. When you get the marquee in place, release the spacebar and keep dragging to modify the size. The spacebar is most helpful when drawing elliptical selections or when drawing a marquee out from the center — this eliminates the guesswork, so you can position your marquees exactly on target.

✦ **Selecting a single-pixel line:** Use the single-row and single-column tools to select a single row or column of pixels. I use these tools to fix screw-ups such as a missing line of pixels in a screen shot, to delete random pixels around the perimeter of an image, or to create perpendicular lines within a fixed space.

✦ **Constraining the aspect ratio:** If you know you want to create an image that conforms to a certain height/width ratio — called an *aspect ratio* — you can constrain either a rectangular or an elliptical marquee so the ratio between height and width remains fixed, no matter how large or small a marquee you create. To accomplish this, press Enter when the marquee tool is active to display the Marquee Options palette, shown in Figure 11-2. Then select Constrained Aspect Ratio from the Style pop-up menu. Enter the desired ratio values into the Width and Height option boxes. For example, if you want to crop an image to the ratio of a 640 × 480-pixel screen, enter 4 and 3, respectively, into the Width and Height option boxes and press Enter to confirm your changes. Then select the area of the image you want to retain and choose Image ➪ Crop.

Figure 11-2: Select the Constrained Aspect Ratio option in the Marquee Options palette to constrain the width and height of a marquee.

✦ **Sizing the marquee numerically:** If you're editing a screen shot or some other form of regular or schematic image, you may find specifying the size of a marquee numerically helpful. To do so, select the Fixed Size option from the Style pop-up menu and enter size values into the Width and Height option boxes. To match the selection to a 640 × 480-pixel screen, for example, just change the Width and Height values to 640 and 480.

✦ **Drawing feathered selections:** A Feather option box is available when you use either of the marquee tools. To *feather* a selection is to blur its edges beyond the automatic anti-aliasing afforded to most tools. For more information on feathering, refer to the "Softening selection outlines" section later in this chapter.

✦ **Creating jagged ellipses:** By default, elliptical selection outlines are anti-aliased. If you don't want anti-aliasing — you might prefer harsh edges when editing screen shots or designing screen interfaces — deselect the Anti-aliased check box. (This option is dimmed when you use the rectangular marquee because anti-aliasing is always on for this tool.)

Tip

Frequently, Photoshop's lack of geometric shape tools throws novices for a loop. In fact, such tools do exist — you simply don't recognize them. To draw a rectangle or ellipse in Photoshop, draw the shape as desired using the rectangular or elliptical marquee tool. Then choose Edit ➪ Fill or Edit ➪ Stroke, respectively, to color the interior or outline of the selection. You can also fill the selection using the Delete-key and Backspace-key techniques discussed in Chapter 9. It's that easy.

Free-form outlines

In comparison to the rectangular and elliptical marquee tools, the lasso tool provides a rather limited range of options. Generally speaking, you drag in a free-form path around the image you want to select. The few special considerations are as follows:

✦ **Feathering and anti-aliasing:** To adjust the performance of the lasso tool, press Enter while the lasso tool is selected to display the Lasso Options palette shown in Figure 11-3. Just as you can feather rectangular and elliptical marquees, you can feather selections drawn with the lasso tool. You can also soften the edges of a lasso outline by selecting the Anti-aliased check box.

Note

Be aware, although you can adjust the feathering of any selection after you draw it by choosing Select ➪ Feather, you must specify antialiasing before you draw a selection. Unless you have a specific reason for doing otherwise, leave the Anti-aliased check box turned on (as it is by default).

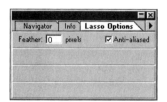

Figure 11-3: Double-click the lasso tool icon to access the veritable truckload of options shown here.

✦ **Drawing polygons:** If you press and hold the Alt key, the lasso tool works like a standard polygon tool. (*Polygon,* incidentally, means a shape with multiple straight sides.) With the Alt key down, you click to specify corners in a free-form polygon, as shown in Figure 11-4. If you want to add curves to the selection outline, drag with the tool while still pressing the Alt key. Photoshop closes the selection outline the moment you release both the Alt key and the mouse button.

Tip

If you make a mistake while creating a selection outline with the polygonal lasso, you can press Delete to eliminate the last segment you drew. Keep pressing Delete to eliminate more segments in the selection outline. This technique works until you close the selection outline and it turns into marching ants. After that, use the techniques discussed later in this chapter to adjust your selection outline.

Tip

You can extend a polygon selection outline to the absolute top, right, or bottom edges of an image. Just Alt+click with the lasso tool outside the Image window or, if the Image window is larger than the image, on the background canvas surrounding the image. Or you can click the scroll bars. Figure 11-4 illustrates the idea.

✦ **The polygonal lasso tool:** If you don't want to bother with pressing the Alt key, you can, instead, use Photoshop 4's new polygonal lasso tool. Press the L key when the lasso is active to switch to the polygonal lasso tool. Then click inside the image to set corners in the selection. Click the first point in the selection or double-click with the tool to complete the selection outline.

Tip

To create free-form curves with the polygonal lasso tool, press the Alt key and drag.

Adobe added the polygonal lasso to Photoshop 4 because of the new role of the Alt key. If no portion of the image is selected, it's no trick to Alt+click with the standard lasso to draw a straight-sided selection. But if some area in the image is selected, pressing Alt tells Photoshop that you want to subtract from the selection outline. For this reason, it's often easier to use the polygonal lasso (although you still can make it work by pressing Alt *after* you click with the lasso tool, as I explain in the "Ways to Change Selection Outlines" later in this chapter).

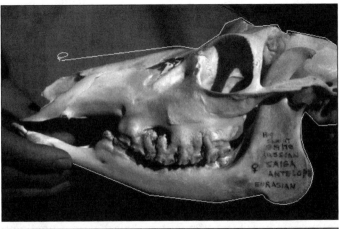

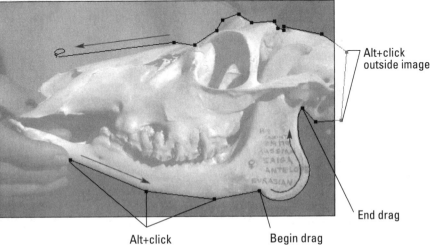

Alt+click
outside image

End drag

Alt+click   Begin drag

Figure 11-4: Alt+click with the lasso tool to create corners in a selection outline, shown as black squares in the bottom image. Drag to create free-form curves. Surprisingly, you can Alt+click outside the image to add corners outside the boundaries of the Image window.

The world of the wand

Using the magic wand tool is a no-brainer, right? You just click with the tool and it selects all the neighboring colors that fall within a selected range. The problem is getting the wand to recognize the same range of colors you see onscreen. For example, if you're editing a photo of a red plate against a pink tablecloth, how do you tell the magic wand to select the plate and leave the tablecloth alone?

Adjusting the performance of the wand is, sadly, pretty tricky and unsatisfying. If you press Enter when the magic wand is active, you see three options inside the Magic Wand Options palette, as shown in Figure 11-5. The Anti-aliased option softens the selection, as it does for the lasso tool. The Tolerance value determines the range of colors the tool selects when you click with it in the Image window. And the Sample Merged check box enables you to take all visible layers into account when defining a selection.

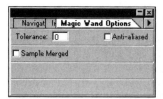

Figure 11-5: Use these options to specify the range of colors you want to select the next time you use the magic wand tool.

Adjusting the tolerance

By now you already understand what's up with the Anti-aliased option, so I'll start with Tolerance. You may have heard the standard explanation for adjusting the Tolerance value: You can enter any number from 0 to 255 in the Tolerance option box. Enter a low number to select a small range of colors; increase the value to select a wider range of colors.

Nothing is wrong with this explanation — in its own small way, the explanation is accurate — but it doesn't provide one iota of information you couldn't glean on your own. If you really want to understand this option, you must dig a little deeper.

When you click a pixel with the magic wand tool, Photoshop first reads the brightness value assigned to that pixel by each of the color channels. If you're working with a grayscale image, Photoshop reads a single brightness value from the one channel only; if you're working with an RGB image, it reads three brightness values, one each from the red, green, and blue channels; and so on. Because each color channel permits 8 bits of data, brightness values range from 0 to 255.

Next, Photoshop applies the Tolerance value, or simply *tolerance,* to the pixel. The tolerance describes a range that extends in both directions — lighter and darker — from each brightness value.

Suppose you're editing a standard RGB image. The tolerance is set to 32 (as it is by default); you click with the magic wand on a turquoise pixel, whose brightness values are 40 red, 210 green, and 170 blue. Photoshop adds and subtracts 32 from each brightness value to calculate the magic wand range that, in this case, is 8 to 72 red, 178 to 242 green, and 138 to 202 blue. Photoshop selects any pixel that both falls inside this range *and* can be traced back to the original pixel via an uninterrupted line of other pixels, which also fall within the range.

From this information, you can draw the following basic conclusions about the magic wand tool:

✦ **Creating a contiguous selection:** The magic wand selects a contiguous region of pixels emanating from the pixel on which you click. If you're trying to select land masses on a globe, for example, clicking St. Louis selects everything from Juneau to Mexico City. It doesn't select London, though, because the cities are separated by an ocean of water that doesn't fall within the tolerance range.

✦ **Clicking midtones maintains a higher range:** Because the tolerance range extends in two directions, you cut off the range when you click a light or dark pixel, as demonstrated in Figure 11-6. Consider the two middle gradations: In both cases, the tolerance is set to 60. In the top gradation, I clicked a pixel with a brightness of 140, so Photoshop calculated a range from 80 to 200. But when I clicked a pixel with a brightness value of 10, as in the bottom gradation, the range shrank to 0 to 70. Clicking a medium-brightness pixel, therefore, permits the most generous range.

✦ **Selecting brightness ranges:** Many people have the impression the magic wand selects color ranges. The magic wand, in fact, selects brightness ranges within color channels. So if you want to select a flesh-colored region — regardless of shade — set against an orange or red background, roughly equivalent in terms of brightness values, you probably should use a different tool.

✦ **Selecting from a single channel:** If the magic wand repeatedly fails to select a region of color that appears unique from its background, try isolating that region inside a single-color channel. You'll probably have the most luck isolating a color on the channel that least resembles it. For example, to select the yellow Sasquatch Xing sign shown in Color Plate 11-1, I switched to the blue channel (Ctrl+3). Because yellow contains no blue, and the brambly background contains quite a bit of blue — as demonstrated in the last example of Figure 11-7 — the magic wand can distinguish the two relatively easily. Experiment with this technique and it will prove even more useful over time.

32 (default)   60   100

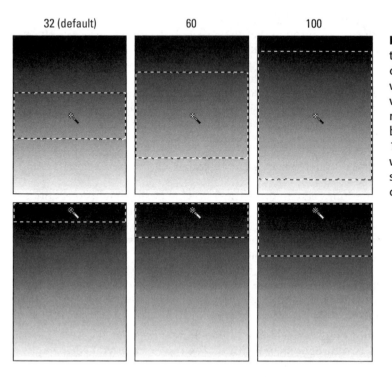

Figure 11-6: Note the results of clicking a pixel with a brightness value of 140 (top row) and a brightness value of 10 (bottom row) with the tolerance set to three different values.

Red   Green   Blue

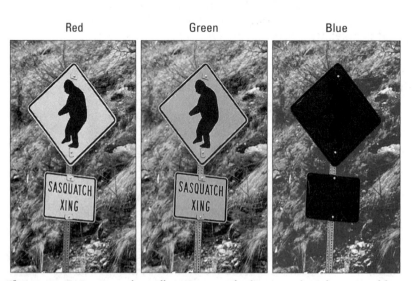

Figure 11-7: Because the yellow Sasquatch sign contains almost no blue, it appears most clearly distinguished from its background in the blue channel. So the blue channel is the easiest channel in which to select the sign with the magic wand.

Making the wand see beyond a single layer

The final option in the Magic Wand Options palette, the Sample Merged option, enables you to create a selection based on pixels from different layers (see Chapter 13). For example, returning to my previous land mass example, suppose you set Europe on one layer and North America on the layer behind it. The two continents overlap. Normally, if you clicked inside Europe with the magic wand tool, the wand would select an area inside Europe without extending out into the area occupied by North America. This is because the wand doesn't even see the contents of other layers; anything outside Europe is an empty void. We're talking pre-Columbus Europe here.

If you select the Sample Merged option, though, things change. Suddenly, the wand can see all the layers you can see. If you click Europe, and if North America and Europe contain similar colors, the wand selects across both shapes.

Mind you, the Sample Merged option does not permit the wand to select images on two separate layers. Strange as this may sound, no selection tool can pull off this feat. Every one of the techniques explained both in this chapter and in all of Part III is applicable to only one layer at a time. Sample Merged merely allows the wand to draw selection outlines that appear to encompass colors on many layers.

What good is this? Well, suppose you want to apply an effect to both Europe and North America. With the help of Sample Merged, you can draw a selection outline that encompasses both continents. After you apply the effect to Europe, you can switch to the North America layer — the selection outline remains intact — and then reapply the effect.

Ways to Change Selection Outlines

If you don't draw a selection outline correctly the first time, you have two options. You can either draw it again from scratch, which is a real bore, or you can change your botched selection outline, which is likely to prove the more efficient solution. You can deselect a selection, add to a selection, subtract from a selection, and even select the unselected stuff and deselect the selected stuff. (If this sounds like a load of nonsense, keep reading.)

Quick changes

Some methods of adjusting a selection outline are automatic: You choose a command and you're done. The following list explains how a few commands — all members of the Select menu — work:

✦ **Hide Edges (Ctrl+H):** Get those marching ants out of my face! We're all grown-ups, right? Do we really need constant streams of marching ants to tell us what we've selected? We were there; we remember. My point is, although visible selection outlines can be helpful sometimes, they can as readily impede your view of an image. When they annoy you, press Ctrl+H. Press Ctrl+H again if you later need to see the selection outline.

✦ **Deselect (Ctrl+D):** You can deselect the selected portion of an image in three ways. You can select a different portion of the image; click anywhere in the Image window with the rectangular marquee tool, the elliptical marquee tool, or the lasso tool; or choose Select ➪ None. Remember, though, when no part of an image is selected, the entire image is susceptible to your changes. If you apply a filter, choose a color-correction command, or use a paint tool, you affect every pixel of the foreground image.

✦ **Inverse (Ctrl+Shift+I):** Choose Select ➪ Inverse to reverse the selection. Photoshop deselects the portion of the image previously selected and selects the portion of the unselected image. This way, you can begin a selection by outlining the portion of the image you want to protect, rather than the portion you want to affect.

Manually adding and subtracting

Ready for some riddles? When editing a portrait, how do you select both eyes without affecting any other portion of the face? Answer: By drawing one selection and then tacking on a second selection. How do you select a doughnut and leave the hole behind? Answer: Encircle the doughnut with the elliptical marquee tool, and then use the same tool to subtract the center.

Photoshop enables you to whittle away at a selection, add pieces on again, whittle away some more, ad infinitum, until you get it exactly right. Short of sheer laziness or frustration, no reason exists why you can't eventually create the selection outline of your dreams:

✦ **Adding to a selection outline:** To increase the area enclosed in an existing selection outline, Shift+drag with one of the marquee or lasso tools. You also can Shift+click with the magic wand tool or Shift+click with one of the marquee tools when the Fixed Size option is active (as described back in the "Geometric selection outlines" section earlier in this chapter).

✦ **Subtracting from a selection outline:** To take a bite from an existing selection outline, press the Alt key while using one of the selection tools.

Photoshop 4.0

Some of you longtime Photoshop users are probably sitting there with your mouths hanging open. "Alt to subtract? How could Adobe do such a thing?" After six years of using the Ctrl key to subtract, this was my reaction. But like it or not, the change is set in stone. From this day on, you press the Ctrl key to get the move tool, and you use Alt to subtract from a selection.

✦ **Intersecting one selection outline with another:** Another way to subtract from an existing selection outline is to Shift+Alt+drag around the selection with the rectangular marquee, elliptical marquee, or lasso tool. You also can Shift+Alt+click with the magic wand tool. Shift+Alt+dragging instructs Photoshop to retain only the portion of an existing selection that also falls inside the new selection outline. I frequently use this technique to confine a selection within a rectangular or elliptical border.

Photoshop 4.0

Although the old Ctrl+key tasks have switched to Alt, Photoshop 4 hasn't entirely abandoned faithful users of previous versions. The program now presents you with special cursors to show you what you're doing. Say you've selected part of an image and the lasso tool is active. When you press the Shift key, Photoshop appends a little plus sign to the lasso cursor to show you're about to add. When you press Alt, you see a little minus sign. Press Shift+Alt to get an *x* for *intersect*. Watching your cursors will make the transition easier.

Using Shift and Alt like a pro

The expanded roles of the Shift and Alt keys in adding, subtracting, and intersecting selection outlines can interfere with your ability to take advantage of other functions of the selection tools. For example, when no portion of an image is selected, you can Shift+drag with the rectangular marquee tool to draw a square. But after a selection is active, Shift+dragging adds a rectangle — not a square — to the selection outline.

The trick is to learn when to press the Shift and Alt keys. Sometimes you must press the key before you begin your drag; sometimes you must press the key after you begin the drag, but before you release. For example, to add a square to a selection outline, Shift+drag, release Shift while keeping the mouse button pressed, and press Shift again to snap the rectangle to a square. The same goes for adding a circle with the elliptical marquee tool.

A few other techniques follow that you'll do well to master. They sound pretty elaborate, I admit, but with a little practice, they become second nature (so does tightrope walking, but don't let that worry you):

✦ To subtract a square or circle from a selection, Alt+drag, release Alt, press Shift, drag until you get it right, release the mouse button, and then release Shift.

✦ To add a rectangle or ellipse and draw from the center outward, Shift+drag, release Shift, press the Alt key, and hold Alt until after you release the mouse button. You can even press the spacebar during the drag to move the marquee around, if you like.

✦ To subtract a marquee drawn from the center outward, Alt+drag, release Alt, press Alt again, and hold the key down until after you release.

✦ What about drawing a straight-sided selection with the lasso tool? To add a straight-sided area to an existing selection, Shift+drag with the tool for a short distance. With the mouse button still down, release Shift and press the Alt key. Then click around as you normally would, while keeping the Alt key down.

✦ To subtract a straight-sided area, Alt+drag with the lasso, release Alt, press Alt again, and click around with the tool.

If you can't manage the last two lasso-tool techniques, then switch to the polygonal lasso instead. In fact, the reason Adobe provided the polygonal lasso tool was to accommodate folks who don't want to deal with pressing the Alt key seven times during a single drag.

Adding and subtracting by command

Photoshop provides several commands under the Select menu that automatically increase or decrease the number of selected pixels in an image according to numerical specifications. The commands in the Select ➪ Modify submenu work as follows:

✦ **Border:** This command selects an area of a specified thickness around the perimeter of the current selection outline and deselects the rest of the selection. For example, to select a 6-point-thick border around the current selection, choose Select ➪ Modify ➪ Border, enter 6 into the Width option box, and press Enter. But what's the point? After all, if you want to create an outline around a selection, you can accomplish this in fewer steps by choosing Edit ➪ Stroke. The Border command, however, broadens your range of options. You can apply a special effect to the border, move the border to a new location, or even create a double-outline effect by first applying Select ➪ Modify ➪ Border and then Edit ➪ Stroke.

✦ **Smooth:** This command rounds off the sharp corners and weird anomalies in the outline of a selection. When you choose Select ➪ Modify ➪ Smooth, the program asks you to enter a Sample Radius value. Photoshop smoothes out corners by drawing little circles around them, and the Sample Radius value determines the radius of these circles. Larger values result in smoother corners.

The Smooth command is especially useful in combination with the magic wand. After you draw one of those weird, scraggly selection outlines with the wand tool, use Select ➪ Modify ➪ Smooth to smooth out the rough edges.

✦ **Expand and Contract:** Both of these commands do exactly what they say, either expanding or contracting the selected area by 1 to 16 pixels. For example, if you want an elliptical selection to grow by 8 pixels, choose Select ➪ Modify ➪ Expand, enter 8, and call it a day. These are extremely useful commands I'll refer to several times throughout the book.

Both Expand and Contract have a flattening effect on a selection. To round things off, apply the Smooth command with a Sample Radius value equal to the number you just entered into the Expand Selection or Contract Selection dialog box. You'll end up with a pretty vague selection outline, but what do you expect from automated commands?

In addition to the Expand command, Photoshop provides two older commands — Grow and Similar — that increase the area covered by a selection outline. Both commands resemble the magic wand tool because they measure the range of eligible pixels by way of a Tolerance value. In fact, the commands rely on the same Tolerance value found inside the Magic Wand Options palette. So if you want to adjust the impact of either command, you must first select the magic wand icon in the Toolbox:

✦ **Grow:** Choose Select ➪ Grow to select all pixels that both neighbor an existing selection and resemble the colors included in the selection, in accordance with the Tolerance value. In other words, Select ➪ Grow is the command equivalent of the magic wand tool. If you feel constrained because you can only click one pixel at a time with the magic wand tool, you may prefer to select a small group of representative pixels with a marquee tool, and then choose Select ➪ Grow to initiate the wand's magic. (If you're familiar with previous versions of Photoshop, be aware the old Ctrl+G keyboard shortcut has been reassigned to Layer ➪ Group with Previous.)

✦ **Similar:** Another member of the Select menu, the Similar command works like the Grow command, except the pixels needn't be adjacent to one another. When you choose Select ➪ Similar, Photoshop selects any pixel that falls within the tolerance range, regardless of the location of the pixel in the foreground image.

One of the best applications for the Similar command is to isolate a complicated image set against a consistent background whose colors are significantly lighter or darker than the image. Consider Figure 11-8, which features a dark and ridiculously complex foreground image set against a continuous background of medium-to-light brightness values. Although the image features sufficient contrast to make it a candidate for the magic wand tool, I would never in a million years recommend using this tool; too many of the colors in the foreground image are discontinuous. The following steps explain how to separate this image using the Similar command in combination with a few other techniques I've described thus far.

Steps: Isolating a Complex Image Set Against a Plain Background

1. **Use the rectangular marquee tool to select some representative portions of the background.** In Figure 11-8, I selected the lightest and darkest portions of the background along with some representative shades in between. Remember, you make multiple selections by Shift+dragging with the tool.

Figure 11-8: Before choosing Select ➪ Similar, select a few sample portions of the background, so Photoshop has something on which to base its selection range.

2. **Double-click the magic wand tool icon to display the Tolerance option box.** For my image, I entered a Tolerance value of 16, a relatively low value, in keeping with the consistency of the background. If your background is less homogenous, you may want to enter a higher value. Make certain you turn on the Anti-aliased check box.

3. **Choose Select ➪ Similar.** Photoshop should select the entire background. If Photoshop fails to select all the background, choose Edit ➪ Undo (Ctrl+Z) and use the rectangular marquee tool to select more portions of the background. You may also want to increase the Tolerance value in the Magic Wand Options palette. If Photoshop's selection bleeds into the foreground image, try reducing the Tolerance value.

4. **Choose Select ➪ Inverse.** Or press Ctrl+Shift+I. Photoshop selects the foreground image and deselects the background.

5. **Modify the selection as desired.** If the detail you want to select represents only a fraction of the entire image, Shift+Alt+drag around the portion of the image you want to retain using the lasso tool. In Figure 11-9, I Shift+Alt+dragged with the polygonal lasso tool to draw a straight-sided outline around the selection.

Figure 11-9: Shift+Alt+drag with the polygonal lasso tool to intersect the area you want to select with a straight-sided outline.

6. **Congratulations, you've isolated your complex image.** Now you can filter your image, colorize it, or perform whatever operation inspired you to select this image in the first place. For myself, I wanted to super-impose the image onto a different background. To do so, I copied the image to the Clipboard (Ctrl+C), opened the desired background image, and then pasted the first image into place (Ctrl+V). The result, shown in Figure 11-10, still needs some touching up with the paint and edit tools, but it's not half bad for an automated selection process.

Photoshop 4.0

Whenever you introduce a selection into another image — by copying and pasting or by dragging the selection and dropping it into another Image window — Photoshop 4 automatically assigns the selection to a new layer. This is a great safety mechanism, which prevents you from permanently affixing the selection to its new background. But this also means you can't save the image in a file format other than the native Photoshop format without first flattening the image. For the big, new story on layers, read Chapter 13.

Figure 11-10: The completed selection superimposed onto a new background

Softening selection outlines

You can soften a selection in two ways. The first method is anti-aliasing, introduced in the "Rasterizing an Illustrator or FreeHand file" section of Chapter 4. Anti-aliasing is an intelligent and automatic softening algorithm, which mimics the appearance of edges you'd expect to see in a sharply focused photograph.

Note   Where did the term *anti-alias* originate? Well, to *alias* an electronic signal is to dump essential data, thus degrading the quality of a sound or image. Anti-aliasing boosts the signal and smoothes the rough spots in a way that preserves the overall quality.

When you draw an anti-aliased selection outline in Photoshop, the program calculates the hard-edged selection at twice its actual size. The program then shrinks the selection in half using bicubic interpolation (described in the "General preferences" section of Chapter 2). The result is a crisp image with no visible jagged edges.

The second softening method, feathering, is more dramatic. Feathering gradually dissipates the selection outline, giving it a blurry edge. Photoshop accommodates partially selected pixels; feathering fades the selection both inward and outward from the original edge.

You can specify the number of pixels affected either before or after drawing a selection. To feather a selection before you draw it, double-click the marquee or lasso tool icon and enter a value into the Feather option box in the Options palette. To feather a selection after drawing it, choose Select ➪ Feather. Or press the new keyboard shortcut, Ctrl+Shift+D. (Why *D* for feather? Because it Dissipates the selection, naturally.)

The Feather Radius value determines the approximate distance over which Photoshop fades a selection, measured in pixels in both directions from the original selection outline. Figure 11-11 shows three selections lifted from the image at the bottom of the figure. The first selection is anti-aliased only. I feathered the second and third selections, assigning Feather Radius values of 4 and 12, respectively. As you can see, a small feather radius makes a selection appear fuzzy; a larger radius makes it fade into view.

Figure 11-11: Three clones selected with the elliptical marquee tool. The top image is anti-aliased and not feathered, the next is feathered with a radius of 4 pixels, and the third is feathered with a radius of 12 pixels.

The math behind the feather

A few eagle-eyed readers have written to ask me why feathering blurs a selection outline more than the number of pixels stated in the Feather Radius value. A radius of 4 pixels actually affects a total of 20 pixels: 10 inward and 10 outward. The reason revolves around Photoshop's use of a mathematical routine called the *Gaussian bell curve,* which exaggerates the distance over which the selection outline is blurred.

Figure 11-12 demonstrates the math visually. The top-left image shows a hard-edged elliptical selection filled with white against a black background. To its right is a side view of the ellipse, in which black pixels are short and white pixels are tall. (Okay, so it's a really a graph, but I didn't want to scare you.) Because no gray pixels are in the ellipse, the side view has sharp vertical walls.

The bottom-left image shows what happens if I first feather the selection with a radius of 4 pixels and then fill it with white. The side view now graphs a range of gray values, which taper gradually from black to white. See those gray areas on the sides (each labeled Diameter)? Those are the pixels that fall into the 8-pixel diameter, measured 4 pixels in and out from the original selection outline. These gray areas slope in straight lines.

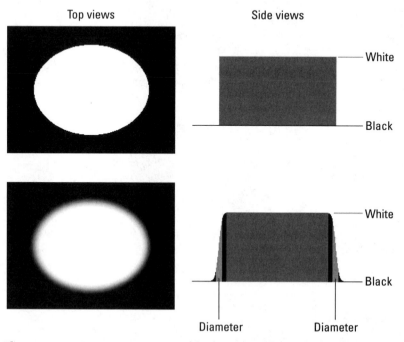

Figure 11-12: Here are some graphic demonstrations of what happens when you feather a selection. Photoshop tapers the ends of the feathered selections (shown by the black areas, bottom right) to prevent your eye from easily detecting where the feathering starts and stops.

The rounded areas of the side view — painted black — are the Gaussian bell curves. These are appended onto the radius of the feather to ensure smooth transitions between the blurry edges and the selected and deselected pixels. Programs that do not include these extra Gaussian curves, such as Corel Photo-Paint for Windows, end up producing ugly feathered selections that appear to have sharp, incongruous edges.

Tip

If exact space is an issue, you can count on the Feather command affecting about 2.7 times as many pixels as you enter into the Feather Radius option box, both in and out from the selection. That's a total of 5.4 times as many pixels as the radius in all.

If this is more than you wanted to know, cast it from your mind. Feathering makes the edges of a selection fuzzy — 'nuff said.

Putting feathering to use

You can use feathering to remove an element from an image while leaving the background intact, a process described in the following steps. The image described in these steps, shown in Figure 11-13, is a NASA photo of a satellite with the Earth in the background. I wanted to use this background with another image, but to do so I first had to eliminate that satellite. By feathering and cloning a selection outline, I covered the satellite with a patch so seamless you'd swear the satellite was never there.

Steps: Removing an Element from an Image

1. **Draw a selection around the element using the lasso tool.** The selection needn't be an exact fit; in fact, you want it rather loose, so allow a buffer zone of at least six pixels between the edges of the image and the selection outline.

2. **Drag the selection outline over a patch in the image.** Now that you've specified the element you want to remove, you must find a patch, that is, some portion of the image to cover the element in a manner that matches the surrounding background. In Figure 11-14, the best match seemed an area just below and to the right of the satellite. To select this area, move the selection outline independently of the image merely by dragging it with the lasso tool. (In Photoshop 4, dragging a selection with a selection tool moves the outline without affecting the pixels.) Make certain you allow some space between the selection outline and the element you're trying to cover.

3. **Choose Select ➪ Feather.** Or press Ctrl+Shift+D. Enter a small value (8 or less) in the Feather Radius option box — just enough to make the edges fuzzy. (I entered 3.) Then press Enter to initiate the operation.

Figure 11-13: Your mission, if you choose to accept it, is to remove the satellite by covering it with selections cloned from the background.

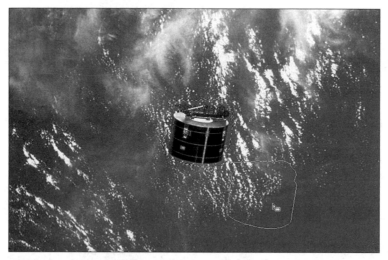

Figure 11-14: After drawing a loose outline around the satellite with the lasso tool, I dragged the outline to select a portion of the background.

4. **Clone the patch onto the area you want to cover.** Select the move tool by pressing the V key. Then Alt+drag the feathered selection to clone the patch and position it over the element you want to cover, as shown in Figure 11-15. To align the patch correctly, choose Select ➪ Hide Edges (Ctrl+H) to hide the marching ants and then nudge the patch into position with the arrow keys.

Figure 11-15: Next, I used the move tool to Alt+drag the feathered selection over the satellite. Sadly, the patch was imperfect and required further adjustments.

5. **Repeat as desired.** My patch was only partially successful. The upper-left corner of the selection matches clouds in the background, but the lower-right corner is dark and cloudless, an obvious rift in the visual continuity of the image. The solution: Try again. With the lasso tool, I drew a loose outline around the dark portion of the image and dragged it up and to the left as shown in Figure 11-16.

6. **It's all déjà vu from here on.** I chose Select ➪ Feather, entered 6 into the Feather Radius option box — thus allowing the clouds a sufficient range to taper off — and pressed Enter. I then selected the move tool and Alt+dragged the feathered patch over the dark, cloudless rift. Finally, I nudged, nudged, nudged with the arrow keys, and voilà, no more satellite. Figure 11-17 shows $200 million worth of hardware vaporized in less than five minutes.

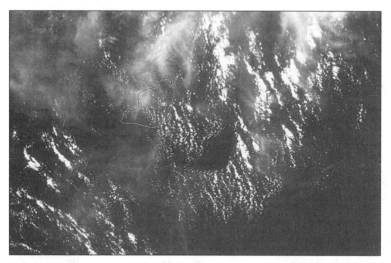

Figure 11-16: I used the lasso tool to draw a new outline around the dark, cloudless portion of the patch. Then I dragged the outline to a different spot in the background.

Figure 11-17: I selected a new bit of cloudy sky and placed it over the formerly cloudless portion of the patch. Satellite? What satellite?

Moving and Duplicating Selections

The previous steps showed how you can move either the selected pixels or the empty selection outline to a new location. Now it's time to examine these techniques in greater depth.

The new role of the move tool

In Photoshop 4, you must use the move tool to move the selected pixels. No longer is it acceptable merely to drag inside the selection with the marquee, lasso, or wand tool, as in Version 3 and earlier. The move tool is no longer an elective feature; now it's your only option.

You can select the move tool at any time by pressing the V key (for *mooV*). The advantage of the move tool is no chance exists to deselect an image or harm the selection outline. Drag inside the selected area to move the selection; drag outside the selection to move the entire layer, selection included. I explain layers in more detail in Chapter 13.

Tip   To access the move tool on a temporary basis, press and hold the Ctrl key. The move tool remains active as long as Ctrl is pressed. This shortcut works when any tool except the hand or pen tool is active. Assign this shortcut to memory at your earliest convenience. Believe me, you'll spend a lot of time Ctrl+dragging in Photoshop 4.

Previewing the move

If you start in dragging (or Ctrl+dragging) a selection, Photoshop displays the outline of the selected area during a move, as shown in the top image in Figure 11-18. But you can also preview the selected pixels in all their splendor as you move them, as shown in the bottom image in the figure. As you might expect, this slows down the screen refresh speed. This also prevents you from viewing the portion of the image behind the selection. But times occur when this capability comes in extremely handy.

Tip   To preview a selection as you move it, click and hold on the selection before you move the mouse. The hourglass cursor appears. The moment the cursor changes back to the standard move cursor — which may happen quickly if you're using a speedy system — you can start dragging.

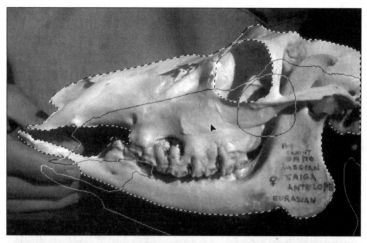

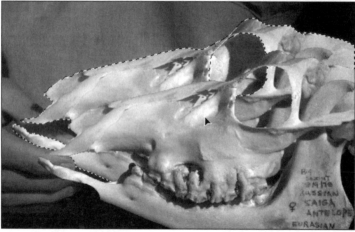

Figure 11-18: You can drag a selection right off the bat to see only its outline (top) or you can press and hold the mouse button for a moment before beginning your drag to preview the selection (bottom).

Making precise movements

Photoshop provides three methods for moving selections in prescribed increments. In each case, the move tool is active, unless otherwise indicated:

✦ First, you can nudge a selection in 1-pixel increments by pressing an arrow key on the keyboard or nudge in 10-pixel increments by pressing Shift with an arrow key. This technique is useful for making precise adjustments to the position of an image.

To nudge a selected area when the move tool is not active, press Ctrl with an arrow key. Press Ctrl and Shift with an arrow key to move in 10-pixel increments. Once the selection is floating — that is, after your first nudge — you can let up on the Ctrl key and use only the arrows (assuming a selection tool is active).

✦ Second, you can press Shift during a drag to constrain a move to some 45-degree direction — that is, horizontally, vertically, or diagonally.

✦ And third, you can use the Info palette to track your movements and to help locate a precise position in the image. To display the Info palette, choose Window ➪ Show Info or press F8. Figure 11-19 shows the Info palette as it appears in Photoshop 4. The first section of the Info palette displays the color values of the image area beneath your cursor. When you move a selection, the other eight items in the palette monitor movement, as follows:

• **X, Y:** These values show the coordinate position of your cursor. The distance is measured from the upper-left corner of the image in the current unit of measure. The unit of measure in Figure 11-19 is pixels.

• **ΔX, ΔY:** These values indicate the distance of your move as measured horizontally and vertically.

• **A, D:** The A and D values reflect the angle and direct distance of your drag.

• **W, H:** These values reflect the width and height of your selection.

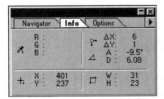

Figure 11-19: The Info palette provides a world of numerical feedback when you move a selection.

Cloning a selection

When you move a selection, you leave a hole in your image in the background color, as shown in the top half of Figure 11-20. If you prefer, instead, to leave the original in place during a move, you have to *clone* the selection — that is, create a copy of the selection without upsetting the contents of the Clipboard. Photoshop offers several different ways to clone a selection:

✦ **Alt+dragging:** When the move tool is active, press the Alt key and drag a selection to clone it. The bottom half of Figure 11-20 shows a selection I Alt+dragged three times. (Between clonings, I changed the gray level of each selection to make them more identifiable.)

✦ **Ctrl+Alt+dragging:** If some tool other than the move tool is active, Ctrl+Alt+drag the selection to clone it. This is probably the technique you'll end up using most often.

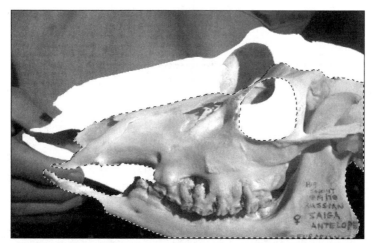

Figure 11-20: When you move a selection, you leave a gaping hole in the selection's wake (top). When you clone an image, you leave a copy of the selection behind. To make a point, I cloned the selection in the bottom image three times.

✦ **Alt+arrowing:** When the move tool is active, press Alt in combination with one of the arrow keys to clone the selection and nudge it one pixel away from the original. If you want to move the image multiple pixels, Alt+arrow the first time only. Then nudge the clone using the arrow key alone. Otherwise, you'll create a bunch of clones you can't undo.

✦ **Ctrl+Alt+arrowing:** If some other tool is active, press Ctrl and Alt with an arrow key. Again, press only the Alt key the first time, unless you want to create a string of clones.

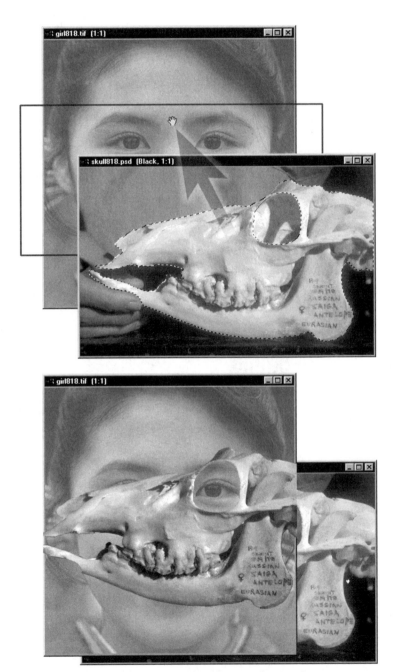

Figure 11-21: Use the move tool to drag a selection from one open window and drop it into another (top). This creates a clone of the selection in the receiving window (bottom).

✦ **Drag-and-drop:** Like about every other program on the planet, Photoshop enables you to clone a selection between documents by dragging it with the move tool from one open window and dropping it in another, as demonstrated in Figure 11-21. As long as you manage to drop into the second window, the original image remains intact and selected in the first window. My advice: Don't worry about exact positioning during a drag-and-drop; first get it into the second window and then worry about placement.

Note

You can drag-and-drop multiple layers if you link the layers first. For more information on this subject, see "Linking layers" in Chapter 13.

✦**Shift+drop:** If the two images are exactly the same size — pixel for pixel — press the Shift key when dropping the selection to position it in the same spot from which it came in the original image. This is called *registering the selection.*

Tip

If an area is selected in the destination image, Shift+dropping positions the selection you're moving in the center of the selection in the destination image. This tip works regardless of whether the two images are the same size.

✦ **Ctrl+drag-and-drop:** Again, if some other tool than the move tool is selected, you must press the Ctrl key when you drag to move the selected pixels from one window to the other.

Moving a selection outline independently of its contents

After all this talk about the move tool and the Ctrl key, you may wonder what happens if you drag a selection with the marquee, lasso, or wand, as in the good old days. The answer is, you move the selection outline independently of the image. This technique serves as yet another means to manipulate inaccurate selection outlines. It also enables you to mimic one portion of an image inside another portion of the image or inside a completely different Image window.

In the top image in Figure 11-22, I used the marquee tool to drag the skull outline down and to the right, so it only partially overlapped the skull. Note, the image itself remains unaltered. I then lightened the new selection, applied a few strokes to set it off from its background, and gave it stripes, as shown in the bottom image. For all I know, this is exactly what a female Russian Saiga antelope looks like.

Tip

You can nudge a selection outline independently of its contents by pressing an arrow key when a selection tool is active. Press Shift with an arrow key to move the outline in 10-pixel increments.

The great news about the revised role of the selection tools is you can drag-and-drop empty selection outlines between images. Just drag the selection from one image and drop it into another, as demonstrated in the first example of Figure

11-21. The only difference is just the selection outline gets cloned; the pixels remain behind. This is a great way to copy pixels back and forth between images. You can set up an exact selection in Image A, drag it into Image B with the marquee tool, move it over the pixels you want to clone, and Ctrl+drag-and-drop the selection back into Image A. This is slick as hair grease, I'm telling you.

So remember, the selection tools now affect only the selection outline. The selection tools never affect the pixels themselves; that's the move tool's job.

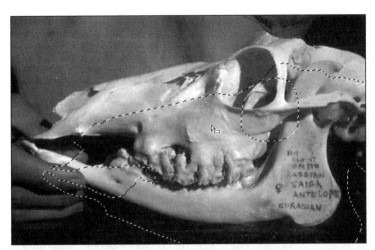

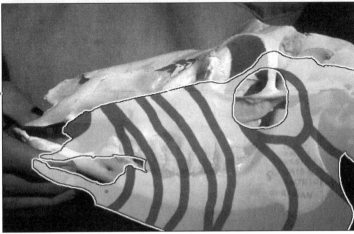

Figure 11-22: Drag a selection with a selection tool to move the outline independently of its image (top). Wherever you drag the selection outline becomes the new selection (bottom).

Floating a selection

In Photoshop 4, floating selections are almost dead, but not quite. First, a *floating selection* is a selection that hovers above the surface of the image. The beauty of a floating selection is you can move it and apply fills using the Delete or Backspace key, all without affecting the underlying image itself. Then you can mix the floating selection with the underlying image by adjusting the Opacity slider bar in the Layers palette. You can also select a blend mode from the pop-up menu in the upper-left corner of the Layers palette.

In Photoshop 4, you can float a selection in one of two ways:

✦ **Move:** When you move a selection by Ctrl+dragging it or pressing Ctrl with an arrow key, Photoshop floats the selection at its new location.

✦ **Clone:** Whether you clone a selection by Ctrl+Alt+dragging it or by pressing Ctrl and Alt in combination with an arrow key, Photoshop floats the cloned selection.

Conversely, all the following techniques *defloat* a selection — that is, drop it in place again — making the image itself susceptible to changes. In Photoshop 4, this list has grown much longer:

✦ **Deselect:** Because a floating selection must remain selected to remain floating, choosing Select ➪ None (Ctrl+D) defloats a selection. Likewise, any operation with the added effect of deselecting an image, such as selecting a different portion of the image, changing the canvas size, or choosing File ➪ Revert, defloats the selection.

✦ **Add to the selection:** If you add to a selection outline by pressing Shift while using any of the selection tools (or adding a path to a selection outline from the Make Selection dialog box, as I'll describe shortly), Photoshop defloats the image. You can subtract from a selection outline and intersect it, however, without defloating it.

✦ **Automatically adjusting the selection outline:** All the commands in the Select menu that affect the shape of a selection outline — including Inverse, Feather, Grow, Similar, and the commands in the Select ➪ Modify submenu — set down the selection. Like Shift+dragging with a selection tool, these commands add pixels to the selection outline, which invariably requires a defloat.

✦ **Paint or edit inside a selection:** If you so much as click in a selection with a paint or edit tool, Photoshop drops the selection.

✦ **Stroke the selection:** Photoshop automatically defloats a selection when you apply Edit ➪ Stroke.

✦ **Apply a filter or color correction:** One of my favorite things to do in previous versions of Photoshop was to float a selection, apply a filter, and then mix it with the underlying original to achieve a more subtle effect. Now, if you apply a filter or color correction to a floater, the floater drops. Phooey.

Luckily, Photoshop 4 offers several workarounds, including the new Filter ➪ Fade command, which I discuss in Chapter 15.

✦ **Editing a mask:** Photoshop automatically defloats a selection when you switch to the quick mask mode, whether or not you edit the mask. For more information on this wonderful feature, read Chapter 12.

✦ **Layer ➪ Defloat:** You can drop a selection by choosing Layer ➪ Defloat or by pressing the new keyboard equivalent, Ctrl+E (for, "Eke, I just dropped my floater!").

Photoshop 4.0

Why this new hostility toward floaters (which never did anyone any harm)? Adobe wants you to get in the habit of using layers. By taking away most of the advantages of floaters, you're left with no other choice. Layers are great and they have many advantages over floaters (as you'll learn in Chapter 13). But I honestly see no reason why floaters had to be undercut so radically. Thanks for letting me get that off my chest.

If everything dropped a floater, there wouldn't be any use for them at all. Here are a few things you can do to leave your floater hovering in peace:

✦ **Move the floater:** You can move a floating selection by dragging it with the marquee, lasso, wand, or move tool. (No need for the Ctrl key once the selection is floating.) You can also nudge the floaters with the arrow keys, again sans Ctrl.

✦ **Fill the floater:** Press Alt+Delete or Alt+Backspace to fill the floaters with the foreground color. Press Ctrl+Delete or Ctrl+Backspace to fill a floater with the background color. (Don't press Delete on its own, though — that just deletes the floater.) Both Alt+Delete/Alt+Backspace and Ctrl+Delete/Ctrl+Backspace are great ways to establish drop shadows.

✦ **Subtract from the floater:** While a selection is floating, you can chip away portions of it by Alt+dragging with a marquee tool or the lasso tool or by Alt+clicking with the magic wand. The area around which you Alt+drag (or on which you Alt+click) disappears.

✦ **Intersect the floater:** Similarly, you can Shift+Alt+drag with a marquee or lasso tool or Shift+Alt+click with the magic wand tool to specify the portion of the selection you want to retain. Anything not included inside the Shift+Alt+drag or Shift+Alt+click disappears.

✦ **Transform the floater:** You can apply Photoshop 4's new Layer ➪ Free Transform (Ctrl+T) to a floater without dropping it. This command enables you to scale, rotate, slant, and distort a selection in one operation. I cover this and the other excellent transformation features in Chapter 13.

✦ **Change the Opacity:** As in previous versions of Photoshop, you can adjust the transparency of a floater by adjusting the Opacity slider bar or by pressing number keys. Press the 1 key for 10 percent, 2 for 20 percent, and so on, up to 0 for 100 percent. You can also press two numbers in a row to specify an exact Opacity value. Lower Opacity settings make the floater translucent, so you can see through to the pixels below.

✦ **Blend modes:** Select a blend mode from the pop-up menu at the top of the Layers palette to merge the floater with the underlying image in weird and wonderful ways. This topic is so huge, it takes all of Chapter 19 to cover it.

How to Draw and Edit Paths

Photoshop's path tools provide the most flexible and precise ways to define a selection short of masking. But, though a godsend to the experienced user, the path tools represent something of a chore to novices and intermediates. Most people take a while to become comfortable with the path tools because a selection outline must be drawn one point at a time.

Note   If you're familiar with Illustrator's pen tool and other path-editing functions, you'll find Photoshop's tools are nearly identical. Photoshop doesn't provide the breadth of options available in Illustrator — you can't transform paths independently of an image or apply sophisticated path operations in Photoshop, for example — but the basic techniques are the same.

The following pages are designed to get you up and running with paths. I'll explain how you approach drawing a path, how you edit it, how you convert it to a selection outline, and how you stroke it with a paint or edit tool. All in all, you'll learn more about paths than you ever wanted to know.

Paths overview

In Photoshop 4, the path tools are now available in the Toolbox, as shown in Figure 11-23. But the path management options — which enable you to convert paths to selections, fill and stroke paths, and save and delete them — still reside in the Paths palette, also shown in the figure. Together, tools and palette options make up a fully functioning path-drawing environment, which rivals similar features provided by Illustrator or FreeHand.

How paths work

Paths differ from normal selections because they exist on the equivalent of a distinct, object-oriented layer, which sits in front of the bitmapped image. After you have draw a path, this setup enables you to edit it with point-by-point precision to make sure the path meets the exact requirements of your artwork. This also prevents you from accidentally messing up the image, as you can when you edit ordinary selection outlines. After you create the path, you convert it into a standard selection outline before you use it to edit the contents of the image, as explained in the section "Converting and saving paths," later in this chapter.

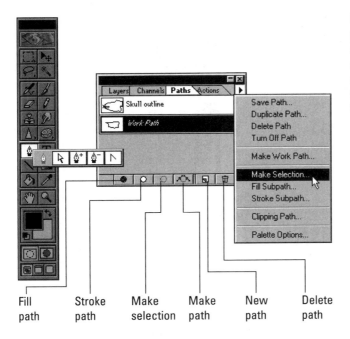

Figure 11-23: The Toolbox provides access to every one of Photoshop's path-drawing tools. To save and organize your paths, display the Paths palette by choosing Window ➪ Show Paths.

Fill path

Stroke path

Make selection

Make path

New path

Delete path

The following steps explain the basic process of drawing a selection outline with the path tools. I explain each step in more detail throughout the remainder of this chapter.

Steps: Drawing a Selection with the Path Tools

1. **Draw the path.** Use the pen tool to draw the outline of your prospective selection. You can select the pen tool by pressing the P key.

2. **Edit the path.** If the outline of the path requires some adjustment, reshape it using the other path tools. You can cycle through the tools by pressing *P*.

3. **Save the path.** When you get the path exactly as you want it, save the path in Photoshop by choosing the Save Path command from the Paths palette menu. Or you can double-click the Work Path item in the scrolling list.

4. **Convert the path to a selection.** You can make the path a selection outline by choosing the Make Selection command. Or press the Enter key on the numeric keypad when a path or selection tool is active.

That's it. After you convert the path to a selection, it works like any of the selection outlines described earlier. You can feather a selection, move it, copy it, clone it, or apply one of the special effects described in future chapters. The path remains intact in case you want to do further editing or to use it again.

Using the Paths palette tools

Before I get into my long-winded description of how you draw and edit paths, here is a quick introduction to the five path tools:

Pen: Use the pen tool to draw paths in Photoshop one point at a time. I explain this tool in detail in the following section. Press the P key to select the tool.

Arrow: This tool enables you to drag points and handles to reshape a path. You can access the arrow tool when any other path tool is active by pressing and holding the Ctrl key. Or press the P key again to make the tool permanently active.

Insert point: Click an existing path to add a point to it. You can access this function when the arrow tool is selected by Ctrl+Alt+clicking on a segment in the path.

Remove point: Click an existing point in a path to delete the point without creating a break in the path's outline. To accomplish this when the arrow tool is selected, Ctrl+Alt+click a point in a path.

Convert point: Click or drag on a point to convert it to a corner or smooth point. You also can drag on a handle to convert the point. Press Ctrl to access the convert point tool when the arrow tool is selected.

Note   The terms *point, smooth point,* and others associated with drawing paths are explained in the upcoming section.

Drawing with the pen tool

When drawing with the pen tool, you build a path by creating individual *points.* Photoshop automatically connects the points with *segments,* which are simply straight or curved lines.

All paths in Photoshop are *Bézier* (pronounced *bay-zee-ay*) paths, meaning they rely on the same mathematical curve definitions that make up the core of the PostScript printer language. The Bézier curve model allows for zero, one, or two levers to be associated with each point in a path. These levers, labeled in Figure 11-24, are called *Bézier control handles* or simply *handles.* You can move each handle in relation to a point, enabling you to bend and tug at a curved segment like a piece of soft wire.

Smooth points

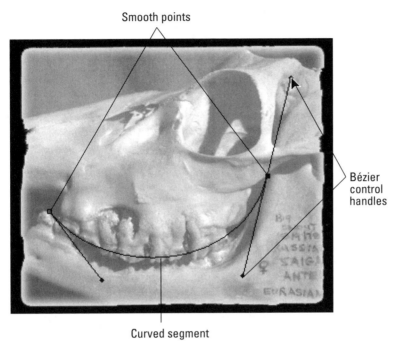

Bézier
control
handles

Curved segment

Figure 11-24: Drag with the pen tool to create a smooth point flanked
by two Bézier control handles.

The following list summarizes how you can use the pen tool to build paths in
Photoshop:

◆ **Adding segments:** To build a path, create one point after another until the
path is the desired length and shape. Photoshop automatically draws a
segment between each new point and its predecessor.

◆ **Closing the path:** If you eventually plan to convert the path to a selection
outline, you need to complete the outline by clicking again on the first point
in the path. Every point will then have one segment entering it and another
segment exiting it. Such a path is called a *closed path* because it forms one
continuous outline.

◆ **Leaving the path open:** If you plan to apply the Stroke Path command
(explained later), you may not want to close a path. To leave the path open,
so it has a specific beginning and ending, deactivate the path by saving it
(choose the Save Paths command from the Paths palette menu). After you
complete the save operation, you can click in the Image window to begin a
new path.

✦ **Extending an open path:** To reactivate an open path, click or drag one of its endpoints. Photoshop draws a segment between the endpoint and the next point you create.

✦ **Joining two open paths:** To join one open path with another open path, click or drag an endpoint in the first path, and then click or drag an endpoint in the second.

Points in a Bézier path act as little road signs. Each point steers the path by specifying how a segment enters it and how another segment exits it. You specify the identity of each little road sign by clicking, dragging, or Alt+dragging with the pen tool. The following items explain the specific kinds of points and segments you can create in Photoshop. See Figure 11-25 for examples.

✦ **Corner point:** Click with the pen tool to create a *corner point,* which represents the corner between two straight segments in a path.

✦ **Straight segment:** Click at two different locations to create a straight segment between two corner points. Shift+click to draw a 45-degree-angle segment between the new corner point and its predecessor.

✦ **Smooth point:** Drag to create a *smooth point* with two symmetrical Bézier control handles. A smooth point ensures that one segment meets with another in a continuous arc.

✦ **Curved segment:** Drag at two different locations to create a curved segment between two smooth points.

✦ **Curved segment followed by straight:** After drawing a curved segment, Alt+click the smooth point you just created to delete the forward Bézier control handle. This converts the smooth point to a corner point with one handle. Then click at a different location to append a straight segment to the end of the curved segment.

✦ **Straight segment followed by curved:** After drawing a straight segment, drag from the corner point you just created to add a Bézier control handle. Then drag again at a different location to append a curved segment to the end of the straight segment.

✦ **Cusp point:** After drawing a curved segment, Alt+drag from the smooth point you just created to redirect the forward Bézier control handle, converting the smooth point to a corner point with two independent handles, sometimes known as a *cusp point.* Then drag again at a new location to append a curved segment that proceeds in a different direction than the previous curved segment.

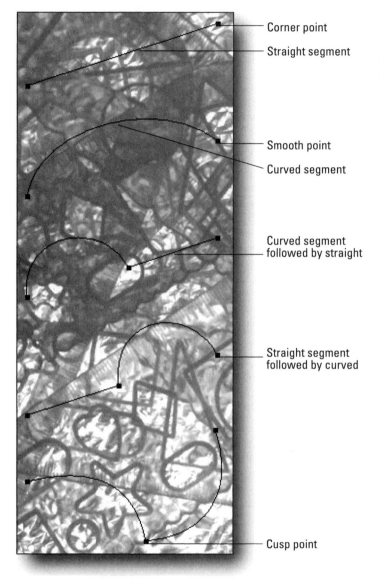

Corner point

Straight segment

Smooth point

Curved segment

Curved segment
followed by straight

Straight segment
followed by curved

Cusp point

Figure 11-25: The different kinds of points and segments you can draw with the pen tool

Reshaping existing paths

As you become more familiar with the pen tool, you'll draw paths correctly the first time around more frequently. But you'll never get it right 100 percent of the time or even 50 percent of the time. From your first timid steps until you develop into a seasoned pro, you'll rely heavily on Photoshop's capability to reshape paths by moving points and handles, adding and deleting points, and converting points to change the curvature of segments. Don't worry if you don't draw a path correctly the first time. The path tools provide all the second chances you'll ever need.

Using the arrow tool

The arrow tool represents the foremost path-reshaping function in Photoshop. After selecting this tool, you can perform any of the following functions:

✦ **Selecting points:** Click a point to select it independently of other points in a path. Shift+click to select an additional point, even if the point belongs to a different path than other selected points. Alt+click a path to select all its points in one fell swoop. You can even marquee points by dragging in a rectangle around them. You cannot, however, apply commands from the Select menu, such as All or None, to the selection of paths.

✦ **Drag selected points:** To move one or more points in a path, select the points you want to move and then drag one of the selected points. All selected points move the same distance and direction. When you move a point while a neighboring point remains stationary, the segment between the two points shrinks, stretches, and bends to accommodate the change in distance. Segments located between two selected or deselected points remain unchanged during a move.

Tip　You can move selected points in 1-pixel increments by pressing arrow keys. If both a portion of the image and points in a path are selected, the arrow keys move the point only. Because paths reside on a higher layer, they take precedence in all functions that might concern them.

✦ **Drag a segment directly:** You also can reshape a path by dragging its segments. When you drag a straight segment, the two corner points on either side of the segment move, as well. As illustrated in Figure 11-26, the neighboring segments stretch, shrink, or bend to accommodate the drag. When you drag a curved segment, though, you stretch, shrink, or bend that segment only, as demonstrated in Figure 11-27.

Tip　When you drag a curved segment, drag from the middle of the segment, approximately equidistant from both its points. This method provides the best leverage and ensures the segment doesn't go flying off in some weird direction you hadn't anticipated.

✦ **Drag a Bézier control handle:** Select a point and drag either of its Bézier control handles to change the curvature of the corresponding segment without moving any of the points in the path. If the point is a smooth point, moving one handle moves both handles in the path. If you want to move a smooth handle independently of its partner, you must use the convert point tool, as discussed in the "Converting points" section later in this chapter.

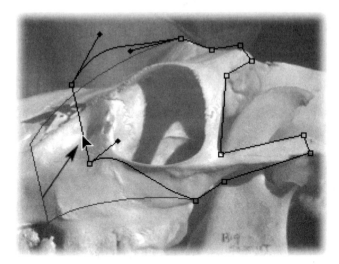

Figure 11-26: Drag a straight segment to move the segment and change the length, direction, and curvature of the neighboring segments.

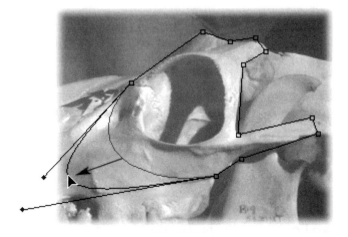

Figure 11-27: Drag a curved segment to change the curvature of that segment only and leave the neighboring segments unchanged.

✦ **Clone a path:** To make a duplicate of a selected path, Alt+drag it to a new location in the Image window. Photoshop automatically stores the new path under the same name as the original.

✦ **Deselect a path:** Click with the arrow tool outside any path to deselect all active paths. Because many options affect the selected path only, deselecting the paths before choosing a command you want to apply to all visible paths is often a good idea.

Tip   Press and hold the Ctrl key to access the arrow tool temporarily when the pen tool or any of the path or edit tools are selected. When you release the Ctrl key, the cursor returns to the selected tool.

Adding and deleting points

The quantity of points and segments in a path is forever subject to change. Whether a path is closed or open, you can reshape it by adding and deleting points, which, in turn, forces the addition or deletion of a segment:

✦ **Appending a point to the end of an open path:** If an existing path is open, you can activate one of its endpoints by either clicking or dragging it with the pen tool, depending on the identity of the endpoint and whether you want the next segment to be straight or curved. Photoshop is then prepared to draw a segment between the endpoint and the next point you create.

✦ **Closing an open path:** You also can use the technique I just described to close an open path. Just select one endpoint, click or drag it with the pen tool to activate it, and then click or drag the opposite endpoint. Photoshop draws a segment between the two endpoints, closing the path and eliminating both endpoints by converting them to *interior points,* which simply means the points are bound on both sides by segments.

✦ **Joining two open paths:** You can join two open paths to create one longer open path. To do so, activate an endpoint of the first path, then click or drag with the pen tool on an endpoint of the second path.

✦ **Inserting a point in a segment:** Select the insert point tool and click anywhere along an open or closed path to insert a point and divide the segment on which you click into two segments. Photoshop automatically inserts a corner or smooth point, depending on its reading of the path. If the point does not exactly meet your needs, use the convert point tool to change it.

Tip   To access the insert or remove point tool, press Ctrl and Alt when using the arrow tool. Ctrl+Alt+click an existing segment to insert a point; Ctrl+Alt+click a point to remove it.

✦ **Deleting a point and breaking the path:** The simplest way to delete a point is to select it with the arrow tool and press either the Delete or Clear key. (You also can choose Edit ➪ Clear, though why you would want to expend so much effort is beyond me.) When you delete an interior point, you delete both segments associated with that point, resulting in a break in the path. If you delete an endpoint from an open path, you delete the single segment associated with the point.

✦ **Removing a point without breaking the path:** Select the remove point tool and click a point in an open or closed path to delete the point and draw a new segment between the two points that neighbor it. The remove point tool ensures no break occurs in a path.

✦ **Deleting a segment:** You can delete a single interior segment from a path without affecting any point. To do so, first click outside the path with the arrow tool to deselect the path. Then click the segment you want to delete and press the Delete key. When you delete an interior segment, you create a break in your path.

✦ **Deleting a whole path:** To delete an entire path, select any portion of it and press the Delete key twice. The first time you press Delete, Photoshop deletes the selected point or segment and automatically selects all other points in the path. The second time you press Delete, Photoshop eliminates everything it missed the first time around.

Converting points

Photoshop enables you to change the identity of an interior point. You can convert a corner point to a smooth point and vice versa. You perform all point conversions using the convert point tool as follows:

✦ **Smooth to corner:** Click an existing smooth point to convert it to a corner point with no Bézier control handle.

✦ **Smooth to cusp:** Drag one of the handles of a smooth point to move it independently of the other, thus converting the smooth point to a cusp.

✦ **Corner to smooth:** Drag from a corner point to convert it to a smooth point with two symmetrical Bézier control handles.

✦ **Cusp to smooth:** Drag one of the handles of a cusp point to lock both handles back into alignment, thus converting the cusp to a smooth point.

Tip   Press the Ctrl key to access the convert point tool temporarily when the arrow tool is selected and positioned over a point.

Filling paths

After you finish drawing a path and getting it exactly as you want it, you can convert it to a selection outline — as described in the upcoming "Converting paths to selections" section — or you can paint it. You can either paint the interior of the path by choosing the Fill Path command from the Paths palette menu, or you can paint the outline of the path by choosing Stroke Path.

The Fill Path command works much like Edit ➪ Fill. After drawing a path, choose the Fill Path command or Alt+click the fill path icon in the lower-left corner of the palette (the one that looks like a filled circle). Photoshop displays a slight variation of the Fill dialog box discussed in Chapter 9, the only difference being the inclusion of two Rendering options. Enter a value into the Feather Radius option box to blur the edges of the fill, as if the path were a selection with a feathered outline. Select the Anti-aliased check box to soften slightly the outline of the filled area.

If one path falls inside another, Photoshop leaves the intersection of the two paths unfilled. Suppose you draw two round paths, one fully inside the other. If you deselect both paths and then choose the Fill Path command, Photoshop fills only the area between the two paths, resulting in the letter *O*.

Caution If the Fill Path command fills only part or none of the path, the path probably falls outside the selection outline. Choose Select ➪ None (Ctrl+D) to deselect the image and then choose the Fill Path command again.

Note If you select one or more paths with the arrow tool, the Fill Path command changes to Fill Subpaths, enabling you to fill the selected paths only. The fill path icon also affects only the selected paths.

Painting along a path

Unlike the Fill Path command, which bears a strong resemblance to Edit ➪ Fill, the Stroke Path command is altogether different than Edit ➪ Stroke. Where Edit ➪ Stroke creates outlines and arrowheads, the Stroke Path command enables you to paint a brush stroke along the contours of a path. This may not sound like a big deal at first, but this feature enables you to combine the spontaneity of the paint and edit tools with the structure and precision of a path.

To paint a path, choose the Stroke Path command from the Paths palette menu to display the Stroke Path dialog box shown in Figure 11-28. In this dialog box, you can choose the paint or edit tool with which you want to stroke the path (which only means to paint a brush stroke along a path). Photoshop drags the chosen tool along the exact route of the path, retaining any tool or brush shape settings that were in force when you chose the tool.

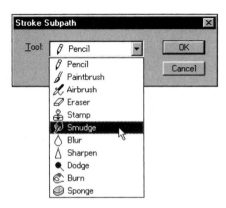

Figure 11-28: Photoshop displays this dialog box when you choose the Stroke Path command while a tool other than a paint or edit tool is selected.

Tip

You can also display the Stroke Path dialog box by Alt+clicking on the stroke path icon, the second icon at the bottom of the Paths palette (labeled back in Figure 11-23). If you prefer to bypass the dialog box, select a paint or edit tool, and then either click the stroke path icon or simply press the Enter key on the numeric keypad. Instead of displaying the dialog box, Photoshop assumes you want to use the selected tool and strokes away.

Note

If the path is selected, the Stroke Path command becomes a Stroke Subpath command. Photoshop then only strokes the selected path, rather than all paths saved under the current name.

The following steps walk you through a little project I created by stroking paths with the paintbrush and smudge tools. Figures 11-29 through 11-31 show the progression and eventual outcome of the image.

Steps: Stroking Paths with the Paintbrush and Smudge Tools

1. **After opening a low-resolution version of a hurricane image, I drew the zigzag path shown in Figure 11-29.** As you can see, the path emits from the eye of the hurricane. I drew the path starting at the eye and working upward, which is important because Photoshop strokes a path in the same direction in which you draw it.

Figure 11-29: I drew this path starting at the eye of the hurricane and working my way upward.

2. **I next saved the path.** I double-clicked the Work Path name in the Paths palette, entered a name for my path, and pressed Enter.

3. **I used the Brushes palette to specify three brush shapes.** Each one had a Roundness value of 40. The largest brush had a diameter of 16, the next largest had a diameter of 10, and the smallest had a diameter of 4.

4. **I double-clicked the paintbrush tool to bring up the Paintbrush Options palette.** Then I set the Fade-out value to 400. Next, I selected the To Background radio button, so Photoshop would draw gradient strokes between the foreground and background colors.

5. **I stroked the path with the paintbrush three times using the Stroke Path command.** I changed the foreground and background colors for each stroke. The first time, I used the largest brush shape and stroked the path from gray to white; the second time, I changed to the middle brush shape and stroked the path from black to white; and the final time, I used the smallest brush shape and stroked the path from white to black. The result of all this stroking is shown in Figure 11-30.

6. **Next, I created two clones of the zigzag path by Alt+dragging the path with the arrow tool.** I pressed the Shift key while dragging to ensure the paths aligned horizontally. I then clicked in an empty portion of the Image window to deselect all paths, so they appeared as shown in Figure 11-30. This enabled me to stroke them all simultaneously in Step 9.

Figure 11-30: After stroking the path three times with the paintbrush tool, I cloned the path twice.

7. **I created a 60-pixel version of my brush shape and reduced its Hardness value to 0 percent.** I then painted a single white spot at the bottom of each of the new paths. I painted a black spot at the bottom of the original path.

8. **I selected the smudge tool.** Then I moved the Pressure slider bar in the Options palette to 98 percent and selected a brush shape with a radius of 16 pixels. At this setting, the tool has a tremendous range, but it eventually fades out.

9. **I pressed Enter on the numeric keypad to apply the smudge tool to all three paths at once.** The finished image appears in Figure 11-31.

Figure 11-31: I stroked all three paths with the smudge tool set to 98 percent pressure to achieve this unusual extraterrestrial-departure effect. At least, I guess that's what it is. It could also be giant space slinkies probing the planet's surface. Hard to say.

Tip

If you're really feeling precise — I think they have a clinical term for that — you can specify the location of every single blob of paint laid down in an image. When the Spacing option in the Brush Options dialog box is deselected, Photoshop applies a single blob of paint for each point in a path. If this isn't sufficient control, I'm a monkey's uncle. (What a terrible thing to say about one's nephew!)

Converting and saving paths

Photoshop provides two commands to switch between paths and selections, both of which are located in the Paths palette menu. The Make Selection command converts a path to a selection outline; the Make Path command converts a selection to a path. And regardless of how you create a path, you can save it with the current image, which enables you not only to reuse the path but also to hide and display it at will.

Converting paths to selections

When you choose the Make Selection command or Alt+click the make selection icon (which looks like a dotted circle, as labeled back in Figure 11-23), Photoshop displays the dialog box shown in Figure 11-32. You can specify whether to anti-alias or feather the selection and to what degree. You can also instruct Photoshop to combine the prospective selection outline with any existing selection in the image. The Operation options correspond to the keyboard functions discussed in the "Manually adding and subtracting" section earlier in this chapter.

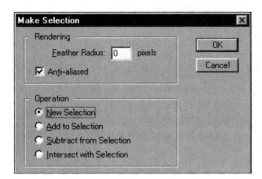

Figure 11-32: When you choose the Make Selection command, you have the option of combining the path with an existing selection.

Photoshop 4 offers several additional ways to convert a path to a selection outline, all of which are more convenient than the Make Selection command:

  ✦ **Press the Enter key on the numeric keypad:** As long as a path or selection tool is active, the Enter key on the numeric keypad converts the path to a selection.

  ✦ **Ctrl+click the path name:** If some other tool is selected, you can Ctrl+click the name of a path in the Paths palette. The path needn't be active.

  ✦ **Shift+Enter or Ctrl+Shift+click:** To add the path to an existing selection, press Shift with one of the above techniques. You can press Shift+Enter (again, you must use the Enter key on the numeric keypad, not the regular Enter key). Or Ctrl+Shift+click a path name in the palette.

  ✦ **Alt+Enter or Ctrl+Alt+click:** Naturally, if you can add, you can subtract. Just press the Alt key with Enter or Ctrl+clicking to subtract the path from the selection.

  ✦ **Shift+Alt+Enter or Ctrl+Shift+Alt+click:** Now we're starting to get into some obscure stuff, but what's possible is possible. You select the intersection of a path and selection outline by pressing a whole mess of keys.

All of these wonderful techniques — most new to Photoshop 4 — have the added advantage of hiding the path when converting the path to a selection. This way, you have full, unobstructed access to your selection outline.

Caution By contrast, the Make Selection command leaves the path onscreen in front of the converted selection. If you try to copy, cut, delete, or nudge the selection, you perform the operation on the path instead.

Converting selections to paths

When you choose the Make Paths command or Alt+click the make path icon (labeled back in Figure 11-23), Photoshop produces a single Tolerance option. Unlike the Tolerance options you've encountered so far, this one is accurate to $\frac{1}{10}$ pixel and has nothing to do with colors or brightness values. Rather, it enables you to specify Photoshop's sensitivity to twists and turns in a selection outline. The value you enter determines how far the path can vary from the original selection. The lowest possible value, 0.5, not only ensures Photoshop retains every nuance of the selection, but it can also result in overly complicated paths with an abundance of points. If you enter the highest value, 10, Photoshop rounds out the path and uses few points. If you plan on editing the path, you probably won't want to venture any lower than 2.0, the default setting.

To bypass the Make Work Path dialog box and turn your selection into a path using the current Tolerance settings, click the make path icon.

Saving paths with an image

As mentioned at the beginning of the paths discussion, saving a path is an integral step in the path-creation process. You can store every path you draw and keep it handy in case you decide later to select an area again. Because Photoshop defines paths as compact mathematical equations, they take up virtually no room when you save an image to disk.

You save one or more paths by choosing the Save Path command from the Paths palette menu or by simply double-clicking the italicized Work Path item in the scrolling list. After you perform the save operation, the path name appears in upright characters. A path name can include any number of separate paths. In fact, if you save a path and then set about drawing another one, Photoshop automatically adds that path in with the saved path. To start a new path under a new name, you first must hide the existing path. Or click the new path icon — the little page at the bottom of the Paths palette — to establish an independent path.

Tip To hide all paths, click the empty portion of the scrolling list below the last saved path name. You can even hide unsaved paths in this way. If you hide an unsaved path and then begin drawing a new one, however, the unsaved path is deleted, never to return again.

Swapping Paths with Illustrator

Photoshop 4 can swap paths directly with Illustrator 6 (and later) and FreeHand 7. All you must do is copy a path to the Clipboard and paste it into the other program. This special cross-application compatibility feature expands and simplifies a variety of path-editing functions. For example, suppose you want to scale and rotate a path:

✦ One way to pull off this feat is to duplicate the image (by choosing Image ➪ Duplicate). Then scale the entire duplicated image using Image ➪ Image Size and rotate it with Image ➪ Rotate Canvas ➪ Arbitrary. Next, drag the transformed path back into the original image.

✦ If you own Illustrator, though, a better way exists. Select the path in Photoshop with the arrow tool and copy it to the Clipboard (Ctrl+C). Then switch to Illustrator, paste the path, and edit as desired. About 95 percent of Illustrator's capabilities are devoted to the task of editing paths — you have far more options at your disposal than in Photoshop. Then when you finish, copy the path again, switch to Photoshop, and paste.

When you paste an Illustrator path into Photoshop, a dialog box offers you the option of rendering the path to pixels — just as you can render an Illustrator EPS document using File ➪ Open — or keeping the path information intact. In other words, you can either turn the path into an image or bring it in as a path, which you can then use as a selection outline. If you want to save the path in the Paths palette, be sure to select the Paste As Paths option.

Tip   Things can get pretty muddled in the Clipboard, especially when you're switching applications. If you copy something from Illustrator, but the Paste command is dimmed inside Photoshop, you may be able to force the issue a little. You may simply need to wake up the Clipboard by opening the Windows 95 Clipbook Viewer (Start ➪ Programs ➪ Accessories ➪ Clipbook Viewer). Don't worry if you see a message about an unsupported format. Just minimize the viewer window and try to paste again. (Computers are kind of slow sometimes. Every once in a while, you must give them a kick in the pants.)

Note   You can copy paths from Photoshop and paste them into Illustrator, regardless of the setting of the Export Clipboard check box in the Preferences dialog box. That option affects pixels only. Paths are so tiny, Photoshop always exports them.

Exporting to Illustrator

If you don't have enough memory to run both Illustrator and Photoshop at the same time, you can export Photoshop paths to disk and then open them in Illustrator. To export all paths in the current image, choose File ➪ Export ➪ Paths to Illustrator. Photoshop saves the paths as a fully editable Illustrator document. This scheme enables you to trace images exactly with paths in Photoshop, and then combine those paths as objects with the exported EPS version of the image inside Illustrator. Whereas tracing an image in Illustrator can prove a little tricky because of resolution differences and other previewing limitations, you can trace images in Photoshop as accurately as you like.

 Note Unfortunately, Illustrator provides no equivalent function to export paths for use in Photoshop; nor can Photoshop open Illustrator documents from disk and interpret them as paths. This means the Clipboard is the only way to take a path created or edited in Illustrator and use it in Photoshop.

 Cross Reference Only about half of Photoshop users own Illustrator. Meanwhile, close to 90 percent of Illustrator users own Photoshop. This is why I cover the special relationship between Illustrator and Photoshop in-depth in Chapter 13 of my Illustrator book. Its prosaic title is *The Illustrator 6 Book* (Peachpit Press, 1996). You'll find out more about using Photoshop with FreeHand in the *Macworld FreeHand 7 Bible* (IDG Books Worldwide, Inc., 1997).

Retaining transparent areas in an image

When you import an image into Illustrator, QuarkXPress, or some other object-oriented program, the image comes in as a rectangle with opaque pixels. Even if the image appeared partially transparent in Photoshop — on a layer, for example — the pixels are filled with white or some other color in the receiving application. These same object-oriented applications, however, do enable you to mask portions of an image you want to appear transparent by establishing a clipping path. Elements that lie inside the clipping path are opaque; elements outside the clipping path are transparent. Photoshop enables you to export an image in the EPS format with an object-oriented clipping path intact. When you import the image into the object-oriented program, it appears premasked with a perfectly smooth perimeter, as illustrated by the clipped image in Figure 11-33.

The following steps explain how to assign a set of saved paths as clipping paths.

Steps: Saving an Image with Clipping Paths

1. **Draw one or more paths around the portions of the image you want to appear opaque.** Areas outside the paths will be transparent.

2. **Save the paths.** Double-click the Work Path name in the Paths palette, enter a name, and press Enter. (Try to use a name that will make sense three years from now when you have to revisit this document and determine what the heck you did.)

3. **Choose the Clipping Path command from the Paths palette menu.** Photoshop displays a dialog box that enables you to select the saved paths you want to assign as the clipping path.

 Note If you like, enter a value into the Flatness option box. This option enables you to simplify the clipping paths by printing otherwise fluid curves as polygons. The Flatness value represents the distance — between 0.2 and 100, in printer pixels — the polygon may vary from the true mathematical curve. A higher value leads to a polygon with fewer sides. This means it looks chunkier, but it also prints more quickly. I recommend a value of 2 or 3. Ted Padova, who runs a service bureau in Ventura, CA, and who has served as technical editor on several of my books, tells me you can go as high as 7 when printing to an imagesetter without seeing the straight edges. I strongly suspect it depends on how much of a perfectionist you are.

4. **Choose File ⇨ Save As and select Photoshop EPS from the Format pop-up menu.** The EPS Format dialog box (shown back in Figure 4-9 of Chapter 4) now includes a Clipping Path pop-up menu. As long as the proper path name appears in the menu — it will if you followed the previous step — you can press the Enter key. An EPS image with masked transparencies is saved to disk.

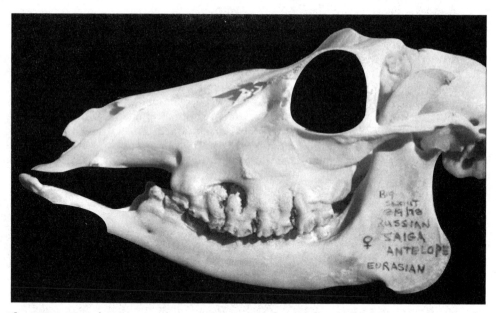

Figure 11-33: I drew one path around the perimeter of the skull and another around the eye socket. After defining the paths as clipping paths, I exported the image in the EPS format, imported it into Illustrator, and set it against a black background for contrast.

Note   PageMaker is capable of handling clipping paths in the TIFF format. If you plan on placing the image in PageMaker, you can save the image in TIFF instead of EPS in Step 4.

Figure 11-34 shows an enhanced version of the clipped skull from Figure 11-33. In addition to exporting the image with clipping paths in the EPS format, I saved the paths to disk by choosing File ➪ Export ➪ Paths to Illustrator. Inside Illustrator, I used the exported paths to create the outline around the clipped image. I also used them to create the shadow behind the image. The white of the eyeball is a reduced version of the eye socket, as are the iris and pupil. The background features a bunch of flipped and reduced versions of the paths. This may look like a lot of work, but the only drawing required was to create the two initial Photoshop paths.

Figure 11-34: It's amazing what you can accomplish by combining scans edited in a painting program with smooth lines created in a drawing program.

 Be prepared for your images to grow by leaps and bounds when imported into Illustrator. The EPS illustration shown in Figure 11-34 consumes six times as much space on disk as the original Photoshop image saved in the TIFF format.

 One more note of caution: When used in excess, clipping paths will present problems on the most sophisticated printing devices. You should only use a clipping path when it's absolutely necessary and cannot be avoided. If you want to place an image against a bitmapped background, for example, do it in Photoshop, not in QuarkXPress or PageMaker. This will invariably speed printing and may mean the difference between whether or not a file prints successfully.

Creating Masks

Selecting Via Masks

Most Photoshop users don't use masks. If my personal experience is any indication, it's not only because masks seem complicated, it's because they strike most folks as being more trouble than they're worth. Like nearly everyone, when I first started using Photoshop, I couldn't even imagine a possible application for a mask. I have my lasso tool and my magic wand. If I'm really in a rut, I can pull out my pen tool. What more could I possibly want?

Quite a bit, as it turns out. Every one of the tools I just mentioned is only moderately suited to the task of selecting images. The lasso tool enables you to create free-form selections, but it can't account for differences in focus levels. The magic wand selects areas of color, but it usually leaves important colors behind and the edges of its selection outlines often appear ragged and ugly. The pen tool is extremely precise, but it results in fairly mechanical outlines, which may appear incongruous with the natural imagery they contain.

Masks offer all the benefits of the other tools. With masks, you can create free-form selections, select areas of color, and generate amazingly precise selections. Masks also address all the deficiencies associated with the selection tools. They can account for different levels of focus, they give you absolute control over the look of the edges, and they create selections every bit as natural as the image itself.

In fact, a mask *is* the image itself. Masks use pixels to select pixels. Masks are your way to make Photoshop see what you see using the data inherent in the photograph. Masks enable you to devote every one of Photoshop's powerful capabilities to the task of creating a selection outline. Masks are, without a doubt, the most accurate selection mechanism available in Photoshop.

Masking defined

For those folks who aren't clear on what a mask is, I'll tell you: A *mask* is a selection outline expressed as a grayscale image.

✦ Selected areas appear white.

✦ Deselected areas appear black.

✦ Partially selected parts of the image appear in gray. Feathered edges are also expressed in shades of gray, from light gray near the selected area to dark gray near the deselected area.

Figure 12-1 shows two selection outlines and their equivalent masks. The top-left example shows a rectangular selection that has been inverted (using Image ⇨ Adjust ⇨ Invert). Below this example is the same selection expressed as a mask. Because the selection is hard-edged with no anti-aliasing or feathering, the mask appears hard-edged, as well. The selected area is white and is said to be *unmasked;* the deselected area is black, or *masked.*

The top-right example in Figure 12-1 shows a feathered selection outline. Again, I've inverted the selection so you can better see the extent of the selection outline. (Marching ants can't accurately express softened edges, so the inversion helps show things off more.) The bottom-right image is the equivalent mask. Here, the feathering effect is completely visible.

When you look at the masks along the bottom of Figure 12-1, you may wonder where the heck the image went. One of the wonderful things about masks is they can be viewed independently of an image, as in Figure 12-1, or with an image, as in Figure 12-2. In the second figure, the mask is expressed as a color overlay. By default, the color of the overlay is a translucent red, like a conventional rubylith. (To see the overlay in its full, natural color, see Color Plate 12-1.) Areas covered with the rubylith are masked (deselected); areas that appear normal — without any red tint — are unmasked (selected). When you return to the standard marching ants mode, any changes you make to your image will affect only the unmasked areas.

Now that you know roughly what masks are (the definition will become progressively clearer throughout this chapter), the question remains, what good are they? Because a mask is essentially an independent grayscale image, you can edit the mask using any of the paint and edit tools discussed in Chapters 8 through 10, any of the filters discussed in Chapters 15 through 17, any of the color correction options discussed in Chapter 18, or about any other function described in any other chapter. You can even use the selection tools, as discussed in the previous chapter. With all these features at your disposal, you can't help but create a more accurate selection outline in a shorter amount of time.

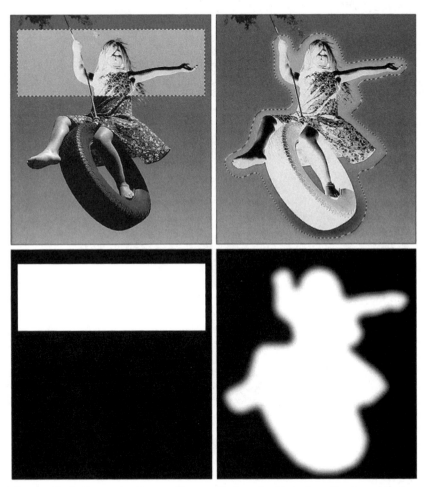

Figure 12-1: Two selection outlines with inverted interiors (top) and their equivalent masks (bottom)

Figure 12-2: Here are the masks from Figure 12-1, shown as they appear when viewed along with an image.

Painting and Editing Inside Selections

Before we immerse ourselves in masking techniques, let's start with a warm-up topic, selection masking. When you were in grade school, perhaps you had a teacher who nagged you to color within the lines. (I didn't. My teachers were more concerned about preventing me from writing on the walls and coloring on the other kids.) At any rate, if you don't trust yourself to paint inside an image because you're afraid you'll screw it up, selection masking is the answer. Regardless of which tool you use to select an image — marquee, lasso, magic wand, or pen — you can paint or edit only the selected area. The paint can't enter the deselected (or protected) portions of the image, so you can't help but paint inside the lines. As a result, all selection outlines act as masks, hence the term *selection masking.*

Figures 12-3 through 12-6 show the familiar skull image subject to some pretty free-and-easy use of the paint and edit tools. (Do you think I ought to lay off the heavy metal or what?) The following steps describe how I created these images using a selection mask.

Steps: Painting and Editing Inside a Selection Mask

1. **I selected the slightly rotting skull of the enchanting Russian Saiga antelope.** You can see the selection outline in such golden oldies as Figures 11-18 and 11-20. If those figures are too remote, just look at the top example in Figure 12-3. For the record, I drew this selection outline using the pen tool.

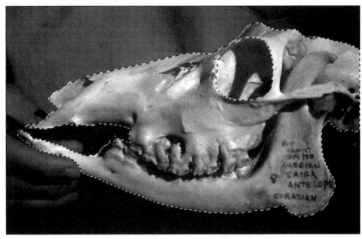

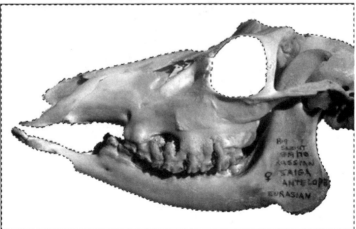

Figure 12-3: After drawing a selection outline around the antelope skull (top), I inversed the selection and deleted the background (bottom).

2. **I reversed the selection with the Inverse command.** I wanted to edit the area surrounding the skull, so I chose Select ⇨ Inverse (Ctrl+Shift+I) to reverse which areas were selected and which were not.

3. **I pressed Ctrl+Delete to fill the selected area with the background color.** In this case, the background color was white — as shown in the bottom half of Figure 12-3.

4. **I painted inside the selection mask.** But before I began, I chose Select ⇨ Hide Edges (Ctrl+H). This enabled me to paint without being distracted by those infernal marching ants. (In fact, this is one of the most essential uses for the Hide Edges command.)

5. **I selected the paintbrush tool and expressed myself.** I selected the 21-pixel soft brush shape in the Brushes palette. With the foreground color set to black, I dragged the paintbrush around the perimeter of the skull to set it apart from its white background, as shown in Figure 12-4. No matter how sloppily I painted, the skull remained unscathed.

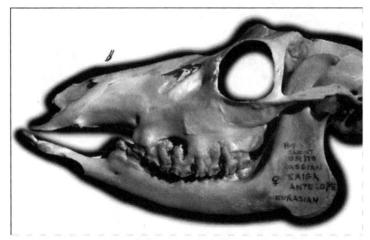

Figure 12-4: I painted inside the selection mask with a 21-pixel soft brush shape.

6. **I next selected and used the smudge tool.** I set the Pressure slider bar inside the Smudge Tool Options palette to 80 percent by pressing the 8 key. I dragged from inside the skull outward 20 or so times to create a series of curlicues. I also dragged from outside the skull inward to create white gaps between the curlicues. As shown in Figure 12-5, the smudge tool can smear colors from inside the protected area, but it does not apply these colors until you go inside the selection. This is an important point to remember, because it demonstrates that although the protected area is safe from all changes, the selected area may be influenced by colors from protected pixels.

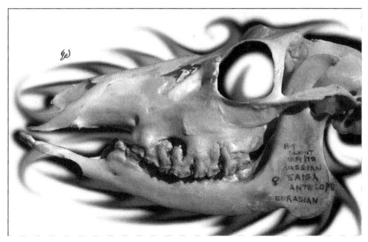

Figure 12-5: Dragging with the smudge tool here smeared colors from pixels outside the selection mask without changing the appearance of those pixels.

7. **I double-clicked the airbrush tool icon in the Toolbox to display the Airbrush Options palette.** Then I selected the Fade check box and set the Fade value to 20, leaving the Transparent option selected in the pop-up menu. I then selected a 60-pixel soft brush shape and, again, dragged outward from various points along the perimeter of the skull. As demonstrated in Figure 12-6, combining airbrush and mask is as useful in Photoshop as it is in the real world.

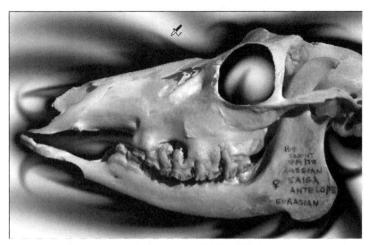

Figure 12-6: I dragged around the skull with the airbrush to distinguish it further from its background. Pretty cool effect, huh? Well, if this is not your cup of tea, maybe you can track down a teenager who will appreciate it.

Working in Quick Mask Mode

Selection masks give you an idea of what masks are all about, but they only scrape the surface. The rest of the discussions in this chapter revolve around using masks to define complex selection outlines.

The most straightforward environment for creating a mask is the *quick mask mode*. In the quick mask mode, a selection is expressed as a rubylith overlay. All the deselected areas in your image appear coated with red and the selected areas appear without red coating, as shown in the middle examples of Color Plate 12-1. You can then edit the mask as desired and exit the mode to return to the standard selection outline. The quick mask mode is — as its name implies — expeditious and convenient, with none of the trappings or permanence of more conventional masks. It's kind of like a fast food restaurant — you use it when you aren't overly concerned about quality and you aim to get in and out in a hurry.

How the quick mask mode works

Typically, you'll at least want to rough out a selection with the standard selection tools before entering the quick mask mode. Then you can concentrate on refining and modifying your selection inside the quick mask, rather than having to create the selection from scratch. (Naturally, this is only a rule of thumb. I violate the rule several times throughout this chapter, but only because the quick mask mode and I are such tight friends.)

To enter the quick mask mode, click the quick mask mode icon, as I've done in Figure 12-7. Or press the Q key. When I pressed *Q* after wreaking my most recent havoc on the extinct antelope skull, I got the image shown in Figure 12-7. The skull receives the mask because it is not selected. (In Figure 12-7, the mask appears as a light gray coating; on your color screen, the mask appears in red.) The area outside the skull looks the same as it always did because it's selected and, therefore, not masked.

Notice the selection outline disappears when you enter the quick mask mode. This is because it temporarily ceases to exist. Any operations you apply affect the mask itself and leave the underlying image untouched. When you click the marching ants mode icon (to the left of the quick mask mode icon) or again press the Q key, Photoshop converts the mask back into a selection outline and again enables you to edit the image.

Note   If you click the quick mask mode icon without seeing anything change onscreen, your computer isn't broken, it simply means you didn't select anything before you entered the mode. When nothing is selected, Photoshop enables you to edit the entire image; in other words, everything's selected. (Only a smattering of commands under the Edit, Layer, and Select menus require something to be selected before they work.) If everything is selected, the mask is white; therefore, the quick mask overlay is transparent and you don't see any difference onscreen. This is another reason it's better to select something before you enter the quick mask mode — you get an immediate sense you're accomplishing something.

Also, Photoshop enables you to specify whether you want the red mask coating to cover selected areas or deselected areas. For information on how to change this setting, see "Changing the red coating," later in this chapter.

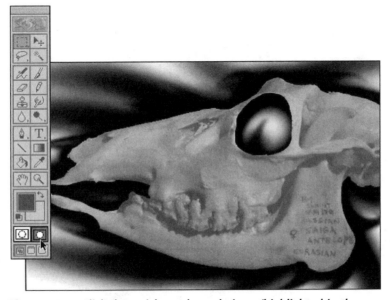

Figure 12-7: Click the quick mask mode icon (highlighted in the Toolbox) to instruct Photoshop to express the selection temporarily as a grayscale image.

Once in the quick mask mode, you can edit the mask in the following ways:

✦ **Subtracting from a selection:** Paint with black to add red coating and, thus, deselect areas of the image, as demonstrated in the top half of Figure 12-8. This means you can selectively protect portions of your image by merely painting over them.

✦ **Adding to a selection:** Paint with white to remove red coating and, thus, add to the selection outline. You can use the eraser tool to whittle away at the masked area (assuming the background color is set to white). Or you can swap the foreground and background colors so you can paint in white with one of the painting tools.

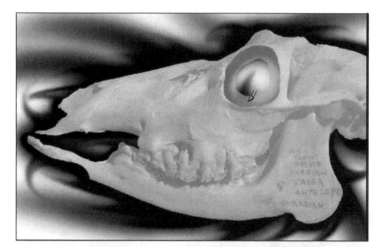

Figure 12-8: After subtracting some of the selected area inside the eye socket by painting in black with the paintbrush tool (top), I feathered the outline by painting with white, using a soft 45-pixel brush shape (bottom).

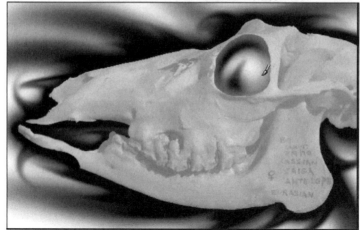

✦ **Adding feathered selections:** If you paint with a shade of gray, you add feathered selections. You also can feather an outline by painting with black or white with a soft brush shape, as shown in the bottom image in Figure 12-8.

✦ **Clone selection outlines:** You can clone a selected area by selecting it with one of the standard selection tools and Ctrl+Alt+dragging it to a new location in the image, as shown in Figure 12-9. Although I use the lasso tool in the figure, the magic wand tool also works well for this purpose. To select an anti-aliased selection outline with the wand tool, set the tolerance to about 10 and be sure the Anti-aliased check box is active. Then click inside the selection. It's that easy.

✦ **Transform selection outlines:** That's right, the quick mask mode provides a method for transforming a selection outline independently of its contents. Enter the quick mask mode, select the mask using one of the standard selection tools, and transform it by choosing Layer ➪ Free Transform or one of the commands from the Layer ➪ Transform submenu. (I discuss these commands in a fair amount of detail in Chapter 13.)

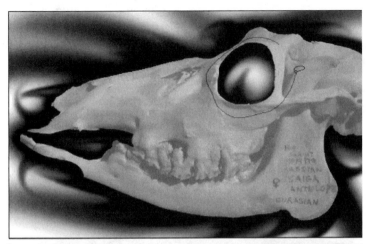

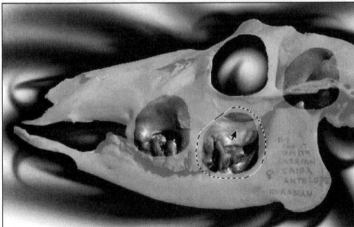

Figure 12-9: To clone the eye socket selection, I lassoed around it (top) and Ctrl+Alt+dragged it (bottom).

These are only a few of the unique effects you can achieve by editing a selection in the quick mask mode. Others involve tools and capabilities I haven't yet discussed, such as filters and color corrections.

When you finish editing your selection outlines, click the marching ants mode icon (to the left of the quick mask mode icon) or press the Q key again to return to the marching ants mode. Your selection outlines again appear flanked by marching ants, and all tools and commands return to their normal image-editing functions. Figure 12-10 shows the results of switching to the marching ants mode and deleting the contents of the selection outlines created in the last examples of the previous two figures.

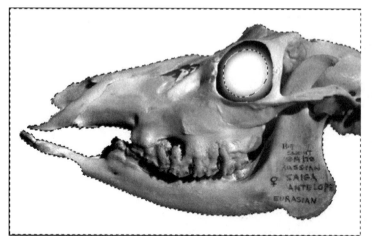

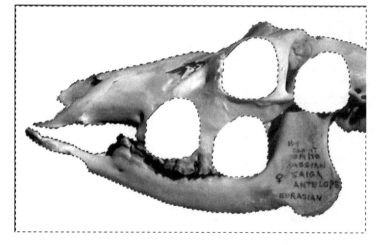

Figure 12-10: The results of deleting the regions selected in the final examples of Figures 12-8 (top) and 12-9 (bottom). Kind of makes me want to rent *It's the Great Pumpkin, Charlie Brown*. I mean, who wouldn't give this antelope a rock?

Tip   As demonstrated in the top example of Figure 12-10, the quick mask mode offers a splendid environment for feathering one selection outline, while leaving another hard-edged or anti-aliased. Granted, because most selection tools offer built-in feathering options, you can accomplish this task without resorting to the quick mask mode. But the quick mask mode enables you to change feathering selectively after drawing selection outlines, something you can't accomplish with Select ➪ Feather. The quick mask mode also enables you to see exactly what you're doing. Kind of makes those marching ants look piddly and insignificant, huh?

Changing the red coating

By default, the protected region of an image appears in translucent red in the quick mask mode, but if your image contains a lot of red, the mask can be difficult to see. Luckily, you can change it to any color and any degree of opacity that you like. To do so, double-click the quick mask icon in the Toolbox (or double-click the Quick Mask item in the Channels palette) to display the dialog box shown in Figure 12-11.

✦ **Color Indicates:** Select the Selected Areas option to reverse the color coating, that is, to cover the selected areas in a translucent coat of red and view the deselected areas normally. Select the Masked Areas option (the default setting) to cover the deselected areas in color.

Tip　　You can reverse the color coating without ever entering the Quick Mask Options dialog box. Simply Alt+click the quick mask icon in the Toolbox to toggle between coating the masked or selected portions of the image. The icon itself changes to reflect your choice.

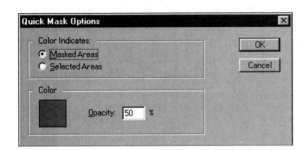

Figure 12-11: Double-click the quick mask mode icon to access the Quick Mask Options dialog box. You then can change the color and opacity of the protected or selected areas when viewed in the quick mask mode.

✦ **Color:** Click the Color icon to display the Color Picker dialog box and select a different color coating. (If you don't know how to use this dialog box, see the "Using the Color Picker" section of Chapter 5.) You can lift a color from the image with the eyedropper after the Color Picker dialog box comes up, but you probably want to use a color that isn't in the image so you can better see the mask.

✦ **Opacity:** Enter a value to change the opacity of the translucent color that coats the image. A value of 100 percent is absolutely opaque.

Change the color coating to achieve the most acceptable balance between being able to view and edit your selection and being able to view your image. For example, the default red coating shows up badly on my grayscale screen shots, so I changed the color coating to light blue and the Opacity value to 65 percent before shooting the screens featured in Figures 12-7 through 12-9.

Gradations as masks

If you think the Feather command is a hot tool for creating softened selection outlines, wait until you get a load of gradations in the quick mask mode. No better way exists to create fading effects than selecting an image with the gradient tool.

Fading an image

Consider the U.S. Capitol building shown in Figure 12-12. Whether you care for the folks who reside inside — personally, I'm sick of all this cynicism about the government, but I'm happy to exploit it for a few cheap laughs — you must admit, this is one beautiful building. Still, you might reckon the structure would be even more impressive if it were to fade into view out of a river of hot Hawaiian lava, like the one to the Capitol's immediate right. Well, you're in luck, because this is one of the easiest effects to pull off in Photoshop.

Figure 12-12: You can use the gradient tool in the quick mask mode to make the Capitol (left) fade out of the lava (right).

Switch to the quick mask mode by pressing the Q key. Then use the gradient tool to draw a linear gradation from black to white. (You can set the gradient style in the Gradient Tool Options palette to either Foreground to Background, or Black, White.) The white portion of the gradation represents the area you want to select. I decided to select the top portion of the Capitol, so I drew the gradation from the top of the second tier to the top of the flag, as shown in the first example of Figure 12-13. Because the gradient line is a little hard to see, I've added a little arrow to show the direction of the drag. (To see the mask in full color, check out the first image in Color Plate 12-2.)

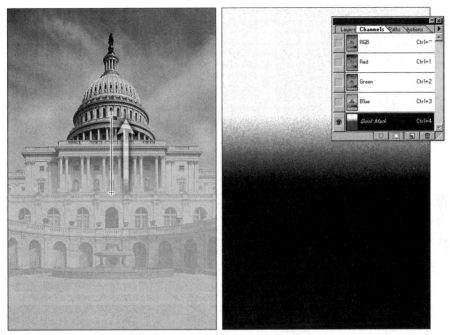

Figure 12-13: After drawing a linear gradation in the quick mask mode near the center of the image (left), I hid the image and applied the Add Noise filter with an Amount of 24 (right).

Banding can be a problem when you use a gradation as a mask. To eliminate the banding effect, therefore, apply the Add Noise filter at a low setting several times. To create the right example in Figure 12-13, I applied Add Noise using an Amount value of 24 and the Uniform distribution option.

Tip

Notice in the right example of Figure 12-13, I've hidden the image so only the mask is visible. As the figure shows, the Channels palette lists the *Quick Mask* in italics. This is because Photoshop regards the quick mask as a temporary channel. You can hide the image and view the mask in black and white by clicking the eyeball in front of the color composite view, in this case RGB. Or just press the tilde key (~) to hide the image. Press the tilde key again to view mask and image together.

To apply the gradation as a selection, I returned to the marching ants mode by again pressing Q. I then Ctrl+dragged the selected portion of the Capitol and dropped it into the lava image to achieve the effect shown in Figure 12-14. I could say something about Congress rising up from the ashes, but I have no idea what I'd mean by this. For the color version of this splendid image, see Color Plate 12-2.

Figure 12-14: The result of selecting the top portion of the Capitol using a gradation mask and then Ctrl+dragging and dropping the selection into the lava image

Applying special effects gradually

You also can use gradations in the quick mask mode to taper the outcomes of filters and other automated special effects. For example, I wanted to apply a filter around the edges of the Lincoln colossus that appears in Figure 12-15. I began by deselecting everything in the image (Ctrl+D) and switching to the quick mask mode. Then I brought up the Gradient Tool Options palette and selected the Foreground to Transparent option from the Gradient pop-up menu.

I pressed the D key to make the foreground color black and the background color white. Then I dragged with the gradient tool from each of the four edges of the image inward to create a series of short gradations that trace around the boundaries of the image, as shown in Figure 12-16. (As you can see, I've hidden the image so you see the mask in black and white.) Because I've selected the Foreground to Transparent option, Photoshop adds each gradation to the last one.

Figure 12-15: This time around, my intention is to surround Lincoln with a gradual filtering effect.

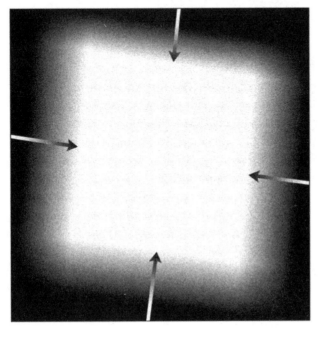

Figure 12-16: Inside the quick mask mode, I dragged from each of the four edges with the gradient tool (as indicated by the arrows).

To jumble the pixels in the mask, I applied Filter ⇨ Noise ⇨ Add Noise with an Amount value of 24. This is the effect that appears in Figure 12-16.

Tip

The only problem is I want to select the outside of the image, not the inside. So I need the edges to appear black and the inside to appear white, the opposite of what you see in Figure 12-16. No problem. All I do is press Ctrl+I (Image ⇨ Adjust ⇨ Invert) to invert the image. Inverting inside the quick mask mode produces the same effect as applying Select ⇨ Inverse to a selection.

Finally, I switched back to the marching ants mode by again pressing Q. Then I applied Filter ⇨ Render ⇨ Clouds to get the atmospheric effect you see in Figure 12-17. Yes, he's Abe the Illusionist — Lincoln as you've never seen him before! Once he gets to Vegas, he'll wipe the floor with David Copperfield.

Figure 12-17: After switching back to the marching ants mode, I chose Filter ⇨ Render ⇨ Clouds to create the foggy effect shown here.

Tip

Notice the corners in the mask in Figure 12-16? These corners are rounded, but you can achieve all kinds of different corner effects with the gradient tool. For harsher corners, select the Foreground to Background option and set the brush mode to Lighten. For some unusual corner treatments, try the Difference and Exclusion brush modes. Wild stuff.

Creating gradient arrows

A few sections ago, Figure 12-13 featured an upward-pointing arrow that faded into view with a dark halo around it. I could have created this arrowhead in a drawing program to get nice sharp points and smooth outlines. But I chose to create it in Photoshop, so I could take advantage of two options drawing programs don't offer: gradient lines and halos. Naturally, you can create both in the quick mask mode.

The following steps explain how to add cool fading arrows to any image, as demonstrated in Figures 12-18 and 12-19. The steps involve the quick mask mode, the gradient tool, the Fill command, and good old Delete.

Steps: Creating Fading Arrows with Halos

1. **Save your image (Ctrl+S).** This is important — you'll be reverting to the deleted image later.

2. **Deselect everything (Ctrl+D) and switch to the quick mask mode (Q).** The image should appear absolutely normal.

3. **Select the line tool (N) and press Enter.** Adjust the line weight and arrowhead settings in the Line Tool Options palette to fit your needs. To create my first arrows (the ones that come inward from the corners in Figure 12-19), I set the Line Width value to 20 and the Width, Length, and Concavity values in the Arrowhead Shape dialog box to 400, 600, and 20, respectively.

4. **Press D to switch to the default colors.**

5. **Draw your line, which will show up in red.** If you don't get it right the first time — as is often the case with this tool — press Ctrl+Z and try again. The beauty of drawing a line in the quick mask mode is you can edit it after the fact without damaging the image. (You could also do the same on a separate layer, but the quick mask mode affords you a little more flexibility in this specific exercise.)

6. **Select the gradient tool (G) and press Enter.** Make sure the Gradient option in the Options palette is set to Foreground to Background, the Type option is set to Linear, and the Opacity slider is set to 100 percent. Then choose Lighten from the brush mode's pop-up menu.

7. **Use the gradient tool to fade the base of the line.** Drag with the gradient tool from the point at which you want the line to begin to fade, down to the base of the line. Try to make the direction of your drag parallel to the line itself, thus ensuring a smooth fade. The first image in Figure 12-18 shows me in the progress of dragging along one of my

arrows with the gradient tool. The small white arrow shows the direction of my drag. (The black line shows the actual cursor you see onscreen.) The second image shows the result of the drag.

Figure 12-18: Drag from the point at which you want the arrow to begin fading to the base of the line (left) parallel to the line itself (indicated here by the white arrow) to fade the line out (right).

8. **Choose Image ⇨ Adjust ⇨ Invert (Ctrl+I).** This inverts the quick mask, thus making the arrow the selected area.

9. **Copy the quick mask to a separate channel.** Drag the *Quick Mask* item in the Channels palette onto the little page icon at the bottom of the palette to copy the quick mask to a permanent mask channel. You'll need it again.

10. **Press Q to switch back to the marching ants mode.** Your arrow appears as a selection outline.

11. **Expand the selection to create the halo.** Choose Select ⇨ Modify ⇨ Expand and enter the desired value, based on the size and resolution of your image. I entered 6 to expand the selection outline 6 pixels.

12. **Choose Select ⇨ Feather (Ctrl+Shift+D).** Enter the same value and press Enter.

13. **Fill the selection with white for a light halo, or black for a dark one.** I wanted a white halo, so I pressed *D* to switch to the default foreground and background colors. Then I pressed Ctrl+Delete to fill the selection with white.

14. **Ctrl+click the Quick Mask Copy item in the Channels palette.** This regains your original arrow-shaped selection outline. (I explain channel masks in detail later in this chapter, but for now, just Ctrl+click.)

15. **Press Shift+Backspace to bring up the Fill dialog box.** Then select Saved from the Use pop-up menu to revert the portion of the image inside the arrows and press Enter.

16. **Float the selection.** Press Ctrl+Alt+up arrow to nudge, clone, and float the selection, and then press the down arrow to nudge it back into place. Change the foreground color to your favorite color and press Alt+Delete or Alt+Backspace to fill the selection.

17. **Choose Multiply from the blend mode pop-up menu in the upper-left corner of the Layers palette.** This burns the colored arrow into the image. Then adjust the Opacity slider to the desired level. I pressed the 4 key to change the Opacity to 40 percent.

After that, I simply kept adding more and more arrows by repeating the process. I saved the image occasionally, so I could create arrows on top of arrows. Most notably, I saved the image before adding the last, big arrow that shoots up from the bottom. Then when I filled the arrow with the saved version, I brought back bits and pieces of a few of the other arrows. (Had I not first saved the image, the arrow fragments behind the big arrow would have disappeared.)

Figure 12-19: I don't know whether this guy's in store for a cold front or what, but if you ever need to annotate an image with arrows, this gradient-arrowhead trick is certainly the way to do it.

Generating Masks Automatically

Another convenient method for creating a mask is the Color Range command under the Select menu. This command enables you to generate selections based on color ranges. You use the familiar eyedropper cursor to specify colors that should be considered for selection, and other colors you want to rule out. The Color Range command is a lot like the magic wand tool, except it enables you to select colors with more precision and to change the tolerance of the selection on the fly.

Using the Color Range command

When you choose Select ➪ Color Range, Photoshop displays the Color Range dialog box shown in Figure 12-20. Like the magic wand combined with the Similar command, Color Range selects areas of related color all across the image, whether or not the colors are immediate neighbors. You click in the Image window to select and deselect colors, as you do with the wand. But rather than adjusting a Tolerance value before you use the tool, you adjust a Fuzziness option any old time you like. Photoshop dynamically updates the selection according to the new value. Think of Color Range as the magic wand on steroids.

Note   So why didn't the folks at Adobe merely enhance the functionality of the magic wand rather than adding this strange command? The Color Range dialog box offers a preview of the mask — something a tool can't do — which is pretty essential for gauging the accuracy of your selection. And the magic wand is convenient, if nothing else. If Adobe were to combine the two functions, you would lose functionality.

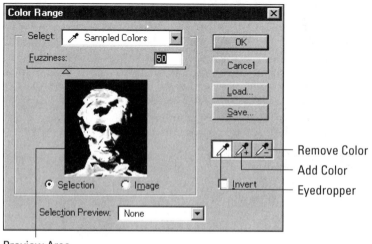

Preview Area

Figure 12-20: The Color Range dialog box enables you to generate a mask by dragging with the eyedropper tool and adjusting the Fuzziness option.

Notice, when you move your cursor outside the Color Range dialog box, it changes to an eyedropper. Click with the eyedropper to specify the color on which you want to base the selection — I call this the base color — as if you were using the magic wand. Or you can click inside the preview area, labeled in Figure 12-20. In either case, the preview area updates to show the resulting mask.

You can also do the following:

✦ **Add colors to the selection:** To add base colors to the selection, select the add color tool inside the Color Range dialog box and click inside the Image window or preview area. You can also access the tool while the standard eyedropper is selected by Shift+clicking (just as you Shift+click with the magic wand to add colors to a selection). You can even Shift+drag with the eyedropper to add multiple colors in a single pass, something you can't do with the wand tool.

✦ **Remove colors from the selection:** To remove base colors from the selection, click with the remove color tool or Alt+click with the eyedropper. You can also drag or Alt+drag to remove many colors at a time.

Tip

If adding or removing a color sends your selection careening in the wrong direction, press Ctrl+Z. Yes, the Undo command works inside the Color Range dialog box as well as out of it.

✦ **Adjust the Fuzziness value:** This option resembles the Tolerance value in the Magic Wand Options palette because it determines the range of colors to be selected beyond the ones on which you click. Raise the Fuzziness value to expand the selected area; lower the value to contract the selection. A value of 0 selects the clicked color only. Unlike changes to Tolerance, however, changing the Fuzziness value adjusts the selection on the fly; no repeat clicking is required, as it is with the wand tool.

Fuzziness and Tolerance also differ in the kind of selection outlines they generate. Tolerance entirely selects all colors within the specified range and adds anti-aliased edges. If the selection were a mask, most of it would be white with a few gray pixels around the perimeter. By contrast, Fuzziness entirely selects only the colors on which you click and Shift+click, and partially selects the other colors in the range. That's why most of the mask is expressed in shades of gray. The light grays in the mask represent the most similar colors; the dark grays represent the least similar pixels that still fall within the Fuzziness range. The result is a tapering, gradual selection, much more likely to produce natural results.

✦ **Reverse the selection:** Select the Invert check box to reverse the selection, changing black to white and white to black. As when using the magic wand, it may be easier to isolate the area you don't want to select than the area you do want to select. When you encounter such a situation, select Invert.

✦ **Toggle the preview area:** Use the two radio buttons below the preview area to control the preview's contents. If you select the first option, Selection, you see the mask that will be generated when you press Enter. If you select the Image option, the preview shows a reduced version of the image.

Tip

You can toggle between the two previews by pressing and holding the Ctrl key. My advice is to leave the option set to Selection and press the Ctrl key when you want to view the image.

✦ **Control the contents of the Image window:** The Selection Preview pop-up menu at the bottom of the dialog box enables you to change what you see in the Image window. Leave the option set to None — the default setting — to view the Image normally in the Image window. Select Grayscale to see the mask on its own. Select Quick Mask to see the mask and image together. Select Black Matte or White Matte to see what the selection would look like against a black or white background.

Although they may sound weird, the Matte options enable you to get an accurate picture of how the selected image will mesh with a different background. Figure 12-21 shows Lincoln's head at the top with the grayscale mask on the right. The mask calls for the shadows in Lincoln's face to be selected, with the highlights deselected. The two Matte views help you see how this particular selection looks against two backgrounds as different as night and day. Use the Fuzziness option in combination with Black Matte or White Matte to come up with a softness setting that will ensure a smooth transition.

✦ **Select by predefined colors:** Choose an option from the Select pop-up menu at the top of the dialog box to specify the means of selecting a base color. If you choose any option besides Sampled Colors, the Fuzziness option and eyedropper tools become dimmed to show they are no longer operable. Rather, Photoshop selects colors based on their relationship to a predefined color. For example, if you select Red, the program entirely selects red and partially selects other colors based on the amount of red they contain. Colors composed exclusively of blue and green are not selected.

The most useful option in this pop-up menu is Out of Gamut, which selects all the colors in an RGB or Lab image that fall outside the CMYK color space. You can use this option to select and modify the out-of-gamut colors before converting an image to CMYK.

✦ **Load and save settings:** Click the Save button to save the current settings to disk. Click Load to open a saved settings file.

When you define the mask to your satisfaction, click the OK button or press Enter to generate the selection outline. Although the Color Range command is more flexible than the magic wand, you can no more expect it to generate perfect selections than any other automated tool. After Photoshop draws the selection outline, therefore, you'll probably want to switch to the quick mask mode and paint and edit the mask to taste.

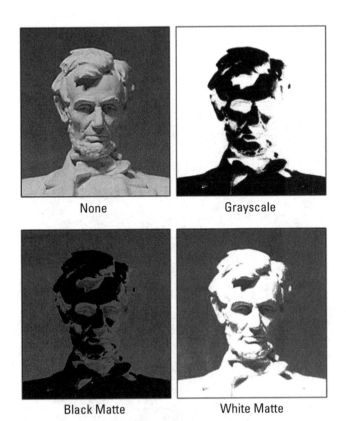

None   Grayscale

Black Matte   White Matte

Figure 12-21: Selecting an option from the Selection Preview pop-up menu changes the way the Color Range command previews the selection in the Image window.

If you learn nothing else about the Color Range dialog box, at least learn to use the Fuzziness option and the eyedropper tools. Basically two ways exist to approach these options. If you want to create a diffused selection with gradual edges, set the Fuzziness option to a high value — 60 or more — and click and Shift+click two or three times with the eyedropper. To create a more precise selection, enter a Fuzziness of 40 or lower and Shift+drag and Alt+drag with the eyedropper until you get the exact colors you want.

Figure 12-22 shows some sample results. To create the left images, I clicked with the eyedropper tool once in Lincoln's face and set the Fuzziness to 160. To create the right images, I lowered the Fuzziness value to 20; then I clicked, Shift+clicked, and Alt+clicked with the eyedropper to lift exactly the colors I wanted. The top examples show the effects of stroking the selections, first with 6-pixel white strokes, and then with 2-pixel black ones. In the two bottom examples, I copied the selections and pasted them against an identical background of — what else? — the Lincoln

Memorial. In all four cases, the higher Fuzziness value yields more generalized and softer results; the lower value results in a more exact but harsher selection.

Fuzziness: 160   Fuzziness: 20

Figure 12-22: After creating two selections with the Color Range command — one with a high Fuzziness value (left) and one with a low one (right) — I alternately stroked the selections (top) and pasted them against a different background (bottom).

A few helpful Color Range hints

Tip

You can limit the portion of an image that Select ➭ Color Range affects by selecting part of the image before choosing the command. When a selection exists, the Color Range command masks only those pixels that fall inside it. Even the preview area reflects your selection. Try it and see.

You can also add or subtract from an existing selection using the Color Range command. Press Shift when choosing Select ➭ Color Range to add to a selection. Press Alt when choosing Color Range to subtract from a selection.

If you get hopelessly lost when creating your selection and you can't figure out what to select and what to deselect, click with the eyedropper tool to start over. This clears all the colors from the selection except the one you click. Or you can press Alt to change the Cancel button to a Reset button. Alt+click the button to return the settings inside the dialog box to those in force when you first chose Select ➭ Color Range.

Creating an Independent Mask Channel

The problem with masks generated via the quick mask mode and Color Range command is they're here one day and gone the next. Photoshop is no more prepared to remember them than it is a lasso or wand selection.

Most of the time, that's okay. You'll only use the selection once, so there's no reason to sweat it. But what if the selection takes you a long time to create? What if, after a quarter hour of Shift+clicking here and Alt+dragging there, adding a few strokes in the quick mask mode, and getting the selection outline exactly right, a slight twitch pulses through your finger and you inadvertently double-click in the Image window with the lasso tool? Good job — not only have you deselected the selection, you've eliminated your only chance to undo the deselection. To coin a euphemism from the world of women's lingerie: You're hosed.

For this reason, you'll probably want to back up your selection if you've spent any amount of time on it. Even if you're in the middle of creating the selection you've been grinding at for quite a while, stop to save it before all heck breaks loose. You wouldn't let a half an hour of image-editing go by without saving, and the rules don't change just because you're working on a selection.

Saving a selection outline to a mask channel

The following steps describe how to back up a selection to an independent mask channel, which is any channel above and beyond those required to represent a grayscale or color image. Mask channels are saved along with the image itself, making it a safe and sturdy solution.

Steps: Transferring a Selection to an Independent Channel

1. **Convert the selection to a mask channel.** One way to do this is to choose Select ⇨ Save Selection, which enables you to save the selection as a mask. The dialog box shown in Figure 12-23 appears, asking you where you want to put the mask. In most cases, you'll want to save the mask to a separate channel inside the current image. To do so, make sure the name of the current image appears in the Document pop-up menu and then select New from the Channel pop-up menu and press Enter.

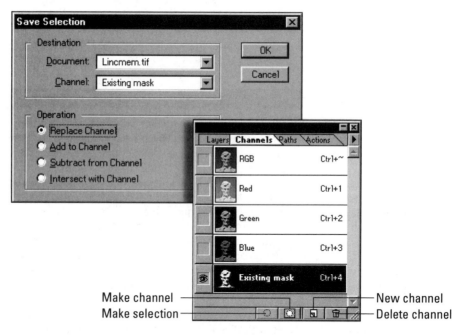

Figure 12-23: The Save Selection dialog box enables you to convert your selection outline to a mask and save it to a new or existing channel.

If you have an old channel you want to replace, select the channel's name from the Channel pop-up menu. The radio buttons at the bottom of the dialog box become available, enabling you to add the mask to the channel, subtract it, or intersect it. These radio buttons work like the equivalent options that appear when you make a path into a selection outline (as discussed in the previous chapter) but, instead, they blend the masks together. The result is the same as if you were adding, subtracting, or intersecting selection outlines, except it's expressed as a mask.

Or you can save the mask to a new document all its own. To do this, choose New from the Document pop-up menu and press Enter.

Tip

Man, what a lot of options! If you only want to save the selection to a new channel and be done with it, you needn't bother with Select ➪ Save Selection. Just click the make channel icon at the bottom of the Channels palette (labeled in Figure 12-23). Photoshop automatically creates a new channel, converts the selection to a mask, and places the mask in the channel.

Regardless of which of these many methods you choose, your selection outline remains intact.

2. **View the mask in the Channels palette.** To do so, click the appropriate channel name in the Channels palette — presumably #2 if you're editing a grayscale image or #4 if you're working in the RGB or Lab mode. In Figure 12-23, I replaced the contents of a channel called Existing Mask, so this is where my mask now resides.

This step isn't the least bit mandatory. It enables you to see your mask and generally familiarize yourself with how masks look. Remember, white represents selection, black is deselected, and gray is partial selection.

To give your channel mask a more specific name, by the way, double-click the channel name in the Channels palette.

3. **Return to the standard image-editing mode by clicking the first channel name in the Channels palette.** Better yet, press Ctrl+1 if you're editing a grayscale image or Ctrl+tilde (~) if the image is in color.

4. **Save the image to disk to store the selection permanently as part of the file.** Only the PICT, TIFF, the World Wide Web formats GIF and PNG, and native Photoshop formats suffice for this purpose. And just the TIFF and native format can handle more than four channels, both accommodating up to 24 channels in all. I generally use the TIFF format when saving images with masks — unless the image contains layers, in which case you have no choice but to save in the Photoshop format.

Caution

When you save a mask with a GIF file, all pixels in the masked area are saved as gray, indicating transparency. In other words, all detail in the masked area goes away.

Tip

If you performed the steps in the "Creating gradient arrows" section earlier in this chapter, you know you can also save a quick mask to its own channel for later use. But in case you missed those steps, or you're saving them for a special occasion, here's how it works. When you enter the quick mask mode, the Channels palette displays an item called *Quick Mask*. The italic letters show the channel is temporary and will not be saved with the image. To clone it to a permanent channel, drag the Quick Mask item onto the new channel icon at the bottom of the Channels palette (the little page labeled in Figure 12-23). Now save the image to the PICT, TIFF, or Photoshop format, and you're backed up.

Converting a mask to a selection

To retrieve your selection later, choose Select ➪ Load Selection. A dialog box nearly identical to the one shown in Figure 12-23 appears, except for the addition of an Invert check box. Select the document and channel containing the mask you want to use. You can add it to a current selection, subtract it, or intersect it. Select the Invert option if you want to reverse the selected and deselected portions of the mask.

Want to avoid the Load Selection command? Ctrl+click the channel name in the Channels palette that contains the mask you want to use. (Note, this has changed in Photoshop 4 — you used to Alt+click in Version 3.) For example, if I Ctrl+clicked the Existing Mask item in Figure 12-23, Photoshop would load the equivalent selection outline into the Image window.

But wait, there's more:

✦ You can press Ctrl+Alt plus the channel number to convert the channel to a selection. For example, Ctrl+Alt+4 would convert the Existing Mask channel shown in the figure.

✦ You can also select the channel and click the far-left mask selection icon at the bottom of the Channels palette. But for my money, this takes too much effort.

✦ To add a mask to the current selection outline, Ctrl+Shift+click the channel name in the Channels palette.

✦ Ctrl+Alt+click a channel name to subtract the mask from the selection.

✦ And Ctrl+Shift+Alt+click to find the intersection.

You can convert color channels to selections as well as mask channels. For example, if you want to select the black pixels in a piece of scanned line art in grayscale mode, Ctrl+click the first item in the Channels palette. This selects the white pixels; press Ctrl+Shift+I (or choose Select ➪ Inverse) to reverse the selection to the black pixels.

Viewing mask and image

Photoshop enables you to view any mask channel along with an image, just as you can view mask and image together in the quick mask mode. To do so, click in the first column of the Channels palette to toggle the display of the eyeball icon. An eyeball in front of a channel name indicates you can see that channel. If you are currently viewing the image, for example, click in front of the mask channel name to view the mask as a translucent color coating, again as in the quick mask mode. Or, if the contents of the mask channel appear by themselves onscreen, click in front of the image name to display it as well.

Using a mask channel is different from using the quick mask mode in that you can edit either the image or the mask channel when viewing the two together. You can even edit two or more masks at once. To decide which channel you want to edit, click the channel name in the palette. To edit two channels at once, click one and Shift+click another. All active channel names appear highlighted.

You can change the color and opacity of each mask independently of other mask channels and the quick mask mode. Click the mask channel name to select one channel only, and then choose the Channel Options command from the Channels palette menu. Or just double-click the mask channel name. (This is not an option when you're editing a standard color channel, such as Red, Green, Blue, Cyan, Magenta, Yellow, Black.) A dialog box similar to the one shown back in Figure 12-11 appears, but this one contains a Name option box so you can change the name of the mask channel. You can then edit the color overlay as described in the "Changing the red coating" section earlier in this chapter.

Tip

If you ever need to edit a selection outline inside the mask channel using paint and edit tools, click the quick mask mode icon in the Toolbox. It may sound a little incestuous — like a play within a play, perhaps — but you can access the quick mask mode even when working within a mask channel. Make sure the mask channel color is different from the quick mask color so you can tell what's happening.

Building a Mask from an Image

So far, everything I've discussed in this chapter has been pretty straightforward. Now it's time to see how the professionals do things. This final section in the chapter explains every step required to create a mask for a complex image — updated especially for this edition of the book. Here's how to select the image you never thought you could select, complete with wispy little details like hair.

Take a gander at Figure 12-24 and you'll see what I mean. I chose this subject not for her good looks or her generous supply of freckles, but for that hair. I mean, look at all that hair. Have you ever seen such a frightening image-editing subject in your life? Not only is this particular girl blessed with roughly 15 googol strands of hair, but every one of them is leaping out of her head at a different level of focus. Can you imagine selecting any one of them with the lasso? No way. Not only does the lasso tool lack sufficient accuracy to pull off this job, but you'd also be fit for an asylum by the time you finished. Furthermore, the hairs are too complex for the magic wand, and no definite edges exist for the Color Range command to latch onto.

Figure 12-24: Have you ever wanted to select hair? Using masks — and a special technique I invented for this purpose — you can.

So what's the solution? Manual masking. Although masking styles vary as widely as artistic style, a few tried-and-true formulas work for everyone. First, you peruse the channels in an image to find the channel that will lend itself best to a mask. You're looking for high degrees of contrast, especially around the edges. Next, you copy the channel and boost the level of contrast using Image ⇨ Adjust ⇨ Levels. (Some folks prefer Image ⇨ Adjust ⇨ Curves, but Levels is more straightforward.) Then you paint inside the lines until you get the mask the way you want it.

The only way to get a feel for masking is to try it out for yourself. The following steps explain exactly how I masked this girl and pasted her against a different background. The final result is so realistic, you'd think she was born there.

Steps: Selecting a Monstrously Complicated Image Using a Mask

1. Browse the color channels. Press Ctrl+1 to see the red channel, Ctrl+2 for green, and Ctrl+3 for blue. (This assumes you're working inside an RGB image. You can also peruse CMYK and Lab images. If you're editing a grayscale image, you have only one channel from which to choose — Black.)

Figure 12-25 shows the three channels in my RGB image. Of the three, the red channel offers the most contrast between the hair, which appears very light, and the background, which appears quite dark.

Red   Blue

Green

Figure 12-25: Of the three color channels, the red channel offers the best contrast between hair and background.

2. **Copy the channel.** Drag the channel onto the little page icon at the bottom of the Channels palette. (I naturally copy the red channel.) Now you can work on the channel to your heart's content without harming the image itself.

3. **Choose Filter ⇨ Other ⇨ High Pass.** The next thing you want to do is to force Photoshop to bring out the edges in the image so you don't have to hunt for them manually. And when you think edges, you should think filters. All of Photoshop's edge-detection prowess is packed into the Filter menu. Several edge-detection filters are available to you — Unsharp Mask, Find Edges, and many others that I discuss in Chapter 15. But the best filter for finding edges inside a mask is Filter ⇨ Other ⇨ High Pass.

High Pass selectively turns an image gray. High Pass may sound strange, but it's quite useful. The filter turns the nonedges completely gray while leaving the edges mostly intact, thus dividing edges and nonedges into different brightness camps, based on the Radius value in the High Pass dialog box. Unlike in most filters, a low Radius value produces a more pronounced effect than a high one, in effect locating more edges.

Figure 12-26 shows the original red channel on left with the result of the High Pass filter on right. I used a Radius of 10, which is a nice, moderate value. The lower you go, the more edges you find and the more work you make for yourself. A Radius of 3 is accurate, but it'll take you an hour to fill in the mask. Granted, 10 is less accurate, but if you value your time, it's more sensible.

Figure 12-26: After copying the red channel (left), I apply the High Pass filter with a Radius value of 10 to highlight the edges in the image (right).

4. **Choose Image ➪ Adjust ➪ Levels (Ctrl+L).** After adding all that gray to the image, follow it up by increasing the contrast. And the best command for enhancing contrast is Levels. Although I discuss this command in-depth in Chapter 18, here's the short version: Inside the Levels dialog box, raise the first Input Levels value to make the dark colors darker, and lower the third Input Levels value to make the light colors lighter. (For now you can ignore the middle value.)

Figure 12-27 shows the result of raising the first Input Levels value to 110 and lowering the third value to 155. As you can see in the left-hand image, this gives me some excellent contrast between the white hairs and black background.

To demonstrate the importance of the High Pass command in these steps, I've shown what would happen if I had skipped Step 3 in the right-hand image in Figure 12-27. Here I've applied the same Levels values as the left image, and yet the image is washed out and quite lacking in edges. Look at that wimpy hair. It simply is unacceptable.

Figure 12-27: Here are the results of applying the Levels command to the mask after the High Pass step (left) and without High Pass (right). As you can see, High Pass has a pronounced effect on the edge detail.

5. **Use the lasso tool to remove the big stuff you don't need.** By way of High Pass and Levels, Photoshop has presented you with a complex coloring book. From here on, it's a matter of coloring inside the lines. To simplify things, get rid of the stuff you know you don't need. All you care about is the area where the girl meets her background — mostly hair and arms. Everything else goes to white or black.

For example, in Figure 12-28, I selected a general area inside the girl by Alt+clicking with the lasso tool. Then I filled it with white by pressing Ctrl+Delete. I also selected around the outside of the hair and filled it with black. At all times, I was careful to stay about 10 to 20 pixels away from the hair and other edges; these I need to brush in carefully with the eraser. (Be sure to press Ctrl+D to eliminate the selection before continuing to the next step.)

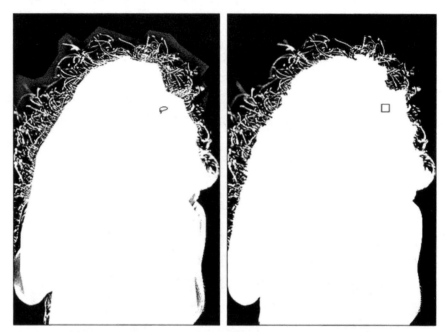

Figure 12-28: To tidy things up a bit, I selected the general areas inside and outside the girl with the lasso tool and filled them with white or black (left). Then I painted inside the lines with the block eraser (right).

6. **Erase inside the lines with the block eraser.** This is the most time-consuming part. You now have to paint inside the lines to make the edge pixels white (selected) or black (not). I like to use the block eraser because it's a hard-edged block. See, Photoshop has already presented me with these lovely and accurate edges. I don't want to gum things up by introducing new edges with a soft paintbrush or airbrush. The block eraser is hard, you can easily see its exact boundaries, and it automatically adjusts as you zoom in and out — affecting fewer pixels at higher levels of magnification, which is what you need. When working in a mask, the eraser always paints in the background color. So use the X key to toggle the background color between white and black.

The second example in Figure 12-28 shows the fruits of my erasing. As you can see, I make a few judgment calls and decide — sometimes arbitrarily — where the hair gets so thick that background imagery won't show through. You may even disagree with some of my eraser strokes. But you know what? It doesn't matter. Despite whatever flaws I may have introduced, my mask is more than accurate enough to select the girl and her unruly hair, as I'll soon demonstrate.

7. **Switch to the color composite view.** Press Ctrl+tilde (~). Or if you're working in a grayscale image, press Ctrl+1. By the way, now is a good time to save the image if you haven't already done so.

8. **Ctrl+click the mask channel to convert it to a selection.** This mask is ready to go prime time.

9. **Ctrl+drag the selection and drop it into a different image.** Figure 12-29 shows the result of dropping the girl into a background of rolling California hills. Thanks to my mask, she looks as natural in her new environment as she did in her previous one. In fact, an uninitiated viewer might have difficulty believing this isn't how she was originally photographed. But if you take a peek at Figure 12-24, you can confirm that Figure 12-29 is indeed an artificial composite. I lost a few strands of hair in the transition, but she can afford it.

Figure 12-29: Thanks to masking, our girl has found a new life in southern California. Now she's ready to finally put on those sunglasses.

The grayscale Figure 12-29 looks great but, in all honesty, your compositions may not fare quite so well in color. When you get a chance, look at the first girl in Color Plate 12-3. Her hair is fringed with blue, an unavoidable holdover from her original blue background. The solution is to brush in the color from her new background. Using the paintbrush tool set to the Color brush mode, you can Alt+click in the background to lift colors from the new background and then paint them into the hair. I also took the liberty of erasing a few of the more disorderly hairs, especially the dark ones above her head. (I used a soft paintbrush-style eraser, incidentally, not the block.) After a minute or two of painting and erasing, I arrived at the second girl in the color plate. Now if that isn't compositing perfection, I don't know what is.

Layers and Transformations

Layers, Layers Everywhere

Layers are Photoshop's most overrated and most underused feature. On one hand, and let's be perfectly clear about this, they add absolutely no functionality to Photoshop. Anything you can accomplish with layers, you can also accomplish without layers. Photoshop artists have been devising fantastic compositions, applying all varieties of selections, and masking and blending images since the program was first released. Wisely, in my opinion, Adobe has yet to make any feature exclusive to layers.

What layers add is flexibility. Because each layer in a composition is independent of other layers, you can change your mind at a moment's notice. Consider Figure 13-1. Here I've compiled the ingredients for a bad day at the doctor's office. (By golly, this may explain the reason for my chronic heartburn.) Each of the bits and pieces of hardware are located on a separate layer, all of which float above the surface of the background X-ray. Even though the pixels from the hardware blend with the X-ray and with each other, I can easily reposition and modify them as the mood strikes me. Photoshop automatically reblends the pixels on the fly.

To show what I mean, I've repositioned and transformed every layer in the second example in Figure 13-1. The MO cartridge is smaller and rotated, the mess of chords hangs up instead of down, and the lock and key are just plain skewed. I can also exchange the order of the layers, merge layers together, and adjust their translucency until I keel over from sheer alternative overload.

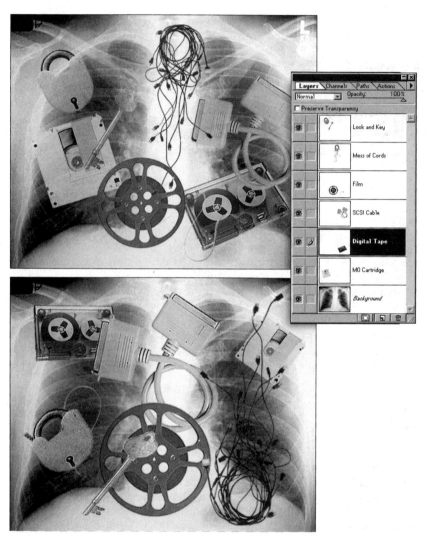

Figure 13-1: So that's what I did with my SCSI cable! Thanks to the flexibility of layers, you can arrange a bunch of images one way one moment (top) and quite differently the next (bottom). Layers enable you to modify a composition without sacrificing quality.

Layers are also uniquely versatile. You can apply three levels of masking to layers — all of which can be in force simultaneously, if you like. You can move and transform multiple layers at a time. And, as I explain in Chapters 18 and 19, you can create a special kind of layer that adjusts the colors in the layers below it and mix layers together using predefined mathematical calculations. Again, you can do it all without layers if you want, but with layers, the world becomes an infinitely editable place.

The basic way layers work remains the same in Photoshop 4 as it did in Version 3. The new Photoshop offers revised transformation capabilities — including numerical transformations — and you can align layers to guides and grids. But the biggest change is a matter of emphasis. Photoshop 4 forces you to use layers, where Photoshop 3 made it entirely optional. The type tool creates a new layer, dragging and dropping a selection with the move tool makes a new layer, the Paste command adds a new layer. Even Edit ➪ Paste Into results in a new layer (now with an automatic layer mask). And, as I mentioned in Chapter 11, many of the benefits of floating selections have been newly relegated to layers.

Photoshop 4 sticks layers in your face. And whether or not you like this change — I think Adobe went a tad overboard — you can't argue with the logic. We should all use layers more often. Layers make it harder to make mistakes, they make it easier to make changes, and they expand your range of options. If a layer might help, little reason exists not to add one. You may not appreciate having to use layers, but at least they're for your own good.

Sending a Selection to a Layer

To its credit, Photoshop enables you to establish a new layer in roughly a billion different ways. If you want to add a selected portion of one image to another image, the easiest method is to Ctrl+drag the selection and drop it into its new home, as demonstrated in Figure 13-2. Photoshop makes you a new layer, lickety-split.

Caution Be sure to Ctrl+drag or use the move tool. If you merely drag the selection with the marquee, lasso, or wand, you drop an empty selection outline into the new Image window.

When you drop the selection, your selection outline disappears. Not to worry, though. Now that the image resides on an independent layer, the selection outline is no longer needed. You can move the layer using the move tool — as you would move a selection. You can even paint inside what was once the selection by selecting the Preserve Transparency check box in the Layers palette. I explain both the move tool and Preserve Transparency in greater detail throughout this chapter.

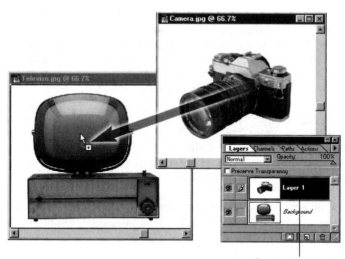

Dropped selection
becomes new layer

Figure 13-2: Ctrl+drag a selection and drop it into a different Image window to introduce the selection as a new layer. As you can see in the Layers palette, the camera becomes a new layer in front of the television.

If you want to clone a selection to a new layer inside the same Image window — useful when performing complex filter routines and color corrections — choose Layer ➪ New ➪ Layer Via Copy. Or press Ctrl+J (the keyboard shortcut for the dead-gone-dead Float command in Photoshop 3).

Other ways to make a layer

Those are only two of many different ways to create a new layer in Photoshop. Here are a few others:

✦ Copy a selection (Ctrl+C) and paste it into another image (Ctrl+V). Photoshop pastes the selection as a new layer.

✦ If you want to relegate a selection exclusively to a new layer, choose Layer ➪ New ➪ Layer Via Cut or press Ctrl+Shift+J. Rather than cloning the selection, Layer Via Cut removes the selection from the background image and places it on its own layer.

✦ To create an empty layer — as when you want to paint a few brushstrokes without harming the original image — choose Layer ➪ New ➪ Layer. Or click the new layer icon at the bottom of the Layers palette (labeled in Figure 13-3).

✦ You can also convert a floating selection — one you've moved or cloned — to a new layer by clicking the new layer icon. Or double-click the *Floating Selection* item in the Layers palette. You can also press Ctrl+Shift+J. (Both double-clicking and pressing Ctrl+Shift+J display dialog boxes, asking you to name the image.)

Photoshop 4.0

Incidentally, you can also create a new layer by choosing New Layer from the Layers palette menu. But this menu has become far less useful in Photoshop 4. As you can see in the wonderfully easy-to-follow Figure 13-3 — can you imagine a more illuminating piece of info art? — nearly all the palette commands are duplicated in the Layer menu. The only unique palette command is Palette Options (circled in the figure), which enables you to change the size of the thumbnails in front of the layer names.

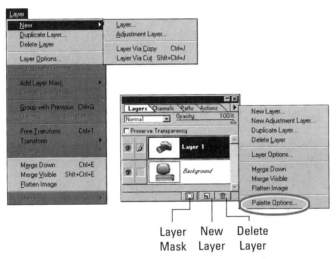

Layer Mask   New Layer   Delete Layer

Figure 13-3: In Photoshop 4, all but one of the commands in the Layers palette menu are duplicated in the Layer menu.

Tip

When you choose the Layer Via Copy or Layer Via Cut command or click the new layer icon, Photoshop automatically names the new layer for you. Unfortunately, the automatic names — Layer 1, Layer 2, and so on — are fairly meaningless and don't help to convey the contents of the layer. (Dammit, Photoshop, don't you know a camera when you see one?) If you want to specify your own name, press the Alt key. Press Ctrl+Alt+J to clone the selection to a layer, hold down Alt and choose Layer via Cut to cut the selection, or Alt+click the new layer icon to create a blank layer. In any case, you'll see the dialog box shown in Figure 13-4. Enter a name for the layer and press Enter. (You can ignore the other options in this dialog box for now.)

When converting a floating selection to a new layer, you can Alt+double-click the Floating Selection item to bypass the dialog box. So Alt works both ways, forcing the dialog box some times and suppressing it others. The only time it produces no effect is when pasting or dropping an image. Too bad — I for one would use it often.

Tip   To rename a layer, double-click its name in the Layers palette. (You can also choose Layer ⇨ Layer Options, but what sane human being would go to all that effort?) Then enter a new name and whack that Enter key.

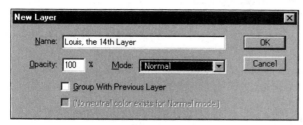

Figure 13-4: Press Alt to force the display of the New Layer dialog box, which enables you to name the new layer.

Duplicating a layer

Cloning a layer isn't a simple matter of Ctrl+Alt+dragging, the way it is with a selection. (Again, I must say, too bad. It should be that easy.) Instead, you clone the layer and then reposition it in two separate operations.

To clone the active layer, you can choose Layer ⇨ Duplicate Layer. But that's the sucker's way. The more convenient way is to drag the layer name you want to clone onto the new layer icon at the bottom of the Layers palette.

To specify a name for the cloned layer or to copy the layer into another image, Alt+drag the layer onto the new layer icon. Always the thoughtful program, Photoshop displays the dialog box shown in Figure 13-5. You can name the cloned layer by entering something into the As option box. To jettison the layer to some other open image, choose the image name from the Document pop-up menu. Or choose New and enter the name for an entirely different image in the Name option box, as the figure shows.

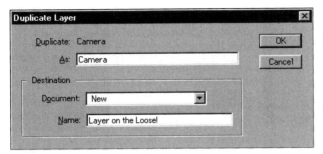

Figure 13-5: You can duplicate the layer into an entirely different image by Alt+dragging the layer onto the new layer icon in the Layers palette.

Working with Layers

Regardless of how you create a new layer, Photoshop lists the layer along with a little thumbnail of its contents in the Layers palette. The new layer's name appears highlighted to show it's active. The little paintbrush icon in front of the layer name also indicates an active layer.

To the left of the paintbrush icon is a column of eyeballs, which invite you to hide and display layers temporarily. Click an eyeball to hide the layer. Click where the eyeball previously was to bring it back and redisplay the layer. Whether hidden or displayed, all layers remain intact and ready for action.

Tip

To view a single layer by itself, Alt+click the eyeball icon before the layer name to hide all other layers. Alt+click in front of the layer again to bring all the layers back into view.

Switching between layers

You can select a different layer by clicking its name in the Layers palette. This layer becomes active, enabling you to edit it. Only one layer may be active at a time in Photoshop — you can't Shift+click to select and edit multiple layers, I'm sorry to say.

If your image contains several layers — like the one back in Figure 13-1 — it might prove inconvenient, or even confusing, to switch from one layer to another in the Layers palette. Photoshop 4, luckily, offers a better way. With any tool, Ctrl+Alt+right-click an element in your composition to go directly to the layer containing the element. For example, Ctrl+Alt+right-clicking the SCSI cable in Figure 13-1 would take me to the SCSI Cable layer.

Why Ctrl+Alt+right-clicking? Here's how it breaks down:

✦ Ctrl gets you the move tool. (If the move tool is already selected, you don't have to press Ctrl because Alt+right-clicking works just fine.)

✦ Right-clicking alone brings up a context-sensitive pop-up menu. When you right-click with the move tool — or Ctrl+right-click with any other tool — Photoshop displays a pop-up menu that lists the layer the image is on and any other layers in the image, as in Figure 13-6. (If a layer is completely transparent at the spot where you right-click, that layer name doesn't appear in the pop-up menu.) Select the desired layer to go there.

✦ The Alt key bypasses the pop-up menu and goes straight to the clicked layer.

Add them all together, and you get Ctrl+Alt+right-click.

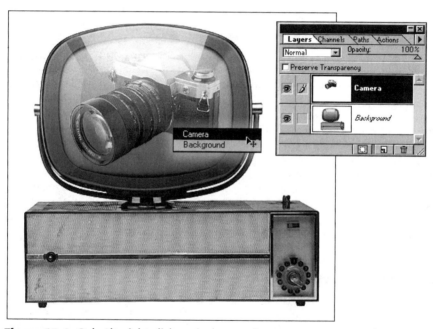

Figure 13-6: Ctrl+Alt+right-click an image to view a pop-up menu. The menu lists the location of the image you've clicked and the background layer.

Switching layers from the keyboard

You can also ascend and descend the layer stack from the keyboard:

✦ **Alt+]:** Press Alt+right bracket to go to the next layer up in the stack. If you're already at the top layer, Photoshop takes you back around to the lowest one.

✦ **Alt+[:** Press Alt+left bracket to go down a layer. If the background layer is active, Alt+[takes you to the top layer.

✦ **Shift+Alt+]:** This takes you to the top layer in the image.

✦ **Shift+Alt+[:** This activates the background layer (or the lowest layer if no background exists).

Photoshop 4.0

Photoshop 3 users note: Every one of these shortcuts has changed in the new version. You used to press Ctrl+bracket and Ctrl+Shift+bracket. Now you use Alt instead.

Understanding transparency

Although the selection outline disappears when you convert a selection to a layer, no information is lost. Photoshop retains every little nuance of the original selection outline — whether it's a jagged border, a little bit of anti-aliasing, or a feathered edge. Anything that wasn't selected is now transparent. The data that defines the opacity and transparency of a layer is called the *transparency mask.*

To see this transparency in action, click the eyeball icon in front of the Background item in the Layers palette. This hides the background layer and enables you to view the new layer by itself. In Figure 13-7, I hid the background TV from Figure 13-6 to view the camera on its own. The transparent areas are covered in a checkerboard pattern. Opaque areas look like the standard image, and translucent areas — where they exist — appear as a mix of image and checkerboard.

Tip

If the checkerboard pattern is hard to distinguish from the image, you can change the appearance of the pattern. Press Ctrl+K and then Ctrl+4 to go to the Transparency & Gamut panel of the Preferences dialog box. Then edit away (as explained back in Chapter 2).

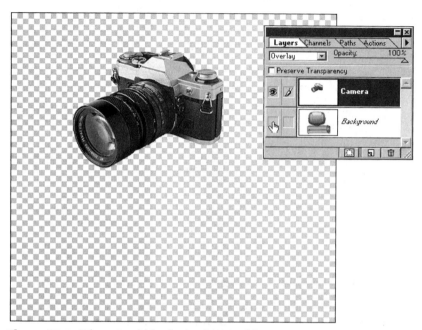

Figure 13-7: When you hide the background layer, you see a checkerboard pattern that represents the transparent portions of the layer.

If you apply an effect to the layer while no portion of the layer is selected, Photoshop changes the opaque and translucent portions of the image, but leaves the transparent region intact. For example, if you press Ctrl+I (or choose Image ➪ Adjust ➪ Invert), Photoshop inverts the image but doesn't change a single pixel in the checkerboard area. If you click in the left column in front of the Background item to bring back the eyeball icon, you may notice a slight halo around the inverted image, but the edge pixels blend with the background image as well as they ever did. In fact, it's exactly as if you applied the effect to a selection, as demonstrated in Figure 13-8. The only difference is this selection is altogether independent of its background. You can do anything you want to it without running the risk of harming the underlying background.

Only a few operations affect the transparent areas of a layer, and most of these are limited to tools. You can paint on transparent pixels to make them opaque. You can clone with the rubber stamp, or smear pixels with the edit tools. But you can send pixels back to transparency using the eraser, as well. All these operations change both the contents of the layer and the composition of the transparency mask.

Tip   You can also fill all pixels by pressing Alt+Delete or Alt+Backspace for the foreground color and Ctrl+Delete or Ctrl+Backspace for the background color. To fill the pixels in a layer without altering the transparency mask, toss in the Shift key. Shift+Alt+Delete (or Backspace) fills the opaque pixels with the foreground color, while Ctrl+Shift+Delete (or Backspace) fills them with the background color. In both cases, the transparent pixels remain every bit as transparent as they ever were.

When a portion of the layer is selected, pressing plain old Delete eliminates the selected pixels and makes them transparent, revealing the layers below.

Figure 13-8: Applying the Invert command to the camera layer inverts only the camera without affecting any of the transparent pixels. The TV remains every bit as visible as ever.

Note   Transparent pixels take up no space in memory, but opaque and translucent pixels do. Thus, a layer containing 25 percent as many pixels as the background layer takes up 25 percent as much space. But if you paint into the transparent area of that same layer, you increase the size of the layer in memory 3K for every RGB pixel you change from transparent to opaque or translucent. Here's the math: A 24-bit pixel consumes exactly 3K in memory, because 1K equals 256 colors to the third power, or 16 million. Obviously, these considerations can have an effect on Photoshop's performance.

Modifying the background layer

At the bottom of the layer stack is the *background layer,* the fully opaque layer that represents the base image. The background image is as low as you go. Nothing can be slipped under the background layer and pixels in the background layer cannot be made transparent, unless you first convert the background to a "normal" layer.

To make the conversion, double-click the background item in the Layers palette. Then enter a name for the new layer — Photoshop suggests Layer 0 — and press Enter. You can now change the order of the layer or erase down to transparency.

In Figure 13-9, I converted the background television to a layer. This particular image (from the PhotoDisc Object Series) included a predrawn path that encircled the TV. I Ctrl+clicked on the path to convert it to a selection outline, and I pressed Ctrl+Shift+I to reverse the selection. Finally, I pressed the Delete key to erase the pixels outside the TV, as the figure demonstrates.

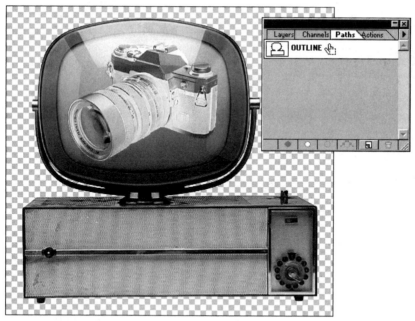

Figure 13-9: After converting the TV image to a layer, I Ctrl+clicked the path, inversed the selection, and pressed the Delete key to reveal the transparent void below.

From this point on, I can reorder the camera and television layers or add layers in back of the TV. I can also introduce a new background layer. (A program like QuarkXPress or PageMaker doesn't recognize Photoshop's transparency, so there's no point in leaving the background transparent. As I mentioned in Chapter 11, if you want to export transparency, you must use a clipping path.)

To add a new background layer, Alt+click the new layer icon at the bottom of the Layers palette. When the New Layer dialog box appears, select the Background option from the Mode pop-up menu, as in Figure 13-10. Then press Enter.

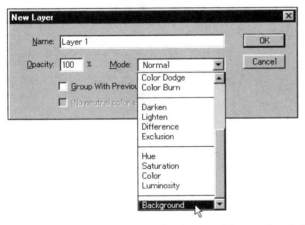

Figure 13-10: To add a new background layer, Alt+click the new layer icon and select the Background option from the Mode pop-up menu.

In Figure 13-11, I added a new background layer. I used the Add Noise and Emboss filters to create a paper texture pattern (as I explained back in Chapter 10). Then I added a drop shadow to match the contours of the TV. (To learn how to create drop shadows, read the "Drop Shadows, Halos, and Spotlights" section later in this chapter.)

Reordering layers

What good would layers be if you couldn't periodically change what's on the top and what's on the bottom? Two ways exist to reorder layers in Photoshop 4. First, you can drag a layer name up or down in the scrolling list to move it forward or backward in layering order. The only trick is to make sure the black bar appears at the point where you want to move the layer before you release the mouse button, as demonstrated in Figure 13-12.

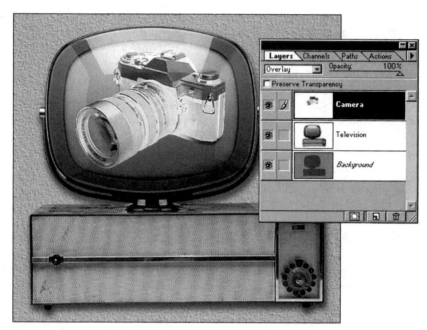

Figure 13-11: I added a background layer behind the television and applied a paper texture and drop shadow to give my composition a little false depth.

Tip

You can even move floating selections by dragging them up and down in the palette. When you do, Photoshop automatically converts the floater to an independent layer. But don't miss that black bar or Photoshop won't move a darn thing.

The second way to reorder layers — by choosing a command from the Layer ➪ Arrange submenu — is new to Photoshop 4. For example, choose Layer ➪ Arrange ➪ Bring Forward to move the active layer up one level; choose Layer ➪ Arrange ➪ Send to Back to move the layer to above the background layer.

You can move faster if you remember the following keyboard shortcuts (all of which perform different functions than they did in Photoshop 3):

✦ **Ctrl+Shift+]:** Press Ctrl+right bracket to move the active layer to the top of the stack.

✦ **Ctrl+Shift+[:** This shortcut moves the active layer to the bottom of the stack, just above the background layer.

✦ **Ctrl+]:** This nudges the layer up one level.

✦ **Ctrl+[:** This nudges the layer down.

The all-important
black bar

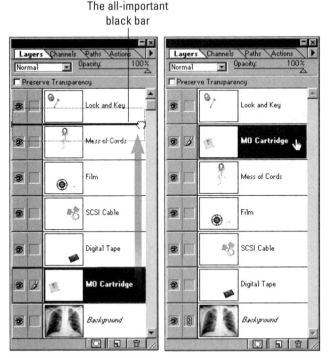

Figure 13-12: Drag the layer between two other layers to make the all-important black bar appear (left) to change the hierarchy of the layer (right).

Note   You can neither reorder the background layer nor move any other layer below the background until you first convert the background to a normal layer, as explained in the previous section.

Automated matting techniques

When you convert an anti-aliased selection to a layer, you sometimes take with you a few pixels from the selection's previous background. These *fringe pixels* can result in an unrealistic outline around your layer that cries out, "This image was edited by a hack." For example, Figure 13-13 shows a magnified detail from my original attempt at creating Figure 13-11. Although the selection outline was accurate, I managed to retain a few white pixels around the edges, as you can see around the outline of the picture tube and arm that holds the tube.

Figure 13-13: This enlarged detail of the TV layer against the textured background shows the fringe pixels left over from the TV's original white background.

You can instruct Photoshop to replace the fringe pixels with colors from neighboring pixels by choosing Layer ➪ Matting ➪ Defringe. Enter the thickness of the perceived fringe in the Width option box to tell Photoshop which pixels you want to replace. To create the image shown in Figure 13-14, I entered a Width value of 1. But even at this low value, the effect is pretty significant, leaving gummy edges in its wake.

Photoshop provides two additional commands under the Layer ➪ Matting submenu: Remove Black Matte and Remove White Matte. Frankly, it's unlikely you'll have much call to use them, but here's the scoop:

✦ **Remove Black Matte:** This command removes the residue around the perimeter of a layer that was lifted from a black background.

✦ **Remove White Matte:** This command removes a white ring around a layer.

Adobe tells me these commands were designed specifically for compositing a scene rendered in a 3D drawing program against a black or white background. But for other purposes, they almost never work. For example, my television is a prime candidate for Remove White Matte — it originated from a white background — and yet it leaves behind more white pixels than the Defringe command set to its lowest setting.

Figure 13-14: Here I used the Defringe command set to a Width value of 1 to replace the pixels around the perimeter of the layer with colors borrowed from neighboring pixels.

Tip   If you encounter unrealistic edge pixels and the automatic matting commands don't solve your problem, you may be able to achieve better results by fixing the edges manually. First, switch to the layer that's giving you fits and Ctrl+click its name in the Layers palette. This creates a tight selection around the contents of the layer. (I tell you more about selecting layers in the "Drop Shadows, Halos, and Spotlights" section later in this chapter.) Then choose Select ➪ Modify ➪ Contract and enter the width of the fringe in the Contract By option box. Next, choose Select ➪ Feather (Ctrl+Shift+D) and enter this same value into the Feather Radius option box. Finally, press Ctrl+Shift+I to inverse the selection and press Delete to eliminate the edge pixels.

Figure 13-15 shows the results of applying this technique to my television. (Figure 13-11 also shows the result at normal size.) By setting the Contract and Feather commands to 1 pixel, I managed to remove the edges without harming the layer itself. And the effect looks better than that produced by the Defringe command (see Figure 13-14).

Blending layers

Photoshop enables you to blend layers with each other like no other program in the business. In fact, Photoshop does such a great job, it takes me an entire chapter — Chapter 19 — to explain these options in detail. I offer this section only by way of introduction, so you're aware of the basics. If you have bigger questions, then Chapter 19 is ready to tell all.

Figure 13-15: Here I removed the edges manually using the Contract, Feather, and Inverse commands. This looks way better than anything Photoshop can do automatically.

The Layers palette offers three basic ways to blend pixels between layers. None of these techniques changes as much as a pixel in any layer, so you can always return and reblend the layers at a later date (see Figure 13-16).

✦ **The Opacity slider bar:** Drag the Opacity slider triangle near the top of the Layers palette to change the opacity of the active layer or floating selection. If you reduce the Opacity value to 50 percent, for example, Photoshop makes the pixels on the active layer translucent, so the colors in the layer mix evenly with the colors in the layer below.

Tip

If any tool other than a painting tool is active — including the selection and navigation tools — you can press a number key to change the Opacity value. Press 1 for 10 percent, 2 for 20 percent, up to 0 for 100 percent. Or you can enter a specific Opacity value by pressing two number keys in a row. For example, press 3 and then 7 for 37 percent.

✦ **The blend mode pop-up menu:** Choose an option from the blend mode pop-up menu to mix every pixel in the active layer with the pixels below it, according to one of several mathematical equations. For example, when you choose Multiply, Photoshop does multiply the brightness values of the pixels and then divides the result by 255, the maximum brightness value. Blend modes use the exact same math as the brush modes covered in Chapter 8. But you can accomplish a lot more with blend modes, which is why I spend so much time examining them in Chapter 19.

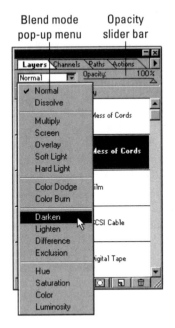

Blend mode pop-up menu

Opacity slider bar

Figure 13-16: The blend mode pop-up menu and the Opacity slider bar enable you to mix layers together without making any permanent changes to the pixels.

✦ **Layer Options:** Choose Layer ➪ Layer Options or double-click a layer name to display the Layer Options dialog box. This dialog box provides access to an Opacity value and a Mode pop-up menu, but it also offers a few unique functions. Using the Blend If slider bars, you can specify which colors are visible in the active layer and which colors show through from the layers behind it. You can also mix the colors using special fuzziness controls and change the slider bar settings for an individual color channel.

This is enough to prepare you for anything I might throw at you between now and Chapter 19. But as I've mentioned four times now, Chapter 19 contains the whole story. (Oops, make that five mentions.)

Fusing several layers into one

Although layers are wonderful and marvelous creatures, they have their price. Layers expand the size of an image in RAM and ultimately lead to slower performance. And as explained in Chapter 4, you can save layered images in only one format, the native Photoshop format.

Photoshop provides several methods for merging layers together (many new to Photoshop 4):

✦ **Merge Down (Ctrl+E):** Choose Layer ➪ Merge Down to merge a layer with the layer immediately below it. When generating screen shots, I use this command 50 or 60 times a day. I paste the screen shot into the Image window, edit the layer as desired, and then press Ctrl+E to set it down. Then I can save the screen shot in any format I like.

Merge Down is the anszwer to Defloat in Photoshop 4. In fact, when you're working with a floating selection, Merge Down changes to Defloat, and both commands share Ctrl+E as a keyboard equivalent.

If the active layer is linked to other layers or part of a clipping group — two conditions I discuss later in this chapter — the Merge Down command changes to Merge Linked or Merge Group, respectively. Again, these commands use Ctrl+E as a shortcut. Merge Down is forever changing to suit the situation.

✦ **Merge Visible (Ctrl+Shift+E):** Choose the Merge Visible command to merge all visible layers into a single layer. If the layer is not visible — that is, if no eyeball icon appears in front of the layer name — Photoshop doesn't eliminate it; the layer simply remains independent.

Tip

To create a merged clone, press the Alt key when applying either Layer ➪ Merge Down or Layer ➪ Merge Visible. Alt+choosing Merge Down (or pressing Ctrl+Alt+E) clones the contents of the active layer into the layer below it. Alt+choosing Merge Visible (or pressing Ctrl+Shift+Alt+E) copies the contents of all visible layers to the active layer.

To copy the merged contents of a selected area, choose Edit ➪ Copy Merged, or press Ctrl+Shift+C. You can then paste the selection into a layer or make it part of a different image.

✦ **Flatten Image:** This command, on the other hand, merges all visible layers and throws away the invisible ones. The result is a single, opaque background layer. Photoshop does not give this command a keyboard shortcut because it's so dangerous. More often than not, you'll want to flatten an image incrementally using the two Merge commands.

Caution

Photoshop suggests you flatten an image when converting from one color mode to another. You can choose not to flatten the image when switching from say, RGB to CMYK, but this may come at the expense of some of the brighter colors in your image.

Dumping layers

You can also merely throw a layer away: Drag the layer name onto the trash can icon at the bottom of the Layers palette. Or click the trash can icon to delete the active layer.

Tip

When you click the trash can icon, Photoshop displays a message asking whether you really want to toss the layer. To give this message the slip in the future, Alt+click the trash can icon.

Saving a flattened version of an image

Only one file format, the native Photoshop format, saves images with layers. If you want to save a flattened version of your image — that is, with all layers fused together into a single image — in some other file format, choose File ➪ Save a Copy (Ctrl+Alt+S) and select the desired format from the Save As pop-up menu. If you select any format other than Photoshop, the program selects and dims the Flatten Image check box in the lower-left corner of the dialog box.

The Save a Copy command neither affects the image onscreen — all layers remain intact — nor changes the name of the image in the Title bar. It merely creates a flattened duplicate of the image on disk.

Drop Shadows, Halos, and Spotlights

A few sections back, I mentioned every layer (except the background) includes a transparency mask; this mask tells Photoshop which pixels are opaque, which are translucent, and which are transparent. And like any mask, Photoshop enables you to convert the transparency mask for any layer — active or not — to a selection outline. In fact, you use the same keyboard techniques you use to convert paths to selections (as explained in Chapter 11) and channels to selections (Chapter 12):

✦ Ctrl+click a layer name to convert the transparency mask to a selection outline. (This replaces the old Ctrl+Alt+T shortcut offered by Photoshop 3).

✦ To add the transparency mask to an existing selection outline, Ctrl+Shift+click the layer name. The little selection cursor includes a plus sign to show you that you're about to add.

✦ To subtract the transparency mask, Ctrl+Alt+click the layer name.

✦ And to find the intersection of the transparency mask and the current selection outline, Ctrl+Shift+Alt+click the layer name.

If you're uncertain you'll remember all these keyboard shortcuts, you can use Select ➪ Load Selection instead. After choosing the command, select the Transparency item from the Channel pop-up menu. (You can even load a transparency mask from another open image if the image is exactly the same size as the one in which you're working.) Then use the Operation radio buttons to merge the mask with an existing selection, as described in the "Converting a mask to a selection" section of Chapter 12.

Selection outlines exist independently of layers, so you can use the transparency mask from one layer to select part of another layer. For example, to select part of the background layer that exactly matches the contents of another layer, you press Shift+Alt+[to descend to the background layer and then Ctrl+click the name of the layer you want to match.

In fact, this is the technique you use to create three of the most sought-after effects in image editing — drop shadows, halos, and spotlights. So now that we've hit on the basics, let's look at a few real-life applications.

Drop shadows

In these first steps, I'll take the dolphin from Figure 13-17 and insert a drop shadow behind it. This might not be the exact subject to which you'll apply drop shadows — sea critters so rarely cast such shadows onto the water's surface — but it accurately demonstrates how the effect works.

Figure 13-17: A dolphin in dire need of a drop shadow

Steps: Creating a Drop Shadow

1. **Select the subject you want to cast the shadow.** In my case, I selected the dolphin by painting the mask shown in Figure 13-18 inside a separate mask channel. These days, I add a mask to nearly every image I create to distinguish the foreground image from its background. I converted the mask to a selection outline by Ctrl+clicking the mask name in the Channels palette and then pressing Ctrl+tilde (~) to switch back to the composite view.

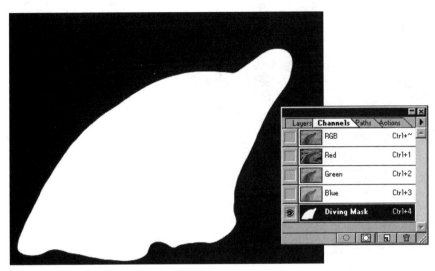

Figure 13-18: This mask separates the dolphin from its watery home.

2. **Send the image to a separate layer by pressing Ctrl+J.** Now that the selection is elevated, you can slip in the drop shadow beneath it.

3. **Retrieve the selection outline for your new layer and apply it to the background layer.** To do this, Ctrl+click the new layer name (presumably Layer 1), then press Shift+Alt+[to switch to the background layer. (Because I saved the mask to a separate channel, I could have, instead, Ctrl+clicked the Mask item in the Channels panel to retrieve the selection. Or I could have pressed Ctrl+Alt+4.)

4. **To create a softened drop shadow — indicative of a diffused light source — choose Select ⇨ Feather.** The Radius value you enter depends on the resolution of your image. I recommend dividing the resolution of your image by 20. When working on a 200 ppi image, for example, enter a Radius value of 10. My image is a mere 140 ppi, so I entered 7. Then press Enter to soften the image.

5. **Press Ctrl+J to send the feathered selection to a new layer.**

6. **Fill the feathered area with black.** If necessary, press *D* to make the foreground color black. Then press Shift+Alt+Delete (or Shift+Alt+Backspace) to fill only the area inside the transparency mask. A slight halo of dark pixels forms around the edges of the image.

7. **Press Ctrl with the arrow keys to nudge the shadow to the desired location.** In Figure 13-19, I nudged the shadow 12 pixels to the right. (Press Ctrl+Shift+arrow key to nudge the shadow 10 pixels.)

Figure 13-19: A drop shadow nudged is 12 pixels due right from the dolphin head, which is situated on the layer above it.

8. **Lower the Opacity setting.** If the shadow is too dark — black lacks a little subtlety — drag the Opacity slider in the Layers palette to change the opacity of the shadow. Or press M to make sure a selection tool is active and then press a number key to change the opacity. I typically press 7 for 70 percent, but I'm probably in a rut.

If you don't like a black drop shadow, you can make a colored one with only slightly more effort. Instead of filling the shadow with black in Step 6, select a different foreground color and press Shift+Alt+Delete (or Shift+Alt+Backspace). For the best result, select a color that is the complimentary opposite of your background color. In Color Plate 13-1, for example, the background is blue, so I selected a reddish orange as the foreground color. Next, choose Multiply from the blend mode pop-up menu on the left side of the Layers palette. This burns the colors in the shadow into those in the image to create a darkened mix. Finally, press a number key to specify the opacity. (In the color plate, I again used 70 percent. I'm definitely in a rut.)

Photoshop 4 includes a predefined Drop Shadow script in the Actions palette. But it applies the drop shadow to the entire image, not just a selected area. If you anticipate you'll add drop shadows often, you might want to create a script of your own using the preceding steps.

Halos

Creating a halo is similar to creating a drop shadow. The only differences are you must expand the selection outline and fill the halo with white (or some other light color) instead of black. The following steps tell all.

Steps: Creating a Downright Angelic Halo

1. **Follow Steps 1 through 3 of the previous instructions.** You'll end up with a version of the selected image on an independent layer and a matching selection outline applied to the background image. (See, I told you this was like creating a drop shadow.)

2. **Expand the selection outline.** Unlike a drop shadow, which is offset slightly from an image, a halo fringes the perimeter of an image pretty evenly. You need to expand the selection outline beyond the edges of the image so you can see the halo clearly. To do this, choose Select ➪ Modify ➪ Expand. You'll be greeted by an Expand By option box. Generally speaking, you want the expansion to match the size of your feathering, so the softening occurs outward. Therefore, I entered 7. (The maximum permissible value is 16; if you want to expand more than 16 pixels, you must apply the command twice.)

3. **Choose Select ➪ Feather and enter the same value you entered in the Expand By option box.** Again, you decide this value by dividing the resolution of your image by 20 (or thereabouts).

4. **Send the selection to a new layer.** Press Ctrl+J.

5. **Fill the halo with white.** Assuming the background color is white, press Ctrl+Shift+Delete or Ctrl+Shift+Backspace.

That's it. Figure 13-20 shows an enlightened-looking dolphin set against a halo effect. I also drew a conventional halo above its head, added some sparklies, and even changed my finned friend's eye using the eyeball brush shape included in the Assorted Brushes document. I mean, if this aquatic mammal's not bound for glory, I don't know who is.

Tip

Incidentally, you needn't create a white halo any more than you must create a black drop shadow. In Step 5, set the background color to something other than white. Then select the Screen option from the blend mode pop-up menu in the Layers palette, thus mixing the colors and lightening them at the same time. If you don't like the effect, select a different background color and press Ctrl+Shift+Delete again. As long as the halo is floating, you can do about anything you want and run no risk of harming the underlying original.

Figure 13-20: Few dolphins reach this level of spiritual awareness, even if you do set them off from their backgrounds using the halo effect. He kind of looks like one of the cast members from *Cocoon*, don't you think?

Spotlights

Now, finally, for the spotlight effect. I use spotlights about a billion times in this book to highlight some special option I want you to look at in a palette or dialog box. I've received so many questions (from fellow authors mostly) on how to perform this effect, I've decided to write the information in this book and be done with it. So here goes.

Steps: Shining a Spotlight on Something Inside an Image

1. **Draw an oval selection inside your image.** Obviously, the best tool for this purpose is the elliptical marquee tool. The selection represents the area where the spotlight will shine. If you don't like where the oval is located, but you basically like its size and shape, drag the outline to a more satisfactory location.

2. **Choose Select ⇨ Feather and enter whatever Radius value you please.** Again, you may want to follow the divide-the-resolution-by-20 rule, but use whatever value you like. (There's no such thing as a wrong Radius value.) To create Figure 13-21, I doubled my Radius value to 14 pixels to create a soft effect.

3. **Press Ctrl+Shift+I.** Most likely, you really want to darken the area outside the spotlight, not lighten the spotlight itself. So choose Select ⇨ Inverse (Ctrl+Shift+I) to swap what's selected and what's not.

4. **Send the selection to a new layer.** That's Ctrl+J, of course.

5. **Fill the transparency mask with black.** With the foreground color set to black, press Shift+Alt+Delete or Shift+Alt+Backspace.

6. **Lower the Opacity setting by pressing a number key.** To get the effect in Figure 13-21, I pressed 6 for 60 percent.

Figure 13-21: Create an elliptical selection, feather it, inverse it, layer it, fill it with black, and lower the opacity to create a spotlight effect like this one.

Actually, the image in Figure 13-21 isn't all that convincing. Although the preceding steps are fine for spotlighting flat images such as screen shots, they tend to rob photographs of some of their depth. After all, in real life, the spotlight wouldn't hit the water in the same way it hits the dolphin. But a way around this exists. You can combine the oval selection outline with the mask used to select the foreground image, thereby eliminating the background from the equation entirely.

Tip

Assuming your image has a mask saved in a separate channel, do this: After establishing the selection and feathering it (Steps 1 and 2), duplicate the mask channel so you don't harm the original. (You do this by dragging the channel name onto the little page icon at the bottom of the Channels palette.) Then choose Select ⇨ Save Selection. Inside the dialog box, select the duplicate mask channel from the Channel pop-up menu and then select the Intersect with Channel radio button. This creates a mask that retains only those areas selected both in the selection outline and the mask. Ctrl+click the revised mask in the Channels palette to convert it to a selection outline and switch to the composite view (Ctrl+tilde). Then perform the preceding Steps 3 through 6 — that is, inverse the selection (Ctrl+Shift+I), send it to a layer (Ctrl+J), fill the transparency mask with black (Shift+Alt+Delete), and change the opacity. Figure 13-22 shows this technique applied to a familiar character.

Figure 13-22: You can mix the feathered selection with the contents of a mask channel to limit the spotlighting effect to the foreground character only.

Caution

Sometimes, the darkness of the area around the spotlight appears sufficiently dark that it starts bringing the spotlighted area down with it. To brighten the spotlight, inverse the selection (Ctrl+Shift+I) so the spotlight is selected again. Then apply the Levels command (Ctrl+L) to brighten the spotlighted area. The Levels command is explained at length in Chapter 18.

Just for fun — what other possible reason would there be? — Color Plate 13-2 shows one result of combining the spotlight effect with the halo effect. I filled the area outside the spotlight with a deep blue. (In this case, a similar color looked better than a complimentary one.) Then, using my original mask, I sent the dolphin to a separate layer and created a yellowish, pinkish halo behind it. Then, I used Edit ⇨ Fill (Shift+Backspace) to return the background image to its original appearance — by selecting the Saved option from the Use pop-up menu in the Fill dialog box — and inverted the background by pressing Ctrl+I. (For the Saved option to work, the saved file must contain a comparable layer.) An interestingly lit dolphin in a radioactive bath is the result.

Moving and Aligning Layers

You can move an entire layer or the selected portion of a layer by dragging inside the Image window with the move tool. Drag inside a selection outline to move only a selection; drag outside the selection to move the entire layer.

As I mention in Chapter 11, you can temporarily access the move tool when some other tool is active by pressing the Ctrl key. To nudge a layer, press Ctrl with an arrow key. Press Ctrl and Shift together to nudge in 10-pixel increments.

If part of the layer disappears beyond the edge of the window, no problem. As long as you don't move your cursor outside the Image window, Photoshop saves even the hidden pixels in the layer, enabling you to drag it into view later. (This only works when moving all of a layer. If you move a selection beyond the edge of the Image window using the move tool, Photoshop clips the selection at the window's edge the moment you deselect it.) If you move your cursor outside the Image window, however, Photoshop thinks you are trying to drag-and-drop pixels from one image to another and responds accordingly.

If you Ctrl+drag the background image — either when no portion of the image is selected or by dragging outside the selection outline — Photoshop automatically converts the background to a new layer (called Layer 0). The area revealed by the move appears as checkerboard transparency. Photoshop saves the hidden portions of the background image in case you ever decide to move the background back into its original position.

Photoshop 4 adds a new feature that speeds layer movements. Select the move tool (by pressing the V key) and then press Enter to display the Move Tool Options palette. You'll find a single Pixel Doubling check box. If you select this check box, Photoshop shows you a low-resolution proxy of the layer as you drag it (or Ctrl+drag it) across the screen. You needn't click and hold to preview the layer as you move it — because Photoshop has fewer pixels to display, it can preview the image right away. Try it.

Pixel Doubling has no effect when you Ctrl+drag selections. It only works when you move entire layers.

Linking layers

Photoshop enables you to move multiple layers at a time. To do so, you must establish a *link* between the layers you want to move and the active layer. Begin by selecting the first layer in the Layers palette you want to link. Then click in the second column to the left of the other layer you want to link. A chain link icon appears in front of each linked layer, as in Figure 13-23. This icon shows the linked layers will move in unison when you Ctrl+drag the active layer. (Note, this only works when nothing is selected. If a portion of the image is selected, the move tool moves only the selection on the active layer.) To break the link, click a link icon, which hides it.

Dragging inside a selection outline moves the selection independently of any linked layers. Dragging outside the selection moves all linked layers.

Tip

To link many layers at a time, drag up and down the link column. To unlink the active layer from all others, click the paintbrush icon in the link column.

Note, when you drag-and-drop linked layers into another document, the layers retain their original orderings. If you hold down Shift when dropping, Photoshop centers the layers in the document. If the document is exactly the same size as the one from which you dragged the layers, the layers drop in the same position they held in the original document. Finally, if something is selected in the document, the dropped layers are centered inside that selection.

Link column

Link icons

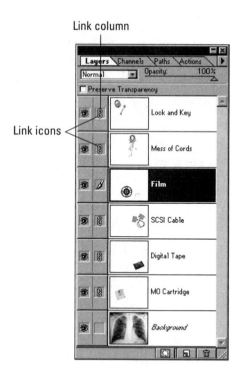

Figure 13-23: Click in the second column in the Layers palette to display or hide link icons. Here I've linked all layers except the background, so I can Ctrl+drag them in unison.

Using guides

Photoshop 4.0

Photoshop 4's new grids and guides enable you to move selections and layers into alignment. Together with the move tool, grids and guides enable you to create rows and columns of image elements, and even align layers by their centers.

To create a guide, press Ctrl+R (View ➪ Show Rulers) to display the horizontal and vertical rulers. Then drag a guideline from the ruler. At the top of Figure 13-24, you can see me dragging a horizontal guide down from the top ruler. Then Ctrl+drag layers and selections in alignment with the guide. In the bottom portion of the figure, I've dragged the MO disk, film reel, and tape — each on different layers — so they snap into alignment at their centers. (The reel has some film hanging from it, which Photoshop considers in calculating the center.) You'll know when the layer snaps into alignment because the move cursor becomes hollow, like the labeled cursor in Figure 13-24.

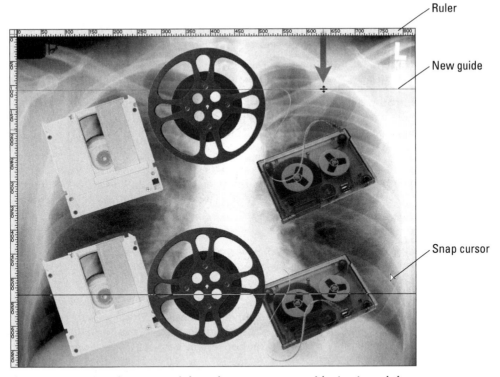

Figure 13-24: Drag from one of the rulers to create a guide (top), and then Ctrl+drag each layer or selection into alignment (bottom).

Guides are pretty straightforward creatures. I mean, you don't have to study them rigorously for years to understand them — a few minutes are all you need to master them. But a few hidden treats exist:

✦ You can show and hide all guides by pressing Ctrl+semicolon (;) or by choosing the Hide (or Show) Guides command from the View menu. When the guides are hidden, layers and selections do not snap into alignment.

✦ You can turn on and off guide snappiness while the guides remain visible by pressing Ctrl+Shift+semicolon (or choosing View ➪ Snap to Guides).

✦ As with all image elements in Photoshop 4, you can move a guide with the move tool. If some other tool is active, Ctrl+dragging also works.

✦ To lock all guides so you can't accidentally move them while you're trying to Ctrl+drag something else, press Ctrl+Alt+semicolon or choose View ➪ Lock Guides. Press Ctrl+Alt+semicolon again to unlock all guides.

Tip ✦ When moving a guide, press the Shift key to snap the guide to the nearest ruler tick mark.

✦ To convert a horizontal guide to a vertical guide, or vice versa, press the Alt key while moving the guide.

✦ If you rotate your document in exact multiples of 90 degrees or flip the image horizontally or vertically, your guides also rotate unless they are locked.

Tip ✦ You can position a guide outside the image if you want. To do so, make the Image window larger than the image. Now you can drag a guide into the empty canvas surrounding the image. You can then snap a layer or selection into alignment with the guide.

✦ To edit the color of the guides, Ctrl+double-click a guide to display the Guides & Grid panel of the Preferences dialog box. You can also change the guides from solid lines to dashed. (This is for screen purposes, by the way. Guides don't print.)

✦ Like paths, Photoshop saves guides with any file format. If you export the image into another program, the guides are invisible. However, the only formats supporting guides on a cross-format basis — that can save your Windows Photoshop guides for use on the Mac — are Photoshop, JPEG, TIFF, and EPS.

✦ If you don't need your guides anymore, choose View ➪ Clear Guides to delete them all in one housekeeping operation. (I wish I had a command like this built into my office — I'd choose Maid ➪ Clear Dust and be done with it.)

Setting up the grid

Photoshop 4.0

Photoshop also offers a grid, which is a regular series of snapping increments. You view the grid — and turn it on — by pressing Ctrl+quote (") or choosing View ➪ Show Grid. Turn the snapping forces of the grid on and off by pressing Ctrl+Shift+quote or choosing View ➪ Snap to Grid.

You edit the grid in the Guides & Grid panel of the Preferences dialog box (which you can get to by pressing Ctrl+K and Ctrl+6 or by Ctrl+double-clicking a guide). I explain how to use these options in the "Guides & Grid" section of Chapter 2. But, for the record, you enter the major grid increments in the Gridline Every option box and enter the minor increments in the Subdivisions option box. For example, in Figure 13-25, I set the Gridline Every value to 50 pixels and the Subdivisions value to 5. This means a moved layer will snap in 10-pixel (50 pixels divide by 5) increments. Figure 13-25 also demonstrates each of the three Style settings.

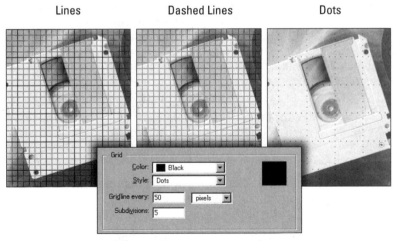

Figure 13-25: Here are the three styles of grid with the Grid Preferences options shown at the bottom.

Applying Transformations

Photoshop and other graphics treat some kinds of edits differently than others. Edits that affect the geometry of a selection or layer are known collectively as *transformations.* These transformations include scaling, rotating, flipping, slanting, and distorting. (Technically, moving is a transformation as well.) Transformations are special because they can affect a selection, a layer, multiple layers, or an entire image at a time.

Transforming the entire image

Photoshop 4 has radically overhauled its transformation capabilities, much for the better. Those transformation commands that affect the entire image are listed in the Image menu; those that affect layers and selections are found in the Layer menu. The following list explains how to apply transformations to every pixel in an image, regardless of whether the image is selected:

✦ **Scale:** To resize the image, use Image ➪ Image Size. Because this command is one of the most essential low-level functions in the program, I covered it way back in Chapter 4.

✦ **Rotate:** To rotate the entire image, choose a command from the Image ➪ Rotate Canvas submenu. To rotate an image scanned on its side, choose the 90° CW or 90° CCW command. (That's clockwise and counterclockwise, respectively.) Choose 180° to spin the image on its head. To enter some other specific value, choose Image ➪ Rotate Canvas ➪ Arbitrary.

To fix a slightly crooked scanned image, select the line tool and set the Line Width value in the Line Tool Options palette to 0. You can then display the Info palette and use the line tool as a measuring device. Because the line weight is 0, you don't do any damage to your image. When you figure out the proper angle, choose Image ➪ Rotate Canvas ➪ Arbitrary and enter it into the Angle option box.

Whenever you apply the Arbitrary command, Photoshop must expand the canvas size to avoid clipping any of your image. This results in background-colored wedges at each of the four corners of the image. You'll either need to clone with the rubber stamp tool to fill in the wedges or to clip them away with the crop tool.

✦ **Flip:** Choose Image ➪ Rotate Canvas ➪ Flip Horizontal to flip the image so left is right and right is left. To flip the image upside-down, choose Image ➪ Rotate Canvas ➪ Flip Vertical.

No command is specifically designed to slant or distort the entire image. In the unlikely event you're keen to do this, you must link all layers and apply one of the commands under the Layer ➪ Transform submenu, as explained in the next section.

Transforming layers and selections

To transform a layer or selection, you can apply one of the commands in the Layer ➪ Transform submenu. Nearly a dozen commands are here, all of which you can explore on your own. I'm not copping out; it's unlikely you'll use any of these commands on a regular basis. (The notable exception is Numeric, which I discuss in the following section.) These commands aren't bad, but one command — Free Transform — is infinitely better.

Photoshop 4.0

Free Transform is one of the best enhancements in Photoshop 4. It enables you to scale, flip, rotate, slant, distort, and move a selection or layer in one continuous operation. This one command enables you to get all your transformations exactly right before pressing Enter to apply the final changes.

To initiate the command, press Ctrl+T or choose Layer ➪ Free Transform. Photoshop surrounds the layer or selection with an eight-handle marquee. You are now in the Free Transform mode, which prevents you from doing anything except transform the image until you apply the operation or cancel it.

Here's how to work in the Free Transform mode:

✦ **Scale:** Drag one of the eight square handles to scale the image inside the marquee. To scale proportionally, Shift+drag a corner handle. To scale about the center, Alt+drag a corner handle.

✦ **Flip:** You can flip the image by dragging one handle past its opposite handle. For example, dragging the left side handle past the right handle flips the image horizontally.

Tip

If you want to perform a simple flip, it's generally easier to choose Layer ➪ Transform ➪ Flip Horizontal or Flip Vertical. Quite surprisingly, you can choose either command while working in the Free Transform mode.

✦ **Rotate:** To rotate the image, drag outside the marquee, as demonstrated in the first example in Figure 13-26. Shift+drag to rotate in 15-degree increments.

✦ **Slant:** Ctrl+drag a side handle (including the top or bottom handle) to slant the image. To constrain the slant, useful for producing perspective effects, Ctrl+Shift+drag a side handle.

✦ **Distort:** You can distort the image by Ctrl+dragging a corner handle. You can tug the image to stretch it in any of four directions.

Tip

To tug two opposite corner handles in symmetrical directions, Ctrl+Alt+drag either of the handles. I show this technique in the second example in Figure 13-26.

✦ **Perspective:** For a one-point perspective effect, Ctrl+Shift+drag a corner handle. To move two points in unison, Ctrl+Shift+Alt+drag a corner handle.

✦ **Move:** Drag inside the marquee to move the image. This is useful when you're trying to align the selection or layer with a background image and you want to make sure the transformations match up properly.

✦ **Undo:** To undo the last modification without leaving the Free Transform mode altogether, press Ctrl+Z.

✦ **Zoom:** You can change the view size by choosing one of the commands in the View menu. You can also use the keyboard zoom shortcuts (Ctrl+spacebar+click, Alt+spacebar+click, Ctrl+plus, Ctrl+minus).

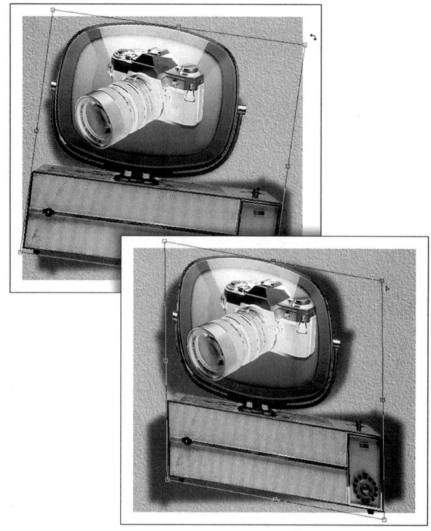

Figure 13-26: After pressing Ctrl+T to initiate the Free Transform command, drag outside the marquee to rotate the layer (top). You can also Ctrl+Alt+drag a corner handle to move the opposite corner handle symmetrically.

✦ **Apply:** Press Enter to apply the final transformation and interpolate the new pixels. You can also double-click inside the marquee. (If the finished effect looks jagged, it's probably because you selected Nearest Neighbor from the Interpolation pop-up menu in the Preferences dialog box. To fix this problem, press Ctrl+Z to undo the transformation, and then press Ctrl+K and select the Bicubic option from the General panel of the Preferences dialog box. And press Ctrl+T to start the transformation over again.)

✦ **Cancel:** To cancel the Free Transform operation, press the Escape key.

Tip

To transform a clone of a selected area, press Alt when choosing the Free Transform command, or press Ctrl+Alt+T. This only works with selected areas — you can't clone an entire layer any more than you can by Alt+dragging with the move tool.

If no part of the image is selected, you can transform multiple layers at a time by linking them, as described in the "Linking layers" section earlier in this chapter. For example, I could have linked the TV and shadow layers to transform the two in unison back in Figure 13-26.

Numerical transformations

To track your transformations numerically, display the Info palette (F8) before applying the Free Transform command. After you initiate Free Transform, you can't change the visible palettes until you complete or cancel the operation.

Or, choose Layer ➪ Transform ➪ Numeric (Ctrl+Shift+T). You can apply this command while working in the Free Transform mode, or apply the entire transformation numerically by pressing Ctrl+Shift+T at the outset. In any case, you get the dialog box shown in Figure 13-27. If you're in the middle of a Free Transform operation, the dialog box reflects the changes you've made so far (except the distortions). Otherwise, Photoshop displays the last settings applied.

For the most part, this dialog box is pretty straightforward. Use the check boxes to decide which kinds of transformations you want to apply. (*Skew* is the same as *slant,* by the way.) The Relative check box controls whether a move is measured relative to the previous position of the element or with respect to the absolute 0,0 coordinate (generally in the upper-left corner of the image).

I imagine most folks will use this dialog box strictly for scaling and rotating. You'd need the spatial awareness of a NASA navigation system to predict a numerical slant.

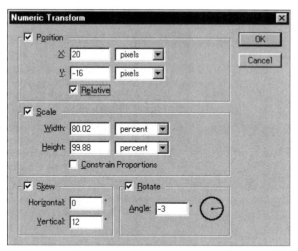

Figure 13-27: Press Ctrl+Shift+T to transform a selection or layer numerically.

Masking and Layers

Layers offer special masking options unto themselves. You can paint inside the confines of a layer as if it were a selection mask; you can add a special mask for a single layer; or you can group multiple layers together and have the bottom layer in the group serve as the mask. Quite honestly, these are the kinds of thoughtful and useful functions I've come to expect from Photoshop. Although they're fairly complicated to use — you must be on your toes once you start juggling layer masks — these functions provide new realms of opportunities.

Preserving transparency

You may have already noticed a little check box called Preserve Transparency near the top of the Layers palette. If not, the option appears spotlighted in Figure 13-28. When checked, it prevents you from painting inside the transparent portions of the layer.

Figure 13-28: The Preserve Transparency check box (upper right) enables you to paint inside the layer's transparency mask without harming the transparent pixels.

Suppose I want to paint inside the girl shown in Figure 13-28. If this were a flat, nonlayered image, I'd have to draw a selection outline carefully around her hair and arms, as I did back in Chapter 12. But there's no need to do this when using layers. Because the girl lies on a different layer than her background, a permanent selection outline tells Photoshop which pixels are transparent and which are opaque. This is the transparency mask.

The first example in Figure 13-29 shows the girl on her own with the background hidden. The transparent areas outside the mask appear in the checkerboard pattern. When the Preserve Transparency option is turned off, you can paint anywhere you want inside the layer. Selecting Preserve Transparency activates the transparency mask and places the checkerboard area off limits.

Figure 13-29: The layered girl as she appears on her own (left) and when airbrushed with the Preserve Transparency check box turned on (right)

The right image in Figure 13-29 shows what happens after I select Preserve Transparency and paint around the girl with the airbrush. (The foreground color is set to white.) Notice, no matter how much paint I may apply, none of it leaks out onto the background.

Although this enlightening discussion pretty well covers it, I feel compelled to share a few additional words about Preserve Transparency:

Tip

✦ You can turn Preserve Transparency on and off from the keyboard by pressing the standard slash character, /, right there on the same key with the question mark. This shortcut was available in Photoshop 3, but few folks knew about it.

✦ Remember, you can fill only the opaque pixels in a layer, whether Preserve Transparency is on or off. Use Ctrl+Shift+Delete (or Ctrl+Shift+Backspace) to fill with the background color, and Shift+Alt+Delete (or Backspace) to fill with the foreground color.

✦ The Preserve Transparency check box is dimmed when the background layer is active because this layer is entirely opaque. There's no transparency to preserve, eh? (That's my impression of a Canadian explaining layer theory, which needs a little work, but I think I'm getting close.)

And, finally, here's a question for all you folks who think you may have Photoshop mastered. Which of the brush modes (explained in Chapter 8) is the exact opposite of Preserve Transparency? The answer is Behind. If you turn off Preserve Transparency and select the Behind brush mode in the Airbrush Options palette, you paint exclusively outside the transparency mask, protecting the opaque pixels. So it follows, when Preserve Transparency is turned on, the Behind brush mode is dimmed.

What this means is Behind is not a true brush mode and should not be grouped with the brush modes. I trust this option will be presented more logically in a future version of Photoshop.

Creating layer-specific masks

In addition to the transparency mask that accompanies every layer (except the background), you can add a mask to a layer to make certain pixels in the layer transparent. Now, you might ask, "Won't simply erasing portions of a layer make those portions transparent?" The answer is yes, but when you erase, you delete pixels permanently. By creating a layer mask, you, instead, make pixels temporarily transparent. You can return several months later and bring those pixels back to life again simply by adjusting the mask. So layer masks add yet another level of flexibility to a program that's already a veritable image-editing contortionist.

To create a layer mask, select the layer you want to mask and choose Layer ➪ Add Layer Mask ➪ Reveal All. Or more simply, click the layer mask icon at the bottom of the Layers palette, as labeled in Figure 13-30. A second thumbnail preview appears to the left of the layer name, also labeled in the figure. A heavy outline around the preview shows the layer mask is active.

To edit the mask, simply paint in the Image window. Paint with black to make pixels transparent. Because black represents deselected pixels in an image, it makes these pixels transparent in a layer. Paint with white to make pixels opaque.

In Photoshop 4, the default foreground and background colors for a layer mask are white and black, respectively. This ensures painting with the paintbrush or airbrush makes pixels opaque, where painting with the eraser makes them transparent, as you would expect.

In Figure 13-30, I created a feathered oval, inversed it, and filled it with black by pressing Ctrl+Delete. This results in a soft vignette around the layer. If I decide I eliminated too much of the hair, not to worry. I merely paint with white to bring it back again.

Link icon   Layer mask
thumbnail

Layer mask icon

Figure 13-30: The black area in the layer mask (which you can see in the thumbnail view, top right) translates to transparent pixels in the layer itself.

Photoshop has gone nuts in the layer mask department, adding lots of bells and whistles to make the function both convenient and powerful. Here's everything you need to know:

✦ **Reveal Selection:** If you select some portion of your layer, Photoshop automatically converts the selection to a layer mask when you click the layer mask icon at the bottom of the palette. The area outside the selection becomes transparent. (The corresponding command is Layer ➪ Add Layer Mask ➪ Reveal Selection.)

Tip

✦ **Hide Selection:** You can also choose to reverse the prospective mask, making the area inside the selection transparent and the area outside opaque. To do this, choose Layer ➪ Add Layer Mask ➪ Hide Selection. Or, better yet, Alt+click the layer mask icon in the Layers palette.

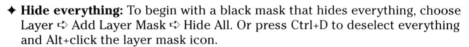
✦ **Hide everything:** To begin with a black mask that hides everything, choose Layer ➪ Add Layer Mask ➪ Hide All. Or press Ctrl+D to deselect everything and Alt+click the layer mask icon.

✦ **View the mask:** Photoshop regards a layer mask as a layer-specific channel. You can actually see it listed in italics in the Channels palette. To view the mask on its own — as a black-and-white image — Alt+click the layer mask thumbnail in the Layers palette. Alt+click again to view the image instead.

✦ **Layer mask rubylith:** To view the mask as a red overlay, Shift+Alt+click the layer mask icon. Or simply press the backslash key, \, above Enter.

After you have both layer and mask visible at once, you can hide the mask by pressing \, or hide the layer and view only the mask by pressing the tilde key (~). So many alternatives!

✦ **Change the overlay color:** Double-click the layer mask thumbnail to access the Layer Mask Display Options dialog box, which enables you to change the color and opacity of the rubylith.

✦ **Turn off the mask:** You can temporarily disable the mask by Shift+clicking the mask thumbnail. (You used to Ctrl+click the thumbnail in Photoshop 3, but this has changed for reasons that will soon become apparent.) A red *X* covers the thumbnail when it's disabled, and all masked pixels in the layer appear opaque. Shift+click again to put the mask in working order again.

✦ **Switch between layer and mask:** As you become more familiar with layer masks, you'll switch back and forth between layer and mask quite frequently, editing the layer one minute, editing the mask the next. You can switch between layer and mask by clicking their respective thumbnails. The icon to the left of the layer/mask item changes to reflect whether the layer or the mask is active. A paintbrush icon indicates the layer is active; a mask icon tells you the mask is the active element.

You can also switch between layer and mask from the keyboard. Press Ctrl+tilde (~) to make the layer active. Press Ctrl+\ to switch to the mask.

✦ **Link layer and mask:** A little link icon appears between the layer and mask thumbnails in the Layers palette. When the link icon is visible, you can move or transform the mask and layer as one. If you click the link icon to turn it off, layer and mask move independently. (You can always move a selected region of the mask or layer independently of the other.)

✦ **Convert mask to selection:** As with all masks in Photoshop 4, you can convert a layer mask to a selection. To do so, Ctrl+click the layer mask icon. Throw in the Shift and Alt keys if you want to add or subtract the layer mask with an existing selection outline.

When, and if, you finish using the mask — you can leave it in force as long as you like — you can choose Layer ➪ Remove Layer Mask. Or just drag the layer mask thumbnail to the trash can icon. Either way, an alert box asks you if you want to discard the mask or permanently apply it to the layer. Click the button that corresponds to your innermost desires.

Pasting inside a selection outline

In the new Photoshop, one command creates a layer mask automatically: Edit ➪ Paste Into (Ctrl+Shift+V). Choose this command to paste the contents of the Clipboard into the current selection, so the selection acts as a mask. Because Photoshop pastes to a new layer, it converts the selection into a layer mask. But here's the interesting part: By default, Photoshop turns off the link between layer and mask. This way, you can Ctrl+drag the layer inside a fixed mask to position the pasted image, as in the old days.

Tip

Once upon a time in Photoshop, a command existed named Edit ➪ Paste Behind. (Or something like that. It might have been Paste in Back. My memory's a little hazy.) The command (whatever its name) pasted a copied image a selection. But while the command is gone, its spirit still lives. Now you press the Alt key when choosing Edit ➪ Paste Into. Photoshop creates a new layer with an inverted layer mask, masking away the selected area.

Masking groups of layers

About now, you may be growing fatigued with the topic of layering masking. But one more option requires your immediate attention. You can group multiple layers into something called a *clipping group,* in which the lowest layer in the group masks the others. Where the lowest layer is transparent, the other layers are hidden; where the lowest layer is opaque, the contents of the other layers are visible.

Note

Despite the similarities in name, a clipping group bears no relation to a clipping path. That is, a clipping group doesn't enable you to prepare transparent areas for import into QuarkXPress and the like.

In Photoshop 4, two ways exist to create a clipping group:

✦ Alt+click the horizontal line between any two layers to group them into a single unit. Your cursor changes to the group cursor labeled in Figure 13-31 when you press Alt; the horizontal line becomes dotted after you click. To break the layers apart again, Alt+click the dotted line to make it solid.

✦ Select the higher of the two layers you want to combine into a clipping group. Then choose Layer ➪ Group with Previous, or press Ctrl+G. To make the layers independent again, choose Layer ➪ Ungroup (Ctrl+Shift+G).

Figures 13-31 and 13-32 demonstrate two steps in a piece of artwork I created for the February 1997 issue of *Macworld* magazine. I had already created some text on an independent layer using the type tool (the subject of the next chapter), and I wanted to fill the text with water. So I added some photographs I shot of a swimming pool to a layer above the text, as shown in Figure 13-31. Then I combined text and pool images into a clipping group. Because the text was beneath the water, Photoshop masked the pool images according to the transparency mask assigned to the text. The result is a water pattern that exactly fills the type, as in Figure 13-32. (For a full-color version of these figures, see Color Plate 13-3.)

Group cursor

Figure 13-31: Alt+click the horizontal line between two layers to group them together.

Figure 13-32: After combining pool water and type layers into a single clipping group, Photoshop applies the type layer's transparency mask to the pool layer.

Note If you're familiar with Illustrator, you may recognize this clipping group metaphor as a relative to Illustrator's clipping path. One object in the illustration acts as a mask for a collection of additional objects. In Illustrator, however, the topmost object in the group is the mask, not the bottom one. So much for consistency.

Amazing Text Stuff

Type Basics

What I'm going to say now will shake you to the core. I'm warning you — this is a biggie. You may want to sit down before you read any further. In fact, after you sit down, you may want to strap yourself in. Maybe go ahead and soundproof the room so no one's alarmed when you scream, "Oh, no, it can't be true!" and "Say it ain't so!"

(Ahem.) Type and graphics are the same thing.

There, there now. I understand. I reacted the same way when I heard the news. Dry your eyes while I explain. You see, your computer treats each character in a word as a little picture. The letter *O,* for example, is a big black oval with a smaller transparent oval set inside it. The only difference between a character of type and a standard graphic is you don't have to draw type; every letter is already drawn for you. So a font is like a library of clip art you can access from the keyboard.

Qualities of bitmapped type

Now that you understand the realities of type, learning Photoshop treats type like any other collection of pixels in an image should come as no surprise. Type legibility is dependent upon the size and resolution of your image.

Figure 14-1, for example, shows four lines of type printed at equal sizes but at different resolutions. If these lines were printed at equal resolutions, each line would be twice as large as the line preceding it. Hence, big type printed at a high resolution yields smooth, legible output, just as a big image printed at a high resolution yields smooth, detailed output. In fact, everything you can say about an image is true of bitmapped type.

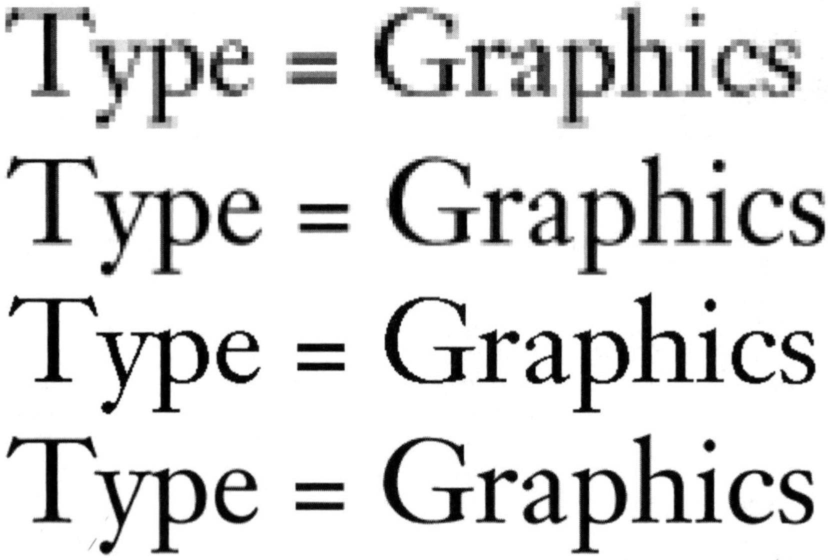

Type = Graphics

Type = Graphics

Type = Graphics

Type = Graphics

Figure 14-1: Four lines of type set in the Type 1 font Janson and printed at different resolutions

You can use both Type 1 (PostScript) and TrueType fonts in Photoshop. To use TrueType fonts, there's nothing extra to do. To use Type 1 fonts, you must install Adobe Type Manager; see Appendix C for details. If you already have ATM installed, make sure it's Version 3 or higher — if not, let the installer put it on. Earlier versions of ATM function less well, or not at all, both with Photoshop and Windows 95.

Another caveat regarding fonts: Be selective when you install them. Under Windows 3.1, both TrueType and Type 1 fonts are stored in WIN.INI, and as that file gets close to 64K in size, strange and unpleasant things can happen. Also, the more fonts you install, the longer it takes Windows 3.1 to load. Type dialog boxes inside programs also can be slowed down by too many fonts. Although Windows 95 stores TrueType font entries in the Registry, you should still keep your total number of installed fonts to under 200 — if nothing else, you can scroll through font lists more quickly. Consider investing in a program such as Ares Software's Font Minder, which enables you to set up groups of fonts you can swap in and out with minimum trouble. Font Minder works with both Windows 3.1 and Windows 95. See Appendix B for further details on font management issues.

The disadvantages of working with type in a painting program are obvious (but I'm going to tell you anyway). First, the resolution of the type is fixed. Rather than matching the resolution of printed text to that of your printer — a function provided by drawing, word processing, and desktop publishing programs, to name a few — Photoshop prints type at the same resolution it prints the rest of the image.

In addition, after you add a line of type to an image, you can't return and add and delete characters from the keyboard as you can in an object-oriented program. If you misspell a word or want to rephrase some text, you must erase the offending characters or words and begin again. In terms of entering type, Photoshop is more likely to remind you of a typewriter and a bottle of correction fluid than a word processor.

Although the disadvantages of creating type in a painting program may initially hamper your progress, the advantages are tremendous. For example, you can do all of the following:

✦ **Create translucent type:** Now that Photoshop 4 automatically creates type on a new layer, you can change the translucency of type more easily than ever by using the Opacity slider bar in the Layers palette. By using this technique, you can merge type and images to create subtle overlay effects, as illustrated in the top example in Figure 14-2.

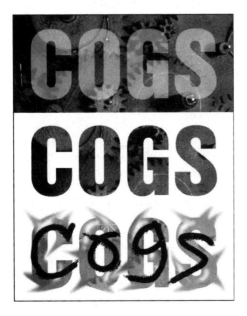

Figure 14-2: Examples of translucent white type (top), type used as a selection (middle), and type enhanced with painting and editing tools (bottom). On the whole, these effects are beyond the means of object-oriented programs.

✦ **Use type as a selection:** Text is ultimately only another variety of a selection outline. You can mask portions of an image (as I did back in Figure 13-32 of Chapter 13) and even select elements and move, copy, or otherwise manipulate them using character outlines, as demonstrated in the middle example in Figure 14-2. I explore this option in detail in the upcoming "Character Masks" section.

✦ **Customize characters:** You also can customize a character of type by converting it to a path, editing the path using the path tools, and converting the path back to a selection outline. Only high-end drawing programs such as Illustrator, FreeHand, and CorelDRAW match this capability.

✦ **Edit type as part of the image:** You can erase type, paint over type, smear type, fill type with a gradation, draw highlights and shadows, and create a range of special text effects that fall well outside the capabilities of an object-oriented program. The last example in Figure 14-2 is one of the *bazillion* possibilities.

✦ **Trade images freely:** If you've ever traded documents over a network or otherwise tried to share a file created in a word processor or desktop publishing program with associates and coworkers, you know what a nightmare fonts can be. If other people's machines aren't equipped with the fonts you used in your document — which seems the case more often than not — your document looks awful on their screens. "What's wrong with this file you gave me?" "Why did you use this font?" And "I liked what you wrote in your report, but it is sure ugly!" are only a few of the responses you can expect. When you work with images, however, your font worries are over, because type in an image is bitmapped. Other users don't need special screen or printer fonts to view your images exactly as you created them. Mind you, I don't recommend you use Photoshop as a word processor, but it's great for creating headlines and short missives you want to fling about the office.

Using the type tool

In a drawing or desktop publishing program, the type tool typically serves two purposes: You can create text or you can edit the characters of existing text by highlighting them and replacing characters or applying formatting commands. Photoshop won't let you reword or reformat text after you add it to an image, however.

Photoshop 4.0

To create text, select the standard type tool (the one that looks like a solid *T*) and click in the Image window. In Photoshop 4, you can select the type tool from the keyboard by pressing the T key. Instead of producing a blinking insertion marker in the window when you click the image, as other graphics programs do, Photoshop displays the Type Tool dialog box shown in Figure 14-3.

Note   Expect to wait a few minutes before you use the type tool for the first time in Photoshop. You'll see a message saying, "Building a font menu. This may take five months or so . . ." (actually, it says "a minute or so" — it only seems like five months). Every program has to load font definitions before it enables you to create type. That's one of the reasons a program like Microsoft Word takes so long to launch. Photoshop waits to build its type library until you use the type tool, thus saving time for folks who never get around to creating type. If you do use the tool, Photoshop must build the library only once per session.

Tip   Photoshop positions the bottom of the text at the spot where you click with the type tool. If you drag with the type tool, you can reposition the type cursor onscreen. Release the button when your cursor is where you want the first character of type to appear. Of course, you can also use the move tool to reposition the text after you create it, as discussed in the upcoming section "Manipulating type on a new layer."

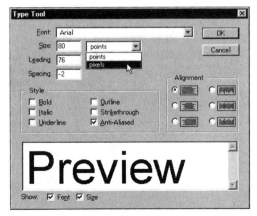

Figure 14-3: To create type in Photoshop, enter it into the Type Tool dialog box, which appears after you click with the type tool. The bottom example shows the type as it appears in the Image window.

Selecting type

When it comes to picking which type to use, be aware of two key issues. First, is the question of whether to use TrueType or PostScript fonts. I don't want to get into font wars here, so I'll just say this: Both formats are sophisticated and capable. Both offer excellent typefaces. Both can coexist in Photoshop and Windows 95. But more high-quality Type 1 fonts exist than TrueType. When Microsoft introduced TrueType with Windows 3.1 and followed it with two extra packages of fonts, it priced the fonts at loss-leader levels. The quality was excellent, but the pricing was way below what would compensate for the amount of work involved in producing such excellent versions. One unconfirmed theory is this strategy represented part of Microsoft's attempt to derail the Type 1 font business in general, and Adobe's in particular. The plan did have the salutary effect of causing Type 1 foundries (including Adobe) to lower their prices. But it also made people think all fonts should be priced so low — which can't be done if the type designers and digitizers are to be compensated fairly for their labors. Think I'm exaggerating? Fire up Macromedia's Fontographer and try to design a font from scratch. You'll change your mind quickly.

A second and related issue is font quality. So far, only Type 1 fonts have the typographic refinements of ligatures, old style numerals, and small caps. If you're serious about typography, you need those refinements — they're a considerable part of what makes digital type avoid looking like digital type. Regardless of which format you choose, though, you should learn about typefaces. Even though your type is rasterized in Photoshop, the garbage in/garbage out principle applies. Use a badly designed face, whether Type 1 or TrueType, and it will look bad in Photoshop. Get to know typefaces and the basics of typography if you want to use type like a pro in Photoshop.

Entering and editing type

At the bottom of the Type Tool dialog box is the text-entry box. You enter and edit the text you want to add to the current image into this box.

You can edit text up to the moment you add it to the image. To make your edits, first select the characters you want to change by dragging over them with the cursor. Then enter new text from the keyboard. To select a whole word, double-click it. You can also cut, copy, and paste text by choosing commands from the Edit menu or using keyboard equivalents.

If the text you are typing reaches the right edge of the text-entry box, the word in progress automatically drops down to the next line. When you click the OK button to exit the dialog box, though, all text appears on the same line unless you specifically entered carriage returns between lines (by pressing the Enter key). Each carriage return indicates the end of one line and the beginning of the next, just as it does when you use a typewriter.

Tip

Get in the habit of clicking the OK button rather than pressing Enter to exit the Type Tool dialog box. You can press Enter to exit the dialog box when the Size, Leading, or Spacing option box is active, but Enter inserts a carriage return when the text-entry box is active.

After you exit the Type Tool dialog box, Photoshop puts your text on a new layer. If your text doesn't look the way you anticipated, press Ctrl+Z or click the trash can icon at the bottom of the Layers palette to delete the new layer. Then start the process over again by clicking with the type tool. When the Type Tool dialog box appears, your previous text is displayed in the text-entry box.

Formatting type

Photoshop formats all text entered into the text-entry box identically according to the specifications in the Type Tool dialog box. You can't select a single character or word in the text-entry box and format it differently than its deselected neighbors.

The formatting options in the Type Tool dialog box work as follows:

✦ **Font:** Select the typeface and type style you want to use from the Font pop-up menu. Or you can select the plain version of the font, such as Times Roman or Helvetica Regular, and apply styles using the Style options.

✦ **Size:** Type size is measured either in points or pixels. You can select the desired measurement from the pop-up menu to the right of the Size option box, as shown in Figure 14-3. If the resolution of your image is 72 ppi, points and pixels are equal. If the resolution is higher, however, a single point may include many pixels. The resolution of Figure 14-3, for example, is 140 ppi, which is why the final text in the image (shown at bottom) is almost twice as large as the 72 ppi text in the dialog box. The moral? Select the points option when you want to scale text according to the image resolution; select pixels when you want to map text to an exact number of pixels in an image.

Note　Type is measured from the top of its *ascenders* — letters like *b, d,* and *h* that rise above the level of most lowercase characters — to the bottom of its *descenders* — letters like *g, p,* and *q* that sink below the baseline. That's the way it's supposed to work, anyway. Characters from fonts in the Adobe Type Library, including those built into all PostScript laser printers and imagesetters, measure only 92 percent as tall as the specified type size.

The top two lines in Figure 14-4 contain 120-pixel type set in the Adobe versions of Times and Helvetica. All characters easily fit inside rectangular outlines that measure exactly 120 pixels tall. By contrast, the third and fourth lines of type are set in equivalent TrueType fonts. These characters are bursting their 120-point rectangular outlines at the seams.

✦ **Leading:** Line spacing or *leading* is the vertical distance between the baseline of one line of type and the baseline of the next line of type within a single paragraph, as illustrated in Figure 14-5. (You must separate lines of type manually by pressing the Enter key in the text-entry box.) Leading is measured in the unit you selected from the Size pop-up menu. If you don't specify a leading value, Photoshop automatically inserts leading equal to 125 percent of the type size.

✦ **Spacing:** Each character in a font carries with it a predetermined amount of *side bearing* that separates it from its immediate neighbors. Although you can't change the amount of side bearing, you can insert and delete the overall amount of space between characters by entering a value into the Spacing option box. Enter a positive value to insert space; enter a negative value to delete space. The value is measured in the unit you selected from the Size pop-up menu.

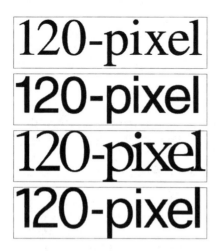

Figure 14-4: From top to bottom, I formatted these lines of type in the PostScript versions of Times and Helvetica and their TrueType equivalents. The PostScript characters fit inside their 120-point rectangular outlines with room to spare; the TrueType characters slightly overlap their outlines.

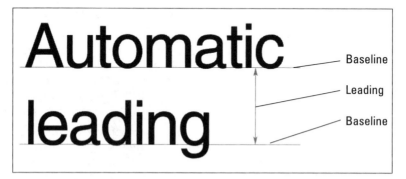

Figure 14-5: Leading is the distance between any two baselines in a single paragraph of text created with the type tool. Here, the type size is 120 pixels and the leading is 150 pixels.

✦ **Style:** Select one or more Style check boxes to specify the type styles you want to apply to your text. If you choose the plain version of a font, the Bold and Italic options call up the bold and italic PostScript or TrueType font definitions. If you apply the Bold option to a font that is already bold, such as Helvetica Bold or Helvetica Black (both shown in Figure 14-6), Photoshop makes the characters slightly heavier. If you apply the Italic option to an already italicized font, such as Helvetica Oblique (again, see Figure 14-6), Photoshop slants the characters even more.

1 Helvetica Regular

2 **Helvetica Regular Bold**

3 **Helvetica Bold**

4 **Helvetica Bold Bold**

5 **Helvetica Black**

6 **Helvetica Black Bold**

7 *Helvetica Regular Italic*

8 *Helvetica Oblique*

9 *Helvetica Oblique Italic*

Figure 14-6: Bolding a plain font produces the same result as choosing the bold version of the font (2 and 3), just as italicizing the plain style is the same as choosing an italicized font (7 and 8). But you can heighten the effects by applying styles to already stylized fonts (4, 6, and 9).

 Caution

The Outline option produces unspeakably ugly results, as demonstrated by the top two examples in Figure 14-7. You can create a better outline style using Edit ➪ Stroke. Press *D* and *X* to make the foreground color white. (You can also Alt+click with the type tool to lift a color with the eyedropper if you like.) Then create your text using the Type Tool dialog box as usual, without selecting Outline. Press *X* to restore black as the foreground color, and press the / key to turn off Preserve Transparency. Finally, choose Edit ➪ Stroke and enter the outline thickness of your choice. Figure 14-7 shows two stroked examples, one with a 1-pixel outline and the other with a 2-pixel outline.

The Shadow option produces equally unattractive results. To create attractive shadowed type, try one of the techniques discussed in the "Character Masks" section of this chapter.

✦ **Anti-aliased:** This Style option is special enough to mention separately. When you select Anti-aliased, Photoshop softens characters by slightly blurring pixels around the perimeter, as shown in Figure 14-8. Unless you want to create very small type or you intend to match the resolution of your output device — printing a 300 ppi image to a 300 dpi printer, for example — select this check box. Photoshop takes longer to produce anti-aliased type, but it's worth it. Unless otherwise indicated, I created all figures in this chapter with the Anti-aliased check box selected.

Figure 14-7: Photoshop's automated outline style, shown here when jagged (first) and anti-aliased (second), is nothing short of hideous. You can get better results by stroking the characters with 1-pixel or 2-pixel outlines (third and bottom).

Antialiased
Jagged as all get out

Figure 14-8: The difference between 120-pixel type when the Anti-aliased option is selected (top line) versus deselected (bottom). Both examples were printed at 190 ppi.

✦ **Alignment:** Select one of these radio buttons to specify the way lines of type in a single paragraph align to the point at which you originally clicked with the type tool. Photoshop offers both horizontal and vertical alignment options. In my opinion, each one of the vertical options is a waste of time, particularly because you have no control over how the text aligns horizontally within the vertical columns. In Figure 14-9, for example, you can see how the characters in each vertical line are always aligned along their left edges. (Incidentally, I used capital letters to show off the vertical alignment options because vertically aligned lowercase letters always look bad, regardless of the program that creates them.)

✦ **Show:** The Type Tool dialog box can preview your settings for the Font, Size, and Style options. Select the Font check box at the bottom of the dialog box to preview font and type style; select the Size check box to preview type size. The size preview is always at 72 ppi, so the size is accurate only if you selected Pixels from the Size pop-up menu. That's why the text outside the dialog box back in Figure 14-3 is larger than the text inside the text entry area. Your settings for the Leading, Spacing, and Alignment options as well as the Anti-aliased check box are not reflected in the preview.

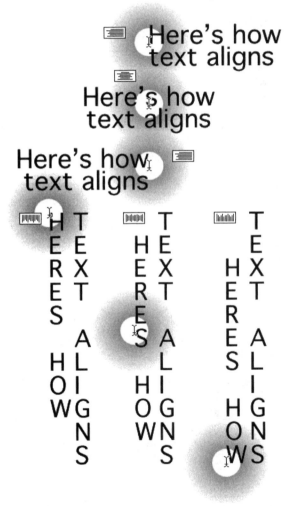

Figure 14-9: A single paragraph of type shown as it appears if you select each of the six Alignment radio buttons. The I-beam cursor shows the point at which I clicked to display the Type Tool dialog box.

Manipulating type on a new layer

After you confirm the contents of the Type Tool dialog box by clicking the OK button, Photoshop 4 places the type on a new layer. You can drag the text layer up and down in the Layers palette, change the Opacity or blend mode, Ctrl+drag the type to move it, transform the type by pressing Ctrl+T, or perform any other operation applicable to a layer. Check out Chapter 13 for the full story.

Now that the type rests on a new layer, you can adjust the kerning without going through all the rigmarole associated with past versions of Photoshop. (Remember how you could Ctrl+drag with the type tool to set down letters in Photoshop 3? That's gone in the new version.) Now you can merely select a letter with the marquee or lasso tool — don't use the magic wand, you'll mess up the edges — and press Ctrl with the left or right arrow tool to nudge the characters into more desirable positions. (Don't worry about selecting the characters perfectly — Photoshop automatically tightens the selection outlines around the characters once you start moving them.)

Photoshop 4 automatically activates the Preserve Transparency check box in the Layers palette for the new text layer. This way, you can paint inside the type without harming the character outlines, just as you could back in Version 3. In the top example of Figure 14-10, I dragged across the characters with the gradient tool; Photoshop automatically isolated the fill to the type. If you want to smear type (as back in Figure 14-2) or otherwise modify the area around the text, turn Preserve Transparency off. To create the bottom example in Figure 14-10, I first filled the characters with white by pressing Ctrl+Delete. Then I pressed the / key to turn off Preserve Transparency, selected the Behind mode in the Airbrush Options palette, and airbrushed with black behind the letters.

Figure 14-10: To paint inside the letters (top), leave Preserve Transparency turned on. To paint in other portions of the layer (bottom), turn off the check box.

Another advantage to having text on a separate layer is it never gets clipped. Have you ever created type that exceeded the boundary of the image? In the old days, Photoshop would clip away the offending characters the second you deselected or defloated the text. So you had to delete the text and try again. Now you can simply increase the size of the canvas using Image ➪ Canvas Size or scale the text down with Free Transform (Ctrl+T). Either way, every character remains intact because the text resides on an independent layer.

Character Masks

Photoshop 4 offers a second type tool. Known as the *type mask tool,* it creates character-shaped selection outlines. You can switch to the type mask tool by pressing the T key when the standard type tool is active. Or select the *T* with the dotted outline from the type tool pop-up menu in the Toolbox.

Generally speaking, the type mask tool works like any other selection tool, except you use the options in the Type Tool dialog box to create the character outlines. Click with the type mask tool to create a new selection outline. Shift+click to add the character outlines to an existing selection. Alt+click to subtract from a selection, and Shift+Alt+click to find the intersection.

The following sections demonstrate a few different ways to use this unusual new tool. Armed with these ideas, you could invent enough additional type effects to keep busy into the next millennium. Honestly, you won't believe the number of effects you can invent by screwing around with type outlines.

Filling type with an image

One of the most impressive and straightforward applications for text in Photoshop is to use the character outlines to select a portion of an image.

Steps: Selecting Part of an Image Using Character Outlines

1. **Open the image you want to mask.**

2. **Create your text.** Select the type mask tool and click in the Image window. Enter the text you want to use as a mask, format it as desired, and click OK to display the type outlines in the Image window. Large, bold characters work best. In Figure 14-11, I used the PostScript font Eras Ultra — an extremely bold type style — with a Size value of 260 and a Spacing value of negative 10.

3. **Drag the character outlines into position.** As with the other selection tools, dragging with the type mask tool moves only the selection outline without affecting the image itself.

4. **Clone the selected portion of the image.** Ctrl+Alt+drag the selected characters to a new location, as demonstrated in Figure 14-12. Or you can Ctrl+drag the selection and drop it into a different Image window to set the text against a new background.

Figure 14-11: The type mask tool produces character-shaped selection outlines you can use to lift portions of an image.

Figure 14-12: The result of Ctrl+Alt+dragging the selected image to an empty part of the Image window

Painting raised type

Instead of cloning the selected image or copying it to a different window, as suggested in Step 4 of the preceding section, you can paint around the character outlines to create a raised text effect, as illustrated in Figure 14-13.

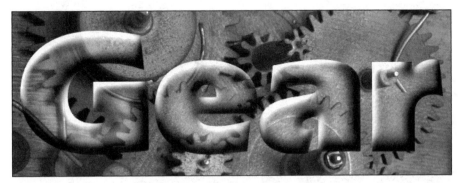

Figure 14-13: Raised type created by painting with the dodge and airbrush tools around the perimeter of the character outlines

To create this image, I carried out the first three steps described in the preceding section. I then prepared the characters by painting inside them with the dodge tool. I used a 65-pixel soft brush shape and selected Shadows from the brush modes pop-up menu (on the left side of the Brushes palette) to concentrate the lightening effect on the dark areas in the image.

As shown in the top image in Figure 14-14, this helps set the letters apart from the rest of the image. To give the letters depth, I pressed *D* to set the foreground color to black; then I used the airbrush tool with a 35-pixel soft brush shape to apply shadows around the lower and right portions of each character, as shown in the middle row of Figure 14-14.

I next switched the foreground color to white and applied highlights around the upper and left portions of characters, which results in the image shown in the bottom row of Figure 14-14.

If you don't consider yourself an artist, you may find the prospect of painting around the edges of characters a little intimidating. But remember, it's next to impossible to make a mistake. Because you're painting inside the selection, no danger exists of harming any portion of the image outside the character outlines. And if you mess up inside the selection, the problem is easily resolved.

If you look closely at the last image in Figure 14-14, for example, you can see in applying white to the arch of the *a*, I accidentally got some on the right corner of the *e*. Hey, nobody's perfect. To fix the problem, all I need to do is select a smaller brush shape and paint over that area of the *e* with black.

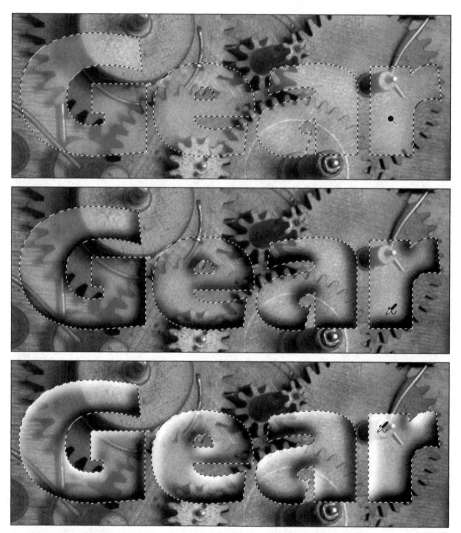

Figure 14-14: After using the dodge tool to lighten the darkest pixels inside the letters (top), I painted in the shadows by airbrushing in black around the right and bottom edges of the letters (middle). Finally, I painted in the highlights by airbrushing in white around the left and top edges of the letters (bottom).

So if you make a mistake, press Ctrl+Z or just keep painting. Try it. The process takes less than an hour and I bet you'll be pleasantly surprised with your results.

Feathering effects

You can feather text outlines as you can feather other kinds of selections. In Figure 14-15, for example, I applied a Feather Radius value of 8 and pressed Ctrl+Delete to fill the selection with white.

Figure 14-15: The result of feathering a text mask and filling it with white

The following steps describe how to create a backlighting effect using Photoshop's feathering capability. Figure 14-16 shows the finished image. The text in the figure appears in front of a plain black background, but you can just as easily apply this technique to an image.

Steps: Using Feathering to Backlight Text

1. **Create a new Image window large enough to accommodate a single line of large text.** I created an image 800 pixels wide × 300 pixels tall.

2. **Fill the entire image with black.** Assuming default colors, press Ctrl+A (Select ➪ All) and Alt+Delete.

3. **Create your text using the type mask tool.** The text in the figure is set in 240-pixel Helvetica Inserat, a member of the Adobe Type Library. Note, you must click twice with the type mask tool; your first click eliminates the selection you created in Step 2, and the second click brings up the Type Tool dialog box.

4. **Position and copy your text.** Drag the selection into the desired location in the Image window and press Ctrl+C.

5. **Feather the selection.** Press Ctrl+Shift+D, enter a number that's about equal to 1/20 the resolution of your image into the Feather Radius option box, and press Enter. My resolution is about 180 ppi, so I entered 9. (Dividing by 20 isn't a hard-and-fast rule — you can use any value that works for your image.)

6. **Press Ctrl+Delete to fill the feathered selection with white.**

7. **Press Ctrl+V to paste the copied text.** As long as you don't deselect the feathered area, the new layer aligns with the feathered type below. Press Ctrl+down arrow key to nudge the selection 3 to 5 pixels. The result appears in the top half of Figure 14-16.

8. **For extra credit, stroke the type with the airbrush.** First, make sure Preserve Transparency is turned on in the Layers palette. Now set the foreground color to 50 percent black and then use the airbrush tool with the 100-pixel soft brush shape to paint a single line across the text. As long as Preserve Transparency is on, you paint exclusively inside the characters. This creates the effect of light seeping through a slightly open door, as shown in the bottom half of Figure 14-16.

Figure 14-16: You can create backlit text by deleting a feathered version of a type mask and then pasting the original, unfeathered type in front (top). A slash of the airbrush gives it some depth (bottom).

Adding drop shadows

I already covered how to create drop shadows in the previous chapter and the process hasn't changed. Still, some minor differences occur when you're working with type, and drop shadows and text go together like ham and eggs, so we might as well take another look. This section examines two methods for adding drop shadows: one involves changing the translucency of type (demonstrated in Figure 14-17); and another relies on feathering (Figure 14-18).

Note   The first steps work only if text and drop shadow are the same color. In the second set of steps, the text and background can be any colors.

Steps: Creating Quick and Easy Hard-edged Drop Shadows

1. **Create your text using the standard type tool.** This technique involves filled type with no feathering, so it's easier to use the standard type tool. (You can use the type mask tool, but it's less convenient.) In Figure 14-17, I used an unusual typeface called Remedy Single from Emigre Graphics. Remedy Single is a pretty wild font, so it lends itself well to this technique, which is by contrast quite simple.

2. **Clone the new layer.** Drag the active layer name in the Layers palette onto the new layer icon at the bottom of the palette.

3. **Nudge the shadow to offset it a few pixels.** To get the effect in Figure 14-17, I pressed Ctrl+down arrow a few times and Ctrl+right arrow a few more times.

4. **Press 4 on the keyboard.** This lowers the opacity of the cloned selection to 40 percent. Even though the translucent clone resides above the original type, it looks like a drop shadow because both layers of type are the same color.

5. **Press Ctrl+Shift+[.** This step is optional — I didn't need it to achieve Figure 14-17. But if you want to paint inside the text or fill it with an image, you need to move the drop shadow in back of the text, which is what Ctrl+Shift+left bracket will do.

Figure 14-17: I took two lines of type set in the font Remedy (yes, those lower characters are part of the font), cloned the type, and changed the opacity of the clone to 40 percent.

The next steps describe a more functional, albeit slightly more complicated, drop shadow technique. The effect is illustrated in Figure 14-18.

Steps: Creating a Feathered Drop Shadow

1. **Create your type, this time using the type mask tool.** Figure 14-18 features my old standby, 240-pixel Helvetica Inserat. Drag the text to move it into the desired position.

2. **Copy the selection to the Clipboard.** Even if your Image window is empty, as mine was, this copies a bunch of white letters.

3. **Feather the character outlines.** Use whatever Feather Radius value you like. I entered 8 because it reminded me of a pleasant year in my childhood and because it was roughly 1/20 of the resolution of the image.

4. **Press Alt+Delete to fill the feathered text with black.** The result is the first example of Figure 14-18. If you want to add a colored shadow to an image, send the selection to a new layer (Ctrl+J) and fill only the feathered characters with the foreground color (Shift+Alt+Delete). Then select Multiply from the blend mode pop-up menu in the Layers palette and change the Opacity as desired. Whatever color you use, the feathered text is ready to serve as the drop shadow.

Figure 14-18: Feather the character outlines and fill them with black to create the drop shadow (top). Then paste the copied version of the text in front of the drop shadow (middle) and paint inside the characters (bottom).

5. **Paste the copied text in front of the drop shadow.** Ctrl+V results in a new layer.

6. **Nudge the layer slightly off center from the shadow.** As always, press Ctrl with a few arrow keys. One possible result appears in the middle example of Figure 14-18. The text is white, so you can see it clearly against the black shadow.

7. **Turn on Preserve Transparency and edit your text.** Photoshop doesn't activate Preserve Transparency automatically because it doesn't know the layer contains text. You can then fill the selected type with a different color or gradation. Or paint inside the character. In the last example of Figure 14-18, I added a pattern with the rubber stamp tool (as discussed in Chapter 10). Then I painted in some wiggly lines with the airbrush tool.

Other Type Options

The type tool puts text on a new layer, and the type mask tool creates character-shaped selection outlines. But these are hardly the big text enhancements many true-blue Photoshop users wanted. Word has it Adobe plans to overhaul text fairly dramatically in Photoshop 5 but, in the meantime, things haven't changed much since Photoshop's early days.

So what are your options? One option is to create your text in Illustrator, FreeHand, or some other drawing program, and then drag-and-drop the text into Photoshop. This way, you can keep the Illustrator or FreeHand file nearby if you need to edit the text in the future. Drawing programs also enable you to create type on a curve and other effects beyond Photoshop's capabilities.

If you don't own Illustrator or FreeHand — or if you're looking for an integrated solution that doesn't require you to leave Photoshop — then you might want to purchase a good third-party plug-in. The best all-around text creation plug-in is PhotoText, part of the $100 PhotoTools collection from Extensis. Shown in Figure 14-19, this is the only plug-in that enables you to modify character spacing, expand or condense type, and apply multiple type styles from one central location inside Photoshop. You'll find a trial demonstration version of PhotoTools along with pricing and contact information on the CD-ROM in the back of this book. Currently, this program isn't available for Windows (which is why I show the Macintosh screen shot in Figure 14-19), but it should be available by the time you read this.

Figure 14-19:
PhotoText from Extensis serves as a fully functioning text-editing environment, complete with a preview of the Image window.

Filters and Special Effects

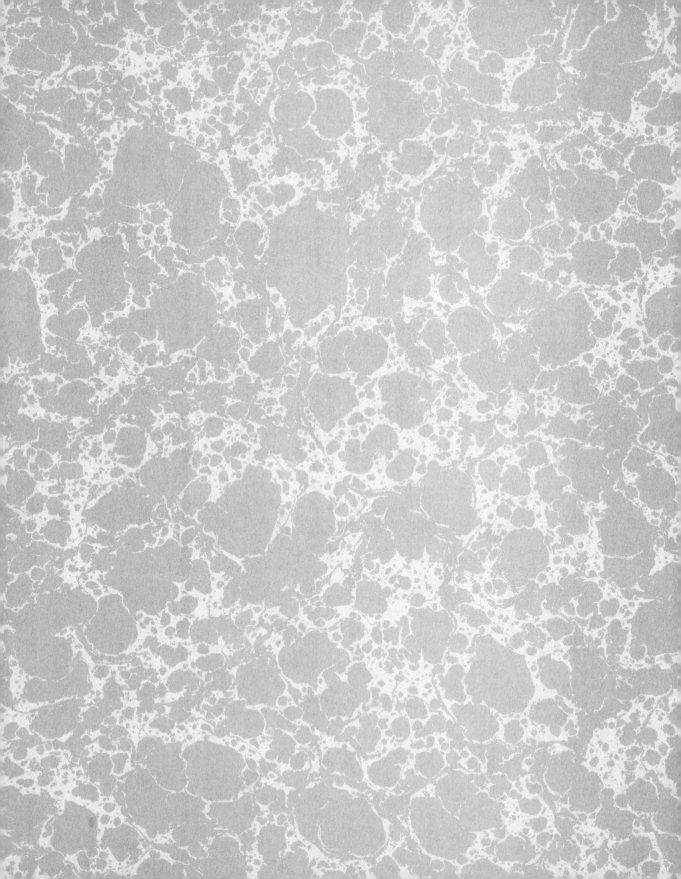

Corrective Filtering

Filter Basics

In Photoshop, *filters* enable you to apply automated effects to an image. Although named after photographer's filters, which typically correct lighting and perspective fluctuations, Photoshop's filters can accomplish a great deal more. You can slightly increase the focus of an image, introduce random pixels, add depth to an image, or completely rip it apart and reassemble it into a *hurky* pile of goo. Any number of special effects are made available via filters.

At this point, a little bell should be ringing in your head, telling you to beware of standardized special effects. Why? Because everyone has access to the same filters you do. If you rely on filters to edit your images for you, your audience will quickly recognize your work as poor or, at least, unremarkable art.

Think of it this way: You're watching MTV. You should be watching VH1 with the rest of the old folks, but when you flipped through the channels, you got stuck on a Peter Gabriel video. Outrageous effects, right? He rides an imaginary roller coaster, bumper cars crash playfully into his face, fish leap over his head. You couldn't be more amused or impressed.

As the video fades, you're so busy basking in the glow, you neglect for a split second to whack the channel changer. Before you know it, you're midway through an advertisement for a monster truck rally. Like the video, the ad is riddled with special effects — spinning letters, a reverberating voice-over slowed down to an octave below the narrator's normal pitch, and lots of big machines filled with little men filled with single brain cells working overtime.

In and of themselves, these special effects aren't bad. A time may even have existed when you thought spinning letters and reverberating voice-overs were hot stuff. But, sometime after you passed beyond preadolescence, you grew tired of these particular effects. Now you associate them with raunchy, local, car-oriented commercials. Certainly, these effects are devoid of substance but, more importantly, they're devoid of creativity.

This chapter and the two that follow are about the creative application of special effects. Rather than trying to show an image subject to every single filter, a service already performed adequately by the manual included with your software, these chapters explain exactly how the most important filters work and offer some concrete ways to use them.

You'll also learn how to apply several filters in tandem and how to use filters to edit images and selection outlines. My goal is not so much to teach you what filters are available — you can learn this by tugging on the Filter menu — but how and when to use filters.

A first look at filters

You access Photoshop's special effects filters by choosing commands from the Filter menu. These commands fall into two general camps: corrective and destructive.

Corrective filters

Corrective filters are workaday tools you use to modify scanned images and to prepare an image for printing or screen display. In many cases, the effects are subtle enough that the viewer won't even notice you applied a corrective filter. As demonstrated in Figure 15-1 and Color Plate 15-1, these filters include those that change the focus of an image, enhance color transitions, and average the colors of neighboring pixels. You'll find these filters in the Filter ➪ Blur, Noise, Sharpen, and Other submenus.

Many corrective filters have direct opposites. Blur is the opposite of Sharpen, Add Noise is the opposite of Median, and so on. This is not to say one filter entirely removes the effect of the other; only reversion commands such as Undo provide this capability. Instead, two opposite filters produce contrasting effects.

Corrective filters are the subject of this chapter. Although they number fewer than their destructive counterparts, I spend more time on them because they represent the functions you're most likely to use on a daily basis.

Unsharp Mask

Gaussian Blur

Median

High Pass

Figure 15-1: This is the gigantic head of fourth century Roman emperor Constantine subject to four corrective filters, including one each from the Sharpen, Blur, Other, and Noise submenus (reading clockwise from upper left).

Destructive filters

The *destructive filters* produce effects so dramatic, they can, if used improperly, completely overwhelm your artwork, making the filter more important than the image itself. For the most part, destructive filters reside in the Filter ⇨ Distort, Pixelate, Render, and Stylize submenus. A few examples of overwhelmed images appear in Figure 15-2 and Color Plate 15-2.

Destructive filters produce way-cool effects, and many people gravitate toward them when first experimenting with Photoshop. But the filters invariably destroy the original clarity and composition of the image. Granted, every Photoshop function is destructive to a certain extent, but destructive filters change your image so extensively, you can't easily disguise the changes later by applying other filters or editing techniques.

Figure 15-2: These are the effects of applying four destructive filters, one each from the Distort, Pixelate, Render, and Stylize submenus (clockwise from upper left). Note, Lens Flare is applicable to color images only, so I had to convert Constantine to the RGB mode before applying the filter.

Wave

Crystallize

Emboss

Lens Flare

Destructive filters are the subject of Chapter 16. Rather than explaining each one of these filters in detail, I provide a general overview.

Effects filters

New to Photoshop 4 is a subset of destructive filters called the *effects filters*. These 47 filters come from the Gallery Effects collection, originally developed by Silicon Beach (the same folks responsible for the old SuperPaint), sold to Aldus Corporation (of PageMaker fame), and finally acquired by Adobe Systems. Not knowing exactly what to do with this grab bag of plug-ins, Adobe first added them to Illustrator 6 and has now made them part of Photoshop 4.

Frankly, I think Adobe should have sentenced Gallery Effects to the same grizzly fate as SuperPaint and other creaky old junk from the Aldus library. Although many of these filters are interesting — and a few might even be useful more than once or twice in a lifetime — they feel tacked on. They weren't developed to satisfy any specific user requirements; they were merely heaped on the Photoshop 4 pile to sweeten the deal.

Little about these filters has changed since Gallery Effects 1.5 came out in 1993. A few filters have been renamed — the old GE Ripple filter is now Ocean Ripple to avoid confusion with Photoshop's own Ripple filter. And one filter, GE Emboss, is gone, presumably because it detracted from the popular Filter ⇨ Stylize ⇨ Emboss. But Adobe hasn't bothered with any meaningful retooling. You can't raise or lower a GE dialog box value using the arrow keys, you can't switch applications when an effects dialog box is visible (both capabilities granted to other filters), and a few of the filters are dreadfully slow.

As a result, I devote only passing attention to the effects filters, explaining those few that fulfill a real need. Of course, I encourage you to experiment and derive your own conclusions. After all, as Figure 15-3 illustrates, these filters do produce intriguing special effects. I mean, Plaster effect is just plain cool. For the record, most of the effects filters reside in the Filter ⇨ Artistic, Brush Strokes, Sketch, and Texture submenus. A few have trickled out into other submenus, including Filter ⇨ Distort ⇨ Diffuse Glow, Glass, and Ocean Ripple; and Filter ⇨ Stylize ⇨ Glowing Edges.

Tip

If your experimentation leads you to the same conclusion as it led me — you can live through most days without the effects filters — you can turn them off to a save a lot of space in RAM, space better devoted to storing pixels. All the effects filters are stored in the Effects folder inside the Adobe/Photoshop/Plugins folder on your hard drive. Move the Effects folder out of the Plugins folder, and all 47 filters will be turned off.

How filters work

When you choose a command from the Filter menu, Photoshop applies the filter to the selected portion of the image. If no portion of the image is selected, Photoshop applies the filter to the entire image. So if you want to filter every nook and cranny of an image, press Ctrl+D and then choose the desired command.

External plug-ins

Some filters are built into the Photoshop application. Others are external modules that reside in the Plugins folder. This enables you to add functionality to Photoshop by purchasing additional filters from third-party collections. Gallery Effects used to be such a collection. Others include PhotoTools from Extensis, Paint Alchemy from Xaos Tools, the Series collections from Andromeda, Eye Candy from Alien Skin, and Kai's Power Tools from MetaTools.

Cutout

Angled Brushes

Figure 15-3: The new effects filters come from Gallery Effects, a little toy surprise Adobe accidentally acquired when it purchased Aldus Corporation. Here we see the impact of one filter each from the Filter ➪ Artistic, Brush Strokes, Sketch, and Texture submenus (clockwise from upper left).

Patchwork

Plaster

If you open the Plugins folder inside the Photoshop folder, you'll see it contains several subfolders. By default, Photoshop places the filters in the Filters and Effects subfolders, but you can place additional filters anywhere inside the Plugins folder. Even if you create a new folder inside the Plugins folder and call it *No Filters Here,* create another folder inside that called *Honest, Fresh Out of Filters,* toss in one more folder called *Carpet Beetles Only,* and put every plug-in you own inside this latest folder, Photoshop sees through your clever ruse and displays the exact filters you always see under their same submenus in the Filter menu. The only purpose of the subfolders is to keep things tidy, so you don't have to look through a list of 6,000 files inside a single Plugins folder (like you did in the old days).

Note In the old days, you had to install third-party plug-ins twice if you wanted to use them both in Photoshop and in other programs. You installed the plug-ins once in Photoshop's Plugins directory, and once in a separate directory for any other programs. You didn't absolutely have to install the plug-ins in that second directory — If you were using, say, Fractal Design Painter, you could just point the program to your Photoshop Plugins directory. But when you tried to use those Photoshop filters in Painter, you got a message saying the filter required Photoshop. Your Plugins menu would be clogged with filters you couldn't use. So, to get around it, you'd do a second install of the plug-ins, putting them in a separate directory, and then point Painter to that directory.

This situation has changed for the better. Adobe has revised the filters from Version 3.04 onward so, in theory, they don't need Photoshop to run if — and it's a big if — the host program supports the 3.04 Plug-ins API. You can direct a program — again, say Painter — to your Photoshop Plugins directory, and it will pick up on the third-party filters and no others.

Previewing filters

For years, the biggest problem with Photoshop's filters was none offered previews to help you predict the outcome of an effect. You just had to tweak your 15,000 meaningless settings and hope for the best. But today, life is much better. Photoshop 3 introduced previews, and Version 4 has made them commonly available to all but the most gnarly filters.

Photoshop offers two previewing capabilities:

✦ **Dialog box previews:** Labeled in Figure 15-4, the 100×100-pixel preview box is now a common feature to all filter dialog boxes. Drag inside the preview box to scroll the portion of the image you want to preview. Move the cursor outside the dialog box to get the square preview cursor (labeled in the figure). Click with the cursor to center the contents of the preview box at the clicked position in the image.

Click the zoom buttons (+ and -) to reduce the image inside the preview box. You can also zoom in by Ctrl+clicking inside the preview box or zoom out by Alt+clicking inside the preview box.

Tip ✦ **Image window previews:** Most corrective filters — as well as a few destructive filters like Mosaic and Emboss — also preview effects in the full Image window. Select the Preview check box to activate this function. While the effect is previewing, a blinking progress line appears under the check box. In Figure 15-4, for example, you can see the bottom of the image still hasn't finished previewing, so the progress line strobes away. If you're working on a relatively poky computer, you'll probably want to turn off this check box to speed the pace at which the filter functions.

Image window   Preview cursor   Preview box   Progress line

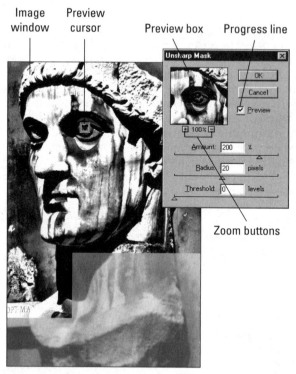

Zoom buttons

Figure 15-4: Most filter dialog boxes enable you to preview the effects of the filter both inside the dialog box and in the Image window.

Note   Incidentally, the Preview check box has no effect on the contents of the preview box. The latter continually monitors the effects of your settings, whether or not you like it.

Tip   Use the Preview check box to compare the before and after effects of a corrective filter in the Image window. Turn the Preview check box on to see the effect; turn it off to see the original image. You can also compare the image in the preview box by clicking in the box. Mouse down to see the old image; release to see the filtered image. It's like an electronic, high-priced, adult version of peek-a-boo. But not nearly as likely to induce giggles.

Even though a dialog box is onscreen and active, you can zoom and scroll the contents of the Image window. Ctrl+click to zoom in, Alt+click to zoom out, and spacebar+drag to scroll. (Before you spacebar+drag, however, make certain an option box isn't active. Otherwise, you add spaces to the value in the option box.) You can also choose commands from the View and Window menus. And feel free to switch applications.

Tip

And one more tip: When you press the Alt key, the Cancel button changes to a Reset button. Alt+click this button to restore the settings that appeared when you first opened the dialog box. (These are not necessarily the factory default settings; they are the settings you last applied to an image.)

Photoshop 4 enhanced the previewing capabilities of several destructive filters, including the likes of Filter ➪ Distort ➪ Ripple and Filter ➪ Stylize ➪ Wind. Even so, seven filters continue to offer no previews whatsoever: Radial Blur, Displace, Color Halftone, Extrude, Tiles, De-Interlace, and Offset. And, of course, single-shot filters — the ones that don't bring up dialog boxes — don't need previews because there aren't any settings to adjust.

Reapplying the last filter

Tip

To reapply the last filter used in the current Photoshop session, choose the first command from the Filter menu or simply press Ctrl+F. If you want to reapply the filter subject to different settings, Alt+choose the first Filter command or press Ctrl+Alt+F to redisplay that filter's dialog box.

Both techniques work even if you undo the last application of a filter. If you cancel a filter while in progress, however, pressing Ctrl+F or Ctrl+Alt+F applies the last uncanceled filter.

Nudging numerical values

Tip

In addition to entering specific numerical values inside filter dialog boxes, you can nudge the values using the up and down arrow keys. When working with percentage values, press an arrow key to raise or lower the value by 1. Press Shift+up arrow or Shift+down arrow to change the value in increments of 10.

If the value accommodates decimal values, it's probably more sensitive to the arrow key. Press an arrow for a 0.1 change; press Shift+arrow for 1.0.

As I mentioned earlier, these tricks don't work in some of the destructive filters dialog boxes, most notably those associated with old Gallery Effects filters.

Fading a filter

In many cases, you apply filters to a selection or image at full intensity — meaning you marquee an area using a selection tool, choose a filter command, enter whatever settings you deem appropriate if a dialog box appears, and then sit back and watch the fireworks.

Photoshop **4.0**

What's so "full intensity" about that? Sounds normal, right? Well, you can reduce the intensity of the last filter applied by choosing the Filter ➪ Fade command or by pressing Ctrl+Shift+F. This command enables you to mix the filtered image with the original, unfiltered one. (This command also works with color corrections, as discussed in Chapter 18.)

As shown in Figure 15-5, the Fade dialog box provides you with the basic tools of image mixing — an Opacity value and a blend mode pop-up menu. To demonstrate the wonders of Filter ➪ Fade, I've applied two particularly destructive Gallery Effects filters to the colossal marble head — Filter ➪ Stylize ➪ Glowing Edges and Filter ➪ Sketch ➪ Note Paper. In the second column of heads, I pressed Ctrl+Shift+F and lowered the Opacity of the two effects to 30 percent. The right-hand images show the effects of two blend modes, Lighten and Overlay.

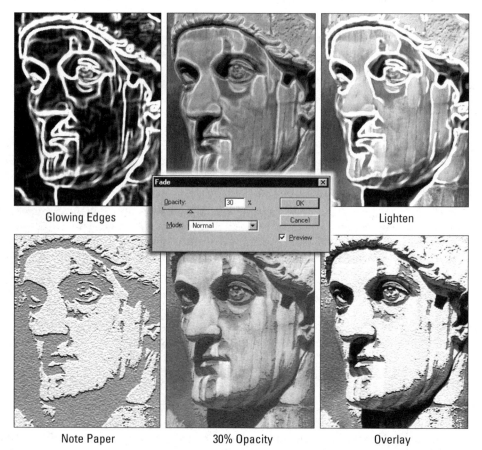

Glowing Edges   Lighten

Note Paper   30% Opacity   Overlay

Figure 15-5: Press Ctrl+Shift+F to mix the filtered image with the unfiltered original. Now, is it me, or is Constantine on Note Paper the spitting image of Rambo? That must be keeping some art historian awake at night.

Creating layered effects

Caution

The drawback of the Fade command is it's only available immediately after you apply a filter (or color correction). If you as much as modify a selection outline after applying the filter, the Fade command dims, only to return when you apply the next filter.

So you may find copying a selection to a separate layer (Ctrl+J) before applying a filter more helpful. This way, you can perform other operations, and even apply many filters in a row, before mixing the filtered image with the underlying original.

Filtering inside a border

And here's another reason to layer before you filter: If your image has a border around it — like the ones shown in Figure 15-6 — you don't want Photoshop to factor the border into the filtering operation. To avoid this, select the image inside the border and press Ctrl+J to layer it prior to applying the filter. The reason is most filters take neighboring pixels into consideration even if they are not selected. By contrast, when a selection floats, it has no neighboring pixels, so the filter affects only the selected pixels.

Figure 15-6 shows the results of applying two filters discussed in this chapter — Unsharp Mask and Motion Blur — when the image is anchored in place and when it's layered. In all cases, the 2-pixel border was not selected. In the left examples, the Unsharp Mask filter leaves a high-contrast residue around the edge of the image, while Motion Blur duplicates the left and right edges of the border. Both problems vanish when the filters are applied to layered images, as seen on the right.

Even if the area outside the selection is not a border per se — perhaps it's only a comparatively dark or light area serving as a visual frame — layering comes in handy. You should always layer the selection unless you specifically want edge pixels calculated by the filter.

Undoing a sequence of filters

Okay, here's one last reason to layer before you filter. Copying an image to a layer protects the underlying image. If you only want to experiment a little, pressing Ctrl+J is often more convenient than taking a snapshot or saving the image for possible reversion. After applying four or five effects to a floating image, you can undo all this automated abuse by Alt+clicking the trash can icon at the bottom of the Layers palette. The underlying original remains unharmed.

Not layered   Layered

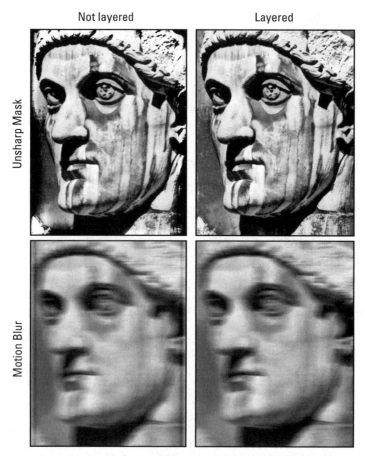

Unsharp Mask

Motion Blur

Figure 15-6: Here are the results of applying two sample filters to images surrounded by borders. In each case, only the image was selected; the border was not selected. Layering the right examples prevented the borders from affecting the performance of the filters.

Heightening Focus and Contrast

If you've experimented at all with Photoshop, you've no doubt had your way with many of the commands in the Filter ➪ Sharpen submenu. By increasing the contrast between neighboring pixels, the sharpening filters enable you to compensate for image elements photographed or scanned slightly out of focus.

The Sharpen, Sharpen More, and Sharpen Edges commands are easy to use and immediate in their effect. You can achieve better results and widen your range of sharpening options, though, if you learn how to use the Unsharp Mask and High Pass commands, which I discuss at length in the following pages.

Using the Unsharp Mask filter

The first thing you should know about the Unsharp Mask filter is it has a weird name. The filter has nothing to do with "unsharpening" — whatever that is — and it is not tied into Photoshop's masking capabilities. The *Unsharp Mask filter* is named after a traditional film compositing technique — also oddly named — that highlights the edges in an image by combining a blurred film negative with the original film positive.

That's all well and good, but most Photoshop artists have never touched a *stat camera* (an expensive piece of machinery, roughly twice the size of a washing machine, used by image editors of the late Jurassic, pre-Photoshop epoch). Even folks like me who used to operate stat cameras professionally never had time to delve into the world of unsharp masking. In addition — and much to the filter's credit — Unsharp Mask goes beyond traditional camera techniques.

To understand Unsharp Mask — or Photoshop's other sharpening filters, for that matter — you first must understand some basic terminology. When you apply one of the sharpening filters, Photoshop increases the contrast between neighboring pixels. The effect is similar to what you see when you adjust a camera to bring a scene into sharper focus.

Two of Photoshop's sharpening filters, Sharpen and Sharpen More, affect whatever area of your image is selected. The Sharpen Edges filter, however, performs its sharpening operations only on the edges in the image — those areas that feature the highest amount of contrast.

Unsharp Mask gives you both sharpening options. It can sharpen only the edges in an image or it can sharpen any portion of an image according to your exact specifications, whether or not it finds an edge. It fulfills the exact purposes as the Sharpen, Sharpen Edges, and Sharpen More commands, but it's much more versatile. Simply put, the Unsharp Mask tool is the only sharpening filter you'll ever need.

When you choose Filter ➪ Sharpen ➪ Unsharp Mask, Photoshop displays the Unsharp Mask dialog box, shown in Figure 15-7, which offers the following options:

✦ **Amount:** Enter a value between 1 and 500 percent to specify the degree to which you want to sharpen the selected image. Higher values produce more pronounced effects.

Figure 15-7: Despite any conclusions you may glean from its bizarre name, the Unsharp Mask filter sharpens images according to your specifications in this dialog box.

✦ **Radius:** This option determines the thickness of the sharpened edge. Low values produce crisp edges. High values produce thicker edges with more contrast throughout the image.

✦ **Threshold:** Enter a value between 0 and 255 to control how Photoshop recognizes edges in an image. The value indicates the numerical difference between the brightness values of two neighboring pixels that must occur if Photoshop is to sharpen those pixels. A low value sharpens lots of pixels; a high value excludes most pixels from the running.

The preview options offered by the Unsharp Mask dialog box are essential visual aids that you're likely to find tremendously useful throughout your Photoshop career. Just the same, you'll be better prepared to experiment with the Amount, Radius, and Threshold options and less surprised by the results if you read the following sections, which explain these options in detail and demonstrate the effects of each.

Specifying the amount of sharpening

If Amount were the only Unsharp Mask option, no one would have any problems understanding this filter. If you want to sharpen an image ever so slightly, enter a low percentage value. Values between 25 and 50 percent are ideal for producing subtle effects. If you want to sharpen an image beyond the point of good taste, enter a value somewhere in the 300 to 500 percent range. And if you're looking for moderate sharpening, try out some value between 50 and 300 percent. Figure 15-8 shows the results of applying different Amount values while leaving the Radius and Threshold values at their default settings of 1.0 and 0, respectively.

If you're uncertain how much you want to sharpen an image, try out a small value, in the 25 to 50 percent range. Then reapply that setting repeatedly by pressing Ctrl+F. As you can see in Figure 15-9, repeatedly applying the filter at a low setting produces a nearly identical result to applying the filter once at a higher setting. For example, you can achieve the effect shown in the middle image in the figure by applying the Unsharp Mask filter three times at 50 percent or once at 250 percent.

I created the top-row results in Figure 15-9 using a constant Radius value of 1.0. In the second row, I lowered the Radius progressively from 1.0 (left) to 0.8 (middle) to 0.6 (right).

Figure 15-8: The results of sharpening an image with the Unsharp Mask filter using eight different Amount values. The Radius and Threshold values used for all images were 1.0 and 0, respectively (the default settings).

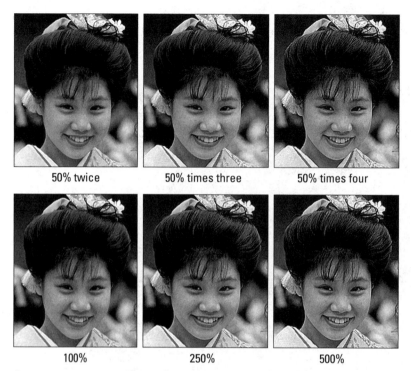

50% twice   50% times three   50% times four

100%   250%   500%

Figure 15-9: Repeatedly applying the Unsharp Mask filter at 50 percent (top row) is nearly equivalent on a pixel-by-pixel basis to applying the filter once at higher settings (bottom row).

The benefit of using small values is they enable you to experiment with sharpening incrementally. As the figure demonstrates, you can add sharpening bit by bit to increase the focus of an image. But you can't reduce sharpening incrementally if you apply too high a value; you must press Ctrl+Z and start again.

Just for fun, Color Plate 15-3 shows the results of applying the Unsharp Mask filter to each of the color channels in an RGB image independently. In each case, the Amount value was set to 300 percent, and the Radius and Threshold values were set to their defaults (1.0 and 0). To heighten the effect, I applied the filter twice to each channel. The top row shows the results of applying the filter to a single channel; in the second row, I applied the filter to two of the three channels (leaving only one channel unfiltered). You can see how the filter creates a crisp halo of color around the rose. Sharpening the red channel creates a red halo, sharpening the red and green channels together creates a yellow halo, and so on. Applying the filter to the red and green channels produced the most noticeable effects because these channels contain the lion's share of the image detail. The blue channel contained the least detail — as is typical — so sharpening it produced the least dramatic results.

If you're a little foggy on how to access individual color channels, read Chapter 5. Incidentally, you can achieve similar effects by sharpening the individual channels in a Lab or CMYK image.

Setting the thickness of the edges

The Unsharp Mask filter works by identifying edges and increasing the contrast around those edges. The Radius value tells Photoshop how thick you want your edges. Large values produce thicker edges than small values.

The ideal Radius value depends on the resolution of your image and the quality of its edges:

✦ When creating screen images — such as Web graphics — use a low Radius value such as 0.5. This results in terrific hairline edges that look so crisp, you'll think you washed your bifocals.

✦ If a low Radius value brings out weird little imperfections — such as grain, scan lines, or JPEG compression artifacts — raise the value to 1.0 or higher. If this doesn't help, don't fret. I include two different sure-fire, image-fixing techniques later in this chapter, one designed to sharpen grainy old photos, and another to accommodate compressed images.

✦ When printing an image at a moderate resolution — anywhere from 120 to 180 ppi — use a Radius value of 1.0. The edges will look a little thick onscreen, but they'll print fine.

✦ For high-resolution images — around 300 ppi — try a Radius of 2.0. Because Photoshop prints more pixels per inch, the edges must be thicker to remain nice and visible.

If you're looking for a simple formula, I recommend 0.1 of Radius for every 15 ppi of final image resolution. This means 75 ppi warrants a Radius of 0.5, 120 ppi warrants 0.8, 180 ppi warrants 1.2, and so on. If you have a calculator, divide the intended resolution by 150 to get the ideal Radius value.

You can, of course, enter higher Radius values — as high as 250, in fact. Higher values produce heightened contrast effects, almost as if the image had been photocopied too many times, generally useful for producing special effects.

Don't take my word for it, though; you be the judge. Figure 15-10 demonstrates the results of specific Radius values. In each case, the Amount and Threshold values remain constant at 100 percent and 0, respectively.

Figure 15-10: These are the results of applying eight different Radius values, ranging from precise edges to gooey.

Figure 15-11 shows the results of combining different Amount and Radius values. You can see a large Amount value helps to offset the softening of a high Radius value. For example, when the Amount is set to 200 percent, as in the first row, the Radius value appears mainly to enhance contrast when raised from 0.5 to 2.0. When the Amount value is lowered to 50 percent, however, the higher Radius value does more to distribute the effect than boost contrast.

200%, 0.5	200%, 2.0	200%, 10.0
100%, 0.5	100%, 2.0	100%, 10.0
50%, 0.5	50%, 2.0	50%, 10.0

Figure 15-11: Note the effects of combining different Amount and Radius settings. The Threshold value for each image was set to 0, the default setting.

For those few folks who are thinking, "By gum, I wonder what would happen if you applied an unusually high Radius value to each color channel independently?" you have only to gaze upon the wondrous Color Plate 15-4. In this figure, I again applied the Unsharp Mask filter to each channel and each pair of channels in the RGB rose image independently. But I changed the Amount value to 100 percent, the Radius value to a relatively whopping 10.0 pixels, and left the Threshold at 0.

To make the splash more apparent, I applied the filter twice to each image. The colors now bound out from the rose, bleeding into the gray background by as much as 10 pixels, the Radius value. Notice how the color fades away from the rose, as if I had feathered it. A high Radius value spreads the sharpening effect and, in doing so, enables the colors to bleed. Because you normally apply the filter to all channels simultaneously, the colors bleed uniformly to create thick edges and high-contrast effects.

Recognizing edges

By default, the Unsharp Mask filter sharpens every pixel in a selection. But you can instruct the filter to sharpen only the edges in an image by raising the Threshold value from 0 to some other number. The Threshold value represents the difference between two neighboring pixels, as measured in brightness levels, that must occur for Photoshop to recognize them as an edge.

Suppose the brightness values of neighboring pixels are 10 and 20. If you set the Threshold value to 5, Photoshop reads both pixels, notes the difference between their brightness values is more than 5, and treats them as an edge. If you set the Threshold value to 20, however, Photoshop passes them by. A low Threshold value, therefore, causes the Unsharp Mask Filter to affect a high number of pixels, and vice versa.

In the top row of images in Figure 15-12, the high Threshold values result in tiny slivers of sharpness that outline only the most substantial edges in the woman's face. As I lower the Threshold value incrementally in the second and third rows, the sharpening effect takes over more and more of the face, ultimately sharpening all details uniformly in the lower-right example.

Using the preset sharpening filters

So how do the Sharpen, Sharpen Edges, and Sharpen More commands compare with the Unsharp Mask filter? First, none of the preset commands enable you to vary the thickness of your edges, a function provided by Unsharp Mask's Radius option. Second, only the Sharpen Edges command can recognize high-contrast areas in an image. And, third, all three commands are set in stone — you can't adjust their effects in any way. Figure 15-13 shows the effect of each preset command and the nearly equivalent effect created with the Unsharp Mask filter.

Sharpening grainy photographs

Having completed my neutral discussion of Unsharp Mask, king of the Sharpen filters, I hasten to interject some commentary, along with a helpful solution to a common sharpening problem.

Figure 15-12: Here are the results of applying nine different Threshold values. To show off the differences best between each image, I set the Amount and Radius values to 500 percent and 2.0, respectively.

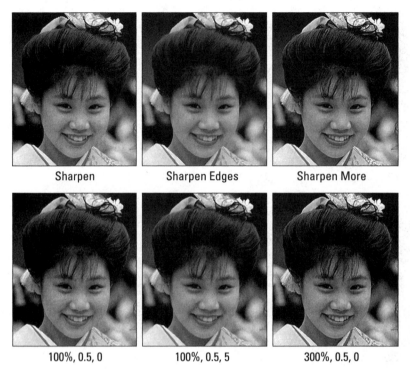

Sharpen	Sharpen Edges	Sharpen More

100%, 0.5, 0	100%, 0.5, 5	300%, 0.5, 0

Figure 15-13: Note the effects of the three preset sharpening filters (top row) compared with the Unsharp Mask equivalents (bottom row). Unsharp Mask values are listed in the following order: Amount, Radius, Threshold.

First, the commentary: Although Amount and Radius are the kinds of superior options that will serve you well throughout the foreseeable future, I urge young and old to observe Threshold with the utmost scorn and rancor. The idea is fine — we can all agree you need some way to draw a dividing line between those pixels you want to sharpen and those you want to leave unchanged. But the Threshold setting is nothing more than a glorified on/off switch resulting in harsh transitions between sharpened and unsharpened pixels.

Consider the picture of prepresidential Dwight D. Eisenhower in Figure 15-14. Like so many vintage photographs, this particular image of Ike is a little softer than we're used to seeing these days. But if I apply a heaping helping of Unsharp Mask — as in the second example in the figure — I bring out as much film grain as image detail. The official Photoshop solution is to raise the Threshold value, but the option's intrinsic harshness results in a pockmarked effect, as shown on the right. Photoshop has simply replaced one kind of grain with another.

Soft

Sharpened, Threshold: 0

Sharpened, Threshold: 2.0

Figure 15-14: The original Ike is a bit soft (left), a condition I can remedy with Unsharp Mask. Leaving the Threshold value set to 0 brings out the film grain (middle), but raising the value results in equally unattractive artifacts (right).

These abrupt transitions are out of keeping with Photoshop's normal approach. Paintbrushes have anti-aliased edges, selections can be feathered, the Color Range command offers Fuzziness — in short, everything mimics the softness found in real life. Yet right here, inside what is indisputably Photoshop's most essential filter, we find no mechanism for softness whatsoever.

While we wait for Photoshop to give us a better Threshold — one with a Fuzziness slider or similar control — you can create a better Threshold using a simple masking technique. Using a few filters, which I explore at greater length throughout this chapter and the next, you can devise a selection outline that traces the essential edges in the image — complete with fuzzy transitions — and leaves the nonedges unmolested. So get out your favorite vintage photograph and follow along with these steps.

Steps: Creating and Using an Edge Mask

1. **Duplicate one of the color channels.** Bring up the Channels palette and drag one of the color channels onto the little page icon. Ike is a grayscale image, so I duplicate the one and only channel.

2. **Choose Filter ➪ Stylize ➪ Find Edges.** As I explain in Chapter 16, the Find Edges filter automatically traces the edges of your image with thick, gooey outlines, ideal for creating edge masks.

3. **Press Ctrl+I or choose Image ➪ Adjust ➪ Invert.** Find Edges produces black lines against a white background, but to select your edges, you need white lines against a black background. The Invert command reverses the lights and darks in the mask, as in the first example in Figure 15-15.

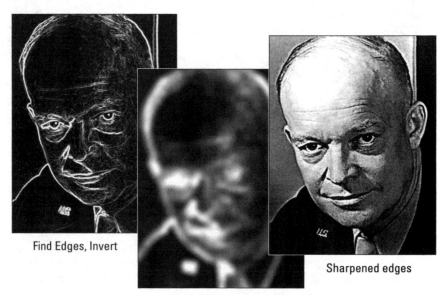

Find Edges, Invert

Find edge mask

Sharpened edges

Figure 15-15: I copy a channel, find the edges, and invert (left). I then apply a string of filters to expand and soften the edges (middle). After converting the mask to a selection outline, I reapply Unsharp Mask with winning results (right).

4. **Choose Filter ➪ Noise ➪ Median.** You need fat, gooey edges, and the current ones are a bit tenuous. To firm up the edges, choose the Median filter, enter a value of 2 (or thereabouts), and press Enter.

5. **Choose Filter ➪ Other ➪ Maximum.** The next step is to thicken the edges. The Maximum filter expands the white areas in the image, serving much the same function in a mask as Select ➪ Modify ➪ Expand serves when editing a selection outline. Enter 4 for the Radius value and press Enter.

6. **Choose Filter ➪ Blur ➪ Gaussian Blur.** Unfortunately, the Maximum filter results in a bunch of little squares that don't do much for our cause.

You can merge the squares into a seamless line by choosing the Gaussian Blur command and entering 4, the same radius you entered for Maximum. Then press Enter.

The completed mask is pictured in the second example of Figure 15-15. Although hardly an impressive sight to the uninitiated eye, you're looking at the perfect edge mask — soft, natural, and extremely accurate.

7. **Return to the standard composite view.** Press Ctrl+tilde (~) in a color image. Because I'm working in a grayscale image, I press Ctrl+1.

8. **Convert the mask to a selection outline.** Ctrl+click the mask name in the Channels palette. Photoshop selects the most essential edges in the image without selecting the grain.

9. **Choose Filter ⇨ Sharpen ⇨ Unsharp Mask.** In the last example in Figure 15-15, I applied the highest permitted Amount value, 500 percent, and a Radius of 2.0.

10. **Whatever values you use, make sure the Threshold is set to 0.** And always leave it at 0 from this day forward.

In case Figures 15-14 and 15-15 are too subtle, I include enlarged views of the great general's eyes in Figure 15-16. The top eyes show the result of using the Threshold value, the bottom eyes were created using the edge mask. Which ones appear sharper and less grainy to you?

Figure 15-16: These are enlarged views of the last examples from Figures 15-14 (top) and 15-15 (bottom). A good edge mask beats the Threshold value every time.

Using the High Pass filter

The High Pass filter falls, more or less, in the same camp as the sharpening filters, but it is not located under the Filter ➪ Sharpen submenu. This frequently overlooked gem enables you to isolate high-contrast image areas from their low-contrast counterparts.

When you choose Filter ➪ Other ➪ High Pass, Photoshop offers a single option: the familiar Radius value, which can vary from 0.1 to 250.0. As demonstrated in Figure 15-17, high Radius values distinguish areas of high and low contrast only slightly. Low values change all high-contrast areas to dark gray and change all low-contrast areas to a slightly lighter gray. A value of 0.1 (not shown) changes all pixels in an image to a single gray value and is, therefore, useless.

Applying High Pass to individual color channels

In my continuing series of color plates devoted to taking the simple beauty of a rose and abusing it but good, Color Plate 15-5 shows the results of applying the High Pass filter set to a Radius value of 10.0 to the various color channels. This application is actually a pretty interesting use for this filter. When applied to all channels at once, High Pass has an irritating habit of robbing the image of color in the low-contrast areas, where the color is most needed. But when applied to a single channel, there's no color to steal. In fact, the filter adds color. For example, because almost no contrast exists in the black shadow of the rose, High Pass elevates the black to gray in each of the affected color channels. The gray in the red channel appears red, the gray in the red channel mixed with the gray in the green channel appears yellow, and so on. As a result, the filter imbues each image with a chalky glow.

Note   I enhanced the High Pass effect slightly in Color Plate 15-5 by increasing the contrast of each affected color channel using the Levels command. Using the three Input option boxes at the top of the Levels dialog box, I changed the first value to 65 and the third value to 190, thereby compressing the color space equally on both the black and white sides. If I hadn't done this, the images would appear more washed out. (Not a lot, but I figure you deserve the best color I can deliver.) For detailed information on the Levels command, read Chapter 18.

Converting an image into a line drawing

The High Pass filter is especially useful as a precursor to Image ➪ Adjust ➪ Threshold, which converts all pixels in an image to black and white (again, covered in Chapter 18). As illustrated in Figure 15-18, the Threshold command produces entirely different effects on images before and after you alter them with the High Pass filter. In fact, applying the High Pass filter with a low Radius value and then issuing the Threshold command converts your image into a line drawing.

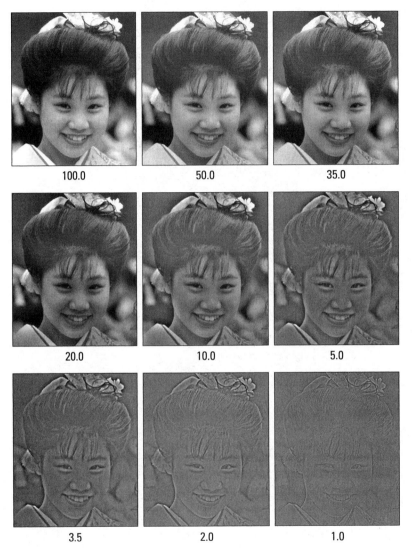

100.0   50.0   35.0

20.0   10.0   5.0

3.5   2.0   1.0

Figure 15-17: The results of separating high- and low-contrast areas in an image with the High Pass filter set at eight different Radius values

In the second row of examples in the figure, I followed Threshold with Filter ➪ Blur ➪ Gaussian Blur (the subject of the next section). I set the Gaussian Blur Radius value to 1.0. Like the Threshold option in the Unsharp Mask dialog box, the Threshold command results in harsh transitions; Gaussian Blur softens them to produce a more natural effect.

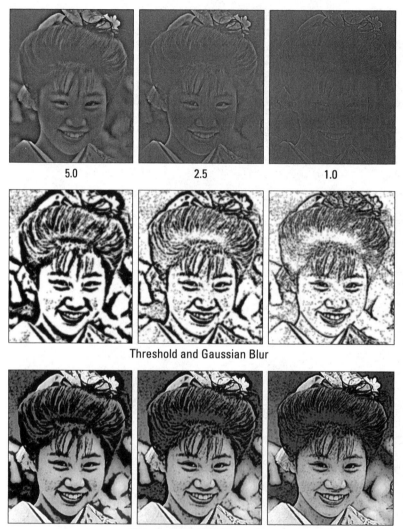

5.0   2.5   1.0

Threshold and Gaussian Blur

Opacity: 45%, Overlay mode

Figure 15-18: Here are several applications of the High Pass filter with low Radius values (top row), followed by the same images subject to Image ⇨ Adjust ⇨ Threshold and Filter ⇨ Blur ⇨ Gaussian Blur (middle). I then layered the second row onto the first and modified the Opacity and blend mode settings.

Why change your image to a bunch of slightly different gray values and then apply a command such as Threshold? One reason is to create a mask, as discussed at length in the "Building a Mask from an Image" section in Chapter 12. (I used Levels instead of Threshold in Chapter 12, but both are variations on the same theme.)

You might also want to bolster the edges in an image. For example, to achieve the last row of examples in Figure 15-18, I layered the images prior to applying High Pass, Threshold, and Gaussian Blur. Then I monkeyed around with the Opacity setting and the blend mode to achieve an edge-tracing effect.

Note I should mention Photoshop provides several automated edge-tracing filters — including Find Edges, Trace Contour, and the Gallery Effects acquisition, Glowing Edges. But High Pass affords more control than any of these commands and enables you to explore a wider range of alternatives. Also worth noting, several Gallery Effects filters — most obviously Filter ⇨ Sketch ⇨ Photocopy — lift much of their code directly from High Pass. Although it may seem a strange effect at first glance, High Pass is one of the seminal filters in Photoshop.

Blurring an Image

The commands under the Filter ⇨ Blur submenu produce the opposite effects of their counterparts under the Filter ⇨ Sharpen submenu. Rather than enhancing the amount of contrast between neighboring pixels, the Blur filters diminish contrast to create softening effects.

Applying the Gaussian Blur filter

The preeminent Blur filter, Gaussian Blur, blends a specified number of pixels incrementally, following the bell-shaped Gaussian distribution curve I touched on in Chapter 11. When you choose Filter ⇨ Blur ⇨ Gaussian Blur, Photoshop produces a single Radius option box, in which you can enter any value from 0.1 to 250.0. (Beginning to sound familiar?) As demonstrated in Figure 15-19, Radius values of 1.0 and smaller blur an image slightly; moderate values, between 1.0 and 5.0, turn an image into a rude approximation of life without my glasses; and higher values blur the image beyond recognition.

Tip Applying the Gaussian Blur filter to a selection in quick mask mode is almost the exact equivalent of feathering the selection in the marching ants mode.

Moderate to high Radius values can be especially useful for creating that hugely amusing *Star Trek* Iridescent Female effect. This is the old *Star Trek,* of course. Captain Kirk meets some bewitching ambassador or scientist who just beamed on board. He takes her hand in sincere welcome as he gives her a lecherous grin and explains how truly honored he is to have such a renowned guest, and so charming to boot, in his transporter room. Then we see it — the close-up of the fetching actress shrouded in a kind of gleaming halo that prevents us from discerning if her lips are chapped or perhaps she's hiding an old acne scar, because some cockeyed cinematographer smeared Vaseline all over the camera lens. I mean, what wouldn't you give to re-create this effect in Photoshop?

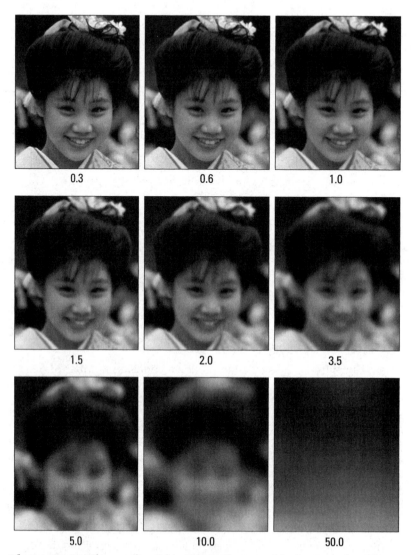

Figure 15-19: The results of blurring an image with the Gaussian Blur filter using eight different Radius values, ranging from slightly out of focus to Bad Day at the Ophthalmologist's office

Unfortunately, I don't have any images of actresses adorned in futuristic go-go boots, so Constantine cum Rambo will have to do in a pinch. The following steps explain how to make the colossal head glow as demonstrated in Figure 15-20.

Steps: The Wondrous Kirk Myopia Effect

1. **Press Ctrl+A to select the entire image.** If you only want to apply the effect to a portion of the image, feather the selection with a radius in the neighborhood of 5 to 8 pixels.

2. **Choose Filter ⇨ Blur ⇨ Gaussian Blur.** Enter some unusually large value into the Radius option box — say, 8.0 — and press Enter.

3. **Press Ctrl+Shift+F to bring up the Fade dialog box.** To achieve the effects shown in Figure 15-20, I reduced the Opacity value to 70 percent, making the blurred image slightly translucent.

4. **You can achieve additional effects by selecting options from the Mode pop-up menu.** For example, I created the upper-right example in the figure by selecting the Screen option, which uses the colors in the filtered image to lighten the original. I created the two bottom examples in the figure by applying the Darken and Lighten options.

Color Plate 15-6 shows an image that's more likely to interest Captain Kirk. It shows a young agrarian woman subject to most of the same settings I applied earlier to Constantine. Again, I applied the Gaussian Blur filter with a Radius of 8.0. Then I used Filter ⇨ Fade Gaussian Blur to adjust the Opacity value and blend mode. The upper-left image shows the Normal mode, but the upper-right image shows the Luminosity mode. In this case, the Screen mode resulted in a washed-out effect, whereas Luminosity yielded an image with crisp color detail and fuzzy brightness values. As a result, some interesting places exist where the colors leap off her checkered dress. As in Figure 15-20, the bottom two images show the effects of the Darken and Lighten modes.

But, you know, as I look at this woman, I'm beginning to have my doubts about her and Captain Kirk. She has Scotty written all over her.

The preset blurring filters

Neither of the two preset commands in the Filter ⇨ Blur submenu, Blur and Blur More, can distribute its blurring effect over a bell-shaped Gaussian curve. For this reason, these two commands are less functional than the Gaussian Blur filter. So you know where they stand in the grand Photoshop focusing scheme, though, Figure 15-21 shows the effect of each preset command and the nearly equivalent effect created with the Gaussian Blur filter.

Normal

Screen

Figure 15-20: After blurring the image, I chose Filter ➪ Fade Gaussian Blur and changed the Opacity value to 70 percent. Then I applied the labeled blend modes to alter the image further.

Darken

Lighten

Anti-aliasing an image

If you have a particularly jagged image, such as a 256-color GIF file, a better way exists to soften the rough edges than applying the Gaussian Blur filter. The best solution is to anti-alias the image. How? After all, Photoshop doesn't offer an Anti-alias filter. Well, think about it. Back in the "Softening selection outlines" section of Chapter 11, I described how Photoshop anti-aliases a brushstroke or selection outline at twice its normal size and then reduces it by 50 percent and applies bicubic interpolation. You can do the same thing with an image.

Figure 15-21: The effects of the two preset blurring filters (top row) compared with their Gaussian Blur equivalents (bottom row), which are labeled according to Radius values

Choose Image ⇨ Image Size and enlarge the image to 200 percent of its present size. Make sure the Resample Image check box is turned on and set to Bicubic. (You can also experiment with Bilinear for a slightly different effect, but don't use Nearest Neighbor.) Next, turn right around and choose Image ⇨ Image Size again, but this time shrink the image by 50 percent.

The top-left example in Figure 15-22 shows a jagged image subject to this effect. I used Image ⇨ Adjust ⇨ Posterize to reduce Moses to four colors. The image is ugly, but it's not unlike the kind of images you may encounter, particularly if you have access to an aging image library. To the right is the same image subject to Gaussian Blur with a low Radius value of 0.5. Rather than appearing softened, the result is just plain fuzzy.

If I, instead, enlarge and reduce the image with the Image Size command, I achieve a true softening effect, as shown in the lower-left example in the figure, commensurate with Photoshop's anti-aliasing options. Even after enlarging and reducing the image four times in a row — as in the bottom-right example — I don't make the image blurry, I simply make it softer.

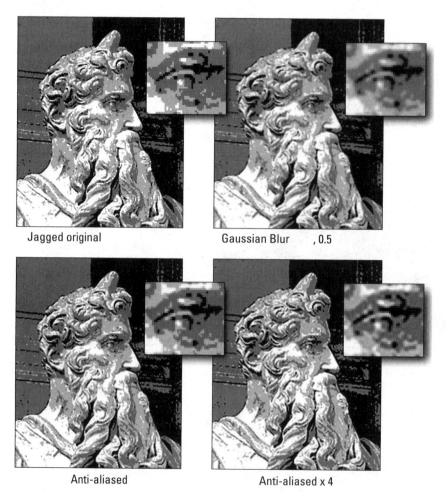

Jagged original   Gaussian Blur   , 0.5

Anti-aliased   Anti-aliased x 4

Figure 15-22: This is a particularly jagged image (top left) followed by the image blurred using a filter (top right). By enlarging and reducing the image one or more times (bottom left and right), I soften the pixels without making them appear blurry. The enlarged details show each operation's effect on the individual pixels.

Directional blurring

In addition to its everyday blurring functions, Photoshop provides two directional blurring filters, Motion Blur and Radial Blur. Instead of blurring pixels in feathered clusters like the Gaussian Blur filter, the *Motion Blur filter* blurs pixels in straight lines over a specified distance. The *Radial Blur filter* blurs pixels in varying degrees depending on their distance from the center of the blur. The following pages explain both of these filters in detail.

Motion blurring

The Motion Blur filter makes an image appear as if either the image or camera was moving when you shot the photo. When you choose Filter ➪ Blur ➪ Motion Blur, Photoshop displays the dialog box shown in Figure 15-23. You enter the angle of movement into the Angle option box. Or you can indicate the angle by dragging the straight line inside the circle on the right side of the dialog box or by clicking the circle itself.

Figure 15-23: Drag the line inside the circle to change the angle of the blur.

You then enter the distance of the movement in the Distance option box. Photoshop permits any value between 1 and 999 pixels. The filter distributes the effect of the blur over the course of the Distance value, as illustrated by the examples in Figure 15-24.

Note   Mathematically speaking, Motion Blur is one of Photoshop's simpler filters. Rather than distributing the effect over a Gaussian curve — which one might argue would produce a more believable effect — Photoshop creates a simple linear distribution, peaking in the center and fading at either end. It's as if the program took the value you specified in the Distance option, created that many clones of the image, offset half the clones in one direction and half the clones in the other — all spaced 1 pixel apart — and then varied the opacity of each.

Using the Wind filter

The problem with the Motion Blur filter is it blurs pixels in two directions. If you want to distribute pixels in one absolute direction or the other, try out the Wind filter, which you can use either on its own or in tandem with Motion Blur.

When you choose Filter ➪ Stylize ➪ Wind, Photoshop displays the Wind dialog box shown in Figure 15-25. You can select from three methods and two directions to distribute the selected pixels. Figure 15-26 compares the effect of the Motion Blur filter to each of the three methods offered by the Wind filter. Notice, the Wind filter does not blur pixels. Rather, it evaluates a selection in 1-pixel-tall horizontal strips and offsets the strips randomly inside the image.

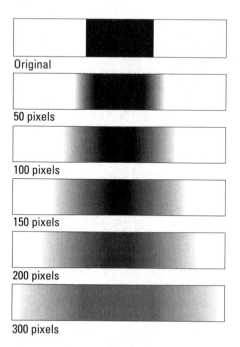

Figure 15-24: This is a single black rectangle followed by five different applications of the Motion Blur filter. Only the Distance value varied, as labeled. A 0-degree Angle value was used in all five examples.

Original

50 pixels

100 pixels

150 pixels

200 pixels

300 pixels

Figure 15-25: Use the Wind filter to distribute a selection randomly in 1-pixel horizontal strips in one of two directions.

To get the best results, try combining the Motion Blur and Wind filters with a translucent selection. For example, to create Figure 15-27, I cloned the entire image to a new layer and applied the Wind command twice, first selecting the Stagger option and then selecting Blast. Next, I applied the Motion Blur command with a 0-degree angle and a Distance value of 30. I then set the Opacity option in the Layers palette to 80 percent and selected Lighten from the blend mode pop-up menu.

Motion Blur

Wind

Figure 15-26: Note the difference between the effects of the Motion Blur filter (upper left) and the Wind filter (other three). In each case, I selected From the Right from the Direction radio buttons.

Blast

Stagger

The result is a perfect blend between two worlds. The motion effect in Figure 15-27 doesn't obliterate the image detail, as the Wind filter does in Figure 15-26. And the motion appears to run in a single direction — to the right — something you can't accomplish using Motion Blur on its own.

Radial blurring

Choosing Filter ⇨ Blur ⇨ Radial Blur displays the Radial Blur dialog box shown in Figure 15-28. The dialog box offers two Blur Method options: Spin and Zoom.

Figure 15-27: Here is the result of combining the Wind and Motion Blur filters with a translucent selection.

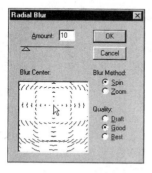

Figure 15-28: Drag inside the Blur Center grid to change the point about which the Radial Blur filter spins or zooms the image.

If you select Spin, the image appears to rotate about a central point. Specify this point by dragging in the grid inside the Blur Center box (as demonstrated in the figure). If you select Zoom, the image appears to rush away from you, as if you were zooming the camera while shooting the photograph. Again, you specify the central point of the Zoom by dragging in the Blur Center box. Figure 15-29 features examples of both settings.

Spin, Draft   Spin, Best

Figure 15-29: These are four examples of the Radial Blur filter set to both Spin and Zoom, subject to different Quality settings (left and right). I specified Amount values of 10 pixels for the Spin examples and 30 for the Zooms. Each effect is centered about the right eye (your right, that is).

Zoom, Draft   Zoom, Best

After selecting a Blur Method option, you can enter any value between 1 and 100 in the Amount option box to specify the maximum distance over which the filter blurs pixels. (You can enter a value of 0, but doing so merely causes the filter to waste time without producing an effect.) Pixels farthest away from the center point move the most; pixels close to the center point barely move at all. Large values take more time to apply than small values. The Radial Blur filter qualifies as one of Photoshop's most time-consuming operations.

Select a Quality option to specify your favorite time/quality compromise. The Good and Best Quality options ensure smooth results by respectively applying bilinear and bicubic interpolation (as explained in the "General preferences" section of Chapter 2). But they also prolong the amount of time the filter spends calculating pixels in your image.

The Draft option diffuses an image, which leaves a trail of loose and randomized pixels, but takes less time to complete. I used the Draft setting to create the left-hand images in Figure 15-29; I selected the Best option to create the images on the right.

Blurring with a threshold

The purpose of the new Filter ➪ Blur ➪ Smart Blur is to blur the low-contrast portions of an image while retaining the edges. This way, you can downplay photo grain, blemishes, and artifacts without harming the real edges in the image. (If you're familiar with Filter ➪ Pixelate ➪ Facet, then knowing Smart Blur is essentially a customizable version of that filter may help.)

The two key options inside the Smart Blur dialog box, shown in Figure 15-30, are the Radius and Threshold slider bars. As with all Radius options, this one expands the number of pixels calculated at a time as you increase the value. Meanwhile, the Threshold value works like the one in the Unsharp Mask dialog box, specifying how different two neighboring pixels must be for them to be considered an edge.

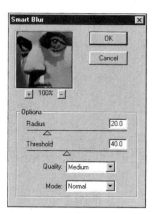

Figure 15-30: The Smart Blur filter enables you to blur the low-contrast areas of an image without harming the edges.

But the Threshold value has a peculiar and unexpected effect on the Radius. The Radius value actually produces more subtle effects if you raise the value beyond the Threshold. For example, look at Figure 15-31. Here is a grid of images subject to different Radius and Threshold values. (The first value below each image is the radius.) In the top row of the figure, the 5.0 radius actually produces a more pronounced effect than its 20.0 and 60.0 cousins. This is because 5.0 is less than the 10.0 threshold, while 20.0 and 60.0 are more.

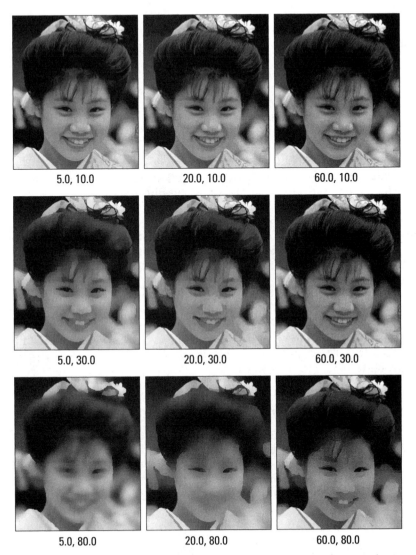

5.0, 10.0	20.0, 10.0	60.0, 10.0
5.0, 30.0	20.0, 30.0	60.0, 30.0
5.0, 80.0	20.0, 80.0	60.0, 80.0

Figure 15-31: Here are combinations of different Radius (first number) and Threshold (second) values. Notice the most dramatic effects occur when the radius is equal to about half the threshold.

The Quality settings control the smoothness of the edges. The High setting takes more time than Medium and Low, but it looks smoother, as well. (All the effects in Figure 15-31 were set to High.) The two additional Mode options enable you to trace the edges defined by the Threshold value with white lines. Overlay Edges shows image and lines, while Edges Only shows just the traced lines. About the only practical purpose for these options is to monitor the precise effect of the Threshold setting in the preview box. Otherwise, the Edges options are clearly relegated to special effects.

Frankly, I'm not convinced Smart Blur is quite ready for prime time. You already know what I think of the Threshold option, and it hasn't become any better here. Without control over the transitions between focused and unfocused areas, things are going to look pretty strange.

Tip   The better way to blur low-contrast areas is to create an edge mask, as I explained back in the "Sharpening grainy photographs" section. Reverse the selection by choosing Select ➪ Inverse and apply the Gaussian Blur filter.

Figure 15-32 shows how the masking technique compares with Smart Blur. In the first image, I applied Unsharp Mask with a Threshold of 20. Then I turned around and applied Smart Blur with a Radius of 2.0 and a Threshold of 20.0, matching the Unsharp Mask value. The result makes Ike look like he has dandruff coming from every pore in his face.

In the second image, I created an edge mask — as explained in the "Creating and Using an Edge Mask" steps — and applied Unsharp Mask with a Threshold of 0. Then I pressed Ctrl+Shift+I to reverse the selection and I applied Gaussian Blur with a Radius of 2.0. The result is a smooth image with sharp edges any president would be proud to hang in the Oval Office.

Softening a selection outline

Gaussian Blur and other Blur filters are equally as useful when editing masks as they are when editing image pixels. As I mentioned earlier, applying Gaussian Blur to a mask has the same effect as applying Select ➪ Feather to a selection outline. But Gaussian Blur affords more control. Where the Feather command affects all portions of a selection outline uniformly, you can apply Gaussian Blur selectively to a mask, enabling you to mix soft and hard edges easily within a single selection outline.

Another advantage to blurring a mask is you can see the results of your adjustments onscreen, instead of relying on the seldom-helpful marching ants. For example, suppose you want to establish a buffer zone between a foreground image and its background. You've managed to select the foreground image accurately — how do you now feather the selection exclusively outward, so no portion of the foreground image becomes selected? Although you can pull off this feat using selection commands like Expand and Feather, it's much easier to apply filters such as Maximum and Gaussian Blur inside a mask. But before I go further, I should back up and explain how Maximum and its pal, Minimum, work.

Figure 15-32: Note the difference between relying on Photoshop's automated Threshold capabilities (left) and sharpening and blurring with the aid of an edge mask (right). Despite the advent of computers, a little manual labor still wins out over automation.

Maximum and Minimum

Filter ➪ Other ➪ Maximum expands the light portions of an image, spreading them outward into other pixels. Its opposite, Filter ➪ Other ➪ Minimum, expands the dark portions of an image. In traditional stat photography, these techniques are known as *spreading* and *choking*.

When you work in the quick mask mode or an independent mask channel, applying the Maximum filter has the effect of incrementally expanding the selected area, adding pixels uniformly around the edges of the selection outline. The Maximum dialog box presents you with a single Radius value, which tells Photoshop how many edge pixels to expand. The exact opposite, the Minimum filter incrementally decreases the size of white areas, which subtracts pixels uniformly around the edges of a selection.

Feathering outward from a selection outline

The following steps describe how to use the Maximum and Gaussian Blur filters to feather an existing selection outline outward so it doesn't encroach on the foreground image.

Steps: Adding a Soft Edge in the Quick Mask Mode

1. **Select the foreground image.** As shown in Figure 15-33, my foreground image is the layered television that figured so heavily into Chapter 13. I convert the layer's transparency mask to a selection outline by Ctrl+clicking the layer's name in the Layers palette.

2. **If you're working on a layer, switch to the background image.** The quickest route is Shift+Alt+[.

3. **Press Q to enter the quick mask mode.** You can create a new mask channel if you prefer, but the quick mask mode is more convenient.

4. **Choose Filter ➪ Other ➪ Maximum.** Enter a Radius value to expand the transparent area into the rubylith. In Figure 15-33, I've entered the highest Radius value permitted, 10 pixels. After pressing Enter, I decided this wasn't enough, so I press Ctrl+Alt+F to bring up the filter again, and further expanded the selection by 4 pixels.

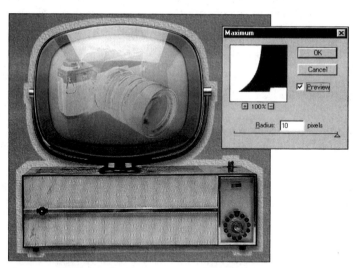

Figure 15-33: The Maximum filter increases the size of the transparent area inside the quick mask mode, thereby expanding the selection outline.

5. **Choose Filter ➪ Blur ➪ Gaussian Blur.** To ensure you don't blur into the foreground image, enter a Radius value no more than half the value you entered into the Maximum dialog box. Altogether, I expanded the selection by 14 pixels, so I entered 7 into the Gaussian Blur dialog box. Photoshop blurs the transparent area, as shown in Figure 15-34.

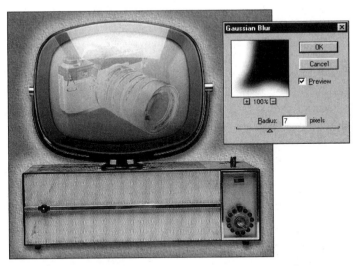

Figure 15-34: Use the Gaussian Blur filter to soften the transparent area, thus feathering the selection outline.

6. **Invert the mask by pressing Ctrl+I.** So far, I've managed to select the TV, but I really want to edit the background. So I press Ctrl+I to invert the mask and inverse the prospective selection.

7. **Press Q to exit the quick mask mode.** Ah, back in the workaday world of marching ants.

8. **Apply the desired effect.** I copied a zebra-skin pattern from another image. Then I chose Edit ➪ Paste Into (Ctrl+Shift+V) to paste the pattern inside the selection. Photoshop created a new layer with layer mask. After Ctrl+dragging the pattern into position, I applied the Overlay blend mode to achieve the effect shown in Figure 15-35.

Thanks to my expanded and softened selection outline, the stripes fade toward the television without ever quite touching it. As I said, you can achieve this effect using Select ➪ Modify ➪ Expand and Feather but, unless you have a special aversion to the quick mask mode, it's easier to be certain of your results when you can see exactly what you're doing.

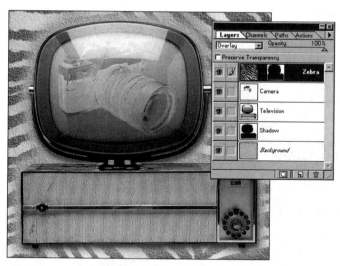

Figure 15-35: I copied some zebra skin from one Image window and pressed Ctrl+Shift+V to paste it into my new selection.

Noise Factors

Photoshop offers four loosely associated filters in its Filter ➪ Noise submenu. One filter adds random pixels — known as *noise* — to an image. The other three, Despeckle, Dust and Scratches, and Median, average the colors of neighboring pixels in ways that theoretically remove noise from poorly scanned images. But in fact, they function nearly as well at removing essential detail as they do at removing extraneous noise. In the following sections, I show you how the Noise filters work, demonstrate a few of my favorite applications, and leave you to draw your own conclusions.

Adding noise

Noise adds grit and texture to an image. Noise makes an image look like you shot it in New York City's Lower East Side and were lucky to get the photo at all because someone was throwing sand in your face as you sped away in your chauffeur-driven, jet-black Maserati Bora, hammering away at the shutter release. In reality, of course, a guy over at Sears shot the photo while you toodled around in your minivan trying to find a store that sold day-old bread. But that's the beauty of Noise. It makes you look cool, even when you aren't.

You add noise by choosing Filter ➪ Noise ➪ Add Noise. Shown in Figure 15-36, the Add Noise dialog box features the following options:

✦ **Amount:** Enter any value between 1 and 999 to specify the amount that pixels in the image can stray from their current colors. The value itself represents a color range rather than a brightness range. For example, if you enter a value of 10, Photoshop can apply any color 10 shades more or less green, more or less blue, and more or less red than the current color. Any value over 255 allows Photoshop to select random colors from the entire 16-million color spectrum. The higher you go above 255, the more likely Photoshop is to pick colors at opposite ends of the spectrum — that is, white and black.

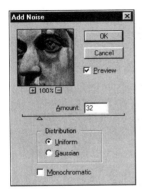

Figure 15-36: The Add Noise dialog box enables you to specify the amount and variety of noise you want to add to the selection.

✦ **Uniform:** Select this option to apply colors absolutely randomly within the specified range. Photoshop is no more likely to apply one color within the range than another, thus resulting in an even color distribution.

✦ **Gaussian:** When you select this option, you instruct Photoshop to prioritize colors along the Gaussian distribution curve. The effect is that most colors added by the filter either closely resemble the original colors or push the boundaries of the specified range. In other words, this option results in more light and dark pixels, thus producing a more pronounced effect.

✦ **Monochromatic:** When working on a full-color image, the Add Noise filter distributes pixels randomly throughout the different color channels. When you select the Monochrome check box, however, Photoshop distributes the noise in the same manner in all channels. The result is *grayscale noise.* (This option does not affect grayscale images; the noise can't get any more grayscale than it already is.)

Figure 15-37 compares three applications of Gaussian noise to identical amounts of Uniform noise. Figure 15-38 features magnified views of the noise so you can compare the colors of individual pixels.

Gaussian, 16   Gaussian, 32   Gaussian, 48

Uniform, 16   Uniform, 32   Uniform, 48

Figure 15-37: The Gaussian option produces more pronounced effects than the Uniform option at identical Amount values.

Noise variations

Normally, the Add Noise filter adds both lighter and darker pixels to an image. If you prefer, though, you can limit the effect of the filter to strictly lighter or darker pixels. To do so, apply the Add Noise filter, and then choose Filter ➪ Fade Add Noise and select the Lighten or Darken blend mode. Or you can copy the image to a new layer, apply the filter, and merge the filtered image with the underlying original.

Figure 15-39 shows sample applications of lighter and darker noise. After copying the image to a separate layer, I applied the Add Noise filter with an Amount value of 100 and selected Gaussian. To create the upper-left example in the figure, I selected Lighten from the blend mode pop-up menu. To create the right example, I selected the Darken mode. In each case, I added a layer of strictly lighter or darker noise, while at the same time, retaining the clarity of the original image.

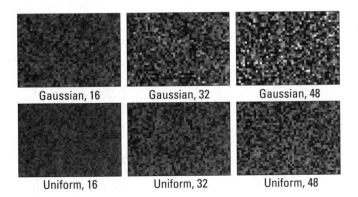

Gaussian, 16 Gaussian, 32 Gaussian, 48

Uniform, 16 Uniform, 32 Uniform, 48

Figure 15-38: These are the upper-left corners of the examples from Figure 15-37 enlarged to four times their original size.

Lighten Darken

Figure 15-39: You can limit the Add Noise filter to strictly lighter (left) or darker (right) noise by applying the filter to a layered clone. To create the rainy and scraped effects (bottom examples), I applied Motion Blur and Unsharp Mask to the noise layers.

Motion Blur, Lighten Motion Blur, Darken

To achieve the streaked noise effects in the bottom example of Figure 15-39, I applied Motion Blur and Unsharp Mask to the layered images. Inside the Motion Blur dialog box, I set the Angle value to -30 degrees and the Distance to 30 pixels. Then I applied Unsharp Mask with an Amount value of 200 percent and a Radius of 1. Naturally, the Threshold value was 0.

Chunky noise

My biggest frustration with the Add Noise filter is you can't specify the size of individual specks of noise. No matter how you cut it, noise only comes in 1-pixel squares. You may know the noise dots can be enlarged in a layer by applying the Maximum or Minimum filter. But, in practice, doing so simply fills in the image because sufficient space doesn't exist between the noise pixels to accommodate the larger dot sizes.

Luckily, Photoshop provides several alternatives. One is the *Pointillize filter,* which adds variable-sized dots and then colors those dots in keeping with the original colors in the image. Although Pointillize lacks the random quality of the Add Noise filter, you can use it to add texture to an image.

To create the top-left image in Figure 15-40, I chose Filter ➪ Pixelate ➪ Pointillize and entered 5 into the Cell Size option box. After pressing Enter to apply the filter, I pressed Ctrl+Shift+F and changed the Opacity value to 50 percent. The effect is rather like applying chunky bits of noise.

The new Gallery Effects filters provide a few noise alternatives. Filter ➪ Sketch ➪ Halftone Pattern adds your choice of dot patterns, as shown in the upper-right example in Figure 15-40. But like all filters in the Sketch submenu, it replaces the colors in your image with the foreground and background colors. Filter ➪ Texture ➪ Grain is a regular noise smorgasbord, enabling you to select from ten different Grain Type options, each of which produces a different kind of noise. The bottom examples in Figure 15-40 show off two of the Grain options, Clumped and Speckled. I used Filter ➪ Fade Grain to reduce the Opacity value for the Speckled effect to 50 percent.

Removing noise with Despeckle

Now for the noise removal filters. Strictly speaking, the Despeckle command probably belongs in the Filter ➪ Blur submenu. The *Despeckle* command blurs a selection and, at the same time, preserves its edges — the idea being unwanted noise is most noticeable in the continuous regions of an image. In practice, this filter is nearly the exact opposite of the Sharpen Edges filter.

The Despeckle command searches an image for edges using the equivalent of an Unsharp Mask Threshold value of 5. It then ignores the edges in the image and blurs everything else with the force of the Blur More filter, as shown in the upper-left image in Figure 15-41.

Pointillize, 50%   Halftone Pattern

Figure 15-40: These are the results of applying several different Add Noise-like filters, including Pointillize, Halftone Pattern, and Grain. A percentage value indicates I modified the Opacity setting in the Fade dialog box.

Grain, Clumped   Speckled, 50%

Averaging pixels with Median

Another command in the Filter ⇨ Noise submenu, the *Median* command removes noise by averaging the colors in an image, one pixel at a time. When you choose Filter ⇨ Noise ⇨ Median, Photoshop produces a Radius option box, into which you can enter any value between 1 and 16. For every pixel in a selection, the filter averages the colors of the neighboring pixels that fall inside the specified radius, ignoring any pixels that are so different they might skew the average, and applies the average color to the central pixel. As verified by Figure 15-41, large values produce the most destructive effects.

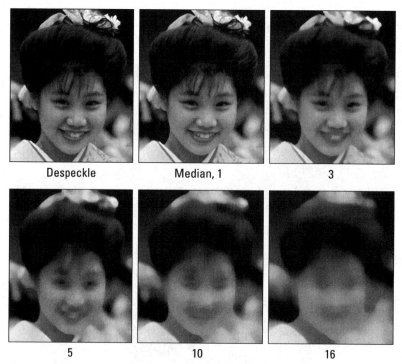

Despeckle   Median, 1   3

5   10   16

Figure 15-41: Note the effects of the Despeckle filter (upper left) and Median filter. The numbers indicate Median filter Radius values.

As with Gaussian Blur, you can achieve some interesting and useful effects by backing off the Median filter with the Fade command. But rather than creating a *Star Trek* glow, Median clumps up details, giving an image a plastic, molded quality, as demonstrated by the examples in Figure 15-42. To create every one of these images, I applied the Median Filter with a Radius of 5 pixels. Then I pressed Ctrl+Shift+F to display the Fade dialog box and lowered the Opacity value to 70 percent. The only difference between one image and the next is the blend mode.

Another difference between Gaussian Blur and Median is Gaussian Blur destroys edges and Median invents new ones. This means you can follow up the Median filter with Unsharp Mask to achieve even more pronounced sculptural effects. I sharpened each one of the examples in Figure 15-42 using an Amount value of 150 percent and a Radius of 1.5.

Normal
Screen

Darken
Lighten

Figure 15-42: After applying the Median filter, I reversed the effect slightly using Filter ➪ Fade Median. Although I varied the blend mode — as labeled beneath the images — the Opacity value remained a constant 70 percent.

Sharpening a compressed image

Digital cameras are the hottest thing in electronic imaging. You can take as many images as you like, download them to your computer immediately, and place them into a printed document, literally minutes after snapping the picture. By the end of this decade, I have little doubt you — yes, you — will own a digital camera.

Unfortunately, the technology is still young. Many brands of digital cameras take exceptional pictures, but most of these high-end devices cost $10,000 or more. Even the Polaroid PDC-2000 — the most affordable quality camera — costs more than $3,000. If you're hoping for a camera under $1,000, you must make do with a consumer model like the Kodak DC50 or the Epson PhotoPC. Even if you pick up this book two years after it's written, and every one of these models has been discontinued, you can expect to pay $200 to $500 for a low-end model.

If you've ever used one of these cameras — only a matter of time, I assure you — you know how difficult it is to sharpen the photographs. Thanks to the stingy supply of pixels and the heavy-handed compression schemes (all based on JPEG), even the daintiest application of the Unsharp Mask filter can reveal a world of ragged edges and unsightly artifacts.

The solution is to firm up the detail and smooth out the color transitions by applying a combination of filters — Median, Gaussian Blur, and Unsharp Mask — to a layered version of the image. The following steps tell all.

Photoshop 4.0 If you own a digital camera, I encourage you to record these steps with the Actions palette, as explained in Chapter 3. This way, you can set Photoshop to open squads of images, batch-process them, and save them in a separate folder, leaving you free to do something fun, like read more of this book.

Steps: Adjusting the Focus of Digital Photos

1. **Select the entire image and copy it to a new layer.** That's Ctrl+A, Ctrl+J. Figure 15-43 shows the image I intend to sharpen, a picture of a friend's child I snapped with a DC40 (the predecessor to the earlier-mentioned DC50). His name, in case you're interested, is Cooper.

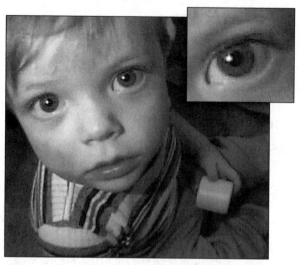

Figure 15-43: I captured this youthful fellow with a low-end digital camera equipped with a removable fish-eye lens. How innocent and happy he looks — obviously not a computer user.

2. **Choose Filter ⇨ Noise ⇨ Median.** After processing several thousand of these images, I've found a Radius value of 2 is almost always the optimal choice. But if the image is particularly bad, a Radius valve of 3 may be warranted.

3. **Choose Filter ⇨ Blur ⇨ Gaussian Blur.** Now that you've gummed up the detail a bit and rubbed out most of the compression, use the Gaussian Blur filter with a Radius of 1.0 to blur the gummy detail slightly. This softens the edges the Median filter creates. (You don't want any fake edges, after all.)

4. **Choose Filter ⇨ Sharpen ⇨ Unsharp Mask.** All this blurring demands some intense sharpening. So apply Unsharp Mask with a maximum Amount value of 500 percent and a Radius of 1.0 (to match the Gaussian Blur radius). This restores most of the definition to the edges, as shown in Figure 15-44.

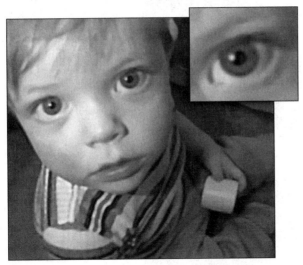

Figure 15-44: Thanks to Median, Gaussian Blur, and Unsharp Mask, Cooper is a much smoother customer. In fact, he's beyond smooth — he's a gummy kid.

5. **Lower the layer's Opacity value.** By itself, the filtered layer is a bit too smooth. So mix the filtered layer with the underlying original with an Opacity value between 30 and 50 percent. I found I could go pretty high, say, 45 percent, with Cooper. Kids have clearly defined details that survive filtering quite nicely.

6. **Merge the image.** Press Ctrl+E to send the layer down.

7. **Continue to correct the image as you normally would.** The examples in Figure 15-45 show the difference between applying the Unsharp Mask filter to the original image (top) and the filtered mixture (bottom). In both cases, I applied an Amount value of 200 percent and a Radius of 1.0. The top photo displays an unfortunate wealth of artifacts — particularly visible in the magnified eye — while the bottom one appears smooth and crisp.

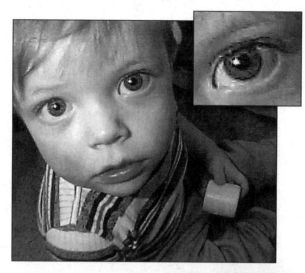

Figure 15-45: Here you can see the difference between sharpening a digital photograph right off the bat (top) and waiting to sharpen until after you've prepared the image with Median, Gaussian Blur, and Unsharp Mask (bottom).

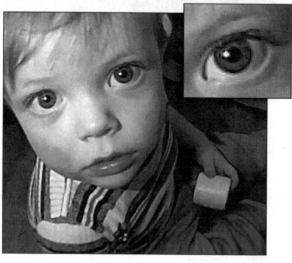

Pinch

Spherize

×2

Color Plate 16-6
The results of using the Pinch (left column) and Spherize (right column) filters to create conical gradations. By the time I captured the first row of images, I had repeated each filter twice. By the second row, I had repeated each filter 12 times. I then mixed the Pinched gradation with the original image using the Soft Light blend mode (bottom left). I cloned the spherized gradation a few times and applied the Screen mode to each (bottom right).

×12

Gradation

Twirl ×3

Flip Horizontal

Rotate 90° CW

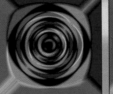

Difference

Rotate 90° CW

Rotate and Flip

and more…

Color Plate 16-7
These two rows of images show a step-by-step experiment in abstract imagery. Starting with a two-color gradation, I convert it to a spiral with Filter ➪ Distort ➪ Twirl. Then I copy the spiral to a layer, flip it, rotate it (top right), apply the Difference mode to achieve the orange image (bottom left). I clone the layer again and rotate it, then I clone a third time and rotate and flip the layer. The final image is the result of tweaking each layer with another distortion filter, including Twirl, Spherize, and ZigZag.

Color Plate 16-8
In this piece, titled Knowing Risk, distortion expert Mark Collen combines a variety of distortion filtering effects to create a surrealistic landscape. The cat, the book, the mongoose, and the twigs are the only scanned images.

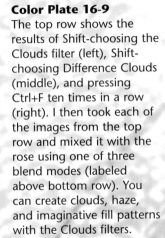

Difference Clouds

× 10

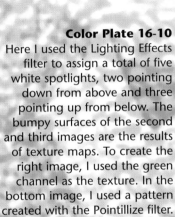

Screen

Hue

Color Plate 16-9
The top row shows the results of Shift-choosing the Clouds filter (left), Shift-choosing Difference Clouds (middle), and pressing Ctrl+F ten times in a row (right). I then took each of the images from the top row and mixed it with the rose using one of three blend modes (labeled above bottom row). You can create clouds, haze, and imaginative fill patterns with the Clouds filters.

Color Plate 16-10
Here I used the Lighting Effects filter to assign a total of five white spotlights, two pointing down from above and three pointing up from below. The bumpy surfaces of the second and third images are the results of texture maps. To create the right image, I used the green channel as the texture. In the bottom image, I used a pattern created with the Pointillize filter.

Color Plate 17-1
Color versions of four Custom filter effects, including (clockwise from upper left) mild sharpening, offset sharpening, edge-detection, and full-color embossing.

Color Plate 17-2
Examples of applying four patterns from the Dispmaps folder with the Displace filter, including (clockwise from upper left) Crumbles, Streaks pattern, Mezzo effect, and Twirl pattern.

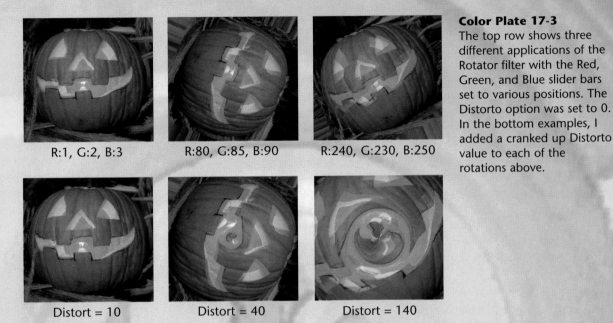

R:1, G:2, B:3   R:80, G:85, B:90   R:240, G:230, B:250

Color Plate 17-3
The top row shows three different applications of the Rotator filter with the Red, Green, and Blue slider bars set to various positions. The Distorto option was set to 0. In the bottom examples, I added a cranked up Distorto value to each of the rotations above.

Distort = 10   Distort = 40   Distort = 140

Color Plate 17-4
Applications of six other filters I created in Filter Factory that you'll find on the CD. Each filter has between 3 and 6 sliders, so there are all sorts of variations you can create.

Channel Mixer   Color Creep   Crisscross

Full Channel Press   Noise Blaster   SuperInvert

Color Plate 18-1
The results of applying the Invert command to a single image in each of the three color modes. I inverted all channels in the RGB and Lab images and all but the black channel in the CMYK image.

RGB   Lab   CMYK

Color Plate 18-2
Here I administered the High Pass filter with a Radius of 3.0, and then applied Threshold separately to each color channel within the three color modes. To smooth the jagged edges, I resampled each image up to 200 percent and then back down to 50 percent using the Image Size command. Then I repeated the process.

RGB   Lab   CMYK

Color Plate 18-3
After cloning the image to a new layer, I applied the High Pass filter and the Posterize command. Then I mixed the layer and the underlying original by choosing each of three overlay modes from the Layers palette. All effects were created with Opacity settings of 100 percent. To make things more colorful, I gave the saturation a healthy boost using the Hue/Saturation command.

Luminosity   Hard Light   Hue

Color Plate 18-4

You can downplay the colors in selected portions of an image by applying Desaturate to convert the pixels to gray values (top left). You can then use Filter ⇨ Fade to reduce the Opacity setting and bring back some colors (top right). Alternatively, you can Invert the selection, choose Filter ⇨ Fade, select the Color blend mode, and lower the Opacity value to 50 percent (bottom left). Raising the Opacity increases the presence of inverted colors (bottom right).

Desaturate

Fade to 50%

Invert and fade to 50%

Invert and fade to 70%

Uncorrected

RGB

Color Plate 18-5

Starting with the uncorrected pumpkin image (top left), I applied Image ⇨ Adjust ⇨ Auto Levels to it in each of the three color modes. The command is really designed for RGB images and tends to mess up CMYK images (lower right). As you folks who live outside Love Canal are probably aware, few pumpkins are fire-engine red.

Lab

CMYK

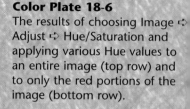

Master, −40°   Master, +20°   Master, +60°

Color Plate 18-6
The results of choosing Image ⇨ Adjust ⇨ Hue/Saturation and applying various Hue values to an entire image (top row) and to only the red portions of the image (bottom row).

Cyan only, −40°   Cyan only, +20°   Cyan only, +60°

Color Plate 18-7
The results of applying various Saturation values to an entire image (top row) and to certain colors — namely cyan and blue — independently of others (bottom row). Without creating a selection or mask, you can isolate colored areas using the Hue/Saturation command. Yes folks, it's just another example of something that wipes the floor with the magic wand.

Master, −50   Master, +50

Master, −90°   Master, +90°

All but cyan
and blue, −100   Cyan and blue, −100
                   All others, +50

Blue areas, 120°   Blue areas, −60°
Other, −50°   Other, 110°

Color Plate 18-8
The results of applying various Hue values to an image when the Colorize option is turned off (top row) and on (bottom row). In the bottom images, I selected the blue areas of the horse with the Color Range command, and then colorized the blue and non-blue areas as indicated by the labels. Notice that while the top two images continue to possess a variety of differently colored pixels, the bottom images contain only two apiece — pink and green.

Color Plate 18-9

These images show the results of correcting images with two of Photoshop's more specialized color commands, Replace Color (top row) and Selective Color (bottom row). The Replace Color command lets you adjust colors while at the same time modifying which pixels are affected and which are not with the help of a Fuzziness option. The Selective Color command adjusts the amount of CMYK ink assigned to predefined color ranges.

Fuzziness, 40

Fuzziness, 200

Red to violet, Relative

Red to violet and
black to white, Absolute

Color Plate 18-10

The effects of applying each of the thumbnails offered in the Variations dialog box to the familiar pumpkin. In each case, the slider bar was set to its default setting of midway between Fine and Coarse with the Midtones radio button selected.

More Green

Lighter

More Yellow

More Cyan

Original

More Red

More Blue

Darker

More Magenta

Color Plate 18-11
Starting with a rather typically washed out image that I shot with a Kodak DC50 (top), I copied the image to a new layer and boosted the saturation with the Hue/Saturation command (second). Then I applied the Median and Gaussian Blur commands and mixed the layer with the underlying original using the Color blend mode and an Opacity value of 70 percent (third). Finally, I used Median, Gaussian Blur, and Unsharp Mask to sharpen the image (bottom).

Original digital photo

Increase saturation to +80

Median, Gaussian Blur, and Color mode

Final sharpened image

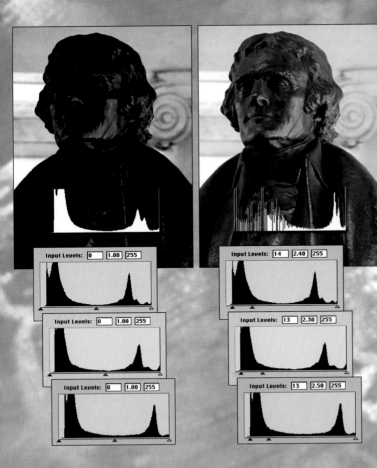

Color Plate 18-12
The celebrated Virginia statesman before (left) and after (right) I corrected him with the Levels command. The white histograms superimposed on Jefferson's chest show the original and corrected distribution of brightness values. The colored histograms illustrate the corrections made to the individual red, green, and blue channels.

Color Plate 18-13
You can use the Curves dialog box to apply gradations as color maps. In the top row, I copied the famous Roman to a new layer, blurred him silly, and applied each of three gradients (saved to disk by Ctrl+Alt+clicking on the Save button in the Gradient Editor dialog box). Then I mixed the images with their underlying originals using the Color blend mode.

Chrome

Blue, Red, Yellow

Spectrum

Color blend mode

Color Plate 18-14
The results of using the Curves command to lighten the colors in the red channel (left), increase the level of contrast in the green channel (middle), and apply an arbitrary color map to the blue channel (right).

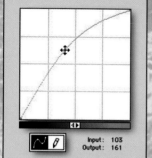
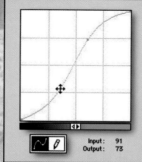
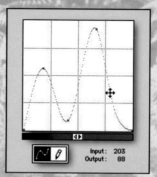

	Input: 103		Input: 91		Input: 203
	Output: 161		Output: 73		Output: 88

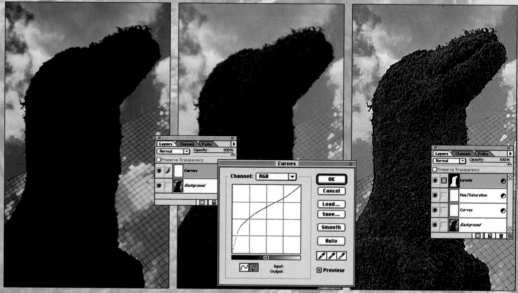

Color Plate 18-15
These images illustrate one way to use adjustment layers to correct the colors in a flat image. After observing that my original image was way too dark (left), I created a new adjustment layer and used the Curves command to lighten the image (middle). I then added two additional layers to increase the saturation levels with Hue/Saturation and correct the brightness levels of the topiary animal with Levels (right).

Color Plate 19-1
Examples of the 17 standard blend
mode options applied to a bright
blue Saturn set against the fiery
backdrop of Jupiter. I also inserted
an 18th Saturn set to the Normal
mode and 50 percent Opacity
(second down, middle column)
just for the sake of comparison.
That, and to take up space.

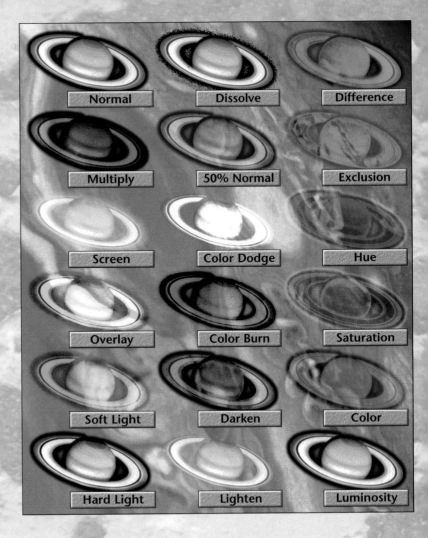

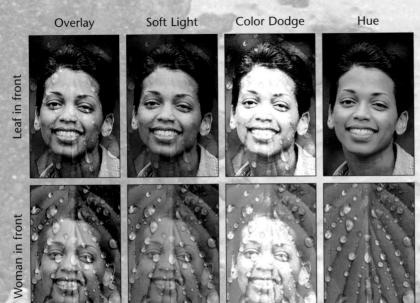

Overlay   Soft Light   Color Dodge   Hue

Leaf in front

Woman in front

Color Plate 19-2
Blend modes change their
meaning depending on which
layer is in front and which is in
back. Here I've taken images of
a woman and a leaf and placed
them on separate layers. In the
top row, the leaf layer is in front,
and in the bottom row, the
woman is in front. The irony is
that every one of these blend
modes favors the layer on
bottom. Only a few — Normal,
Hard Light, and Luminosity —
favor the image on top.

Charcoal

Hard Light

Color

Difference

Original

Soft Light

Color Dodge

Luminosity

Color Plate 19-3
Each column of images shows a progression in which I sandwiched an image filtered with the Charcoal effect (top left) between two originals (bottom left). Each image in the top row shows the filtered image interacting with the original background layered according to the labeled blend mode. The bottom images show the results of adding the top layer of the sandwich and applying another blend mode. For example, applying Difference to the filtered layer and Luminosity to the top layer creates the bottom right effect.

Color Plate 19-4
The top row shows the results of a series of corrective and destructive filters, each of which go a long way toward destroying the detail in my image. But when I insert the filter effect in between two copies of the original image, and then apply the Difference blend mode to the middle and top layers, I bring back much of the detail, as shown in the bottom row. No other technique restores detail quite like a tasty Difference sandwich.

Unsharp Mask

Motion Blur

Lens Flare

Find Edges

Difference sandwich

Color Plate 19-5
For the purpose of comparison, the first image shows the result of compositing an RGB image onto itself using the Hard Light mode. Other examples show the different effects you can achieve by duplicating the image, converting it to the Lab mode, and then mixing it with the original RGB image using the Apply Image command, again set to Hard Light.

RGB on RGB

Lab on RGB

Lightness on RGB

Inverted b on RGB

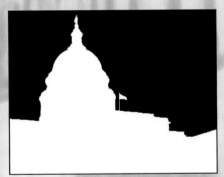

Mask Channel

Hard Light

Color Plate 19-6
After creating a separate mask channel (top left), I used this mask to protect the sky in the target image. Though I used the Apply Image command to apply several compositing effects to the Capitol building, none affected the sky so long as the Mask check box was selected.

Screen

Inverted Difference

Original

System (Macintosh)

System (Windows)

Color Plate 20-1
Examples of a 24-bit image (top left) downgraded using the Indexed Color command. I applied the fixed palettes from the Macintosh and Windows operating systems in the upper middle and right examples. I used the Adaptive option to create the bottom row of images. As you can see, the Adaptive option produces reasonably good results, even at low-color settings.

Adaptive, 8 bits/pixel

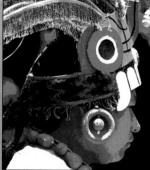
Adaptive, 6 bits/pixel

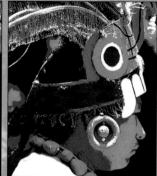
Adaptive, 4 bits/pixel

None, 94K

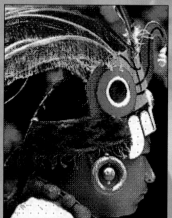
Pattern, 105K

Diffusion, 118K

Color Plate 20-2
Here I reduced the image from Color Plate 20-1 using each of three different Dither options — None, Pattern, and Diffusion. Beside each option name is the size of the file when saved in the GIF format. As you can see, GIF is better suited to compressing an image when no dithering is involved.

These steps work well for sharpening other kinds of compressed imagery, including old photographs you downloaded from the World Wide Web, which you overcompressed without creating backups and images. If applying the Unsharp Mask filter brings out the goobers, try these steps instead.

Cleaning up scanned halftones

Photoshop offers one additional filter in the Filter ⇨ Noise submenu: Dust & Scratches. The purpose of the *Dust & Scratches filter* is to remove dust particles, hairs, scratches, and other imperfections that may accompany a scan. The filter offers two options: Radius and Threshold. As long as the offending imperfection is smaller or thinner than the Radius value and different enough from its neighbors to satisfy the Threshold value, the filter de-enables the spot or line and interpolates between the pixels around the perimeter.

But like so many automated tools, this one works only when conditions are favorable. I'm not saying you shouldn't ever use it — in fact, you may always want to give this filter the first crack at a dusty image. But if it doesn't work, don't get your nose out of joint. Just hunker down and eliminate the imperfections manually using the rubber stamp tool, as explained in the "Touching up blemishes" section of Chapter 10.

Now, as I say, Dust & Scratches was designed to eliminate gunk on a dirty scanner. Moiré patterns are another problem this filter may eliminate. *Moiré patterns* appear when scanning halftoned images from books and magazines. See, any time you scan a printed image, you're actually scanning a collection of halftone dots rather than a continuous-tone photograph. In most cases, the halftone pattern clashes with the resolution of the scanned image to produce rhythmic and distracting moirés.

Caution When scanning published photographs or artwork, take a moment to determine if what you're doing is legal. It's up to you to make sure the image you scan is no longer protected by copyright — most, but not all, works over 75 years old are considered fair game — or that your noncommercial application of the image falls under the fair-use umbrella of commentary or criticism.

The Dust & Scratches filter can be useful for eliminating moirés, particularly if you reduce the Threshold value below 40. But this also goes a long way toward eliminating the actual image detail, as shown in Color Plate 15-7. This figure features an image scanned from a previous issue of *Macworld*. (Because I created the original image, *Macworld* probably won't sue me, but you shouldn't try it.)

The left half of Color Plate 15-7 shows the individual color channels in the image; the right half shows the full-color image. I've blown up a detail in each image so you can better see the pixels in the moiré pattern.

The top example in the color plate shows the original scanned image with its awful moirés. (Actually, I've slightly exaggerated the moirés to account for any printing anomalies; but believe me, with or without enhancement, the image is a mess onscreen.) The middle example shows the same image subject to the Dust & Scratches filter with a Radius of 2 and a Threshold value of 20. The moirés are gone, but the edges have all but disappeared as well. I'm tempted to describe this artwork using adjectives like "soft" and "doughy," and them are fightin' words in the world of image editing.

But what about that bottom example? How did I manage to eliminate the moirés and preserve the detail shown here? Why, by applying the Gaussian Blur, Median, and Unsharp Mask filters to individual color channels.

The first step is to examine the channels independently (by pressing Ctrl+1, Ctrl+2, and Ctrl+3). You'll likely find each one is affected by the moiré pattern to a different extent. In the case of this scan, all three channels need work, but the blue channel — the usual culprit — is the worst. The trick, therefore, is to eliminate the patterns in the blue channel and draw detail from the red and green channels.

To fix the blue channel, I applied both the Gaussian Blur and Median commands in fairly hefty doses. I chose Filter ➪ Blur ➪ Gaussian Blur and specified a Radius value of 1.5 pixels, a rather high value considering the image measures only about 300 pixels tall. Then I chose Filter ➪ Noise ➪ Median and specified a Radius of 2.

The result was a thickly modeled image with no moirés, but little detail. To firm things up a bit, I chose Filter ➪ Sharpen ➪ Unsharp Mask and entered 200 percent for the Amount option and 1.5 for the Radius. I opted for this Radius value because it matches the Radius I used to blur the image. When correcting moirés, a Threshold value of 0 is almost always the best choice. A higher Threshold value not only prevents the sharpening of moiré pattern edges but also ignores real edges, which are already fragile enough.

The green and red channels required incrementally less attention. After switching to the green channel, I applied the Gaussian Blur filter with a Radius of 1.0. Then I sharpened the image with the Unsharp Mask filter set to 200 percent and a Radius value of 0.5. In the red channel (Ctrl+1), I applied Gaussian Blur with a Radius value of 0.5. The gradual effect wasn't enough to warrant sharpening.

When you're finished, switch back to the RGB view (Ctrl+~) to see the combined result of your labors. (Or keep an RGB view of the image up onscreen by choosing Window ➪ New Window.) The focus of the image will undoubtedly be softer than it was when you started. You can cure this to a limited extent by applying discreet passes of the Unsharp Mask filter, say, with an Amount value of 100 percent and a low Radius value. Remember, oversharpening may bring the patterns back to life or even uncover new ones.

Tip   One last tip: Always scan halftoned images at the highest resolution available to your scanner. Then resample the scan down to the desired resolution using Image ➪ Image Size. This step by itself goes a long way toward eliminating moirés.

Full-Court Filtering

Destructive Filters

Corrective filters enable you both to eliminate flaws in an image and to apply special effects. Destructive filters, on the other hand, are devoted solely to special effects. That's why this chapter is actually shorter than its predecessor, even though Photoshop offers nearly twice as many destructive filters as corrective counterparts. Quite simply, destructive filters are less frequently used and, ultimately, are less useful.

Don't get me wrong — these filters are a superb bunch. But because of their more limited appeal, I don't explain each one. Rather, I concentrate on the ones I think you'll use most often, breeze over a handful of others, and let you discover on your own those I ignore.

Note   Remember, all the filters in the Distort submenu, as well as the Lens Flare filter, operate entirely in memory. When you use other filters, you have the benefit of your scratch disk to enable you to do bigger operations than the physical RAM on your system might otherwise enable. Not so with the filters I just mentioned. When they run out of physical RAM, that's it. A workaround of sorts exists: If you're working on a color image, apply the filter in turn to each of the color channels. And for Windows 3.1 users, let me remind you, as a limitation of the Win32s subsystem you're using to run Photoshop, 16MB is the largest block of RAM that can be so allocated. Same workaround as before — but your best bet is to get Windows 95.

A million wacky effects

Oh, heck, I guess I can't ignore half the commands under the Filter menu —
they're not completely useless. But you aren't likely to use them more than once
every lunar eclipse. So only the briefest descriptions of these filters follow:

✦ **Color Halftone:** Located under the Filter ➪ Pixelate submenu, this command
turns an image into a piece of Roy Lichtenstein artwork, with big, comic-
book halftone dots. While scads of fun, the filter is ultimately a novelty that
takes about a year and a half to apply.

✦ **Fragment:** Ooh, it's an earthquake! This lame filter repeats an image four
times in a square formation and lowers the opacity of each to create a sort of
jiggly effect. You don't even have any options to control it. I guess I'm
missing the genius behind Filter ➪ Pixelate ➪ Fragment.

✦ **Lens Flare:** Found in the Render submenu, this filter adds sparkles and halos
to an image to suggest light bouncing off the camera lens. Even though
photographers work their behinds off trying to make sure these sorts of
reflections don't occur, you can add them after the fact. You can select from
one of three Lens Type options, adjust the Brightness slider between 10 and
300 percent (though somewhere around 100 is bound to deliver the best
results), and move the center of the reflection by dragging a point around
inside the Flare Center box.

Tip   If you want to add a flare to a grayscale image, first convert it to the RGB
mode. Then apply the filter and convert back to grayscale (as I did back in
Figure 15-2). The Lens Flare filter is applicable to RGB images only.

Here's another tip suggested by the technical editor, Ted Padova, on the
Macintosh version of this book. Prior to choosing Lens Flare, create a new
layer, fill it with 50 percent gray, and apply the Overlay blend mode. After
applying the filter, you can move it around and vary the Opacity as much as
you like, giving you more control over the final effect.

✦ **Diffuse:** This single-shot filter under the Filter ➪ Stylize submenu dithers the
edges of color, much like the Dissolve brush mode dithers the edges of a soft
brush. The Diffuse filer is moderately useful, but not likely to gain a place
among your treasured few.

✦ **Solarize:** Located in the Stylize submenu — as are the two following filters —
Solarize is easily Photoshop's worst filter. It's only a color-correction effect
that changes all medium grays in the image to 50 percent gray, all blacks and
whites to black, and remaps the other colors to shades in between. (If you're
familiar with the Curves command, the map for Solarize looks like a
pyramid.) The Solarize filter belongs in the Image ➪ Adjust submenu or,
better yet, on the cutting room floor.

✦ **Tiles:** The Tiles filter breaks an image into a bunch of regularly sized, but randomly spaced, rectangular tiles. You specify how many tiles fit across the width and height of the image: A value of 10, for example, creates 100 tiles, and the maximum distance each tile can shift. You can fill the gaps between tiles with foreground color, background color, or an inverted or normal version of the original image. A highly intrusive and not particularly stimulating effect.

✦ **Extrude:** The more capable cousin of the Tiles filter, the Extrude filter breaks an image into tiles and forces them toward the viewer in three-dimensional space. The Pyramid option is fun, devolving an image into a collection of spikes. When using the Blocks option, you can select a Solid Front Faces option that renders the image as a true 3D mosaic. The Mask Incomplete Blocks option simply leaves the image untouched around the perimeter of the selection where the filter can't draw complete tiles.

Actually, I like Extrude. For the sheer heck of it, Color Plate 16-1 shows an example of Extrude applied to one of the sharpened roses from Color Plate 15-4. I set the Type to Blocks, the Size to 10, the Depth to 30 and Random, with both the Solid Front Faces and Mask Incomplete Blocks radio buttons selected. Pretty great, huh? I only wish the filter would generate a selection outline around the masked areas of the image so I could eliminate anything not extruded. It's a wonderful effect, but not one that lends itself to many occasions.

✦ **Diffuse Glow:** The first of the Gallery Effects I mostly ignore, Filter ➪ Distort ➪ Diffuse Glow sprays a coat of dithered, background-colored pixels onto your image. Yowsa, let me at it.

✦ **The Artistic filters:** As a rule, the effects under the Filter ➪ Artistic submenu add a painterly quality to your image. Colored Pencil, Rough Pastels, and Watercolor are examples of filters that successfully emulate traditional mediums. Other filters — Fresco, Smudge Stick, and Palette Knife — couldn't pass for their intended mediums in a dim room filled with dry ice.

✦ **The Brush Strokes filters:** I could argue the Brush Strokes submenu contains filters that create strokes of color. This is true of some of the filters — including Angled Strokes, Crosshatch, and Sprayed Stroke. Others — Dark Strokes and Ink Outlines — generally smear colors, while still others — Accented Edges and Sumi-e — belong in the Artistic submenu. Whatever.

✦ **The Sketch filters:** In Gallery Effects parlance, Sketch means color sucker. Beware: Every one of these filters replaces the colors in your image with the current foreground and background colors. If the foreground and background colors are black and white, the Sketch filter results in a grayscale image. Charcoal and Conté Crayon create artistic effects, Bas Relief and Note Paper add texture, and Photocopy and Stamp are stupid effects you could produce better, and with more flexibility, using High Pass.

Tip

To retrieve some of the original colors from your image after applying a Sketch filter, press Ctrl+Shift+F to bring up the Fade dialog box and try out a few different Mode settings. Overlay and Luminosity are particularly good choices. In Color Plate 16-2, I applied the Charcoal filter with the foreground and background colors set to light blue and dark green. Then I used the Fade command to select the Overlay mode.

✦ **The Texture filters:** As a group, the commands in the Filter ➪ Texture submenu are my favorite effects filters. Craquelure, Mosaic Tiles, and Patchwork apply interesting depth textures to the image. And Texturizer provides access to several scaleable textures and enables you to load your own (as long as the pattern is saved in the Photoshop format), as demonstrated in Figure 16-1. The one dud is Stained Glass, which creates polygon tiles like Photoshop's own Crystallize filter, only with black lines around the tiles.

Certainly, room exists for disagreement about which filters are good and which are awful. After I wrote a two-star *Macworld* review about the first Gallery Effects collection in 1992 — I must admit, I've never been a big fan — a gentleman showed me page after page of excellent artwork he had created with them. Recently, a woman showed me her collection of amazing Lens Flare imagery. I mean, here's a filter that creates a bunch of bright spots, yet this talented person went absolutely nuts with it.

I guess the moral is, just because I think a filter or other piece of software is a squalid pile of unspeakably bad code, this doesn't mean a creative artist can't come along and put it to remarkable use. But this is because you are good; this is not because the filter is good. So if you're feeling particularly creative today, give these filters a try. Otherwise, skip them with a clear conscience.

What about the others?

Some filters don't belong in either the corrective or destructive camp. Take Filter ➪ Video ➪ NTSC Colors and Filter ➪ Other ➪ Offset, for example. Both are examples of commands with no business being under the Filter menu, and both could have been handled much better.

The NTSC Colors filter modifies the colors in your RGB or Lab image for transfer to videotape. Vivid reds and blues, which might otherwise prove unstable and bleed into their neighbors, are curtailed. The problem with this function is it's not an independent color space; it's a single-shot filter that changes your colors and is done with it. If you edit the colors after choosing the command, you may well reintroduce colors incompatible with NTSC devices and, therefore, warrant a second application of the filter. Conversion to NTSC, another light-based system, isn't as fraught with potential disaster as conversion to CMYK pigments, but it still deserves better treatment than this.

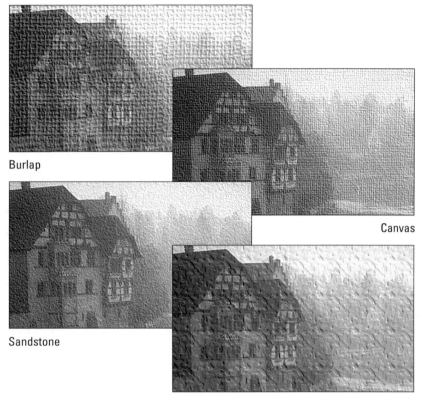

Burlap

Canvas

Sandstone

Random Strokes

Figure 16-1: Filter ➪ Texture ➪ Texturizer enables you to select from four built-in patterns — including the first three shown here — and to load your own. In the last example, I loaded the Random Strokes pattern included with Photoshop.

The Offset command moves an image a specified number of pixels. Why didn't I cover it in Chapter 11 with the other movement options? Because the command actually moves the image inside the selection outline, while it keeps the selection outline stationary. It's as if you pasted the entire image into the selection outline and you were now moving it around. The command is a favorite among fans of channel operations, a topic I cover in Chapter 19. You can duplicate an image, offset the entire thing a few pixels, and then mix the duplicate and original to create highlight or shadow effects. But I much prefer the more interactive control of layering and nudging with the arrow keys. Nowadays, I imagine the Offset filter might find favor with folks who want to automate movements from the Actions palette.

Cross Reference

Among the filters I've omitted from this chapter is Filter ➪ Stylize ➪ Wind, which is technically a destructive filter, but is covered along with the blur and noise filters in Chapter 15. I discussed Filter ➪ Render ➪ Texture Fill in Chapter 10. And, finally, for complete information on the Custom, Displace, and Filter Factory filters, stay tuned for Chapter 17.

As for the other filters in the Filter ➪ Distort, Pixelate, Render, and Stylize submenus, read on to discover all the latest and greatest details.

Third-party filters

In addition to the filters provided by Photoshop, you can purchase all sorts of plug-in filters from other companies. In fact, Photoshop supports its own flourishing cottage industry of third-party solutions.

Cross Reference

The CD at the back of this book includes sample versions of some interesting filters. For complete information on the specific filters and the companies that provide them, read the "Using the CD-ROM" Appendix at the back of this book. Many of the filters are demo versions of the shipping products — this means you can see what they do, but you can't actually apply the effects — or they only work for a limited period of time. I know, it's a drag, but these folks claim they like to make money every once in a while, and I can't say I blame them.

The Pixelate Filters

The new Filter ➪ Pixelate submenu features a handful of commands that rearrange your image into clumps of solid color:

✦ **Crystallize:** The Crystallize filter organizes an image into irregularly shaped nuggets. You specify the size of the nuggets by entering a value from 3 to 300 pixels in the Cell Size option.

✦ **Facet:** The Facet filter fuses areas of similarly colored pixels to create a sort of hand-painted effect.

✦ **Mosaic:** The Mosaic filter blends pixels together into larger squares. You specify the height and width of the squares by entering a value into the Cell Size option box.

✦ **Pointillize:** This filter is similar to Crystallize, except it separates an image into disconnected nuggets set against the background color. As usual, you specify the size of the nuggets by changing the Cell Size value.

The Crystal Halo effect

By applying one of these filters to a feathered selection, you can create what I call the *Crystal Halo effect,* named after the Crystallize filter, which tends to deliver the most successful results. (For a preview of these effects, sneak a peek at Figure 16-2.) The following steps explain how to create a Crystal Halo, using the images in Figures 16-2 and 16-3 as an example.

Steps: Creating the Crystal Halo Effect

1. **Select the foreground element around which you want to create the halo.** Then choose Select ⇨ Inverse to deselect the foreground element and select the background.

2. **Press Q to switch to the quick mask mode.**

3. **Choose Filter ⇨ Other ⇨ Minimum.** As I explained in Chapter 15, this filter enables you to increase the size of the deselected area around the foreground element. The size of the Radius value depends on the size of the halo you want to create. For my part, I wanted a 15-pixel halo. Unfortunately, the Radius option box in the Minimum dialog box can't accommodate a value larger than 10. So I entered 10 the first time. When Photoshop finished applying the filter, I pressed Ctrl+Alt+F to bring up the Minimum dialog box again and entered 5.

4. **Choose Filter ⇨ Blur ⇨ Gaussian Blur.** Then enter a Radius value 0.1 less than the amount by which you increased the size of the deselected area. In my case, I entered 14.9. This will cut into the image slightly, but hardly enough to be visible, as shown in the left image in Figure 16-2.

5. **Choose Filter ⇨ Pixelate ⇨ Crystallize.** Enter a moderate value into the Cell Size option box. I opted for the value 12, slightly larger than the default value. After pressing Enter, you get something along the lines of the selection outline shown in the right image in Figure 16-2. The filter refracts the softened edges, as if you were viewing them through textured glass.

6. **Press Q to switch back to the marching ants mode.** Then use the selection as desired. I merely pressed Ctrl+Delete to fill the selection with white, as shown in the top-left image in Figure 16-3.

Figure 16-2: Create a heavily feathered selection outline (left) and then apply the Crystallize filter to refract the feathered edges (right).

You may find this technique particularly useful for combining images. You can copy the selection and paste it against a different background or copy a background from a different image and choose Edit ➪ Paste Into to paste it inside the crystal halo's selection outline.

Figure 16-3 shows several variations on the Crystal Halo effect. To create the upper-right image, I substituted Filter ➪ Pixelate ➪ Facet for Filter ➪ Pixelate ➪ Crystallize in Step 5. I also sharpened the result to increase the effect of the filter (which nevertheless remains subtle). To create the lower-right image, I applied the Mosaic filter in place of Crystallize, using a Cell Size value of 8. Finally, to create the lower-left image, I applied the Pointillize filter. Because Pointillize creates gaps in a selection, I had to paint inside Moses to fill in the gaps and isolate the halo effect to the background before returning to the marching ants mode.

Creating a mezzotint

A *mezzotint* is a special halftone pattern that replaces dots with a random pattern of swirling lines and worm holes. Photoshop's Mezzotint filter is an attempt to emulate this effect. Although not entirely successful — true mezzotinting options can only be properly implemented as PostScript printing functions, not as filtering functions — they do lend themselves to some interesting interpretations.

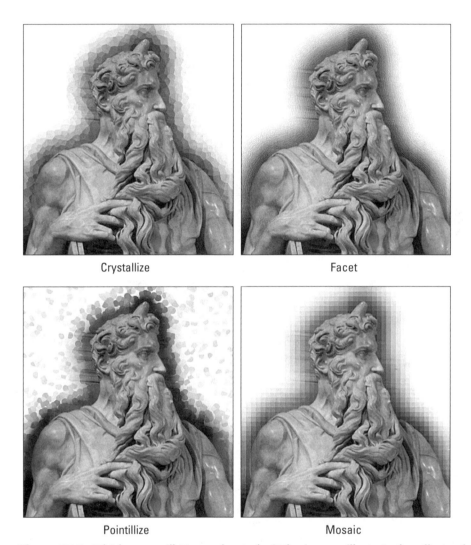

Crystallize

Facet

Pointillize

Mosaic

Figure 16-3: Which aura will Moses don today? The images illustrate the effects of applying each of four filters to a heavily feathered selection in the quick mask mode and pressing Ctrl+Delete.

The filter itself is straightforward. You choose Filter ⇨ Pixelate ⇨ Mezzotint, select an effect from the Type submenu, and press Enter. A preview box enables you to see what each of the ten Type options looks like. Figure 16-4 shows off four of the effects at 230 ppi.

Medium dots   Coarse dots

Short lines   Long strokes

Figure 16-4: The results of applying the Mezzotint filter set to each of four representative effects. These line patterns are on par with the halftoning options offered when you select Mode ⇨ Bitmap, as discussed back in Chapter 5.

To create Figure 16-5, I applied the Mezzotint filter set to the Long Lines effect. Then I used the Filter ⇨ Fade Mezzotint command to mix filtered and original images. I selected Overlay from the Mode pop-up menu and set the Opacity value to 40 percent. The result is a scraped image. (I've decreased the resolution of the image to 180 ppi, so you can see the effect a little more clearly.)

Figure 16-5: To get this effect, I chose Filter ➪ Fade after applying the Mezzotint filter. Then I selected the Overlay mode and set the Opacity slider to 40 percent.

When applied to grayscale artwork, the Mezzotint filter always results in a black-and-white image. When applied to a color image, the filter automatically applies the selected effect independently to each of the color channels. Although all pixels in each channel are changed to either black or white, you can see a total of eight colors — black, red, green, blue, yellow, cyan, magenta, and white — in the RGB composite view. The upper-left example of Color Plate 16-3 shows an image subject to the Mezzotint filter in the RGB mode.

If the Mezzotint filter affects each channel independently, then it follows that the color mode in which you work directly and dramatically affects the performance of the filter. For example, if you apply Mezzotint in the Lab mode, you again whittle the colors down to eight, but a much different eight — black, cyan, magenta, green, red, two muddy blues and a muddy rose — as shown in the top-middle example of Color Plate 16-3. If you're looking for bright happy colors, don't apply Mezzotint in the Lab mode.

In CMYK, the filter produces roughly the same eight colors you get in RGB — white, cyan, magenta, yellow, violet-blue, red, deep green, and black. However, as shown in the top-right example of the color plate, the distribution of the colors is much different. The image appears much lighter and more colorful than its RGB counterpart. This happens because the filter has a lot of black to work with in the RGB mode but little — only that in the black channel — in the CMYK mode.

The bottom row of Color Plate 16-3 shows the effects of the Mezzotint filter after using the Fade command to mix it with the original image. As in Figure 16-4, I chose Overlay from the Mode pop-up menu and set the Opacity value to 40 percent. These three different images were all created using the same filter set to the same effect. Absolutely the only difference is color mode.

Edge-Enhancement Filters

The Filter ➪ Stylize submenu offers access to a triad of filters that enhances the edges in an image. The most popular of these is undoubtedly Emboss, which adds dimension to an image by making it look as if it were carved in relief. The other two, Find Edges and Trace Contour, are less commonly applied, but every bit as capable and deserving of your attention.

Embossing an image

The Emboss filter works by searching for high-contrast edges (like the Sharpen Edge and High Pass filters), highlighting the edges with black or white pixels, and then coloring the low-contrast portions with medium gray. When you choose Filter ➪ Stylize ➪ Emboss, Photoshop displays the Emboss dialog box shown in Figure 16-6. The dialog box offers three options:

✦ **Angle:** The value in the Angle option box determines the angle at which Photoshop lights the image in relief. If you enter a value of 90 degrees, for example, you light the relief from the bottom straight upward. So the white pixels appear on the bottom sides of the edges and the black pixels appear on the top sides. Figure 16-7 shows eight reliefs lit from different angles. I positioned the images so they appear lit from a single source.

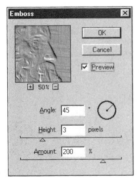

Figure 16-6: The Emboss dialog box enables you to control the depth of the filtered image and the angle from which it is lit.

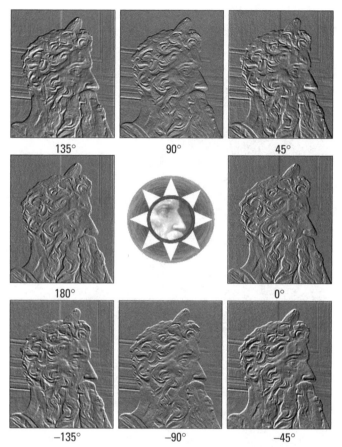

Figure 16-7: Reliefs lighted from eight different angles, in 45-degree increments. In all cases, the central sun image indicates the location of the light source. Height and Amount values of 1 pixel and 250 percent were used for all images.

✦ **Height:** The Emboss filter accomplishes its highlighting effect by displacing one copy of an image relative to another. You specify the distance between the copies using the Height option, which can vary from 1 to 10 pixels. Lower values produce crisp effects, as demonstrated in Figure 16-8. Values above 3 goop up things unless you also enter a high Amount value. Together, the Height and Amount values determine the depth of the image in relief.

Tip

The Height value is analogous to the Radius value in the Unsharp Mask dialog box. You should, therefore, set the value according to the resolution of your image — 1 for 150 ppi, 2 for 300 ppi, and so on.

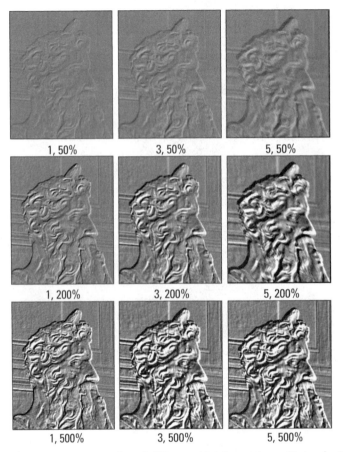

Figure 16-8: Examples of different Height settings (first value) and Amount settings (second value). The Angle value used for each image was 135 degrees.

✦ **Amount:** Enter a value between 1 and 500 percent to determine the amount of black and white assigned to pixels along the edges. Values of 50 percent and lower produce almost entirely gray images, as you can see in the top row of Figure 16-8. Higher values produce sharper edges, as if the relief were carved more deeply.

As a stand-alone effect, Emboss is only okey-dokey. It's one of those filters that makes you gasp with delight the first time you see it, but it never quite lends itself to any practical application after you become acquainted with Photoshop. If you think of Emboss as an extension of the High Pass filter, though, it takes on new meaning. You can use Emboss to edit selection outlines in the quick mask mode, as you might use the High Pass filter. You also can use Emboss to draw out detail in an image.

Figure 16-9 shows the result of using the Fade command immediately after applying the Emboss filter. First, I applied the Emboss filter at an Angle of 135 degrees, a Height of 2 pixels, and an Amount of 250 percent. Then I pressed Ctrl+Shift+F to display the Fade dialog box. To create the left example, I selected Darken from the Mode pop-up menu. This added shadows to the edges of the image, thus boosting the texture without unduly upsetting the original brightness values. I selected the Lighten blend mode to create the right example. In both cases, I set the Opacity value to 70 percent.

Figure 16-9: After applying the Emboss filter, I used my old friend the Fade command to darken (left) and lighten (right) the image.

Tip

To create a color relief effect, apply the Emboss filter and then select the Luminosity option in the Fade dialog box. This retains the colors from the original image while applying the lightness and darkness of the pixels from the filtered selection. The effect looks something like an inked lithographic plate, with steel grays and vivid colors mixing together. An example of this effect at 80 percent Opacity appears in the first example of Color Plate 16-4.

The second example in that same color plate shows a more impressive — if less practical — technique. Rather than applying Luminosity, I chose the Difference mode inside the Fade dialog box. With its hard edges and vivid colors, this image looks like some impossible frame from an educational film on genetic engineering. I can hear the narrator commenting, "Prom dates across America have perked up significantly since scientists discovered how to splice the red rose with a poppy."

Tracing around edges

Photoshop 4 provides three filters that trace around pixels in your image to accentuate the edges, all located in the Filter ➪ Stylize submenu. Longtime users will recognize Find Edges and Trace Contour. The new member of the team is the effects filter Glowing Edges.

✦ **Find Edges:** This filter detects edges similarly to High Pass. Low-contrast areas become white, medium-contrast edges become gray, and high-contrast edges become black, as in the labeled image in Figure 16-10. Hard edges become thin lines; soft edges become fat ones. The result is a thick, organic outline you can overlay onto an image to give it a waxy appearance. To achieve the bottom-left effect in the figure, I chose the Fade ➪ Find Edges command and applied the Overlay mode and an 80 percent Opacity setting. She'll never get her hand off that canning jar as long as she lives.

✦ **Glowing Edges:** This Gallery Effects filter is a variation on Find Edges with two important differences: Glowing Edges produces an inverted effect, changing low-contrast areas to black and edges to white, as in the labeled image in Figure 16-10. The filter also displays a dialog box that enables you to adjust the width, brightness, and smoothness of the traced edges. Glowing Edges is a great backup command. If you aren't satisfied with the effect produced by the Find Edges filter, choose the Glowing Edges command instead and adjust the options as desired. If you want black lines against a white background, press Ctrl+I to invert the effect.

✦ **Trace Contour:** Illustrated on the right side of Figure 16-10, Trace Contour is a little more involved than the others and slightly less interesting. The filter traces a series of single-pixel lines along the border between light and dark pixels. Choosing the filter displays a dialog box containing three options: Level, Upper, and Lower. The Level value indicates the lightness value above which pixels are considered light and below which they are dark. For example, if you enter 128 — medium gray, as by default — Trace Contour draws a line at every spot where an area of color lighter than medium gray meets an area of color darker than medium gray. The Upper and Lower options tell the filter where to position the line — inside the lighter color's territory (Upper) or inside the space occupied by the darker color (Lower).

Figure 16-10: The top row of images demonstrates the effect of the three edge-tracing commands available from the Filter ⇨ Stylize submenu. After applying each command, I used the Fade command to apply the blend modes and Opacity values demonstrated in the bottom row.

Like Mezzotint, Trace Contour applies itself to each color channel independently and renders each channel as a 1-bit image. A collection of black lines surrounds the areas of color in each channel; the RGB, Lab, or CMYK composite view shows these lines in the colors associated with the channels. When you work in RGB, a cyan line indicates a black line in the red channel (no red plus full intensity green and blue becomes cyan). A yellow line indicates a black line in the blue channel, and so on. You get a single black line when working in the grayscale mode.

Creating a metallic coating

The edge-tracing filters are especially fun to use in combination with Filter ➪ Fade. I first got interested in playing with these filters after trying out the Chrome filter included with the first Gallery Effects collection. Now included with Photoshop as Filter ➪ Sketch ➪ Chrome, this filter turns an image into a melted pile of metallic goo. No matter how you apply Chrome, it completely wipes out your image and leaves a ton of jagged color transitions in its wake. It's only useful with color images, and then only if you follow up with the Fade command and the Luminosity mode. Even then, I've never been particularly satisfied with the results.

But it got me thinking: How can you create a metallic coating, with gleaming highlights and crisp shadows, without resorting to Chrome? Find Edges offers a way. First, copy your image to a separate layer. Then apply the Gaussian Blur filter. A Radius value between 1.0 and 4.0 produces the best results, depending on how gooey you want the edges. Then apply the Find Edges filter. Because the edges are blurry, the resulting image is light; so I recommend you darken it using Image ➪ Adjust ➪ Levels (raise the first Input Levels value to 100 or so, as explained in Chapter 18). The blurry edges appear in the top-left example in Figure 16-11.

To produce the bottom-left image, I mixed the layer with the underlying original using the Overlay blend mode and an Opacity of 80 percent. The result is a shiny effect that produces a metallic finish without altogether destroying the detail in the image.

If you decide you like this effect, there's more. The second and third columns of Figure 16-11 show the results of applying Filter ➪ Sketch ➪ Bas Relief and Filter ➪ Artistic ➪ Plastic Wrap. After applying each filter, I chose Filter ➪ Fade, selected the Overlay mode, and set the Opacity value to 80 percent, repeating the effect I applied to the Gaussian Blur and Find Edges layer.

Color Plate 16-5 shows the same effects in color. Starting with an unedited construction worker, I went through the usual calisthenics of selecting and layering the image. Next, I applied Gaussian Blur (3.0 Radius) and Find Edges. The effect was too light, so I chose Image ➪ Adjust ➪ Levels and entered 128 into the first option box. Everything darker than medium gray went to black, uniformly strengthening the effect. The result is the full-color metallic coating shown in the second example in the top row of the color plate. To get the top-right image, I merely selected Overlay from the blend mode pop-up menu in the Layers palette and changed the Opacity value to 80 percent.

In the bottom row of Color Plate 16-5, I really went nuts. In each case, I applied one of three effects filters — Bas Relief, Plastic Wrap, and the infamous Filter ➪ Sketch ➪ Chrome. And each time, I chose Filter ➪ Fade, selected the Luminosity mode, and reduced the Opacity value to 80 percent.

Blur & Find Edges   Bas Relief   Plastic Wrap

Overlay, 80%

Figure 16-11: After applying Gaussian Blur and Find Edges to a layered version of the image (top left), I composited the filtered image with the original using the Overlay mode (bottom left). The second and third columns show similar effects achieved using the effects filters Bas Relief and Plastic Wrap.

Okay, okay, so Chrome still looks more metallic than the other effects, but it also plays havoc with the detail. I'm willing to settle for a more subtle effect if it means I can still recognize my subject when I'm finished.

Distortion Filters

For the most part, commands in the Distort submenu are related because they move colors in an image to achieve unusual stretching, swirling, and vibrating effects. They're rather like the transformation commands from the Layer menu:

They perform their magic by relocating and interpolating colors rather than by altering brightness and color values.

The distinction, of course, is while the transformation commands enable you to scale and distort images by manipulating four control points, the Distort filters provide the equivalent of hundreds of control points, all of which you can use to affect different portions of an image. In some cases, you're projecting an image into a fun-house mirror; other times, it's a reflective pool. You can fan images, wiggle them, and change them in ways that have no correlation to real life, as illustrated in Figure 16-12.

Figure 16-12: This is your image (left); this is your image on distortion filters (right). Three filters, in fact: Spherize, Ripple, and Polar Coordinates.

Distortion filters are powerful tools. Although they are easy to apply, they are extremely difficult to use well. Here are some rules to remember:

✦ **Practice makes practical:** Distortion filters are like complex vocabulary words. You don't want to use them without practicing a little first. Experiment with a distortion filter several times before trying to use it in a real project. You may even want to write down the steps you take, so you can remember how you created an effect.

✦ **Use caution during tight deadlines:** Distortion filters are enormous time-wasters. Unless you know exactly how you want to proceed, you may want to avoid using them when time is short. The last thing you need when you're working under the gun is to get trapped trying to pull off a weird effect.

✦ **Apply selectively:** The effects of distortion filters are too severe to inflict all at once. You can achieve marvelous, subtle effects by distorting feathered and layered selections. Although I wouldn't call the image in Figure 16-12 subtle, no single effect was applied to the entire image. I applied the Spherize filter to a feathered elliptical marquee that included most of the image. I then reapplied Spherize to the eye. I selected the hair and beard and applied the Ripple filter twice. Finally, after establishing two heavily feathered vertical columns on either side of the image in the quick mask mode, I applied the Polar Coordinates filter, which reflected the front and back of the head. Turn the book upside down and you'll see a second face.

✦ **Combine creatively:** Don't expect a single distortion to achieve the desired effect. If one application isn't enough, apply the filter again. Experiment with combining different distortions.

✦ **Save your original:** Never distort an image until you save it. After you start down Distortion Boulevard, the only way to go back is File ➪ Revert. And, as always, it's a good idea to layer the image before applying the filter so you can delete it if you don't like the effect.

Caution

Distortion filters interpolate between pixels to create their fantastic effects. This means the quality of your filtered images is dependent on the setting of the Interpolation option in the General Preferences dialog box. If a filter is producing jagged effects, the Nearest Neighbor option is probably selected. Try selecting the Bicubic or Bilinear option instead.

Reflecting an image in a spoon

Most folks take their first ventures into distortion filters by using Pinch and Spherize. *Pinch* maps an image onto the inside of a sphere or similarly curved surface; *Spherize* maps it onto the outside of a sphere. It's similar to looking at your reflection on the inside or outside of a spoon.

You can apply Pinch to a scanned face to squish the features toward the center or apply Spherize to accentuate the girth of the nose. Figure 16-13 illustrates both effects. It's a laugh, and you feel as though you're onto something no one else thought of before. (At least that's how I felt — but I'm easily amazed.)

You can pinch or spherize an image using either the Pinch or Spherize command. As shown in Figure 16-14, a positive value in the Pinch dialog box produces a similar effect to a negative value in the Spherize dialog box. A slight difference exists between the spatial curvature of the 3D calculations: Pinch pokes the image inward or outward using a rounded cone — we're talking bell-shaped, much like a Gaussian model. Spherize wraps the image on the outside or inside of a true sphere. As a result, the two filters yield subtly different results. Pinch produces a soft transition around the perimeter of a selection; Spherize produces an abrupt transition. If this doesn't quite make sense to you, play with one, try out the same effect with the other, and see which you like better.

Figure 16-13: Constantine does the popular throbbing facial dance — well, it was popular back in 300 A.D. — thanks to the Pinch (left) and Spherize (right) filters.

Another difference between the two filters is Spherize provides the additional options of enabling you to wrap an image onto the inside or outside of a horizontal or vertical cylinder. To try these effects, select the Horizontal Only or Vertical Only options from the Mode pop-up menu at the bottom of the Spherize dialog box.

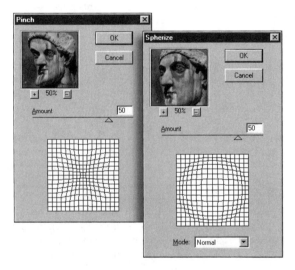

Figure 16-14: Both the Pinch and Spherize dialog boxes enable you to pinch or spherize an image. Pinch wraps on a rounded cone; Spherize wraps onto a sphere.

Tip

Both the Pinch and Spherize filters are applicable only to elliptical regions of an image. If a selection outline is not elliptical in shape, Photoshop applies the filter to the largest ellipse that fits inside the selection. As a result, the filter may leave behind a noticeable elliptical boundary between the affected and unaffected portions of the selection. To avoid this effect, select the region you want to edit with the elliptical marquee tool and then feather the selection before filtering it. This softens the effect of the filter and provides a more gradual transition (even more so than Pinch already affords).

One of the more remarkable properties of the Pinch filter is it enables you to turn any image into a conical gradation. Figure 16-15 illustrates how the process works.

First, blur the image to eliminate any harsh edges between color transitions. Then apply the Pinch filter at full strength (100 percent). Reapply the filter several more times. Each time you press Ctrl+F, the center portion of the image recedes farther into the distance, as shown in Figure 16-15. After ten repetitions, the face in the example all but disappeared.

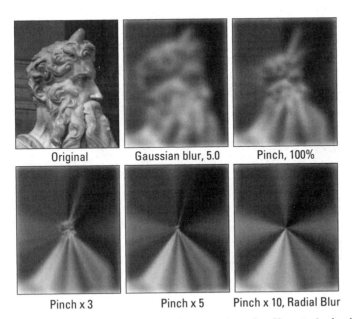

Original   Gaussian blur, 5.0   Pinch, 100%

Pinch x 3   Pinch x 5   Pinch x 10, Radial Blur

Figure 16-15: After applying the Gaussian Blur filter, I pinched the image ten times and applied the Radial Blur filter to create a conical gradation.

Next, apply the Radial Blur filter set to Spin 10 pixels or so to mix the color boundaries a bit. The result is a type of gradation you can't create using Photoshop's gradient tool.

You can also use the Spherize tool set to a negative Amount value to create a conical gradation. Color Plate 16-6 shows off the subtle differences between using the Pinch and Spherize filters for this purpose. The left examples were created with Pinch; the right examples with Spherize. The first row shows the effect of applying each filter twice set to 100 and -100 percent, respectively. The spherized face is larger, showing the Spherize filter works more slowly, but it also grabs more edge detail. The second row shows the results of 12 repetitions of each filter. Although the two gradations are similar, the spherized one contains a hundred or so extra streaks. In the last row, I mixed the gradation with the original image using different blend modes. The Soft Light mode was responsible for the alarming conical-sunburn effect on the left. I repeated the filter four times using the Screen mode to get the right image. "Look, Ma, I had a sprinkler system installed on my helmet!"

Twirling spirals

The Twirl filter rotates the center of a selection while leaving the sides fixed in place. The result is a spiral of colors that looks for all the world as if you poured the image into a blender set to a slow speed.

When you choose Filter ➪ Distort ➪ Twirl, Photoshop displays the Twirl dialog box, shown in Figure 16-16. Enter a positive value from 1 to 999 degrees to spiral the image in a clockwise direction. Enter a negative value to spiral the image in a counterclockwise direction. As you are probably aware, 360 degrees make a full circle, so the maximum 999-degree value equates to a spiral that circles around approximately three times, as shown in the bottom right example in Figure 16-17.

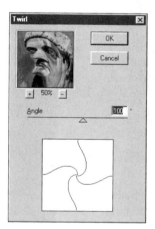

Figure 16-16: The Twirl dialog box enables you to create spiraling images.

Tip   The Twirl filter produces smoother effects when you use lower Angle values. So you're better off applying a 100-degree spiral ten times rather than applying a 999-degree spiral once, as verified by Figure 16-17.

In addition to creating ice-cream swirls like those shown in Figure 16-17, you can use the Twirl filter to create organic images virtually from scratch, as witnessed by Figures 16-18 and 16-19.

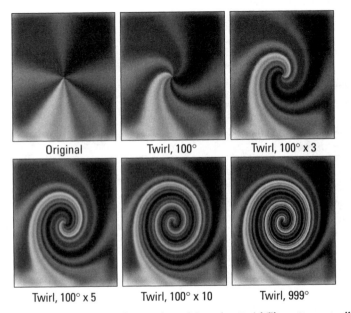

| Original | Twirl, 100° | Twirl, 100° x 3 |
| Twirl, 100° x 5 | Twirl, 100° x 10 | Twirl, 999° |

Figure 16-17: The effects of applying the Twirl filter. Repeatedly applying the Twirl filter at a moderate value (bottom middle) produces a smoother effect than applying the filter once at a high value (bottom right).

To create the images shown in Figure 16-18, I used the Spherize filter to flex the conical gradation vertically by entering 100 percent in the Amount option box and selecting Vertical Only from the Mode pop-up menu. After repeating this filter several times, I eventually achieved a stalactite-stalagmite effect, as shown in the center example of the figure. I then repeatedly applied the Twirl filter to curl the flexed gradations like two symmetrical hairs. The result merges the simplicity of pure math with the beauty of bitmapped imagery.

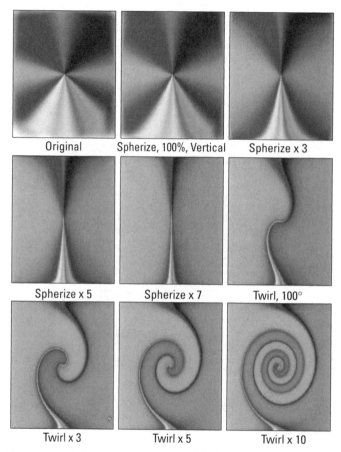

Original | Spherize, 100%, Vertical | Spherize x 3

Spherize x 5 | Spherize x 7 | Twirl, 100°

Twirl x 3 | Twirl x 5 | Twirl x 10

Figure 16-18: You can create surprisingly naturalistic effects using distortion filters exclusively.

Figure 16-19 illustrates a droplet technique designed by Mark Collen. I took the liberty of breaking down the technique into the following steps.

Steps: Creating a Thick-liquid Droplet

1. **Press the D key.** As it has so many times in the past, the D key again restores the default foreground and background colors. Good effort, D key.

2. **Select a square portion of an image.** Drag with the rectangular marquee tool while pressing the Shift key.

3. **Drag inside the selection outline with the gradient tool.** Drag a short distance near the center of the selection from upper left to lower right, creating the gradation shown in the top-left box in Figure 16-19. (To create the effect shown the figure, set the Gradient option to Foreground to Background in the Gradient Tool options palette.)

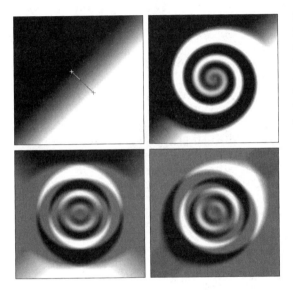

Figure 16-19: Although they appear to be the result of the ZigZag filter, these images were created entirely by using the gradient tool, the Twirl filter, and some transformations.

4. **Choose the Twirl filter and apply it at -360 degrees so the spiral moves counterclockwise.** To create the top-right image in the figure, I applied the Twirl filter three times. Each repetition of the filter adds another ring of ripples.

5. **Press Ctrl+J to copy the selection to a layer.**

6. **Choose Layer ➪ Transform ➪ Flip Horizontal.**

7. **Lower the Opacity value to 50 percent.** Select the rectangular marquee tool and then press 5. The result appears in the lower-left example in Figure 16-19.

8. **Choose Layer ➪ Transform ➪ Rotate 90° CW.** This rotates the layer a quarter turn, thus creating the last image in the figure. You can achieve other interesting effects by choosing Lighten, Darken, and others from the brush modes pop-up menu.

Now, if a few twirls and transformations can produce an effect this entertaining in black and white, imagine what you can do in color. On second thought, don't imagine; check out Color Plate 16-7 instead. The first row in this eight-part color plate is nothing more than a color version of Figure 16-19, intended merely to set the scene. As you can see, I've created a gradation using two complementary colors, blue and yellow. In the fifth example (lower left), I apply the Difference blend mode to the layer and return the Opacity setting to 100 percent. Next, I clone that layer and rotate it another 90 degrees clockwise to produce the sixth example. The Difference blend mode remains in effect for this cloned layer as well. Not satisfied, I clone that layer, rotate it another 90 degrees, and flip it horizontally. The result, also subject to Difference, is the seventh example. Then, for the coup de grâce, I randomly apply the Twirl, Spherize, and ZigZag filters to the layers to mutate the concentric rings into something a little more interesting.

If that went a little fast for you, not to worry. More important than the specific effect is this general category of "distortion drawings." A filter like Pinch or Twirl enables you to create wild imagery without ever drawing a brushstroke or scanning a photograph. If you can do this much with a simple two-color gradation, think what you can do if you throw in a few more colors. Pixels are little more than fodder for these powerful functions.

Creating concentric pond ripples

I don't know about you, but when I think of zigzags, I think of cartoon lighting bolts, wriggling snakes, scribbles — anything that alternately changes directions along an axis, like the letter Z. The ZigZag filter does arrange colors into zigzag patterns, but it does so in a radial fashion, meaning the zigzags emanate from the center of the image, like spokes in a wheel. The result is a series of concentric ripples. If you want parallel zigzags, check out the Ripple and Wave filters, described in the next section. (The ZigZag filter creates ripples, and the Ripple filter creates zigzags. Go figure.)

When you choose Filter ➪ Distort ➪ ZigZag, Photoshop displays the ZigZag dialog box shown in Figure 16-20. The dialog box offers the following options:

✦ **Amount:** Enter an amount between negative and positive 100 in whole-number increments to specify the depth of the ripples. If you enter a negative value, the ripples descend below the surface. If you enter a positive value, the ripples protrude upward. Examples of three representative Amount values appear in Figure 16-21.

✦ **Ridges:** This option box controls the number of ripples in the selected area and accepts any value from 1 to 20. Figure 16-22 demonstrates the effect of three Ridges values.

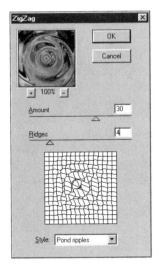

Figure 16-20: The ZigZag dialog box enables you to add concentric ripples to an image, as if the image were reflected in a pond into which you dropped a pebble.

✦ **Pond Ripples:** This option is a cross between the two that follow. Pond Ripples moves pixels outward and rotates them around the center of the selection to create circular patterns. As demonstrated in the top rows of Figures 16-21 and 16-22, this option truly results in a pond-ripple effect.

✦ **Out From Center:** When you select this option, Photoshop moves pixels outward in rhythmic bursts according to the value in the Ridges option box. Because the gradation image I created in Figure 16-14 was already arranged in a radial pattern, I brought in Moses to demonstrate the effect of the Out From Center option, as shown in the second rows of Figures 16-21 and 16-22.

✦ **Around Center:** Select this option to rotate pixels in alternating directions around the circle without moving them outward. This is the only option that produces what I would term a zigzag effect. The last rows of Figures 16-21 and 16-22 show the effects of the Around Center option.

Creating parallel ripples and waves

Photoshop provides four means to distort an image in parallel waves, as if the image were lying on the bottom of a shimmering or undulating pool. Of the four, the ripple filters — which include Ripple, Ocean Ripple, and Glass — are only moderately sophisticated, but they're also relatively easy to apply. The fourth filter, Wave, affords you greater control, but its options are among the most complex Photoshop has to offer.

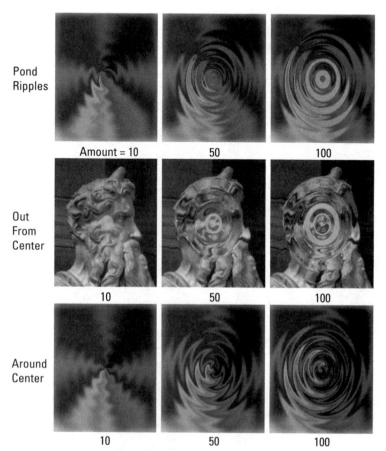

Pond Ripples — Amount = 10 / 50 / 100

Out From Center — 10 / 50 / 100

Around Center — 10 / 50 / 100

Figure 16-21: The effects of the ZigZag filter subject to three Amount values and the Pond Ripples, Out From Center, and Around Center settings. In all cases, the Ridges value was 5.

The Ripple filter

To use the Ripple filter, choose Filter ➪ Distort ➪ Ripple. Photoshop displays the Ripple dialog box shown in Figure 16-23. You have the following options:

✦ **Amount:** Enter an amount between negative and positive 999 in whole-number increments to specify the width of the ripples from side to side. Negative and positive values change the direction of the ripples but, visually speaking, they produce identical effects. The ripples are measured as a ratio of the Size value and the dimensions of the selection — all of which translates to "Experiment and see what happens." You can count on getting ragged effects from any value over 300, as illustrated in Figure 16-24.

Pond
Ripples

Out
From
Center

Around
Center

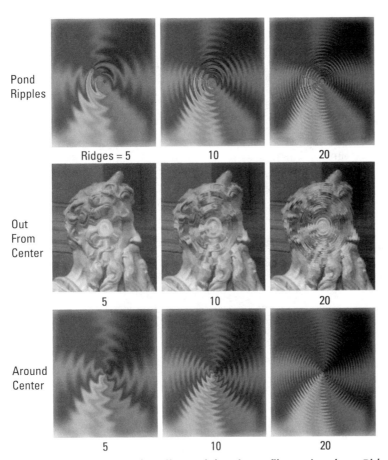

Ridges = 5   10   20

5   10   20

5   10   20

Figure 16-22: The effects of the ZigZag filter using three Ridges values and each of the three Style pop-up menu options. In all cases, the Amount value was 20.

Figure 16-23: The Ripple filter makes an image appear as if it were refracted through flowing water.

✦ **Size:** Select one of the three options in the Size pop-up menu to change the length of the ripples. The Small option results in the shortest ripples and therefore the most ripples. As shown in the upper-right corner of Figure 16-24, you can create a textured glass effect by combining the Small option with a high Amount value. The Large option results in the longest and fewest ripples.

Tip

You can create a blistered effect by overlaying a negative ripple onto a positive ripple. Try this: First, copy the selection. Then apply the Ripple filter with a positive Amount value — say, 300. Next, paste the copied selection and apply the Ripple filter at the exact opposite Amount value, in this case, –300. Press 5 to change the Opacity slider bar to 50 percent. The result is a series of diametrically opposed ripples that cross each other to create teardrop blisters.

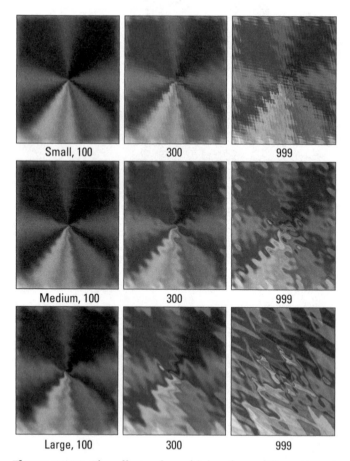

Small, 100   300   999

Medium, 100   300   999

Large, 100   300   999

Figure 16-24: The effects of combining three different Ripple filter Amount values with three different Size settings

Ocean Ripple and Glass

The Ocean Ripple and Glass filters are gifts from Gallery Effects. Both filters emulate the effect of looking at an image through textured glass. These two distorters so closely resemble each other, they would be better merged into one. But where the effects filters are concerned, interface design is as fickle and transitory as the face on the cover of *Tiger Beat* magazine.

The Ocean Ripple and Glass dialog boxes appear joined at the hip in Figure 16-25. While the names and effects of the specific slider bars vary, the only real difference between the two filters is Ocean Blur subscribes to a fixed ripple texture and Glass enables you to switch out the texture by selecting from a pop-up menu.

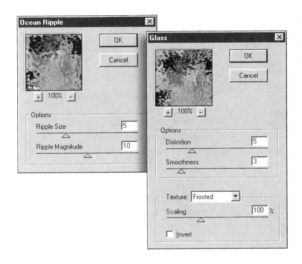

Figure 16-25: The new Ocean Ripple and Glass effects filters are two birds of a feather, ultimately born from the same yolk.

To guide you in your experimentations, Figure 16-26 shows the Pinch gradation subject to several Ocean Blur settings. The first number represents the Ripple Size value (listed first in the dialog box); the second number in the figure represents the Ripple Magnitude value. As you can see, you can vary the Size value with impunity. But raise the Magnitude value and you're looking through sculpted glass.

The Wave filter

Now that you've met the ripple family, it's time to ride the Wave. I could write a book on this filter alone. It wouldn't be very big, nobody would buy it, and I'd hate every minute of it, but you never know what a freelancer will do next. Keep an eye out for *Wave Filter Bible* at your local bookstore.

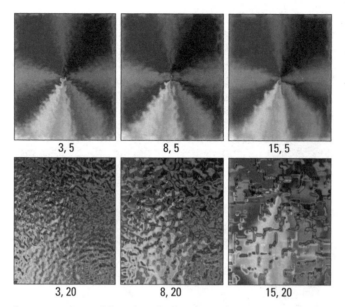

3, 5   8, 5   15, 5

3, 20   8, 20   15, 20

Figure 16-26: Raising the Ripple Size value (first number in each pair) spreads out the effect, while raising the Ripple Magnitude (second number) adds more depth and contrast to the ripples.

In the meantime, choose Filter ➪ Distort ➪ Wave (that's the easy part) to display the Wave dialog box shown in Figure 16-27. Photoshop presents you with the following options, which make applying a distortion almost every bit as fun as operating an oscilloscope:

✦ **Number of Generators:** Right off the bat, the Wave dialog box boggles the brain. A friend of mine likened this option to the number of rocks you throw in the water to start it rippling. One generator means you throw in one rock to create one set of waves, as demonstrated in Figure 16-28. You can throw in two rocks to create two sets of waves (see Figure 16-29), three rocks to create three sets of waves, and all the way up to a quarry full of 999 rocks to create, well, you get the idea. If you enter a high value, however, be prepared to wait a few years for the preview to update.

✦ **Wavelength and Amplitude:** Beginning to feel like you're playing with a ham radio? The Wave filter produces random results by varying the number and length of waves (Wavelength) as well as the height of the waves (Amplitude) between minimum and maximum values, which can range anywhere from 1 to 999. (The Wavelength and Amplitude options, therefore, correspond in theory to the Size and Amount options in the Ripple dialog box.) Figures 16-28 and 16-29 show examples of representative Wavelength and Amplitude values.

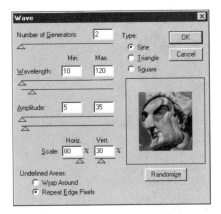

Figure 16-27: The Wave dialog box enables you to wreak scientific havoc on an image. Put on your pocket protector, take out your slide rule, and give it a whirl.

✦ **Scale:** You can scale the effects of the Wave filter between 1 and 100 percent horizontally and vertically. All the effects featured in Figures 16-28 and 16-29 were created by setting both Scale options to 15 percent.

✦ **Undefined Areas:** The Wave filter distorts a selection to the extent that gaps may appear around the edges. You can either fill those gaps by repeating pixels along the edge of the selection, as in the figures, or by wrapping pixels from the left side of the selection onto the right side and pixels from the top edge of the selection onto the bottom.

✦ **Type:** You can select from three kinds of waves. The Sine option produces standard sine waves that rise and fall smoothly in bell-shaped curves, just like real waves. The Triangle option creates zigzags that rise and fall in straight lines, like the edge of a piece of fabric cut with pinking shears. The Square option has nothing to do with waves at all but, instead, organizes an image into a series of rectangular groupings, reminiscent of Cubism. You might think of this option as an extension of the Mosaic filter. Figures 16-28 and 16-29 demonstrate all three options.

✦ **Randomize:** The Wave filter is random by nature. If you don't like the effect you see in the preview box, click the Randomize button to stir things up a bit. You can keep clicking the button until you get an effect you like.

Distorting an image along a curve

The Distort command, which isn't discussed elsewhere in this book, creates four corner handles around an image. You drag each corner handle to distort the selected image in that direction. Unfortunately, you can't add other points around the edges to create additional distortions, which can be frustrating if you're trying to achieve a specific effect. If you can't achieve a certain kind of distortion using Layer ➪ Transform ➪ Distort, the Shear filter may be your answer.

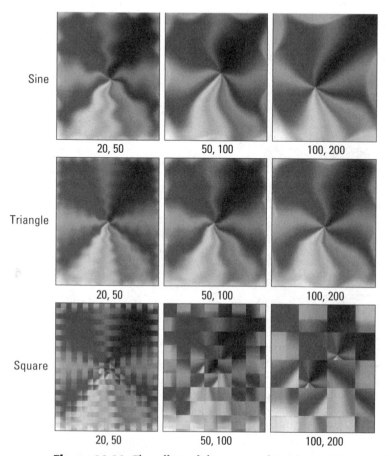

Figure 16-28: The effect of three sets of Maximum Wavelength (first value) and Amplitude (second value) settings when combined with each of the three Type settings. The Number of Generators value was 1 in all cases.

Shear distorts an image along a path. When you choose Filter ➪ Distort ➪ Shear, you get the dialog box shown in Figure 16-30. Initially, a single line with two points at either end appears in the grid at the top of the box. When you drag the points, you slant the image in the preview. This plus the name of the filter is Shear — Adobe's strange term for skewing (it appears in Illustrator as well) — leads many users to dismiss the filter as nothing more than a slanting tool. But in truth, it's more versatile than that.

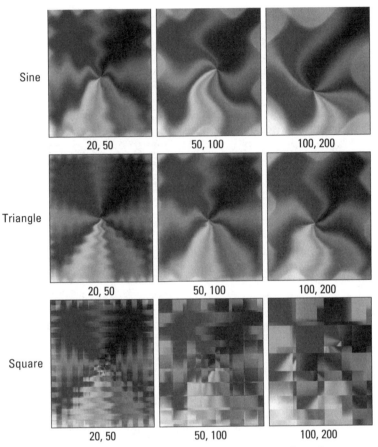

Sine

20, 50   50, 100   100, 200

Triangle

20, 50   50, 100   100, 200

Square

20, 50   50, 100   100, 200

Figure 16-29: The only difference between these images and their counterparts in Figure 16-28 is the Number of Generators value used for all images was 2.

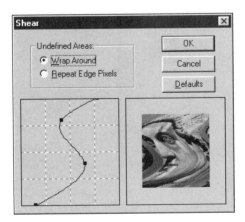

Figure 16-30: Click the grid line in the left corner of the Shear dialog box to add points to the line. Drag these points to distort the image along the curve.

You can add points to the grid line simply by clicking it. A point springs up every time you click an empty space in the line. Drag the point to change the curvature of the line and distort the image along the new curve. Or you can simply click at the spot in the grid where you want to add the point. To delete a point, drag it off the left or right side of the grid. To delete all points and return the line to its original vertical orientation, click the Defaults button.

The Undefined Areas options work just as they do in the Wave dialog box (described in the preceding section). You can either fill the gaps on one side of the image with pixels shoved off the opposite side by selecting Wrap Around or you can repeat pixels along the edge of the selection by selecting Repeat Edge Pixels.

Changing to polar coordinates

The Polar Coordinates filter is another one of those gems many folks shy away from because it doesn't make much sense at first glance. When you choose Filter ➪ Distort ➪ Polar Coordinates, Photoshop presents two radio buttons, as shown in Figure 16-31. You can either map an image from rectangular to polar coordinates or from polar to rectangular coordinates.

All right, time for some global theory. The first image in Figure 16-32 shows a stretched detail of the world map. Although a tad simplistic, this map falls under the heading of a Mercator projection, meaning Greenland is all stretched out of proportion, looking as big as the United States and Mexico combined.

The reason for this has to do with the way different mapping systems handle longitude and latitude lines. On a spherical globe, lines of latitude converge at the poles. On a Mercator map, they run absolutely parallel. Because the Mercator map exaggerates the distance between longitude lines as you progress away from the equator, it likewise exaggerates the distance between lines of latitude. The result is a map that becomes infinitely enormous at each of the poles.

Figure 16-31: In effect, the Polar Coordinates dialog box enables you to map an image onto a globe and view the globe from above.

Figure 16-32: The world from the equator up expressed in rectangular (left) and polar (right) coordinates

When you convert the map to polar coordinates (by selecting the Rectangular to Polar radio button in the Polar Coordinates dialog box), you look down on it from the extreme north or south pole. This means the entire length of the top edge of the Mercator map becomes a single dot in the exact center of the polar projection. The length of the bottom edge of the map wraps around the entire perimeter of the circle. The second example in Figure 16-32 shows the result. As you can see, the Rectangular to Polar option is just the thing for wrapping text around a circle.

If you select the Polar to Rectangular option, the Polar Coordinates filter produces the opposite effect. Imagine for a moment that the conical gradation shown in the upper-left corner of Figure 16-33 is a fan spread out into a full circle. Now imagine closing the fan, breaking the hinge at the top, and spreading out the rectangular fabric of the fan. The center of the fan unfolds to form the top edge of the fabric, and what was once the perimeter of the circle is now the bottom edge of the fabric. Figure 16-33 shows two examples of what happens when you convert circular images from polar to rectangular coordinates.

Tip   The Polar Coordinates filter is a great way to edit gradations. After drawing a linear gradation with the gradient tool (as discussed in Chapter 9), try applying Filter ➪ Distort ➪ Polar Coordinates with the Polar to Rectangular option selected. (Rectangular to Polar turns it into a radial gradation, sometimes with pretty undesirable results.) You get a redrawn gradation with highlights at the bottom of the selection. Press Ctrl+F to reapply the filter to achieve another effect. You can keep repeating this technique until jagged edges start to appear. Then press Ctrl+Z to return to the last smooth effect.

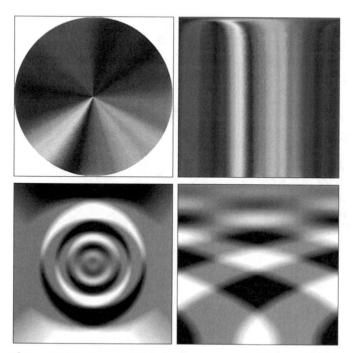

Figure 16-33: Two familiar circular images (left) converted from polar to rectangular coordinates (right). The top example is simple enough that you can probably predict the results of the conversion in your head. The lower example looks cool, but you'd need a brain extension to predict the outcome.

Distorting an image inside out

The following exercise describes how to achieve a sizzling, parting-of-the-Red-Sea effect. Although it incorporates several distortion filters, the star of the effect is the Polar Coordinates filter, which is used to turn the image inside out and then convert it back to polar coordinates after flipping it upside down. No scanned image or artistic talent is required. Rumor has it Moses puts in a guest appearance in the final image.

This effect is the brainchild of Mark Collen, easily the most authoritative distortion expert I've had the pleasure of knowing. I already mentioned his name in this chapter, in connection with the "Creating a Thick-liquid Droplet" steps. To be perfectly honest, I probably should have mentioned him more because many of the ideas conveyed in this chapter were based on long, expensive telephone conversations with Mark.

At any rate, Figures 16-34 through 16-39 show the progression of the image through the following steps, starting with a simplistic throwback to Dada (the art movement, not the family member) and continuing to the fabled sea rising in billowing streams. Color Plate 16-8 shows one of Mark's most vivid images, which was created in part using many of the techniques from the following steps. Obviously, Mark used a few other filtering and nonfiltering techniques to create his image but, gee whiz, folks, you can't expect the guy to share everything he knows in one fell swoop. Mark has to make a living, after all.

Steps: The Parting-of-the-Red-Sea Effect

1. **Draw some random shapes in whatever colors you like.** My shapes appear against a black background in Figure 16-34, but you can use any shapes and colors you like. To create each shape, I used the lasso tool to draw the outline of the shape and pressed Alt+Delete to fill the lassoed selection with the foreground color. The effect works best if a lot of contrast exists between your colors.

Figure 16-34: Draw several meaningless shapes with the lasso tool and fill each with a different color.

2. **Choose Image ⇨ Rotate Canvas ⇨ 90° CCW.** In Step 3, you'll apply the Wind Filter to add streaks to the shapes you created, as shown in Figure 16-35. Because the Wind filter creates horizontal streaks only, and your goal is to add vertical streaks, you must temporarily reorient your image before applying the filter.

3. **Choose Filter ➭ Stylize ➭ Wind.** Select Blast and From the Left and press Enter. To randomize the image in both directions, choose the Wind filter again and select Blast and From the Right.

4. **Choose Image ➭ Rotate ➭ 90° CW.** This returns the image to its original orientation.

5. **Choose Filter ➭ Blur ➭ Motion Blur.** Enter 90 degrees into the Angle option and use 20 pixels for the Distance option. This blurs the image vertically to soften the blast lines, as in Figure 16-35.

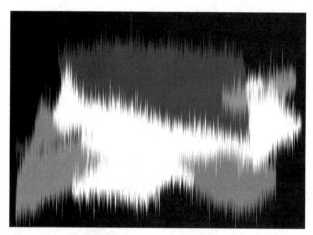

Figure 16-35: The result of rotating the image a quarter turn, blasting it in both directions with the Wind filter, rotating it back into place, and applying the Motion Blur filter vertically.

6. **Choose Filter ➭ Distort ➭ Wave.** Then enter the values shown in Figure 16-36 into the Wave option box. Most of these values are approximate. You can experiment with other settings if you like. The only essential value is 0 percent in the Vert. option box, which ensures the filter waves the image in a horizontal direction only.

7. **Choose Filter ➭ Distort ➭ Ocean Ripple.** I entered 15 for the Ripple Size and 5 for the Ripple Magnitude to get the effect shown in Figure 16-37.

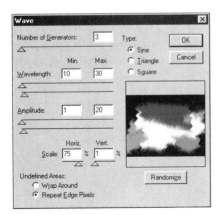

Figure 16-36: Apply these settings from the Wave dialog box to wave the image in a vertical direction only.

8. **Expand the canvas size.** To perform the next step, the Polar Coordinates filter needs lots of empty room in which to maneuver. If you filled up your canvas like I did, choose Image ⇨ Canvas Size and add 200 pixels both vertically and horizontally. The new canvas size, with generous borders, appears in Figure 16-37.

Figure 16-37: After applying the Ripple filter, use the Canvas Size command to add a generous amount of empty space around the image.

9. **Choose Filter ➪ Distort ➪ Polar Coordinates.** So far, you've probably been a little disappointed by your image. I mean, it's just this disgusting little hairy thing that looks like a bad rug or something. Well, now's your chance to turn it into something special. Choose Filter ➪ Distort ➪ Polar Coordinates and select the Polar to Rectangular radio button. Photoshop, in effect, turns the image inside out, sending all the hairy edges to the bottom of the screen. Finally, an image worth waiting for.

10. **Choose Image ➪ Rotate Canvas ➪ Flip Vertical.** This turns the image upside down. As I believe Hemingway said, the hair also rises, as shown in Figure 16-38. This step prepares the image for the next major polar conversion, due in the year 2096.

Figure 16-38: Convert the image from polar to rectangular coordinates to turn it inside out. Then flip it vertically to prepare it for the next polar conversion.

11. **Use the rectangular marquee tool to select the central portion of the image.** Leave about 50 pixels along the top and bottom of the image deselected, as well as 100 pixels along both sides. Then feather the selection with a 15-pixel radius.

12. **Press Ctrl+F to reapply the Polar Coordinates filter using the same settings as before.** Okay, so it happened before 2096. How could I have known? The pixels inside the selection now billow into a fountain.

13. **Add Moses to taste.** The finished image appears in Figure 16-39.

Figure 16-39: Marquee the central portion of the image with a heavily feathered selection outline, convert the selection from rectangular to polar coordinates, and put Moses into the scene. My, doesn't he look natural in his new environment?

Adding Clouds and Spotlights

In a way, you can think of all five filters in the Filter ➪ Render submenu as lighting filters. You can use Clouds and Difference Clouds to create a layer of haze over an image. Lens Flare creates light flashes and reflections (as I mentioned earlier). Lighting Effects lights an image as if it were hanging on a gallery wall. You can even use the unremarkable Texture Fill command to add an embossed texture to a piece lighted with the Lighting Effects filter. Together, these five suggest a new category called *creative filters*, but it's too early to tell.

Creating clouds

If you've played with the Clouds filters at all, you probably thought, "Hmf," and gave them up for a screwy feature Adobe's programmers decided to add in lieu of some meatier functions. Certainly these filters don't qualify as groundbreaking, but they're not at all bad and can yield some pretty entertaining results.

Clouds create an abstract and random haze of color between the foreground and background colors. Difference Clouds works exactly like layering the image, applying the Clouds filter, and selecting the Difference blend mode in the Layers palette.

Why on earth should this filter make special provisions for a single blend mode? Because you can create cumulative effects. Try this: Select blue as the foreground color and then choose Filter ➪ Render ➪ Clouds. Ah, just like a real sky, huh? Now choose Filter ➪ Render ➪ Difference Clouds. It's like some kind of weird Halloween motif, all blacks and oranges. Press Ctrl+F to repeat the filter. Back to the blue sky. Keep pressing Ctrl+F over and over and notice the results. A pink cancer starts invading the blue sky; a green cancer invades the orange one. Multiple applications of the Difference Clouds filter generate organic oil-on-water effects.

Tip

To strengthen the colors created by the Clouds filter, press Shift when choosing the command. This same technique works when using the Difference Clouds filter as well. In fact, I don't know of any reason not to Shift+choose these commands, unless you have some specific need for washed-out effects.

Color Plate 16-9 shows some pretty entertaining applications of the Clouds filters. With the foreground and background colors set to blue and orange, respectively, I applied the Clouds filter to a layered copy of the rose image. For maximum effect, I Shift+chose the filter to create the top-left image in the color plate. I then Shift+chose the Difference Clouds filter to create the purple montage in the figure, and pressed Ctrl+F ten times to achieve the top-right image. Looks to me like I definitely have something growing in my Petri dish.

Yeah, so really groovy stuff, right? Shades of "Purple Haze" and all that. But now that I've created this murky mess, what the heck do I do with it? Composite it, of course. The bottom row of Color Plate 16-9 shows examples of mixing each of the images from the top row with the original rose. In the left example, I chose the Overlay option from the blend mode pop-up menu in the Layers palette. In the middle example, I chose the Screen mode. And in the last example, I chose Hue. This last one is particularly exciting, completely transforming the colors in the rose while leaving the gray (and, therefore, unsaturated) background untouched. Without a mask, without anything but a rectangular marquee, I've managed to precisely color the interior of the rose.

Lighting an image

Photoshop is definitely venturing into 3D drawing territory with the Lighting Effects filter. This complex function enables you to shine lights on an image, color the lights, position them, focus them, specify the reflectivity of the surface, and even create a surface map. In many ways, it's a direct lift from Fractal Design Painter. But whereas Painter provides predefined paper textures and light refraction effects that bolster the capabilities of its excellent tool, Photoshop offers better controls and more lighting options.

Note   The Lighting Effects filter is applicable exclusively to RGB images.

When you choose Filter ➪ Render ➪ Lighting Effects, Photoshop displays what is easily its most complex dialog box, as shown in Figure 16-40. The dialog box has two halves: one in which you actually position light with respect to a thumbnail of the selected image, and one that contains about a billion intimidating options. Between us, I think Adobe could have done a better job, but the dialog box is functional.

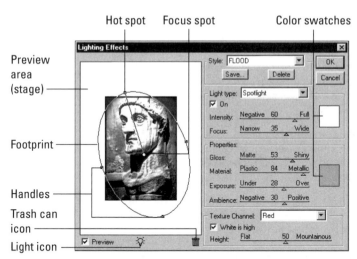

Figure 16-40: The Lighting Effects dialog box enables you to light an image as if it were hanging in a gallery, lying on a floor, or, perhaps, resting too near a hot flame.

No bones about it, this dialog box is a bear. The easiest way to apply the filter is to choose one of the predefined lighting effects from the Style pop-up menu at the top of the right side of the dialog box, see how it looks in the preview area, and — if you like it — press Enter to apply the effect.

But if you want to create your own effects, you'll have to work a little harder. Here are the basic steps involved in creating a custom effect.

Steps: Lighting an Image

1. **Drag from the light icon at the bottom of the dialog box into the preview area to create a new light source.** I call this area the stage because it's as if the image is painted on the floor of a stage and the lights are hanging above it.

2. **Select the kind of light you want from the Light Type pop-up menu.** It's just below the Style pop-up menu. You can select from Directional, Omni, and Spotlight:

   ✦ *Directional* works like the sun, being a general, unfocused light that hits a target from an angle.

   ✦ *Omni* is a bare light bulb hanging in the middle of the room, shining in all directions from a center point.

   ✦ And *Spotlight* is a focused beam that is brightest at the source and tapers off gradually.

3. **Specify the color of the light by clicking the top color swatch.** You can also muck about with the Intensity slider bar to control the brightness of the light. If Spotlight is selected, the Focus slider becomes available. Drag the slider toward Narrow to create a bright laser of light; drag toward Wide to diffuse the light and spread it over a larger area.

4. **Move the light source by dragging at the *focus point* (the colored circle in the stage).** When Directional or Spotlight is selected, the focus point represents the spot at which the light is pointing. When Omni is active, the focus point is the actual bulb. (Don't burn yourself.)

5. **If Directional or Spotlight is active, you can change the angle of the light by dragging the hot spot.** The *hot spot* represents the location in the image liable to receive the most light. When you use a Directional light, the hot spot appears as a black square at the end of a line joined to the focus point. The same holds true when you edit a Spotlight; the confusing thing is there are four black squares altogether. The light source is joined to the focus point by a line, the three *handles* are not.

Tip   To make the light brighter, drag the hot spot closer to the focus point. Dragging the hot spot away from the focus point dims the light by increasing the distance it must travel. It's like putting a flashlight in the living room when you're in the garage — the light gets dimmer as you move farther away from it.

6. **With Omni or Spotlight in force, you can edit the elliptical footprint of the light.** When Omni is in force, a circle surrounds the focus point. When editing a Spotlight, you see an ellipse. Either way, this shape represents the *footprint* of the light, which is the approximate area of the image affected by the light. You can change the size of the light by dragging the handles around the footprint. Enlarging the shape is like raising the light source. When the footprint is small, the light is close to the image, so it's concentrated and bright. When the footprint is large, the light is high above the image, so it's more generalized.

Tip   When editing the footprint of a Spotlight, Shift+drag a handle to adjust the width or height of the ellipse without affecting the angle. To change the angle without affecting the size, Ctrl+drag a handle.

7. **Introduce more lights as you see fit.** You can take advantage of a bunch of different techniques as you add and subtract lights from the stage. Press the Tab key to switch from one light to the next. You can duplicate a light in the stage by Alt+dragging its focus point. To delete the active light, press the Delete key. Or, if you prefer, you can drag the focus point onto the trash can icon at the bottom of the dialog box.

8. **Change the Properties and Texture Channel options as you see fit.** I explain these in detail after the steps.

9. **If you want to save your settings for future use, click the Save button.** Photoshop invites you to name the setup, which then appears as an option in the Style pop-up menu. If you want to eliminate one of the presets, select it from the pop-up menu and click the Delete button.

10. **Press Enter to apply your settings to the image.**

That's almost everything. The only parts I left out are the Properties and Texture Channel options. The *Properties slider bars* control how light reflects off the surface of your image:

✦ **Gloss:** Is the surface dull or shiny? Drag the slider toward Matte to make the surface flat and nonreflective, like dull enamel paint. Drag the slider toward Shiny to make it glossy, as if you had slapped on a coat of lacquer.

✦ **Material:** This option determines the color of the light that reflects back off the image. According to the logic employed by this option, Plastic reflects back the color of the light; Metallic reflects the color of the object itself. If only I had a bright, shiny plastic thing and a bright, shiny metal thing, I could check to see if this logic holds true in real life (like maybe that matters).

✦ **Exposure:** I'd like this option better if you could vary it between Sun Block 65 and Melanoma. Unfortunately, the more prosaic titles are Under and Over, exposed, that is. This option controls the brightness of all lights like a big dimmer switch. You can control a single selected light using the Intensity slider, but the Exposure slider offers the added control of changing all lights in the stage area and the ambient light (described next) together.

✦ **Ambience:** The last slider enables you to add *ambient light,* which is a general, diffused light that hits all surfaces evenly. First, select the color of the light by clicking the color swatch to the right. Then drag the slider to cast a subtle hue over the stage. Drag toward Positive to tint the image with the color in the swatch; drag toward Negative to tint the stage with the swatch's opposite. Keep the slider set to 0 — dead in the center — to cast no hue.

The Texture Channel options enable you to treat one channel in the image as a *texture map,* a grayscale surface in which white indicates peaks and black indicates valleys. (As long as White is High is selected, that is. If you deselect that option, everything flips, and black becomes the peak.) It's as if one channel has a surface. By selecting a channel from the pop-up menu, you create an emboss effect, much like that created with the Emboss filter, except much better because you can light the surface from many angles at once, and it's in color to boot.

Choose a channel to serve as the embossed surface from the pop-up menu. Then change the Height slider to indicate more or less Flat terrain or huge Mountainous cliffs of surface texture.

Color Plate 16-10 shows an image lit with a total of five spotlights, two from above and three from below. In the first example, I left the Texture Channel option set to None. In the second example, I selected the green channel as the surface map. And in the third example, I filled a separate mask channel with a bunch of white and black dollops using Filter ➪ Pixelate ➪ Pointillize, then I selected the mask from the Texture Channel pop-up menu in the Lighting Effects dialog box. The result is a wonderfully rough paper texture.

Constructing Homemade Effects

Creating a Custom Effect

If my wife were here right now, she might be tempted to say something diplomatic like, "Deke, dear, I think our guests are growing a teeny bit tired of the subject of filters. Perhaps this would be a good time to move on to a new subject." To which I would respond, "Nonsense! Folks love to listen to me drone on and on about filters. I can't imagine anything more intriguing, can you? Speaking of which, is there any beer left in this house? (Urp.)" Whether you share my fascination with filters, don't get up and go home, because I've yet to tell you about three very important filters — Custom, Displace, and the Filter Factory — that enable you to create your own custom-tailored special effects.

Fully understanding the Custom and Displace filters requires some mathematical reasoning skills — and even if you're a math whiz, you'll probably have occasional difficulty predicting the outcomes of these filters. Using the Filter Factory requires flat-out programming skills. If math isn't your bag, if number theory clogs up your synapses to the extent you feel like a worthless math wimp, by all means don't put yourself through the torture. Skip all the mathematical background in this chapter and read the "Applying Custom Values" and "Using Displacement Maps" sections to try out some specific, no-brainer effects.

Cross Reference If you have no desire to learn the Filter Factory, you can experiment with some filters I programmed using this plug-in. On the CD-ROM at the back of this book, you'll find several fully functioning filters, all of which include interactive slider bars and previews. If you copy the filters (found in the Filters/Torment folder on the CD) to your Plugins folder and launch Photoshop, you'll see my filters in the Filter ➪ Tormentia submenu. (These filters torment your image in a demented way, hence, *Tormentia.* I also considered *Tormento,* but that sounds like something you'd put on your pizza.) I explain what the filters do and how they work in Appendix E.

On the other hand, if you're not scared silly of math and you want to understand how to create effects of your own eventually, read on, you hearty soul.

The Custom filter

The Custom command enables you to design your own *convolution kernel,* which is a variety of filter in which neighboring pixels get mixed together. The kernel can be a variation on sharpening, blurring, embossing, or a half dozen other effects. You create your filter by entering numerical values into a matrix of options.

When you choose Filter ➪ Other ➪ Custom, Photoshop displays the dialog box shown in Figure 17-1. It sports a 5 × 5 matrix of option boxes followed by two additional options, Scale and Offset. The matrix options can accept values from negative to positive 999. The Scale value can range from 1 to 9,999, and the Offset value can range from negative to positive 9,999. The dialog box includes Load and Save buttons so you can load settings from disk and save the current settings for future use.

Like most of Photoshop's filters, the Custom filter also includes a constantly updating preview box, which you'll have lots of time to appreciate if you decide to try your hand at designing your own effects. Select the Preview check box to view the effect of the kernel in the Image window as well.

Here's how the filter works: When you press Enter to apply the values in the Custom dialog box to a selection, the filter passes over every pixel in the selection, one at a time. For each pixel being evaluated — which I'll call the PBE, for short — the filter multiplies the PBE's current brightness value by the number in the center option box (the one containing a 5 in Figure 17-1). To help keep things straight, I'll call this value the CMV, for *central matrix value.*

The filter then multiplies the brightness values of the surrounding pixels by the surrounding values in the matrix. For example, Photoshop multiplies the value in the option box above the CMV by the brightness value of the pixel above the PBE. It ignores any empty matrix option boxes and the pixels they represent.

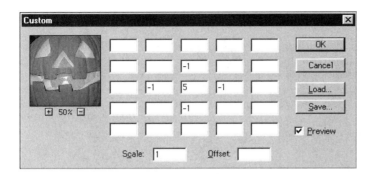

Figure 17-1: The Custom dialog box enables you to design your own convolution kernel by multiplying the brightness values of pixels.

Finally, the filter totals the products of the multiplied pixels, divides the sum by the value in the Scale option, and adds the Offset value to calculate the new brightness of the PBE. It then moves on to the next pixel in the selection and performs the calculation all over again. Figure 17-2 shows a schematic drawing of the process.

Perhaps seeing all of this spelled out in an equation will help you understand the process. Then again, perhaps not — but here it comes anyway. In the following equation, NP stands for *neighboring pixel* and MV stands for the corresponding *matrix value* in the Custom dialog box.

New brightness value = (((PBE x CMV) + (NP1 x MV1) + (NP2 x MV2) + . . .) ÷ Scale) + Offset

Luckily, Photoshop calculates the equation without any help from you. All you have to do is punch in the values and see what happens.

Custom filter advice

Now obviously, if you go around multiplying the brightness value of a pixel too much, you end up making it white. And a filter that turns an image white is pretty darn useless. The key, then, is to filter an image and, at the same time, maintain the original balance of brightness values. To achieve this, be sure the sum of all values in the matrix is 1. For example, the default values in the matrix shown back in Figure 17-1 are 5, -1, -1, -1, and -1, which add up to 1.

If the sum is greater than 1, use the Scale value to divide the sum down to 1. Figures 17-3 and 17-4 show the results of increasing the CMV from 5 to 6 and then to 7. This raises the sum of the values in the matrix from 1 to 2 and then to 3.

In Figure 17-3, I entered the sum into the Scale option to divide the sum back down to 1 (any value divided by itself is 1, after all). The result is Photoshop maintains the original color balance of the image and, at the same time, filters it slightly differently. When I did not raise the Scale value, the image became progressively lighter, as illustrated in Figure 17-4.

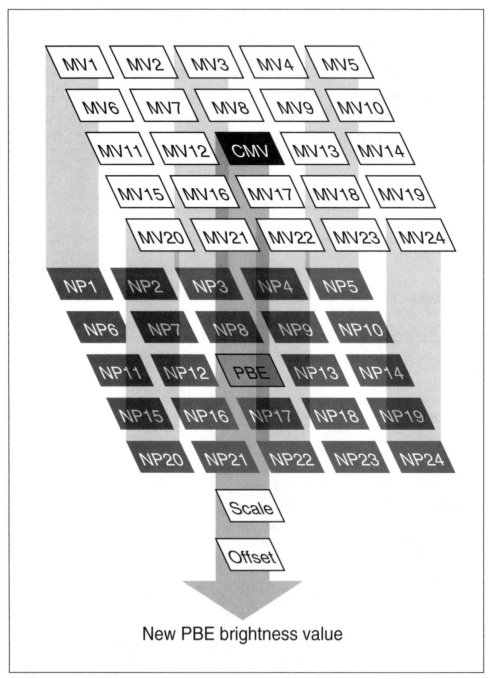

Figure 17-2: The Custom filter multiplies each matrix value by the brightness value of the corresponding pixel, adds the products together, divides the sum by the Scale value, adds the Offset value, and applies the result to the pixel being evaluated.

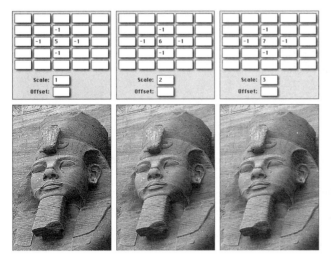

Figure 17-3: Raising the Scale value to reflect the sum of the values in the matrix maintains the color balance of the image.

If the sum is less than 1, increase the CMV until the sum reaches the magic number. For example, in Figure 17-5, I lowered the values to the left of the CMV and then above the CMV by 1 apiece to increase the sharpening effect. To ensure the image did not darken, I also raised the CMV to compensate. When I did not raise the CMV, the image turned black, as shown in Figure 17-6.

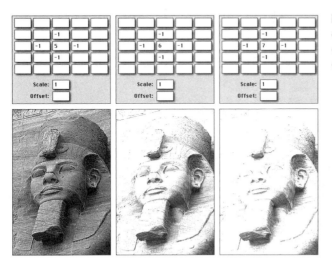

Figure 17-4: Raising the sum of the matrix values without counterbalancing it in the Scale option lightens the image.

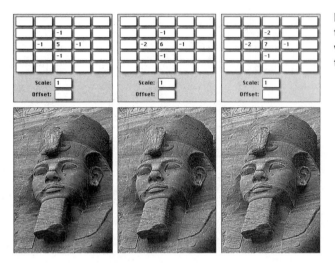

Figure 17-5: Raising the CMV to compensate for the lowered values in the matrix maintains the color balance of the image.

Tip

Although a sum of 1 provides the safest and most predictable filtering effects, you can use different sums, such as 0 and 2, to try out more destructive filtering effects. If you do, be sure to raise or lower the Offset value to compensate. For some examples, see the "Non-1 variations" section.

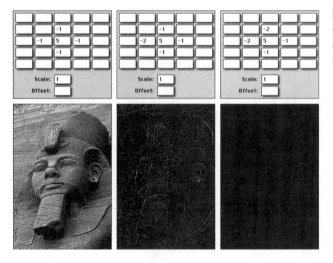

Figure 17-6: Lowering the sum of the matrix values without counterbalancing them with the CMV darkens the image.

Applying Custom Values

The following sections show you ways to sharpen, blur, and, otherwise, filter an image using specific matrix, Scale, and Offset values. My sincere hope is, by the end of the Custom filter discussions, you not only will know how to repeat my examples, but also how to apply what you've learned to design special effects of your own.

Symmetrical effects

Values that are symmetrical both horizontally and vertically about the central matrix value produce sharpen and blur effects:

✦ **Sharpening:** A positive CMV surrounded by symmetrical negative values sharpens an image, as demonstrated in the first example of Figure 17-7. Figures 17-3 through 17-6 also demonstrate varying degrees of sharpening effects.

✦ **Blurring:** A positive CMV surrounded by symmetrical positive numbers — balanced, of course, by a Scale value as explained in the preceding section — blurs an image, as demonstrated in the second example of Figure 17-7.

✦ **Blurring with edge-detection:** A negative CMV surrounded by symmetrical positive values blurs an image and adds an element of edge-detection, as illustrated in the last example of the figure. These effects are unlike anything provided by Photoshop's standard collection of filters.

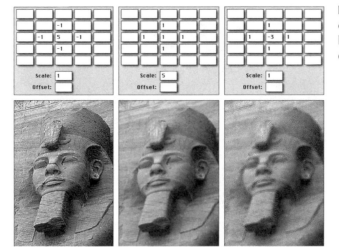

Figure 17-7: Symmetrical values can result in sharpening (left), blurring (middle), and edge-detection (right) effects.

Sharpening

The Custom command provides as many variations on the sharpening theme as the Unsharp Mask filter. In a sense, it provides even more, for whereas the Unsharp Mask filter requires you to sharpen an image inside a Gaussian radius, you get to specify exactly which pixels are taken into account when you use the Custom filter.

To create Unsharp Mask-like effects, enter a large number in the CMV and small values in the surrounding option boxes, as demonstrated in Figure 17-8. To go beyond Unsharp Mask, you can violate the radius of the filter by entering values around the perimeter of the matrix and ignoring options closer to the CMV, as demonstrated in Figure 17-9.

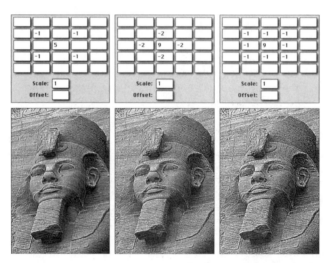

Figure 17-8: To create severe sharpening effects, enter a CMV just large enough to compensate for the negative values in the matrix.

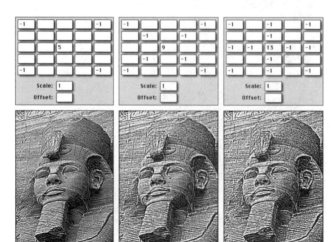

Figure 17-9: To heighten the sharpening effect even further, enter negative values around the perimeter of the matrix.

You can sharpen an image using the Custom dialog box in two basic ways. First, you can enter lots of negative values into the neighboring options in the matrix and then enter a CMV just large enough to yield a sum of 1. This results in radical sharpening effects, as demonstrated throughout the examples in Figures 17-8 and 17-9.

Second, you can tone down the sharpening by raising the CMV and using the Scale value to divide the sum down to 1. Figures 17-10 and 17-11 show the results of raising the CMV to lessen the impact of the sharpening effects performed in Figures 17-8 and 17-9.

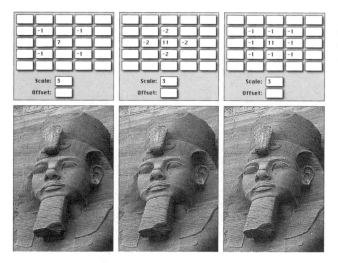

Figure 17-10: To sharpen more subtly, increase the central matrix value and then enter the sum into the Scale value.

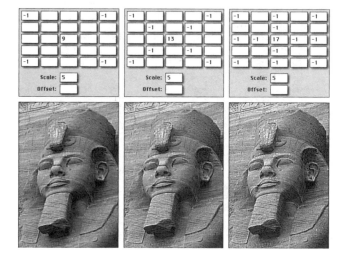

Figure 17-11: When you soften the effect of radical sharpening, you create a thicker, higher contrast effect, much as when raising the Radius value in the Unsharp Mask dialog box.

Blurring

The philosophy behind blurring is much the same as that behind sharpening. To produce extreme blurring effects, enter lots of values or high values into the neighboring options in the matrix, enter 1 into the CMV, and then enter the sum into the Scale option. Examples appear in Figure 17-12. To downplay the blurring, raise the CMV and the Scale value by equal amounts. In Figure 17-13, I used the same neighboring values as in Figure 17-12, but I increased the CMV and the Scale value by 3 apiece.

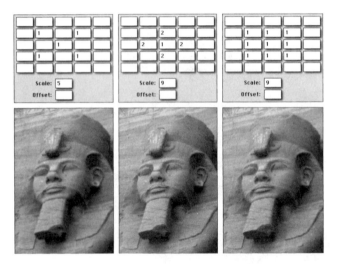

Figure 17-12: To create severe blurring effects, enter 1 for the CMV and fill the neighboring options with 1s and 2s.

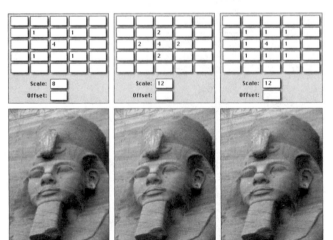

Figure 17-13: To blur more subtly, increase the central matrix value and the Scale value by equal amounts.

Edge-detection

Many of you are probably beginning to get the idea by now but, in case you're the kind of person who believes friends don't let friends do math, I'll breeze through this one more time in the venue of edge-detection. If you really want to see those edges, enter 1s and 2s into the neighboring options in the matrix and then enter a CMV small enough — it's a negative value, after all — to make the sum 1. Examples appear in Figure 17-14 for your viewing pleasure.

To lighten the edges and bring out the blur, raise the CMV and enter the resulting sum into the Scale option box. The first example in Figure 17-15 pushes the boundaries between edge-detection and a straight blur.

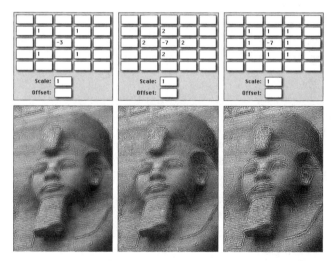

Figure 17-14: To create severe edge-detection effects, enter a negative CMV small enough to compensate for the positive values in the matrix.

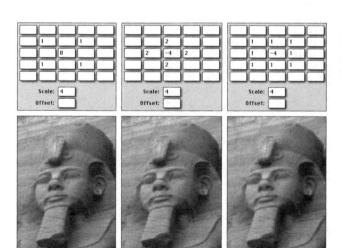

Figure 17-15: To blur the edges, increase the central matrix value and then enter the sum into the Scale value.

Non-1 variations

Every image shown in Figures 17-7 through 17-15 is the result of manipulating matrix values and using the Scale option to produce a sum total of 1. Earlier in this chapter, I showed you what can happen if you go below 1 (black images) or above 1 (white images). But I haven't shown you how you can use non-1 totals to produce interesting, if somewhat washed out, effects.

The key is to raise the Offset value, thereby adding a specified brightness value to each pixel in the image. By doing this, you can offset the lightening or darkening caused by the matrix values to create an image with half a chance of printing.

Lightening overly dark effects

The first image in Figure 17-16 uses nearly the exact values used to create the extreme sharpening effect in the last image of Figure 17-8. The only difference is the CMV is 1 lower (8, down from 9), which, in turn, lowers the sum total from 1 to 0.

The result is an extremely dark image with hints of brightness at points of high contrast. The image looks okay onscreen — actually, it looks pretty cool because of all those little starlike sprinkles in it — but it's likely to fill in during the printing process. If the first image in Figure 17-16 looks like anything but a vague blob of blackness, it's a credit to the printer of this book. Most printers who didn't have a giant publisher breathing down their necks would have kissed this image good-bye, and rightly so. It's too darn dark.

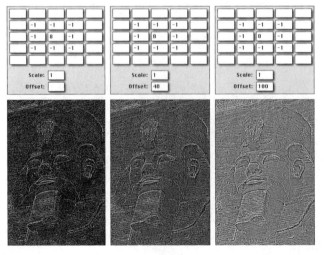

Figure 17-16: Three examples of sharpening effects with sum totals of 0. I lightened the images incrementally by entering positive values into the Offset option box.

To prevent the image from filling in and to help head off any disputes with your printer, lighten the image using the Offset value. Photoshop adds the value to the brightness level of each selected pixel. A brightness value of 255 equals solid white, so you don't need to go too high. As illustrated by the last example in

Figure 17-16, an Offset value of 100 is enough to raise most pixels in the image to a medium gray. Figure 17-17 shows the results of lightening an overly dark edge-detection effect using the Offset value.

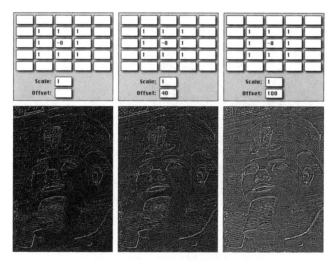

Figure 17-17: Three examples of edge-detection effects with sum totals of 0. I lightened the image incrementally by using progressively higher Offset values.

Darkening overly light effects

You also can use the Offset value to darken filtering effects with sum totals greater than 1. The images in Figures 17-18 and 17-19 show sharpening and edge-detection effects whose matrix totals amount to 2. On their own, these filters produce effects that are too light. However, as demonstrated in the middle and right examples in the figures, you can darken the effects of the Custom filter to create high-contrast images by entering a negative value into the Offset option box.

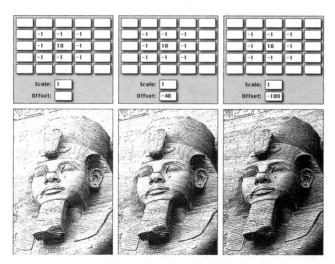

Figure 17-18: Three examples of sharpening effects with sum totals of 2. I darkened the images incrementally by entering negative values into the Offset option box.

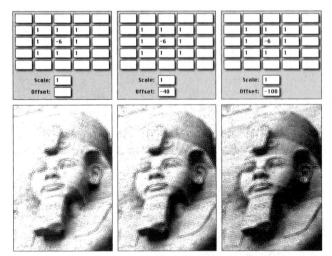

Figure 17-19: Three examples of edge-detection effects with sum totals of 2. I darkened the images incrementally with progressively lower Offset values.

Using extreme offsets

If a brightness value of 255 produces solid white, and a brightness value of 0 is solid black, why in blue blazes does the Offset value permit any number between negative and positive 9,999, a number 40 times greater than solid white? Because the matrix options can force the Custom filter to calculate brightness values much darker than black and much lighter than white. Therefore, you can use a very high or very low Offset value to boost the brightness of an image in which all pixels are well below black or diminish the brightness when all pixels are way beyond white.

Figure 17-20 shows exaggerated versions of the sharpening, blurring, and edge-detection effects. The sum totals of the matrixes are -42, 54, and 42, respectively. Without some help from the Offset value, each of these filters would turn every pixel in the image black (in the case of the sharpening effect) or white (blurring and edge-detection). But as demonstrated in the figure, using enormous Offset numbers brings out those few remaining brightness values. The images are so polarized, there's hardly any difference between the three effects, except the first image is an inverted version of the other two. The difference is even less noticeable if you lower the Opacity of the effect using Filter ➪ Fade, as demonstrated in the second row of examples in Figure 17-20.

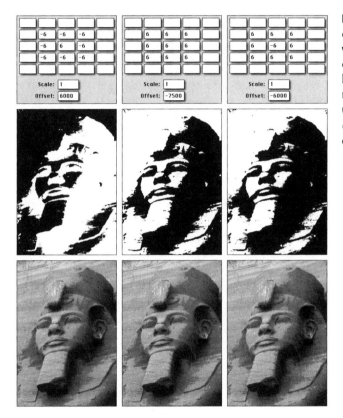

Figure 17-20: You can create high-contrast effects by exaggerating all values in the matrix and then compensating by entering a very high or very low Offset value (top row). When you back off the effect using Filter ➪ Fade Custom (bottom row), these dramatic effects are barely discernible.

Other custom effects

By now, I hope you understand what an absolute trip the Custom filter can be, provided you immerse yourself in the old adventurous spirit. Quite honestly, I could keep showing you ways to use the Custom filter for another 20 or 30 pages. But then my publisher would come unglued because I'd never finish the book, and you'd miss the pleasure of discovering variations on your own.

Nonetheless, you're probably wondering what happens if you go absolutely berserk, in a computer geek sort of way, and start entering matrix values in unusual, or even arbitrary, arrangements. The answer is, as long as you maintain a sum total of 1, you achieve some pretty interesting and even usable effects. Many of these effects will be simple variations on sharpening, blurring, and edge-detection.

Directional blurs

Figure 17-21 shows examples of entering positive matrix values all in one row, all in a column, or in opposite quadrants. As you can see, as long as you maintain uniformly positive values, you get a blurring effect. By keeping the values lowest in the center and highest toward the edges and corners, though, you can create directional blurs. The first example resembles a slight horizontal motion blur, the second looks like a slight vertical motion blur, and the last example looks like it's vibrating horizontally and vertically.

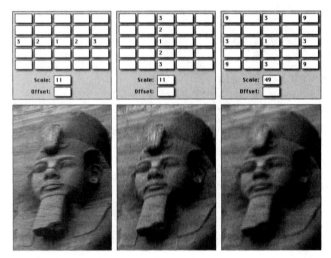

Figure 17-21: Enter positive matrix values in a horizontal formation (left) or vertical formation (middle) to create slight motion blurs. By positioning positive values in opposite corners of the matrix, you create a vibrating effect (right).

Directional sharpening

To sharpen edges selectively in an image based on the angles of the edges, you can organize negative and positive matrix values into rows or columns. For example, to sharpen only the horizontal edges in an image, fill the middle row of matrix options with positive values and the rows immediately above and below with negative values, as demonstrated in the left example in Figure 17-22. Similarly, you can sharpen only the vertical edges by entering positive values in the middle column and flanking the column on the left and right with negative values, as shown in the middle example in the figure. In the last example, I arranged the positive values along a diagonal axis to sharpen only the diagonal edges.

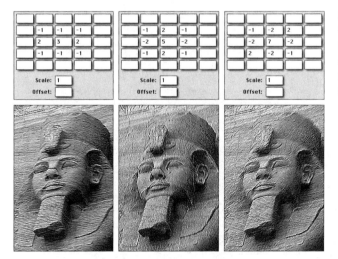

Figure 17-22: Arrange positive values in a row (left), column (middle), or along a diagonal axis (right) to sharpen horizontal, vertical, and diagonal edges exclusively.

You can even combine directional sharpening with directional blurring. Figure 17-23 shows the first example from Figure 17-22 blurred both horizontally and vertically. To blur the image horizontally, as in the middle example of Figure 17-23, I added positive values to the extreme ends of the middle row, thereby extending the range of the filter and creating a sort of horizontal jumbling effect. To blur the image vertically, as in the final example of the figure, I added positive values to the ends of the middle column.

Embossing

So far, we aren't going very nuts, are we? Despite their unusual formations, the matrix values in Figures 17-21 through 17-23 still manage to maintain symmetry. Well, now it's time to lose the symmetry, which typically results in an embossing effect.

Figure 17-24 shows three variations on embossing, all of which involve positive and negative matrix values positioned on opposite sides of the CMV. (The CMV happens to be positive merely to maintain a sum total of 1.)

This type of embossing has no hard-and-fast light source, but you might imagine the light comes from the general direction of the positive values. When I swapped the positive and negative values throughout the matrix (all except the CMV), I approximated an underlighting effect, as demonstrated by the images in Figure 17-25.

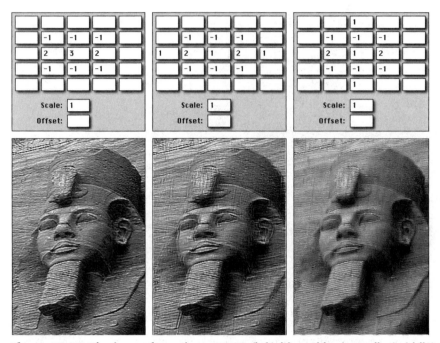

Figure 17-23: The image from Figure 17-22 (left) blurred horizontally (middle) and vertically (right)

In truth, it's not so much a lighting difference as a difference in edge enhancement. White pixels collect on the side of an edge represented by positive values in the matrix; black pixels collect on the negative-value side. So when I swapped the locations of positive and negative values between Figures 17-24 and 17-25, I changed the distribution of white and black pixels in the filtered images.

Embossing is the loosest of the Custom filter effects. As long as you position positive and negative values on opposite sides of the CMV, you can distribute the values in almost any way you see fit. Figure 17-26 demonstrates three entirely arbitrary arrangements of values in the Custom matrix. Figure 17-27 shows those same effects downplayed by raising the CMV and entering the sum of the matrix values into the Scale option box.

Incidentally, the main advantage of using the Custom filter rather than using Filter ➪ Stylize ➪ Emboss to produce embossing effects is Custom preserves the colors in an image, while Emboss sacrifices color and changes low-contrast portions of an image to gray. Color Plate 17-1 shows the matrix values from the first example of Figure 17-26 applied to a color image. It also shows examples of other Custom effects, including variations on sharpening and edge-detection.

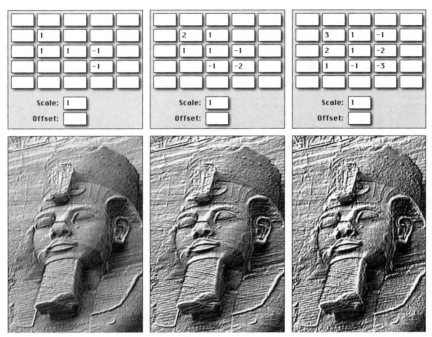

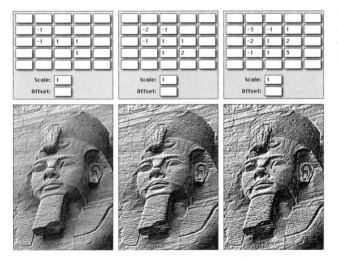

Figure 17-24: You can create embossing effects by distributing positive and negative values on opposite sides of the central matrix value.

Figure 17-25: Change the location of positive and negative matrix values to change the general direction of the light source.

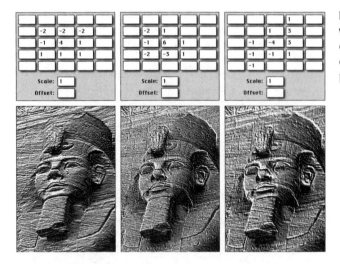

Figure 17-26: You can create whole libraries of embossing effects by experimenting with different combinations of positive and negative values.

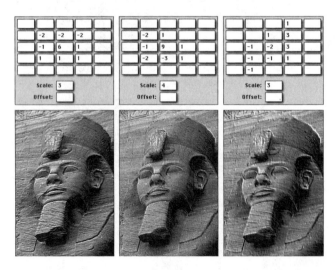

Figure 17-27: To emboss more subtly, increase the central matrix value and the Scale values by equal amounts.

If you become enthralled with convolution kernels and you feel compelled to explore them in more detail, you may want to check out a $200 plug-in called KPT Convolver from MetaTools. Although steeply priced, Convolver enables you to explore convolutions using a more intuitive interface and without using any math. Convolver doesn't do anything you can't already do with the Custom filter, but it can simultaneously apply different convolutions to separate color channels and enable you to investigate filtering possibilities you aren't likely to discover on your own.

Displacing Pixels in an Image

Photoshop's second custom effects filter is Filter ➪ Distort ➪ Displace, which enables you to distort and add texture to an image by moving the colors of certain pixels in a selection. You specify the direction and distance the Displace filter moves colors by creating a second image called a *displacement map,* or *dmap* (pronounced *dee-map*) for short. The brightness values in the displacement map tell Photoshop which pixels to affect and how far to move the colors of those pixels:

✦ **Black:** The black areas of the displacement map move the colors of corresponding pixels in the selection a maximum prescribed distance to the right and/or down. Lighter values between black and medium gray move colors a shorter distance in the same direction.

✦ **White:** The white areas move the colors of corresponding pixels a maximum distance to the left and/or up. Darker values between white and medium gray move colors a shorter distance in the same direction.

✦ **Medium gray:** A 50 percent brightness value, such as medium gray, ensures the colors of corresponding pixels remain unmoved.

Suppose I create a new Image window the same size as the scan of the Egyptian temple carving I've used about 60 times in this chapter. This new image will serve as the displacement map. I divide the image into four quadrants. As shown in the middle example of Figure 17-28, I fill the upper-left quadrant with black, the lower-right quadrant with white, and the other two quadrants with medium gray. (The arrows indicate the direction in which the quadrants will move colors in the affected image. They do not actually appear in the dmap.)

When finished, I save the dmap to disk in the native Photoshop format so the Displace filter can access it. I then return to the Egyptian carving image, choose Filter ➪ Distort ➪ Displace, edit the settings as desired, and open the dmap from disk. The result is the image shown in the last example of Figure 17-28. In keeping with the distribution of brightness values in the dmap, the colors of the pixels in the upper-left quadrant of the carving image move rightward, the colors of the pixels in the lower-right quadrant move to the left, and the colors in the upper-right and lower-left quadrant remain intact.

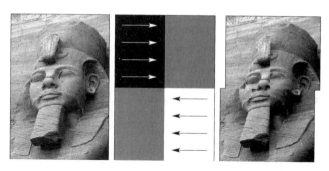

Figure 17-28: The Displace filter moves colors in an image (left) according to the brightness values in a separate image, called the displacement map (middle). The arrows indicate the direction the map moves colors in the image (right).

Note　A dmap must be a color or grayscale image; you must save the dmap in the native Photoshop file format and turn on the 2.5 Compatibility option found on the Saving Files panel of the Preferences dialog box. The Displace command does not recognize PICT, TIFF, or any of the other nonnative (albeit common) file formats. Who knows why? Those programmers move in mysterious ways.

At this point, you likely have two questions: How do you use the Displace filter, and why in the name of all that is good would you possibly want to use it? The hows of the Displace filter are covered in the following section. To discover some whys — which should, in turn, help you dream up some whys of your own — read the "Using Displacement Maps" section later in this chapter.

Displacement theory

Like any custom filtering effect worth its weight in table salt — an asset that has taken something of a nose dive in the recent millennium — you need a certain degree of mathematical reasoning skills to predict the outcome of the Displace filter. Although I was a math major in college (well, actually, I double-majored in math and fine arts, and I must admit to paying the lion's share of attention to the latter), I frankly was befuddled by the results of my first few experiments with the Displace command. Don't be surprised if you are, as well. With some time and a modicum of effort, though, you can learn to anticipate the approximate effects of this filter.

Direction of displacement

Earlier, I mentioned — and I quote — "The black areas of the displacement map move . . . colors . . . to the right and/or down . . . the white areas move . . . colors . . . to the left and/or up." Yikes, talk about your fragmented quotations. I think I'll sue! Anyway, the point is, you may have wondered to yourself what all this "and/or" guff was all about. "Is it right or is it down?" you may have puzzled, and rightly so.

The truth is, the direction of a displacement can go either way. It's up to you. If you like right, go with it. If you like down, don't let me stop you. If you like both together, by all means, have at it.

Beginning to understand? No? Well, it works like this: A dmap can contain one or more color channels. If the dmap is a grayscale image with one color channel only, the Displace filter moves colors that correspond to black areas in the dmap both to the right and down, depending on your specifications in the Displace dialog box. The filter moves colors that correspond to white areas in the dmap both to the left and up.

Figure 17-29 shows two examples of an image displaced using a single-channel dmap, which appears on the left side of the figure. (Again, the arrows illustrate the directions in which different brightness values move colors in the affected image. They are not part of the dmap file.) I displaced the middle image at 10 percent and the right image at 20 percent. The colors in the right image travel twice the distance as those in the middle image, therefore, but all colors travel the same direction. (The upcoming section "The Displace dialog box" explains exactly how the percentage values work.)

Figure 17-29: The results of applying a single-channel displacement map (left) to an image at 10 percent (middle) and 20 percent (right)

However, if the dmap contains more than one channel — whether it's a color image or a grayscale image with an independent mask channel — the first channel indicates horizontal displacement, and the second channel indicates vertical displacement. All other channels are ignored. So the Displace filter moves colors that correspond to black areas in the first channel of the dmap to the right and colors that correspond to white areas to the left. (Again, this depends on your specifications in the Displace dialog box.) The filter then moves colors that correspond to the black areas in the second channel downward and colors that correspond to white areas upward.

Figure 17-30 shows the effect of a two-channel dmap on our friend, the pharaoh. The top row shows the appearance and effect of the first channel on the image at 10 percent and 20 percent. The bottom row shows the appearance and effect of the second channel.

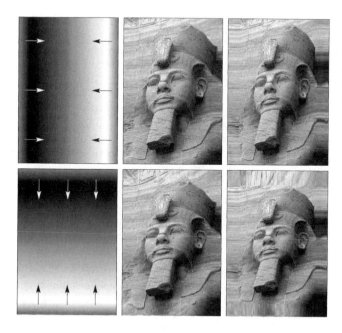

Figure 17-30: The horizontal (top row) and vertical (bottom row) results of applying a two-channel displacement map (left column) to an image at 10 percent (middle) and 20 percent (right)

Brightness value transitions

If you study Figure 17-30 for any length of time, you'll notice a marked stretching effect around the edges of the image, particularly around the two right images. This is an effect you want to avoid.

The cause of the effect is twofold: First, the transition from gray to black and gray to white pixels around the perimeter of the dmap is relatively quick, especially compared with the gradual transitions in the central portion of the image. Second, transitions — reading from left to right, or top to bottom — produce a more noticeable effect when they progress from light to dark than from dark to light. The reason for this is these transitions follow the direction of Photoshop's displacement algorithm. (I know, when I throw in a word like *algorithm*, everybody's eyes glaze over, but try to stick with me.)

For example, in the light-to-dark transition on the left side of the first-channel dmap in Figure 17-30, one gray value nudges selected colors slightly to the right, the next darker value nudges them an extra pixel, the next darker value another pixel, and so on, resulting in a machine gun displacement effect that creates a continuous stream of the same colors over and over again. Hence, the big stretch.

Get it? Well, if not, the important part is this: To avoid stretching an image, make your dmap transitions slow when progressing from light to dark and quick when progressing from dark to light. For example, in the revised dmap channels shown in the left column of Figure 17-31, the gray values progress slowly from gray to black, abruptly from black to gray to white, and then slowly again from white to gray. Slow light to dark, fast dark to light. The results are smoother image distortions, as demonstrated in the middle and right columns of the figure.

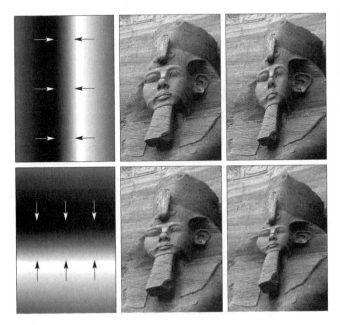

Figure 17-31: Changing the speeds of color transitions in the two-channel displacement map (left column) created smoother image distortions at both the 10 percent (middle) and 20 percent (right) settings.

The Displace dialog box

When you choose Filter ➪ Distort ➪ Displace, Photoshop displays the Displace dialog box. ("Displays the Displace" is the modern equivalent of "Begin the Beguine," don't you know.) As shown in Figure 17-32, the Displace dialog box provides the following options:

✦ **Scale:** You can specify the degree to which the Displace filter moves colors in an image by entering percentage values into the Horizontal Scale and Vertical Scale option boxes. At 100 percent, black and white areas in the dmap each have the effect of moving colors 128 pixels. That's 1 pixel per each brightness value over or under medium gray. You can isolate the effect of a single-channel dmap vertically or horizontally — or ignore the first or second channel of a two-channel dmap — by entering 0 percent into the Horizontal or Vertical option box, respectively.

Figure 17-33 shows the effect of distorting an image exclusively horizontally (top row) and vertically (bottom row) at each of three percentage values: 5 percent, 15 percent, and 30 percent. In each case, I used the two-channel dmap from Figure 17-31.

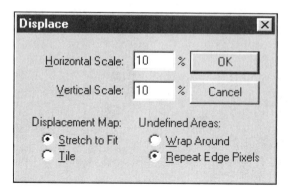

Figure 17-32: Use these options to specify the degree of distortion, how the filter matches the displacement map to the image, and how it colors the pixels around the perimeter of the selection.

Figure 17-33: Here are the results of applying the Distort filter exclusively horizontally (top row) and exclusively vertically (bottom row) at 5 percent (left column), 15 percent (middle), and 30 percent (right).

✦ **Displacement Map:** If the dmap contains fewer pixels than the image, you can either scale it to match the size of the selected image by selecting the Stretch to Fit radio button or repeat the dmap over and over within the image by selecting Tile. Figure 17-34 shows a small two-channel dmap that contains radial gradations. In the first column, I stretched the dmap to fit the image. In the second column, I tiled the dmap. To create both examples in the top row, I set the Horizontal Scale and Vertical Scale values to 10 percent. To create the bottom-row examples, I raised the values to 50 percent.

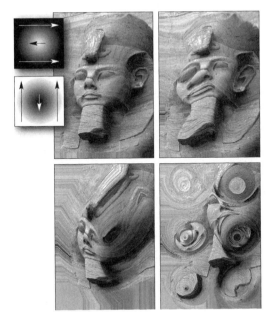

Figure 17-34: Using a small, two-channel dmap (offset top left), I stretched the dmap to fit (left column) and tiled it (right column) at 10 percent (top row) and 50 percent (bottom row).

✦ **Undefined Areas:** These radio buttons enable you to tell Photoshop how to color pixels around the outskirts of the selection that are otherwise undefined. By default, the Repeat Edge Pixels radio button is selected, which repeats the colors of pixels around the perimeter of the selection. This can result in extreme stretching effects, as shown in the middle example of Figure 17-35. To repeat the image inside the undefined areas instead, as demonstrated in the final example of the figure, select the Wrap Around option.

Tip

The Repeat Edge Pixels setting was active in all displacement map figures prior to Figure 17-35. In these cases, I frequently avoided stretching effects by coloring the edges of the dmap with medium gray and gradually lightening or darkening the brightness values toward the center.

Figure 17-35: After creating a straightforward, single-channel displacement map (left), I applied the filter subject to two different Undefined Areas settings, Repeat Edge Pixels (middle) and Wrap Around (right).

After you finish specifying options in the Displace dialog box, press Enter to display a variation of the Open dialog box, where you can select the displacement map saved to disk. Only native Photoshop documents show up in the scrolling list.

Using Displacement Maps

So far, all the displacement maps demonstrated involve gradations of one form or another. Gradient dmaps distort the image over the contours of a fluid surface, like a reflection in a fun-house mirror. In this respect, the effects of the Displace filter closely resemble those of the Pinch and Spherize filters described in the last chapter. But the more functional and straightforward application of the Displace filter is to add texture to an image.

Creating texture effects

Figure 17-36 shows the results of using the Displace filter to apply nine of the patterns from the Dispmaps folder inside the Photoshop/Plugins/Filters folder. Color Plate 17-2 shows the effects of applying four of the patterns to color images. Introduced in Chapter 10, this folder contains repeating patterns Adobe designed especially with the Displace filter in mind.

As shown in the figure and color plate, most of these patterns produce the effect of viewing the image through textured glass — an effect known in high-end graphics circles as *glass refraction*. Those few patterns containing too much contrast to pass off as textured glass — including Fragment layers, Mezzo effect, and Schnable effect — can be employed to create images that appear as if they were printed on coarse paper or even textured metal.

To view each of the textures from the Displacement Maps folder on its own, see Figure 10-14 in the "How to create patterns" section of Chapter 10. Like Figure 17-36, Figure 10-14 is labeled so you can easily match texture and effect.

When using a repeating pattern — including any of the images inside the Displacement Maps folder — as a dmap, be sure to select the Tile radio button inside the Displace dialog box. This repeats the dmap rather than stretching it out of proportion.

I also explained in Chapter 10 that you can create your own textures from scratch using filtering effects. I specifically described how to create a stucco texture by applying the Add Noise filter three times in a row to an empty image and then using the Emboss filter to give it depth. (See the "Using filters" item in the "How to create patterns" section.) This texture appears in the first example of Figure 17-37. I applied the texture at 2 percent and 10 percent to create the windblown middle and right examples in the figure.

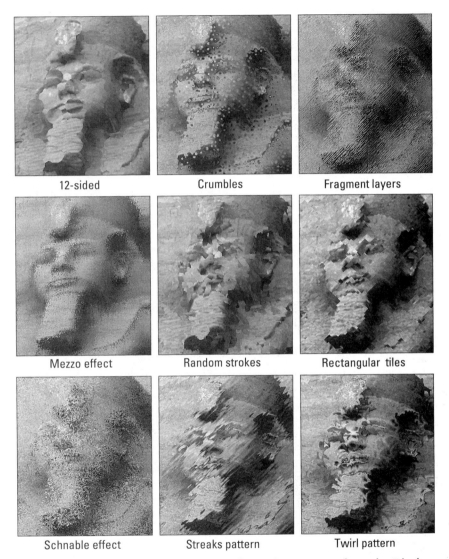

Figure 17-36: These are examples of applying nine patterns from the Displacement Maps folder with the Displace filter at 10 percent horizontally and vertically.

Figure 17-37: After creating a stucco texture with the Add Noise and Emboss filters (left), I applied the texture as a displacement map at 2 percent (middle) and 10 percent (right).

The stucco pattern is only one of an infinite number of textures you can create using filters. In fact, stucco is a great base texture on which to build. For example, to create the wavy texture that starts off the first row of Figure 17-38, I softened the stucco texture by applying the Gaussian Blur filter with a 0.3-pixel radius. I then applied the Ripple filter twice with the Large option selected and an Amount value of 100. That's all there was to it.

To create the second texture in the figure, I applied the Crystallize filter at its default Cell Size value of 10. Believe me, I could go on creating textures like this forever and, more importantly, so could you. The images in the second and third columns of Figure 17-38 show the results of applying the textures with the Displace filter at 2 percent and 10 percent, respectively.

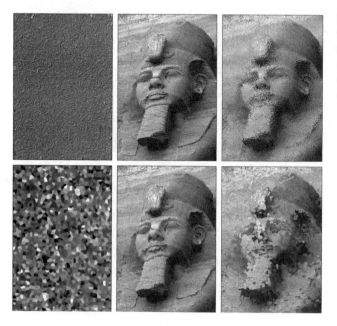

Figure 17-38: After creating two textures with the Add Noise, Emboss, and Ripple filters (first column), I applied the textures as displacement maps at 2 percent (middle) and 10 percent (right).

In the final analysis, any pattern you design for use with the rubber stamp tool is equally applicable for use with the Displace filter. Furthermore, of the two options — rubber stamp and Displace — the latter is more likely to yield the kind of textured effects that will leave your audience begging, pleading, and scraping for more.

Displacing an image onto itself

I throw in this technique just for laughs. Personally, I can't get enough of *Dr. Strangelove*. That's why I call this the *Make My Day at the Atomic Café* effect. Warning: This effect features simulated melting Egyptian carvings. If you find them unnerving, you have a very soft stomach.

The Make My Day at the Atomic Café effect involves nothing more than using an image as its own displacement map. First, make sure the image you want to distort is saved to disk in the native Photoshop format with the 2.5 Compatibility option turned on. Then choose Filter ➪ Distort ➪ Displace, specify the desired settings, and select the version of the image saved to disk. Figure 17-39 shows three applications of this effect, once applied at 10 percent exclusively horizontally, the next at 10 percent vertically, and the last at 10 percent in both directions.

Figure 17-39: See Egypt, have a blast. Here I applied the pharaoh image as a displacement map onto itself at 10 percent horizontally (left), 10 percent vertically (middle), and 10 percent in both directions.

As a variation, save the image in its original form. Then choose Image ➪ Map ➪ Invert (Ctrl+I) and save the inverted image to disk under a different name. Open the original image and use the Displace filter to apply the inverted image as a displacement map. Figure 17-40 shows some results.

Figure 17-40: These are the results of applying an inverted version of the pharaoh as a displacement map onto the original image at 10 percent horizontally (left), 10 percent vertically (middle), and 10 percent in both directions.

If you really want to blow an image apart, apply Horizontal Scale and Vertical Scale values of 50 percent or greater. The first row of Figure 17-41 shows a series of 50 percent applications of the Displace filter. I took the liberty of sharpening each image to heighten the effect. In the second row, I applied the filter and used Filter ⇨ Fade with the Opacity value set to 10 percent. In this way, I retained the detail of the original image while still managing to impart a smidgen of sandblasting.

Figure 17-41: Here are the results of displacing the pharaoh image with itself at 50 percent horizontally, 50 percent vertically, and 50 percent in both directions (top row), followed by the same effects after I used Filter ⇨ Fade with an Opacity value of 10 percent (bottom row).

Using the Filter Factory

If you've made it this far through the chapter, I just want to say one thing about the Filter Factory: It's incredibly powerful and capable of doing far, far more than any filter I've described. But it's also difficult to use — so difficult, in fact, that it makes everything I've discussed in the previous pages look incredibly easy and transparently obvious. The Filter Factory tests the abilities of the most experienced Photoshop user.

Note

Before you can use the Filter Factory, you must install the Filter Factory plug-in in your Plugins folder. The Filter Factory is included only on the Photoshop CD-ROM and does not install during the normal installation process. You'll find the Filter Factory folder — named Ffactory — inside the Goodies/Plug_ins folder on the CD-ROM. Simply copy the folder to the Photoshop Plugins folder on your hard drive.

Choose Filter ➪ Synthetic ➪ Filter Factory to display the Filter Factory dialog box, shown in Figure 17-42. This must be the scariest dialog box ever put before a Photoshop user. Yours is probably even more scary. The R option box contains a little *r*, the G option box contains a little *g*, and the B option box contains a little *b*. Throw in a few arbitrarily named slider bars, and you have the perfect formula for striking terror in the unsuspecting image-editor's heart.

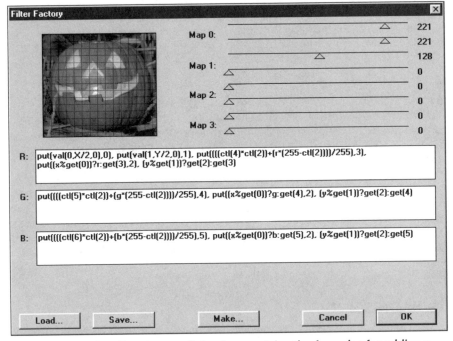

Figure 17-42: The Filter Factory dialog box contains the formulas for adding a series of grid lines to an image.

Note   If the command is dimmed, it's because you're not in the RGB mode. Like the Light Flare and Lighting Effects filters, Filter Factory is applicable to RGB images only.

Now I must make something perfectly clear: There's no way I can describe every nuance of programming a custom filter with the Filter Factory in less than 100 pages. So, to keep the story short and sweet, I'll explain the most important functions and variables, walk you through the process of creating a moderately amusing effect, and show you how to save your work as a fully functioning filter. If you're serious about using the Filter Factory, I suggest you also read the sparse PDF documentation Adobe includes on its CD-ROM. It isn't the kind of thing you simply read through and ingest immediately, and some of the formulas are inaccurate (in my version, anyway), but at least it lists all the variables, operators, and functions permitted in the programming language. You may also want to load the settings I've included on my CD and study my work. If you find a useful operation, feel free to copy and paste it into a filter of your own. It isn't stealing; it's research.

How the Factory works

To use this filter, you enter formulaic *expressions* into the R, G, and B option boxes. Each option box represents what you're doing to the red, green, or blue color channel. You can also integrate the slider bars at the top of the dialog box into your formulas. When you convert the formulas into a filter, you can specify which slider bars to include in the filter's own dialog box, enabling the user to modify the settings. You needn't use the slider bars, but without them you get a single-shot filter like Photoshop's Sharpen More or Facet effects.

Tip   The Load and Save buttons enable you to load formulas from disk or save them for later use or for editing. If you've had a long, hard day and it's time to go home — or you're already home and you want to go to bed — don't forget to save the formulas to disk. Every time you restart Photoshop, the Filter Factory reverts to its original useless values of *r*, *g*, and *b*.

The Make button creates a filter (as I'll discuss more later). The problem is, you can't open a filter with the Filter Factory once you've created it. So if you ever want to modify a setting or two — and believe me, you will — be sure to save the settings separately using the Save button. I recommend saving filter and settings under the same name in different folders to eliminate as much confusion as possible.

The expressions

Like the Custom filter, the Filter Factory evaluates each pixel in each channel one at a time and then finishes up by sending a new brightness value to that pixel. So in the following discussions, I'll take advantage of the same acronym I used earlier in this chapter — PBE, to indicate the *pixel being evaluated.*

You change the brightness of the PBE using three kinds of expressions — variables, operators, and functions. Here's the scoop on each.

Variables

You can enter two kinds of values into a Filter Factory option box — hard-and-fast numbers, such as 3 and 17, and variables. *Variables* are single letters, which represent values that are forever changing. The *r* that first appears in the R option box, for example, represents the brightness value that currently occupies the PBE in the red channel. So by entering *r* in the R option box, you tell Photoshop to change the red PBE to its current color, which is no change whatsoever. It's just Adobe's way of creating a clean slate in which you can work.

All variables reset to a new value every time the filter advances from one pixel to the next. The most important variables are as follows:

✦ **r, g, and b:** The brightness value currently assigned to the PBE in the red channel is *r*. The green value of the PBE is *g*; the blue value is *b*. Why the heck would you want access to any of these values? Why, to mix them, of course. For example, if you enter *(r*g)/255* in the R option box — that's all you have to enter — you multiply the red value by the green value, divide the result by 255, and put the result in the filtered red channel. The final product is identical to copying the contents of the green channel, pasting it onto the red channel, and choosing the Multiply overlay mode. Try it out and see.

✦ **c:** This variable represents the brightness value of the PBE in the current channel, whatever that may be. In the R option box, *c* is identical to *r*. So the equation *(c*g/255)* means *(r*g/255)* in the R channel and *(b*g/255)* in the B channel.

✦ **x and y:** The horizontal coordinate of the PBE is saved to *x*. This value is measured in pixels from the left edge of the image. The vertical coordinate is *y*, as measured from the top of the image. These values are useful for shifting pixels around or mixing neighboring pixels together (as you can with the Custom command).

✦ **X and Y:** The total width of the image is *X*, the total height is *Y*. So *X-x* calculates the distance from the PBE to the right edge.

You can also use other variables: The letter *m*, for example, measures the distance from the PBE to the exact center of the image, and *d* is the angle from the PBE to the center pixel (measured from 0 to 1,024, so 255 is equivalent to 90 degrees). But *r, g, b, c, x, y, X,* and *Y* are the variables you'll use most often.

Operators

Operators include arithmetic signs, such as plus and minus, as well as relational symbols, such as < and >. They also include logical operations. For example, *?* tells the Filter Factory to complete the following operation only if the previous expression holds true and, if it is false, complete the operation after the colon (:). For example, the expression *x<(X/2)?r:g* means if the PBE is inside the left side of the image, color it with the red channel value. If not, color it with the green value. The following are the most important operators:

✦ **+, -, *, and /:** These symbols stand for plus, minus, multiply, and divide. The Filter Factory always handles multiply and divide operations before plus and minus operations. So the equation *4+8/2* equals 8, not 6.

✦ **%:** Use the percentage sign to retain the remainder from a division equation. For example, *11%4* equals 3.

✦ **(and):** Parentheses tell the Filter Factory to complete the equation inside the parentheses before completing others. The equation *(4+8)/2* equals 6 because 4 and 8 are added before dividing by 2.

✦ **<, >, <=, and >=:** These symbols mean less than, greater than, less than or equal to, and greater than or equal to. All four are used primarily within conditional operations like the one I mentioned at the beginning of this section.

✦ **==, =!:** Two equal signs in a row mean "equal to." An equal sign and an exclamation point mean "not equal to." Again, use these inside conditional operations.

✦ **?:** Here's the conditional operation, as I explained earlier.

Again, these aren't all the possible operators, just the best of them. But I should mention one additional operator: The comma separates phrases in an expression, sort of like a period separates sentences. The phrase after the final comma is the one the Filter Factory applies to the PBE. All previous phrases are used for calculation purposes only. You can see how this works in the step-by-step example that's coming up right after the discussion of functions.

Functions

All *functions* are composed of three letters followed by numbers, variables, and equations inside parentheses. For example, *abs(x-X)* finds the absolute value of the equation inside the parentheses, which means you get a positive result whether the answer to the equation is positive or negative. (Because negative brightness values simply become black, this can be useful.)

Rather than simply listing the functions, I'll explain them in groups. First, two functions use holding cells. In typical programming, you store the results of incremental equations in variables, but in the Filter Factory, variables are used by the filter only. You get 10 numbered cells, ranging from 0 to 9. The two functions that work with cells are *put,* to place a number inside a cell, and *get,* to retrieve it. It's similar to copying and pasting with 10 tiny Clipboards. The expression *put(r+b,0)* puts the result of the equation *r+b* into cell 0. Conversely, *put(r+b,1)* puts it in cell 1, and so on. The expression *get(0)/2* would retrieve the result of *r+b* and divide it by 2.

The function *src* retrieves information about a specific pixel in your image. For example, *src(x+5,y+5,0)* returns the brightness of the pixel 5 pixels to the right and 5 pixels down from the PBE. What is the last 0 for? This tells the function to get the value from the red channel. The green channel is 1, the blue channel is 2, mask channels are 3 through 9.

Similar to *src, rad* finds out the brightness value of a pixel in a certain channel based on its distance and direction from the center of the image. For example, if you enter *rad(d-16,m-16,0)* into the red channel, you rotate the contents of the channel 16 increments (about 6 degrees) counterclockwise and distort its center outward. The upcoming step-by-step example uses this function.

The function *rnd* generates a random number between two extremes, which is great for creating noise. The expression *rnd(r,g)* generates a random value between the red brightness value of the PBE and the green brightness of the PBE.

Evaluating the sliders

These next functions — *ctl* and *val* — get their own headline because they're so important. They evaluate how a user of your filter sets the slider bars. The function *ctl* simply retrieves the setting of a specified slider bar. There are eight slider bars in all, numbered 0 to 7 from top to bottom. (The sliders labeled Map 0 are, therefore, sliders 0 and 1; Map 1 includes sliders 2 and 3; and so on.) Each slider can be adjusted from 0 to 255. So if the first slider bar is set to 128, the function *ctl(0)* retrieves the number 128. You can then change the impact of your filter by moving the slider in real time. For example, if you enter *r*ctl(0)/255* in the R option box, you multiply the red value of the PBE by the setting of the top slider divided by 255. This makes the red channel black when the slider is set to 0, normal when the slider is set to 255, and darker shades when set to any increment in between.

The *val* function evaluates the setting of a slider bar within a specified range. For example, *val(0,15,-15)* takes the setting of the top slider, translates it to 15 when it's at 0, and translates it to -15 when it's at 255. As you can see, this function enables you to translate the data within any specified range, even making the low values high and vice versa. This is useful when you don't want the entire range of data from 0 to 255 to mess up the results of your equations.

Touring the factory

Okay, now for a little hands-on action. The steps will be short and straightforward, but the results are both useful and interesting. I encourage you to try these steps. Even if you've been sitting there with your jaw hanging open throughout the entire chapter, even if you haven't the slightest idea what you're doing, you can create a fully functioning filter.

The steps show you how to create the Rotator filter included on the CD-ROM at the back of the book. For a sneak peek at the havoc you can wreak with this filter, look at Color Plate 17-3. Talk about your incentives!

Steps: Creating a Filter Inside the Factory

1. **Open an RGB image or convert some other image to the RGB mode.** This filter yields interesting results even when applied to grayscale images converted to RGB.

2. **Choose Filter ➪ Synthetic ➪ Factory.** Set all the slider bars back to 0, just in case somebody's been fooling around with them.

3. **Enter *rad(d-(4*ctl(0)),m,0)* into the R option box.** The first argument in the expression — *d-(4*ctl(0))* — subtracts four times the value of the top slider bar from the angle variable *d*. Why four times? Because the slider only offers 256 increments, and the filter measures a full circle in 1,024 increments — 256 times 4 equals 1,024, thus enabling you to translate the slider values to a full circle.

   Meanwhile, *d* is the angle of the current pixel from the center and *m* is the distance from the pixel to the center. So *rad(d-(4*ctl(0)),m,0)* tells the filter to lift the brightness from the pixel in a counterclockwise direction from the PBE. The result is the red channel rotates in the opposite direction — clockwise. Drag the slider bar and you'll see this is true.

4. **Insert the phrase *-ctl(4)/2* after the m so the expression reads *rad(d-(4*ctl(0)),m-ctl(4)/2,0).*** You'll use the second and third slider bars — *ctl(1)* and *ctl(2)* — for rotating the other two channels. But I think I'd like to use the fifth slider bar for distorting the image. Why not the fourth channel? Because the first three sliders will be devoted to rotation. The distortion slider will be logically different, so it might be nice to create a blank space between the rotation and distortion sliders. Not using slider four is the way to do this.

   By changing the expression to *rad(d-(4*ctl(0)),m-ctl(4)/2,0),* you tell Photoshop to subtract half the value from the fourth slider from the distance-from-center variable, thus shoving the pixels outward as you drag the fifth slider bar (the top of the two labeled Map 2). Give it a try.

5. **Copy the R expression and paste it into G.** Select the entire expression in the R option box, copy it by pressing Ctrl+C, tab to the G option box, and press Ctrl+V to paste. Then change the *ctl(0)* function to *ctl(1)* and the final number after the comma from a *0* to a *1,* so it reads *rad(d-(4*ctl(1)),m-ctl(4)/2,1).* Now the expression takes rotation data from the second slider bar and lifts its colors from the green channel. The result is a rotating green channel.

6. **Tab to the B option box and press Ctrl+V again.** Change *ctl(0)* to *ctl(2)* and change the final *0* to a *2.* The result is *rad(d-(4*ctl(2)),m-ctl(4)/2,2).* Just to make sure you haven't fallen behind, Figure 17-43 shows all three expressions exactly as they should appear.

   Tip A little yellow triangle to the left of the R, G, or B option boxes, by the way, is Photoshop's way of telling you your formula contains some sort of error — a missing parenthesis or some other faux pas.

7. **Click the Save button and save your settings to disk.** Use the name *ROTATE2.AFS* to distinguish this filter from the one already included on the CD. (AFS is the file extension assigned to settings files.)

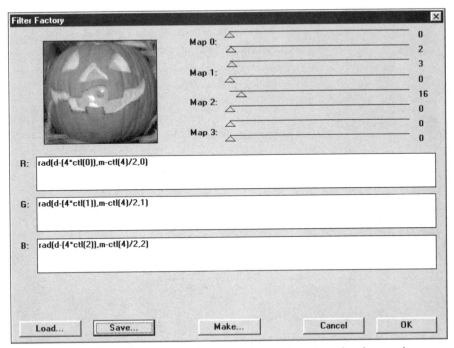

Figure 17-43: These three expressions enable you to rotate the three color channels independently using the first three slider bars and to distort the image using the fifth slider.

8. **Adjust the sliders to set the defaults.** Before you turn this sucker into its own filter, make sure the sliders are set as you want them to appear by default. Every time you open the new filter for the first time during a Photoshop session, these slider values will appear as they do now. You may want to set all sliders to 0 so the user starts from square one, but that's completely up to you.

9. **Click the Make button to convert your code into a filter.** Clicking Make displays the dialog box shown in Figure 17-44. Enter the submenu in which you want the filter to appear in the Category option box. If you want it to appear with the rest of the *Photoshop Bible* filters, enter Tormentia. Enter the name of the filter, Rotator Copy, in the Title option box. Then enter copyright and author information in the next two option boxes. (Go ahead, give yourself credit. You've earned it.) Enter the filename for the filter in the Filename option box (remember, it's a good idea to give the filter the same name you used when saving the formula to disk in Step 7 — in this case, ROTATE2.) As indicated to the right of the Filename option box, Photoshop assigns the extension .8BF to filter files.

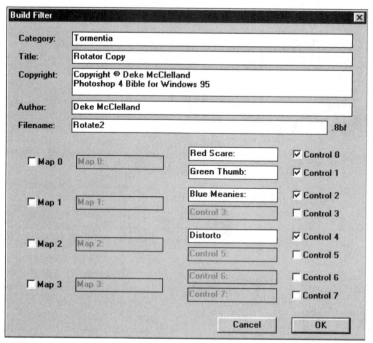

Figure 17-44: Click the Make button to display this dialog box, which enables you to name your filter, assign it to a submenu, and select the slider bars you want to appear in the final dialog box.

10. **Select a Control check box for every slider you want to appear in your final filter.** The Control check boxes along the right side represent the slider bars inside the Filter Factory dialog box. Select the check boxes for Control 0, Control 1, Control 2, and Control 4. Then name them appropriately. My suggested names appear in Figure 17-44, but they may be a little too clever for your tastes.

Caution   Watch out: The Filter Factory enables you to select any of the slider check boxes, whether or not they were used in your formulas. If you're not careful, you can activate a slider bar with no function.

11. **When you're finished, press Enter.** Photoshop displays an alert message announcing it has successfully created the filter. Click the Cancel button to escape the Filter Factory dialog box.

12. **Quit Photoshop and relaunch it.** Open an RGB image — like the Filter Factory itself, any filter you create in the factory is applicable to RGB images only — and choose your newest command, Filter ⇨ Tormentia ⇨ Rotator Copy. The dialog box should look something like the one shown in Figure 17-45. Notice the gaps between the Blue Meanies and Distorto

sliders. Nice logical grouping, huh? Feel free to drag the controls and apply the filter as much as you want. It's alive!

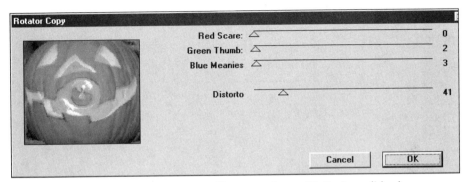

Figure 17-45: The new Rotator Copy filter complete with its four slider bars

To see a demonstration of your powerful new filter, check out Color Plate 17-3, in which I applied the filter six times at various settings. The top row shows the effect of rotating the channels to different degrees with the Distorto option set to 0. The bottom row shows the same rotation values, but with the Distorto slider turned up to various volumes. It's not the most practical filter on Earth, but it's diverting. You might even find something to do with it. Of course, you probably don't need two copies of the same filter hanging around on your hard drive, so if you created Rotator Copy in the above steps, I heartily suggest you delete the duplicate filter.

Tip

By the way, those sliders have a tendency to move around after you finish dragging them. It's irritating. If you're interested in achieving an exact value, click at the location where you want to move the slider triangle. The triangle jumps in place. Then click, click, click to get the slider triangle right where you want it.

Cross Reference

If you want practical filters, check the ones I've included on the CD. Most are much more complicated than the one you created in the steps, but they all use the variables, operators, and functions described in this chapter. Open the settings files to look at my code. (Just click the Load button inside the Filter Factory dialog box.) To whet your appetite, look at Color Plate 17-4, which shows all but one of the remaining filters on the CD applied to the pumpkin. (The one that wouldn't fit is Ripping Pixels, which creates a random value between the brightness of the pixel in one channel and that of one of the other channels, creating a highly customizable noise effect.) These are only sample applications, most of them using the default slider bar settings. Obviously, jillions of other variations are possible. Have loads of fun.

Corrections, Composites, and the Web

Mapping and Adjusting Colors

What Is Color Mapping?

Color mapping is a fancy name for shuffling colors around. For example, mapping Color A to Color B simply means taking all the A-colored pixels and converting them to B-colored pixels. Photoshop provides several commands that enable you to map entire ranges of colors based on their hues, saturation levels, and, most frequently, brightness values.

Color effects and corrections

Why would you want to change colors around? Here's one reason: to achieve special effects. You know those psychedelic horror movies that show some guy's hair turning blue while his face turns purple and the palms of his hands glow a sort of cornflower yellow? A grayscale version of this very effect appears in the second example of Figure 18-1. Although not the most attractive effect by modern standards — you may be able to harvest more tasteful results if you put your shoulder to the color wheel — psychedelic qualifies as color mapping for the simple reason that each color shifts incrementally to a new color.

But the more common reason to map colors is to enhance the appearance of a scanned image or digital photograph, as demonstrated in the third example in Figure 18-1. In this case, you're not creating special effects — you're just making straightforward color adjustments, known in the biz as *color corrections*. Scans are never perfect, no matter how much money you spend on a scanning device or a service bureau. Scans can always benefit from tweaking and subtle adjustments, if not outright overhauls, in the color department.

Figure 18-1: Nobody's perfect, and neither is the best of scanned photos (left). You can modify colors in an image to achieve special effects (middle) or simply fix the image with a few well-targeted color corrections (right). Too bad Photoshop hasn't delivered on its promised Remove Excessive Jewelry filter.

Remember, though, Photoshop can't make something from nothing. In creating the illusion of more and better colors, most of the color-adjustment operations you perform actually take some small amount of color away from the image. Somewhere in your image, two pixels that were two different colors before you started the correction change to the same color. The image may look ten times better, but it will, in fact, be less colorful than when you started.

This principle is important to remember because it demonstrates that color mapping is a balancing act. The first nine operations you perform may make an image look progressively better, but the tenth may send it into decline. No magic formula exists, unfortunately. The amount of color mapping you need to apply varies from image to image. But if you follow my usual recommendations — use the commands in moderation, know when to stop, and save your image to disk before doing anything drastic — you should be fine.

Photoshop 4.0

Photoshop 4 offers a new color correction option that ensures you never make a mistake. You can now add a special layer of color correction information that affects all layers below it. Known as an *adjustment layer*, this is quite possibly Version 4's best enhancement. For more information about adjustment layers, read the "Adjustment Layers" section near the end of this chapter.

The good, the bad, and the wacky

Photoshop 4 stores all its color mapping commands — 14 in all — under the Image ➪ Adjust submenu. These commands fall into three basic categories:

✦ Commands such as Invert and Threshold are quick-and-dirty color mappers. They don't fix images, but they can be useful for creating special effects and adjusting masks.

✦ Brightness/Contrast and Color Balance are true color correction commands, but they sacrifice functionality for ease of use. If I had my way, these commands would be removed from the Image ➪ Adjust submenu and thrown in the dust heap.

✦ The third, more complicated variety of color correction commands, provide better control, but they take a fair amount of effort to learn. Levels, Curves, and Hue/Saturation are examples of color correcting at its best and most complicated.

This chapter contains little information about the second category of commands for the simple reason that some of them are inadequate and ultimately a big waste of time. Exceptions exist, of course — Auto Levels is a decent quick fixer, and Variations offers deceptively straightforward sophistication — but Brightness/ Contrast and Color Balance are frankly beneath contempt. They are as liable to damage your image as fix it, making them quite dangerous in a dull, pedestrian sort of way. I know because I spent my first year with Photoshop relying exclusively on Brightness/Contrast and Color Balance, all the while wondering why I couldn't achieve the effects I wanted. Then, one happy day, I spent about half an hour learning Levels and Curves, and the quality of my images skyrocketed. So wouldn't you rather learn it right in the first place? I hope so, because the die is cast.

Quick Color Effects

Before we get into all the high-end gunk, however, I'll take a moment to explain the first category of commands, all of which happen to occupy one of the lower sections in the Image ➪ Adjust submenu. These commands — Invert, Equalize, Threshold, and Posterize — produce immediate effects that are either difficult to duplicate or not worth attempting with the more full-featured commands.

Invert

When you choose Image ➪ Adjust ➪ Invert (Ctrl+I), Photoshop converts every color in your image to its exact opposite, just as in a photographic negative. As demonstrated in Figure 18-2, black becomes white, white becomes black, fire becomes water, good becomes evil, Imelda Marcos goes barefoot, and the brightness value of every primary color component changes to 255 minus the original brightness value.

Note   This is not the proper way to convert a scanned color photographic negative to a positive, by the way, because of issues involving the orange cast produced by the film itself.

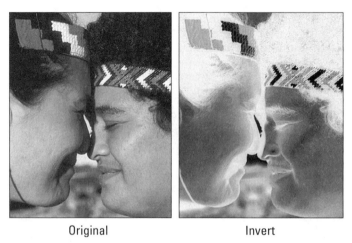

Original   Invert

Figure 18-2: An image before the advent of the Invert command (left) and after (right)

Image ➪ Adjust ➪ Invert is about the only color mapping command that retains every single drop of color in an image. (The Hue/Saturation command also retains colors under specific conditions.) If you apply the Invert command twice in a row, you arrive at your original image.

When you're working on a full-color image, the Invert command simply inverts the contents of each color channel. This means the command produces different results when applied to RGB, Lab, and especially CMYK images. Color Plate 18-1 shows the results of inverting a single image in each of these modes. The RGB and Lab images share some similarities, but you find all kinds of subtle differences if you study the backgrounds and the basic colors of the faces.

Inverting in CMYK is much different. Typically, the Invert command changes much of a CMYK image to black. Except in rare instances — such as in night scenes — the black channel contains lots of light shades and few dark shades. So when you invert the channel, it becomes extremely dark. To reverse this effect, I inverted only the cyan, magenta, and yellow channels in the right example of Color Plate 18-1. (I did this by inverting the entire image and then going to the black channel

— Ctrl+4 — and pressing Ctrl+I again.) Although this approach is preferable to inverting the black channel, it prevents the blacks in the hair and shadows from turning white (which would be the only portions even remotely light had I inverted the black channel as well).

So you know, when I refer to applying color corrections in the CMYK mode, I mean applying them after choosing Mode ➪ CMYK Color. Applying corrections in the RGB mode when Mode ➪ CMYK Preview is active produces the same effect as when CMYK Preview is not selected; the only difference is the onscreen colors are curtailed slightly to fit inside the CMYK color space. You're still editing inside the same old red, green, and blue color channels, so the effects are the same.

Cross Reference

As I mentioned back in Chapter 12, inverting the contents of the mask channel is the same as applying Select ➪ Inverse to a selection outline in the marching ants mode. In fact, this is one of the most useful applications of the filter. If you're considering inverting a color image, however, I strongly urge you to try out the SuperInvert filter I created for the CD. It enables you to invert each channel independently and incrementally. Any setting under 128 lessens the contrast of the channel: 128 makes it completely gray, and any value over 128 inverts it to some degree.

Equalize

Equalize is the smartest, and at the same time least useful, of the Image ➪ Adjust pack. When you invoke this command, Photoshop searches for the lightest and darkest color values in a selection. Then it maps the lightest color in all the color channels to white, maps the darkest color in the channels to black, and distributes the remaining colors to other brightness levels in an effort to distribute pixels evenly over the entire brightness spectrum. This doesn't mean any one pixel will actually appear white or black after you apply Equalize; rather, one pixel in at least one channel will be white and another pixel in at least one channel will be black. In an RGB image, for example, the red, green, or blue component of one pixel would be white, but the other two components of that same pixel might be black. The result is a higher contrast image with white and black pixels scattered throughout the color channels.

If no portion of the image is selected when you choose Image ➪ Adjust ➪ Equalize, Photoshop automatically maps out the entire image across the brightness spectrum, as shown in the upper-right example of Figure 18-3. If you select a portion of the image before choosing the Equalize command, however, Photoshop displays a dialog box containing the following two radio buttons:

✦ **Selected Area Only:** Select this option to apply the Equalize command strictly within the confines of the selection. The lightest pixel in the selection becomes white, the darkest pixel becomes black, and so on.

✦ **Entire Image Based on Area:** If you select the second radio button, which is the default setting, Photoshop applies the Equalize command to the entire image based on the lightest and darkest colors in the selection. All colors in the image that are lighter than the lightest color in the selection become white, and all colors darker than the darkest color in the selection become black.

The bottom two examples in Figure 18-3 show the effects of selecting different parts of the image when the Entire Image Based on Area option is in force. In the left example, I selected a dark portion of the image, which resulted in over-lightening of the entire image. In the right example, I selected an area with both light and dark values, which boosted the amount of contrast between highlights and shadows in the image.

The problem with the Equalize command is it relies too heavily on some pretty bizarre automation to be of much use as a color correction tool. Certainly, you can create some interesting special effects. But if you'd prefer to adjust the colors automatically in an image from black to white, regardless of the color mode and composition of the individual channels, choose Image ➪ Adjust ➪ Auto Levels (Ctrl+Shift+L). If you want to adjust the tonal balance manually and, therefore, with a higher degree of accuracy, the Levels and Curves commands are tops. I explain all of these commands at length later in this chapter.

Threshold

I touched on the Threshold command a few times in previous chapters. As you may recall, Threshold converts all colors to either black or white based on their brightness values. When you choose Image ➪ Adjust ➪ Threshold, Photoshop displays the Threshold dialog box shown in Figure 18-4. The dialog box offers a single option box and a slider bar, either of which you can use to specify the medium brightness value in the image. Photoshop changes any color lighter than the value in the Threshold option box to white, and changes any color darker than the value to black.

The dialog box also includes a graph of all the colors in the image — even if only a portion of the image is selected. This graph is called a *histogram*. The width of the histogram represents all 256 possible brightness values, starting at black on the left and progressing through white on the right. The height of each vertical line in the graph demonstrates the number of pixels currently associated with that brightness value. Therefore, you can use the histogram to gauge the distribution of lights and darks in your image. This may seem weird at first, but with enough experience, the histogram becomes an invaluable tool, enabling you to corroborate the colors you see onscreen.

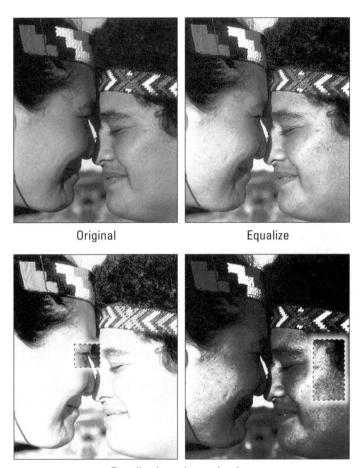

Original   Equalize

Equalize based on selection

Figure 18-3: Here is an image before (top left) and after (top right) applying the Equalize command when no portion of the image is selected. You can also use the brightness values in a selected region as the basis for equalizing an entire image (bottom left and right).

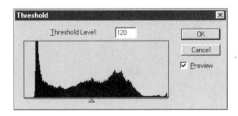

Figure 18-4: The histogram in the Threshold dialog box shows the distribution of brightness values in the selection.

Tip   Generally speaking, you achieve the best effects if you change an equal number of pixels to black as you change to white (and vice versa). So rather than moving the slider bar to 128, which is the medium brightness value, move it to the point at which the area of the vertical lines to the left of the slider triangle looks roughly equivalent to the area of the vertical lines to the right of the slider triangle.

The upper-left example in Figure 18-5 shows the result of applying the Threshold command with a Threshold Level value of 120 (as in Figure 18-4). Although this value more or less evenly distributes black and white pixels, I lost a lot of detail in the dark areas.

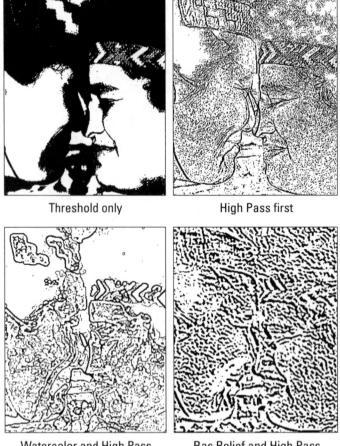

Threshold only   High Pass first

Watercolor and High Pass   Bas Relief and High Pass

Figure 18-5: By itself, the Threshold command tends to deliver flat results (top left). To express the detail better, apply High Pass and other filters prior to choosing Threshold.

As you may recall from my "Using the High Pass filter" discussion in Chapter 15, you can use Filter ➪ Other ➪ High Pass in advance of the Threshold command to retain areas of contrast. In the upper-left image in Figure 18-5, I applied the High Pass filter with a radius of 1.0 pixel, followed by the Threshold command with a value of 125. In the two bottom images, I first chose an effects filter — Filter ➪ Artistic ➪ Watercolor on the left and Filter ➪ Sketch ➪ Bas Relief on the right — then I applied High Pass with a radius of 1.0 pixel followed by the Threshold command.

If the Threshold effects in Figure 18-5 are a bit austere, first clone the image to a layer and then mix the layer with the underlying original. Figure 18-6 shows all the effects from Figure 18-5 applied to layers subject to the Overlay blend mode and 50 percent Opacity. In each example, the translucent selection helps to add contrast and reinforce details in the original image.

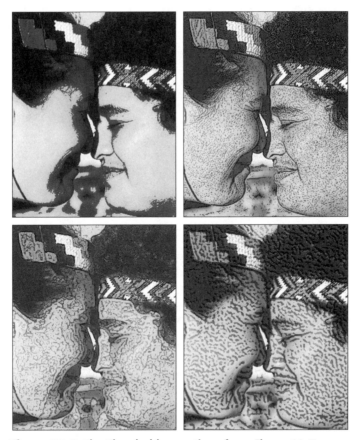

Figure 18-6: The Threshold operations from Figure 18-5 are applied to separate layers, blended with the Overlay mode and an Opacity value of 50 percent.

If you want to achieve a colorful Threshold effect, try applying the Threshold command independently to each color channel. In an RGB image, for example, press Ctrl+1 and then apply Image ➪ Adjust ➪ Threshold. Then press Ctrl+2 and repeat the command, and press Ctrl+3 and do it again. Color Plate 18-2 shows examples of what happens when I apply High Pass (with a radius of 3.0) and Threshold to independent color channels in the RGB, Lab, and CMYK modes. To soften the transitions and to avoid trapping problems, I resampled each image up and down a few times, as described back in the "Anti-aliasing an image" section of Chapter 15.

Posterize

The Posterize command is Threshold's rich cousin. Whereas Threshold boils down an image into two colors only, Posterize can retain as many colors as you like. You can't control how colors are mapped, however, as you can when you use Threshold. The Posterize dialog box does not provide a histogram or slider bar. Instead, Posterize automatically divides the full range of 256 brightness values into a specified number of equal increments.

To use the Posterize command, choose Image ➪ Adjust ➪ Posterize and enter a value into the Levels option box. The Levels value represents the number of brightness values the Posterize command retains. Higher values result in subtle color adjustments; lower values produce more dramatic effects. The first example in Figure 18-7 shows an image subject to a Levels value of 8.

By now, you may be thinking, "By golly, if Posterize is so similar to Threshold, I wonder how it works when applied after the High Pass filter?" Well, you're in luck, because this is exactly the purpose of the second example in Figure 18-7. Here I chose the High Pass filter and entered 3.0 for the radius. Then I applied the Posterize command with the same Levels value (8) as before.

Now, in case you've tried this same effect on your full-color image and thought, "Yech, this looks terrible — half the color just disappeared," the key is to apply High Pass and Posterize to a layered version of the image and then mix the effect with the underlying original. Color Plate 18-3 shows the results of applying the High Pass filter with a radius of 3.0 and the Posterize command with a setting of 8 to the layered clone and then compositing the layer and underlying original using each of three overlay modes from the Layers palette. The Luminosity option applies only the lights and darks in the layered image, allowing the colors in the underlying image to show through; Hard Light strengthens the light and dark shades; and Hue applies the colors from the layer with the saturation and brightness values from the original. After flattening each image, I increased the saturation of the colors using Image ➪ Adjust ➪ Hue/Saturation (Ctrl+U), which I discuss in an upcoming section.

Posterize   High Pass first

Figure 18-7: This is an image subject to the Posterize command with a Levels value of 8 (left). You can retain more detail in an image by applying the High Pass filter before using Posterize (right).

Quick Corrections

Photoshop offers two quick correctors under the Image ➪ Adjust submenu, which I want to discuss before entering into the larger world of advanced color correction. Both are single-shot commands that alter your image without any dialog boxes or special options. The first, Desaturate, sucks the saturation as of a selection and leaves it looking like a grayscale image. The second, Auto Levels, automatically increases the contrast of an image according to what Photoshop deems as the ideal brightness values.

Sucking saturation

Little reason exists to apply the Desaturate command to an entire image; you can just as easily choose Image ➪ Mode ➪ Grayscale to accomplish the same thing and dispose of the extra channels that would otherwise consume room in memory and on disk. I know of only two reasons to sacrifice all colors in the RGB mode:

✦ You want to retain the option of applying RGB-only filters, such as Lens Flare, Lighting Effects, and anything created with the Filter Factory.

✦ You intend to downsize the colors using Image ➪ Mode ➪ Indexed Colors and save the final image in the GIF format for use on the World Wide Web (as I discuss in Chapter 20).

But mostly, you use Desaturate to rob color from discrete selections or independent layers, neither of which the Grayscale mode can accommodate. For example, in Color Plate 18-4, I used Select ⇨ Color Range to select all of the pumpkin except the eyes and mouth and a few speckly bits here and there. (I could have used the quick mask mode to tweak the selection and get it just right, but it didn't strike me as particularly important in this case.) I then applied Image ⇨ Adjust ⇨ Desaturate (Ctrl+Shift+U) to achieve the first example. To create the top-right pumpkin, I chose Filter ⇨ Fade Desaturate and changed the Opacity value to 50 percent, bringing back some of the original colors from the full-color original and achieving an only slightly desaturated pumpkin.

Tip

In case you missed that last paragraph, you can use Filter ⇨ Fade (Ctrl+Shift+F) to back off the effects of any command under the Image ⇨ Adjust submenu. As always, the Fade command is available immediately after you apply the color correction; if you so much as alter a selection outline, Fade goes dim.

Desaturate isn't the only way to suck colors out of an image. You can also invert the colors and mix them with their original counterparts to achieve a slightly different effect. The bottom row of Color Plate 18-4 shows what I mean. In the lower-left example, I applied Invert (Ctrl+I) to my same Color Range selection. Then I pressed Ctrl+Shift+F, changed the Opacity setting to 50 percent, and — here's the important part — selected Color from the Mode pop-up menu.

Note the inverted and mixed colors are slightly different than the desaturated tones in the pumpkin above. When set to the Color blend mode, the colors in the inverted image should theoretically cancel the colors in the underlying original. The Invert command doesn't change the saturation of the pixels, however, so the saturation is the same of the inverted and original pixels. As a result, some colors from the underlying image are allowed to show through, as the bottom-left image shows.

The bottom-right example shows what happened when I changed the Opacity to 70 percent, thus favoring the inverted colors. Why'd I do that? Maybe I just like blue pumpkins. Or more likely, I had a fourth spot to fill in the figure, and a blue pumpkin seemed like the guy to fill it.

Note

By the way, you may be wondering why Adobe selected Ctrl+Shift+U as the keyboard shortcut for Desaturate. Well, Desaturate is actually a renegade element from the Hue/Saturation command, which enables you to raise and lower saturation levels to any degree you like. The shortcut for Hue/Saturation is Ctrl+U — for *hUUUUe,* don't you know — so Desaturate is Ctrl+Shift+U.

Auto contrast correction

Image ⇨ Adjust ⇨ Auto Levels (Ctrl+Shift+L) goes through each color channel and changes the lightest pixel to white, changes the darkest pixel to black, and stretches out all the shades of gray to fill out the spectrum. In Figure 18-8, I started with a drab and murky image. But when I applied Auto Levels, Photoshop pumped up the lights and darks, bolstering the contrast. Although I would argue the corrected image is too dark, it's not half bad for an automated, no-brainer command you just choose and let rip.

Figure 18-8: A grayscale image before (left) and after (right) applying the Auto Levels command

Unlike the Equalize command, which considers all color channels as a whole, Auto Levels looks at each channel independently. So as with the Invert command, the active color mode has a profound effect on Auto Levels. Color Plate 18-5 shows our friendly jack o' lantern prior to color corrections, followed by the same image corrected with Auto Levels in the RGB, Lab, and CMYK modes. Quite frankly, the RGB image is the only acceptable one. The Lab image is far too orange, and the CMYK image is too dark, thanks to the exaggeration of the black channel. Auto Levels has also darkened the cyan channel, turning the pumpkin a bright red one rarely sees in today's sincere pumpkin patches.

Like Invert, Equalize, and other automatic color mappers, Auto Levels is designed specifically for use in the RGB mode. If you use it in CMYK, you're more likely to achieve special effects than color correction.

Note   The Auto Levels command serves the same purpose and produces the same effect as the Auto button in the Levels dialog box. You shouldn't really rely on either. What you should do is read the rest of this chapter and learn about the bigger and better color correction commands.

Hue Shifting and Colorizing

The following sections cover commands specifically designed to change the distribution of colors in an image. You can rotate the hues around the color spectrum, change the saturation of colors, adjust highlights and shadows, and even tint an image. Two of these commands — Hue/Saturation and Selective Color — are applicable exclusively to color images. The other two — Replace and Variations — can be applied to grayscale images, but are not the best solutions. Although both enable you to select specific ranges of brightness values you want to edit, they apply their corrections with less finesse than either the Levels or Curves commands, both of which are discussed toward the end of the chapter.

Tip Before I go any further, I should mention one awesome little bit of advice. Remember how Ctrl+Alt+F redisplays the last filter dialog box so you can tweak the effect? Well, a similar shortcut is available when you're applying color corrections. Press the Alt key when choosing any of the commands described throughout the rest of this chapter to display that command's dialog box with the settings last applied to the image. If the command has a keyboard equivalent, just add Alt to restore the last settings. Ctrl+Alt+U, for example, brings up the Hue/Saturation dialog box with the settings you last used.

Using the Hue/Saturation command

The Hue/Saturation command provides two functions. First, it enables you to adjust colors in an image according to their hues and saturation levels. You can apply the changes to specific ranges of colors or modify all colors equally across the spectrum. And second, the command enables you to colorize images by applying new hue and saturation values while retaining the core brightness information from the original image.

This command is perfect for colorizing grayscale images. I know, I know, Woody Allen wouldn't approve, but with some effort, you can make Ted Turner green with envy. Just scan him and change the Hue value to 140 degrees.

When you choose Image ➪ Adjust ➪ Hue/Saturation (Ctrl+U), Photoshop displays the Hue/Saturation dialog box, shown in Figure 18-9. Before I explain how to use this dialog box to produce specific effects, let me briefly introduce the options:

✦ **Master:** Select the Master option to adjust all colors in an image to the same degree. If you prefer to adjust some colors in the image differently than others, select one of the color radio buttons along the left side of the dialog box. In the RGB and CMYK modes, the dialog box offers the R (Red), Y (Yellow), G (Green), C (Cyan), B (Blue), and M (Magenta) options, as shown in Figure 18-9. In the Lab mode, two radio buttons bite the dust, leaving Y (Yellow), G (Green), B (Blue), and M (Magenta), each of which represents an extreme end of the *a* or *b* spectrum.

You can specify different slider bar settings for every one of the color ranges. For example, you might select R (Red) and move the Hue slider triangle to +50 and then select Y (Yellow) and move the Hue triangle to -30. All radio buttons are dimmed when you select the Colorize check box.

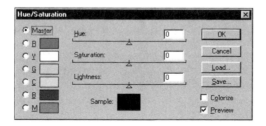

Figure 18-9: The Hue/Saturation dialog box enables you to adjust the hues and saturation values in a color image or to colorize a grayscale image.

✦ **Hue:** The Hue slider bar measures colors on the 360-degree color circle, as explained back in the "HSB" section of Chapter 5. When the Master radio button is selected, you can adjust the Hue value from negative to positive 180 degrees.

When one of the other color radio buttons is active in the RGB or CMYK mode, the Hue value can vary from negative to positive 60 degrees, because each of the colors is 60 degrees from either of its neighbors in the color wheel. (Red is 60 degrees from yellow, which is 60 degrees from green, and so on.) When a color radio button is active in the Lab mode, the Hue value can vary from negative to positive 90 degrees, thanks to Lab's specialized color organization.

Regardless of mode, letters appear at either end of the Hue slider when any option except Master is selected. The letters indicate the effect of moving the slider triangle in either direction. For example, if you select R (Red), the letters M and Y flank the slider, indicating a negative value maps red pixels toward magenta, while a positive value maps red pixels toward yellow.

✦ **Saturation:** Normally, the Saturation value can vary from negative to positive 100. The only exception occurs when the Colorize check box is active, in which case saturation becomes an absolute value, measured from 0 to 100.

Note

Photoshop precedes positive values in the Hue, Saturation, and Lightness option boxes with plus signs (+) to show you are adding to the current color attributes of the pixels. When you select Colorize, the plus signs disappear from all but the Lightness value, because hue and saturation become absolute values you apply to pixels, rather than adding to or subtracting from existing pixel colors.

✦ **Lightness:** You can darken or lighten an image by varying the Lightness value from negative to positive 100.

Caution   Because this value invariably changes all brightness levels in an image to an equal extent — whether or not Colorize is selected — it permanently dulls highlights and shadows. You'll, therefore, most likely, want to avoid this option like the plague and rely instead on the Levels or Curves command to edit brightness and contrast.

✦ **Sample:** This color swatch serves as a guidepost. Really, it's pretty redundant, because you can monitor the effects your settings have on an image by selecting the Preview check box. But if you want to see the impact of your settings on one color in particular, you can isolate it by clicking that color in the Image window with the eyedropper cursor. (The cursor automatically changes to an eyedropper when you move it outside the Hue/Saturation dialog box and into the Image window.)

✦ **Load/Save:** As in all the best color correction dialog boxes, you can load and save settings to disk in case you want to reapply the options to other images. These options are especially useful if you find a magic combination of color correction settings that accounts for most of the color mistakes produced by your scanner.

✦ **Colorize:** Select this check box to apply a single hue and a single saturation level to the entire selection, regardless of how it was previously colored. All brightness levels remain intact, though you can adjust them incrementally using the Lightness slider bar (a practice I do not recommend, as I mentioned earlier).

✦ **Preview:** Select the Preview check box to update the image continually every time you adjust a setting.

Tip   You can restore the options in the Hue/Saturation, Levels, and Curves dialog boxes to their original settings by Alt+clicking the Reset button. (The Cancel button changes to Reset when you press the Alt key.)

Adjusting hue and saturation

All right, now that you know how the options work, it's time to give them a whirl. One caveat before I launch into things: Grayscale figures won't help you one whit in understanding the Hue/Saturation options, so I refer you a few times to three color plates. You may want to slap a sticky note on the page that contains Color Plates 18-6, 18-7, and 18-8 before you begin reading, so you can easily flip back and forth between text and figures.

Changing hues

When the Colorize check box is inactive, the Hue slider bar shifts colors in an image around the color wheel. It's as if the pixels were playing a colorful game of musical chairs, except none of the chairs disappear. If you select the Master radio button and enter a value of +60 degrees, for example, all pixels stand up, march one-sixth of the way around the color wheel, and sit down, assuming the colors of their new chairs. A pixel that was red becomes yellow, a pixel that was yellow becomes green, and so on. The top row of Color Plate 18-6 shows the result of applying various Hue values to a single image. Note, in each case, all colors in the image change to an equal degree.

Note

As long as you select only the Master option and edit only the Hue value, Photoshop retains all colors in an image. In other words, after shifting the hues in an image +60 degrees, you can later choose Hue/Saturation and shift the hues -60 degrees to restore the original colors.

If you select any radio button other than Master, the musical chairs, metaphor breaks down a little. All pixels that correspond to the color you select move to the exclusion of other pixels in the image. The pixels that move must, well, sit on the nonmoving pixels' laps, meaning you sacrifice colors in the image.

For example, I edited the images in the second row of Color Plate 18-6 by applying Hue values while only the C (Cyan) radio button was selected. (In other words, I didn't apply Hue changes in combination with any other radio button.) All pixels that included some amount of cyan shifted to new hues according to the amount of cyan the pixels contained; all noncyan pixels remained unchanged. Despite the fact that the Hue values in each column of the color plate are identical, the colors in the horse changed less dramatically when C (Cyan) was selected than when I used the Master option. Even the pixels in the primarily cyan areas contain trace amounts of blue, which is excluded from the C (Cyan) hue adjustments.

Changing saturation levels

When I was a little kid, I loved watching my grandmother's television, because she kept the Color knob cranked at all times. The images appeared to leap off the screen, like they were radioactive or something. Way cool. Well, the Saturation option works just like that Color knob. I don't recommend you follow my grandmother's example and send the saturation for every image through the roof, but it can prove helpful for enhancing or downplaying the colors in an image. If the image looks washed out, try adding saturation; if colors leap off the screen so everybody in the image looks like they're wearing neon makeup, then subtract saturation.

Note

Just as the Saturation option works like the Color knob on a TV set, the Hue value serves the same purpose as the Tint knob, and the Lightness value works like the Brightness knob. It looks like your mother was wrong when she told you sitting on your behind and staring at the TV wasn't going to teach you anything.

The top row of Color Plate 18-7 shows the results of applying Saturation values when the Master option is selected. As you can see, all colors in the image fade or fortify equally. By applying the Saturation values to specific color options only, however, you can selectively fade and fortify colors, as demonstrated in the second row of the color plate. The lower-left image in the color plate shows the result of selecting each color radio button — except C (Cyan) and B (Blue) — in turn and lowering the Saturation to -100, which translates to no saturation whatsoever, or all grays. Only grays, cyans, and blues are left. In the lower-right image, I lowered the Saturation for C (Cyan) and B (Blue) to -100 and raised the saturation of all other colors to +50, thus eliminating the image's most prominent colors and enhancing the remaining weaker ones.

The Saturation option is especially useful for toning down images captured with low-quality scanners that exaggerate certain colors. Back in the early years, I used to work with a model that would digitize flesh tones in varieties of vivid oranges and red. I couldn't for the life of me figure out how to peel the colors off the ceiling until I tried the Saturation option in the Hue/Saturation dialog box. By selecting the R (Red) radio button and dragging the slider down to about -50, I was usually able to eliminate the problem. You can, too.

Correcting out-of-gamut colors

Another common use for the Saturation option is to prepare RGB images for process-color printing. As I explained in Chapter 5, many colors in the RGB spectrum are considered *out of gamut,* meaning they fall outside the smaller CMYK color space. Photoshop now provides a means for recognizing such colors while remaining inside the RGB color space. Choose View ➪ Gamut Warning (Ctrl+Shift+Y) to color all out-of-gamut colors with gray (or some other color you specify using the Preferences command). The pixels don't actually change to gray; they just appear gray onscreen as long as the command is active. To turn View ➪ Gamut Warning off, choose the command again.

How do you eliminate such problem colors? Well, you have three options:

✦ Let Photoshop take care of the problem automatically when you convert the image by choosing Image ➪ Mode ➪ CMYK Color. This tactic is risky because Photoshop simply cuts off colors outside the gamut and converts them to their nearest CMYK equivalents. What was once an abundant range of differently saturated hues becomes abruptly flattened, like you gave it some kind of cruel buzz haircut. Choosing View ➪ CMYK Preview (Ctrl+Y) while working in the RGB color space gives you an idea of how dramatic the buzz can be. Sometimes the effect is hardly noticeable, in which case no additional attention may be warranted. Other times, the results can be disastrous.

✦ Another method is to scrub away with the sponge tool. In Chapter 8, I discussed how much I dislike this alternative, and despite the passage of ten chapters, I haven't changed my mind. Although it theoretically offers selective control — you just scrub at areas that need attention until the gray pixels created by the Gamut Warning command disappear — the process leaves too much to chance and, frequently, does more damage than simply choosing Image ➪ Mode ➪ CMYK Color.

✦ The third and best solution involves the Saturation option inside the Hue/Saturation dialog box.

No doubt this last item comes as a huge surprise, given I decided to broach the whole out-of-gamut topic in the middle of examining the Saturation option. But try to scoop your jaw off the floor long enough to peruse the following steps, which outline the proper procedure for bringing out-of-gamut colors back into the CMYK color space.

Steps: Eliminating Out-of-Gamut Colors

1. **Create a duplicate of your image to serve as a CMYK preview.**
   Choose Image ➪ Duplicate to create a copy of your image. Then choose View ➪ CMYK Preview or press Ctrl+Y. This image represents what Photoshop will do with your image if you don't make any corrections whatsoever. It's good to have around for comparative purposes.

2. **Return to your original image and choose Select ➪ Color Range.**
   Then select the Out Of Gamut option from the Select pop-up menu and press Enter. You have now selected all the nonconformist antigamut pixels throughout your image. These radicals must be expunged.

3. **To monitor your progress, choose View ➪ Gamut Warning to display the gray pixels.** Oh, and don't forget to press Ctrl+H to get rid of those pesky ants.

4. **Press Ctrl+U to display the Hue/Saturation dialog box.**

5. **Lower the saturation of individual color ranges.** Don't change any settings while Master is selected; it's not exact enough. Rather, experiment with selecting individual color radio buttons and lowering the Saturation value. The Hue slider can sometimes be useful as well. Every time you see one of the pixels change from gray to color, it means another happy pixel has joined the CMYK pod. You may want to shout, "It's pointless to resist the invasion of the gamut snatchers!" and laugh mockingly just to make your work more entertaining.

Tip

Keep an eye on the duplicate image in the CMYK preview mode. If you edit a color in your original image and render it less colorful than the CMYK preview, it means you're doing damage you could avoid by simply choosing Image ➪ Mode ➪ CMYK Color. For example, if you drag the Saturation slider down to -35 for Y (Yellow) and notice the revived pixels in the original image have become noticeably less colorful than their counterparts in the duplicate, nudge the slider back up to brighten the colors. If you can't seem to find an equitable solution, try selecting a different color radio button and editing it. Or try nudging the Hue slider and see what happens. Be patient; this takes a little time.

6. **When only a few hundred sporadic gray spots remain onscreen, click the OK button to return to the Image window.** Bellow imperiously, "You may think you have won, you little gray pixels, but I have a secret weapon!" Then choose Image ➪ Mode ➪CMYK Color and watch as Photoshop forcibly thrusts them into the gamut.

Mind you, the differences between your duplicate image and the one you manually turned away from the evil empire of RGB excess will be subtle, but they may prove enough to produce a better-looking image with a wider range of colors.

Cross Reference

If the Hue/Saturation command doesn't seem to be working out, try using the Variations command or the Levels and Curves commands, as explained later in this chapter. The Variations command goes so far as to display the out-of-gamut pixels inside its previews and hide its gamut warning as colors come into the fold.

Avoiding gamut-correction edges

The one problem with the previous steps is the Color Range command selects only the out-of-gamut pixels without even partially selecting their neighbors. As a result, you desaturate out-of-gamut colors while leaving similar colors fully saturated, an effect that can produce visual edges in an image.

Tip

One solution is to insert a step between Steps 2 and 3 in which you do the following: Change the Tolerance value in the Magic Wand Options palette to, say, 12. Next, choose Select ➪ Similar, which expands the selected area to incorporate all pixels that fall within the Tolerance range. Finally, choose Select ➪ Feather and enter a value that's about a quarter of the Tolerance value — in this case, 3.

This solution isn't perfect — ideally, the Color Range option box wouldn't dim the Fuzziness slider when you choose Out Of Gamut — but it does succeed in partially selecting a few neighboring pixels without sacrificing too many of the out-of-gamut bunch.

Colorizing images

When you select the Colorize check box in the Hue/Saturation dialog box, the options in the dialog box perform differently. Returning to that wonderful musical chairs analogy, the pixels no longer walk around a circle of chairs; they all get up and go sit in the same chair. Every pixel in the selection receives the same hue and the same level of saturation. Only the brightness values remain intact to ensure the image remains recognizable.

The top row of Color Plate 18-8 shows the results of shifting the hues in an image in two different directions around the color wheel. In each case, the Colorize option is turned off. The second row shows similar colors applied separately to the blue and nonblue portions of the image using the Colorize option. (I selected these regions using the Color Range command.) The colors look similar within each column in the color plate. The Hue values are different in the shifted images than those in the colorized images, however, because the shifted colors are based on relative adjustments while the colorized changes are absolute.

In most cases, you only want to colorize grayscale images or bad color scans because colorizing ruins the original color composition of an image. You probably also want to lower the Saturation value to somewhere in the neighborhood of 50 to 80. All the colors in the second-row images in Color Plate 18-8 err on the high side, with Saturation values of 80.

Tip

To touch up the edges of a colorized selection, change the foreground color to match the Hue and Saturation values you used in the Hue/Saturation dialog box. You can do this by choosing the HSB Sliders command from the Color palette menu and entering the values into the H and S option boxes. Set the B (Brightness) value to 100 percent. Then select the paintbrush tool and change the brush mode in the Paintbrush Options palette to Color. And paint away.

Shifting selected colors

The Replace Color command enables you to select an area of related colors and adjust the hue and saturation of that area. When you select Image ➪ Adjust ➪ Replace Color, you get a dialog box much like the Color Range dialog box. Shown in Figure 18-10, the Replace Color dialog box varies in only a few respects: It's missing the Select and Selection Preview pop-up menus and it offers three slider bars, taken right out of the Hue/Saturation dialog box.

In fact, this dialog box works exactly as if you were selecting a portion of an image using Select ➪ Color Range and editing it with the Hue/Saturation command. There is no functional difference whatsoever. The Replace Color and Color Range dialog boxes even share the same default settings. If you change the Fuzziness value in one, the default Fuzziness value of the other changes as well. It's like they're identical twins or something.

So why does the Replace Color command even exist? Because it enables you to change the selection outline and apply different colors without affecting the image in any way. Just select the Preview check box to see the results of your changes onscreen, and you're in business.

The top row of Color Plate 18-9 shows two effects created by selecting an area and changing the Hue value to +148 and the Saturation value to -12 (as in Figure 18-10). In the first example, I selected the pumpkin face by setting the Fuzziness value to 40 and clicking and Shift+clicking a few times with the eyedropper tool. In the right example, I clicked just once in the area behind the pumpkin and changed the Fuzziness to 200, the maximum setting. I was able to experiment freely without once leaving the dialog box or redrawing the selection outline.

Figure 18-10: The Replace Color dialog box works like the Color Range dialog box described back in Chapter 12, with a few Hue/Saturation options thrown in.

If you're not clear on how to use all the options in the Replace Color dialog box, read the "Generating Masks Automatically" section in Chapter 12. It tells you all about the eyedropper tools and the Fuzziness option.

Shifting predefined colors

The Selective Color command enables you to adjust the colors in CMYK images. You can use the command when working on RGB or Lab images, but because it enables you to adjust the levels of cyan, magenta, yellow, and black inks, Selective Color makes more sense in the CMYK color space.

Frankly, I'm not keen on the Selective Color command. For general image editing, the Variations command provides better control and more intuitive options. Adobe created the Selective Color command to accommodate traditional press managers who prefer to have direct control over ink levels rather than monkeying around with hue, saturation, and other observational color controls. If Selective Color works for you, great. But if it never quite gels, don't get hung up on it. You can accomplish all this and more with the Variations command, described in the next section.

Choosing Image ➪ Adjust ➪ Selective Color brings up the dialog box shown in Figure 18-11. To use the dialog box, choose the predefined color you want to edit from the Colors pop-up menu, and then adjust the four process-color slider bars to change the predefined color. When the Relative radio button is selected, you add or subtract color, much as if you were moving the color around the musical chairs using the Hue slider bar. When you select Absolute, you change the predefined color to the exact value entered into the Cyan, Magenta, Yellow, and Black option boxes. The Absolute option is, therefore, much like the Colorize check box in the Hue/Saturation dialog box.

If you examine it closely, you notice the Selective Color dialog box is much like the Hue/Saturation dialog box. You have access to predefined colors in the form of a pop-up menu instead of radio buttons, and you can adjust slider bars to alter the color. The key differences are the pop-up menu enables you to adjust whites, medium grays (Neutrals), and blacks — options missing from Hue/Saturation — and the slider bars are always measured in CMYK color space.

The bottom row of Color Plate 18-9 includes two examples that show how this dialog box works. To create the first, I chose Red from the Colors pop-up menu and dragged the Cyan slider bar all the way up to +100 percent and the Yellow slider all the way down to -100 percent. I also selected the Relative radio button, which retains a lot of pink in the pumpkin's face. To create the second example, I reapplied the same colors, but selected the Absolute radio button, making the entire pumpkin purple. I also chose Black from the Colors pop-up menu and dragged the Black slider to -100 percent.

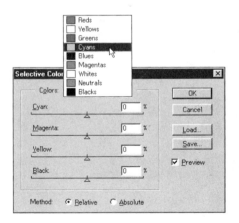

Figure 18-11: Select a predefined color from the Colors pop-up menu and adjust the slider bars to change that color.

Tip

As I mentioned at the outset, the Selective Color command produces the most predictable results when you're working on a CMYK image. For example, when you drag the Cyan slider triangle to the right, you're actually transferring brightness values to the cyan channel. You have to watch for a few anomalies, though, particularly when editing Black. In the CMYK mode, areas of your image that appear black include not only black, but also shades of cyan, magenta, and yellow, resulting in what printers call a *rich black* (or saturated black). To change black to white, as I did in the lower-right example of Color Plate 18-9, you must set the Black slider to -100 percent and also set the Cyan, Magenta, and Yellow sliders to the same value.

Using the Variations command

The Variations command is at once Photoshop's most essential color correction function and its funkiest:

✦ On one hand, you can adjust hues and luminosity levels based on the brightness values of the pixels. This gives you a selective degree of control unmatched by Hue/Saturation. You can also see what you're doing by clicking little thumbnail previews (see Figure 18-12), which takes much of the guesswork out of the correction process.

✦ On the other hand, the Variations dialog box takes over your screen and prevents you from previewing corrections in the Image window. Furthermore, you can't see the area outside of a selection, which proves disconcerting when making relative color adjustments.

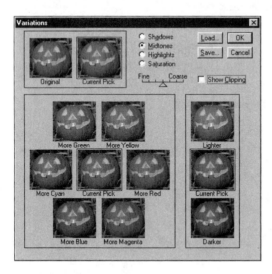

Figure 18-12: Click the thumbnails to shift the colors in an image; adjust the slider bar in the upper-right corner to change the sensitivity of the thumbnails; and use the radio buttons to determine which part of an image is selected.

Variations is, therefore, best suited to correcting an image in its entirety. Here's how it works: To infuse color into the image, click one of the thumbnails in the central portion of the dialog box. The thumbnail labeled More Cyan, for example, shifts the colors toward cyan. The thumbnail even shows how the additional cyan will look when added to the image. In case you're interested in seeing how these thumbnails actually affect a final printed image in the CMYK color space, check out Color Plate 18-10.

Now notice each thumbnail is positioned directly opposite its complementary color. More Cyan is across from More Red, More Blue is across from More Yellow, and so on. In fact, clicking a thumbnail not only shifts colors toward the named color, but away from the opposite color. For example, if you click More Cyan and then click its opposite, More Red, you arrive at the original image.

Note

Although this isn't exactly how the colors in the additive and subtractive worlds work — cyan is not the empirical opposite of red — the colors are theoretical opposites, and the Variations command makes the theory a practicality. After all, you haven't yet applied the color to the image, so the dialog box can calculate its adjustments in a pure and perfect world. Cyan and red ought to be opposites so, for the moment, they are.

To control the amount of color shifting that occurs when you click a thumbnail, move the slider triangle in the upper-right corner of the dialog box. Fine produces minute changes; Coarse creates massive changes. To give you an idea of the difference between the two, you have to click a thumbnail about 40 times when the slider is set to Fine to equal one click when it's set to Coarse.

The radio buttons at the top control which colors in the image are affected. Select Shadows to change the darkest colors, Highlights to change the lightest colors, and Midtones to change everything in between.

Note

In fact, if you're familiar with the Levels dialog box — as you will be when you read "The Levels command" section later in this chapter — the first three radio buttons have direct counterparts in the slider triangles in the Levels dialog box. For example, when you click the Lighter thumbnail when the Highlights option is selected in the Variations dialog box, you perform the same action as moving the white triangle in the Levels dialog box to the left — that is, you make the lightest colors in the image even lighter.

The Saturation radio button enables you to increase or decrease the saturation of colors in an image. Only one thumbnail appears on either side of the Current Pick image — one that decreases the saturation, and another that increases it. The Variations command modifies saturation differently than Hue/Saturation — where Hue/Saturation will push the saturation of a color as far as it will go, Variations attempts to modify the saturation without changing overall brightness values. As a result, an image saturated with Hue/Saturation will look lighter than one saturated with Variations.

As you click the options — particularly when modifying saturation — you may notice weird colors spring up inside the thumbnails. These brightly colored pixels are gamut warnings, highlighting colors that exceed the boundaries of the current color space. For example, if you're working in the RGB mode, these colors extend beyond the RGB gamut. Although the colors won't actually appear inverted as they do in the dialog box, it's not a good idea to exceed the color space because it results in areas of flat color, just as when you convert between the RGB and CMYK spaces. To view the thumbnails without the weirdly colored pixels, turn off the Show Clipping check box. (Incidentally, this use of the word *clipping* — Photoshop's third use, in case you're counting — has nothing to do with paths or masks.)

Enhancing colors in a compressed image

Now that you know every possible way to adjust hues and saturation levels in Photoshop, it's time to discuss some of the possible stumbling blocks. The danger of rotating colors or increasing the saturation of an image is you can bring out some unstable colors. Adjusting the hues can switch ratty pixels from colors your eyes aren't sensitive to — particularly blue — into colors your eyes see well — reds and greens. Drab color can also hide poor detail, which becomes painfully obvious when you make the colors bright and vivid.

Consider the digital photograph featured in Color Plate 18-11. Snapped in Copley Square in Boston with a Kodak DC50, the original image at the top of the color plate is drab and lifeless. If I use the Hue/Saturation command to pump up the saturation levels, a world of ugly detail rises out of the muck, as shown in the second example. (Obviously, I've taken the saturation a little too high, but only to demonstrate a point.) The detail would have faired no better if I had used the Variations command to boost the saturation.

Unstable colors may be the result of JPEG compression, as in the case of the digital photo. Or you may have bad scanning or poor lighting to thank. In any case, you can fix the problem using our friends the Median and Gaussian Blur commands, as I explain in the following steps.

If you work with heavily compressed images on a regular basis, you may want to record these steps with the Actions palette, as explained in Chapter 3. Unlike the "Adjusting the Focus of Digital Photos" steps back in Chapter 15, you won't want to apply these steps to every digital photograph you take — or even most of them — but they come in handy more often than you may think.

Steps: Boosting the Saturation of Digital Photos

1. Select the entire image and copy it to a new layer. It seems like half of all Photoshop techniques begin with Ctrl+A and Ctrl+J.

2. **Press Ctrl+U to display the Hue/Saturation dialog box.** Then raise the Saturation value to whatever setting you desire. Don't worry if your image starts to fall apart — that's the whole point of these steps. Pay attention to the color and don't worry about the rest. In the second example in Color Plate 18-11, I raised the Saturation to +80.

3. **Choose Filter ➪ Noise ➪ Median.** As you may recall from the last module, Median is the preeminent JPEG image fixer. A radius value of 4 or 5 pixels works well for most images. You can take it even higher when working with resolutions of 200 ppi or more. I used 5. This destroys the detail, but that's not important. The color is all that matters.

4. **Choose Filter ➪ Blur ➪ Gaussian Blur.** As always, the Median filter introduces its own edges. And this is one case where you don't want to add any edges whatsoever. So blur the heck out of the layer. I used a radius of 4.0, just one pixel less than my Median radius value.

5. **Select Color from the blend mode pop-up menu in the Layers palette.** Photoshop mixes the gummy, blurry color with the crisp detail underneath. I also lowered the Opacity to 70 percent to produce the third example in Color Plate 18-11.

My image was still a little soft, so I applied the digital-photo sharpening steps from Chapter 15. After flattening the image, I pressed Ctrl+A and Ctrl+J again to copy it to yet another new layer. (I could have also pressed Alt while choosing Layer ➪ Merge Visible to copy the previous layers to a new one.) Then I applied the Median, Gaussian Blur, and Unsharp Mask filters, flattened the image one last time, and sharpened the image to taste. The finished result appears at the bottom of Color Plate 18-11. Although a tad bit too colorful — Boston's a lovely city, but it's not quite this resplendent — the edges look every bit as good as they did in the original photograph, and in many ways better.

Making Custom Brightness Adjustments

The Lighter and Darker options in the Variations dialog box are preferable to the Lightness slider bar inside the Hue/Saturation dialog box because you can specify whether to edit the darkest, lightest, or medium colors in an image. But neither command is adequate for making precise adjustments to the brightness and contrast of an image. Photoshop provides two expert-level commands for adjusting the brightness levels in both grayscale and color images:

✦ The Levels command, which is ideal for most color corrections, enables you to adjust the darkest values, lightest values, and midrange colors for the entire selection or independently within each color channel.

✦ The Curves command, which is great for creating special effects and correcting images that are beyond the help of the Levels command. Using the Curves command, you can map every brightness value in every color channel to an entirely different brightness value.

Note A controversy seems to be brewing in the back rooms of some print houses and art shops over which command is better, Levels or Curves. Based on a few letters I've received over the years, it seems some folks consider Curves as the better command, and Levels about as useful as Brightness/Contrast.

This is most certainly not the case, however. Levels enables you to enter numerical values, and it includes a histogram so you can better gauge how your adjustments will affect the image. Meanwhile, Curves enables you to map out more than three significant points (the Levels limit) on a graph. The point is, both commands have their advantages, and both offer practical benefits for intermediate and advanced users alike.

No substitute exists for a good histogram, so I prefer to use Levels for my daily color correcting. If you can't quite get the effect you want with Levels, or you know you need to map specific brightness values in an image to other values, use Curves. The Curves command is the more powerful function, but it is also more cumbersome than Levels.

The Levels command

When you choose Image ➪ Adjust ➪ Levels (Ctrl+L), Photoshop displays the Levels dialog box shown in Figure 18-13. The dialog box offers a histogram, as explained in the "Threshold" section earlier in this chapter, as well as two sets of slider bars with corresponding option boxes and a few automated eyedropper options in the lower-right corner. You can compress and expand the range of brightness values in an image by manipulating the Input Levels options and then mapping those brightness values to new brightness values by adjusting the Output Levels options.

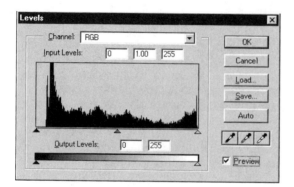

Figure 18-13: Use the Levels dialog box to map brightness values in the image (Input Levels) to new brightness values (Output Levels).

The options in the Levels dialog box work as follows:

✦ **Channel:** Select the color channel you want to edit from this pop-up menu. You can apply different Input Levels and Output Levels values to each color channel. The options along the right side of the dialog box affect all colors in the selected portion of an image, however, regardless of which Channel option is active.

✦ **Input Levels:** Use these options to modify the contrast of the image by darkening the darkest colors and lightening the lightest ones. The Input Levels option boxes correspond to the slider bar immediately below the histogram. You map pixels to black (or the darkest Output Levels value) by entering a number from 0 to 255 into the first option box or by dragging the black slider triangle. For example, if you raise the value to 55, all colors with brightness values of 55 or less in the original image become black, darkening the image as shown in the first example of Figure 18-14.

You can map pixels at the opposite end of the brightness scale to white (or the lightest Output Levels value) by entering a number from 0 to 255 into the last option box or by dragging the white slider triangle. If you lower the value to 200, all colors with brightness values of 200 or greater become white, lightening the image as shown in the second example of Figure 18-14. In the last example of the figure, I raised the first value and lowered the last value, thereby increasing the amount of contrast in the image.

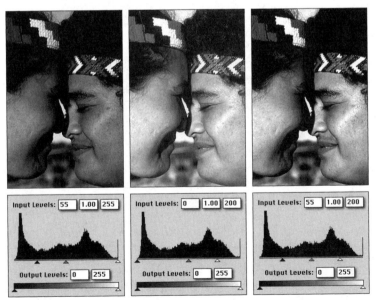

Figure 18-14: These are results of raising the first Input Levels value to 55 (left), lowering the last value to 200 (middle), and combining the two (right).

Tip

One of my favorite ways to edit the Input Levels values is to press the up and down arrow keys. Each press of an arrow key raises or lowers the value by one. Press Shift with an arrow key to change the value in increments of ten.

✦ **Gamma:** The middle Input Levels option box and the corresponding gray triangle in the slider bar (shown highlighted in Figure 18-15) represent the gamma value, which is the brightness level of the medium gray value in the image. The gamma value can range from 0.10 to 9.99, with 1.00 being dead-on medium gray. Any change to the gamma value has the effect of decreasing the amount of contrast in the image by lightening or darkening grays without changing shadows and highlights. Increase the gamma value or drag the gray slider triangle to the left to lighten the medium grays (also called *midtones*), as in the first and second examples of Figure 18-16. Lower the gamma value or drag the gray triangle to the right to darken the medium grays, as in the last example in the figure.

You can also edit the gamma value by pressing the up and down arrow keys. Pressing an arrow key changes the value by 0.01, while pressing Shift+arrow changes the value by 0.10. I can't stress enough how useful this technique is. I rarely do anything except press arrow keys inside the Levels dialog box now.

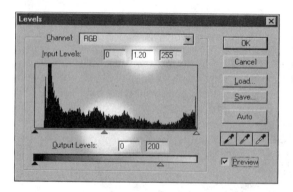

Figure 18-15: I highlighted the gamma options by selecting everything but the highlighted areas and applying the values shown in the previous figure.

✦ **Output Levels:** Use these options to curtail the range of brightness levels in an image by lightening the darkest pixels and darkening the lightest pixels. You adjust the brightness of the darkest pixels — those that correspond to the black Input Levels slider triangle — by entering a number from 0 to 255 into the first option box or by dragging the black slider triangle. For example, if you raise the value to 55, no color can be darker than that brightness level (roughly 80 percent black), which lightens the image as shown in the first example of Figure 18-17. You adjust the brightness of the lightest pixels — those corresponding to the white Input Levels slider triangle — by entering a number from 0 to 255 into the second option box or by dragging the white slider triangle. If you lower the value to 200, no color can be lighter than that brightness level (roughly 20 percent black), darkening the image as shown in the second example of Figure 18-17. In the last example of the figure, I raised the first value and lowered the second value, thereby dramatically decreasing the amount of contrast in the image.

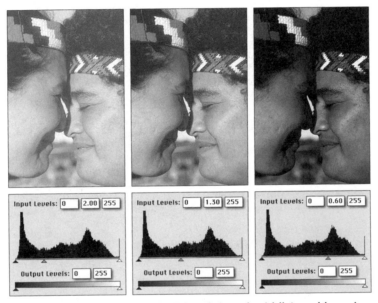

Figure 18-16: The results of raising (left and middle) and lowering (right) the gamma value to lighten and darken the midtones in an image

Tip

You can fully or partially invert an image using the Output Levels slider triangles. Just drag the black triangle to the right and drag the white triangle to the left past the black triangle. The colors flip, whites mapping to dark colors and blacks mapping to light colors.

✦ **Load/Save:** You can load and save settings to disk using these buttons.

✦ **Auto:** Click the Auto button to map the darkest pixel in your selection to black and the lightest pixel to white automatically, just like Image ⇨ Adjust ⇨ Auto Levels. Photoshop actually darkens and lightens the image by an extra half a percent, in case the darkest and lightest pixels are statistically inconsistent with the rest of the image.

To enter a percentage of your own, Alt+click the Auto button (the button name changes to Options) to display the Auto Range Options dialog box shown in Figure 18-18. Enter higher values to increase the number of pixels mapped to black and white; decrease the values to lessen the effect. The first two examples in Figure 18-19 compare the effect of the default 0.50 percent values to higher values of 5.00 percent. (Strictly for comparison purposes, the last image in the figure demonstrates the effect of the Equalize command applied to the entire image.)

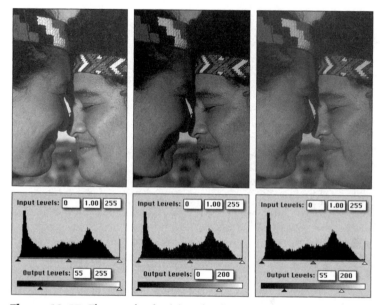

Figure 18-17: The result of raising the first Output Levels value to 55 (left), lowering the second value to 200 (middle), and combining the two (right)

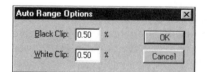

Figure 18-18: Alt+click the Auto button to change the extent to which Photoshop closes the range of black and white pixels.

Note   Any changes made inside the Auto Range Options dialog box also affect the performance of the Auto Levels command. At all times, the effects of the Auto button and Auto Levels command are absolutely identical.

✦ **Eyedroppers:** Select one of the eyedropper tools in the Levels dialog box and click a pixel in the Image window to adjust the color of that pixel automatically. If you click a pixel with the black eyedropper tool (the first of the three), Photoshop maps the color of the pixel and all darker colors to black. If you click a pixel with the white eyedropper tool (last of the three), Photoshop maps it and all lighter colors to white. Use the gray eyedropper tool (middle) to change the exact color you click to medium gray and adjust all other colors in accordance. For example, if you click a white pixel, all white pixels change to medium gray and all other pixels change to even darker colors.

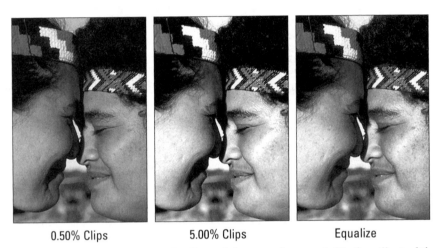

0.50% Clips   5.00% Clips   Equalize

Figure 18-19: Note the default effect of the Auto button (left), the effect of the Auto button after raising the Clip values (middle), and the effect of the Equalize filter (right).

Tip

One way to use the eyedropper tools is to color-correct scans without much messing around. Include a neutral swatch of gray with the photograph you want to scan. (If you own a Pantone swatch book, Cool Gray 5 or 6 is your best bet.) After opening the scan in Photoshop, choose the Levels command, select the gray eyedropper tool, and click the neutral gray swatch in the Image window. This technique won't perform miracles, but it will help you to distribute lights and darks in the image more evenly. You then can fine-tune the image using the Input Levels and Output Levels options.

✦ **Preview:** Select this option to preview the effects of your settings in the Image window.

To give you a sense of how the Levels command works, the following steps describe how to improve the appearance of an overly dark, low-contrast image such as the first example in Color Plate 18-12. Thanks to natural lighting and the dark color of the stone, this statue of Thomas Jefferson is hardly recognizable. Luckily, you can bring out the highlights using Levels.

Steps: Correcting Brightness and Contrast with the Levels Command

1. **Press Ctrl+L to display the Levels dialog box.** The histogram for the Jefferson image appears superimposed in white in front of the great man's chest. As you can see, most of the colors are clustered together on the left side of the graph, showing far more dark colors exist than light ones.

2. **Press Ctrl+1 to examine the red channel.** Assuming you're editing an RGB image, Ctrl+1 displays a histogram for the red channel. The channel-specific histograms appear below Jefferson, colorized for your viewing pleasure.

3. **Edit the black Input Levels value as needed.** Drag the black slider triangle to below the point at which the histogram begins. In the case of Jefferson, you can see a spike in the histogram about one-half pica in from the left side of the graph. I dragged the black triangle directly underneath that spike, changing the first Input Levels value to 14, as you can see in the red histogram on the right side of Color Plate 18-12.

4. **Edit the white Input Levels value.** Drag the white slider triangle to below the point at which the histogram ends. In the color plate, the histogram features a tall spike on the far right side. This means a whole lot of pixels are already white. I don't want to create a flat hot spot, so I leave the white triangle alone.

5. **Edit the gamma value.** Drag the gray triangle to the gravitational center of the histogram. Imagine the histogram is a big mass, and you're trying to balance the mass evenly on top of the gray triangle. Because my histogram is weighted too heavily to the left, I had to drag the gray triangle far to the left, until the middle Input Levels value changed to 2.40, which represents a radical shift.

6. **Repeat Steps 2 through 5 for the green and blue channels.** Your image probably has a significant preponderance of red about it. To fix this, you need to edit the green and blue channels in kind. The graphs on the right side of Color Plate 18-12 show how I edited my histograms. Feel free to switch back and forth between channels as much as you like to get everything just right.

7. **Press Ctrl+tilde (~) to return to the composite RGB histogram.** Once you get the color balance right, you can switch back to the composite mode and further edit the Input Levels. I typically bump up the gamma a few notches — to 1.2 or so — to account for dot gain.

You may notice your RGB histogram has changed. Although the histograms in the individual color channels remain fixed, the composite histogram updates to reflect the red, green, and blue modifications. I've superimposed the updated histogram in white on the corrected Jefferson on the right side of Color Plate 18-12. As you can see, the colors are now better distributed across the brightness range.

8. **Press Enter to apply your changes.** Just for fun, press Ctrl+Z a few times to see the before and after shots. Quite the transformation, eh?

Tip   If you decide, after looking at the before and after views, you could do a better job, undo the color correction. Then press Ctrl+Alt+L to bring up the Levels dialog box with the previous settings intact. Now you can take up where you left off.

The Curves command

If you want to map any brightness value in an image to absolutely any other brightness value — no holds barred, as they say at the drive-in movies — you want the Curves command. When you choose Image ➪ Adjust ➪ Curves (Ctrl+M), Photoshop displays the Curves dialog box, shown in Figure 18-20, which offers access to the most complex and powerful color correction options on the planet.

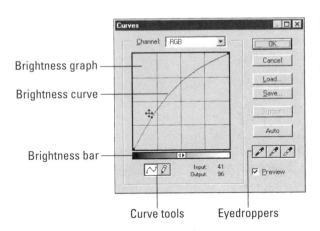

Figure 18-20: The Curves dialog box enables you to distribute brightness values by drawing curves on a graph.

Briefly, here's how the options work:

✦ **Channel:** Surely you know how this option works by now. You select the color channel you want to edit from this pop-up menu. You can apply different mapping functions to different channels by drawing in the graph below the pop-up menu. But, as is always the case, the options along the right side of the dialog box affect all colors in the selected portion of an image, regardless of which Channel option is active.

✦ **Brightness graph:** The brightness graph is where you map brightness values in the original image to new brightness values. The horizontal axis of the graph represents input levels; the vertical axis represents output levels. The brightness curve charts the relationship between input and output levels. The lower-left corner is the origin of the graph (the point at which both input and output values are 0). Move right in the graph for higher input values, up for higher output values. Because the brightness graph is the core of this dialog box, upcoming sections explain it in more detail.

✦ **Brightness bar:** The brightness bar shows the direction of light and dark values in the graph. When the dark end of the brightness bar appears on the left, colors are measured in terms of brightness values, in which case the colors in the graph proceed from black on the left to white on the right, as demonstrated in the left example of Figure 18-21. Therefore, higher values produce lighter colors. This is my preferred setting because it measures colors in the same direction as the Levels dialog box.

If you click the brightness bar, white and black switch places, as shown in the second example of Figure 18-21. The result is Photoshop measures the colors in terms of ink coverage, from 0 percent of the primary color to 100 percent of the primary color. Higher values now produce darker colors. If you click the brightness bar in the process of drawing a curve, the curve automatically flips to retain any changes you made, as the figure illustrates.

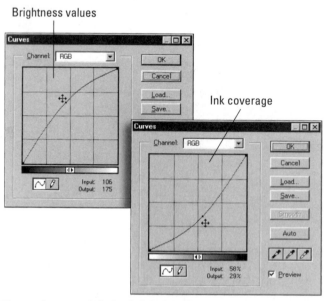

Figure 18-21: Click the brightness bar to change the way in which the graph measures color: by brightness values (left) or by ink coverage (right).

✦ **Curve tools:** Use the curve tools to draw the curve inside the brightness graph. Click in the graph with the point tool (on the left, selected by default) to add a point to the curve. Drag a point to move it. To delete a point, drag it outside the boundaries of the graph. The pencil tool (on the right) enables you to draw free-form curves simply by dragging inside the graph, as shown in Figure 18-22.

Tip

You can draw straight lines with the pencil tool by clicking at one location in the graph and Shift+clicking at a different point, just as you can when using the real pencil tool in the Image window.

✦ **Input/Output numbers:** The input and output numbers monitor the location of your cursor in the graph according to brightness values or ink coverage, depending on the setting of the brightness bar.

✦ **Load/Save:** Use these buttons to load and save settings to disk.

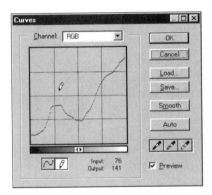

Figure 18-22: Use the pencil tool to draw free-form lines in the brightness graph. If the lines appear rough, you can soften them by clicking the Smooth button.

Tip

Okay, here's the weirdest tip in all of Photoshop. It's not very practical, but it's about as wild as you can get. You can use a gradation as a Curves map. First, click the Edit button in the Gradient Tool Options palette, select one of the more garish gradients, like Spectrum. Then Ctrl+Alt+click the Save button to save the gradient as a Curves file. Open the file in the Curves dialog box, and stand back and watch the fireworks.

In the psychedelic Color Plate 18-13, I cloned Constantine to a new layer and applied a heavy dose of Gaussian Blur. Then I used the Curves command to apply one of three gradients. In the bottom row, I mixed each of the fantastic Images with its underlying original using the Color blend mode.

✦ **Smooth:** Click the Smooth button to smooth out curves drawn with the pencil tool. Doing so leads to smoother color transitions in the Image window. This button is dimmed except when you use the pencil tool.

✦ **Auto:** Click this button to map the darkest pixel in your selection to black and the lightest pixel to white automatically. Photoshop throws in some additional darkening and lightening according to the Clip percentages, which you can edit by Alt+clicking the button.

✦ **Eyedroppers:** Photoshop actually enables you to use a fourth eyedropper from the Curves dialog box. If you don't select any eyedropper tool (or you click in the graph to deselect the current eyedropper) and move the cursor out of the dialog box into the Image window, you get the standard eyedropper cursor. Click a pixel in the image to locate the brightness value of that pixel in the graph. A circle appears in the graph, and the input and output numbers list the value for as long as you hold down the mouse button, as shown in the first example in Figure 18-23.

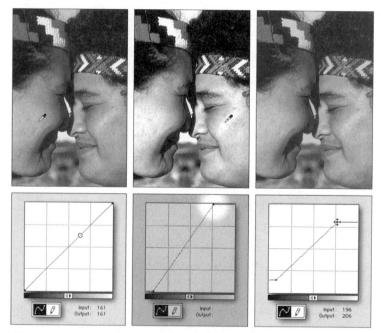

Figure 18-23: Use the standard eyedropper cursor to locate a color in the brightness graph (left). Click with one of the eyedropper tools from the Curves dialog box to map the color of that pixel in the graph (middle). You can then edit the location of the point in the graph by dragging it (right).

The other eyedroppers work as they do in the Levels dialog box, mapping pixels to black, medium gray, or white. For example, the second image in Figure 18-23 shows the white eyedropper tool clicking a light pixel, thereby mapping that value to white, as shown in the highlighted portion of the graph below the image. You can further adjust the brightness value of that pixel by dragging the corresponding point in the graph, as demonstrated in the last example of the figure.

✦ **Preview:** Select this option to preview your settings in the Image window.

Continuous curves

Caution

All discussions in the few remaining pages of this section assume the brightness bar is set to edit brightness values (in which case the gradation in the bar lightens from left to right). If you set the bar to edit ink coverage (the bar darkens from left to right), you can still achieve the effects I describe, but you must drag in the opposite direction. For example, if I tell you to lighten colors by dragging upward, you drag downward. In a backward world live the ink coverage people.

When you first enter the Curves dialog box, the brightness curve appears as a straight line strung between two points, as shown in the first example of Figure 18-24, mapping every input level from white (the lower-left point) to black (the upper-right point) to an identical output level. If you want to perform seamless color corrections, the point tool is your best bet because it enables you to edit the levels in the brightness graph while maintaining a continuous curve.

To lighten the colors in the selected portion of the image, click near the middle of the curve with the point tool to create a new point, and then drag the point upward, as demonstrated in the second example of Figure 18-24. To darken the image, drag the point downward, as in the third example.

Create two points in the curve to boost or lessen the contrast between colors in the image. In the first example of Figure 18-25, I created one point near the white point in the curve and another point close to the black point. I then dragged down on the left point and up on the right point to make the dark pixels darker and the light pixels lighter, which translates to higher contrast.

In the second example of the figure, I did just the opposite, dragging up on the left point to lighten the dark pixels and down on the right point to darken the light pixels. As you can see in the second image, this lessens the contrast between colors, making the image more gray.

In the last example in Figure 18-25, I bolstered the contrast with a vengeance by dragging the right point down and to the left. This has the effect of springing the right half of the curve farther upward, thus increasing the brightness of the light pixels in the image.

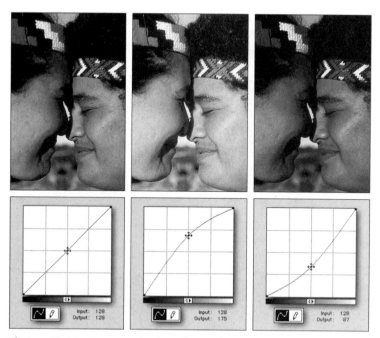

Figure 18-24: Create a single point in the curve with the point tool (left) and then drag it upward (middle) or downward (right) to lighten or darken the image evenly.

Arbitrary curves

You can create some mind-numbing color variations by adjusting the brightness curve arbitrarily, mapping light pixels to dark, dark pixels to light, and in-between pixels all over the place. In the first example of Figure 18-26, I used the point tool to achieve an arbitrary curve. By dragging the left point severely upward and the right point severely downward, I caused dark and light pixels alike to soar across the spectrum.

If you're interested in something a little more subtle, try applying an arbitrary curve to a single channel in a color image. Color Plate 18-14, for example, shows an image subject to relatively basic color manipulations in the red and green channels, followed by an arbitrary adjustment to the blue channel.

Although you can certainly achieve arbitrary effects using the point tool, the pencil tool is more versatile and less inhibiting. As shown in the second example of Figure 18-26, I created an effect that would alarm Carlos Castaneda just by zigzagging my way across the graph and clicking the Smooth button.

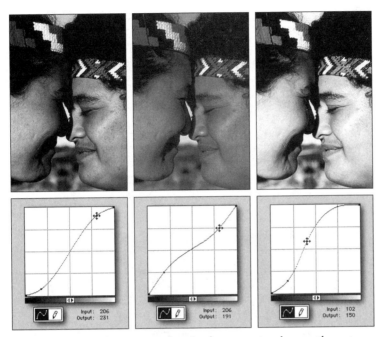

Figure 18-25: Create two points in the curve to change the appearance of contrast in an image, whether by increasing it mildly (left), decreasing it (middle), or boosting it dramatically (right).

Figure 18-26: These arbitrary brightness curves were created using the point tool (left) and the pencil tool (right).

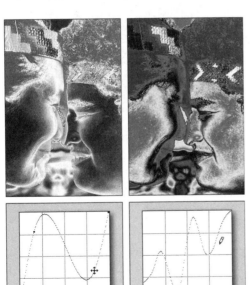

In fact, the Smooth button is an integral part of using the pencil tool. Try this little experiment: Draw a bunch of completely random lines and squiggles with the pencil tool in the brightness graph. As shown in the first example of Figure 18-27, your efforts will most likely yield an unspeakably hideous and utterly unrecognizable effect.

Next, click the Smooth button. Photoshop automatically connects all portions of the curve, miraculously smoothing out the color-mapping effect and rescuing some semblance of your image, as shown in the second example of the figure. If the effect is still too radical, you can continue to smooth it out by clicking additional times on the Smooth button. I clicked the button twice more to create the right image in Figure 18-27. Eventually, the Smooth button restores the curve to a straight line.

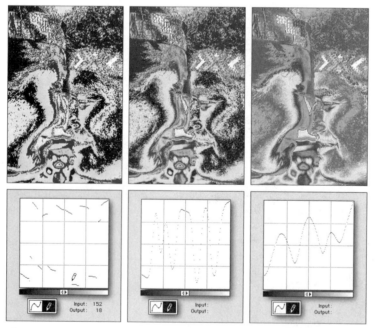

Figure 18-27: After drawing a series of completely random lines with the pencil tool (left), I clicked the Smooth button once to connect the lines into a frenetic curve (middle) and then twice more to even out the curve, thus preserving more of the original image (right).

Adjustment Layers

Every one of the commands I've discussed in this chapter is applicable to a single layer at a time. If you want to correct the colors in multiple layers, you have to create a special kind of layer called an *adjustment layer*. New to Photoshop 4, adjustment layers are layers that contain mathematical color correction information. The layer applies its corrections to all layers below it, without affecting any layers above.

You can create an adjustment layer in one of two ways:

✦ Choose Layer ⇨ New ⇨ Adjustment Layer.

✦ Ctrl+click the new layer icon at the bottom of the Layers palette.

Either way, Photoshop displays the New Adjustment Layer dialog box shown in Figure 18-28. This dialog box contains the standard Name, Opacity, and Mode options that accompany any kind of layer. But you also get a Type pop-up menu, which offers some of Photoshop's most important color correction commands. Select the kind of color correction you want to apply from the menu, and then press Enter.

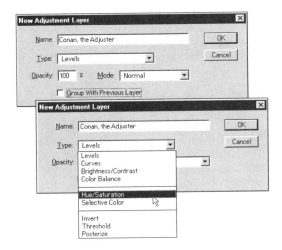

Figure 18-28: The New Adjustment Layer dialog box, as it appears normally (top) and with Type pop-up menu unfurled (bottom)

Photoshop then displays the dialog box for the selected correction (unless you choose Invert, which does not offer a dialog box). Change the settings as desired and press Enter as you normally would. The completed color correction appears as a new layer in the Layers palette. In Figure 18-29, for example, I've added a total of three adjustment layers. Photoshop marks adjustment layers with half-black circles, so you can readily tell them apart from image layers.

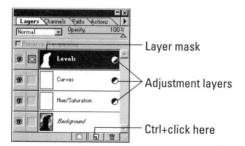

Figure 18-29: Here I've created three layers of color correction in front of a single background image.

The advantages of layer-based corrections

Now at this point, you may think, "Big whoop. You can apply corrections to multiple layers. That doesn't seem like such a great feature." Not only would that be an unkind assessment of adjustment layers — hey, computer code has feelings, too — but an inaccurate assessment as well. I've said before this is Photoshop 4's most important new feature, and here's why:

✦ **Forever editable:** As long as the adjustment layer remains intact — stored in the native Photoshop format, of course — you can edit the color correction over and over again without damaging the underlying pixels. Unlike standard color corrections, which make permanent alterations to selected pixels, adjustment layers are temporary in nature. On the slightest whim, you can double-click the layer name in the palette to bring up the color correction dialog box, complete with the settings currently in force. Tweak the settings as the mood hits you and press Enter to make changes on the fly. You can't get any more flexible than this.

✦ **Flexible layer masking:** You can also adjust the affected area to your heart's content. An adjustment layer covers the entire image like an adjustable wall-to-wall carpet. You modify the affected area by painting inside the layer. The layer doesn't contain any pixels of its own, so painting in an adjustment layer changes its layer mask. Paint with black to remove the correction from an area, use white to paint the correction back in.

Tip

In fact, if a selection is active when you create a new adjustment layer, Photoshop automatically creates a layer mask according to the selection outline. For example, in Color Plate 18-15, I selected the topiary dinosaur before creating the Levels layer. Photoshop thoughtfully converted my selection into a mask, as labeled in Figure 18-29. And like any layer mask, I can edit it well into the future without any adverse side effects.

✦ **Reorder your corrections:** As with any layers, you can shuffle adjustment layers up and down in stacking order. For example, if you decide you don't want the correction to affect a specific layer, just drag the adjustment layer to a level in the Layers palette below the layer you want to exclude. If you're juggling multiple adjustment layers, as in Figure 18-29, you can shuffle the adjustment layers to change the order in which they're applied. You can even use the standard keyboard shortcuts, Ctrl+[and Ctrl+].

✦ **Fade corrections:** You can fade a standard color correction right after you apply it using Filter ⇨ Fade. But you can fade a correction applied with an adjustment layer any old time. Just change the Opacity and blend mode settings in the Layers palette.

✦ **Correct with blend modes:** Some folks prefer to correct overly light or dark images using blend modes. Take an image, copy it to a new layer, and apply the Multiply mode to darken the layer or Screen to lighten it. The problem with this trick is it increases the size of the image in memory. Duplicating the image to a new layer requires Photoshop to double the size of the image in RAM.

Tip

Adjustment layers enable you to apply this same technique without adding pixels to RAM. Create a new adjustment layer with the Levels option selected. After the Levels dialog box comes up, press Enter to ignore it. Now select Multiply or Screen from the blend mode pop-up menu in the Layers palette. The adjustment layer serves as a surrogate duplicate of the layers below it, mocking every merged pixel. And it doesn't add so much as a K to the file size. It's an image-editing miracle — layers without the pain.

Note

You can make an adjustment layer part of a clipping group so your color corrections only apply to the layers in that group. This way, you can apply the color correction where you want it — you don't have to apply it to every pixel in all the layers beneath the adjustment layer.

Correcting a flat image using layers

Although many artists will use this new feature to edit multilayer compositions, adjustment layers are equally applicable to flat photos. Originally printed in the February 1996 issue of *Macworld* magazine, Color Plate 18-15 shows an image shot with a Polaroid PDC-2000 and corrected using a total of three color corrections, layered one on top of the other. (Much of this text also comes from that same article.) At first glance, the original photo on the left side of the color plate is a textbook example of what happens if you ignore backlighting. But as you have probably figured out by now, an image that appears black may actually contain several thousands of colors just itching to get out. Adjustment layers make it easier than ever to free these colors and make them fully visible to the world.

Because my image was in such rotten shape, I decided to start with the expert Curves command. I Ctrl+clicked the new layer icon and selected Curves from the Type pop-up menu. Then I used the pencil tool in the Curves dialog box to draw a radical upswing on the left side of the graph, dramatically lightening the blacks right out of the gate. I clicked the Smooth button a few times to even out the color transitions, as demonstrated in the second example in Color Plate 18-15.

All this lightening resulted in some very washed-out colors (a typical side effect), so I created a second adjustment layer using the Hue/Saturation command. By raising the Saturation value, I quickly breathed a little enthusiasm into these tired old hues — a sufficient amount, in fact, to make it clear how soft the focus was. So I went back to the original image layer and applied the Unsharp Mask filter. Had it not been for the advent of adjustment layers, I would have had to sharpen the image before color correcting it, making it impossible to gauge the results accurately, or sharpen the image after correcting, which might bring out compression artifacts and other undesirable anomalies. With adjustment layers, however, I can sharpen and correct at the same time, giving no operation precedent over the other.

The hedge monster remained a little dark, so I selected it with the Color Range command and then created a third adjustment layer for the Levels command. Using Levels, I quickly enhanced the brightness and contrast of the green beast, bringing him out into the full light of day. As I mentioned earlier, Photoshop automatically generated a layer mask for my selection, which appears as a tiny white silhouette in the Layers palette.

To be fair, I should mention that adjustment layers are not an original invention for Photoshop. Just as Painter/X2 offered bitmapped layers more than a year before Photoshop, Live Picture introduced correction layers two years prior to the arrival of Photoshop 4. Live Picture's layers also enable you to sharpen, blur, and distort underlying pixels temporarily, three operations currently beyond Photoshop's reach. My guess is Photoshop will continue to grow in this direction in the future. The day you can apply filters with adjustment layers is the day this feature will be complete.

The Wonders of Blend Modes

Mixing Images Together

Fifty ways must exist to combine and compare differently colored pixels in Photoshop. So far, we've seen how you can smear and blur pixels into each other, select pixels using other pixels, layer pixels in front of pixels, compare a pixel to its neighbors using automated filters, and map the colors of pixels to other colors. Any time you edit, mask, composite, filter, or color correct an image, you're actually breeding the image with itself or with other images to create a new and unique offspring.

This chapter explores the final and ultimate experiment in Photoshop's great genetics laboratory. *Blend modes,* also called *calculations,* enable you to mix the color of a pixel with that of every pixel in a straight line beneath it. A single blend mode is as powerful as a mask, a filter, and a color map combined and, best of all, it's temporary. As long as one image remains layered in front of another, you can replace one calculation with another as easily as you change a letter of text in a word processor.

To appreciate the most rudimentary power of blend modes, consider Figure 19-1. The first image shows a terrestrial thrill seeker composited in front of the Apollo crew's old stomping grounds. Both layers are as opaque as if you had cut them out with scissors and glued them together. (Granted, you'd have to be skilled with scissors.) The anti-aliased edges of the parachute mix slightly with the moon pixels below them. But beyond that, every pixel is a digital hermit, steadfastly avoiding interaction.

The second image in Figure 19-1 paints a different picture. Here I've created several clones of the parachute and moon and mixed them together using Photoshop's considerable array of calculation capabilities. Although I used just two images, I composited them onto ten layers, only one of which — the background layer — was fully opaque. I don't know if it's moon men invading Earth or the other way around but, whatever it is, it wouldn't have been possible without blend modes and their ilk.

Figure 19-1: Layers enable you to combine images from different sources (left), but blend modes enable you to mix images together to create intriguing, if sometimes unexpected, interactions (right).

Photoshop gives you three ways to mix images:

✦ **The Layers palette:** You can combine a floating selection or an independent layer with underlying pixels using the Opacity slider and blend mode pop-up menu, both members of the Layers palette. Figure 19-2 shows these two illustrious items in the context of the layers list for Figure 19-1. To learn everything there is to know about the Opacity slider and blend mode pop-up menu, read the next section.

Figure 19-2: This is the list of layers in the Invasion Moon composition, with blend mode pop-up menu proudly displayed on the right.

✦ **The Blend If sliders:** You can double-click a layer name in the Layers palette to display the Layers Options dialog box. Many of the options in this dialog box are found elsewhere, but the two slider bars at the bottom are unique. They enable you to drop colors out of the active layer and to force colors to show through from layers below. This is one of Photoshop's oldest, finest, and to least-used features, as I discuss later in the "Dropping Out and Forcing Through" section.

✦ **Channel operations:** The so-called channel operations enable you to combine two open images of identical size or one image with itself. Photoshop offers two commands for this purpose: Image ⇨ Apply Image and Image ⇨ Calculations. Unusually complex and completely lacking in sizing and placement functions, these commands provide access to two unique blend modes named Add and Subtract. Simply put, unless a technique involves the Add or Subtract mode, or you want to clone two images into a third image window, you can mix images with greater ease, flexibility, and feedback using the Layers palette. For more on this lively topic, see the "Using Channel Operation Commands" section later in this chapter.

Blend modes are not Photoshop's most straightforward feature. A time may even come when you utter the words, "Blend modes are stupid." They demand a generous supply of experimentation and, even then, they'll fool you. As a former math major, I well understand the elementary arithmetic behind Photoshop's calculations. And yet, despite roughly a decade of experience with blend modes in Photoshop and other programs, I frequently am surprised by their outcome.

The key, therefore, is to combine a basic understanding of how blend modes and other compositing features work with your natural willingness to experiment. Sometime when you don't have a deadline looming over your head, take some multilayered composition you have lying around and hit it with a few calculations. Even if the end result is a disaster you wouldn't share with your mother, let alone a client, you can consider it time well spent.

Using Opacity and Blend Modes

This is not the first time in this book I've touched on the Opacity slider or the blend mode pop-up menu. And given that the Layer palette's blend modes mimic the brush modes — both in name and in function — discussed in "The 18 paint tool modes" section near the end of Chapter 8, we're covering some familiar territory. But you'll soon find a significant difference exists between laying down a single color with a brush and merging the hundred or so thousand colors that inhabit a typical layer. This difference is the stuff on the following pages.

Note Incidentally, both the Opacity and blend mode options are dimmed when you're working on the background layer or in a single-layer image. There's nothing underneath, so there's no point in mixing.

Changing the Opacity setting

The Opacity slider is the easiest of the layer mixers to understand. It enables you to mix the active layer with the layers below in prescribed portions. The Opacity slider is sort of like mixing a drink. Suppose you pour one part vermouth and four parts gin into a martini glass. (Any martini enthusiast knows that's too much vermouth, but bear with me on this one.) The resulting beverage is ⅕ vermouth and ⅘ gin. If the vermouth were a layer, you could achieve the same effect by setting the Opacity to 20 percent. This implies 20 percent of what you see is vermouth and the remaining 80 percent is underlying gin.

When any selection or navigation tool is active, you can change the Opacity setting for a layer or floating selection from the keyboard. Press a single number key to change the Opacity in 10-percent increments. That's 1 for 10 percent, 2 for 20 percent, up to 0 for 100 percent — in order along the top of your keyboard — as it has been since the olden days. But, aye, here's the new rub. In Photoshop 4, you can press two keys in a row to specify an exact two-digit Opacity value. Yes, I know, I already mentioned this in Chapter 13, but it bears repeating.

The shy and retiring Behind and Clear

After that enlightening bit of repetitious information, it's time to move on to the more complicated realm of blend modes. There are, in fact, 19 blend modes in all. But most of the time, you only see 17. The two you're missing are Behind and Clear, and they are available only after you establish a floating selection on a layer.

Try this: Create a layer and put some stuff on it. To see the effects of the Behind and Clear modes better, make sure some portion of the layer is transparent, and the layer looks different than its background. Then select part of the layer and press Ctrl+Alt+arrow key. (Any arrow key will do.) You now have a floating selection on a layer. Check out the blend mode pop-up menu in the Layers palette; you will find Behind and Clear in the third and fourth positions.

Just like the Behind mode available for brushes, the Behind blend mode enables you to tuck the floating selection behind the opaque portions of the active layer. In other words, the floating selection is allowed to fill the transparent and translucent areas of the active layer only.

Note

As I mentioned in Chapter 13, Behind is the opposite of Preserve Transparency. So if the Preserve Transparency check box is turned on, Behind has no effect.

The Clear mode uses the floating selection to cut a hole in the active layer. It's like having a little hole you can move around independently of the pixels, without danger of harming them.

You know that scene in *Yellow Submarine* where the Fab Four are making fun of that poor little marsupial dude with the long, mustard-colored nose? After they finish labeling him a "Nowhere Man" — hey, give him a break, guys, maybe his priorities are different — the creature announces he has a hole in his pocket. He then takes the hole out, puts it on the floor, and it becomes a hole in the floor. Later, the holes multiply — I can't remember why — and all the guys sail through the holes, singing some other song with nothing to do with the plot, which was already in short supply. Granted, it's a pointless movie — as this is a pointless analogy — but the concept is absolutely the same as Photoshop's Clear mode. Clear turns a floating selection into a portable hole in the active layer.

Tip

This feature is especially useful for clipping holes into a layer using character outlines. Create some text with the type mask tool, press Ctrl+Alt+arrow to float the text, and convert it to a bunch of holes by choosing the Clear mode. If you suddenly become concerned that you've lost part of the layer, don't panic. Choose the Normal mode and the original pixels come back into play.

The remaining 17 blend modes

The remaining 17 blend modes are available whether you're editing a layer or a floating selection. But it seems like a lot of excess verbiage to keep saying "layer or floating selection" over and over again, so any time I say "layer" in the following list, you'll know I mean both.

Also, when I allude to a little something called a *composite pixel,* I mean the pixel color that results from all the mixing going on in back of the active layer. For example, your document may have hoards of layers with all sorts of blend modes in effect, but as long as you work on, say, layer 23, Photoshop treats the image formed by layers 1 through 22 as if it were one flattened image filled with a bunch of static composite pixels.

As you read through this plethora of blend mode descriptions, you can check out examples of the blend modes in Color Plate 19-1. Here we have a bunch of layered photographs of Saturn composited against the stormy gaseous planet of Jupiter. Although the planets aren't to scale — I understand both bodies are several times larger than this book, for example — they do a fair job of showing the effects of the various blend modes.

✦ **Normal:** In combination with an Opacity setting of 100 percent, this option displays every pixel normally in the active layer, regardless of the colors of the underlying image. Figure 19-3 shows a banner positioned on a single layer composited in front of a stucco texture created on the Background layer. The blend mode in force is Normal. (The drop shadow, incidentally, is merely an artistic embellishment that exists on the background layer.)

When you use an Opacity of less than 100 percent, the color of each pixel in the active layer is averaged with the composite pixel in the layers behind it according to the Opacity value.

Figure 19-3: An active layer containing the banner image and drop shadow subject to the Normal blend mode and an Opacity setting of 100 percent

✦ **Dissolve:** This option specifically affects feathered or softened edges. If the active layer is entirely opaque with hard edges, this option has no effect. If the selection is anti-aliased, the effect is generally too subtle to be of much use. The Dissolve option randomizes the pixels in the feathered portion of an active layer, as shown in the top example of Figure 19-4. It also randomizes pixels of hard- or soft-edged selections when the Opacity value is set below 100 percent, as shown in the second example in the figure.

✦ **Multiply:** To understand the Multiply and Screen modes, you must use a little imagination. So here goes: Imagine the active layer and the underlying image are both photos on transparent slides. The Multiply mode produces the same effect as holding those slides up to the light, one slide in front of the other. Because the light has to travel through two slides, the outcome is invariably a darker image that contains elements from both images. An example of the Multiply blend mode appears in Figure 19-5.

✦ **Screen:** Still have those transparent slides from the Multiply analogy? Well, place them both in separate projectors and point them at the same screen, and you'll get the same effect as Screen. Rather than creating a darker image, as you do with Multiply, you create a lighter image, as demonstrated in Figure 19-6 and Color Plate 19-1.

Figure 19-4: The Dissolve option applied to an opaque floating selection with heavily feathered edges (top) and to a second selection set to 40 percent opacity (bottom)

Figure 19-5: The Multiply blend mode produces the same effect as holding two overlapping transparencies up to the light. It always results in a darker image.

You can use the Screen blend mode to emulate film that has been exposed multiple times. Ever seen Thomas Eakin's pioneering *Jumping Figure,* which shows rapid-fire exposures of a naked man jumping from one location to another? Each shot is effectively screened onto the other, lightening the film with every exposure. The photographer was smart enough to limit the exposure time so he didn't overexpose the film; likewise, you should only apply Screen when working with images that are sufficiently dark, so you avoid overlightening.

Figure 19-6: The Screen mode produces the same effect as shining two projectors at the same screen. It always results in a lighter image.

✦ **Overlay, Soft Light, and Hard Light:** You can't separate these guys. All three multiply the dark colors in the active layer and screen the light colors into the composite pixels in the layers below. But they apply their effects to different degrees. Overlay favors the composite pixels, while Hard Light favors the layered pixels. (In fact, the two are direct opposites.) Soft Light is a washed-out version of Hard Light that results in a low-contrast effect.

Figure 19-7 shows all three blend modes applied to a single banner layer on the left. I then duplicated the banner layer with blend mode still in force to get the effects on the right. As these examples demonstrate, the modes effectively tattoo one image onto the image behind it. Even after multiple repetitions of the banners in the figure, the stucco texture still shows through, as if the banner were appliquéd onto it.

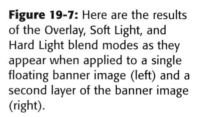

Figure 19-7: Here are the results of the Overlay, Soft Light, and Hard Light blend modes as they appear when applied to a single floating banner image (left) and a second layer of the banner image (right).

Overlay

Soft Light

Hard Light

I recommend starting with the Overlay mode any time you want to mix both the active layer and the layers behind it to create a reciprocal blend. By this, I mean a blend that mixes the colors evenly without eliminating any of the detail in either layer. After you apply Overlay, vary the Opacity to favor the composite pixels. I've said it before and I'll say it again, Overlay is Photoshop's most practical blend mode, the one you should always try first.

If you can't quite get the effect you want at lower Opacity settings, switch to the Soft Light mode and give that a try. On the other hand, if the Overlay mode at 100 percent seems too subtle, switch to Hard Light. You can even clone the layer to darn well emblazon the layer onto its background, as in the bottom-right image in Figure 19-7.

✦ **Color Dodge:** When you apply the Color Dodge mode, each color in the layer becomes a brightness value multiplier. Light colors like white produce the greatest effect, and black produces no effect. As a result, Color Dodge is Photoshop's most dramatic whitening agent, the equivalent of applying bleach to colored fabric. When applied to the banner layer in Figure 19-8, it exaggerates the stucco texture, resulting in a rougher effect than either Screen or the upcoming Lighten.

Figure 19-8: Color Dodge uses the active layer to bleach the pixels in the layer below. Nothing is subtle about this effect.

✦ **Color Burn:** If Color Dodge is bleach, then Color Burn is charcoal dust. It uses the colors in the active layer to reduce brightness values, resulting in a radical darkening effect. Like Color Dodge, the Color Burn mode creates a chalky effect when applied to the banner in Figure 19-9. You may also want to sneak a peek at Color Plate 19-1; this illustrates that both Color Dodge and Color Burn saps the colors from your images more surely than any other blend modes. If you want a high-contrast stamping effect, these are the blend modes to use.

✦ **Darken:** When you select this option, Photoshop applies colors in the active layer only if they are darker than the corresponding pixels below. Remember, Photoshop compares the brightness levels of pixels in a full-color image on a channel-by-channel basis. So, although the red component of a pixel in the active layer may be darker than the red component of the underlying composite pixel, the green and blue components, may be lighter. In this case, Photoshop would assign the red component, but not the green or blue, thereby subtracting some red and making the pixel slightly more turquoise. Compare the predictable grayscale example in Figure 19-10 to its more challenging color counterpart in Color Plate 19-1.

Figure 19-9: Color Burn sears an image charcoal black. No other darkening mode is this gritty or severe.

Figure 19-10: The same active layer subject to the Darken blend mode. Only those pixels in the selection that are darker than the pixels in the underlying stucco texture remain visible.

✦ **Lighten:** If you select this option, Photoshop applies colors in the active layer only if they are lighter than the corresponding pixels in the underlying image. Again, Photoshop compares the brightness levels in all channels of a full-color image. Examples of the Lighten blend mode appear in Figure 19-11 and Color Plate 19-1.

✦ **Difference and Exclusion:** The Difference mode was available in Photoshop 3, but Exclusion is new to Version 4. Even so, the two are kindred blending spirits.

Figure 19-11: Our friend, the active layer, subject to the Lighten blend mode. Only those pixels in the selection that are lighter than the pixels in the underlying stucco texture remain visible.

Difference inverts lower layers according to the brightness values in the active layer. White inverts the background absolutely, black doesn't invert it at all, and all the other brightness values invert it to some degree in between. As a result, the stucco shows through the black areas of the lion heads in Figure 19-12, while the light areas of the banner have inverted the texture nearly to black.

Exclusion works like Difference, except for one, er, difference. Shown in the second example of Figure 9-12, Exclusion sends medium-colored pixels to gray, creating a lower contrast effect, just as Soft Light is a low-contrast version of Hard Light.

Tip

One of my favorite uses for the Difference and Exclusion modes is to create a Difference sandwich, in which you sandwich a filtered version of an image between two originals. I explain this technique and others in the upcoming section "Sandwiching a filtered image."

✦ **Hue:** The Hue mode and the following three blend modes make use of the HSL color model to mix colors between active layer and underlying image. When you select Hue, Photoshop retains the hue values from the active layer and mixes them with the saturation and luminosity values from the underlying image. An example of this mode appears in the right column of Color Plate 19-1.

Note

I don't include grayscale figures for the Hue, Saturation, Color, and Luminosity blend modes for the simple reason these modes affect color images only. In fact, all four options are dimmed when you're editing a grayscale image.

✦ **Saturation:** When you select this option, Photoshop retains the saturation values from the active layer and mixes them with the hue and luminosity values from the underlying image. This mode rarely results in anything but subtle effects, as demonstrated by the bright orange Saturn in Color Plate 19-1. You'll usually want to apply it in combination with some other blend mode. For example, after applying a random blend mode to a layer, you might duplicate the layer and then apply the Saturation mode either to boost or downplay the colors, much like printing a gloss or matte coating over the image.

✦ **Color:** This option combines hue and saturation. Photoshop retains both the hue and saturation values from the active layer and mixes them with the luminosity values from the underlying image. Because the saturation portion of the Color mode has such a slight effect, Color frequently produces an almost identical effect to Hue. For example, the Hue and Color versions of Saturn in Color Plate 19-1 are similar, with the former appearing only slightly less bright than the latter.

✦ **Luminosity:** The Luminosity blend mode retains the lightness values from the active layer and mixes them with the hue and saturation values from the underlying image. An example of this mode appears in the lower-right corner in Color Plate 19-1. Here Saturn appears every bit as clearly defined as the Normal example in the upper-left corner, but it assumes the orange color of its Jupiterian background. So just as the Color mode uses the layer to colorize its background, the Luminosity mode uses the background to colorize the layer.

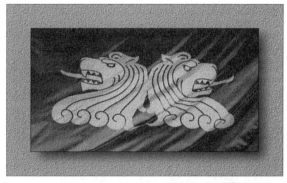

Difference

Figure 19-12: When you apply the Difference mode (top), white pixels invert the pixels beneath them, while black pixels leave the background untouched. The Exclusion mode (bottom) performs a similar effect, but instead of inverting medium colors, it changes them to gray.

Exclusion

Blend mode madness

Remember that scene in *Amadeus* where Mozart is telling the king about some opera he's writing — "Marriage of Franz Joseph Haydn" or something like that — and he's bragging about how many folks he has singing on stage at the same time? Remember that scene? Oh, you're not even trying. Anyway, you can do the same thing with Photoshop. Not with melody or recitative or anything like that, but with imagery. Just as Mozart might juggle several different melodies and harmonies at once, you can juggle layers upon layers of images, each filtered differently and mixed differently with the images below it.

Predicting the outcome of these monumental compositions takes a brain the magnitude of Mozart's. But screwing around with different settings takes no intelligence at all, which is where I come in.

The hierarchy of blend modes

The most direct method for juggling multiple images is sandwiching. By *sandwiching,* I mean placing a heavily filtered version of an image between two originals. This technique is based on the principle that most blend modes — all but Multiply, Screen, Difference, and Exclusion — change depending on which of two images is on top.

For example, Figure 19-13 shows two layers, A and B, and what happens when I blend them with the Overlay mode. When the leaf is on top, as in the third example, the Overlay mode favors the woman; but when the woman appears on the top layer, the Overlay mode favors the leaf.

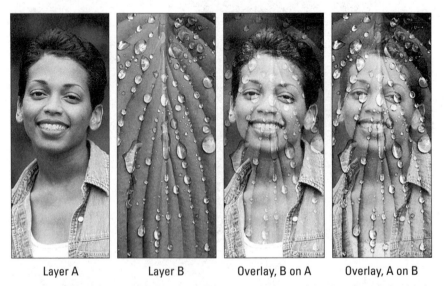

Layer A   Layer B   Overlay, B on A   Overlay, A on B

Figure 19-13: After establishing two layers, woman and leaf, I placed the leaf on top and applied Overlay to get the third image. Then I switched the order of the layers and applied the Overlay mode to the woman to get the last image.

As I mentioned earlier, the Overlay mode always favors the lower layer. Its opposite, Hard Light, favors the active layer. Therefore, I could have achieved the exact effect shown in the third example of Figure 19-13 by placing the leaf underneath and setting the woman layer to Hard Light. Flip-flop the layers and apply Hard Light to the leaf to get the last example.

Other blend modes have opposites, as well. Take the Normal mode, for example. When you apply Normal, whichever image is on top is the one you see. If you change the Opacity, however, you reveal the underlying image. At 50 percent Opacity, it doesn't matter which image is on top. The color of every pair of pixels in both images is merely averaged. So an inverse relationship exists. If the filtered image is on top, an Opacity setting of 25 percent produces the same effect as if you reversed the order of the images and changed the Opacity to 75 percent.

The other obvious opposites are Color and Luminosity. If I were to position the green leaf in front of the woman and apply Color, the woman would turn green. The same thing would happen if I placed the woman in front and applied Luminosity.

The moral of this minutia is, the order in which you stack your layers is as important as the blend modes you apply. Even filters that have no stacking opposites — Soft Light, Color Dodge, Hue, and others — will produce different effects depending on which layer is on top. For your general edification, Figure 19-14 and, possibly more enlightening, Color Plate 19-2 show a few examples.

Sandwiching a filtered image

When you sandwich a filtered image between two originals — which, as you may recall, is what all this is leading up to — you can lessen the effect of the filter and achieve different effects than those I discussed in Chapter 15. Layers and blend modes give you the flexibility to experiment as much as you want and for as long as you please.

In Color Plate 19-3, I copied the woman's face to a new layer and then applied Filter ➪ Sketch ➪ Charcoal with the foreground color set to dark purple and the background color set to green. The top row of images in the color plate show what happened when I used three different blend modes — Hard Light, Color, and Difference — to mix the Charcoal image with the underlying original.

I next cloned the background layer and moved it above the Charcoal layer, so the filtered image resided between two originals, creating a sandwich. The originals are the bread of the sandwich, and the Charcoal layer is the meat (or the eggplant, for you vegetarians). The bottom row demonstrates the effects of applying each of three blend modes to the top slice of bread, which interacts with the blend mode applied to the Charcoal meat shown above. For example, in the second column, I applied the Hard Light mode to the filtered image to achieve the top effect. Then I created the top layer and applied the Soft Light mode to get the bottom effect.

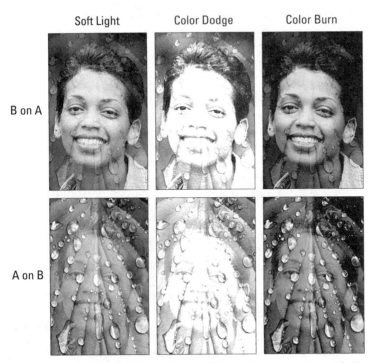

Soft Light   Color Dodge   Color Burn

B on A

A on B

Figure 19-14: Examples of a few additional blend modes with the leaf on the front layer (top row) and the woman in front (bottom row)

Creating a Difference sandwich

Ask your local deli guy, and he'll tell you everyone has a favorite sandwich. Where blend modes are concerned, my favorite is the Difference sandwich. By applying Difference to both the filtered layer and the cloned original on top, you effectively invert the filter into the original image and then reinvert the image to create a more subtle and utterly unique effect.

Figure 9-15 and Color Plate 19-4 show a small sampling of the several thousand possible variations on the Difference sandwich theme. In the top rows of both figures, I've vigorously applied a series of standard filters — so vigorously, in fact, that I've pretty well ruined the image. But no fear. By stacking it on top of the original, cloning the original on top of it, and applying the Difference mode to both layers, you can restore much of the original image detail, as shown in the bottom examples of the two figures. (I corrected the colors of the images by adding an adjustment layer on top of the sandwich but, otherwise, you see the effects in their raw form.)

Note A few notes about the Difference sandwich. First of all, the effect doesn't work nearly so well if you start reducing the Opacity values. Second, try using the Exclusion mode instead of Difference if you want to lower the contrast. And finally, Difference is one of those few blend modes that produces the same effect, regardless of how you order the layers. This means you can filter either the middle layer or the bottom layer in the sandwich and get the exact effect. But the top layer must be the original image.

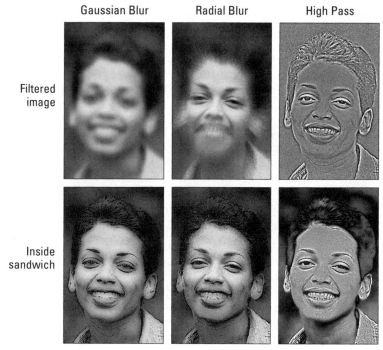

Figure 19-15: Three different filtering effects as they appear on their own (top row) and when inserted into a Difference sandwich (bottom row)

Dropping Out and Forcing Through

When you double-click a layer name in the Layers palette, Photoshop displays the Layer Options dialog box shown in Figure 19-16. In addition to enabling you to name a layer, change the Opacity value, and do some other stuff I've already covered in this book, you can drop out pixels in the active layer and force through pixels from lower layers according to their brightness values.

Photoshop 4.0

This feature has gone through more changes than a chameleon. In Photoshop 2.0, the Paste Controls dialog box was designed specifically to accommodate pasted images. In Photoshop 2.5, the Composite Controls dialog box was the only way to apply blend modes. Photoshop 3.0 did away with this dialog box for floating selections and made it exclusively applicable to layers. In Version 3.0.5, it once again became available for floaters (mostly because I complained, I think — no one else seemed to care). And now in Photoshop 4.0, floating selections are once again out of the picture. Sometimes I miss those old days.

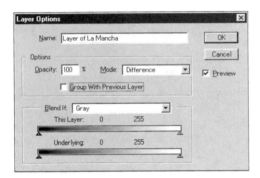

Figure 19-16: When editing a layer, you can access a dialog box of options to mix the colors selectively in the active layer with the colors in the image below.

After that bit of unnecessary nostalgia, let me take this opportunity to announce the Layer Options dialog box offers the following eight options, which have changed little over time:

✦ **Name:** Use this option box to change the layer name that appears in the Layers palette.

✦ **Opacity:** The Opacity option box enables you to specify the translucency of the active layer. This option works identically to the Opacity slider bar in the Layers palette.

✦ **Mode:** Here's where you select one of the 17 blend modes you could already access in the Layers palette pop-up menu.

✦ **Group with Previous Layer:** Select this option to combine the active layer and the one below it into a clipping group, as discussed in the "Masking groups of layers" section of Chapter 13. I ignored this option in Chapter 13 because it's easier to Alt+click the horizontal line between the two layers to convert them to a clipping group.

✦ **Blend If:** Select a color channel from the Blend If pop-up menu to apply the effects of the slider bars beneath the menu to one color channel independently of the others. When the Gray option is active, as it is by default, your changes affect all color channels equally. (To my knowledge, this is the only instance where Gray means all color channels; elsewhere, Gray means a gray composite, like Gray, should mean.) For the record, the Opacity value and Mode option affect all channels, regardless of the color channel you select from Blend If.

✦ **This Layer:** This slider bar enables you to exclude ranges of colors according to brightness values in the active layer. When you exclude colors by dragging the black triangle to the right or the white triangle to the left, the colors disappear from view.

✦ **Underlying:** This slider forces colors from the underlying layers to poke through the active layer. Any colors not included in the range set by the black and white triangles cannot be covered and are, therefore, visible regardless of the colors in the active layer.

✦ **Preview:** Select the Preview check box to update the Image window continually every time you adjust a setting.

The slider bars are far too complicated to explain in a bulleted list. To learn more about these options, as well as the Blend If pop-up menu, read the following sections.

Color exclusion sliders

Drag the triangles along the This Layer slider bar to abandon those pixels in the active layer whose colors fall within a specified range of brightness values. You can abandon dark pixels by dragging the left slider triangle or light pixels by dragging the right slider triangle. Figure 19-17 shows examples of each. To create the top example, I dragged the left slider bar until the value immediately to the right of the This Layer label read 50, thereby deleting pixels whose brightness values were 50 or less. To create the bottom example, I dragged the right slider triangle until the second value read 180, deleting pixels with brightness values of 180 or higher.

Drag the triangles along the Underlying slider bar to force pixels in the underlying image to show through if they fall within a specified brightness range. To force dark pixels in the underlying image to show through, drag the left slider triangle; to force light pixels to show through, drag the right slider triangle.

To achieve the effect in the top example in Figure 19-18, I dragged the left slider triangle until the value immediately to the right of the Underlying label read 120, forcing the pixels in the stucco pattern with brightness values of 120 or lower to show through. In the second example, I dragged the right slider triangle until the second value read 180, uncovering pixels at the bright end of the spectrum.

Figure 19-17: These are the results of moving the left This Layer slider triangle to 50 (top) and, after Alt+clicking on the Reset button, dragging the right slider triangle to 180 (bottom).

Fuzziness

The problem with abandoning and forcing colors with the slider bars is you achieve some pretty harsh color transitions. Both Figures 19-17 and 19-18 bear witness to this fact. Talk about your jagged edges! Luckily, you can soften the color transitions by abandoning and forcing pixels gradually over a fuzziness range, which works much like the Fuzziness value in the Color range dialog box, leaving some pixels opaque and tapering others off into transparency.

To taper off the opacity of pixels in either the active layers or the underlying image, Alt+drag one of the triangles in the appropriate slider bar. The triangle splits into two halves, and the corresponding value above the slider bar splits into two values separated by a slash, as demonstrated in Figure 19-19.

The left triangle half represents the beginning of the fuzziness range — that is, the brightness values at which the pixels begin to fade into or away from view. The right half represents the end of the range — that is, the point at which the pixels are fully visible or invisible.

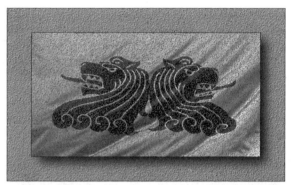

Figure 19-18: These are the results of moving the left Underlying slider triangle to 120 (top) and then resetting the left triangle back to 0 and moving the right triangle to 180 (bottom).

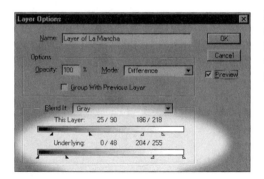

Figure 19-19: Alt+drag a slider triangle to split it in half. You can then specify a fuzziness range across which brightness values will gradually fade into transparency.

Figures 19-20 and 19-21 show softened versions of the effects from Figures 19-17 and 19-18. In the top example of Figure 19-20, for example, I adjusted the range of the left This Layer slider triangle so the value immediately to the right of the This Layer label read 30/70. The result is a much smoother effect than achieved in the top example in Figure 19-17. In the bottom example of Figure 19-20, I changed the range of the right This Layer slider triangle so the second value read 120/230.

Figure 19-20: The results of adjusting the fuzziness range of the left This Layer slider triangle to 30/70 (top) and that of the right This Layer slider triangle to 120/230 (bottom)

In Figure 19-21, I applied fuzziness ranges with the Underlying slider. In fact, both examples in the figure are the result of applying the same value, 120/180, to opposite Underlying slider triangles. In the top example, all brightness values under 120 gradually extending to values up to 180 show through the active layer. In the second example, all brightness values above 180 gradually extending down to 120 show through. The resulting two images look much like sand art. (The next thing you know, I'll be showing you how to create string art and black velvet Elvises.)

Color channel options

The options in the Blend If pop-up menu are applicable exclusively to the settings you apply using the This Layer and Underlying slider bars. When you work with a grayscale image, the Blend If pop-up menu offers one option only — Black — meaning the Blend If option has no effect on grayscale editing. When you work in the RGB, CMYK, or Lab mode, however, the Layer Options dialog box enables you to abandon and force ranges of pixels independently within each color channel.

To do so, select a color channel from the Blend If pop-up menu and then set the slider triangles as desired. Each time you select a different Blend If option, the slider triangles retract to the positions at which you last set them for that color channel.

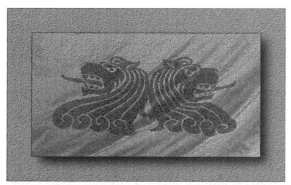

Figure 19-21: The results of adjusting the fuzziness range of both the left (top) and right (bottom) Underlying slider triangles to 120/180

Using Channel Operation Commands

Image ➪ Apply Image and Image ➪ Calculations provide access to Photoshop's *channel operations,* which composite one or more channels with others according to predefined mathematical calculations. Although once hailed as Photoshop's most powerful capabilities, channel operations have been eclipsed by the standard and more accessible functions available from the Layers and Channels palettes. One day, I suspect Adobe will scrap Apply Image and Calculations altogether. But until that day, I will dutifully document them both.

The Apply Image and Calculations commands enable you to merge one or two identically sized images using 12 of the 17 blend modes discussed earlier, plus 2 additional modes: Add and Subtract. In a nutshell, the commands duplicate the process of dragging and dropping one image onto another (or cloning an image onto a new layer) and using the blend mode and Opacity settings in the Layers palette to mix the two images together.

Although Apply Image and Calculations are more similar than different, each command fulfills a specific — if not entirely unique — function:

✦ **Apply Image:** This command takes an open image and merges it with the foreground image (or takes the foreground image and composites it onto itself). You can apply the command to either the full-color image or one or more of the individual channels.

✦ **Calculations:** The Calculations command works on individual channels only. It takes a channel from one image, mixes it with a channel from another (or the same) image, and puts the result inside an open image or in a new Image window.

The primary advantage of these commands over other, more straightforward compositing methods, is they enable you to access and composite the contents of individual color channels without a lot of selecting, copying and pasting, cloning, floating, and layering. You also get two extra blend modes, Add and Subtract, which may prove useful on a rainy day.

The Apply Image and Calculations commands provide previewing options so you can see how an effect will look in the Image window. But thanks to the sheer quantity of unfriendly options offered by the two commands, I suggest you use them on an occasional basis. The Calculations command can be a handy way to combine masks and layer transparencies to create precise selection outlines. And Apply Image is good for compositing images in different color models, such as RGB and Lab (as I explain in the "Mixing images in different color modes" section later in this chapter).

But, if your time is limited and you want to concentrate your efforts on learning Photoshop's most essential features, feel free to skip Apply Image and Calculations. I assure you, you won't be missing much.

The Apply Image command

Channel operations work by taking one or more channels from an image, called the *source,* and duplicating them to another image, called the *target.* When you use the Apply Image command, the foreground image is always the target, and you can select only one source image. Photoshop then takes the source and target, mixes them together, and puts the result in the target image. So the target image is the only image the command actually changes. The source image remains unaffected.

When you choose Image ➪ Apply Image, Photoshop displays the dialog box shown in Figure 19-22. Notice you can select from a pop-up menu of images to specify the Source, but the Target item — listed above the Blending box — is fixed. This is the active layer in the foreground image.

If this sounds a little dense, think of it this way: The source image is the floating selection, and the target is the underlying original. Meanwhile, the Blending options are the blend modes pop-up menu and Opacity slider in the Layers palette.

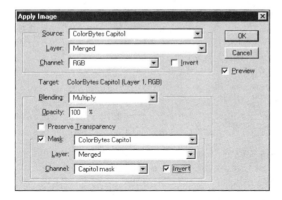

Figure 19-22: The Apply Image command enables you to mix one source image with a target image and make the result the new target.

Using the Apply Image command is a five-step process. You can always simply choose the command and hope for the best, but you'll get the most use from it if you do the following:

Steps: Applying the Apply Image Command

1. **Open the two images you want to mix.** If you want to mix the image with itself to create some effect, open the one image.

2. **Make sure the two images are exactly the same size, down to the last pixel.** Use the crop tool and Image Size command as necessary. (You needn't worry about this step when mixing an image with itself.)

3. **Inside the target image, switch to the channel and layer you want to edit.** If you want to edit all channels, press Ctrl+tilde (~) to remain in the composite view.

Tip When you're editing a single channel, I strongly advise you to display all channels onscreen. For example, after pressing Ctrl+1 to switch to the red channel, click in front of the RGB item in the Channels palette to display the eyeball icon and show all channels. Only one channel is active, but all are visible. This way, you can see how your edits inside the Apply Image dialog box will affect the entire image, not only the one channel.

4. **Select the portion of the target image you want to edit.** If you want to affect the entire image, don't select anything.

5. **Choose Image ⇨ Apply Image and have at it.**

Obviously, the last step is a bit more difficult than it sounds. That's why I've put together the following list to explain how all those options in the Apply Image dialog box work:

✦ **Source:** The Source pop-up menu contains the name of the foreground image, as well as any other images that are both open and exactly the same size as the foreground image. If the image you want to merge is unavailable, you must not have paid much attention to Step 2. Press Escape to cancel, resize and crop as needed, choose Image ⇨ Apply Image, and try again.

✦ **Layer:** This pop-up menu lists all layers in the selected source image. If the image doesn't have any layers, Background is your only option. Otherwise, select the layer containing the prospective source image. Select Merged to mix all visible layers in the source image with the target image.

✦ **Channel:** Select the channels you want to mix from this pop-up menu. Both composite views and individual color and mask channels are included. Remember, you'll be mixing these channels with the channels you made available in the target image before choosing the command.

For example, if the target image is an RGB image shown in the full-color composite view, and you choose RGB from the Channel pop-up menu in the Apply Image dialog box, Photoshop mixes the red, green, and blue channels in the source image with the corresponding red, green, and blue channels in the target image. If you switched to the red channel before choosing Apply Image and then selected the RGB option, however, the program mixes a composite grayscale version of the RGB source image with the red channel in the target and leaves the other target channels unaffected.

✦ **Selection, Transparency, and Layer Mask:** If a portion of the source image is selected, the pop-up menu offers a Selection option, which enables you to apply the selection outline as if it were a grayscale image, just like a selection viewed in the quick mask mode. If you selected a specific layer from the Layer pop-up menu, you'll find a Transparency option that represents the transparency mask. If the layer includes its own layer mask, a Layer Mask option also appears.

None of the three options is particularly useful when you work in the composite view of the target image; you'll usually want to apply the Selection, Transparency, or Layer Mask option only to a single channel, as described in "The Calculations command" section toward the end of this chapter. (For an exception, see the upcoming tip.)

✦ **Invert:** Select this check box to invert the contents of the source image before compositing it with the target image. This option enables you to experiment with different effects. The last example in Color Plate 19-5, for example, shows one use for the Invert check box. I inverted the *b* channel before compositing it with the RGB image to create an early dawn effect.

✦ **Target:** You can't change this item. It merely shows which image, channels, and layers are affected by the command.

✦ **Blending:** This pop-up menu offers access to 12 of the blend modes I discussed in "The remaining 17 blend modes" section earlier in this chapter. The Dissolve, Hue, Saturation, Color, and Luminosity options are missing. (Darken and Lighten have inexplicably been renamed Darker and Lighter, though they work just the same.) Two additional options, Add and Subtract, are discussed in the "Add and Subtract" section later in this chapter.

✦ **Opacity:** By now, I gather you're well aware of how this one works.

✦ **Preserve Transparency:** When you're editing a layer in the target image, that is, you activated a specific layer before choosing Image ➪ Apply Image, the Preserve Transparency check box becomes available. Select it to protect transparent portions of the layer from any compositing, much as if the transparent portions were not selected and, therefore, masked.

✦ **Mask:** Select this option to mask off a portion of the source image. I already mentioned you can specify the exact portion of the target image you want to edit by selecting that portion before choosing the Apply Image command. But you can also control which portion of the source image is composited on top of the target through the use of a mask. When you select the Mask check box, three new pop-up menus and an Invert check box appear at the bottom of the Apply Image dialog box. For complete information on these options, see the upcoming "Compositing with a mask" section.

✦ **Result:** If you press the Alt key when choosing Image ➪ Apply Image, Photoshop appends one additional option — the Result pop-up menu — at the end of the Apply Image dialog box. This option enables you to send the result of the operation to a separate Image window, layer, or channel. This can be useful if you don't want to upset the contents of the foreground window, if you want to send the result to a separate layer for further compositing, or if you only want to edit a mask. (This last operation is generally made easier by the Calculations command, as described in the "Combining masks" section near the end of this chapter.)

Tip   One of my favorite reasons to Alt+choose Apply Image is to convert a mask in one image to a selection outline in another image of equal size. You can accomplish this without the Apply Image command by converting the mask to a selection and then dragging and dropping it, but Apply Image enables you do this in one step.

Here's how it works: Go to the receiving image — the one into which you want to transfer the selection — and Alt+choose Apply Image. (Be sure nothing in the image is already selected, or the Result pop-up menu will not appear.) Select the identically sized image that contains the mask from the Source pop-up menu, choose the mask channel name from the Channel pop-up menu, and choose Normal from the Blending menu. Then choose Selection from the Result pop-up menu and press Enter.

Mixing images in different color modes

Tip

Throughout my laborious explanations of all those options in the Apply Image dialog box, I've been eagerly waiting to share with you the command's one truly unique capability. Image ⇨ Apply Image is the only way to composite RGB and Lab images while leaving them set to their separate color modes. For example, you could mix the lightness channel from the Lab image with the red channel from the RGB image, the *a* channel with the green channel, and the *b* channel with the blue channel. By contrast, you'd have to composite the channels one at a time if there were no Apply Image command. (If you were simply to drag-and-drop a Lab image into an RGB image, Photoshop would automatically convert the image to the RGB color space, which results in a different effect.)

To help make things a little more clear, Color Plate 19-5 shows four examples of an image composited onto itself using the Hard Light blend mode (which you select from the Blending pop-up menu, as I'll cover shortly). The first example shows the result of selecting the RGB image as both source and target. As always, this exaggerates the colors in the image and enhances contrast, but retains the same basic color composition as before.

The other examples in the color plate show what happened when I duplicated the image by choosing Image ⇨ Duplicate, converted the duplicate to the Lab mode (Mode ⇨ Lab Color), and then composited the Lab duplicate with the RGB original. To do this, I switched to the RGB image, chose Image ⇨ Apply Image, and selected the Lab image from the Source pop-up menu. In the top-right example, I chose Lab from the Channel pop-up menu to blend each of the Lab channels with one of the RGB channels — lightness with red, and so on. Although I stuck with the Hard Light blend mode, you can see the effect is different. In the bottom-left example, I chose Lightness from the Channel pop-up menu, which mixed the lightness channel with all three RGB channels. And in the bottom-right image, I chose *b* from the Channel pop-up menu and selected the Invert check box, which inverted the *b* channel before applying it.

Note

You cannot mix an entire CMYK image with an RGB or Lab image because the images contain different numbers of channels. In other words, while you can mix individual channels from CMYK, RGB, and Lab images, you can't intermix the channels — cyan with red, magenta with green, and so on. In other words, CMYK does not appear as an option inside the Channel pop-up menu when you edit an RGB image. In other words . . . oh, nuts, that's enough.

Compositing with a mask

I said I'd go into a little more depth about the Mask option in this section, and now it's time to pay up. All the Mask option does is provide a method for you to import only a selected portion of the source image into the target image. Select the Mask check box and choose the image that contains the mask from the pop-up menu on the immediate right. As with the Source pop-up menu, the Mask menu lists only those images that are open and are the exact size as the target image. If necessary, select the layer on which the mask appears from the Layer pop-up menu. Then select the specific mask channel from the final pop-up menu. This needn't be a mask channel; you can use any color channel as a mask.

After you select all the necessary options, the mask works like so: Where the mask is white, the source image shows through and mixes in with the target image, just as if it were a selected portion of the floating image. Where the mask is black, the source image is absent, as if you had Ctrl+dragged around that portion of the floating selection with the lasso or some other selection tool, leaving the target entirely protected. Gray values in the mask mix the source and target with progressive emphasis on the target as the grays darken.

If you prefer to swap the masked and unmasked areas of the source image, select the Invert check box at the bottom of the dialog box. Now, where the mask is black, you see the source image; where the mask is white, you don't.

The first example in Color Plate 19-6 shows a mask I used to select the Capitol dome while protecting the sky. I prepared this mask and put it in a separate mask channel. In the other examples in the color plate, I again composited the RGB and Lab versions of the image — as in the previous section — using various blend modes. No matter how dramatically the Apply Image command affected the dome, the sky remained unscathed, thanks to the mask. If the Mask option had not been turned on, for example, the top-right image in Color Plate 19-4 would have looked exactly like the corresponding image in Color Plate 19-3.

You can even use a selection outline or layer as a mask. If you select some portion of the source image before switching to the target image and choosing Image ⇨ Apply Image, you can access the selection by choosing — what else? — Selection from the Channel pop-up menu at the bottom of the dialog box. Those pixels from the source image that fall inside the selection remain visible; those that do not are transparent. Use the Invert check box to inverse the selection outline. To use the boundaries of a layer selected from the Layer pop-up menu as a mask, choose the Transparency option from the Channel menu. Where the layer is opaque, the source image is opaque (assuming the Opacity option is set to 100 percent, of course); where the layer is transparent so, too, is the source image.

Add and Subtract

The Add and Subtract blend modes found in the Apply Image dialog box (and also in the Calculations dialog box) work a bit like the Custom filter that I discussed in Chapter 17. However, instead of multiplying brightness values by matrix numbers and calculating a sum, as the Custom filter does, these modes add and subtract the brightness values of pixels in different channels.

The Add option adds the brightness value of each pixel in the source image to that of its corresponding pixel in the target image. The Subtract option takes the brightness value of each pixel in the target image and subtracts the brightness value of its corresponding pixel in the source image. When you select either Add or Subtract, the Apply Image dialog box offers two additional option boxes, Scale and Offset. Photoshop divides the sum or difference of the Add or Subtract mode by the Scale value (from 1.000 to 2.000) and then adds the Offset value (from negative to positive 255).

If equations will help, here's the equation for the Add blend mode:

Resulting brightness value = (Target + Source) ÷ Scale + Offset

And here's the equation for the Subtract mode:

Resulting brightness value = (Target — Source) ÷ Scale + Offset

If equations only confuse you, remember this: The Add option results in a destination image that is lighter than either source; the Subtract option results in a destination image that is darker than either source. If you want to darken the image further, raise the Scale value. To darken each pixel in the target image by a constant amount, which is useful when applying the Add option, enter a negative Offset value. If you want to lighten each pixel, as when applying the Subtract option, enter a positive Offset value.

Applying the Add command

The best way to demonstrate how these commands work is to offer an example. To create the effects shown in Figures 19-24 and 19-25, I began with the two images shown in Figure 19-23. The first image, Capitol Gray, is your everyday, average grayscale image. The second image, Capitol Blur, took a little more work. I applied Filter ➪ Other ➪ Minimum to enlarge the dark regions of the image by a radius of 3 pixels and applied the Gaussian Blur filter with a radius of 6.0 pixels. I next used the Levels command to change the second Output Levels values to 140, thus uniformly darkening the image. (The Add and Subtract commands work best when neither target nor source contains large areas of white.) Finally, for the sheer heck of it, I drew in some clouds and lightning bolts with the airbrush and smudge tools.

 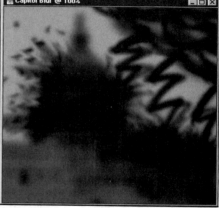

Figure 19-23: The target (left) and source (right) used to create the effects shown in Figures 19-24 and 19-25

After switching to the Capitol Gray image and choosing Image ⇨ Apply Image, I selected the Capitol Blur image from the Source pop-up menu. I was working with flat, grayscale images, so I didn't have to worry about the Layer and Channel options. I selected the Add option from the Blending pop-up menu and accepted the default Scale and Offset values of 1 and 0, respectively, to achieve the first example in Figure 19-24. Because the skies in both the target and source images were medium gray, they added up to white in the resulting image. The black areas in the source image helped prevent the colors inside the building from becoming overly light.

Unfortunately, the image I created was a bit washed out. To improve the quality and detail of the image, I changed the Scale value to 1.2 to downplay the brightness values slightly and entered an Offset value of -60 to darken the colors uniformly. The result of this operation is the more satisfactory image shown in the second example of Figure 19-24.

Figure 19-24: Here are two applications of the Add blend mode on the images from Figure 19-23, one subject to Scale and Offset values of 1 and 0 (left) and the other subject to values of 1.2 and -60 (right).

Applying the Subtract command

To create the first example in Figure 19-25, I selected the Subtract option from the Blending pop-up menu, once again accepting the default Scale and Offset values of 1 and 0, respectively. This time, the sky turns pitch black because I subtracted the medium gray of the Capitol Blur image from the medium gray of the Capitol Gray image, leaving no brightness value at all. The building, however, remains a sparkling white because most of that area in the Capitol Blur image is black. Subtracting black from a color is like subtracting 0 from a number — it leaves the value unchanged.

The image seemed overly dark, so I lightened it by raising the Scale and Offset values. To create the second image in Figure 19-25, I upped the Scale value to 1.2, just as in the second Add example, which actually darkened the image slightly. Then I changed the Offset value to 60, thus adding 60 points of brightness value to each pixel. This second image is more likely to survive reproduction with all detail intact.

The difference between Subtract and Difference

I've already shown examples of how the Difference mode inverts one image using the brightness values in another. But the math behind Difference is actually similar to that behind Subtract. Like Subtract, the Difference option subtracts the brightness values in the source image from those in the target image. However, instead of treating negative values as black, as Subtract does, or enabling you to compensate for overly dark colors with the Scale and Offset options, Difference changes all calculations to positive values.

Figure 19-25: Here are two applications of the Subtract command on the images from Figure 19-23, one subject to Scale and Offset values of 1 and 0 (left) and the other subject to values of 1.2 and 60 (right).

If the brightness value of a pixel in the target image is 20 and the brightness value of the corresponding pixel in the source image is 65, the Difference option performs the following equation: 20 — 65 = -35. It then takes the absolute value of -35 (or, in layman's terms, hacks off the minus sign) to achieve a brightness value of 35. Pretty easy stuff, huh?

Any divergence between the Subtract and Difference options becomes more noticeable on repeated applications. The top row of Figure 19-26, for example, shows the effect of applying the Subtract mode (left) versus the Difference mode (right). As before, I applied these commands to the Capitol Gray and Capitol Blur images from Figure 19-23.

As far as perceptible differences between the two images are concerned, the pixels that make up the bushes in the lower-left corner of each image and those of the clouds along each image's right side are on the rebound in the Difference example. In effect, they became so dark, they are again lightening up. But that's about the extent of it.

In the second row of Figure 19-26, I applied the Subtract and Difference options a second time. Using the top-left example in the figure as the target and the Capitol Blur image as the source, I achieved two different results. When calculating the colors of the pixels in the sky, the Difference blend mode apparently encountered sufficiently low negative values that removing the minus signs left the sky ablaze with light. Everything dark is light again.

Figure 19-26: Repeated applications of the Subtract (left column) and Difference (right column) commands

716   Part VI ✦ Corrections, Composites, and the Web

The Calculations command

Although its options are nearly identical, the Calculations command performs a slightly different function than Apply Image. Rather than compositing a source image on top of the current target image, Image ⇨ Calculations combines two source channels and puts the result in a target channel. You can use a single image for both sources, a source and the target, or all three. The target needn't be the foreground image (although Photoshop previews the effect in the foreground image window). And the target can even be a new image. But the biggest difference is, instead of affecting entire full-color images, the Calculations command affects only individual color channels. Only one channel changes as a result of this command.

Choosing Image ⇨ Calculations displays the dialog box shown in Figure 19-27. Rather than explaining this dialog box option by option — I'd end up wasting 35 pages and repeating myself every other sentence — I'll attack the topic in a little less-structured fashion.

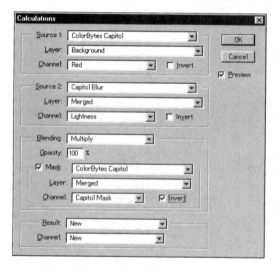

Figure 19-27: Use the Calculations command to mix two source channels and place them inside a new or existing target channel.

When you arrive inside the dialog box, you select your source images from the Source 1 and Source 2 pop-up menus. As with Apply Image, the images must be exactly the same size. You can composite individual layers using the Layer menus. Select the channels you want to mix together from the Channel options. In place of the full-color options — RGB, Lab, CMYK — each Channel menu offers a Gray option, which represents the grayscale composite of all channels in an image.

The Blending pop-up menu offers the same 14 blend modes — including Add and Subtract — found in the Apply Image dialog box. But remembering how the Calculations dialog box organizes the source images when working with blend modes is important. The Source 1 image is equivalent to the source when using the Apply Image command (or the active layer when compositing); the Source 2 image is equivalent to the target (or the underlying original). Therefore, choosing the Normal blend mode displays the Source 1 image. The Subtract command subtracts the Source 1 image from the Source 2 image.

Half of the blend modes perform identically, regardless of which of the two images is Source 1 and which is Source 2. The other half — including Normal, Overlay, Soft Light, and Hard Light — produce different results based on the image you assign to each spot. But as long as you remember Source 1 is the active layer — hey, it's at the top of the dialog box, right? — you should be okay.

Tip   The only one that throws me off is Subtract, because I see Source 1 at the top of the dialog box and naturally assume Photoshop will subtract Source 2, which is beneath it. Unfortunately, this is the exact opposite of how it really works. If you are similarly confused and set up the equation backward, you can reverse it by selecting both Invert options. Source 2 minus Source 1 results in the same effect as an inverted Source 1 minus an inverted Source 2. (After all, the equation (255 — Source 1) — (255 — Source 2), which represents an inverted Source 1 minus an inverted Source 2, simplifies down to Source 2 — Source 1. If math isn't your strong point, don't worry. I was only showing my work.)

As you can in the Apply Image dialog box, you can specify a mask using the Mask options in the Calculations dialog box. The difference here is the mask applies to the first source image and protects the second one. So where the mask is white, the two sources mix together normally. Where the mask is black, you see the second source image only.

The Result options determine the target for the composited channels. If you select New from the Result pop-up menu, as in Figure 19-27, Photoshop creates a new grayscale image. Or, you can stick the result of the composited channels in any channel inside any image that is the same size as the source images.

Combining masks

As described for the Apply Image command, Selection, Transparency, and Layer Mask may be available as options from any of the Channel pop-up menus. But here they have more purpose. You can composite layer masks to form selection outlines, selection outlines to form masks, and all sorts of other pragmatic combinations.

Figure 19-28 shows how the Calculations command sees selected areas. Whether you're working with masks, selection outlines, transparency masks, or layer masks, the Calculations command sees the area as a grayscale image. So in Figure 19-28, the white areas are selected or opaque, and the black areas are deselected or transparent.

Assuming I've chosen Image ⇨ Calculations and selected the images using the Source 1 and Source 2 options, the only remaining step is to select the proper blend mode from the Blending pop-up menu. Screen, Multiply, and Difference are the best solutions. The top row in Figure 19-29 shows the common methods for combining selection outlines. In the first example, I added the two together using the Screen mode, as in the previous steps. In fact, Screening masks and adding selection outlines are exact equivalents. To subtract the Source 1 selection from Source 2, I inverted the former (by selecting the Invert check box in the Source 1 area) and applied the Multiply blend mode. To find the intersection of the two masks, I simply applied Multiply without inverting.

Source 1   Source 2

Figure 19-28: These are two selections expressed as grayscale images (aka masks). The left image is the first source, and the right image is the second.

But the Calculations command doesn't stop at the standard three — add, subtract, and intersect. The bottom row of Figure 19-29 shows three methods of combining selection outlines that are impossible using keyboard shortcuts. For example, if I invert the Source 1 mask and combine it with the Screen mode, I add the inverse of the elliptical selection and add it to the polygonal one. The Difference mode adds the portion of the elliptical selection that doesn't intersect the polygonal one and subtracts the intersection. And inverting Source 1 and then applying Difference retains the intersection, subtracts the portion of the polygonal selection that is not intersected, and inverts the elliptical selection where it does not intersect. These may not be options you use every day, but they are extremely powerful if you can manage to wrap your brain around them.

Depending on how well you've kept up with this discussion, you may be asking yourself, "Why not apply Lighter or Add in place of Screen, or Darker or Subtract in place of Multiply?" The reason becomes evident when you combine two soft selections. Suppose I blurred the Source 2 mask to give it a feathered edge. Figure 19-30 shows the results of combining the newly blurred polygonal mask with the elliptical mask using a series of blend modes. In the top row, I added the two selection outlines together using the Lighter, Add, and Screen modes. Lighter results in harsh corner transitions, while Add cuts off the interior edges. Only Screen does it just right. The bottom row of the figure shows the results of subtracting the elliptical mask from the polygonal one by occasionally inverting the elliptical mask and applying Darker, Subtract, and Multiply. Again, Darker results in sharp corners. The Subtract mode eliminates the need to invert the elliptical marquee, but it brings the black area too far into the blurred edges, resulting in an overly abrupt interior cusp. Multiply ensures all transitions remain smooth as silk.

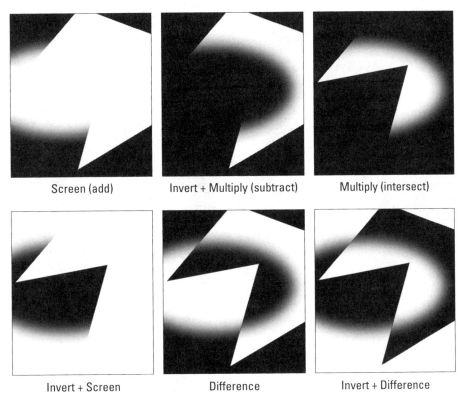

| Screen (add) | Invert + Multiply (subtract) | Multiply (intersect) |

| Invert + Screen | Difference | Invert + Difference |

Figure 19-29: Starting with the masks shown in Figure 19-28, I combined them in traditional (top row) and nontraditional (bottom row) ways using the Calculations command.

The reason for the success of the Screen and Multiply modes is they mix colors together. Lighter and Darker simply settle on the color of one source image or the other — no mixing occurs — hence, the harsh transitions. Add and Subtract rely on overly simplistic arithmetic equations — as I explained earlier, they merely add and subtract brightness values — which result in steep fall-off and build-up rates; in other words, cliffs of color transition exist where there should be rolling hills. Both Screen and Multiply soften the transitions using variations on color averaging that makes colors incrementally lighter or darker.

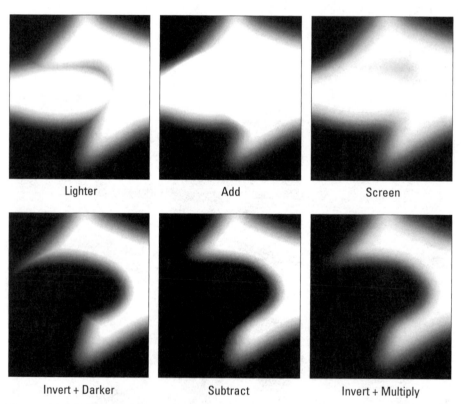

Lighter	Add	Screen

Invert + Darker	Subtract	Invert + Multiply

Figure 19-30: When adding softened selections (top row) and subtracting them (bottom row), the Screen and Multiply modes provide the most even and continuous transitions.

Creating Graphics for the Web

The World of Web Imagery

The Internet may well be the most chaotic, anarchic force ever unleashed on the planet. It has no boundaries, has no unifying purpose, is controlled by no one, and is owned by everyone. It's also incomprehensibly enormous, larger than any single government or business entity on the planet. If the ten richest men in the world pooled their resources, they still couldn't purchase all the computers and cables that keep the Internet alive. In terms of pure size and volume, the Web makes the great thoroughfares of the Roman empire look like a paperboy's route.

As a result, it's impossible to get a bead on the World Wide Web. With several million hands in the pie, and several million more hands groping for a slice, the Web is as subject to casual comprehension as are the depths of the oceans, the infinity of the cosmos, or the meaning of life. And the Web mutates faster than any of those forces. Something just changed while you were reading the last sentence. An important new Web technology hit the market during the sentence you're reading now. It's enough to drive any sane human bonkers.

Fortunately, I'm not altogether sane, so I find the Web quite intriguing. Even so, whatever I write today will, no doubt, change by the time you read this. We may all have the

Internet cabled into our homes, animation and video images may rule the day, and the Web as I presently know it, may be stone-cold dead. All of this will happen gradually, of course — even lightning-fast changes take some time to occur. And were a new technology to come along that combined the power of Java, the versatility of HTML, and the ease of use of a bar of soap, every one of the untold millions of Web content providers would continue to create their millions of different pages in millions of different ways. The most brilliant of technologies is forever mitigated by the willingness of humans to adapt to it.

I include the preceding by way of a disclaimer for the general thesis of this chapter, which is simply this: Bitmapped graphics rule the Web. Sure, text-based content, file libraries, and hyperlinks are the main stock and trade of the Internet, but the graphics are what make the Web intelligible and invite us to come back for more. Graphics have brought the masses to the Web, images account for 90 percent of all Web graphics, and Photoshop is the world's number-one image editor. As a result, Photoshop has become as inextricably linked to the Web as Netscape Navigator, Adobe PageMill, RealAudio, and a hundred other programs. It's just another happy accident in Photoshop's unexpected runaway success.

The smaller, the speedier

If you have any experience with the Web, you know small images are speedy images. By "small," I don't mean small in physical size (although this often helps). I mean small in terms of disk space. A 20K image that fills your screen takes less time to download and display than a 50K file no larger than a sticky note. It's the act of getting the data through the cables and phone lines that takes the time; by comparison, the time it takes your browser software to interpret the data is insignificant.

Therefore, the main focus of this chapter is file size. How can you squish the finest graphics you're capable of creating into the smallest amount of disk space with the least amount of sacrifice? This is the single most important challenge facing Web artists today. And while the Webwide world is certain to change by the time you read this, I have a sneaking suspicion that small and speedy will remain the watchwords for some time.

Preparing screen images

Many Web artists come from a background in print media and, while much of what you've learned while preparing printed photographs is equally applicable to online artwork, differences do exist. Foremost among them, you never need worry about converting images to the CMYK color space. All Web graphics are RGB (or a subset of indexed colors or gray values). This is extremely good news, because it means, for once in the history of electronic publishing, what you see onscreen is really, truly, what you're going to get.

Well, almost. Ignoring the differences in the ways people perceive colors and the variances in ambient light from one office or study to the next, measurable differences exist between monitors. Some monitors produce highly accurate colors, others — especially older screens — are entirely unreliable. But more importantly, some screens display images more brightly than others.

The typical Macintosh user with an Apple-brand monitor, for example, is cursed with a very bright screen. Apple monitors — and many non-Apple brands developed for the Mac — are calibrated to a gamma of 1.8. Meanwhile, most PC monitors are calibrated to 2.2, which is roughly equivalent to a standard television.

Note Higher gamma values translate to darker displays because they indicate degrees of compensation. That is, an image must be lightened only to 1.8 on the Mac to look as light as an image corrected to 2.2 on the PC.

So how do you make sure visitors to your Web site aren't confronted by overly light images, regardless of what platform they use? The solution is to strike a compromise. Choose Image ⇨ Adjust ⇨ Levels (Ctrl+L) and lower the gamma (the middle Input Levels value) to between .8 and .85. The result is an image that appears slightly dark on your monitor and slightly light on a Mac screen, as illustrated in Figure 20-1.

Slightly light for Mac   Slightly dark for PC

Figure 20-1: An image viewed on a typical Macintosh screen (left) looks lighter than when viewed on a PC screen (right).

More rules of Web imagery

Here are a few more items to remember when creating Web graphics:

✦ **Resolution doesn't matter:** Regardless of the Resolution value you enter into the Image Size dialog box, the Web browser displays one image pixel for every screen pixel (unless you specify an alternative image size in your HTML file). All that counts, therefore, is the pixel measurements — the number of pixels wide by the number of pixels tall.

✦ **GIF, JPEG, and PNG:** GIF and JPEG are the file formats of choice for Web graphics. GIF supports only 256 colors, so it's better for high-contrast artwork and text. JPEG applies lossy compression, so it's better for photographs and other continuous-tone images. The upstart format is PNG, which is essentially a 24-bit version of GIF designed for small, full-color images you don't want to compress.

✦ **Indexing colors:** Before you can save an image in the GIF format, you must reduce the number of colors to 256 or fewer. Photoshop uses a technique called *indexing* — this reassigns colors according to a fixed index — which serves much the same purpose as the index in the back of this book.

Tip

✦ **Turn off image previews:** To keep your file sizes as small as possible, turn off the Save Thumbnail check box in the Save dialog box when you save your image.

By recognizing which formats to use when and how best to reduce colors, you can better ensure that visitors to your Web site will spend less time sitting on their hands and more time enjoying your site. I explain the fine points of the file formats and color indexing in the following sections.

Saving JPEG Images

When it comes to saving photographic images, no format results in smaller file sizes than JPEG. As explained in gory detail in Chapter 4, the JPEG format decreases the file size by applying a lossy compression scheme that actually redraws details in the image. Inside the JPEG Options dialog box, select lower Quality settings to put the screws to the image and squish it as low as it will go. But in doing so, you also sacrifice image detail. (Revisit the first color plate in this book, Color Plate 4-1, to see an example of JPEG compression at work.)

To show you how well the JPEG format works, Figure 20-2 shows a series of images saved in the JPEG and GIF formats, along with their file sizes. The original file consumed 62K in memory. Yet by lowering the Quality setting to Medium, I got the file size down to 28K on disk. To accomplish similar savings using the GIF format, I had to reduce the color palette to 3 bits, or a mere 8 colors. (For the record, this same file saved in the PNG format consumed 63K on disk.) As you can plainly see in the enlarged details, applying JPEG compression has a less destructive effect on the appearance of the image than reducing the color palette.

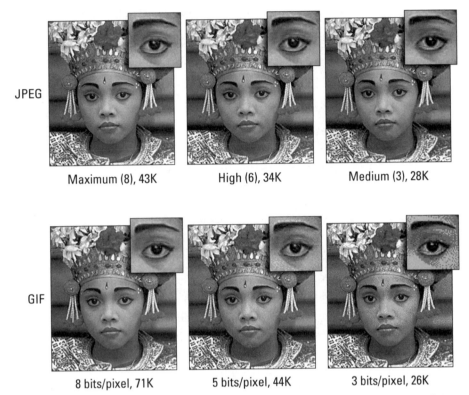

JPEG

Maximum (8), 43K   High (6), 34K   Medium (3), 28K

GIF

8 bits/pixel, 71K   5 bits/pixel, 44K   3 bits/pixel, 26K

Figure 20-2: JPEG compression produces smaller file sizes with less impact than reducing the color palette and saving in GIF. The number in parentheses indicates the Quality value entered into the JPEG Options dialog box.

Note
When determining the file size of your image, refer to the size given in the Open dialog box and not the one showing in the Preview box at the bottom of the Image window. The number in the Open dialog box is the size of the image on disk, and the number in the Preview box is the size of the image in memory. You're concerned with the size on disk in this situation.

When you save a JPEG image, Photoshop displays the JPEG Options dialog box shown in Figure 20-3. Here's how the options contained inside affect Web images:

✦ **Image Options:** Use the Quality option to specify the amount of compression applied to your image. Lower values mean smaller file sizes and more JPEG compression gook. Many experts say Medium (3) is the best setting for Web graphics, but I think it looks pretty awful, especially onscreen. I prefer a Quality value of 5 or better.

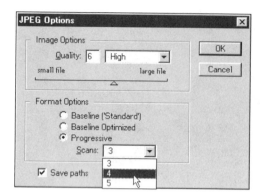

Figure 20-3: Select the Baseline Optimized or Progressive radio button when saving a JPEG image for use on the Web.

Photoshop 4.0

✦ **Format Options:** Most Web browsers support two variations on the JPEG format. The so-called *baseline* (or *sequentially displayed*) format displays images in line-by-line passes onscreen, left to right, top to bottom. The *progressive* JPEG format displays an image onscreen in multiple passes, enabling visitors to your page to get an idea of how an image looks right off the bat, without waiting for the entire image to arrive.

To save a baseline image for use on the Web, select Baseline Optimized. This format includes better Huffman encoding that makes the file even smaller than Baseline ("Standard"). You can generally reduce the file size by 5 to 10 percent using this option. Select the Progressive option to save an image that gradually appears onscreen in passes.

✦ **Scans:** If you select the Progressive radio button, you can pick a number of passes from the Scans pop-up menu. A higher value results in a faster display of the initial image on your page, but it may also take longer to display completely onscreen because of all the incremental refreshing. (Some browsers are smart enough not to redisplay individual JPEG scans if they already have received data for subsequent ones.) A medium value of 4 is probably best, but it doesn't particularly matter.

A fair amount of debate exists over whether you should use progressive JPEG (and other incremental display options such as GIF interlacing). Certainly, some older Web browsers don't support progressive JPEG files, but this is not much of a problem these days. More controversial, some artists believe progressive JPEGs are somehow tacky, because they have a rough appearance in the first few passes.

If this bothers you, and you don't want the viewer to see your image until it's in the final form, select Baseline Optimized. But if you want my opinion, this would do your visitors a disservice. By providing an immediate, unfinished pass at your image, you're giving the viewer an early right of refusal. And this is what the Web's all about — providing the viewer with the tools of page customization and navigation. I mean, heck, guests can turn your graphics completely off if they like. If you get too hung up on making your visitors see things your way, you'll go bonkers. Too many things are out of your control.

Preparing and Saving GIF Images

So much for JPEG, now on to GIF. The GIF format came into being during a time when only the super savvy owned 1,200 Bps modems. It supports a maximum of 8 bits per pixel (256 colors) and uses LZW compression, just like TIFF. GIF comes in two varieties, known by the snappy monikers 87a and 89a, with the latter supporting transparent pixels.

Frankly, GIF is getting a little long in the tooth. Most online pundits figure PNG will replace GIF in the next few years. But, for the time being, GIF is an extremely popular and widely supported format. And despite obvious limitations, GIF has its uses. GIF is a much better format than JPEG for saving high-contrast line art or text. Figure 20-4 shows two versions of the same image; the top image was saved in the JPEG format, and the bottom one was saved in GIF. As you can see, the JPEG compression utterly ruins the image. And I had to reduce the Quality setting to 0 — the absolute minimum — to get the file size down to 16K. Meanwhile, saving the image in the GIF format sacrificed no detail whatsoever and resulted in a file size of 18K. GIF's LZW compression is well-suited to high-resolution artwork with large areas of flat color.

Figure 20-4: The JPEG format creates weird patterns in high-contrast images (top) and saves relatively little space on disk. Meanwhile, GIF keeps the sharp edges intact (bottom).

But before you can save a color image in the GIF format, you have to reduce the number of colors using Image ➪ Mode ➪ Indexed Color. The following section explains how this command works.

Incidentally, the Indexed Color command isn't the only way to decrease color palettes. If you find the command doesn't quite meet your needs, then you may want to invest in a color-management utility. The $400 DeBabelizer from Equilibrium is the absolute master of color reduction, although it is expensive and extraordinarily difficult to use.

Using the Indexed Color command

Choose Image ➪ Mode ➪ Indexed Color to display the dialog box shown in Figure 20-5. This command enables you to strip an image of all but its most essential colors. Photoshop then generates a color *look-up table* (or *LUT*), which describes the few remaining colors in the image. The LUT serves as an index, which is why the process is called *indexing*.

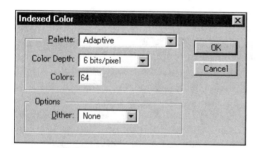

Figure 20-5: Use the Palette options to select the kinds of colors that remain in the image. Use the Color Depth option to specify how many colors remain.

For some reason, Photoshop doesn't enable you to index grayscale, Lab, or CMYK images. If the Indexed Color command is dimmed, choose Image ➪ Mode ➪ RGB to convert the image to the RGB mode, and then choose Image ➪ Mode ➪ Indexed Color.

Don't expect to edit your image after you index it. Most of Photoshop's functions — including the gradient tool, all the edit tools, and the filters — refuse to work. Others, like feathering and the paintbrush and airbrush tools, don't work like they should. If you plan on editing an 8-bit image much in Photoshop, convert it to the RGB mode, edit as desired, and then switch back to the indexed color mode when you finish.

Now that all the warnings and special advice are out of the way, the following sections explain how to use the options inside the Indexed Color dialog box. Enjoy.

Specifying the palette

The first pop-up menu — Palette — tells Photoshop how to compute the colors in the look-up table. You'll usually want to select the Adaptive option, as in Figure 20-5. But, so you're prepared to be all you can be, the following list explains how each of the options works:

✦ **Exact:** If the image already contains fewer than 256 colors, the Exact option appears by default. This only occurs if you've created an extremely high-contrast image — such as a screen shot — or you're working from an image that originated as grayscale. If Exact is selected, press Enter and let the command do its stuff. No sense messing with a good thing.

✦ **System:** Photoshop 4 now offers two System options used by the Macintosh and Windows operating systems. The only reason to use either of these options is if you want to add a bit of imagery to the system. For example, you always want to select the System (Windows) option when creating a wallpaper pattern or a custom file icon. Color Plate 20-1 shows examples of a 24-bit image downsized to the Mac and Windows system palettes.

✦ **Web:** To make things as confusing as possible, Netscape and other Web browsers include their own color palettes. This is a 216-color LUT that mostly includes colors found in both the Mac and Windows system palettes. If you're afraid most of your guests own old 8-bit monitors, Web might be the best choice. But I still argue in favor of Adaptive. The image will look far better on 16-bit and better monitors (which, these days, represents the majority), and it won't look that much worse on an 8-bit screen.

✦ **Uniform:** This is the dumbest option of all. It merely retains a uniform sampling of colors from the spectrum. I've never heard of anyone finding a use for the Uniform option — but, as always, I welcome your suggestions.

✦ **Adaptive:** The Adaptive option selects the most frequently used colors in your image, which typically delivers the best possible results. Because Adaptive ignores all system and Web palettes, images downsized with this option look best on high-color monitors, as I previously mentioned. To demonstrate how much better they look, the bottom row of Color Plate 20-1 shows three images subject to the Adaptive palette at various Color Depth settings. Even with a mere 64 and 16 colors, the middle and right images look as good or better than the 256-color system-palette images above them.

Tip

You can influence the performance of the Adaptive option by selecting an area of your image before choosing the Indexed Color command. Photoshop will then favor the selected area when creating the palette. For example, when indexing the image in Color Plate 20-1 down to the 8-color palette (bottom right), I selected the fellow's face to avoid losing all the flesh tones.

✦ **Custom:** Select the Custom option to load a look-up table from disk. This option is useful when creating multimedia content, but rarely serves any purpose for Web graphics. You can save a custom palette using Image ⇨ Mode ⇨ Color Table, as I explain in this chapter.

✦ **Previous:** The Previous option uses the last look-up table created by the Indexed Color command. If you're trying to create a series of high-contrast graphics you want to look as homogenous as possible, this is the option to use. The Previous option is dimmed unless you have used the Indexed Color command at least once during the current session.

Color depth

Select a value from the Color Depth pop-up menu to specify the number of colors you want to retain in your image. Fewer colors result in smaller GIF files. I generally try 6 bits/pixel first, which result in 64 colors. If this looks okay, I press Ctrl+Z and try 5 bits/pixel; if not, I press Ctrl+Z and try 7 bits/pixel. This is all a matter of getting the colors as low as they can go without becoming ugly. The bottom row in Color Plate 20-1 shows examples of the same image with 256, 64, and 16 colors.

Note

Like all computer programs, Photoshop measures color in terms of *bit depth*. As I've mentioned several times in this book, an 8-bit image translates to 256 colors. Photoshop computes this figure by taking the number 2 and multiplying it by itself the number of times specified by the bit depth; 24-bit means 2 to the 24th power, which is 16 million; 4-bit means 2 to the 4th power, which is 16. You don't need to know this to select an option from a pop-up menu — Photoshop constantly keeps you apprised of the number of colors in the Colors option box — but sometimes it's nice to see what the program's doing.

Dither

Use the Dither pop-up menu to specify how Photoshop distributes the indexed colors throughout the image:

✦ **None:** If you select None, Photoshop maps each color in the image to its closest equivalent in the look-up table, pixel for pixel. This results in the harshest color transitions. But as I'll explain in a moment, this is frequently the preferable option.

✦ **Pattern:** This option is available only if you select System (Macintosh) from the Palette options. But even then, avoid this like the plague, because it dithers colors in a geometric pattern. Look to the lower-left example of Figure 20-6 and the middle image in Color Plate 20-2 for examples.

✦ **Diffusion:** The Diffusion option dithers colors randomly to create a naturalistic effect, as shown in the lower-right example of Figure 20-7 and the last image in Color Plate 20-2.

After looking at Figure 20-7 and Color Plate 20-2, you might be inclined to think Diffusion is the option of choice. Not necessarily. In most cases, None is the better option. First, None results in smaller GIF files (as Color Plate 20-2 shows). Because

LZW is better-suited to compressing uninterrupted expanses of color, harsh transitions mean speedier images. Second, if a guest views your page on an 8-bit monitor, the system will dither the image automatically (assuming you selected Adaptive from the Palette pop-up menu). System dithering on top of Diffusion dithering gets incredibly messy; system dithering on its own, however, is acceptable.

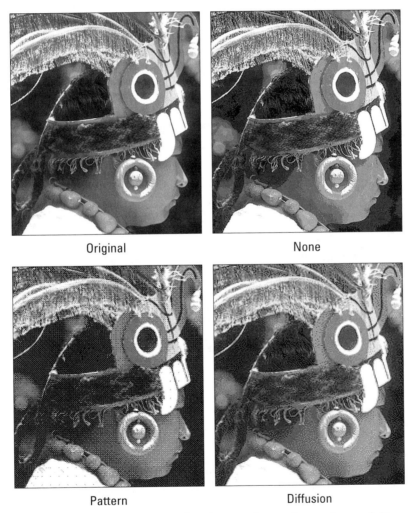

Original   None

Pattern   Diffusion

Figure 20-6: These are the results of converting an image (upper left) using each of the three Dither options: None, Pattern, and Diffusion.

Editing indexed colors

As I said earlier, Adaptive is generally the best choice when creating Web graphics, because it scans each image for the most essential colors. But even the Adaptive option doesn't get things 100 percent right. On occasion, Photoshop selects some colors that look noticeably off base.

To replace all occurrences of one color in an indexed image with a different color, choose Image ➪ Mode ➪ Color Table. The ensuing Color Table dialog box, shown in Figure 20-7, enables you to edit the contents of the LUT selectively. To edit any color, click it to display the Color Picker dialog box. Then select a different color and press Enter to go back to the Color Table dialog box. Then press Enter again to close the Color Table dialog box and change every pixel colored in the old color to the new color.

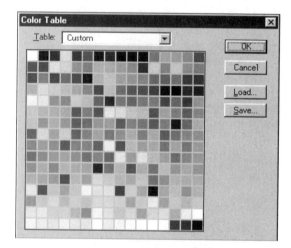

Figure 20-7: Use the Color Table dialog box to modify the colors in an indexed image.

The Color Table dialog box also enables you to open and save palettes and select predefined palettes from the Table pop-up menu. What the Color Table dialog box doesn't enable you to do is identify a color from the image. For example, if you're trying to fix a color in your image, you can't display the Color Table dialog box, click the color in the image, and have the dialog box show you the corresponding color in the look-up table. The only way to be sure you're editing the correct color, and be forewarned, this is a royal pain in the behind, is to slog through the following steps, which begin before you choose Image ➪ Mode ➪ Color Table.

Steps: Editing a Specific CLUT Color

1. **Use the eyedropper tool to click the offending color in the image.** This makes it the foreground color.

2. **Click the foreground color icon to display the specs for the color in the Color Picker dialog box.** Write down the RGB values on a piece of paper, the palm of your hand, or a bald friend's scalp. (Don't edit the color inside the Color Picker dialog box at this time. If you do, you just change the color without changing any pixel in the image associated with that color.) Press Escape to leave the dialog box.

3. **Choose Image ➪ Mode ➪ Color Table.**

4. **Click a color that looks like it might be the right one.** After the Color Picker appears, compare the color's RGB numbers to those you wrote down. If they match, boy, did you ever luck out. Go ahead and edit the color as desired. If the RGB values don't match, press the Escape key to return to the Color Table dialog box and try again. And again. And again.

Tip

To create a *color ramp* — that is, a gradual color progression — drag, rather than click, the colors in the palette to select multiple colors at a time. Photoshop then displays the Color Picker dialog box, enabling you to edit the first color in the ramp. After you select the desired color and press Enter, the Color Picker reappears, this time asking you to edit the last color in the ramp. After you specify this color, Photoshop automatically creates the colors between the first and last colors in the ramp in even RGB increments.

Saving the completed GIF image

When it comes time to save your GIF image, you can save it in either the GIF87a or 89a format. To save a GIF87a image — where all pixels are opaque — choose File ➪ Save As and select the CompuServe GIF option from the Save As pop-up menu. After you press Enter, Photoshop presents you with two options: Normal and Interlaced. If you want the Web browser to display the image in incremental passes — similar to a progressive JPEG image — select Interlaced. Otherwise, select Normal.

On the other hand, if you want your GIF image to include transparent pixels, thereby permitting viewers to see through portions of the image to the Web page background pattern, you need to export the image to the GIF89a format. Choose File ➪ Export ➪ GIF89a Export to display the similarly named dialog box shown in Figure 20-8. Here you'll find an Interlace check box, which you can turn on or off as desired. There's also a Caption check box that enables you to save a caption created with File ➪ File Info. The only purpose for this is to let image-cataloging programs search for the file by keywords. The caption does not appear in the HTML file.

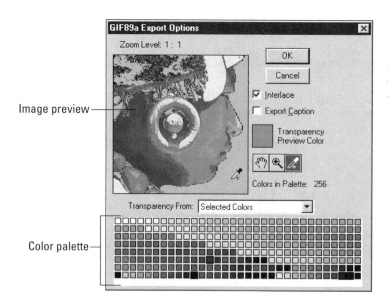

Image preview ———

Color palette —

Figure 20-8: Click with the eyedropper cursor to make colors in the image transparent, as I have with the pixels outside the man's face.

All this is well and good, but the real purpose of the GIF89a Export dialog box is to make pixels transparent:

✦ Click a pixel in the image preview or on one of the swatches in the following color palette to make that color transparent. Keep clicking to add more transparent colors. Photoshop surrounds the transparent color swatches with heavy outlines.

✦ Ctrl+click a color to bring it back from transparency and return it to opacity again.

✦ You can scroll the preview by pressing the spacebar and dragging inside it. Zoom in by Ctrl+spacebar+clicking. Zoom out by selecting the zoom icon and then Alt+clicking. Or you can zoom out by spacebar+Alt+clicking (be sure to press the spacebar first).

✦ By default, Photoshop changes the transparent pixels to gray. But if gray is a popular color in your image, this may make editing the image later difficult. Because Photoshop has no method for expressing GIF transparency — the checkerboard method only works for native Photoshop files — the transparent pixels appear gray in color when you open and edit the image. So I recommend you take the extra precaution of changing the transparent pixels to some way-out color, like bright yellow or green. To do this, click the swatch labeled Transparency Preview Color (just below the check boxes) and select a new color in the Color Picker.

Tip   ✦ If your image contains a mask channel, you can use the mask to define the transparent areas in the image. Select the mask name from the Transparency From pop-up menu in the GIF89a Export Options dialog box. The black areas of the mask translate to transparency; the white areas are opaque. Remember, GIF can handle only two levels of opacity — on and off, with no room for translucency. So if the mask includes gray pixels, the dark gray pixels become transparent and the light gray pixels become opaque.

Cross Reference   For examples of transparent pixels, you might want to check out my site at `http://www.dekemc.com`. Every single graphic includes some transparent pixels, enabling the drop shadows and other gradual elements to blend in with the background.

Saving PNG Images

New Technology   The newest Web image format is currently the *Portable Network Graphics* format, or PNG (pronounced *ping*). Developed by a panel of independent graphics experts, PNG was designed specifically to outperform and, ultimately, to replace GIF. PNG supports 24-bit and 48-bit images, enables you to include mask channels for gradual transparency control, and — perhaps most importantly — is not patented. Starting in 1995, Unisys, the developer of GIF, began to charge royalties to Web software developers. PNG, meanwhile, is free for all, which is why some folks claim PNG unofficially stands for "PNG, Not GIF."

PNG files are typically larger than comparable JPEG or GIF images because a PNG file does not include JPEG's lossy compression, and it can contain more colors than a GIF image. (The exception is when you save a grayscale or indexed PNG file, which is frequently smaller than the same file saved in GIF.) So PNG is generally best suited to small images — buttons and thumbnails — with fine details you don't want mangled by JPEG compression.

Photoshop supports any RGB, grayscale, or indexed image in the PNG format. PNG doesn't support layers (of course), but it does enable you to include a single mask channel. Assuming the browser supports extra PNG channels, the mask defines the opacity and transparency of the image on the page. PNG graphics can even be translucent (as defined by gray areas in the mask channel), a terrific advantage over GIF and JPEG.

When you save a PNG image, Photoshop displays the dialog box shown in Figure 20-9. Here you can select the kind of interlacing and compression you want to apply:

✦ **Interlace:** The PNG format offers the strangely named *Adam7* interlacing. Adam7 draws your image onscreen in seven passes, drawing the image in blocks and filling in the pixels between blocks. If you want interlacing, select Adam7. If you don't, turn it off.

Figure 20-9: When saving a PNG file, Photoshop offers you some peculiar options found nowhere else in the program.

✦ **Filter:** These options enable you to specify the way in which Photoshop applies PNG's special *zlib* compression scheme. This particular scheme compresses data in blocks and the Filter options enable you to specify the way in which the blocks are calculated. Even when armed with this knowledge, only one option, None, makes any sense. None turns off the compression. The other options enable you to tweak the compression for the minimum possible file size.

See, GIF's LZW compression can actually lead to an increase in file size in some cases. To avoid this, PNG gives you a sufficient number of compression options to ensure smaller files. You can certainly experiment with the options to see which one gives you the smallest results. But unless you're absolutely obsessed by small file size — we're talking about saving a few hundred bytes at most — select Adaptive and let the compression to do its magic without your help.

Caution   Before you rush out to save an image to the PNG format, however, you must realize support is thus far spotty. Currently, none of the major HTML page-creation programs — including PageMill, Claris HomePage, Netscape Navigator Gold, and others — support PNG, and the major browser programs — Netscape Navigator and Microsoft Internet Explorer — offer only limited support. (Netscape 3, for example, requires you to add a plug-in, such as Siegel and Gale's PNG Live.) All this will change, of course. I imagine PNG support will become fairly universal by, say, the beginning of 1998. But in the meantime, PNG is more interesting than practical.

Appendixes

Hardware for Photoshop

Contributed by Robert Phillips

Some Philosophy

What's that P-word doing here? What on earth does it have to do with Photoshop, let alone a hardware section? In my not-so-humble view, everything! I put it here because philosophy is implicit in all five appendixes and, to make sure you get it, I'll keep referring to Appendix A. Trust me, it's not gratuitous academia.

Think about how you get computer information, whether in print, online, or from friends (obviously you don't consult with enemies). How many times have you seen a magazine shout "100 Hot Tips for Windows 95" or an online posting "Here's a great tip for using Photoshop as a word processor!" lately? Seems everyone is in the tip business.

But in the computer world, the tail (or tip) is wagging the dog. An incredible undigested, free-floating mass of disorganized information (as my favorite Roman poet, Ovid, put it, *indigestaque moles*). A profusion of confusion. As if you had all your various Photoshop images scattered over your drive partitions in multiple directories — you'd spend all your time trying to find and organize them, rather than using them. Same thing for tips. So many tips are floating around, your mind numbs, and you wind up using none of them. But if you think a bit about computers generally — and Windows 95 and Photoshop specifically — you can do the tip equivalent of keeping all your Photoshop files on one drive. Traditionally, when societies began to pass on all their knowledge as isolated snippets of information in encyclopedias, those societies were not long for this world. Apocalyptic enough for you? Good. Let's begin!

You should think of computers and their operating systems as inherently unstable. If you've ever read any detailed descriptions of how a microprocessor processes a command like *add 2 and 2,* you'll still be shaking your head, even more if you know how the microprocessors and hard drives and whatever are built. One little glitch, one mote of dust and — nada! Same thing goes for software. So many possible ways exist for the code to interact, it's impossible for even the most rigorous QA to catch all potential bugs; this lends truth to the current industry wheeze: *There's no such thing as a bug-free Windows application.*

Note   That QA acronym means *Quality Assurance.* It's cyberspeak for the toiling technicians who spend their days searching for multiligate creatures and swatting them.

This is, I think, the fundamental philosophy. Anything you add to your hardware or software has potential instability. Obviously, you have to add some things — a keyboard and monitor are kind of nice to have. But the more you add, the more you're upping the instability quotient. I've seen this oh-so-many times in my sysop capacity on CompuServe's ADOBEAPPS forum. Someone is having wicked problems with Photoshop. The usual fast-relief answers don't work, so I ask to see a report from MSD—Microsoft Diagnostics — MSD.EXE, which lives in your Windows directory. Oh-so-many times, that person's system looks like, well, the bottom of a Shake 'N Bake bag. Chained AUTOEXEC.BAT and CONFIG.SYS files, multiple pieces of hardware clamoring for hardware interrupts — enough to make even angels weep, let alone a mortal sysop.

Of course, you have a personal relationship with your computer. This is as it should be, and this explains why so many people go to such lengths with wallpaper, color schemes, and screen savers.

Note   But this does not explain why many network administrators are so interested in removing those items from computers on their LANs. I read in the description of a seminar for network administrators: "You'll never have to see your users' unauthorized wallpaper again." Some people just don't get it.

You probably don't have the luxury of dedicating one computer to Photoshop and nothing else. And, hey, you spent your money, you want to compute *your* way! Well, I must tell you, you can't have it all. A lot, yes, but not all. Not if you want a stable system. You have to prioritize. Put on the extra hardware you must have to use Photoshop and forget the rest. This means *favor a digitizing tablet over a sound card.* Or, if you have both and need to attach a CD-ROM drive, *favor using an industry-standard SCSI card over IDE the SCSI connection that comes with many sound cards.* Same thing for software-ware. If you're on Windows 3.1, forget about alternatives to Program Manager, such as Norton Desktop. It's a fine program, and many have no problems using it with less-demanding *business productivity* applications. Forget, too, about programs that can burrow deep into your hardware system, such as third-party screen savers. As good as they are (I'm a big fan of After Dark), in a Photoshop environment you're asking for trouble. Forget about any number of apparently Microsoft-sanctioned doodads, such as the cursor wrap feature of the Microsoft Mouse Intellipoint drivers, Windows 95 doodads (such as animated cursors), or (if you have Microsoft Plus!) full window drag. You'll also be better off using the default "standard" WIndows 95 mouse driver.

Grinch enough for you? I'm not trying to deprive you of all fun, but I am trying to show you the practical consequences of the philosophy I've enunciated. All the examples I've given can destabilize your working environment for Photoshop. I've helped people solve Photoshop-specific problems arising from each one. Further, I practice all of what I've preached. The results? I've pushed Photoshop relentlessly ever since it first appeared in version 2.5 for Windows. I tend to have about one *General Protection Fault* (GPF) — that's a nice way of saying *Abandon All Hope Until Ye Restart* — a month at most, unless I'm running a beta test.

Let me tell you, briefly, about something that happened shortly after Photoshop 2.5 for Windows shipped. An able, regular member of the then-ADOBE forum (now ADOBEAPPS) on CompuServe was having wicked problems. He got the strange message that he had physical RAM problems. At first we thought this was only Photoshop being funky, because none of his diagnostics programs reported any problem with physical RAM. But, after some serious troubleshooting, it turned out he *did* have a bad ram chip (SIMM), which led us to christen Photoshop as *the ultimate hardware diagnostic tool*. Photoshop probably makes the heaviest, most mercilessly relentless demands you could imagine on your system. The more stable your system, the better your odds of not seeing Photoshop in its, er, *diagnostic* capacity.

So, back to where we started. Think about the philosophy of stability as you contemplate both hardware and software issues. You still can have some fun — a lot of fun. Tinker with your wallpaper, tinker with your Desktop color schemes — it's perfectly safe. Tinker with native Windows 95 screen savers (many fine ones already are online). That, too, is perfectly safe. Let the rest go. You'll be doing you, and yours, a terrific favor. Or, as Sergeant Phil Esterhaus put it on *Hill Street Blues,* "Let's be careful out there."

Hardware overview

Hardware makes me nervous. Every time I have to "go under the hood," I steel myself, gulp, and make sure I have Tylenol handy. I just want to get the hardware installed and running and get back to my software comfort zone. Sounds odd? I've written WIN.INI files from scratch, and I'll hack the Registry in a trice. Moving programs and editing Master Boot Records (MBRs) is no problem. But seating a new card in an expansion slot makes me nervous. For even the most apparently trivial hardware matters, I shamelessly truckle to the hardware oriented, affectionately known as *Gearheads.*

I suspect you're probably like me. You just want your computer to "start me up." But it is hardware, and you, like myself, have to live with it. So here are some insights I've gleaned during my illustrious career as a hardware-phobe. This isn't an introduction to what computers are, or the differences between a hard drive and a floppy drive. Plenty of good books, and endless magazine articles, are available for that. Rather, it's to help you get a quick handle on hardware considerations specific to Photoshop and Windows 95. These aren't the only possible opinions, but I know these are valid and I know these can work.

Buying a Computer

Hey, I said this wasn't an introduction to computers! What's up? Simple — you may be entering the digital universe for the first time. How do you sort through all those vendors hawking their machines as screaming state-of-the-art, best-of-breed (and other buzz phrases) ad nauseam? You may realize you need a more substantial machine than your current one, because it isn't cost-effective to upgrade. What you do next will materially affect how you feel about Photoshop and Windows 95, and how effectively you use them.

A time existed when IBM was the standard, and people who used their boxes walked tall. Those who used a clone were always a tad apologetic, as if admitting granddad was an alcoholic. No longer. IBM still makes fine PCs, but now it's only one brand of many. The erstwhile clones have multiplied and taken over the PC world. So the first principle is to consider IBM if its products suit your needs. But don't limit yourself.

You'll see a dizzying variety of names in reviews or advertisements. Some names will keep recurring. Some will have snazzy advertisements, but never appear in reviews. It's a cacophony out there. Here's how to make a symphony:

✦ **Read reviews relentlessly and widely.** You'll find variations in what the reviewers like, but certain manufacturers will keep reappearing. Make a list.

✦ **Read the manufacturers' advertisements.** Compare prices and features. Make more lists.

✦ **Talk to people.** Ask everyone you can find. Ask friends, ask enemies. If you're in your dentist's office and happen to see a Fizzy Swiggles-brand Pentium, ask how they like it.

✦ **Ask online.** Many major vendors have sections on the major online services. Right now, the most and the best are on CompuServe. This is also a factor in your buying decision; if you need support, online is often far faster and more effective than even the most finely tuned support lines. Remember, vendor forums, by their nature, will attract people with problems. See what kind of problems people report and the vendor's response.

✦ **Call the manufacturers.** You've done enough research. *Ahem*. This implies ordering over the phone and waiting for FedEx or UPS. Right — I've bought three computers that way with nary a hitch. I've seen people with the sad prejudice that *mail order equals junk* ease on down to their local computer superstore and bring home a gawldurned mess. I've nothing against those stores, but I've found mail/phone-order merchandise is as good, with more configuration options and (often) more technically savvy advice.

✦ **Listen carefully to your would-be sales representatives.** How willing are they to take time to explain? To go the little bit extra? If they go all distant on you when they hear you're not a purchasing agent of a Fortune 500 company, move on; it's your money, so why should you pay for abuse? If you have a bad experience, but you're otherwise leaning toward a particular manufacturer, call again. Sometimes it can take several sales reps before you find one with whom you can work. This is important. Regardless of your technical level, you're going to need some hand-holding, so it's best to feel good at the start.

✦ **Ask about the hardware.** Who makes the monitor? The video card? The motherboard? (Often the best motherboards are made by the chip manufacturer.) Look at the reviews and ask online. You're not obliged to purchase everything from one source. My current Pentium was offered with a perfectly good video card, but not one I thought appropriate for my use of Photoshop. So I purchased the card elsewhere. True, it cost me a little more overall, but I got precisely the card I wanted. You also want to ask carefully if it's an Original Equipment Manufacturer (OEM) version; that is, one the hardware maker produces to order for the computer vendor. If it is, you have some thinking to do. Typically, the OEM versions have all the functionality you need. But it gets dicey when you're looking for support. Some manufacturers directly support their OEM cards, and others demand you go to your computer vendor.

✦ **Look for a company on the way up.** Not just starting out, but not one that's riding high on major commercial success. Hungry, growing companies will take pains to give you value and assemble your machine with care. If they're too new, they'll be understaffed and still trying to figure out how to be vendors. If they're too established, they may be so overwhelmed, they don't have time to do this extra (much as they might like to). I'm not slamming either the brand new or the well-established companies. Many buy from them with satisfaction. But I've used the buy-from-the-hungry principle over the years for a 386, 486, and a Pentium, and I've seen any number of people do likewise. Maybe I've been lucky, but I haven't had a second's down time or trouble with any of them. Even the 386 is currently going strong.

Some Hardware Specifics

I want to discuss some specific hardware considerations for Photoshop and Windows 95 that will keep you out of trouble and enable you to use Photoshop most efficiently. This isn't intended to be all-inclusive — I've even totally bypassed one area, printers, because that could take an entire book. For an excellent extended discussion of Windows 95 hardware issues, see Woody Leonhard & Barry Simon, *The Mother of All Windows 95 Books* (Addison Wesley), Chapter 6. More on this book and *Windows 95 SECRETS* (IDG Books Worldwide, Inc.), by Brian Livingston and Davis Straub, at the end of Appendix B.

Memory

If you've followed all the media on Windows 95, you probably know the Received Wisdom that Windows 95 will run tolerably in 8MB of RAM and well in 16MB. 16MB is the *sweet spot* (I *hate* that phrase, but it's so common, I have to use it). Beyond that, you're getting into diminishing returns for your hardware dollar. This is all true, until Photoshop enters the picture.

On either Mac or PC, Photoshop is probably the most memory-hungry critter you'll ever invite in. I know of no one on either platform who says "I have more than enough memory for Photoshop." Rather, all will say they're getting by, but the ideal is in the future. Sort of like athletes on "getting in shape." Being *in shape* is something they're aiming for, but they'll never admit to in the present.

For Photoshop, then, the sweet spot information does not apply for several good reasons. Certain Photoshop filters, for example, operate entirely in memory. Short-sheet them on memory and they won't work. Apart from those filters, Photoshop can operate on images larger than its available memory by using the *scratch disk* (see Chapter 2) as virtual (physical) memory; that is, using hard disk space to emulate RAM. It does work, but it's slower than running entirely in RAM, and the disk-thrashing can drive you crazy. Adobe knows what it's saying when it recommends physical RAM of three to five times the size of the image on which you'll be working.

In short, more is more. You can get Photoshop to run in memory just a tad under the recommended minimum (which varies by version and operating system), but you have to jack your system around so much, and you will find Photoshop so slow, that it's nothing you should try. You will find it wanting for any kind of productivity, and as much more as you can get. Trust me, I was functional, sort of, with 16MB on my 486, but that was before I got 32MB on my Pentium. And by Photoshop standards, even my 32MB is low end.

Fixed storage media—the hard drive

Obviously, you'll be using a hard drive. If you've been in computing as long as I have, you'll remember when computers came with two floppy drives, and you could run WordPerfect from one of them. You'll also remember when a hard drive cost in excess of $1,000. Luckily, times have changed.

SCSI or EIDE?

The perennial question. It's true SCSI offers the most flexibility and speed. You can run your drive off a SCSI card internally and daisy-chain various external devices, such as a CD-ROM and scanner. It's also true SCSI offers the largest drives — 8GB ones are common.

But there are tradeoffs. With SCSI, you get involved with such matters as SCSI-2, Fast SCSI, and SCSI-3. You get involved with cabling. You also get involved with drivers (Photoshop is notoriously sensitive both to SCSI cabling and drivers); sometimes, the latest and greatest will fix a problem, and sometimes it will cause a problem.

EIDE is certainly fast — I've yet to see anyone complain they couldn't do their work on an EIDE drive. Of course, some users want to wring every nanosecond of speed from their computers. But I think the speed gains are illusory and offset quickly when problems strike. Problems can lie around the corner in an all-SCSI system — a cable glitch, a funky driver, an IRQ conflict.

Caution Timing tests and benchmarks are fine up to a point. But don't get caught in the morass of shaving half seconds off a benchmark or comparing PC benchmarks with Macintosh benchmarks. No matter how good the benchmark, it can't reflect how an individual works — your usage may be entirely different. More importantly, you can become obsessed with shaving fractions of seconds from benchmark results. That may be fine if you're a Gearhead but, hey, you're a Photoshopper!

You can have the best of both worlds. Get EIDE and save yourself some trouble, unless you're sure you're going to need 8GB of space. You can still run your SCSI devices from a SCSI card; that's exactly how my CD-ROM and scanner are working now. If I ever want to bite the SCSI drive bullet, I'm set.

Working smarter with drive partitions

Regardless of how you decide the SCSI/EIDE issue, now you have your monster drive. Chances are it's at least 1GB and, most likely, it's larger. Resist the temptation to have one C: partition to cover the entire drive, easy and tempting though it may seem. Depending on how you work, it may not enable you or your drive to work to maximum efficiency.

It all has to do with cluster size and the use of disk space. DOS stores files in *clusters* (units of memory space). Cluster sizes are directly related to the size of the partition (or unpartitioned drive). One cluster can't hold two different files, so bigger clusters mean more unusable memory space. Suppose your new computer has a 1.6GB EIDE drive, which is the largest drive of this kind currently available and popular. If you have only one partition (C:), you'll have 32K clusters, which will probably be a big waste of space. Here's why. Say you have a 1K text file. To store it, DOS will need one cluster. Fine, but remember you have 32K clusters. This means physically to store your 1K file, DOS will use 32K of physical space, in this case meaning you've lost the use of 31K of storage space. There's no way you can steal that space for another file. You can do the math as easily as I can. If you have a lot of small files, you'll be wasting an enormous amount of physical space.

At the other extreme, you can have 2K clusters, provided your partitions are under 127.9MB in size. Using our example 1K file again, you'd only have 1K of wasted space, not 63K. Much better. The tradeoff, though, is you have multiple partitions, and you'll need quite a number of letters to account for your drives. You may not like tracking all those drive letters. I don't mind, but that's just me.

You may be convinced, though, about my wasted space argument and have a 4GB SCSI drive all set to partition into 126MB chunks. Wrong again. DOS only gives you as many drive letters as the letters of the alphabet. The letters A and B are reserved for floppy drives; starting with the letter C, you've 24 letters. (23, usually, because your CD-ROM drive will take a letter). So, you have 23 or 24 left. Do the math again; you'll run out of drive letters if you try to partition that entire 4GB drive into 126MB chunks. Besides, you may not like the idea of trying to keep a large number of drive letters straight in your head (see Figure A-1). Have you had enough? There *is* a way out, which I'm going to tell you.

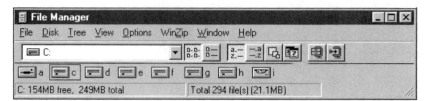

Figure A-1: Two different ways to partition a 1.6GB drive. Clusters of 2K give you many drive letters (top), while clusters of 4K give you fewer drive letters (bottom). Notice the difference in partition sizes — each is at the maximum for the given cluster size.

If you're dedicating your machine to Photoshop and will produce large image files (triple-digit megs and all that), go ahead and have one C: partition. While some files will waste space with 64K clusters, those big image files won't. Figure A-2 gives a graphic representation of this, using the *PC* magazine utility CHKDRIVE, which displays the efficiency of a drive with various cluster sizes. In the upper example, I've analyzed my data drive (E:), and in the lower, I've analyzed a drive with only ten 18MB image files. Notice with the upper example how rapidly and how far the storage efficiency drops; with only a few large files, efficiency remains high on the lower example drive.

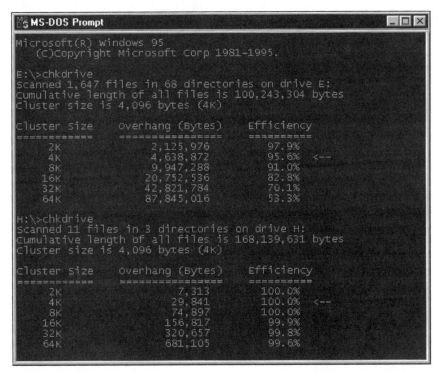

```
MS-DOS Prompt                                            _ □ ✕

Microsoft(R) Windows 95
    (C)Copyright Microsoft Corp 1981-1995.

E:\>chkdrive
Scanned 1,647 files in 68 directories on drive E:
Cumulative length of all files is 100,243,304 bytes
Cluster size is 4,096 bytes (4K)

Cluster Size      Overhang (Bytes)        Efficiency
============      ================        ==========
     2K              2,125,976               97.9%
     4K              4,638,872               95.6%   <--
     8K              9,947,288               91.0%
    16K             20,752,536               82.8%
    32K             42,821,784               70.1%
    64K             87,845,016               53.3%

H:\>chkdrive
Scanned 11 files in 3 directories on drive H:
Cumulative length of all files is 168,139,631 bytes
Cluster size is 4,096 bytes (4K)

Cluster Size      Overhang (Bytes)        Efficiency
============      ================        ==========
     2K                  7,313              100.0%
     4K                 29,841              100.0%   <--
     8K                 74,897              100.0%
    16K                156,817               99.9%
    32K                320,657               99.8%
    64K                681,105               99.6%
```

Figure A-2: Wasted space quickly adds up on a drive with many small files, but doesn't on a drive with a few large files, even with larger cluster sizes.

Besides, you don't want to try to save a 200MB file to a 126MB partition, unless you're fond of *Insufficient disk space* messages.

But, if you're like me, you also need to use applications other than Photoshop with your computer. So let's talk trade-off. On my current machine with its 1.6GB drive, I could have 126MB partitions, but then I'd have drive letters through R:, which means I'd run out of partition letters if I put in a second 1.6GB drive. But larger clusters mean more wasted space, so I compromised. My partitions are under the 4K cluster cutoff figure of 250MB, which means I have partitions through I: (the CD-ROM is J:) and plenty of space for another drive partitioned similarly. Or, I could have made several partitions 256MB, with one large 500MB partition for all those images. The former would be efficient with the 4K clusters, while the latter, with its 64K clusters, would also be efficient because I'd be storing only my large images there. Look at Figures A-1 and A-2 again to remind yourself how cluster size affects storage efficiency.

Think about your files and how you'll be using Photoshop and your computer. Cases may occur for having one large partition, but make sure it's by your choice and not because you or your vendor are taking the path of least resistance.

Compression

I can sum up my advice here in one word: *Don't*. I'm not referring to compression of groups of files by using PKZIP. I'm referring to drivewide or hard diskwide compression.

It's true the compression that comes with Windows 95, especially the Plus! Package, is about as good as it gets. It's also true any number of people will say they've used compression, whether from Microsoft or a third-party vendor, without problems. I still say: *Don't*.

Consider my previous philosophy: *Compression is one more layer where things can go haywire*. I've seen this happen to people all too often. Photoshop QA goes into fits when you mention compression to it. Hard drives are inexpensive these days and you will be far better off adding or replacing than introducing the possible havoc of any disk-compression scheme.

Removable media

Ready for some more heresy? I don't use a tape backup. I don't knock those who do, but it's one more piece of hardware to juggle in your system. Windows 95 support is only starting to appear. In light of this, if you have an absolute, total disaster (not likely, but anything's possible) with Windows 95, you could be in a position where you can't access your tape backup. Thus, I advise against this false sense of security. It's far easier to copy my smaller files to floppies (or compress a number of them with PKZIP and then place them on a floppy). For larger files, I can use PKZIP's capability to *span* a file over several floppies. For really large files, I use my Bernoulli.

Windows 95 has a minimal backup program. To perform scheduled backups, you need the extra capability that comes with the Plus! Package. Arcada Backup and Colorado Backup are out. Both are functional, but their installation setup wizards can sometimes go a little crazy. Exercise caution.

Of Bernoullis and SyQuests . . .

Right now this is chaotic. Removable media drives from both manufacturers are available in sizes from 44MB up to 135MB, and larger ones are beginning to appear. A series of new, smaller drives from Bernoulli and SyQuest have become hot items because their pricing (near $200) has made them virtual commodities.

Older Bernoullis and SyQuests have been virtual mainstays for getting large files to service bureaus. The former have been more prevalent on the PC side, the latter on the Mac side. Given their expense, if you're planning to purchase one, checking with your service bureau first would be wise.

The newer ZIP drives from Bernoulli are a special case because they come in SCSI versions and other versions that attach to your parallel port. Even if your service bureau doesn't support them, you still may be able to use them (thanks to industry columnist Jim Seymour for this tip): *purchase two.* One for your production use, the other to take with your files to the service bureau — be sure to ask for it back.

I mentioned this in Chapter 2, but it's worth repeating here. I don't want you totally to wear out your fingers thumbing around because you need them for mousing in Photoshop. You can use a Bernoulli or SyQuest as your scratch-disk volume. It will be slower than if you'd used your hard drive, and you must be sure you have a disk loaded in it. That said, to do so, add the following line to your PHOTOS30.INI file:

```
AllowRemovableScratch=1
```

If you're using Photoshop 3.04, that .INI file resides in your Windows directory. If you're using 3.05, it resides in the Photoshop directory, in a subdirectory called PREFS.

If you're upgrading from Windows 3.1 and you're using the parallel-port ZIP drive, remove it before installing Windows 95 (unless you want to forget about printing). After the installation, reconnect the ZIP drive and install its Windows 95 drivers.

CD-ROM

Chances are, if you've bought a computer recently, it came with an internal CD-ROM drive. If you haven't, or it didn't, you should acquire one as soon as possible. This isn't *doodaditis,* it's common sense. Programs such as Adobe Photoshop offer many extra goodies on their CD-ROM versions — demos, stock art, filters. Books like this one are bursting with all sorts of extras on their CD-ROMs. Virtually all stock art and photos come on CD-ROM. Without a CD-ROM drive, you'll be unnecessarily limited.

Read reviews and talk to people before making your decision. *Internal* versus *external* is a thorny question. The internal drive can save you some space, but you have to take your computer apart if you need to change a jumper or dip switch. CD-ROM drives that enable you to put multiple discs in one caddy are starting to appear, but beware — some of them map each CD-ROM to a drive letter and chew into your DOS memory to do it. Under Windows 95, DOS is not dead. Programs need access to the *lower DOS* (640K) area. If you mortgage it too many times, you'll find some programs won't open and some hardware (scanners, notoriously) won't run. Although some will argue otherwise, I can't agree you should look for a caddyless CD-ROM, which means more handling of the precious silver discs and more chances for an accident.

The fastest drives right now are 12X (12-*times-standard* speed), but slower ones are considerably less expensive and will serve you well for Photoshop work.

Don't feel you're losing face or speed if you must use real mode drivers for your CD-ROM and its SCSI card; Microsoft's hype is a bit out of hand there. But use protected mode (Windows 95) drivers if you can. During installation, sometimes your CD-ROM and SCSI card will not be detected. You can select Add New Hardware from Windows 95's Control Panel to see a list of SCSI cards. Choose your card and follow the prompts; you will find this installs the card's driver and also enables recognition of your CD-ROM drive. (Assuming it's supported, as a large number are.) After you have protected mode CD-ROM support, you can *REM* out (precede the line of code with REM to keep it from running) the MSCDEX, SCSI driver, and CD-ROM driver references in your AUTOEXEC.BAT and CONFIG.SYS files.

Finally, it's now becoming possible to burn your own CD-ROM disks; various packages exist for under $2,000 and begin at about $500. Traditionally, burning a CD-ROM has been a nightmare. You need a dedicated SCSI hard drive and lots of internal fortitude. Initial reviews of these new packages suggest these matters have improved considerably, so I recommend you closely follow these promising new developments.

Input

As the name implies, *input* deals with getting what you want into Photoshop, whether it's a keyboard command, a photo of Aunt Matilda, or a squiggly pattern you want to draw. The keyboard will not suffice. You need at least one further input device (mouse, digitizing tablet), and you'll almost certainly want a scanner. Input devices enable you to get your materials into Photoshop and to get your commands into Photoshop, too.

Keyboards and mice

Both of these are personal decisions, and not ones to be made lightly. You'll use both all the time, so you want a keyboard and a mouse that feel right to you.

Keyboards come with varying degrees of hardness and softness when you press the keys. Sounds colloquial, but those are the best words I can find. Hard keyboards make a distinct click when you press the keys and they have a bit of resistance. Soft keyboards make a muted click and feel, well, soft. I personally prefer the hard keyboards and use those by IBM and Northgate. The softer keyboards that come with so many computers drive me crazy. But you may feel exactly the opposite. Strike a few keys. You'll know almost immediately whether you have to go shopping.

Note

There's something else about keyboards: *the position of the function keys*. The original IBM PC keyboard (yup, that was my first computer, right along with two floppy drives and a green monochrome monitor) had the function keys in a neat column at the left. It was incredibly easy to use. With the AT-class computers, everything changed. The function keys were arranged in a row across the top. Unfortunately, virtually all keyboards, except those by Northgate, use this arrangement. To whomever created it, I have a load of moldy prunes to deliver.

Same rules apply to mice — try before you buy. I personally like the Microsoft 2.0 mouse and its ergonomic shaping, but I have large hands. You may want a smaller mouse from another manufacturer.

Caution

If you've purchased a Microsoft mouse recently, chances are it came with the Intellipoint 1.1 drivers (sometimes referred to as 10.1, to keep them in line with the 8.X and 9.X drivers that came out previously for Windows 3.1), which are Windows 95-aware. Those drivers offer — increasing across version numbers — an incredible series of doodads, such as cursor wrap, mouse focus, and the like. These extras can function variably anywhere in Windows 95 and can sometimes cause problems in Photoshop. I advise against using them. Use only the Windows 95 drivers that came with your installation. Incidentally, Microsoft is aware of these problems and is, reportedly, working on a fix.

Caution

Here comes the second mouse warning! If you upgraded over an existing Windows 3.1 installation, your system may or may not be using your earlier Microsoft mouse drivers. I advise against it. Those earlier drivers did offer the famous (notorious) cursor wrap, which did not get along well with Photoshop under Windows 3.1 — the notorious *Growstub* error message appeared. You can still get that error under Windows 95 if you're using the earlier drivers. My advice is to forgo the cursor wrap and use the native Windows 95 drivers. This may take some fiddling. Depending on how your mouse was set up previously, Windows 95 may or may not have recognized its drivers. Get help from some of the sources listed at the end of Appendix B.

Scanners

Scanners (along with the digitizing tablets discussed in the next section) are your most important input devices. They open a whole world of possibilities. If you can get something onto a scanner, you can digitize and manipulate it in Photoshop. Some of those possibilities may not be entirely legal. Although you can scan and tinker with whatever you like in the privacy of your computer room, copyright issues are important if you're going to do anything with an image beyond private use.

Caution   Please be careful and seek competent legal advice when using images.

A time existed when flatbed scanners were the high end and any number of us managed with hand-held scanners. I have fond memories of my Logitech; some of my best line art scans came from it. But in this day and age (especially if you're a Photoshopper), the prices have dropped so low, you have no reason to put off buying a color flatbed scanner.

Color scanners all have their own characteristics, which can be equally pleasing or irritating to their owners. Here, again, you should read reviews (*many* reviews) and hang out where scanner gurus gather. I recommend frequenting CompuServe's DTPFORUM, which has an entire section devoted to scanners.

Prices tend to go up with resolution. You can do an enormous amount with the 400 dpi, typically offered by the under $1,000 scanners. If you're aiming for high-end color work, you'll need more resolution; this means spending money for a more powerful flatbed, breaking your piggy bank for a drum scanner or, at the least, paying money to have a drum scan done for you. If you're new to scanning, I think you'll be happy with the 400-dpi scanners currently available.

What about transparency scanning? Many scanners offer transparency adapters. The results are mixed. I've heard excellent reports about one manufacturer and terrible reports about another. I'd advise caution before you spring for a transparency adapter. If you don't, you have two choices. You can have your service bureau do it (prices are reasonable, so this might be your method of choice if you don't have to scan many slides), or you can purchase a dedicated slide scanner, such as one by Nikon or Polaroid.

Getting a good scan is an art in itself. Much of this book has to do with ways to tweak Photoshop images for precisely those reasons. But I want to focus here on getting your scanner operational.

Scanners often come with their own dedicated cards, but they will also run off standard SCSI cards. I personally favor the latter, despite my previous, otherwise harsh, words about SCSI. But, I've used the dedicated cards without problem. The key word, though, is TWAIN. Wiseacres like to say the acronym means Technology Without Any Interesting Name, but that's unfair and untrue. In 1992, several major firms founded the Working Group for TWAIN. They took the T-word from the idea of uniting input devices and programs — the twain shall meet (get it?). But what's in a name? You want to know what it means to you.

In pre-TWAIN days, every program needed its own chunk of code to enable it to interface with the scanner drivers and, sometimes, even a special program-specific driver. It was a nightmare. TWAIN involves a standard API the programmers can implement directly. Then, all you need is a TWAIN-compliant scanner (which virtually all currently available are) and the TWAIN module from the scanner maker and you're up and running. End of nightmare? Well, it was but, then, it wasn't.

All of this was relatively fine under Windows 3.1 and even under Windows 95 with a 16-bit program, such as Photoshop 2.5 or 2.5.1. But along came Photoshop 3.0/3.01, and no one could scan anymore. This was something Microsoft didn't exactly trumpet along with its mantra *32-bits is better*. A 16-bit anything can't talk to a 32-bit something directly — it's all in the *bitness* (to coin a phrase). No 32-bit scanner drivers or TWAIN modules existed, none were forthcoming from Microsoft (unlike the case for Windows NT), and none still are, because Microsoft left it up to the scanner manufacturers to do their 32-bittedness.

Of course, cries of anguish occurred, and then along came Photoshop 3.04 with its *thunking layer. Thunking* (honestly, I didn't make up the term — it's programmer-speak) allows a 16-bit whatever to talk to a 32-bit program, whether third-party plug-in filters or TWAIN modules. Other manufacturers followed suit, and you could use TWAIN to run your 16-bit scanner software and TWAIN32 to run 32-bit scanner software (if you had any — some manufacturers actually were ready with them shortly after Windows 95 shipped).

Then along came the TWAIN_32 standard of the *universal thunker*. This promised to simplify things because it allows one command, TWAIN_32, for both 16-bit and 32-bit scanner modules. Well, almost — some scanner manufacturers had rushed to update their modules to work under the old dispensation and now found them broken under this latest wrinkle. My advice is to try your scanner with TWAIN (16-bit driver) or TWAIN_32 (16- or 32-bit driver). Chances are, those will do it. TWAIN32 (note absence of underscore) is best saved for specific cases on advice of your scanner manufacturer.

Caution   Hewlett Packard scanners need a bit of extra discussion because they're omnipresent. Protected Mode scanner drivers have recently become available, and many users rushed to them because they were eager to eliminate CONFIG.SYS, which they were keeping around just to load the scanner driver. Besides, they'd bought into the 32-bit mantra. Thing is, when they got to Photoshop 3.04, they found problems. There was no more scanner. It seems the new driver conflicted with Adobe's thunking layer. Now the drivers would work if the thunking layer was eliminated, but this meant *sayonara* to the 16-bit plug-in filters, which were also getting thunked. Reports now indicate TWAIN_32 gives you both (TWAIN_32 comes with Photoshop 3.05 and is available for download from Adobe). At the same time, I've regularly followed reports of those using these new drivers, and I haven't felt compelled to venture into this. I don't mind having a real-mode driver rattling around if it means I can scan reliably. I don't need a CONFIG.SYS file, either. I can load it via WINSTART.BAT (a dodge not well-known) and the excellent freeware, DEVICE.COM, widely available online as DEVICE.ZIP. I suppose I will ultimately upgrade, but I'm not entirely impressed with the stability and ease of installation of the new drivers.

Finally, are the TWAIN modules themselves. This is important, because how you control the scan will affect what you have to do with Photoshop. Figure A-3 illustrates DeskScan from Hewlett Packard. The module is certainly capable.

Figure A-3: The Hewlett Packard TWAIN module, DeskScan

The third-party program Ofoto 2.0 gives you far more calibration options; nice extra features, such as automatic moiré removal; and, in general, can improve the quality of your scans to a quantum degree. The downside is it's stand-alone, which means you either save your scan and then open it in Photoshop or take it over via the Clipboard. Ofoto doesn't support an enormously wide range of scanners. Still, if your scanner is among those supported, it's the best thing you can do for your scans. See Figure A-4, which illustrates the expanded range of scanning options.

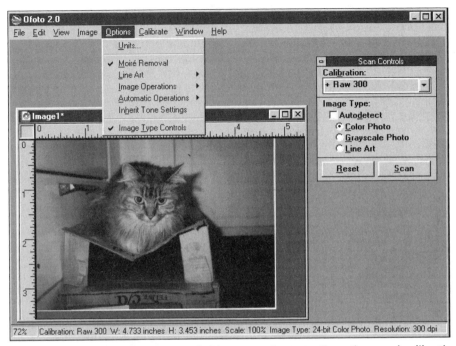

Figure A-4: Ofoto 2 offers a remarkable range of automatic options and calibration settings.

Digitizing tablets

A digitizing tablet could be your other most important Photoshop peripheral. As the title implies, you draw with the tablet's pen and watch your strokes appear on the screen. Programs such as Photoshop and Painter can reflect changes in your drawing speed and pressure, and support is beginning to appear for the erasing function in the newest generation of Wacom tablets.

Several excellent manufacturers of digitizing tablets exist. I'm going to break with my general policy of shunning specific hardware recommendations and advise you to get a Wacom, for a simple reason: Wacom is currently the industry standard. Programmers write with Wacom in mind, which means your best chance of having a tablet work as it should is with a Wacom (more on this in a second). Other tablets inevitably follow the Wacom standard but, well, you see my point. It's much like the case with PostScript. There's genuine Adobe PostScript, and there are the clones. Many of the clones are excellent, but the standard is still different enough, and important enough, that you should stick with it.

But wait! I talked as if it could be dubious to get a tablet to work. That's right. I don't want to frighten you, but I want to be honest. I see some users get their tablets working perfectly from the first install, while others, with identical systems, never seem to have them working right. I don't necessarily want to blame the end users for that. It's something of a black art; it took me the better part of an hour on the phone with a Wacom technician to get my tablet working under Windows 3.1.

I can share some general information with you. Windows 95 and Windows NT only support the Wintab standard with Photoshop. Under Windows 3.1, it's the Penwin standard. You want to be sure your tablet's drivers, as well as your video drivers, are in accord with this.

The good news is most users do get their tablets working, but it may take you some frustration to get there.

Video capture

Traditionally, hardware for video input has been more for the Adobe Premiere crowd. But something is now causing great excitement: Snappy. Snappy plugs into your parallel port and accepts video output from a television, a VCR, or a camcorder; you can capture a frame and take it straight into Photoshop.

Output

As the word *output* suggests, this is how you get your work from Photoshop. Minimally, of course, that means to your screen. This is, perhaps, obvious, because without screen output, you can't work in Photoshop! But it isn't quite that obvious. Hardware can greatly influence what you see onscreen and, thus, not only how you work, but the quality of your work.

Video cards

Photoshop absolutely requires a 256-color (or greater) display mode or it refuses to open. Although this may seem a gratuitous statement, I regularly get queries from people who get the error message because they're using 16-color drivers. Don't think if you're working in less than 24-bit color mode that your file information will be consequently less. Nope. You'll be saving 24-bit color files (unless you've selected the Indexed Color mode in Photoshop) regardless.

Here's what I think. You want a minimum of 2MB video memory (this is dedicated memory on the video card — it has nothing to do with your computer's main RAM, sometimes called VRAM, sometimes WRAM, sometimes even DRAM — don't worry about acronyms this time), upgradable to 4MB. The 2MB enables you to have 24-bit color at 800×600 screen size and 16-bit (64,000 colors) at $1,024 \times 768$ screen size. With the 4MB, you can have 24-bit color at $1,024 \times 768$, and even get into serious colors at even larger sizes, assuming your monitor is big enough to keep you away from the ophthalmologist. The possibilities — and prices — go up with more video memory. I won't discuss those because if you know you want them, you know at least as much as I do.

What about ISA or VLB or PCI? (Again, don't worry about the acronyms.) ISA was the old standard, while VLB and PCI represent newer, accelerated bus specifications that allow the card and computer to talk to each other with fewer bottlenecks. Two years ago, VLB was all the rage; right now, about all you can find is PCI. Your choice of card depends on whether you have an older computer with VLB or a newer one with PCI — either is capable.

What about *legacy hardware?* (That's another cyberphrase I hate.) Many older cards have native support in Windows 95, but the manufacturers have been in no hurry to produce newer drivers and Windows 95-specific Control Panel add-ons. Thus, while the ATI Graphics Pro Turbo has both, the ATI Graphics Ultra Pro (still a fine card) does not. In contrast, the Matrox Millennium is already on its second revision (see Figure A-5).

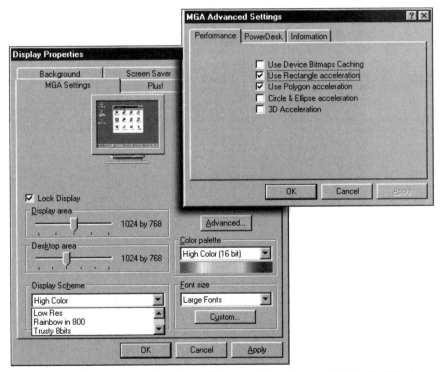

Figure A-5: The Matrox Millennium video card has its own tab in the Windows 95 Control Panel.

Here's some general advice: check with the Web or ftp site of your card manufacturer for the latest drivers for Windows 95 or NT *before* you spend time on the phone with tech support about a "Photoshop redraw bug."

Monitors

Monitors are subjective. Larger is better, but the depth of your pockets is a consideration. The big price jump occurs after the 17-inch size. Desktop real estate is another consideration. The bigger the monitor, the heavier and more space hungry.

That said, I think 15 inches should be your minimum size and, if you can manage it, 17 inches. With a 17-inch monitor, you can do good work at 1,024 × 768 and have several windows open at the same time. This isn't nearly as possible with a 15-inch monitor, although you can do it (bifocal contingent speaking loudly here).

Beyond this, ask and look. Especially look. Some monitors have certain characteristics some users love and others hate. I personally go crazy looking at monitors with Trinitron tubes, but any number of people I respect love them. Let your eyes tell you. After all, you're going to look at your monitor for a long, long time.

Keeping Things Humming

This is a judgment call. Hardware and software interact. Matters dealing most specifically with hardware appear here, while matters involving software appear in the next appendix.

Something big and important

What I'm going to tell you now, I've seen often and even experienced a few times. But I've never seen it discussed, probably because it's so obvious. Often the most obvious points need discussion, though.

Here's the scenario: Photoshop has been humming along for you. You're right on schedule for your production deadline. You get a well-earned night's sleep and fire up Windows 95 in the morning, and something starts going wrong. You may have difficulty getting into Windows 95, or you may get that far, but not into Photoshop. You may get into Photoshop, but not much further. In short, you have a problem.

You go crazy. You're sure everything was fine when you powered down for the night. Has some gremlin gone into the works while you were sleeping?

Stop a second and do some serious thinking. In the course of your last session, did you do something, anything at all, to your system? In my own case, after doing intensive Photoshop work, I tend to say, *Hey, I'm on track. It's time to have some fun. I want to put that new program on, tweak a few Windows 95 settings, and play a game.* Often, you do this and forget about it. One of the things you did (we hope not more than one) had systemwide impact. You didn't see it at the time but, now that you've restarted Windows 95, whatever you did has taken effect.

This is shockingly easy to do. It happened to me as I worked on this appendix. In my case, I put on my recently arrived shipping copy of Fractal Design's Painter 4.0. The screen colors went haywire. I know such things can happen with 64K video drivers using bitmap caching, so I went into my Matrox control panel and turned the bitmap caching off. No luck. I nosed through Painter's documentation and saw a Preferences setting for turning Painter's bitmap was caching off, which I turned off. Guess what happened the next morning? I called up this appendix in Word for Windows 95, typed in some purple prose, and couldn't see it. I typed some more and still couldn't see it. I backspaced and I could see it. Even odder, when starting a new document, I had no problems seeing what I'd typed. Yikes! Did this mean I had to become a Word for Windows 95 guru? Finally, I remembered I'd turned off my video bitmap caching globally and neglected to turn it back on after I'd found the tweak I needed to do inside Painter. Aha! I went to the Matrox control panel, turned the bitmap caching back on, and my prose, purple and otherwise, no longer disappeared. I'd simply forgotten one of my late-night twiddles.

Learn from this. Don't do anything of importance after you're done for the day. Power down and take a well-earned rest.

Disappearing hardware

This doesn't come from anything you've done — it comes from something you haven't done. Windows 95 looks at hardware dynamically. If it sees 32-bit drivers installed for a particular piece of hardware, but that hardware hasn't been used recently, it can, apparently, just disappear from Control Panel ➪ System ➪ Device Manager. This is by design. It's the same principle that allows Windows 95 to recognize when you've added new hardware. See Figure A-6.

It can give you a horrible turn. Don't panic. Your hardware isn't dead; it may just be sleeping. Make sure your hardware is turned on, and then, in Device Manager, click the Refresh button. If you're lucky, your missing hardware will magically reappear. In the worst case, it will reappear with a big yellow question mark, which means you must reinstall the drivers.

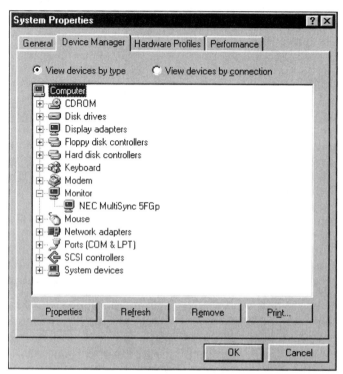

Figure A-6: Device Manager with everything working properly

This happens most often with external CD-ROM drives (you may have powered it down to save wear and tear) or scanners (same reasons). Moral of the story — if you have devices that use 32-bit drivers, keep them turned on. If they use 16-bit drivers, you needn't keep them turned on. Incidentally, I use 16-bit scanner drivers for this reason, too (in addition to the ones I enumerated in the previous Scanners section). Call me nervous but, because I'm not scanning all the time, I don't want to keep my scanner on all the time. The 16-bit drivers suit me fine.

Device Manager

Check Control Panel ➪ System ➪ Device Manager regularly (look at Figure A-6 again). Yellow question marks are warnings. Red circles with the slash can be serious; this symbol means a piece of hardware isn't running as it should. In the case of your hard drive, this can be serious. You may well be running with real-mode generic drivers, and your system may be at a crawl. If you see one of those red doodads, start reading your documentation and talking to technical support people. Finally, if you've recently installed new hardware drivers, highlight the hardware item, click the Properties button, and then click in the resultant dialog

box (the Driver tab). You can tell if the drivers you *thought* were installed are
installed. See Figure A-7.

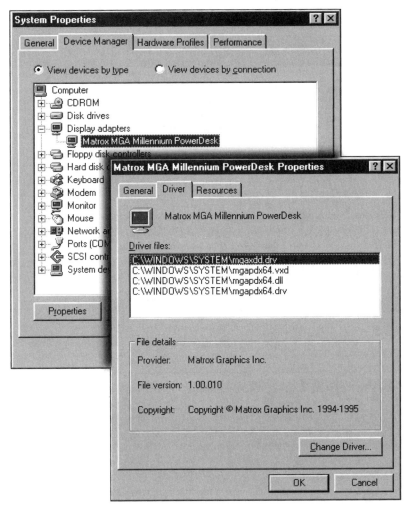

Figure A-7: All my Matrox video drivers are present and accounted for in
the Driver dialog box.

Another tab you should check in the System dialog box is Performance. When you
first bring it up, it will tell you if your system is running as well as possible. If your
system isn't at its best, Performance will usually tell you what to do. Most often, it
tells you to install 32-bit CD-ROM drivers. Follow the advice you get. You're aiming

to read "Your system is configured for optimal performance." While you're there, click, in turn, File System and CD-ROM. As good as Windows 95 is at detecting hardware, it doesn't always detect the speed of your CD-ROM correctly. If it hasn't, change as appropriate. See Figure A-8.

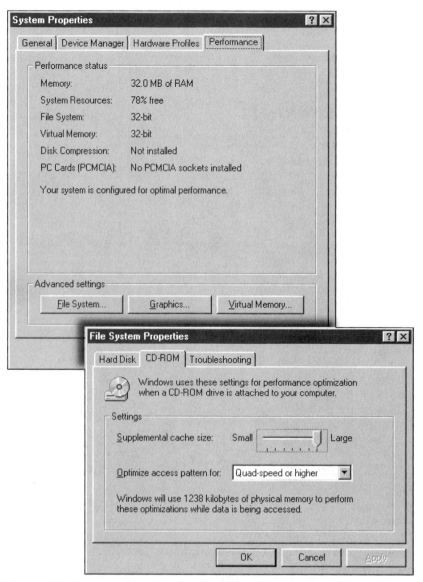

Figure A-8: Windows 95 originally thought my Plextor CD-ROM was dual speed. I fixed this easily in the Performance tab.

I advise you to leave the other tabs and buttons alone, unless you're having serious hardware problems, know exactly what you're doing, or have been told to do something.

Under no circumstances change anything about hardware in the Registry (more on that big no-no in Appendix B), unless you're anxious to have a dead system.

Keeping Things Tidy

Photoshop uses only the largest block of free contiguous space in the partition for its scratch disk. You can have a 100MB partition with a scratch disk of 1MB or less if this partition shares space with 50MB of severely fragmented files.

Even if you have a dedicated scratch disk partition, your scratch disk capacity can disappear. When you crash, your scratch disk becomes a large .TMP file and stays in the partition. With enough of these, your scratch disk capacity and efficiency plummet.

How to stay tidy

✦ **BEST: Dedicate one partition for the scratch disk.** You can do absolutely nothing to extract data from a .TMP file. Kill them and bid good riddance. Regularly run either CHKDSK with the /f switch or Scandisk to eliminate lost clusters and cross-linked files, which are only eating space. Before running either of these, check your documentation.

✦ **GOOD: Regularly maintain a scratch disk's shared partition.** Watch for .TMP files, per the preceding item. Run the aforementioned utilities and add a disk defragmenter. You want to defragment and optimize the space, so you have the largest possible amount of contiguous free space. This is because the DOS file system, even under Windows 95, does not necessarily write files contiguously. It often writes files on a space-available basis, especially if you have some free space caused by file deletions.

Tip

Tell Windows 95 to use a fixed-size for the swap by setting the min and max sizes at equal values. Use a value of 2.5x physical RAM size to start.

What to use

I use the tools that come with Microsoft's Plus! Package. I run them automatically via the System Agent (SAGE), shown in Figure A-9.

Don't take my word for this. See what others are saying and make your own decision.

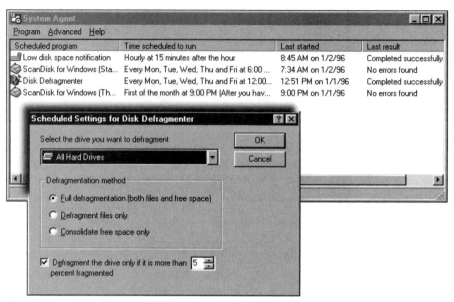

Figure A-9: The System Agent (SAGE) that comes with the Windows 95 Plus! Package allows automatic scheduling of disk maintenance.

Tips for NT users

All the Windows 95 hints apply. If you're running NT, you should use a machine with a good brand-name SCSI card. To use EIDE or IDE with NT is a crime. A good idea is to have the NT swap file on a different physical disk drive from the Photoshop scratch files. Putting them on two different partitions on the same disk won't cut it. If you're getting new disks for NT swap or Photoshop scratch space, consider getting multiple small drives and using disk array striping instead of getting one large disk. Prices are such that it could work out nearly the same, but the performance gains can be significant.

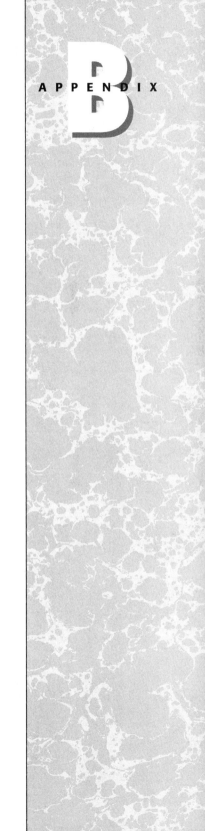

Software and Photoshop

Contributed by Robert Phillips

Sounds redundant, doesn't it? After all, Photoshop is software. What this appendix does is get you going with the other major piece of software — Windows 95 — with a few looks at some other relevant programs along the way. I'm not going into competition with the many fine Windows 95 books already published. Rather, I want to share some ideas for working smarter and safer with Photoshop under Windows 95.

Installing Windows 95

Two ways exist to install Windows 95: Either as the first thing to go down on your C: partition (see the upcoming section "Fresh installation"), or with an existing Windows 3.1 installation or alongside an existing Windows 3.1 installation (see the following section "Upgrade installation"). In this last instance, you can either install over Windows 3.1 or install Windows 95 into a separate directory and then *dual boot* (start the one you want). Actually, you have more choices — you can have Windows 95, Windows NT, and OS/2. I'm omitting details on this last scenario. If you have those operating systems and know you want to do it, you either know how or you know how to find out. Both life and this book are too short.

Upgrade installation

If you're nervous, you can dual boot with Windows 3.1. Thus, you can get into Windows 95 gradually. You will have to reinstall your applications into Windows 95, but this may be a small price to pay for your sanity.

You can install over Windows 3.1. The advantage is you get to keep all your previously existing program groupings (the groups from the Windows 3.1 Program Manager will reappear on your Start menu in Windows 95). The disadvantage is you probably have all sorts of gunk hanging around your Windows system area, such as .INI files and .DLLs from long-gone programs. No uninstaller, no matter how good, can keep your system totally clean.

Fresh installation

If you install absolutely fresh, you lose all the gunk. You do have to reinstall your programs, but this is a great time for housekeeping. I've been amazed at how many programs I really don't need. And my Windows 95 speed increased at least one-third when I lost the gunk. The downside is you must be extra careful while preparing to install.

Do this, regardless

The following items will help you get a reliable installation of Windows 95 with minimum risk to your data and your system.

Back up Windows 3.1

Whichever course of action you choose, you need to do this. I'm cautious. I don't trust any tape backup or believe installing with dual boot leaves Windows 3.1 absolutely clean forever. I don't even trust the Windows 95's installer option of backing up Windows 3.1.

Find another partition on your drive and make some .ZIP files. Four, to be precise. One for \WINDOWS, one for \WINDOWS\SYSTEM, one for \WINDOWS\SYSTEM\ WIN32S, and one for \DOS. The reasons for the first two backups are obvious. You want Win32s backed up because the Windows 95 installer removes many of those files. You want DOS backed up because the installer will zap many of your DOS files if you're installing over Windows 3.1 (a text file with Windows 95 tells you which ones; it's many but by no means all; I think it's easier just to back up what you have). Why do I use .ZIP files? I find them the most reliable for this sort of work. If you want to be super cautious, use PKZIP's disk-spanning option to copy those .ZIP files to floppies.

Create a bootable floppy

Whether you're doing an absolutely clean install or installing into/alongside a current Windows 3.1, you need this floppy. If you don't have two, make them now. I say this because a disk can mysteriously go south, and you don't want to be stuck. Using the File Manager command to make a system disk is easiest (remember: make TWO!). Now, go out to regular DOS and *test each disk* in turn to boot your system. Next, you should add certain files to both disks, although I sincerely hope you will need to use only one of them. The one you need to use is SYS.COM. If you need to return to pre-W95 DOS rapidly, all you must do is boot from the disk and run SYS C: from the A: prompt (more on all this later). In addition, put the following files on both of your startup disks: FORMAT, FDISK, DEBUG, XCOPY, EDIT, and QBASIC.EXE. Make a subdirectory labeled STARTUP and copy your current AUTOEXEC.BAT, CONFIG.SYS, WIN.INI, and SYSTEM.INI files there. Finally, you'd do well to create your own floppy that can boot DOS <u>and</u> has your SCSI drives on it.

You should do both of the preceding, regardless of how you're planning to install Windows 95. Until you get comfortable with (or fanatic about) Windows 95, they'll save your sanity.

Installing

Although I personally favor doing a clean install, my editor and I have decided against doing a walkthrough here — and, likewise, against detailing the other methods. Are we feeling mean-spirited? Nope — just practical. This is a book about Photoshop, with some pointers on Windows 95; you wouldn't be pleased to have a book about Windows 95 with some pointers on Photoshop, now would you? Excellent books are available that tell it all. For the whole story, see *Windows 95 SECRETS* and *The Mother of All Windows 95 Books* (see details at the end of this appendix).

If you're using the upgrade package to do a clean install, make sure you have the first floppy of your original Windows 3.1 package handy. Because you'll be doing an *upgrade* install, the installer will want proof you're legal. If you install over Windows 3.1, it could sniff out the proof. Because you aren't, it can't sniff — it will ask you early on to insert that floppy. If you received Windows 3.1 on a CD-ROM, find out how to produce Disk 1 from it. Substantial evidence supports the fact that you can't insert the CD-ROM and keep the "sniffer" happy. More than one install has aborted.

This may not happen to you — my average has been 50 percent. Sometimes, at the very end of a CD-ROM-based installation, you'll get the mysterious message that *Windows 95 can't access your CD-ROM to finish its installation.* What this means is the earlier hardware detection phase didn't find what it needed. Don't panic. Let it finish installing, and then boot off the bootable floppy, copy your CD-ROM and SCSI drivers to the root directory, and compose AUTOEXEC.BAT and CONFIG.SYS files with the appropriate references. Reboot and then you can access your CD-ROM via the real-mode drivers. Typically, you'll find the printer setup is all that was left undone. Now, go into the Control Panel, select the Add New Hardware applet, follow the Wizard, and all should be fine. Remember to delete those files you created in your root directory.

In general, during the install, let the installer detect appropriate hardware. You may find when it reports to you that it missed your monitor type; when it gives you the summary you will have the option to change it. For installation, I strongly urge you to select the last option (Custom), because I never trust default choices. Go through each section and be sure to click the Details button to add exactly what you want. In particular, some new wallpaper and new screen savers exist, which you'll probably want. Choose other items depending on your needs and your computer's capabilities. Don't feel this is all carved in stone. You can add other items later through the Control Panel's Add Programs item.

I've found the actual install fairly trouble free, but some users have not. If your system simply stops responding (give it plenty of time), don't be afraid to follow the Microsoft suggestion to turn your computer off and then back on again. You're not damaging anything — the Windows 95 installer has kept a disk record of what it must do. Once you actually get into Windows 95 for the first time, the installer will do a lot of setting up (it will tell you what it's doing). After it's finished, reboot. Even though you don't have to, this is an excellent precaution.

Using Windows 95

The following tips will help you become comfortable with the Windows 95 operating system (and help you steer clear of some pitfalls).

The desktop

The very first thing to do is go into My Computer or Explorer, head for your WINDOWS directory, find WINFILE.EXE, click the right mouse button, and drag the file to your desktop. Release the button and accept the default of *Create a Shortcut* from the pop-up menu. You just created a shortcut for File Manager.

Your shortcut is identified as a shortcut by the little arrow on its icon. (Yes, the little arrow may clobber the icon's look — not so in the case of File Manager, but it could make you *mondo* cranky if that arrow obscures part of an icon you've spent hours crafting.) Ways exist to change the arrow to something else or make it disappear. *Don't change it.* Much as you may hate those little arrows, they can save you from yourself. If you eliminate the arrows, you'll have no tool except your memory to distinguish between shortcuts and actual files. Do you trust your memory? Do you trust your reflexes late at night? I don't. Let those arrows be.

Tip
You can create shortcuts by doing other kinds of dragging, too. But you can get into trouble, depending on whether you're dragging a document or an executable file. Use the right mouse button — you'll always get the pop-up menu and you'll always have the chance to make certain you're creating a shortcut. (You definitely do not want to move an executable file to your Desktop; other kinds of dragging can move executable files too easily and accidentally.)

Caution   Of course, you can delete shortcuts, either by highlighting and using the Delete key, or by using the right mouse button and selecting Delete from the pop-up menu. But then you'll be asked if it's okay to delete the file. You may, as I once did, panic: *Are you deleting the shortcut only or the underlying file?* The wording of the question is ambiguous. In reality, you're only deleting the shortcut — the underlying file is still wherever it lives. But I had to query Microsoft before I felt entirely comfortable. See Figure B-1.

Tip   You may not like Windows 95's habit of labeling your new shortcut with the prefatory words *Shortcut to.* Allegedly, if you delete those words often enough, Windows 95 wises up. My Windows 95 has never gotten those smarts. I still must manually eliminate those words. Although I'm not big on keyboard shortcuts, F2 is helpful here.

Of course, you can use the right mouse button for much more. Right-click anywhere on the Desktop, and choose Properties. You can easily configure your color, wallpaper, screen saver, or monitor.

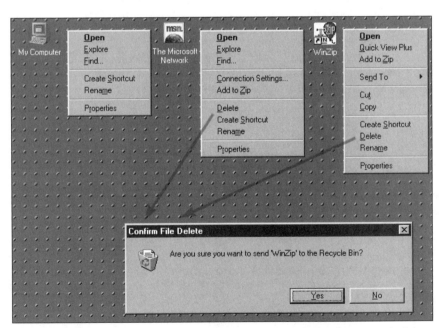

Figure B-1: Not everything on your Desktop is created equal. You can't delete some things (left). Windows 95 puts certain full executables on your Desktop (center) — these you can delete. And you can delete shortcuts (right). But notice that either deletion will produce the same confirmation dialog box (bottom). The secret is in the icon. Notice the absence of an arrow in the center icon, the presence in the right icon — the former's an executable, the latter's only a shortcut.

Tip

When selecting your screen saver, you may notice some of the choices from Windows 3.1 have a grayed-out Configure button. Microsoft changed the format of Windows 95 .SCR savers a bit, so this is a common occurrence. If you can't wait for a Windows 95 version of your favored saver, you can still configure it. Use Explorer to find it in your WINDOWS directory and then right-click it. You'll see a Configure option on the pop-up menu like the one at the bottom of Figure B-2.

Tip

The icon here is a misnomer. Every book on Windows 95 should have at least one Stupid Trick. But I couldn't ask for a Stupid Trick icon because we know Photoshop is a serious program! Here's my nomination. Right-click your Desktop, select the Screen Saver tab, scroll down to Flying Windows, and press the Settings button. Ramp up the Warp speed setting to Fast and set the Density to its maximum (75). On a fast Pentium . . . well, I told you this was a Stupid Trick. My first and last.

While you're in a shortcut mood, try this one. Use Explorer, go to the Start Menu and then to Programs. Drag a shortcut to this onto the Desktop. This shortcut enables you to edit and rearrange your programs on the Start Menu with the least amount of fuss. Alternative: Right-click the Start button, select Explore, right-click Programs, select Create Shortcut, and then drag Shortcut to Programs to the Desktop. See Figure B-3.

While you're in Desktop mode, look at Recycle Bin. By default, it uses 10 percent of your drive space. This may be too large. Right-click Properties and set it back to something more reasonable (I use 5 percent).

Managing files

Whether under DOS or Windows-whatever, file management is a highly personal matter. Some swear by doing all their chores on the command line. Some swear by File Manager — and some swear at it. Windows 95 offers two more objects of affection or disdain — Explorer and My Computer — and a host of right-mouse button functionality besides. So many choices, so little time!

I won't try to push one method of file management on you. Although I'll talk about mine, chances are my method won't be yours. What I want to do is give you a brief idea of some of the possibilities. Far more permutations exist than I could begin to cover, so look at my suggestions in the "Getting Help" section at the end of this appendix.

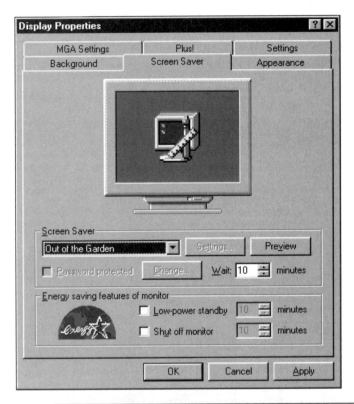

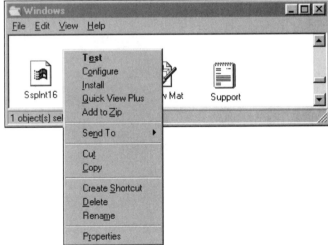

Figure B-2: This 16-bit screen saver apparently can't be configured in Control Panel (top). Do it in Explorer (bottom).

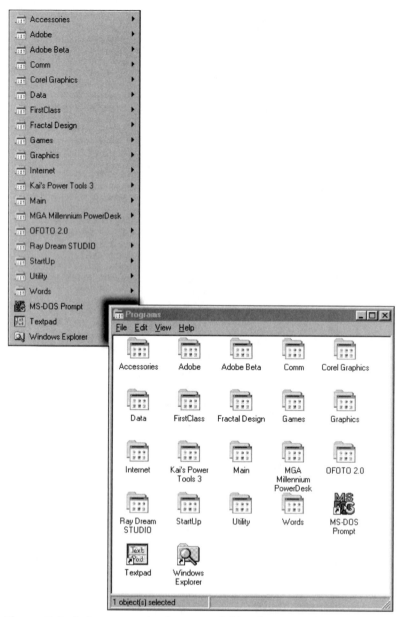

Figure B-3: A shortcut to the Programs folder (bottom) gives you ready editing of the Start Menu (top).

File Manager

Everyone loved to complain about this under Windows 3.1 — many praised (with some justification) the file-management facilities of Norton Desktop or PC Tools. I appreciate all those positions, but I never found File Manager to be the nasty rotten thing that led some to dub it File *Mangler*. I used Outside/In from SCC, a series of file viewers that hooked right in (SCC has become a part of Inso Corporation and now makes QuickView Plus, which I'll discuss shortly). WinZip (discussed later) attached to my menu bar and gave me all the compression functionality I needed. If I felt I needed more, I could always roll my own via WinBatch.

You may be mourning or celebrating the apparent loss of File Manager in Windows 95. Not so fast! It's still there; the installation program just hasn't set up an icon for it. You'll find a new version of WINFILE.EXE in your Windows directory. Of course, if you hate File Manager and have already decided My Computer and Explorer are the greatest things since sliced bread, you'll leave it buried there. The first thing I did was create a shortcut to File Manager on my Desktop. I use it about half the time; the other half I click my way through My Computer and Explorer.

My Computer and Explorer

Okay, I admit it. I didn't take to either of these during the beta, and they're still not my favorites. I like doing drag-and-drop on drive icons, which File Manager makes so easy. I like having two windows open so easily and then changing drives with a click on the icons. I know all sorts of ways exist to soup up these gizmos — I've tried any number of them, and I'm still not a convert. I want to manage my files without thinking about how I do it. For me, nothing beats File Manager most of the time. But I see these new incarnations have their uses.

Putting them together

When I'm moving large numbers of files or checking what's what, I use File Manager. If I'm working intensively with a group of project files in one directory (or several subdirectories branching from one), I keep Explorer windows open on my Desktop for the directories, so I can use the Send To option on the right-button menu. This makes copying to a floppy a virtual snap.

Tip   You can send files elsewhere, of course. To any program you'd like. For example, you may want to choose opening a .PSD file in either Photoshop or Painter. No problem. Place shortcuts to those programs in the Send To directory, and you have 'em. (See Figure B-4.) This is particularly useful if you find some program has overwritten all your file associations. For example, Corel Photo-Paint seems to think you'll want to open all your graphics files in it. Some nerve! Hacking through the Registry to fix this is both time-consuming and dangerous. Doctoring the Send To choices is quick and easy.

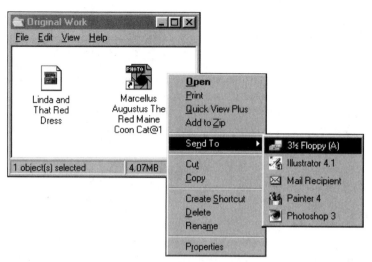

Figure B-4: Customize the Send To pop-up menu to have freedom of choice for opening your graphics files.

Tip

You may look for a newly moved, copied, or downloaded file in a directory you're viewing and not see it. Don't panic — if you put it there, it's there. Whether in Explorer or File Manager, press the F5 key to refresh; you'll see your file. (In some cases, it will be the last file in Explorer, out of alphabetical order.)

File viewers

If you installed Windows 95 from CD-ROM, you had the option of installing Quick View file viewers, which you can bring up by right-clicking a file. If you didn't, you can still download them from Microsoft directly or from Microsoft's many online presences. But you may want to view many more file types than this apparently meager selection.

Two choices exist. QuickView Plus, from Inso Corporation, expands the file viewing capability astronomically; it's easily installed and intuitive to use. I found QuickView Plus a winner from day one of its beta. The second choice is MasterSoft's Viewer 95, which offers similar viewing capabilities. Each program works well, each operates somewhat differently, and each has slightly different features. You can't go wrong with either one.

Norton Navigator

This program is omnipresent. Unlike Norton Utilities for Windows 95, which I've not installed because I consider it too unstable, I've used Navigator. In its first incarnation it was very slow — Symantec has since released a patch and slipstreamed it into shipping copies.

With the patch, it runs just fine on my Pentium with 32MB of memory. On my 486-66 with 16MB of memory, it's a different story. Others have reported this same sort of differential. There's a lot to like about Norton Navigator, but I don't personally find it offers enough to justify space on my drive. You may feel differently — consider it if you have the hardware to support it.

Application Issues

In the Windows 3.1 world, every application seemed to have its own way of installing. Microsoft's attempt to impose standard installation methodologies, via its Windows 95 Logo Program, is thus all to the good. But you still need to think about installing. Here are some selected considerations that may improve the quality of your installing life.

Installing

If you're installing a Windows 3.1 application and the installer won't work with Start ➪ Run, try running the installer out of File Manager. If it's a Win32s application, you can sometimes fool it with a text file in your WINDOWS directory. Name the file WIN32S.INI and put the following two lines in it:

```
[Win32s]
Version=1.20.123.0
```

You may need to tinker with those numbers because the Win32s subsystem is constantly evolving. Check with your application vendor before doing this, though. Many have recommended precisely this workaround — and Microsoft has recommended it, too.

Increasing numbers of Windows 95 applications come on CD-ROM, and more have an Auto Play function; insert the CD-ROM, hear the drive whir, hear some music (if you have a sound card), and see a splash screen. You may not like this, and you may want the old-fashioned method of finding the install program on the CD-ROM and proceeding from there. I've found some CD-ROM install programs simply do not work straight from Auto Play, but they work fine the old-fashioned way. You can do two things:

✦ **Disable for a particular CD-ROM:** Depress the Shift key while inserting the CD-ROM. Your Auto Play setting remains intact.

✦ **Disable Auto Play globally:** Go into Device Manager, select the specific CD-ROM drive, select Properties, and uncheck the Auto Play box.

Regardless, I don't trust installers. I don't trust uninstallers. I don't trust the uninstall routines Windows 95 applications use. I want to know precisely what's going where, and I've found a hands-on approach works the best.

Adobe products

✦ **Adobe Illustrator:** In Versions 4 through 4.03, it may not open at all. It may open and then display a message about a damaged or missing *ruler font file*. As far as I can tell, this message is harmless. But these versions of Illustrator aren't entirely stable under Windows 95 (Version 4.1 was tweaked for stability and also adds TrueType font support). I recommend upgrading to Version 6 or 7.

✦ **Adobe Type Manager:** You should have at least 4.0, which is the current shipping version, included with Photoshop. You may be able to run at earlier levels, but you're asking for trouble.

Caution

By the time you read this, ATM may be incrementally higher and, sometimes, those increments contain more changes than the numbering implies. Commendably, Adobe seems perpetually to be tweaking ATM, which is all to the good, given its importance and operation from deep inside Windows. I strongly advise you to stay current with ATM at all times.

✦ **PageMaker:** Version 5 runs, but 6 and 6.5 are Windows 95 logo compliant. 6.5 is good and inexpensive (as upgrades go) and has many new features. Do yourself a favor and upgrade.

✦ **Photoshop:** 3/3.01 was not entirely happy with Windows 95. Upgrade to 4.0, the version currently shipping.

The Major No-No — Hacking the Registry

I've given this a heading all by itself. It's impossible to overemphasize how dangerous this can be. PC people are an inventive lot; despite that it's harder to get at the Registry than to WIN.INI and SYSTEM.INI, you may be tempted to try. *Don't.* I'll explain.

The good old days — .INI files

It's true that if you messed up editing WIN.INI or SYSTEM.INI, you might render Windows nonfunctional. But you always had a safety net — text files. If they kept Windows from starting, you could stay in straight DOS, bring up a text editor, and undo your changes. Another safety feature existed, too: The .INI files had been around so long that editing and mistakes were all thoroughly documented.

The Registry — happy days are here again?

The safety net is gone. The Registry, which supplants most of the functions of WIN.INI and SYSTEM.INI (and, according to Microsoft's plan, will ultimately render them irrelevant), isn't a text file at all. It's a binary file you change by using the Regedit utility. You can't scan whole sections at once; you must navigate through *keys, subkeys,* and the like. Sometimes, one application buries entries in several places, so it's hard to read and harder to edit. Make a mistake in the wrong area and *anything* can happen. Windows 95's hidden backup can't save you, either. You may have to do a hack that brings down your system; before you realize it, Windows 95 may change your hacked registry, save it as your backup copy, and delete your last good Registry backup. This is quite possible — Windows 95 always seems to be writing to the Registry. Of course, you can save the whole Registry elsewhere, or you can save the section you're working on via the Export command. But if you don't remember to export each section you twiddle, you have a problem.

Think I'm gloomy? It gets worse. Microsoft's documentation for the Registry is pitiful. I have a theory about this. Windows 95 is designed to shield the user from as much as possible; Microsoft doesn't want people buying trouble. But sometimes hacking the Registry is the only way to get *out* of trouble, and Microsoft isn't making this any easier for you.

Various third-party information is appearing (some by knowledgeable Windows 95 users and programmers). I don't use any of it. Although I greatly respect the knowledge of those who have found some truly ingenious hacks, I don't think anyone (even Microsoft) fully understands how the Registry interacts with the rest of the operating system.

Is it really worth risking your system so the Start menu has stickier submenus, or doesn't fly up so fast, or so windows don't *explode* from a minimized state? Hacks are around for these and other things. Do as you will, but you won't have me for company if you venture down this path now. A day will come when we can hack safely. But that day hasn't yet dawned.

About Drivers

Latest isn't necessarily greatest. I've scattered references throughout the book to give specific examples of this. Sometimes latest is truly greatest, but sometimes a newer driver will break something that previously worked fine. So here's my driver advice:

✦ **Troll for drivers:** You could die of senility waiting for the manufacturer to send them automatically. Drivers tend to turn up first on the manufacturer's BBS and/or WWW page. Later they hit the online services.

✦ **If you have Internet access, try the manufacturer's WWW or FTP site:** This particularly applies to video drivers. A new driver comes out, and the BBS has a perpetual busy signal. This is not the manufacturer's fault — do you know how many eager beavers are out there? But you can almost always get onto their Internet sites immediately.

✦ **Keep your old drivers:** As I just mentioned, you may need them. Especially for diagnostics. I keep mine for at least a year.

Getting Help

The documentation Microsoft provides with Windows 95 is, well, skimpy. Even with the help files, you're probably need more. Here are some starting points.

Online

All the major services offer Windows 95 areas. I particularly like MSWIN95 on CompuServe, but the areas on The Microsoft Network and the Adobe areas on America Online are worthy, too. A proliferation of Windows 95 pages are also on the World Wide Web. I hesitate to mention any here. The Web changes constantly, so any address is unreliable. I think the safest strategy is using Yahoo! (www.yahoo.com). Yahoo! is probably the fastest route to an up-to-date listing. And, of course, there's always www.adobe.com. You can get to the most commonly used Adobe Photoshop Web sites right from Photoshop itself from the Help ⇨ Adobe Photoshop Home Page menu.

The printed word

The following items are a few of the most important printed resources for living and working with Windows 95.

Periodicals

Tips are everywhere. Articles are everywhere. Some are useful, some are redundant, some are just plain wrong (not many, luckily). If you must have tips, and more of them, any computer publication you choose will be spawning them on a monthly basis. You don't need me to tell you which publications to read.

But I'd like to tell you about one source that is less well-known. Brian Livingston, whose Windows 95 book I've mentioned before and will again in the next section, has a regular Windows 95 column in *InfoWorld*. Brian is privy to all manner of information, tips, and ideas — his range is breathtaking. You may qualify for a free subscription to that weekly newspaper. If you don't, most large libraries carry it.

It's worth subscribing just for Brian's weekly column. (Incidentally, IDG Books Worldwide, Inc., is part of the same company that publishes *InfoWorld*.)

Books

For the last time: Get *Windows 95 SECRETS,* by Brian Livingston and Davis Straub (IDG Books Worldwide, Inc.). Brian's books on Windows 3.1 took me from novice to, well, let's be modest and say less-than-novice status. *Windows 95 SECRETS* is just as good. If you want to flesh out my brief comments on Explorer, here's your nirvana. It comes with a superb CD-ROM, too.

You may also want *The Mother of All Windows 95 Books,* by Woody Leonhard and Barry Simon (Addison-Wesley). This book also has a fine CD-ROM. The book's emphases are so different from *SECRETS,* it can hardly be viewed as competing.

Of course, the *Windows 95 Resource Kit* (Microsoft Press) is another necessity. It's big, it's incomplete, it's frustrating. But it's all Microsoft is saying publicly about Windows 95, so it's a key resource. But it isn't a joy to read; *SECRETS* is.

Installing Photoshop 4

The process of installing Photoshop is well documented in the user manual, and it's remarkably straightforward. So rather than waste valuable pages slogging through a step-by-step discussion, I'll touch on the few areas I think might prove helpful.

Note   You install Photoshop 4 by running the setup utility found on the CD-ROM included inside the box. Most folks already know this, but to eliminate any confusion, I do not provide the Photoshop software on the CD-ROM included with this book. This book is intended to teach you how to use the software; you must purchase the program itself from a software reseller. The program costs roughly 15 times as much as this book, so you can see how it might be tough to include it.

Before You Install

Wait! Don't pop that CD into your CD-ROM drive just yet. Before you install Photoshop 4, you should take a few precautionary steps:

+ **Inventory your disk space:** The installation instructions ask you to have at least 20MB of free disk space. When I look at my Photoshop directory, I see about 8MB of space taken up, but this doesn't mean Adobe is wrong. Installers need a certain amount of overhead on disk space for decompressing files. And the installer needs to put certain files in your Windows directory and subdirectories. This will vary depending on your operating system. If you use Windows 3.1, you need room for the Win32s subsystem. In addition, regardless of operating system, you need room on that driver for the 1MB of color management files that go into a Photocd subdirectory of the main Windows directory. If you don't have enough free space, the installer will give you an *insufficient disk space* error message.

For absolute safety, I recommend having 20MB free on the drive you choose for Photoshop. That's more than you absolutely need, but it ensures you won't get an incomplete installation.

✦ **Turn off the nonessentials:** Close all running programs, any little doodads you may be running from the StartUp Group or from the RUN and LOAD lines of WIN.INI, and any screen savers. Most important, turn off any virus checker. Some installers will balk or abort an install if a virus checker is running.

✦ **Run a disk inventory program:** Here's one for the paranoid in the crowd (like me). Before you install Photoshop, set up a disk inventory program — that is, a program that takes a snapshot of your Windows drive and the drive you intend for Photoshop (which may be one and the same, of course). After installation, you run the program again, and it provides you with a report of the differences between your pre-install and post-install drive.

I offer this recommendation for several reasons. First, I never entirely trust uninstall routines. And I like to know what goes where — if I later need to troubleshoot a problem in some program, and I've narrowed things down to a .DLL that has been overwritten, I can bring up my install records and usually find which program is guilty.

Several excellent shareware programs are included on the CD-ROM that comes with *Windows 95 SECRETS* by Brian Livingston and Davis Straub (IDG Books Worldwide, Inc.). You might also want to try the excellent freeware program In Control 3, which you can find on the Internet at the following URL: www.zdnet.com/~pcmag/download/utils/inctrl3.htm. In Control 3 is available for Windows 95 and Windows NT; for a Windows 3.1 version, download In Control 2 from www.zdnet.com/~pcmag/download/utils/inctrl2.htm.

After taking these better safe than sorry steps, you're ready to install Photoshop in earnest.

Installing Photoshop

As I promised earlier, I'm not going to waste time or paper repeating the clear-cut installation instructions you can find in the *Getting Started* booklet that comes with Photoshop. Rather, I'd like to offer some helpful annotations:

✦ **The Installer splash screen:** After you slip the CD into your CD-ROM drive, the installer utility takes over your computer and displays an initial screen with four buttons. Click the Install Adobe Photoshop button to move on.

Tip

If the installer doesn't run automatically when you put it in your CD-ROM drive, you can jump start the installer by choosing Run from the Windows 95 Start menu (or from Program Manager, if you're using Windows 3.1), and then running this program file: D:\Photoshop\Disk1\Setup.exe. This program file takes you directly to the Photoshop setup and welcome screen, discussed next.

✦ **The Welcome Screen:** The next thing you see. Read it and move on.

✦ **The Name/Company/Serial Number screen:** Time to get interactive. If this is a new installation, use the serial number that comes on the card inside your Photoshop box. If it's an upgrade, use your previous serial number. Note, those are zeroes in the strings of digits — you never need to type the letter *O*.

✦ **Setup Type:** You'll be given a choice of installations: *Typical, Compact, Custom.* If, like me, you want to be the one who determines what does and doesn't get slapped onto your hard drive, choose Custom. The default destination directory will be on your C drive; if you want to install Photoshop on some other drive, click the Browse button and select the drive.

Note

The Compact installation merely installs Photoshop with none of the additional files. Typical installs everything, including the sample files needed to run the Photoshop tutorial. The Custom option enables you to choose which components of Photoshop you want to install. Granted, you don't have much flexibility — you can't pick and choose which filter files you want to install, for example — but at least you have a tiny modicum of control. Unless you're short on disk space, install everything but the Sample Files item. Yes, the tutorial is nice, but you don't need no stinkin' tutorial. That's why you bought this book, right?

If you're really tight on disk space, you may decide you can do without the Duotone Files as well (see Chapter 7 for information on printing duotones). Unfortunately, leaving off these files only saves a tiny bit of space — you'll probably still need to do some house cleaning on your hard drive to free up some space.

✦ **Select Program Folder:** Because I use Adobe applications all the time, I already have an Adobe program group. Surely you do, too? But if not, set this as the folder of choice.

✦ **Start Copying Files:** Your chance to confirm your choices and to back out if you've had second thoughts. Double-check this screen carefully before moving on.

✦ **Registration:** After the installer is finished, you're given the opportunity to register your copy of the program by modem. Personally, I almost never register. Maybe I'm lazy, maybe I'm paranoid, maybe I figure my name's already on enough mailing lists. But if you want to be apprised when new versions of Photoshop come out, you have to let Adobe know where you are.

Tip If you forget to install something, don't worry. You can always reinstall a single item later. Just rerun the installer, choose the Custom install option, select the items you want to install, and send the installation process on its merry way.

Installing the Extras

The Install utility doesn't necessarily install everything you may need to use Photoshop. For example, included on the CD-ROM are Adobe Type Manager 3.02, a bunch of stock photos, plus some additional goodies.

To get to these extras, click the Explore This CD-ROM button on the Photoshop Installer welcome screen to head out to the Windows 95 Explorer. Or click Exit to Desktop to quit the installer, and launch Explorer yourself. Then install the various components on the Photoshop CD as follows:

✦ **ATM 3.02:** You may be able to do without Adobe Type Manager (ATM) if you only intend to use TrueType fonts. But if you want to use Type 1 PostScript fonts in Photoshop, you must have ATM installed. If you have a version earlier than 3, definitely install the newer version that comes with Photoshop. To install ATM, open the ATM302 folder, and then double-click the Install.exe item. Restart your computer after installation to kick ATM into gear.

Note ATM should be available by the time you read this, but it isn't included on the Photoshop CD. The version of ATM on the Photoshop CD absolutely, positively, will not run on Windows NT.

✦ **Goodies:** Inside the Goodies folder, you'll find an Actions folder that contains predefined scripts for the Actions palette (Chapter 3); a Gradients folder that stores predefined gradations (Chapter 9); and a Textures folder with textures for the Lighting Effects filter (Chapter 16). Copy the folders you find intriguing to the Photoshop/Plugins folder on your hard drive.

✦ **Plug_Ins:** Also inside the Goodies folder is a folder named Plug_ins, which contains plug-ins that support the Amiga IFF, Ham, MacPaint, and PixelPaint formats, as discussed in Chapter 4. If you want to use them (not very likely), copy them to the Plugins folder on your hard drive.

The Plug_Ins folder also contains the files you need to run the Filter Factory, described in Chapter 17, which enables you to create your own custom filters. If you want to learn how to use this wonderful, but complex, feature, copy the Ffactory folder into the Plugins folder on your hard drive.

✦ **Stockart:** As its name implies, this folder contains a bunch of stock art images you can use to practice your Photoshop techniques. You needn't install these files — you can open them right from the CD from inside Photoshop.

Note   If you examine the Photoshop directory on your hard drive, you'll notice each folder contains several subfolders of its own, purely for organizational purposes. You can move things around if you like, as long as you don't move the files in the Plugins folder out of that folder. (In other words, you can move a file from the Filters folder in the Plugins folder to the Extensions folder inside that same folder, but you shouldn't move the file outside the Plugins folder.) If you do, you'll prevent that file from loading when you start up Photoshop, which, in turn, will make that feature unavailable.

Photograph Credits

The images used in this book came from all kinds of sources. The following list cites the figures or color plates in which a photograph appears. Following the figure number is the name of the photographer and the company from which the photo was licensed. In each case, the photographer holds the copyright. If the photograph comes from a CD collection, the product name appears in italics along with, or instead of, a photographer, and the company holds the copyright. If no company is listed, the photo was licensed from the photographer directly.

To all who contributed their photography, my heartfelt thanks.

Images	Photographer/Product	Company
Figures 2-2, 2-4, and 2-5	*Antistock*	Digital Stock
Figure 2-9	*Natural World*	Digital Stock
Figure 2-10	*Natural World*	Digital Stock
Figure 3-1	*Business & Commerce*	Digital Stock
Figure 4-1	*Urban Graffiti*	Digital Stock
Figure 4-13	*V. 11, Retro Americana*	PhotoDisc
Figure 4-19	*Urban Graffiti*	Digital Stock
Figures 4-21, 4-22, and 4-24	*Urban Graffiti*	Digital Stock
Figure 4-25	*Sport & Leisure*	Digital Stock

Images	Photographer/Product	Company
Color Plate 4-1	*V. 9, Holidays & Celebrations*	PhotoDisc
Color Plate 4-2	The Studio Dog, *Studio Geometry Background Series I*	PhotoDisc
Figures 5-6, 5-8, and 5-9	me, with a Polaroid PDC-2000	
Figures 6-2, 6-3, 6-4, and 6-6	*Water Sports*	Digital Stock
Color Plates 6-1 through 6-3	*Water Sports*	Digital Stock
Figure 7-5	*V. 11, Retro Americana*	PhotoDisc
Figure 7-6	Denise McClelland	
Figure 7-15	Mark Collen	
Color Plate 7-1	Mark Collen	
Figure 8-5	*Signature Series 16, Everyday People*	PhotoDisc
Figures 8-6 through 8-8, 8-29, and 8-30	Russell McDougal	
Figures 8-13 and 8-14	*V. 5, World Commerce & Travel*	PhotoDisc
Figure 8-15	*V. 12, Food & Dining*	PhotoDisc
Color Plate 8-1	*V. 12, Food & Dining*	PhotoDisc
Color Plate 8-2	*V. 5, World Commerce & Travel*	PhotoDisc
Color Plates 8-4 through 8-6	*Fine Art Series 1, European Paintings*	PhotoDisc
Figure 9-2	*V. 30, Contemporary Cuisine*	PhotoDisc
Figures 9-4, 9-11, 9-23, and 9-25 (dog)	*Object Series 18, Everyday Animals*	PhotoDisc
Figures 9-4, 9-11, 9-23, and 9-25 (hydrant)	me, with a Polaroid PDC-2000	
Figures 9-6 and 9-7	*Vol. 11, Retro Americana*	PhotoDisc
Figures 9-23 through 9-25 (fly)	*V. 8, Bugs & Butterflies*	MetaTools
Color Plate 9-1	*V. 30, Contemporary Cuisine*	PhotoDisc
Color Plate 9-3	*Signature Series 14, Cultural Arts*	PhotoDisc
Figures 10-2 through 10-5, 10-12, and 10-22	Denise McClelland	
Figures 10-6 and 10-7	Russell McDougal	

Images	Photographer/Product	Company
Figures 10-8 through 10-11	Michael Probst	Reuter
Figures 10-17 through 10-20	*V. 23, Far Eastern Business & Culture*	PhotoDisc
Figures 11-4, 11-18, 11-20 through 11-22, 11-24 through 11-27, 11-33, and 11-34	*V. 4, Technology & Medicine*	PhotoDisc
Figure 11-7	*V. 16, US Landmarks and Travel*	PhotoDisc
Figures 11-8 through 11-10	Russell McDougal	
Figures 11-11, 11-29 through 11-31	*V. 4, Technology & Medicine*	PhotoDisc
Figures 11-13 through 11-17	*V. 4, Technology & Medicine*	PhotoDisc
Figure 11-21 (face)	*V. 5, World Commerce & Travel*	PhotoDisc
Color Plate 11-1	*V. 16, US Landmarks and Travel*	PhotoDisc
Figures 12-1 and 12-2	*Sport & Leisure*	Digital Stock
Figures 12-3 through 12-10	*V. 4, Technology & Medicine*	PhotoDisc
Figures 12-12 through 12-14 (Capitol)	*Washington D.C.*	Digital Stock
Figures 12-12 and 12-14 (lava)	*Fire & Ice*	Digital Stock
Figures 12-15, 12-17, 12-20 through 12-22	*Washington D.C.*	Digital Stock
Figures 12-18 and 12-19	*Volume 11, Retro Americana*	PhotoDisc
Figures 12-24 through 12-29	*Children & Teens*	Digital Stock
Color Plate 12-1	*Sport & Leisure*	Digital Stock
Color Plate 12-2 (Capitol)	*Washington D.C.*	Digital Stock
Color Plate 12-2 (lava)	*Fire & Ice*	Digital Stock
Color Plate 12-3 (girl)	*Children & Teens*	Digital Stock
Color Plate 12-3 (background)	*Southern California*	Digital Stock
Figure 13-1 (x-ray)	*V. 29, Modern Technologies*	PhotoDisc
Figures 13-1, 13-24, and 13-25	*Object Series 15, InfoMedia*	PhotoDisc
Figures 13-2, 13-6 through 13-9, 13-11,13-13 through 13-15, 13-26	*Object Series 15, InfoMedia*	PhotoDisc
Figures 13-17, 13-19 through 13-22	*V. 6, Nature & the Environment*	PhotoDisc

Images	Photographer/Product	Company
Figures 13-28 through 13-30	*Children & Teens*	Digital Stock
Figures 13-31 and 13-32	me, with a Polaroid PDC-2000	
Color Plates 13-1 and 13-2	*V. 6, Nature & the Environment*	PhotoDisc
Color Plate 13-3	me, with a Polaroid PDC-2000	
Figures 14-2, 14-11 through 14-15	Carlye Calvin, *Sampler One*	Color Bytes
Figure 14-19	*Characters & Expressions*	Digital Stock
Figures 15-1 through 15-7, 15-20, 15-23, 15-25 through 15-27, 15-29, 15-30, 15-36, 15-39, 15-40, and 15-42	*Italy*	Digital Stock
Figures 15-8 through 15-13, 15-17 through 15-19, 15-21, 15-31, 15-37, and 15-41	*V. 23, Far Eastern Business & Culture*	PhotoDisc
Figures 15-14 through 15-16, and 15-32	*World War II*	Digital Stock
Figure 15-22	*V. 5, World Commerce & Travel*	PhotoDisc
Figures 15-33 through 15-35	*Object Series 15, InfoMedia*	PhotoDisc
Figure 15-35 (zebra pattern)	Nick Koudis, *Background Series 5, Wackgrounds*	PhotoDisc
Figures 15-43 through 15-45	me, with a Kodak DC40	
Color Plates 15-1 and 15-2	*Italy*	Digital Stock
Color Plates 15-3 through 15-5	*V. 9, Holidays & Celebrations*	PhotoDisc
Color Plate 15-6	*V. 5, World Commerce & Travel*	PhotoDisc
Figure 16-1	*Central Europe*	Digital Stock
Figure 16-2 through 16-9, 16-12, 16-15, 16-21, 16-22, and 16-39	*V. 5, World Commerce & Travel*	PhotoDisc
Figures 16-13, 16-14, 16-16, 16-23, 16-27, 16-30, and 16-40	*Italy*	Digital Stock
Figures 16-10 and 16-11	*V. 11, Retro Americana*	PhotoDisc
Color Plates 16-1 through 16-4, and 16-9	*V. 9, Holidays & Celebrations*	PhotoDisc
Color Plate 16-5 and 16-6	*V. 7, Business & Occupations*	PhotoDisc
Color Plate 16-8	Mark Collen	

Images	Photographer/Product	Company
Color Plate 16-10	*Antistock*	Digital Stock
Figures 17-1, 17-42, 17-43, and 17-45	*V. 9, Holidays & Celebrations*	PhotoDisc
Figures 17-3 through 17-31, and 17-33 through 17-41	*V. 5, World Commerce & Travel*	PhotoDisc
Color Plates 17-1 and 17-2	*Flowers*	Digital Stock
Color Plates 17-3 and 17-4	*V. 9, Holidays & Celebrations*	PhotoDisc
Figure 18-1	*V. 25, Government & Social Issues*	PhotoDisc
Figures 18-2, 18-3, 18-5 through 18-7, 18-14, 18-16, 18-17, 18-19, and 18-23 through 18-27	*V. 5, World Commerce & Travel*	PhotoDisc
Figures 18-8, 18-10, and 18-12	*V. 9, Holidays & Celebrations*	PhotoDisc
Color Plates 18-1 through 18-3, and 18-6 through 18-8	*Antistock*	Digital Stock
Color Plates 18-4, 18-5, 18-9, and 18-10	*V. 9, Holidays & Celebrations*	PhotoDisc
Color Plate 18-11	me, with a Kodak DC50	
Color Plate 18-12	*V. 25, Government & Social Issues*	PhotoDisc
Color Plate 18-13	*Italy*	Digital Stock
Color Plate 18-14	*V. 5, World Commerce & Travel*	PhotoDisc
Color Plate 18-15	me, with a Polaroid PDC-2000	
Figure 19-1 (parachute)	*Active Lifestyles 2*	Digital Stock
Figure 19-1 (moon)	*Space & Exploration*	Digital Stock
Figures 19-3 through 19-12, 19-17, 19-18, 19-20, and 19-21	Russell McDougal	
Figures 19-13 through 19-15 (woman)	*V.28, People, Lifestyles, & Vacations*	PhotoDisc
Figures 19-13 and 19-14 (leaf)	*V.26, Homes & Gardens*	PhotoDisc
Figures 19-23 through 19-26	Carlye Calvin, *Sampler One*	Color Bytes
Color Plate 19-1	*Space & Exploration*	Digital Stock
Color Plates 19-2 through 19-4	*V.28, People, Lifestyles, & Vacations*	PhotoDisc

Images	Photographer/Product	Company
Color Plate 19-2 (leaf)	*V.26, Homes & Gardens*	PhotoDisc
Color Plates 19-5 and 19-6	Carlye Calvin, *Sampler One*	Color Bytes
Figure 20-1	*V. 35, Business Today*	PhotoDisc
Figure 20-2	*Indigenous Peoples*	Digital Think
Figure 20-6 and 20-8	*V. 5, World Commerce & Travel*	PhotoDisc
Color Plates 20-1 and 20-2	*V. 5, World Commerce & Travel*	PhotoDisc
Backgrounds for all color plates	Nick Koudis, Jim Grant, The Studio Dog, Skan/9, *Background Series,* KPT Power Photos	PhotoDisc HSC Software

Using the CD-ROM

To access the images and documents included on the CD-ROM, insert the CD into your CD-ROM drive. Open My Computer and double-click the icon for your CD-ROM drive. The window pops open and displays the following seven folders:

✦ **Gallery:** This folder contains original artwork that was created using Photoshop. The eight artists represented have a range of styles and techniques, and you can get some great ideas from looking at their images. These images are only for viewing purposes.

✦ **Images:** This folder contains both high-resolution and low-resolution images from stock photo agencies PhotoDisc and Digital Stock.

✦ **Filters:** Two folders are within this folder: One is labeled Macintosh; the second is labeled Windows. Each contains Photoshop filters and demo software from a variety of vendors, including Extensis, Alien Skin, and Andromeda Software. The Tormentia filters described in Chapter 17 are also found here. To use any of these filters, drag them into the Plugins folder on your hard drive.

✦ **Macworld:** This folder contains an article originally published in *Macworld* magazine.

✦ **DigThink:** This folder contains information from DigitalThink, a company that offers classes in Photoshop via the Web.

✦ **Acrobat:** This folder contains the items you need to install an Acrobat reader on your hard drive. The reader will enable you to read PDF files, including those from Extensis.

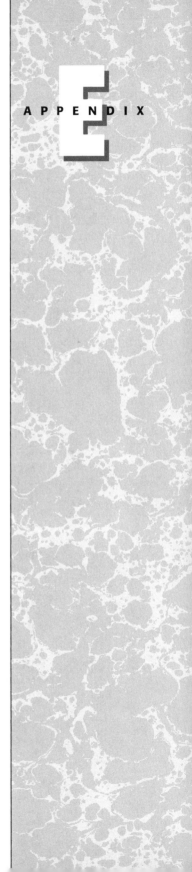

✦ **Digimarc:** This folder contains information about an innovative new service that embeds an electronic copyright into any image. If you distribute a lot of images electronically, you may want to check out Digimarc.

Gallery

These folders contain images created by artists who use Photoshop as one of the tools of their trade. These images are provided as inspirational material only; they are not for commercial use and the artists retain all copyrights to their work.

To view these images, first start up Photoshop, and then open the image inside Photoshop. A number of the artists have included Details files; check these out for information on how the images were created, the artists' thoughts about their work, and contact information. To access the Details files, open them in your favorite word processor.

✦ **Jeff Brice:** Jeff is a Seattle-based digital artist/illustrator. He's worked for *Wired* magazine, Adobe, Hewlett Packard, Scribner, *Time, Newsweek,* Fidelity, J. P. Morgan, DEC, and many more editorial and corporate clients. Jeff tries to apply his background in fine arts to his illustration work. His work can be seen in the newly published "Mind Grenades," by Hardwired.

✦ **Steve Campbell:** Steve has been redefining and reinventing himself as a digital fine artist, having been twice selected to exhibit in Fractal Design's yearly Art Expo traveling gallery and winning prizes three years in a row in the MicroPublishing/Iris Digital Art contest, with awards ceremonies held yearly at Seybold, San Francisco. His work has been featured on the 1995 Adobe Graphics Sampler, and can also be seen in *Painting With Computers,* from Rockport Publishing.

✦ **Christopher Ching:** Based in Manhattan, New York, Chris is an illustrator whose pictures are simple, conceptually distilled. Subtle Photoshop effects are an integral part of his illustration work.

✦ **Kevin Curry:** Kevin is an illustrator based in Albuquerque, New Mexico. His work has appeared in national publications, including *Macworld* and *PC World.*

✦ **Diane Fenster:** Cover artist Diane Fenster from Pacifica, California, creates both fine art and illustration. Her style is an innovative combination of her own 35mm photography, video, still video, and scanned imagery. Diane's fine art has been exhibited internationally and her images appear in numerous publications and CDs, including the Aperture monograph "Metamorphoses: Photography In The Electronic Age." She is a guest lecturer at many seminars and conferences and her work was exhibited at the SIGGRAPH 95 Art & Design show. Diane's illustration style is an outgrowth of the explorations she has taken with her personal work; her commissions range from editorial to advertising to Web.

✦ **Larry Goode:** Larry graduated from the University of Texas at Austin in 1985 with a BFA in Painting and Drawing. After working freelance at several Austin design firms, he was hired as a designer for Fuller, Dyal, and Stamper (FD&S) in 1987. At FD&S, Larry began teaching himself the Macintosh and exploring Photoshop and other applications. In 1995, he joined forces with longtime friend and business associate, Ranulfo Ponce, to form Design Island, a four-person design shop, where the emphasis is on illustration, multimedia, and graphic design.

✦ **Ranulfo Ponce:** Ranulfo is a partner in Design Island, a multitalented corporation in the fields of graphic design, environmental graphics, multimedia, illustration, and Web page and site design. He studied technical illustration for five years with an additional five years' experience in graphic design, environmental graphics, and production. Ranulfo is also the driving force in the multimedia area of Design Island.

✦ **Greg Vander Houwen:** Greg is a principal in the computer graphics firm, Interact. He has a background in video, computers, photography, and apple farming. Greg's award-winning imagery has been shown internationally, and his clients include Microsoft, Adobe, and Apple. He also lectures on image compositing, special FX, retouching, and illustration. Greg is an artist by nature and an illustrator by trade. He also enjoys philosophizing during an occasional lunar eclipse.

Images

The Images folder contains two folders, named DigStock and PhotDisc:

✦ **DigStock:** Digital Stock Corporation has provided us with a number of high-resolution images (pictured in Figure E-1), as well as several hundred low-resolution images. Each one of the high-resolution images comes from the figures of this book, enabling you to experiment with the very images you see on the printed page. Wow, talk about planning! To open any of the images, first start Photoshop and then open the image inside the program. Digital Stock has provided these files to give you a feel for its extensive collection of stock photography. For a catalog containing thousands of images, follow the instructions in the text file, called FreeOffr. To read this file, open it in your favorite word processor.

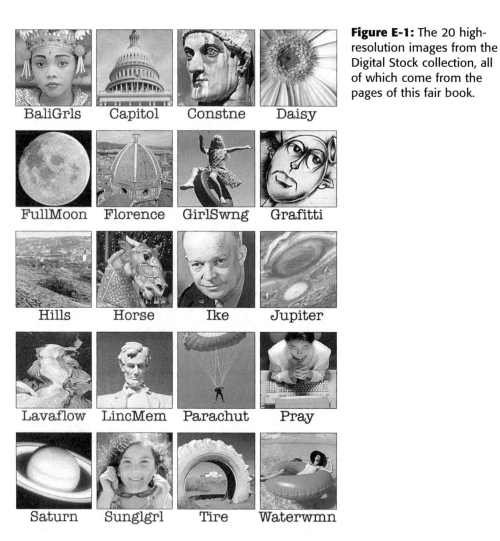

Figure E-1: The 20 high-resolution images from the Digital Stock collection, all of which come from the pages of this fair book.

BaliGrls   Capitol   Constne   Daisy

FullMoon   Florence   GirlSwng   Grafitti

Hills   Horse   Ike   Jupiter

Lavaflow   LincMem   Parachut   Pray

Saturn   Sunglgrl   Tire   Waterwmn

✦ **PhotDisc:** Three folders are in the PhotDisc folder. The first includes 20 high-resolution images that come from the book. See them again in Figure E-2. You can use these images to re-create the examples in the book or to create your own effects. The folder called Low-res contains several thousand low-resolution images from the company's extensive image library. Finally, the folder titled More contains information on the company, in the form of a Web page. To look at this file, you must have a Web browser, such as Netscape Navigator or Microsoft's Internet Explorer. The images in the Hi-res folders from both Digital Stock and PhotoDisc include a limited-use license. You can use the images in your publications and original artwork, but you cannot sell or give away electronic versions of the files. The other images, including those in the Low-res folders, are for placement and experimentation only. You are not authorized to use them in artwork or post them electronically. If you are interested in using any of these images, you must purchase the desired image directly from Digital Stock or PhotoDisc.

Figure E-2: The 20 high-resolution images from the PhotoDisc collection, which I have featured in pivotal locations throughout this book.

Filters

Two folders are here: One is called Macintosh, and the other is Windows. All the filters included in the Windows folder are also included in the Macintosh folder, so I'll explain the Windows contents first.

Windows (and Macintosh)

You can find the following plug-ins in both the Windows and Macintosh folders.

Alien Skin

Alien Skin has provided both Mac and Windows users with a demo version of Cutout, one of the ten filters included in their plug-in collection, The Black Box 2. The demo is the same as the commercial version of Cutout, except a splash screen appears each time the demo is run. Dismiss the splash screen by clicking it. If you're a Mac user, you can install the demo by double-clicking the icon labeled Install Cutout Demo 2.1. Windows users should run the file called Setup32.exe.

Andromeda

Andromeda Software has generously provided samples of its Series 1, Series 2, and Series 3 filters for both Macintosh and Windows users. Andromeda has also offered information on its newest filters, Series 4 and Velociraptor. For directions on installing these filters, please open the Read Me files included in each folder in your favorite word processor.

✦ **Series 1:** This folder contains the Circular Multiple Images filter/plug-in, which is one of ten in the Andromeda Series 1 Photography Filters. The filter is fully operational. Try successive applications of the filter on the same image and vary Intensity (opacity) and Areas to create stunning kaleidoscopic effects.

✦ **Series 2:** The 3D Demo filter in this folder has a fully operational interface and Preview Window, although the output (OK button) has been disabled. Use this filter to wrap your image on 3D surfaces; rotate and shade the image and surface, and even view the surface from any angle.

✦ **Series 3:** The Series 3 Screens filter (which I awarded a rare five-star review in *Macworld* magazine) offers special effects screening for grayscale images. In this version, the interface and Preview windows are operational, but the output button has been disabled. For help getting started with this filter, check out the Quickstart tutorial included in the folder. You can use any word processor to read the Quickstart file.

✦ **Series 4:** Series 4 Techtures is a product that enables you to apply textures to images, while Velociraptor is a motion trails plug-in. These folders contain

Read Me files, which describe the filters, images created using the filters, and pictures of the filter interfaces.

Tormentia

This is a collection of eight filters I created using the Filter Factory, explained in Chapter 17. To learn what each of these filters does, read the Tormentia.txt file included in the Tormentia folder. On Windows machines, this file is best opened in Microsoft Word. The strange-looking characters are apostrophes that didn't translate properly. Sorry about that.

Extensis

You will find Extensis folders in both the Windows and Macintosh Filters folders.

Macintosh

This folder contains two files, a Read Me and Extensis's licensing agreement, as well as two folders, one named Software and one called Extensis Info. The Software folder includes demo versions of Extensis products including Intellihance 2.0.1, PhotoTools 1.0, and PhotoNavigator.

✦ **Intellihance:** This is an intelligent photo-correction plug-in that corrects images so simply even a child could use it. This demo enables you to run Intellihance up to five times per session. You must quit and relaunch Photoshop if you wish to continue using Intellihance. You can run Intellihance on a total of 30 images before it fully expires. To install this software, double-click the Intellihance installer.

✦ **PhotoTools:** Here is a collection of eight Photoshop plug-ins, including four modules to create commonly used special effects automatically. PhotoTools also includes customizable toolbars and a special tips module chock full of Photoshop 4 insights by yours truly. (I've been told PhotoTools is helpful - but I should stop. I'm making me blush.) This demo version will function fully for 30 days, and then it'll poop out and die. To install it, double-click the Install PhotoTools icon.

✦ **PhotoNavigator:** This bit of freeware enables you — quickly and accurately — to navigate your way around large images. A rather well-known secret is this filter was the inspiration for Photoshop 4's new Navigator palette. In fact, I only include PhotoNavigator so you can compare it to the Navigator palette and say, "Well, well!" or words to that effect. Feel free to give it to some poor slob who's still using Photoshop 3.

Extensis has also included demo versions of DrawTools (a collection of color, moving, and shaping plug-ins for Illustrator and FreeHand), PageTools (for PageMaker), QX-Tools 2.0 (for QuarkXPress), CyberPress (an HTML export XTension for QuarkXPress), AstroByte BeyondPress 2.0 (another HTML export module for XPress), and Fetch (an image-cataloging database).

You can also find information about all the products of Extensis in the folder named Extensis Info. Here you'll find an HTML page you can read with your favorite browser and a PDF order form you can open with Adobe Acrobat (included on this CD).

Windows
This folder contains demo versions of Intellihance 2.0, PhotoTools 1.1, and PageTools 2.0 and 2.0.1.

Datastream Imaging (Macintosh only)
This folder contains information about, as well as one filter from, WildRiverSSK, a collection of seven Photoshop filters. The included filter is DekoBoko, which in Japanese means convex/concave. This filter creates 3D style frames. To install DekoBoko, drag the file named WRSSK DekoBoko1.0e to the filters folder inside your Photoshop folder.

Macworld
This folder contains an article originally published in the hallowed pages of the finest trade publication on Earth, *Macworld* magazine. "Copyright and the Visual Arts" comes from the October 1996 issue of *Macworld*. Written by my capable pal, Marjorie Baer, it explains copyright infringement and how to avoid it. You can open the article in your favorite Web browser.

DigThink
This folder contains HTML files from DigitalThink, a company that offers classes in Java, C++, and other topics over the Web. They also have a first-rate Photoshop class, authored by a guy named Deke. To learn more about this and other classes from DigitalThink, open the index.html document in your favorite Web program.

Acrobat
This folder contains everything you need to install the Acrobat reader, which enables you to read the PDF files contained on the CD-ROM. To install the reader, double-click the Acrobat Installer icon.

Digimarc

Photoshop 4 supports a digital watermarking feature called *PictureMarc* from a company called Digimarc. PictureMarc enables you to embed special copyright information into any image you distribute electronically. The embedding modifies the pixels in your image, but it's designed to be invisible, or as near to invisible as possible. People who look at your artwork can then view the copyright information by simply choosing a command; they cannot, however, eliminate the copyright as they might if you had entered it into the File Info dialog box.

The one tickle is you must register with Digimarc before you can take advantage of this service. Although Adobe has officially endorsed the PictureMarc service, I haven't decided what I think of it. So rather than writing about it here, I chose to include these HTML pages from DigiMarc and let you investigate for yourself.

Cross Platform Notes

Macintosh users should ignore the Autorun.inf and Ph4bible.ico files. These are strictly for Windows, so don't bother trying to open them. Similarly, Windows users should ignore the Icon_ files. These are only for the Mac folks.

Index

(continued)

Installing the CD-ROM

Insert the CD-ROM into your CD-ROM drive.

Windows users: Open My Computer and double-click the icon for your CD-ROM drive.

Mac users: Double-click the CD icon that appears on your desktop.

Please see Appendix E for more information on using the CD-ROM.

IDG BOOKS WORLDWIDE, INC.
END-USER LICENSE AGREEMENT

READ THIS. You should carefully read these terms and conditions before opening the software packet(s) included with this book ("Book"). This is a license agreement ("Agreement") between you and IDG Books Worldwide, Inc. ("IDGB"). By opening the accompanying software packet(s), you acknowledge that you have read and accept the following terms and conditions. If you do not agree and do not want to be bound by such terms and conditions, promptly return the Book and the unopened software packet(s) to the place you obtained them for a full refund.

1. **License Grant.** IDGB grants to you (either an individual or entity) a nonexclusive license to use one copy of the enclosed software program(s) (collectively, the "Software") solely for your own personal or business purposes on a single computer (whether a standard computer or a workstation component of a multiuser network). The Software is in use on a computer when it is loaded into temporary memory (RAM) or installed into permanent memory (hard disk, CD-ROM, or other storage device). IDGB reserves all rights not expressly granted herein.

2. **Ownership.** IDGB is the owner of all right, title, and interest, including copyright, in and to the compilation of the Software recorded on the disk(s) or CD-ROM ("Software Media"). Copyright to the individual programs recorded on the Software Media is owned by the author or other authorized copyright owner of each program. Ownership of the Software and all proprietary rights relating thereto remain with IDGB and its licensers.

3. **Restrictions On Use and Transfer.**

   (a) You may only (i) make one copy of the Software for backup or archival purposes, or (ii) transfer the Software to a single hard disk, provided that you keep the original for backup or archival purposes. You may not (i) rent or lease the Software, (ii) copy or reproduce the Software through a LAN or other network system or through any computer subscriber system or bulletin-board system, or (iii) modify, adapt, or create derivative works based on the Software.

   (b) You may not reverse engineer, decompile, or disassemble the Software. You may transfer the Software and user documentation on a permanent basis, provided that the transferee agrees to accept the terms and conditions of this Agreement and you retain no copies. If the Software is an update or has been updated, any transfer must include the most recent update and all prior versions.

4.   **Restrictions On Use of Individual Programs.** You must follow the individual requirements and restrictions detailed for each individual program in the "About the Disk or CD" section of this Book. These limitations are also contained in the individual license agreements recorded on the Software Media. These limitations may include a requirement that after using the program for a specified period of time, the user must pay a registration fee or discontinue use. By opening the Software packet(s), you will be agreeing to abide by the licenses and restrictions for these individual programs that are detailed in the "About the Disk or CD" section and on the Software Media. None of the material on this Software Media or listed in this Book may ever be redistributed, in original or modified form, for commercial purposes.

5.   **Limited Warranty.**

    (a)   IDGB warrants that the Software and Software Media are free from defects in materials and workmanship under normal use for a period of sixty (60) days from the date of purchase of this Book. If IDGB receives notification within the warranty period of defects in materials or workmanship, IDGB will replace the defective Software Media.

    (b)   **IDGB AND THE AUTHOR OF THE BOOK DISCLAIM ALL OTHER WARRANTIES, EXPRESS OR IMPLIED, INCLUDING WITHOUT LIMITATION IMPLIED WARRANTIES OF MERCHANTABILITY AND FITNESS FOR A PARTICULAR PURPOSE, WITH RESPECT TO THE SOFTWARE, THE PROGRAMS, THE SOURCE CODE CONTAINED THEREIN, AND/OR THE TECHNIQUES DESCRIBED IN THIS BOOK. IDGB DOES NOT WARRANT THAT THE FUNCTIONS CONTAINED IN THE SOFTWARE WILL MEET YOUR REQUIREMENTS OR THAT THE OPERATION OF THE SOFTWARE WILL BE ERROR FREE.**

    (c)   This limited warranty gives you specific legal rights, and you may have other rights that vary from jurisdiction to jurisdiction.

6.   **Remedies.**

    (a)   IDGB's entire liability and your exclusive remedy for defects in materials and workmanship shall be limited to replacement of the Software Media, which may be returned to IDGB with a copy of your receipt at the following address: Software Media Fulfillment Department, Attn.: *Photoshop 4 For Windows 95® Bible*, IDG Books Worldwide, Inc., 7260 Shadeland Station, Ste. 100, Indianapolis, IN 46256, or call 1-800-762-2974. Please allow three to four weeks for delivery. This Limited Warranty is void if failure of the Software Media has resulted from accident, abuse, or misapplication. Any replacement Software Media will be warranted for the remainder of the original warranty period or thirty (30) days, whichever is longer.

(b) In no event shall IDGB or the author be liable for any damages whatsoever (including without limitation damages for loss of business profits, business interruption, loss of business information, or any other pecuniary loss) arising from the use of or inability to use the Book or the Software, even if IDGB has been advised of the possibility of such damages.

(c) Because some jurisdictions do not allow the exclusion or limitation of liability for consequential or incidental damages, the above limitation or exclusion may not apply to you.

7. **U.S. Government Restricted Rights.** Use, duplication, or disclosure of the Software by the U.S. Government is subject to restrictions stated in paragraph (c)(1)(ii) of the Rights in Technical Data and Computer Software clause of DFARS 252.227-7013, and in subparagraphs (a) through (d) of the Commercial Computer—Restricted Rights clause at FAR 52.227-19, and in similar clauses in the NASA FAR supplement, when applicable.

8. **General.** This Agreement constitutes the entire understanding of the parties and revokes and supersedes all prior agreements, oral or written, between them and may not be modified or amended except in a writing signed by both parties hereto that specifically refers to this Agreement. This Agreement shall take precedence over any other documents that may be in conflict herewith. If any one or more provisions contained in this Agreement are held by any court or tribunal to be invalid, illegal, or otherwise unenforceable, each and every other provision shall remain in full force and effect.

HIGH-IMPACT DESIGNS
START WITH HIGH-QUALITY IMAGES.

Digital Stock offers thousands of outstanding, royalty-free stock images on CD ROM. Each high-resolution image is drum-scanned and perfect for everything from multimedia to full-page print. A disc of 100 images is just $249. Order our Starter Pak and receive a Catalog Disc and Catalog Book for just $19.95. Call 1-800-545-4514 or visit our web site.

IDG BOOKS WORLDWIDE REGISTRATION CARD

Title of this book: Photoshop® for Windows® 95 Bible

My overall rating of this book: ❑ Very good [1] ❑ Good [2] ❑ Satisfactory [3] ❑ Fair [4] ❑ Poor [5]

How I first heard about this book:

❑ Found in bookstore; name: [6] _____

❑ Advertisement: [8] _____

❑ Word of mouth; heard about book from friend, co-worker, etc.: [10] _____

❑ Book review: [7] _____

❑ Catalog: [9] _____

❑ Other: [11] _____

What I liked most about this book:
_____
_____

What I would change, add, delete, etc., in future editions of this book:
_____
_____

Other comments:
_____

Number of computer books I purchase in a year: ❑ 1 [12] ❑ 2-5 [13] ❑ 6-10 [14] ❑ More than 10 [15]

I would characterize my computer skills as: ❑ Beginner [16] ❑ Intermediate [17] ❑ Advanced [18] ❑ Professional [19]

I use ❑ DOS [20] ❑ Windows [21] ❑ OS/2 [22] ❑ Unix [23] ❑ Macintosh [24] ❑ Other: [25]_____
(please specify)

I would be interested in new books on the following subjects:
(please check all that apply, and use the spaces provided to identify specific software)

❑ Word processing: [26] _____

❑ Data bases: [28] _____

❑ File Utilities: [30] _____

❑ Networking: [32] _____

❑ Other: [34] _____

❑ Spreadsheets: [27] _____

❑ Desktop publishing: [29] _____

❑ Money management: [31] _____

❑ Programming languages: [33] _____

I use a PC at (please check all that apply): ❑ home [35] ❑ work [36] ❑ school [37] ❑ other: [38] _____

The disks I prefer to use are ❑ 5.25 [39] ❑ 3.5 [40] ❑ other: [41]_____

I have a CD ROM: ❑ yes [42] ❑ no [43]

I plan to buy or upgrade computer hardware this year: ❑ yes [44] ❑ no [45]

I plan to buy or upgrade computer software this year: ❑ yes [46] ❑ no [47]

Name: _____ Business title: [48] _____ Type of Business: [49] _____

Address (❑ home [50] ❑ work [51]/Company name: _____)

Street/Suite# _____

City [52]/State [53]/Zipcode [54]: _____ Country [55] _____

❑ **I liked this book!** You may quote me by name in future IDG Books Worldwide promotional materials.

My daytime phone number is _____

IDG BOOKS

THE WORLD OF COMPUTER KNOWLEDGE

❏ YES!

Please keep me informed about IDG's World of Computer Knowledge.
Send me the latest IDG Books catalog.